MW00345874

APA
Dictionary
of
Statistics
and Research
Methods

Ψ

APA
Dictionary
of
Statistics
and Research
Methods

Sheldon Zedeck, PhD
Editor in Chief

American Psychological Association
Washington, DC

Published by
American Psychological Association
750 First Street, NE
Washington, DC 20002
www.apa.org

To order
APA Order Department
P.O. Box 92984
Washington, DC 20090-2984
Tel: (800) 374-2721; Direct: (202) 336-5510
Fax: (202) 336-5502; TDD/TTY: (202) 336-6123
Online: www.apa.org/pubs/books/
E-mail: order@apa.org

In the U.K., Europe, Africa, and the Middle East, copies may be ordered from
American Psychological Association
3 Henrietta Street
Covent Garden, London
WC2E 8LU England

AMERICAN PSYCHOLOGICAL ASSOCIATION STAFF
Gary R. VandenBos, PhD, Publisher
Julia Frank-McNeil, Senior Director, APA Books
Theodore J. Baroody, Director, Reference, APA Books
Patricia D. Mathis, Senior Reference Development Editor, APA Books

Typeset in Aylesbury, England, by Market House Books, Ltd.
Printer: United Book Press, Baltimore, MD
Cover Designer: Naylor Design, Washington, DC

Library of Congress Cataloging-in-Publication Data

APA dictionary of statistics and research methods / Sheldon Zedeck, editor in chief ; Lisa L. Harlow, Shelley A. Blozis, A. T. Panter, associate editors.
  pages cm
  ISBN-13: 978-1-4338-1533-1
  ISBN-10: 1-4338-1533-8
  1. Psychology—Research—Methodology. 2. Statistics—Methodology. I. Zedeck, Sheldon.
  BF76.5.A7263 2013
  150.72'7—dc23
                              2013017131

British Library Cataloguing-in-Publication Data
A CIP record is available from the British Library.

The citation for this publication is American Psychological Association. (2014). *APA dictionary of statistics and research methods*. Washington, DC: Author.

Printed in the United States of America
First Edition

DOI: 10.1037/14336.000

I dedicate this volume to the memory of my parents, Judith and Hyman; to the support and love from my brother Morris and his wife Ellen; to my mentors and colleagues who influenced my data analytic and research perspectives, particularly Carol Vale, Robert M. Guion, Patricia Cain Smith, Edwin E. Ghiselli, and Geoffrey Keppel; to my wife Marti, our children, and their spouses—Cindy and Jason Singer, Jason and Stacey Skura Zedeck, and Tracy; and to my grandchildren, Molly, Ella, Lilly, Aidan, and Noah, all of whom have played a statistically and practically significant role in my life.

—*Sheldon Zedeck*

I dedicate this volume and boundless gratitude to previous statistical mentors who got me started, particularly Peter Bentler, George Huba, and Edward Stearns; and to my husband, Gary, and daughter, Rebecca, who keep me going.

—*Lisa L. Harlow*

I dedicate this volume to my mentor and the driving inspiration of my work in quantitative methods, Robert Cudeck, and to the three most precious people in my life: Richard, Faustino, and Maximiliano, who give endless support and encouragement.

—*Shelley A. Blozis*

I dedicate this volume to my most inspirational quantitative mentors, Jeffrey S. Tanaka and Lyle V. Jones, and to my loving family—Nechama, Yaakov, George, Danielle, Michaela, Jonathan, Joshua, Giulia, Dara, Sarajane, and most of all my dad.

—*A. T. Panter*

Contents

Preface

The *APA Dictionary of Statistics and Research Methods* builds on a strong core of lexicographical reference works published in the past seven years by APA Books. APA inaugurated this collection with the parent *APA Dictionary of Psychology* (2006)—the culmination of some ten years of research and lexicographic activity. A resource of 25,000 entries, it won critical endorsement from both the publishing and reference library communities.

Two derivative works followed almost immediately: the abridged *APA Concise Dictionary of Psychology* (2008; available both in print and as an app for iPhone, iPad, and Android), whose 10,000 entries were selected for a more general readership, and the student version, the *APA College Dictionary of Psychology* (2009), which features 5,000 entries that are essential for psychology advanced placement high-school students and university-level psychology majors alike.

A third derivative (and the first with a subdisciplinary focus) followed in 2012: the *APA Dictionary of Clinical Psychology* (available in print and via Kindle). Its 11,000 entries directly address the needs of clinical psychologists, whether they work in health and mental health clinics, in independent and group practices, or as consultants to professionals in such fields as medicine, law, social work, and consumer relations. The content focuses on clinical training, clinical supervision, and the diagnosis, treatment, and prevention of emotional and behavioral disorders, with definitions describing the biological, developmental, social, and individual-difference underpinnings of health and mental health.

A fourth derivative, again subdisciplinary in nature, was published in 2013: The *APA Dictionary of Lifespan Developmental Psychology* is specifically tailored to offer scholars and students balanced coverage (in some 7,500 entries) in such core areas as developmental theory; genetics; and the biosocial, cognitive, and psychosocial perspectives of development. Entries span all the stages of life, from birth through childhood; through adolescence; and through the early, middle, and late periods of adulthood.

To some degree, editorial work on each of the derivatives noted above resulted in changes to APA's overall collection of dictionary terms, whether those changes are revisions or updates of entries that appeared in the parent dictionary or whether they are entirely new entries added to offer a more complete representation of the evolving lexicon of psychology.

The *APA Dictionary of Statistics and Research Methods,* however, has been something of a more consciously advanced enterprise in the development of our series. Although partially derived from the original corpus of terms in the parent dictionary, the work may more accurately be seen as APA's first endeavor to create an entirely new reference in this subarea—one that stands on its own and one that reaches out beyond psychology in its applicability to allied social, behavioral, and health sciences.

Evolution of the *APA Dictionary of Statistics and Research Methods*

In March 2009, the APA publisher began a search for an editor in chief (EIC) for a long-planned dictionary that would focus specifically on the two vital and related areas of statistics and research methods. The goal was to generate a focused specialty product that would use the content-specific corpus from the *APA Dictionary of Psychology* as a base but more than double the coverage to some 4,000 entries. Sheldon Zedeck (see About the Editorial Board, p. xvi) was the publisher's first choice to take the task in hand.

Zedeck began the process by identifying potential associate editors (AEs), both to help develop the project and to serve as peer reviewers and entry drafters. Because the dictionary is intended to cover *all* of psychology, and whereas the EIC's fields of specialization are industrial and organizational psychology and psychometrics, Zedeck undertook the task of identifying candidates who would bring diverse breadth and expertise to the project. To do so, he conducted a survey of all of the then-current editors of APA scholarly journals, asking them, in turn, to identify colleagues and journal peer reviewers who were methods and data analysis experts and upon whom the journal editors relied to review submitted articles that are especially centered on methodology or data analysis issues or that require special expertise from these perspectives. Specifically, the EIC requested that the journal editors identify, from among their most reliable reviewers, those whom they considered (a) most knowledgeable across different strategies and approaches, (b) highly articulate in explaining (communicating) shortcomings in strategy or analysis in plain English, (c) able to recognize alternative methods and strategies that would be more appropriate than those presented in article manuscripts, and (d) up-to-date in the latest methods and data analytic strategies.

The result of this survey was the identification and recruitment of five distinguished scholars: Daniel J. Bauer, Shelley A. Blozis, Lisa L. Harlow, Jay Myung, and A. T. Panter. All five editors were involved in the initial determination of which entries would constitute the corpus of this work (see Selection of Terms to Define, p. xi). Drs. Bauer and Myung were not able to continue beyond this first stage due to other commitments. Drs. Harlow, Blozis, and Panter, however, continued their roles as AEs throughout the entire editorial process (see their brief biographical descriptions, p. xvi) and were involved both in the review and editing of entries inherited from the parent *APA Dictionary of Psychology* and in the drafting of entirely new entries.

Selection of Terms to Define

The first task for the editorial team was to review more than 8,000 headwords (i.e., terms to define) collected for consideration by APA Reference staff from the original *APA Dictionary of Psychology*, other dictionaries, handbooks, articles in the APA journal *Psychological Methods*, and similar scholarly sources. The EIC divided the complete list of these potential headwords into three sections and assigned two members of the editorial team per section to assess which headwords should be included in the new dictionary. Each member independently ranked the headwords for their importance using the following coding system:

1. a basic concept in the field that is essential to understanding the topic area and must be included not only in the current specialty dictionary but also in any revised edition of the larger parent dictionary;
2. a more focused concept in the field that enhances understanding and should be included in the current specialty dictionary but not necessarily in the larger parent dictionary;
3. an outdated, overly detailed, or narrowly applicable concept that is inappropriate for the desired overall length and intended level of readership and thus should be omitted from the final product but nonetheless retained in the "consideration pool" for possible future use; or
4. a term that is not related to psychology in any way and should be deleted altogether from the consideration pool.

The rank codes were further defined for the editorial team as follows:

Rank 1: Essential vocabulary. Identify as Rank 1 all *essential* terms in current use that have a precise meaning to psychological research and the statistical analysis of psychological data. Thus, Rank 1 terms represent basic concepts without which one could not understand these fields. A term's use may be determined from its current prevalence in both scholarly and general psychological literature, its supporting relevance to key terms in the same literature, or both. Generally, Rank 1 terms are superordinate, comprising vocabulary that is the basis from which other words derive or to which they refer (relate back).

Also identify as Rank 1 any current terms in the culture at large that nonetheless significantly factor into psychological research and data analysis, even if these terms are controversial, misunderstood, or misused. For example, the term *power* is a general one with a commonly understood meaning, but it is applied much more specifically within data collection and analysis, both to refer to a mathematical notation indicating the number of times a quantity is multiplied by itself and to refer to the probability that the null hypothesis will be rejected when the alternative hypothesis is true.

Rank 2: Useful vocabulary. Identify as Rank 2 all *specific, more focused* terms in current use that have a precise meaning to psychological research and the statistical analysis of psychological data. In other words,

Rank 2 terms are those that provide more detailed knowledge of these fields but without which one still has a reasonably complete theoretical understanding. For example, complex alternative forms of the basic analysis of variance, such as the *between-subjects analysis of variance* and the *fixed-effects analysis of variance,* typically should be ranked a 2.

Rank 2 terms may also be those that are in the process of falling out of usage and generally are now understood by another name (e.g., *Brown–Spearman formula,* which is now typically referred to as the *Spearman–Brown prophecy formula*), those that have major historical importance to the development of the field or of its constructs (e.g., *hypothetico-deductive method,* which often appears in student or other literature dealing with the history and philosophy of psychology and related domains), or those that are so new as not to have yet gained widespread usage in the field (e.g., *experimenter biosocial effect*).

Rank 3: Unnecessary vocabulary. Identify as Rank 3 any terms that are *too specialized* or otherwise overly concentrated to be widely applicable within the field. For example, the term *between-subjects factorial analysis of variance,* a very specific combination of several other types of analysis of variance techniques, should be ranked a 3, because the separate entries for its component concepts (*analysis of variance, between-subjects analysis of variance,* and *factorial analysis of variance*) on their own are sufficient to enable a reader to understand the meaning of this more complicated, highly detailed concept.

Also identify as Rank 3 all terms that are *obsolete* within or *tangential* to psychological research and the statistical analysis of psychological data. In other words, Rank 3 terms are those that are no longer in use in these fields at all, rarely if ever appearing in current literature (e.g., *aftertest*), and those belonging primarily to other fields (e.g., quality management, economics) with minimal or no connection to psychology or its domains (e.g., *integer programming*).

During the ranking process, the editors researched various sources (particularly APA's *PsycINFO* database) to identify terms that were frequently used in the past decade. The EIC also responded to questions and comments from APA Reference and made general notes that would subsequently be helpful as definitions were finalized.

As each member of the pair of reviewing editors completed his or her batch of entries, the rankings were collated and the entire team was provided with the collective results for the purpose of resolving ranking discrepancies. If after further review the AEs still could not agree, the EIC resolved the ranking discrepancies, generally through mediation among the rankers.

In addition to ranking existing headwords, each editor was asked to identify new terms or words not on the list provided by APA Reference. Identification of such terms was achieved by relying on the editorial board members' expertise, as well as by examining vocabulary from a variety of professional sources, including scholarly journals, recent monographs, current handbooks, desk references, and other academic publications. These terms, too, were ranked. The entire selection process resulted in the retention of somewhat fewer than 5,000 headwords.

Editorial Process

In autumn 2010, the editorial board began to review, edit, and write definitions according to the following directives:

1. provide the *what*, *why*, and *how* for each term;
2. provide examples where possible;
3. use plain English instead of jargon; and
4. avoid the overuse of complicated formulas and equations.

A fifth directive was to consider whether an entry would benefit from a graphical or tabular illustration. Although there are clearly many entries that would benefit from graphical display, due to space considerations APA Reference ultimately researched and selected approximately 110 entries for illustration.

In spring 2012, the board presented its final set of definitions to APA Reference and Market House Books Ltd, the dictionary compiling professionals in the United Kingdom with whom APA Reference has worked on all its dictionaries to date. APA and Market House jointly began a final editorial and preproduction phase, generally cleaning up the copy in terms of redundant compounds, variant terms, and proper lexicographical format. In the end, some 4,080 entries were finalized for inclusion.

Future Perspectives

It is commonplace among those in the field of lexicography to assert that a dictionary—*any* dictionary, but *especially* a first edition—is a work-in-progress, the only limitations upon the future of which are the publishing company's continued interest in keeping the work alive and current and its ability to locate and task the appropriate people to provide solid content and stylistic expertise for revised and new editions.

We therefore issue this first edition of the *APA Dictionary of Statistics and Research Methods* with an eye to these potential limitations and with the recognition that, although all parties have collectively done the best they could—given the temporal imperatives of scholarly publishing—there is always room for correction and improvement. We are, in fact, proud of our work and send it out into the world confident that it is a very strong start, that it offers greater and better coverage than the competition of which we are aware, and that we fully intend to keep the work a living project in future generations.

To assist us in this task, we invite you to contact APA Reference at books@apa.org to note errors of omission, inaccuracies, infelicities of phrasing, new vocabulary, and omitted senses. As always, we welcome your thoughtful appraisal and suggestions.

Acknowledgments

The development and production of a dictionary requires an extraordinary amount of effort and collaboration with many participants. Our experiences as the editor and as publisher of this dictionary benefitted immensely from an incredible group of colleagues and staff who devoted many hours in guidance, consultation, demonstrated patience, fortitude, and energy. It is difficult to express our true appreciation to the many participants in a short space, but, to start, we want to acknowledge the associate editors: Shelley Blozis, Lisa Harlow, and Abigail Panter. This team contributed invaluable wisdom to the generation of the plan for the dictionary, spent endless hours reviewing potential entries, and spent even more hours writing and revising definitions. We also want to acknowledge the contribution of the consulting editors, Dan Bauer and Jay Myung, for their efforts in reviewing entries for possible inclusion in the dictionary. On the project genesis and development side, we owe gratitude and thanks to Ted Baroody (Director, Reference, APA Books) and to Trish Mathis (Senior Reference Development Editor, APA Books), who worked with the editorial team from day one, helping to generate the structure for the dictionary, reviewed drafts on process and procedure, and provided wise feedback on any issue requested throughout the project; they performed their tasks with grace and support that resulted in the final product being a personally rewarding partnership. Finally, we thank our consummately professional U.K. editorial and production team at Market House Books. We want to thank all of these participants for their support, encouragement, and wisdom.

Sheldon Zedeck, PhD
Editor in Chief

Gary R. VandenBos, PhD
Publisher

Editorial Staff

Editor in Chief

Sheldon Zedeck, PhD

Associate Editors

Lisa L. Harlow, PhD
Shelley A. Blozis, PhD
A. T. Panter, PhD

Consulting Editors

Daniel J. Bauer, PhD
Jay Myung, PhD

Senior Editor (American Psychological Association)

Patricia D. Mathis

Senior Editors (Market House Books, Ltd)

Jonathan Law
Elizabeth Martin

Assistant Editor (American Psychological Association)

Kristen L. Knight

Editor in Chief, *APA Dictionary of Psychology*

Gary R. VandenBos, PhD

About the Editorial Board

Sheldon Zedeck, PhD, is a professor of psychology and of the Graduate School at the University of California, Berkeley, and the 2010 recipient of The Berkeley Citation for distinguished service to the campus. He is an industrial/organizational psychologist who has published articles on the topics of moderator variables, selection and validation, test fairness, high-stakes testing, statistical banding, performance appraisal, assessment centers, stress, and work and family issues. He has coauthored texts on data analysis and measurement theory. He is former editor of the *Journal of Applied Psychology* (2003–2008) and the editor in chief for the *APA Handbook of Industrial and Organizational Psychology* (2010). His research on law school admissions received the 2011 Smashing Bias Research Award (with M. Shultz) from the Level Playing Field Institute for the Promotion of Outstanding Research on Ensuring Fairness From the Classroom to the Boardroom.

Lisa L. Harlow, PhD, is a professor of psychology at the University of Rhode Island, whose focus is on increasing interest, retention, performance, and diversity in quantitative science. Since obtaining her doctorate in 1985 from the University of California, Los Angeles, she has authored more than 75 publications on multivariate methods and applications. She is editor of *Psychological Methods* (2014–2019), current editor of the *Multivariate Applications Series*, and former associate editor of *Structural Equation Modeling*. She is also a past president of APA Division 5 (Evaluation, Measurement, and Statistics) and of the Society of Multivariate Experimental Psychology. Her honors include the Jacob Cohen Award for Distinguished Contributions to Teaching and Mentoring; a Distinguished Fellowship at the Institute for Advanced Study, University of Melbourne, Australia; and a Fulbright Scholar Award at York University, Toronto, Canada.

Shelley A. Blozis, PhD, is an associate professor of psychology at the University of California at Davis. She is a quantitative psychologist, obtaining her doctorate from the University of Minnesota, who has published articles on mixed models for longitudinal data and methods for missing data. She has served on the editorial board of *Psychological Methods* since 2003.

A. T. Panter, PhD, is the Bowman and Gordon Gray Distinguished Professor of Psychology at the University of North Carolina at Chapel Hill. She develops instruments, research designs, and data-analytic strategies for applied research questions in higher education, personality, and health. She is an American Psychological Association fellow, a member of the Graduate Record Examinations Advisory Board, and a former member of a Social Security Administration advisory panel to revise occupational information systems used for disability determination. She and three other colleagues conducted the Educational Diversity Project to examine links among race and other factors and educational diversity in law students around the U.S., and she has coedited books on research design and quantitative methods, including the *APA Handbook of Research Methods in Psychology* (2012), the *Handbook of Ethics in Quantitative Methodology* (2011), and *The Sage Handbook of Methods in Social Psychology* (2004).

Quick Guide to Format

accuracy *n.* **1.** lack of error or BIAS in a measure; the more accurate the measure, the closer the measurement is to the TRUE SCORE for an individual. **2.** a measure of performance on a task, usually defined as the proportion of correct responses. **—accurate** *adj.*

Akaike's information criterion (AIC) a SUMMARY STATISTIC used in comparing the relative GOODNESS OF FIT of two or models for a given set of data, while taking into account the number of parameters in each model. The model with the lowest AIC is considered the best among all models specified. [Hirotsugu **Akaike** (1927–2009), Japanese statistician]

autocorrelation *n.* the situation in which values of a variable measure over time are correlated with other values of the same series separated from them by a specific interval. This often occurs with economic or demographic data. Autocorrelations are generally assumed to be linear relationships and may be presented graphically in an **autocorrelogram** (or **correlogram**) or formulaically in an **autocorrelation function (ACF)**. Also called **serial correlation**. See TIME-SERIES ANALYSIS.

axis *n.* (*pl.* **axes**) a fixed reference line in a coordinate system. See also ABSCISSA; ORDINATE.

Aa

A-B-A-B-A design a type of SINGLE-CASE DESIGN having five consecutive phases: a baseline condition in which no treatment is present (Phase A), a treatment condition in which a manipulation is introduced (Phase B), a return to the no-treatment condition (Phase A), a reintroduction of the treatment (Phase B), and a subsequent return to the no-treatment condition (Phase A). It is an extension of the A-B-A-B DESIGN that provides stronger causal evidence of a relationship between the treatment and a consequential change in the DEPENDENT VARIABLE by removing the treatment a second time. See also A-B-A DESIGN; A-B-A-C-A DESIGN.

A-B-A-B design a type of SINGLE-CASE DESIGN having four phases: a baseline condition in which no treatment is present (Phase A), a treatment condition in which a manipulation is introduced (Phase B), a return to the no-treatment condition (Phase A), and a subsequent reintroduction of the treatment (Phase B). In evaluating the treatment twice, the A-B-A-B design helps to establish causality by providing evidence of a repeated relationship between the introduction and removal of the treatment and a consequential change in the DEPENDENT VARIABLE. See also A-B-A-B-A DESIGN; A-B-A DESIGN.

A-B-A-C-A design a type of SINGLE-CASE DESIGN having five consecutive phases: a baseline condition in which no treatment is present (Phase A), a treatment condition in which a manipulation is introduced (Phase B), a return to the no-treatment condition (Phase A), a new treatment condition in which a different manipulation is introduced (Phase C), and a subsequent return to the no-treatment condition (Phase A).

The A-B-A-C-A design helps to establish the effects on the DEPENDENT VARIABLE of alternating treatments by evaluating the relationship between the introduction and removal of one treatment and a subsequent introduction and removal of a second treatment. See also A-B-A-B-A DESIGN.

A-B-A design a type of SINGLE-CASE DESIGN having three phases: a baseline condition in which no treatment is present (Phase A), a treatment condition in which a manipulation is introduced (Phase B), and a return to the no-treatment condition (Phase A). The design allows for evaluation of the introduction of the treatment by comparing the DEPENDENT VARIABLE between the first two phases (A-B sequence) as well as evaluation of the removal of the treatment by comparing the dependent variable between the last two phases (B-A sequence). This greatly reduces the possibility of a coincidental treatment effect, which may occur in the simpler A-B DESIGN. See also A-B-A-B-A DESIGN; A-B-A-B DESIGN.

A-B design the simplest SINGLE-CASE DESIGN, comprising a pretreatment or baseline phase (Phase A) followed by a treatment phase (Phase B). Although it allows for evaluation of the treatment's effect by comparing the DEPENDENT VARIABLE during the two phases, the design does not provide evidence of causality since it does not establish a repeated relationship between the introduction and removal of the treatment and a consequential change in the dependent variable (compare A-B-A DESIGN). See also PRETEST–POSTTEST DESIGN.

abduction *n.* the process of studying an event or phenomenon in order to generate possible explanatory hypotheses. The object is to determine which hypotheses should be tested, rather than which should be adopted as correct. —**abduct** *vb.*

ability level an index of achievement or performance that reports the absolute or relative ability of the participant in relation to the trait or characteristic being assessed.

ability parameter (symbol: θ) in ITEM RESPONSE THEORY, a theoretical value that represents a person's capability or probable performance on a task. It is assumed that test takers possess some degree of underlying ability, and that for each individual at each ABILITY LEVEL there is a specific ITEM CHARACTERISTIC CURVE defining the probability of responding correctly.

ability scale a set of values that represent increasingly higher levels of performance on a test or set of tasks. Ability scales are ORDINAL measures, as the distances between any two adjacent scale values are not equal and the value of zero is arbitrary. See also DIFFICULTY SCALE.

abscissa *n.* the horizontal coordinate in a graph or data plot; that is, the *x*-axis. See also ORDINATE.

absolute deviation the distance between a data point and a measure of CENTRAL TENDENCY, such as the mean. The absolute deviation does not indicate the direction of difference. For example, if the mean is 10 a value of 18 and one of 2 both show an absolute deviation from the mean of 8; the signs associated with +8 and –8 are ignored.

absolute difference the distance between two numeric values disregarding whether this is positive or negative. The absolute difference thus provides no information about relative magnitude. For example, the absolute difference between 11 and 20 is 9, as is the absolute difference between 13 and 4.

absolute error the degree to which an observation is inaccurate without specification of whether it errs by being too high or too low. Absolute error is computed as the average ABSOLUTE DIFFERENCE between the intended or expected value and the actual value. See also CONSTANT ERROR; RANDOM ERROR.

absolute frequency see FREQUENCY.

absolute measurement a measurement made directly and independently of comparison with other measurements. An absolute measurement of an individual's height, for instance, would yield a single definitive value that need not be assessed relative to another person to be meaningful. Compare RELATIVE MEASUREMENT.

absolute rating scale a type of assessment instrument in which the targets (e.g., people, objects) are not compared with other targets or a standard stimulus but are judged in absolute terms. For instance, a respondent may be presented with the options *excellent, good, fair,* and *poor* and asked to choose the one that best describes his or her current state of health. Compare COMPARATIVE RATING SCALE.

absolute true score 1. a value for a random variable that exists independently of any test used to measure the variable. For example, an individual has an absolute true score for blood pressure or cholesterol level regardless of the accuracy of any tests used to measure these scores. **2.** an average score that is derived from testing every member of a population (e.g., every child of a certain age in the state), rather than one derived from a sample of that population.

absolute value a number considered without regard to its algebraic sign (i.e., whether it is positive or negative). For example, assume that for each person in a weight management program there was a number indicating the difference between the current week's weight and the weight on the previous week. This could reveal a negative number (e.g., –1) if the person lost one pound; conversely it could be a positive value (e.g., +1) if the person weighed one pound more than last week. If the absolute value of the weight difference was taken, it would simply reveal a difference of 1 pound, without any indication of whether it was plus or minus. Also called **modulus**.

absolute zero a value on a measurement scale that denotes the complete absence of the measured characteristic. A RATIO SCALE has an absolute zero, whereas an INTERVAL SCALE does not. Also called **true zero**.

absorbing state a condition from which there is no possibility of transitioning to another condition. In a sequence of events such as a MARKOV CHAIN, for example, a state is absorbing if there is zero probability of leaving that state once it has been obtained. Compare TRANSIENT STATE.

accelerated failure time model in SURVIVAL ANALYSIS, a model in which the response variable is a known transformation of the time until the event of interest occurs. When this transformation is the LOGARITHM, the model is referred to more specifically as a **censored linear regression model**. In aging research, for example, an investigator might use an accelerated failure time model to evaluate whether a specific intervention increases lifespan.

accelerated longitudinal design see COHORT-SEQUENTIAL DESIGN.

acceleration n. in mathematics and statistics, the rate of change in the SLOPE of a function or the rate of change in one variable as a function of an increase in a second variable. Compare DECELERATION.

acceptance region the range of values for a test statistic that leads to acceptance of the NULL HYPOTHESIS, such that the ALTERNATIVE HYPOTHESIS is rejected as a valid explanation for observed data. Compare CRITICAL REGION.

acceptance–rejection method see REJECTION METHOD.

acceptance sampling a process in which a random sample is chosen from a larger group of items and used to make a decision about the quality of the items in that group. Acceptance sampling is often used in commerce to test the quality of merchandise in a batch: A random sample from the batch is inspected and the results used to determine whether the batch as a whole meets desired standards or whether it fails to meet standards and should be rejected as defective. Also called **lot acceptance sampling**.

accessible adj. in a MARKOV CHAIN, describing a state j that there is a possibility of reaching from another state i in some number of steps. —**accessibility** n.

accidental sampling see CONVENIENCE SAMPLING.

accrual rate the rate at which something accumulates. For example, the accrual rate of volunteers to participate in a research study may be documented and used to help determine how best to recruit individuals for similar studies in the future.

accuracy n. **1.** lack of error or BIAS in a measure; the more accurate the measure, the closer the measurement is to the TRUE SCORE for an individual. **2.** a measure of performance on a task, usually defined as the proportion of correct responses. —**accurate** adj.

ACE abbreviation for ALTERNATING CONDITIONAL EXPECTATION.

ACES abbreviation for ACTIVE CONTROL EQUIVALENCE STUDY.

ACF abbreviation for AUTOCORRELATION function.

acquiescent response set see YEA-SAYING.

action research socially useful and theoretically meaningful research developed and carried out in response to a social issue or problem, results of which are applied to improve the situation

A

(e.g., by changing existing or developing new public policies).

active control equivalence study (**ACES**) a three-group experimental design in which one group receives the treatment of interest, a second group receives a comparable standard treatment, and a third CONTROL GROUP receives a PLACEBO. The two treatment groups are compared to each other to assess their equivalence and also are compared to the placebo group to evaluate the efficacy of the treatments.

active control trial a two-group experimental design in which one group receives the treatment under study and the second group receives a comparable standard treatment. Although efficacy generally is best evaluated by comparing a treatment to a PLACEBO, active control trials are used in situations when withholding treatment from individuals by assigning them to a placebo group is not ethical. Compare PLACEBO CONTROLLED TRIAL.

active deception intentionally misleading research participants by giving them false information in order to get more valid results. For example, a researcher might present participants with incorrect correlations between gender and performance in different academic subject areas before testing whether such hypothetical statistics affect subsequent performance on different achievement tests. Also called **deception by commission**. Compare PASSIVE DECEPTION. See DECEPTION RESEARCH.

activity log a diary kept by a researcher or research participant of activities in various settings. An activity log may include information about the location of the participant by time period (e.g., at home, at work, traveling) and whether the time is spent alone or with family, friends, or work associates. An activity log as a method of obtaining a record of events generally is superior to interviews based on a participant's memory.

actuarial *adj.* in medicine, describing an approach to diagnosis and treatment that uses data about previous events to estimate the likelihood of a particular outcome. An actuarial approach will rely on statistically established relationships to reach conclusions or make decisions about, say, which approach to use in treating a particular disorder. Compare CLINICAL.

acyclic digraph see DIRECTED ACYCLIC GRAPH.

AD abbreviation for average deviation. See MEAN ABSOLUTE DEVIATION.

adaptation period a period of time during which a research participant becomes accustomed to the materials, instruments, or equipment to be used in a study or reaches a certain performance level. Adaptation periods help reduce the influence of situational novelty on a participant's behavior.

adaptive cluster sampling an ADAPTIVE SAMPLING scheme that also involves an element of CLUSTER SAMPLING. The study population is divided into a number of equally sized clusters, one of which is randomly drawn and examined. If the units in the set meet the predetermined criteria, then adjacent sets are chosen and evaluated. If the adjacent sets also meet the criteria, they too are added to the sample and additional sets are selected. The process continues until cases are found that do not meet the criteria.

adaptive method any procedure tailored to a given problem or situation. Examples of adaptive methods include ADAPTIVE TESTING, in which items change in response to an examinee's performance, and ALGORITHMS that adjust to a given data problem to optimize performance of the algorithm in that particular instance.

adaptive sampling a method of sampling data in which information from past outcomes is used to reduce the chances of collecting future data that correspond to poor outcomes. A group of individuals randomly chosen from the population of interest is evaluated and the information gathered is used to concentrate additional selection efforts where they are most likely to be successful. For example, if a researcher is interested in studying a certain animal of a particular age, he or she could first assess a subset of animals from a given geographical area and then target further sampling efforts in the specific portions of that area shown to possess the most animals meeting the criteria.

adaptive testing a testing technique designed to adjust to the response characteristics of individual examinees by presenting items of varying difficulty based on the examinee's responses to previous items. The process continues until a stable estimate of the ABILITY LEVEL of the examinee can be determined. See also ITEM RESPONSE THEORY.

added-variable plot a method of displaying data in which the variance remaining in a response or DEPENDENT VARIABLE after it has been predicted by one or more INDEPENDENT VARIABLES is plotted against the variance remaining after a new independent variable is added. In other words, added-variable plots show the result of adding another variable to the model while taking into account the effects of the other independent variables already in the model. Also called **partial regression plot**.

addition rule a maxim of probability theory stating that the likelihood of observing a set of distinct events is equal to the sum of the probabilities of observing the individual events. Also called **addition law; or rule**. Compare MULTIPLICATION RULE.

additive *adj.* characterized or produced by addition. For example, a FUNCTION is said to be additive when the quantities defining it may be summed to obtain a meaningful result. An additive function is also known as a LINEAR FUNCTION. Compare NONADDITIVE.

additive effect the constant effect of one PREDICTOR VARIABLE on a DEPENDENT VARIABLE across all levels of other related predictors. Thus, the total effect of all predictors is equal to the sum of their individual effects, with no INTERACTION EFFECT.

additive model a description of the relationship between a response variable and a set of predictor variables in which the effect of each predictor is assumed to be the same across all levels of the other predictors in the model. Thus, the combined effect of all predictors is determined by summing their individual effects.

additive scale a scale with all points distributed equally so that a meaningful result can be obtained by addition (e.g., a metric ruler).

additivity test a method used to evaluate whether the effects of each of a set of predictor or INDEPENDENT VARIABLES on a DEPENDENT VARIABLE are constant across all levels of the other predictors included in the model. A significant result from this test indicates that the relationship of interest is not an ADDITIVE EFFECT but is characterized by one or more INTERACTION EFFECTS between the independent variables.

adequate sample a SAMPLE that adequately represents the larger population from which it was drawn in terms of size, being large enough to provide satisfactory PRECISION by minimizing the possibility of chance affecting the data obtained.

ad hoc for a particular purpose or in response to some particular event or occurrence. For example, an **ad hoc committee** is convened on a short-term basis to address a single problem, and an **ad hoc hypothesis** is an explanation of a particular phenomenon, rather than a general theory. [Latin, literally: "to this"]

adj R² symbol for ADJUSTED R².

adjusted effect the effect of a predictor or INDEPENDENT VARIABLE on a response or DEPENDENT VARIABLE after the influence of one or more other predictors has been removed. For example, a researcher might find that education level predicts income via the MEDIATOR of residential area; an adjusted effect would be one without the influence of the mediator included.

adjusted mean 1. in ANALYSIS OF VARIANCE, the average score value (MEAN) obtained after removing all differences that can be accounted for by COVARIATES. **2.** a mean value obtained after removing any OUTLIERS.

adjusted R the correlation between scores on a response or DEPENDENT VARIABLE and the values predicted by a set of INDEPENDENT VARIABLES, after accounting for the number of predictors and the number of observations involved in the calculation. See also MULTIPLE CORRELATION COEFFICIENT.

adjusted R^2 (symbol: adj R^2; R^2_{adj}) the square of the correlation between scores on a response or DEPENDENT VARIABLE and the values predicted by a set of INDEPENDENT VARIABLES after accounting for the number of predictors and the number of observations involved in the calculation. It gives the proportion of the variance in a response that is accounted for by its relationship with the predictors and yields a better estimate of the population variance than the ADJUSTED R upon which it is based. In an ANALYSIS OF VARIANCE or MULTIPLE REGRESSION the adjusted R^2 often is known as EPSILON SQUARED. Also called **shrunken R^2**. See also COEFFICIENT OF MULTIPLE DETERMINATION.

adjusted standard deviation for a set of scores, a measure of the DISPERSION of these scores about the mean after taking into account the fact that this mean is an estimate of the true value in a larger population of interest. It is calculated in the same manner as the STANDARD DEVIATION generally except that $N - 1$ is used as the denominator in the formula instead of N (where N = sample size), thus providing an unbiased estimate of the POPULATION STANDARD DEVIATION.

adjusted variance the square of the ADJUSTED STANDARD DEVIATION. The adjusted variance is an unbiased estimate of the POPULATION VARIANCE.

adjusting for baseline a method of accounting for preexisting differences between individuals or groups prior to examining the effect of a treatment or experimental condition. For example, a researcher may wish to determine whether a certain training program improves a person's performance on a task. He or she might adjust for baseline by administering the individual a practice test to determine the initial performance level before holding a series of training sessions and then administering a posttest to determine the new performance level. If the DIFFERENCE SCORE between the two tests is significantly dissimilar there is some evidence that performance is improved after the training session.

admissible hypothesis a HYPOTHESIS that is logically possible and open to empirical testing given a specific set of conditions.

adoption study a research design that investigates the relationships among genetic and environmental factors in the development of personality, behavior, or disorder by comparing the similarities of biological parent–child pairs with those of adoptive parent–child pairs.

AEq abbreviation for AGE EQUIVALENT.

age calibration a process in which a test score is assigned a value so that the score may be interpreted relative to other test takers in the same age range.

age cohort see COHORT.

age effect in research, any outcome associated with being a certain age. Such effects may be difficult to separate from COHORT EFFECTS and PERIOD EFFECTS.

age equivalent (AEq) a measure of development or performance expressed in terms of the average chronological age at which the observed score is obtained. For example, assume a student obtains a score of 95 on a particular test, a value typical of the average performance of students in the eighth grade. Thus, the age equivalent of 95 is 13, the age of most eighth graders. Also called **age-equivalent score; test age**.

age-equivalent scale a system for expressing test scores in terms of the chronological ages at which the scores are typically obtained.

age-grade scaling a method of standardizing a test by establishing norms based on a sample of children who are of the typical chronological age for their grade in school.

agglomerative clustering a procedure used to combine separate entities into homogeneous sets (clusters) by forming pairs of similar entities and then pairing these pairs until all are merged into one large group. That is, in agglomerative clustering one focuses initially upon each individual or object and moves progressively "upward" to combine them into a single, agglomerative group or cluster. It is one of two types of HIERARCHICAL CLUSTERING, the other being DIVISIVE CLUSTERING. Also called **agglomerative hierarchical clustering; bottom-up (hierarchical) clustering; hierarchical agglomerative clustering**.

aggregate data scores or observations that have been re-expressed by a SUMMARY STATISTIC. Calculating the arithmetic average of a set of test scores obtained over time for each individual in a group and then using each person's single average score as representative of their test performance would be an example of aggregating data.

aggregation *n.* in statistics, a process of combining and summarizing a set of scores into a smaller set of scores that capture an aspect of the original set. See AGGREGATE DATA. Compare DISAGGREGATION. —**aggregate** *vb.* —**aggregative** *adj.*

aggregation problem the difficulty of drawing conclusions or making inferences about an individual on the basis of data for a group or population. See ECOLOGICAL FALLACY.

agreement coefficient see COEFFICIENT OF AGREEMENT.

AH abbreviation for ALTERNATIVE HYPOTHESIS.

AID abbreviation for AUTOMATIC INTERACTION DETECTOR.

Akaike's information criterion (AIC) a SUMMARY STATISTIC used in comparing the relative GOODNESS OF FIT of two or more models for a given set of data, while taking into account the number of parameters in each model. The model with the lowest AIC is considered the best among all models specified. [Hirotsugu **Akaike** (1927–2009), Japanese statistician]

algorithm *n.* a well-defined procedure or set of rules that is used to solve a particular problem or conduct a series of computations, usually in a limited number of steps. —**algorithmic** *adj.*

alienation coefficient see COEFFICIENT OF ALIENATION.

allocation ratio a ratio of the number of individuals assigned to one treatment condition to the number assigned to a different condition that serves to maximize the ability of a statistical test to detect a difference in a measured outcome between the conditions.

allocation rule see CLASSIFICATION RULE.

all-possible-subsets multiple correlation a measure of the degree of association between an outcome variable and its corresponding predicted value based on a given set of predictors from an analysis in which all possible subsets from a finite pool of predictors have been evaluated. See ALL-POSSIBLE-SUBSETS REGRESSION.

all-possible-subsets regression a method for predicting an outcome variable based on a series of equations formed by all possible subsets of predictors from a finite pool of predictors. The "best" subset is identified using criteria established by the researcher, such as the value of AKAIKE'S INFORMATION CRITERION or of the COEFFICIENT OF MULTIPLE DETERMINATION. Also called **all-possible-subsets multiple regression; setwise regression**.

alpha (symbol: α) *n.* **1.** the likelihood of incorrectly rejecting a statement or hypothesis concerning a characteristic of a population. More specifically, it is the probability of incorrectly rejecting a true NULL HYPOTHESIS (i.e., committing a TYPE I ERROR) in research. Although the value of alpha is chosen by the investigator based on what is deemed acceptable for a particular study, alpha values of .05 and .01 are commonly used. **2.** a measure of RELIABILITY for a set of responses to a test or measure. See CRONBACH'S ALPHA.

alpha coefficient see CRONBACH'S ALPHA.

alpha error see TYPE I ERROR.

alpha level see SIGNIFICANCE LEVEL.

alternate form a set of test items that are developed to be similar to another set of test items, so that the two sets represent different versions of the same test. Each item set is intended for the same purpose (i.e., measures the same concept) and is administered in the same manner. In order to demonstrate that one test is an alternate form of the other, a researcher usually must show that there is matching content (each test has the same number of each kind of item) and that FACTOR LOADINGS and MEA-

SUREMENT ERRORS are approximately the same across the two versions. Also, each version should yield similar score distributions (i.e., similar MEANS and STANDARD DEVIATIONS). Alternate forms of a test can be used to measure its reliability (see ALTERNATE-FORMS RELIABILITY). Also called **alternative test form; comparable form; equivalent form; parallel form**.

alternate-forms reliability a measure of the consistency and freedom from error of a test, as indicated by a CORRELATION COEFFICIENT obtained from responses to two or more ALTERNATE FORMS of the test. Also called **comparable-forms reliability; equivalent-forms reliability; parallel-forms reliability**.

alternating conditional expectation (**ACE**) an algorithm designed to obtain optimal TRANSFORMATIONS in data analysis. In MULTIPLE REGRESSION, for example, where a response or DEPENDENT VARIABLE is predicted by several INDEPENDENT VARIABLES and where it is assumed that the effects of each of the predictors are constant, ACE may be used to find a transformation that maximizes the proportion of variance in one variable that is explained by the others.

alternating treatments design a type of study in which the experimental condition or treatment assigned to the participant changes from session to session or within sessions. For example, a researcher comparing two methods for eliminating the disruptive classroom behavior of a student might have the teacher use one method throughout the morning and the other method throughout the afternoon and then evaluate the student's behavior with each technique.

alternative hypothesis (**AH**; symbol: H_1, H_a) a statement that is contrasted with or contradicts the NULL HYPOTHESIS as an explanation for observed data. Generally, it is a scientific prediction of significant results in HYPOTHESIS TEST-

ING; that is, an alternative hypothesis posits meaningful differences or relationships between the variables under investigation.

alternative hypothesis distribution a theoretical set of plausible values of a characteristic under certain assumptions that is compared to its corresponding NULL DISTRIBUTION in the process of conducting a POWER ANALYSIS.

alternative test form see ALTERNATE FORM.

AML abbreviation for ASYMMETRIC MAXIMUM LIKELIHOOD.

analogue observation a response recorded from a participant in an ANALOGUE STUDY designed to induce a particular behavior in a controlled environment, such as a laboratory or clinic. Compare NATURALISTIC OBSERVATION; SELF-MONITORING OBSERVATION.

analogue sample a group of individuals selected for inclusion in a study who possess the symptoms of a particular disorder but who have not sought treatment for the disorder. For example, a researcher may use college students with mild problems resembling those seen in outpatient clinical settings and expose them to specific therapy techniques to study their responses.

analogue study a study intended to induce a particular behavior under controlled environmental conditions that resemble or approximate the real-world situation of interest. Examples include the use of hypnosis, drugs, and sensory deprivation in a laboratory setting to induce brief periods of abnormal behavior that simulate those of psychopathological conditions. Also called **analogue design**; **analogue experiment**; **analogue research**.

analysis of covariance (**ANCOVA**) an extension of the ANALYSIS OF VARIANCE that adjusts for the influence of a COVARIATE in testing whether there is a significant difference between means of two or more groups on one or more INDEPENDENT VARIABLES. In other words, it is a statistical method of studying the responses of different groups to a DEPENDENT VARIABLE that adjusts for the influence of a variable that is not being investigated but nonetheless is related to the dependent variable and thus may influence the study results. An analysis of covariance is appropriate in two types of cases: (a) when experimental groups are suspected to differ on a background-correlated variable in addition to the differences attributed to the experimental treatment (i.e., the analysis corrects for chance differences between groups that arise when participants are assigned randomly to the treatment groups) and (b) where adjustment on a covariate can increase the precision of the experiment (i.e., reduce the ERROR TERM). For example, suppose a researcher analyzes whether there is a difference in learning among three types of instruction—in-class lecture, online lecture, and textbook only. He or she divides a random selection of adult students into three groups, implements the different instruction types, and administers the same test to all participants to determine how much they learned. If the researcher knows each participant's educational background, he or she could use an analysis of covariance to adjust the treatment effect (test score) according to educational level, which would reduce the observed variation between the three groups caused by variation in education levels rather than by the instruction itself.

analysis of covariance structures a method of examining the relationships among a set of variables with regard to how each one varies according to variation in the others. It is similar to STRUCTURAL EQUATION MODELING but distinguished by its emphasis on simultaneous variation (i.e., covariance). Also called **covariance structure analysis**.

analysis of unweighted means see UNWEIGHTED MEANS ANALYSIS.

analysis of variance (**ANOVA**) a statistical method of studying the variation in responses of two or more groups on a DEPENDENT VARIABLE. ANOVAs test for significant differences among the mean response values of the groups and can be used to isolate both the joint INTERACTION EFFECTS and the separate MAIN EFFECTS of INDEPENDENT VARIABLES.

analysis of weighted means a method of comparing samples of unequal sizes in which the data for each group are averaged in a manner that takes into account the differing number of observations contributing to the calculation. See WEIGHTED AVERAGE.

analysis unit see UNIT OF ANALYSIS.

analytic approach any method based on breaking down a complex process into its parts so as to better understand the whole. For example, a researcher studying cognition in children might identify such component skills as problem solving, reasoning, imagination, and memory; examine each in turn; and then detemine how they interact. Compare SYNTHETIC APPROACH.

analytic induction a QUALITATIVE RESEARCH strategy for developing and testing a theory in which the researcher tentatively defines a phenomenon, creates a hypothesis to explain it, and examines a single specific occurrence of the phenomenon in order to confirm or refute the hypothesis. If the hypothesis is confirmed, additional cases are examined until a sufficient degree of certainty about the correctness of the hypothesis is obtained and the study may be concluded. If the hypothesis is not confirmed, the phenomenon is redefined or the hypothesis revised so as to accommodate the findings.

anchor *n.* a number or descriptive quality used as a point of reference for making a subjective judgment. For instance, a study participant may be asked to rate his or her health on a scale that uses an upper anchor labeled *perfect health*.

anchor test a set of test items used as a reference point in comparing ALTERNATE FORMS of a test. One alternate form is administered to one group of participants, another is administered to a different group, and the items comprising the anchor test are administered to both groups. Scores on each alternate form are then compared with scores on the anchor test.

ANCOVA acronym for ANALYSIS OF COVARIANCE.

Andersen–Gill model an extension of the COX REGRESSION ANALYSIS model that is used in SURVIVAL ANALYSIS for data that show LEFT CENSORING, time-varying COVARIATES, recurrent events, and discontinuous intervals of risk. [Per Kragh **Andersen** (1952–), Danish statistician; Richard D. **Gill** (1951–), British-born Dutch mathematician]

Anderson–Darling test see DARLING TEST. [Theodore W. **Anderson** (1918–), U.S. mathematician; Donald A. **Darling** (1915–), U.S. mathematician]

Andrews plot a method for displaying multidimensional data using only two dimensions in which one curve is generated for each row of data, as in the hypothetical illustration overleaf. Here f(*t*) is a function derived for an observation (e.g., occupation type) that is based on multiple variables (e.g., education required, starting salary, promotion opportunities). The different values of *t* indicate the similarity of the three occupations shown. [David F. **Andrews**, Canadian statistician]

and rule see MULTIPLICATION RULE.

anecdotal method an investigational technique in which informal verbal reports of incidents casually observed are accepted as useful information. The anecdotal method is scientifically inadequate but can offer clues as to areas of investigation that warrant more systematic, controlled research.

angular transformation see ARC SINE TRANSFORMATION.

animal rights the belief that animals

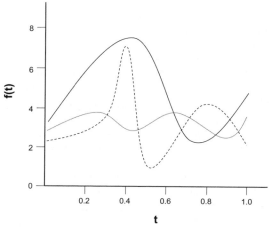

f(t) (vertical axis)

t (horizontal axis)

Andrews plot

should be treated with respect and be free from exploitation and abuse by humans. Animal research is monitored in many universities and other organizations by an animal care committee, whose purpose is to ensure the humane care and use of animals by assuring compliance with federal and state regulations and by supporting veterinary oversight and continuing education and training.

anonymity *n.* a principle of research ethics stating that the identity of a study participant should remain unknown. Relatedly, CONFIDENTIALITY applies to situations in which a participant's identity is known but should not be disclosed by the researcher.

ANOVA acronym for ANALYSIS OF VARIANCE.

ANOVA summary table a table pre-

senting the most important DESCRIPTIVE STATISTICS obtained from an ANALYSIS OF VARIANCE (ANOVA). It typically provides the DEGREES OF FREEDOM, the SUM OF SQUARES, the MEAN SQUARE, the F RATIO, and the SIGNIFICANCE LEVEL associated with each effect studied, as in the example below.

Ansari–Bradley test a NONPARAMETRIC procedure for determining the equivalence of two samples without requiring that the variables of interest have a NORMAL DISTRIBUTION. Rather, it assumes the middle values of the distributions are equal and evaluates whether the DISPERSIONS are equal, whether the scores within each sample are independent, and whether the shapes of the distributions are identical.

Anscombe residual a particular type

Source	df	SS	MS	F	p
Lecture topic (L)	2	1,200	600	21.18	< .001
Presentation method (P)	1	2,200	2,200	77.66	< .001
L × P interaction	2	700	350	12.35	< .001
Error	60	1,700	28.33		

ANOVA summary table

of error or unexplained variance in a response variable that does not require the values of the response variable to follow a NORMAL DISTRIBUTION. It is used with GENERALIZED LINEAR MODELS. [Francis J. Anscombe (1918–2001), British statistician]

antecedent variable any variable that precedes a response variable. For example, in REGRESSION ANALYSIS it is the INDEPENDENT VARIABLE, in a MEDIATIONAL PROCESS it is the intervening variable, and in PATH ANALYSIS it is the variable beginning a chain of causal links. Compare CONSEQUENT VARIABLE.

antedependence *n.* a relationship among multiple values of a response variable observed over time such that each value depends upon one or more previous values. See AUTOCORRELATION.

A-optimal design a research design in which the set of INDEPENDENT VARIABLES causing the least average variance in a DEPENDENT VARIABLE is chosen from a larger pool of possible variables for predicting values of that variable. See also D-OPTIMAL DESIGN; E-OPTIMAL DESIGN.

a posteriori denoting conclusions derived from observations or other manifest occurrences: reasoning from facts. Compare A PRIORI. [Latin, "from the latter"]

a posteriori comparison see POST HOC COMPARISON.

apparatus *n.* any instrument or equipment used in an experiment or other research.

apparent error rate the inaccuracy that can be observed when applying a REGRESSION EQUATION hypothesizing associations among a set of variables to a set of actual data points. An estimate of how well the model fits the data, the apparent error rate often underestimates the true error rate.

apparent limit the lower or upper bound of a CLASS INTERVAL within which a data point may fall. For example, in displaying ages from 1 to 100, a researcher may use intervals such as 1–10, 11–20, and so forth. The values determining the intervals (e.g., 1 and 10) are the apparent limits.

applied research studies conducted to solve real-world problems, as opposed to studies that are carried out to develop a theory or to extend basic knowledge. Examples include ACTION RESEARCH and EVALUATION RESEARCH. Compare BASIC RESEARCH.

applied science research conducted to serve a practical human purpose rather than with the purpose of extending knowledge for its own sake. Compare BASIC SCIENCE.

applied statistics the use of statistical methods and procedures to understand data in psychology, sociology, economics, and other disciplines. Compare THEORETICAL STATISTICS.

apprehensive-subject role behavior displayed by a research participant who dislikes being evaluated or is otherwise anxious about the study but nonetheless tries to do well and convey a positive impression. Compare FAITHFUL-SUBJECT ROLE; GOOD-SUBJECT ROLE; NEGATIVISTIC-SUBJECT ROLE.

approximate bootstrap confidence method a procedure in which many subsets of an observed sample data set are used to produce a range of plausible values for a population characteristic, such as the MEAN or VARIANCE. It is less computationally involved than similar BOOTSTRAPPING methods.

approximation *n.* the process of obtaining a value that is at least close to the desired or actual value. For example, one might round a measurement to the nearest decimal place for ease of subsequent calculations. The degree of inaccuracy inherent to this process is known as **approximation error**.

a priori denoting conclusions derived

from premises or principles: deducing from prior assumptions. Compare A POS-TERIORI. [Latin, "prior to"]

a priori comparison any examination in which two or more quantities are compared in accordance with plans established prior to conducting the research study. For example, even before data are collected, a researcher might hypothesize that two groups given personal instruction would show better mean performance on a task compared to those who receive only written instruction. Thus, he or she could decide in advance to compare the combined personal instruction groups to the written instruction group. The researcher might also decide ahead of time to compare one personal instruction group with the other as an additional a priori comparison. Also called **a priori contrast**; **planned comparison** (or **contrast**). Compare POST HOC COMPARISON.

aptitude–treatment interaction (**ATI**) see TRAIT–TREATMENT INTERACTION.

arbitrary constant in an equation, an undetermined quantity whose value is unchanged across units so as to ensure the solution conforms to certain requirements.

arbitrary origin a value chosen as a reference point for other values. In some calculations, it is convenient to express a set of scores as DEVIATIONS about an arbitrarily chosen point of origin (such as the MEAN of a distribution) to ease later computational burdens.

arbitrary weight a WEIGHT used to assign different levels of importance to different entities that is not specific to a procedure or data set.

archival data information about past events, behaviors, and other phenomena that are stored in a relatively permanent form, particularly as used in ARCHIVAL RESEARCH. Also called **archival records**.

archival research the use of books,

journals, historical documents, and other existing records or data available in storage in scientific research. Archival research allows for unobtrusive observation of human activity in natural settings and permits the study of phenomena that otherwise cannot easily be investigated. A persistent drawback, however, is that causal inferences are always more tentative than those provided by laboratory experiments. Also called **archival method**.

arc sine transformation a means of changing proportional data to approximate a NORMAL DISTRIBUTION: Percentages that denote counts or frequencies are converted into a new set of scores whose distribution assumes a bell-shaped curve. The process minimizes variances across the different groups being compared and allows for the application of certain analytic techniques requiring that normality and other AS-SUMPTIONS be met. Also called **angular transformation**; **arcsine transformation**; **inverse sine transformation**.

area sampling a method of selecting individuals for research in which specific neighborhoods, streets, homes, or other geographic areas are designated in advance as the source of participants.

area under the curve (**AUC**) in a graphical display of a DISTRIBUTION, the region between the plotted function and the horizontal x-axis. It is used in such calculations as determining the probability of the occurrence of specific values of a RANDOM VARIABLE.

argument n. a sequence of propositions that provides logical reasons for accepting a conclusion as valid or true. A single one of these statements is referred to as a **premise**.

ARIMA model acronym for AUTORE-GRESSIVE INTEGRATED MOVING-AVERAGE MODEL.

arithmetic mean see MEAN.

arithmetic progression a sequence of numbers in which the difference between consecutive numbers is a fixed value. For example, the numbers 1, 5, 9, 13, and 17 form an arithmetic progression. Also called **arithmetic sequence**; **arithmetic series**.

ARMA model abbreviation for AUTO-REGRESSIVE MOVING-AVERAGE MODEL.

AR model abbreviation for AUTORE-GRESSIVE MODEL.

array *n.* any ordered arrangement of data, particularly a two-dimensional grouping of data into rows and columns. The following listing of students' scores on a test is an example of a simple array:

Student A	55
Student B	76
Student C	81
Student D	82
Student E	89
Student F	90
Student G	90
Student H	90
Student I	94
Student J	98

The concept may be extended to more than two dimensions.

artifact *n.* an experimental finding that is not a reflection of the true state of the phenomenon of interest but rather is the consequence of a flawed design or analytic error. For example, characteristics of the researcher (e.g., expectations, personality) or the participant (e.g., awareness of the researcher's intent, concern over being evaluated) are common sources of artifacts. See also CONFOUND; DEMAND CHARACTERISTICS.

ascertainment bias error in selecting individuals or units for a sample, such that those units selected are not representative of the relevant population. For example, a medical researcher who studies a sample of patients that omits certain types of people who have the disorder of interest is likely to obtain results having an ascertainment bias. The term is often preferred over SAMPLING BIAS in clinical contexts.

Aspin–Welch–Satterthwaite test (**AWS test**) a statistical method used to evaluate the NULL HYPOTHESIS regarding the differences between two sample means when the population variances are not equal. It is a proposed solution to the BEHRENS–FISHER PROBLEM and thus may not be appropriate when data are not normal. Also called **Aspin–Welch test**; **Welch test**. [Alice A. **Aspin**; B. L. **Welch**, British statistician; F. E. **Satterthwaite**]

assessment *n.* in research, a systematic process of obtaining information from participants and using it to make inferences or judgments about them.

assessment–classification model a system in which a profile of scores is used to evaluate and group individuals, as opposed to using a score average or some other summary measure. For example, members of a human resources department at an organization might first determine the characteristics of job candidates and analyze the requirements of different types of jobs at the company, then classify or match specific people with specific job types.

assessment instrument any test, interview, questionnaire, or other tool for the evaluation of ability, achievement, interests, personality, psychopathology, or the like.

assessment research the study of an organizational unit in order to understand its functioning and make recommendations for improvements or changes. See also EVALUATION RESEARCH.

association *n.* the degree of statistical dependence or relationship between two or more phenomena. See also CORRELATION; STRENGTH OF ASSOCIATION. **—associative** *adj.* **—associational** *adj.*

association analysis see CORRELATION ANALYSIS.

association model a method used to

study the strength of relationship between a predictor variable and a response variable where values for the latter take the form of ORDINAL DATA. More specifically, it tests for STATISTICAL INDEPENDENCE between the variables.

assumption *n.* one or more conditions that need to be met in order for a statistical procedure to be fully justified from a theoretical perspective. For example, ANALYSIS OF VARIANCE assumes HOMOGENEITY OF VARIANCE and independence of observations, among other criteria. If the assumptions were to be violated to an extreme extent, the results would be invalid. See also ROBUSTNESS.

assumption of equal variance see HOMOGENEITY OF VARIANCE.

assumption of independence the ASSUMPTION that scores in one data set are unrelated to scores in another data set.

assumption of normality the ASSUMPTION that a set of scores follow a particular function described by a bell-shaped curve (i.e., the NORMAL DISTRIBUTION).

asymmetrical confidence interval a range of plausible values for an unknown population characteristic the upper and lower bounds of which are not equidistant from the center of the range. Thus, each side of the CONFIDENCE INTERVAL is distinct from the other. Compare SYMMETRICAL CONFIDENCE INTERVAL.

asymmetrical distribution any nonnormal distribution: a set of ordered scores in which the frequency of values is not equal above and below the center or midpoint of the set. If one divides the distribution at its MEAN, the arrangement of scores differs across the two halves. See SKEWNESS. Compare SYMMETRICAL DISTRIBUTION.

asymmetrical test 1. any of various statistical methods used to evaluate an entity whose range of values is not assumed to be uniformly arranged about a midpoint. **2.** an infrequent synonym of DIRECTIONAL TEST.

asymmetric maximum likelihood (**AML**) an alternative method of model fitting in REGRESSION ANALYSIS. It is a form of MAXIMUM LIKELIHOOD used when there is a high degree of scatter or dispersion around the REGRESSION LINE.

asymmetry *n.* SKEWNESS: the condition in which the values of a data set are not arranged equally around a center point. Compare SYMMETRY. —**asymmetrical** *adj.*

asymptote *n.* a straight line that defines the limit of a curve, such that the curve continues to approach but never reaches the line. The concept of asymptote is often invoked in relation to the learning curve. Participants in learning studies often show a steady improvement in performance that then levels off as the curve approaches asymptote; any further improvements will be minimal, regardless of further practice or training.

asymptotically unbiased describing a statistical procedure that on average yields an increasingly true population value as the number of observations upon which it is based increases. Thus, an **asymptotically unbiased estimator** on average yields a correct calculation of a population characteristic as the sample size used approaches infinity.

asymptotic curve a curved line possessing an upper or lower limit (the ASYMPTOTE) that is approached but never reached.

asymptotic distribution a THEORETICAL DISTRIBUTION that takes the form of an ASYMPTOTIC CURVE when plotted. Asymptotic distributions are used in hypothesis testing, for example, to generate theoretically derived competing distributions such as the NULL DISTRIBUTION and the ALTERNATIVE HYPOTHESIS DISTRIBUTION.

asymptotic method any statistical procedure for estimating a population quantity that becomes more accurate as the number of observations involved in the calculation increases. Asymptotic methods use assumptions—including EFFICIENCY, NORMALITY, and SYMMETRY—that generally are not absolutely true for finite samples but that become steadily more true as sample sizes increase. Also called **large-sample method**.

ATI abbreviation for aptitude–treatment interaction. See TRAIT–TREATMENT INTERACTION.

attention-placebo control group a set of research participants who are given an inert treatment (PLACEBO) with cognitive requirements resembling those of the actual treatment under investigation. Their responses function as a psychologically neutral condition against which to assess the effectiveness of the treatment under study. For example, a researcher investigating a new imagery-based stroke therapy would need to ensure all participants have the same experience, regardless of the experimental group into which they are placed, in order to attribute any differences in outcome to the therapy. By replicating the nonactive characteristics necessary for delivery of the therapy, the researcher thus ensures the members of an attention-placebo control group are subject to the same time, attention, and other cognitive demands as they would be had they received the actual treatment.

attenuation *n.* an underestimation of the size of an effect or relationship due to poor measurement or RESTRICTION OF RANGE. See also CORRECTION FOR ATTENUATION.

attribute testing the assessment of the abilities or skills possessed by a research participant prior to the participant's involvement in a research study.

attribute variable a preexisting characteristic of a study participant, such as ethnic background or age, that is not changed during the course of the research but is considered in conjunction with an experimental manipulation or intervention. Attribute variables may be CATEGORICAL or CONTINUOUS.

attrition *n.* the loss of study participants over time. Attrition may occur for a variety of reasons (e.g., the nature of the data being collected, participant relocation, aversive or costly data collection procedures) and can threaten the EXTERNAL VALIDITY and INTERNAL VALIDITY of research. It also creates the potential for BIAS—individuals who drop out may have unique characteristics that are relevant to the phenomenon of interest such that the remaining sample is no longer representative of the population—and may reduce the POWER of statistical analyses.

AUC abbreviation for AREA UNDER THE CURVE.

audit *n.* an evaluation of a service, intervention, or outcome. In research it refers to an examination of the soundness of a study's findings.

auditory test any test intended to evaluate a person's hearing ability. For example, one might measure the difference in time between presentation of a sound and a participant's response, such as pressing a specific letter on a keyboard.

autocorrelation *n.* the situation in which values of a variable measured over time are correlated with other values of the same series separated from them by a specific interval. This often occurs with economic or demographic data. Autocorrelations are generally assumed to be linear relationships and may be presented graphically in an **autocorrelogram** (or **correlogram**) or formulaically in an **autocorrelation function** (ACF). Also called **serial correlation**. See TIME-SERIES ANALYSIS.

autocovariance *n.* in a STOCHASTIC PROCESS, the COVARIATION of a variable with earlier or later versions of itself.

Covariance implies that the variability is linear as opposed to nonlinear.

automatic interaction detector (**AID**) a method of accounting for variation in a single response variable using a set of predictors. Values of the response variable are sequentially broken down into smaller and relatively more homogeneous subsets according to one or more of the predictor variables that best achieve this goal. See also CHI-SQUARE AUTOMATIC INTERACTION DETECTOR.

autoregression *n.* a pattern of relationship between repeated measures of a variable taken over time, such that the variable as observed at one point in time is predicted by the variable observed at one or more earlier points in time. See TIME-SERIES ANALYSIS.

autoregressive integrated moving-average model (**ARIMA model**) a strategy for modeling and forecasting TIME-SERIES DATA that are presumed to have a steady underlying trend. It is an extension of the AUTOREGRESSIVE MOVING-AVERAGE MODEL that examines the differences between successive values in the time series instead of the values themselves. Also called **Box–Jenkins model**.

autoregressive model (**AR model**) a model used to represent TIME SERIES that demonstrate AUTOREGRESSION, that is, where each successive observation depends, at least in part, on one or more previously observed values.

autoregressive moving-average model (**ARMA model**) a strategy for modeling and forecasting TIME-SERIES DATA that involve AUTOCORRELATION. Incorporating components of both an AUTOREGRESSIVE MODEL and a MOVING-AVERAGE MODEL, it relies on two patterns of relationship between observations of a variable taken over time: The first allows a score at one point in time to be predicted by a previously observed score, and the second allows a score at one point in time to be predicted by an unobserved score at a previous occasion. ARMA models incorporating additional space–time variation are called SPACE–TIME AUTOREGRESSIVE MOVING-AVERAGE MODELS.

available-case analysis see PAIRWISE DELETION.

average *n.* see MEAN.

average absolute deviation see MEAN ABSOLUTE DEVIATION.

average deviation (**AD**) see MEAN ABSOLUTE DEVIATION.

average error the typical degree to which a series of observations are inaccurate with respect to an absolute criterion (e.g., a standard weight or length) or a relative criterion (e.g., the mean of the observations within a given condition).

average-linkage clustering a multivariate procedure for grouping individuals or entities into clusters (homogeneous groups) on the basis of a set of relevant variables. Each individual is assigned to his or her own cluster initially and at each subsequent step the most similar pair of clusters are merged into a new group. The process continues until all individuals have been combined into one large cluster. The process may be mapped in a DENDROGRAM. Average-linkage clustering is one of several forms of AGGLOMERATIVE CLUSTERING procedures. Also called **group-average clustering**. Compare COMPLETE-LINKAGE CLUSTERING; SINGLE-LINKAGE CLUSTERING.

averages law see LAW OF LARGE NUMBERS.

AWS test abbreviation for ASPIN–WELCH–SATTERTHWAITE TEST.

axis *n.* (*pl.* **axes**) a fixed reference line in a coordinate system. See also ABSCISSA; ORDINATE.

Bb

background variable see SUBJECT VARIABLE.

back-to-back stem-and-leaf plot a variation of a STEM-AND-LEAF PLOT in which the trailing digits (leaves) from two data sets are displayed on either side of the same central column of initial values (stem). The leaf values from one data set are given on the right-hand side while those of the second group are shown on the left-hand side. For example, consider the following hypothetical sets of test scores obtained by participants on two different occasions:

79 79 83 83 86 87 92 99

and

80 81 82 83 87 87 90 99

The back-to-back stem-and-leaf plot for these values is

```
        | 7 | 9 9
0 1 2 3 7 7 | 8 | 3 3 6 7
      0 9 | 9 | 2 9
```

back-translation see TRANSLATION AND BACK-TRANSLATION.

backward elimination a technique used in REGRESSION ANALYSIS in which the goal is to forecast an outcome or response variable according to a subset of predictor variables narrowed down from a large initial set. In background elimination, all available predictors are included originally and then examined one at a time, with any predictors that do not contribute in a statistically meaningful manner systematically dropped until a predetermined criterion is reached. Also called **backward deletion; backward selection; stepdown selection**. See also STEPWISE REGRESSION.

bagplot *n.* an extension of a BOX-AND-WHISKER PLOT to two variables, simultaneously summarizing the data for both and showing the degree of relationship between them. It includes a filled square or other shape indicating the MEDIAN of the scores, a **bag** or shaded polygon encircling the middle 50% of scores, a **loop** or differently shaded polygon encircling the remaining data points, and a **fence** or curve marking the edge of the loop beyond which any OUTLIERS are displayed. The DISPERSION of the data points is indicated by the size of the bag, while the shape and orientation of the bag indicate SKEWNESS and correlation, respectively. A generic example is given opposite.

Balaam's design an experimental approach in which participants are divided into four groups and experience different conditions or treatments (A and B) in one of four possible sequences: AA, BB, AB, or BA. More specifically, in one sequence participants receive the first treatment over two periods, in a second sequence participants receive the second treatment over two periods, in a third sequence participants receive the first treatment in the first period and the second treatment in the second period, and in the fourth sequence participants receive the second treatment in the first period and the first treatment in the second period. A type of CROSSOVER DESIGN, Balaam's design is used in studies in which a treatment CARRYOVER EFFECT is anticipated. [L. N. **Balaam**, Australian biometrician]

balanced design any research design in which the number of observations or measurements obtained in each experimental condition is equal. For example, a health researcher interested in exercise and depression would be using a bal-

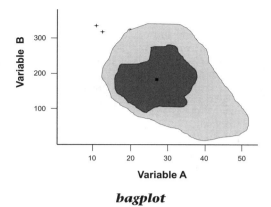

bagplot

anced design if he or she examined 50 people who exercise less than 30 minutes per day, 50 people who exercise between 30 and 60 minutes per day, and 50 people who exercise more than 60 minutes per day.

balanced Latin square a type of study design in which multiple conditions or treatments are administered to the same participants over time. It is a form of LATIN SQUARE that must fulfill three criteria: Each treatment must occur once with each participant, each treatment must occur the same number of times for each time period or trial, and each treatment must precede and follow every other treatment an equal number of times. For example, consider the following balanced Latin square for an experimental design involving four treatments (A, B, C, and D) and four people:

| | Treatment Order | | | |
	1	2	3	4
Participant 1	A	B	D	C
Participant 2	B	C	A	D
Participant 3	C	D	B	A
Participant 4	D	A	C	B

As shown, one person receives the treatments in the sequence A, B, D, and then C; a second person receives them in the sequence B, C, A, and D; a third person receives them in the sequence C, D, B, and A; and a fourth person receives them in the sequence D, A, C, and B.

balanced longitudinal data observations or measurements collected from the same individuals on multiple occasions and within the same time frame for each period. For example, a researcher may survey all of the children in a particular classroom at 9 a.m., 12 p.m., and 3 p.m. on a particular day. If, however, the researcher were to survey some of the children at 9 a.m., some at 12 p.m., and some at 3 p.m., then the observations would be **unbalanced longitudinal data**.

balanced repeated replication (**BRR**) a statistical procedure used to calculate the variance associated with an estimated value for a population PARAMETER. In this method, the data set is divided into two equal portions and the parameter calculated for one of those halves. The original full data set is then divided a second time and a new parameter calculation obtained, with the process continuing a given number of times to generate a set of estimates from which a measure of the variance can be calculated for the entire data set. BRR is similar to other resampling techniques, such as BOOTSTRAPPING and the JACKKNIFE, but uses half of the sample at a time and also takes into account complex sample characteristics.

balanced replication 1. a strategy for conducting a study at two or more locations in which the different conditions

B

or treatments are randomly assigned to participants and administered the same number of times at each location. **2.** an occasional synonym for BALANCED REPEATED REPLICATION.

balanced scale a test or survey in which, for each possible response, there is a response that means the opposite. A rating scale with the four alternatives *very poor*, *poor*, *good*, and *very good* is an example, as is a set of survey questions in which half of the questions characterize a particular trait (e.g., perceived stress level) in one direction (e.g., low) and the other half characterize the trait in the opposite direction (e.g., high).

balancing score a score used for MATCHING participants in a treatment group and a comparison group on some variable, with the goal of forming groups that have identical distributions of values for that variable. A PROPENSITY SCORE is an example.

band chart a type of LINE GRAPH in which different subsets of data for the same variable are displayed in different shaded areas or strata. For example, a band chart might present overall weekly sales of a company's product as well as the portion of such that were completed online and the portion completed through calls to the customer service department. Also called **stratum chart**.

banding a strategy for personnel selection, whereby scores on an employment test are broken into bands based on its RELIABILITY, STANDARD ERROR OF MEASUREMENT, and STANDARD ERROR OF ESTIMATE. Banding assumes that there is substantial unreliability in any single observed score and that candidates who score within the same band are equally qualified. Consequently, hiring decisions are made from within band ranges, in contrast to traditional approaches that choose the highest scorer first, the next highest scorer second, and so forth.

bar graph a graph in which bars of varying height with spaces between them are used to display data for variables defined by qualities or categories. For example, to show the political affiliations of Americans, the different parties would be listed on the *x*-axis, and the height of the bar rising above each party would represent the number or proportion of people in that category. Also called **bar chart**; **bar diagram**. See also HISTOGRAM.

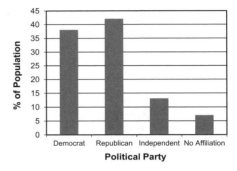

Bartlett's correction a modification applied to improve the quality of the statistic obtained from the LIKELIHOOD-RATIO TEST, which is used to evaluate hypotheses about the relationships among a set of variables. Also called **Bartlett's adjustment** (**factor**). [Maurice Stevenson **Bartlett** (1910–2002), British statistician]

Bartlett test for eigenvalues in PRINCIPAL COMPONENTS ANALYSIS, a procedure used to test for HOMOGENEITY OF VARIANCE across a set of EIGENVALUES. [Maurice Stevenson **Bartlett**]

Bartlett test for equality of variance a procedure used to determine whether variation across two or more groups is equal, this being a critical assumption in ANALYSIS OF VARIANCE and many other parametric methods. The Bartlett test is sensitive to scores that are not from a NORMAL DISTRIBUTION. Also called **Bartlett–Box test**; **Bartlett test for homogeneity of variance**; **Bartlett's test**. [Maurice Stevenson **Bartlett**; George E. P. **Box** (1919–), British statistician]

Bartlett test of sphericity a method often used in FACTOR ANALYSIS or PRINCIPAL COMPONENTS ANALYSIS to determine whether variables in a population are unrelated. Specifically, the test is used to assess whether a population CORRELATION MATRIX has ones along the diagonal and zeros for the remaining elements, a pattern that implies that all of the variables in the set are uncorrelated with each other. See also MAUCHLY'S SPHERICITY TEST. [Maurice Stevenson **Bartlett**]

baseline *n.* data or information obtained prior to or at the onset of a study (e.g., before introduction of an intervention) that serves as a basis for comparison with data collected at a later point in time so as to assess the effects of particular manipulations or treatments. For example, a memory researcher may measure how many words from a list participants remember initially and then compare that figure to the number of words they remember following the use of a new mnemonic technique (i.e., the experimental manipulation).

baseline assessment a process of obtaining information about a participant's status (e.g., ability level, psychological well-being) before exposure to an intervention, treatment, or other study manipulation. The information so obtained is compared to data gathered during the course of the research in order to identify any effects associated with the study conditions.

baseline characteristic any of various qualities of a participant that are assessed prior to a study or intervention as they may potentially influence outcome measures. For example, a researcher evaluating the effect of a new stress-reduction technique on health status may examine such baseline characteristics as sex, age, and ethnicity.

baseline hazard function in SURVIVAL ANALYSIS, the SURVIVAL FUNCTION obtained for an at-risk individual when all COVARIATES are set at zero.

basement effect see FLOOR EFFECT.

base rate the naturally occurring frequency of a phenomenon in a population. An example is the percentage of students at a particular college with major depressive disorder. This rate is often contrasted with the rate of the phenomenon under the influence of some changed condition in order to determine the degree to which the change influences the phenomenon.

base year a 12-month period used as a reference in constructing an index. A base year is chosen (e.g., 2012) and set to some arbitrary value (e.g., 100), and differences between that base year and other years are then calculated to determine the amount of change.

basic research research conducted to obtain greater understanding of a phenomenon, explore a theory, or advance knowledge, with no consideration of any direct practical application. Also called **pure research**. Compare APPLIED RESEARCH.

basic science scientific research or theory that is concerned with knowledge of fundamental phenomena and the laws that govern them, regardless of the potential applications of such knowledge. Also called **fundamental science; pure science**. Compare APPLIED SCIENCE.

bathtub curve a type of SURVIVAL CURVE that has a specific shape with three major parts: an initial decreasing trend, which is followed by a relatively stable and unchanging trend, which in turn is followed by an increasing trend.

Bayes estimator a rule for estimating the value of a population characteristic that is based on both empirically obtained data and one's prior expectations regarding the parameter of interest. For example, to estimate the mean student score on a particular test using this method, one would not only analyze the scores of a sample of students but also take into account whatever information is already available about values on that variable in the population. [Thomas **Bayes** (1702–1761), British mathematician and theologian]

Bayes factor in BAYESIAN theory, a quantification of the extent to which sample data favor one model over another: It is the probability of obtaining a given set of observed data assuming that the NULL HYPOTHESIS is true, divided by the probability of obtaining the same data assuming that a contradictory ALTERNATIVE HYPOTHESIS is true. Small values are taken as evidence against the null hypothesis, as they indicate that obtained observations are relatively more likely under the alternative hypothesis. Also called **Bayes ratio**. [Thomas **Bayes**]

Bayesian *adj.* denoting an approach to statistical inference and probability that enables previously known (a priori) information about a population characteristic of interest to be incorporated into the analysis. In Bayesian methods, estimated quantities thus are based in part on empirical data (i.e., what was actually observed) and in part on collective or individual knowledge about what to expect in the population (as captured in a PRIOR DISTRIBUTION). See also POSTERIOR DISTRIBUTION. [Thomas **Bayes**]

Bayesian confidence interval see CREDIBLE INTERVAL. [Thomas **Bayes**]

Bayesian controversy the long-running debate about the relative merits of the two major perspectives in statistics and probability, namely, the BAYESIAN approach and the FREQUENTIST approach. [Thomas **Bayes**]

Bayesian inference a method of drawing conclusions about a characteristic of a population using both sample data and previously known information about that characteristic. It relies upon BAYES THEOREM to derive POSTERIOR DISTRIBUTIONS from obtained observations and PRIOR DISTRIBUTIONS. Compare FREQUENTIST INFERENCE. [Thomas **Bayes**]

Bayesian information criterion (**BIC**) in BAYESIAN statistics, a summary value used in comparing the relative fit of one model to another for a given set of data. Although adding to the complexity of a model often will improve fit to a set of data, the Bayesian information criterion adds a penalty for each such addition, such that relative model fit also is judged in terms of model parsimony (simplicity). [Thomas **Bayes**]

Bayesian model averaging (**BMA**) a BAYESIAN approach to data analysis in which two or more models are considered to account for patterns in observed data and the level of certainty (i.e., PRIOR DISTRIBUTION) associated with each model is examined and combined to yield a single POSTERIOR DISTRIBUTION for the set of models as a whole. The technique can be applied to any set of plausible models of a certain class (e.g., structural equation models, regression models). [Thomas **Bayes**]

Bayesian network a graphical representation of a set of RANDOM VARIABLES and their probabilistic relationships that takes into account uncertainty in the proposed system. For example, a Bayesian network could display the likeliness of being diagnosed with a particular illness given the presence of various symptoms. [Thomas **Bayes**]

Bayes theorem a formula for calculating the probability that an event will occur that allows for the acquisition of new information regarding that event. For example, consider the probability that an individual will have a stroke within the next year. Using Bayes theorem, one could take an estimate of this probability based on general population data for that individual's age group (i.e., the PRIOR PROBABILITY) and revise it to account for the results of that person's stress tests and other cardiological markers, creating what is known as the POSTERIOR PROBABILITY. [Thomas **Bayes**]

BC*a* (**BC*a***) abbreviation for BIAS-COR-

RECTED ACCELERATED PERCENTILE IN-TERVAL.

B coefficient see REGRESSION COEFFI-CIENT.

before–after design see PRETEST–POSTTEST DESIGN.

behavioral profile an overall representation of the behavioral characteristics of a participant or group of participants in a test or experiment, often used to study patterns and trends.

behavioral science any of various disciplines devoted to the scientific study of human and animal actions and reactions using systematic observation and experimentation. Psychology, sociology, and anthropology are examples.

behavior checklist a list of actions, responses, or other behaviors that are to be recorded each time they are observed, as by an experimental investigator, study participant, or clinician.

behavior coding a method of recording observations in which defined labels are used by specially trained individuals to denote specific qualities and characteristics of behaviors as they are witnessed. For example, a developmental researcher might use the following coding scheme for infant vocalizations: (1) vowels; (2) syllables (i.e., consonant–vowel transitions); (3) babbling (a sequence of repeated syllables); and (4) other (e.g., cry, laugh, vegetative sounds). Behavior coding systems typically are specific to a given study and the behaviors under investigation.

behavior diary a detailed log of a person's activities or responses as recorded by a trained observer or the individual him- or herself, usually on a regular basis over a specified interval of time. For example, a behavior diary might be used to log a study participant's activities over a 24-hour period.

behavior observation the recording or evaluation of the ongoing behavior of one or more research participants by one or more observers. Behavior observation may be carried out live or through video media and often involves the use of rating scales, checklists, or charts.

behavior rating use of a scale to assess the degree to which an individual displays one or more behaviors in a given situation.

behavior sampling a data collection method in which the behaviors of one or more individuals are observed and recorded during a designated period of time. Observations can be made in either a natural or a research setting, and they may be conducted over multiple time periods with or without the awareness of the individual being observed.

Behrens–Fisher problem the problem of comparing the means of two samples drawn from different populations when the variances of these populations are not assumed to be equal. In other words, the problem involves the difficulty of making statistical inferences in the absence of equal population variances. The Behrens–Fisher problem may be addressed in many ways, such as by using a T TEST to estimate a PROBABILITY LEVEL (p value) or by using CONFIDENCE INTERVALS to estimate the range of uncertainty around the mean difference. [W. U. **Behrens**; Sir Ronald Aylmer **Fisher** (1890–1962), British statistician]

bell curve the characteristic curve obtained by plotting the values of a NORMAL DISTRIBUTION. The shape resembles a cross-sectional representation of a bell (i.e., a large rounded central peak tapering off on either side). Also called **bell-shaped distribution**.

Bentler–Bonett index in STRUCTURAL EQUATION MODELING, a value that reflects the degree to which a hypothesized pattern of relationships among variables is consistent with the observed pattern in a specific data set, relative to an alternative pattern that assumes that the variables are entirely unrelated to one another. It differs from the Bentler comparative FIT INDEX (CFI) in being normed. Also called **normed fit index** (**NFI**). [Peter M. **Bentler**, U.S. quantitative psychologist; Douglas G. **Bonett**, U.S. psychometrician]

Bernoulli distribution a theoretical distribution of the number of trials required before the first success is obtained in a BERNOULLI PROCESS. Such a distribution is defined by two values: 0 and 1. Usually a value of 0 is used to denote a failure (i.e., the item of interest does not occur) and a value of 1 is used to denote a success (i.e., the item of interest does occur). On this basis, the likeliness of a success is denoted as p and the likeliness of a failure is denoted as $q = 1 - p$. For example, a single toss of a coin has a Bernoulli distribution with $p = 0.5$ (where 0 = heads and 1 = tails). A Bernoulli distribution is a special case of a BINOMIAL DISTRIBUTION. [Jacques **Bernoulli** (1654–1705), Swiss mathematician and scientist]

Bernoulli process a sequence of unrelated events whose outcome values can only be equal to 0 or 1 (denoting either failure or success) with each outcome having the same probability. For example, the results from tossing a coin a given number of times when the conditions for each toss of the coin are identical could be described as a Bernoulli process. In other words, a Bernoulli process is a sequence of BERNOULLI TRIALS. [Jacques **Bernoulli**]

Bernoulli's theorem see LAW OF LARGE NUMBERS. [Jacques **Bernoulli**]

Bernoulli trial a single experiment in which the only two possible outcomes are success or failure. Usually a value of 0 is used to denote a failure (i.e., the item of interest does not occur) and a value of 1 is used to denote a success (i.e., the item does occur). A sequence of Bernoulli trials is known as a BERNOULLI PROCESS. See also BERNOULLI DISTRIBUTION. [Jacques **Bernoulli**]

Bernoulli variable a variable that can take on only one of two possible values indicating either success or failure. Usually a value of 0 is used to denote a failure and a value of 1 is used to denote a success. See BERNOULLI PROCESS; BERNOULLI DISTRIBUTION. [Jacques **Bernoulli**]

Bessel's correction an adjustment used to reduce bias when calculating the VARIANCE and STANDARD DEVIATION in a sample. Specifically, it is the use of $n - 1$ instead of n in the denominator of the computational formulas used to compute these values, where n is the number of observations in the sample. [Friedrich Wilhelm **Bessel** (1784–1846), German-born Russian astronomer and mathematician]

best estimator the statistic obtained from a sample data set that over repeated sampling exhibits the least amount of variance relative to other statistics in estimating the corresponding value in the larger population.

best fit the theoretical pattern that best accounts for the relationships among variables in a data set. For example, a REGRESSION EQUATION having the best fit to sample data is the one that minimizes differences between observed and predicted values. On a SCATTERPLOT, a **line of best fit** provides a visual depiction of this pattern, allowing extrapolation to values not part of the original data set. It is important to note that the best-fitting pattern is not necessarily the one that generated the observed data, as other patterns not considered may provide a superior fit.

best linear unbiased estimator (**BLUE**) the LINEAR EQUATION that most accurately characterizes the relationship between an outcome variable and a set of predictor variables when applied to a sample data set. Thus, the quantity obtained from a BLUE on average equals the quantity in the larger population from which it is derived and over repeated sampling has the least amount of variation relative to other procedures. See also GAUSS–MARKOV THEOREM.

beta (symbol: β) *n.* **1.** the likeliness of committing a TYPE II ERROR in research. **2.** the effect of a predictor variable on an outcome variable, such as in REGRESSION ANALYSIS or STRUCTURAL EQUATION MODELING.

beta coefficient the multiplicative constant in a REGRESSION ANALYSIS that indicates the change in an outcome variable associated with the change in a predictor variable after each has been standardized to have a distribution with a mean of 0 and a STANDARD DEVIATION of 1. A beta coefficient controls for the effect of other predictors included in the analysis and thus allows for direct comparison of the individual variables despite differences in measurement scales (e.g., salary measured in dollars and educational degree measured in years of schooling). Also called **beta weight**; **standardized regression coefficient**.

beta distribution a family of PROBABILITY DISTRIBUTIONS whose values range from 0 to 1 and whose shape is defined by two quantities (parameters) referred to as α and β. A beta distribution provides the likelihood of obtaining each of the possible values within the 0, 1 range.

beta error see TYPE II ERROR.

beta level the likeliness of failing to reject the NULL HYPOTHESIS when it is in fact false; that is, the probability of making a TYPE II ERROR. The beta level for a given statistical procedure is related to the POWER of that procedure (β level = 1 − power).

beta weight see BETA COEFFICIENT.

between-groups analysis of variance see BETWEEN-SUBJECTS ANALYSIS OF VARIANCE.

between-groups degrees of freedom in an ANALYSIS OF VARIANCE for data from a BETWEEN-SUBJECTS DESIGN, the number of groups to be compared minus one. For example, the between-groups DEGREES OF FREEDOM in a study examining the effectiveness of four different therapies for depression would be 3 (i.e., one less than the number of therapy groups being examined). This quantity is used to calculate the BETWEEN-GROUPS MEAN SQUARE. Also called **between-conditions degrees of freedom**; **between-subjects degrees of freedom**; **between-treatments degrees of freedom**. Compare WITHIN-GROUPS DEGREES OF FREEDOM.

between-groups design see BETWEEN-SUBJECTS DESIGN.

between-groups mean square in an ANALYSIS OF VARIANCE, an index of the variance among the different levels of the INDEPENDENT VARIABLE being analyzed: It is calculated by dividing the BETWEEN-GROUPS SUM OF SQUARES by the BETWEEN-GROUPS DEGREES OF FREEDOM. The between-groups mean square forms the numerator of the F RATIO. Also called **between-conditions mean square**; **between-groups variance**; **between-subjects mean square**; **between-subjects variance**; **between-treatments mean square**; **between-treatments variance**; **mean square between**. Compare WITHIN-GROUPS MEAN SQUARE.

between-groups sum of squares in an ANALYSIS OF VARIANCE, a quantity that is used to determine the BETWEEN-GROUPS MEAN SQUARE. It is calculated by adding together the squared differences between each group average (MEAN) in a set and the overall average (GRAND MEAN), with each squared difference weighted by the number of members in the respective group. Also called **between-conditions sum of squares**; **between-subjects sum of squares**; **between-treatments sum of squares**. Compare WITHIN-GROUPS SUM OF SQUARES.

between-groups variance see BETWEEN-GROUPS MEAN SQUARE.

between-subjects analysis of variance an examination of the variance in a set of data obtained from a study in which a different group of participants is randomly assigned to each condition. In this procedure, the researcher determines how much of the variance in the obtained data is due to the influence of the variables under investigation and how much is due to random differences among the group members. For example, a researcher studying how amount of daily walking (e.g., none, 30 minutes, 60 minutes, 90 minutes) affects quality of sleep might divide participants into different groups that each walk for one of the specified lengths of time and then evaluate the results using a between-subjects analysis of variance. Also called **between-groups analysis of variance**; **independent-groups analysis of variance**; **independent-measures analysis of variance**; **independent-samples analysis of variance**. Compare WITHIN-SUBJECTS ANALYSIS OF VARIANCE.

between-subjects degrees of freedom see BETWEEN-GROUPS DEGREES OF FREEDOM.

between-subjects design a study in which individuals are assigned to only one treatment or experimental condition and each person provides only one score for data analysis. For example, in a between-subjects design investigating the efficacy of three different drugs for treating depression, one group of depressed individuals would receive one of the drugs, a different group would receive another one of the drugs, and yet another group would receive the remaining drug. Thus, the researcher is comparing the effect each medication has on a different set of people. Also called **between-groups design**; **independent-groups design**; **independent-measures design**; **independent-samples design**. Compare WITHIN-SUBJECTS DESIGN.

between-subjects factor in an ANALYSIS OF VARIANCE, an INDEPENDENT VARIABLE with multiple levels, each of which is assigned to or experienced by a distinct group of participants. In a study examining weight loss, for example, the different amounts of daily exercise under investigation would be a between-subjects factor if each was undertaken by a different set of people. Also called **between-subjects variable**.

between-subjects mean square see BETWEEN-GROUPS MEAN SQUARE.

between-subjects sum of squares see BETWEEN-GROUPS SUM OF SQUARES.

between-subjects variable see BETWEEN-SUBJECTS FACTOR.

between-subjects variance see BETWEEN-GROUPS MEAN SQUARE.

Bhattacharya distance (Bhattacharyya distance) a measure of the degree of similarity between two PROBABILITY DISTRIBUTIONS. A Bhattacharya distance of 1 indicates that the two distributions are completely different, whereas a Bhattacharya distance of 0 indicates that the two distributions are probabalistically the same. [A. **Bhattacharya**, Indian statistician]

bias *n.* **1.** systematic error arising during SAMPLING, data collection, or data analysis. See BIASED ESTIMATOR; BIASED SAMPLING. **2.** any deviation of a measured or calculated quantity from its actual (true) value, such that the measurement or calculation is unrepresentative of the item of interest. **3.** any tendency or preference, such as a RESPONSE BIAS. —**biased** *adj.*

bias-corrected accelerated percentile interval (BCa; BC$_a$) a method of obtaining a CONFIDENCE INTERVAL for a quantity of interest in which BOOTSTRAPPING procedures are used to enhance EFFICIENCY and ROBUSTNESS. This may be necessary where sample sizes are small. For example, in determining a BCa for a POPULATION MEAN, a researcher would draw a subset of values from the larger set of observed scores, determine the confidence interval for that subset, return the values to the larger pool, and then repeat the process numerous times. He or she would then calculate a single overall confidence interval from the set of intervals obtained.

biased estimator a value obtained from sample data that consistently under- or overestimates the true quantity in the larger population of interest. In other words, a biased estimator is one whose value on average differs from the value of the PARAMETER it purports to represent. Also called **biased statistic**. Compare UNBIASED ESTIMATOR.

biased sampling selecting individuals or other study units from a population in such a manner that the resulting sample is not representative of the population. Compare UNBIASED SAMPLING. See also SAMPLING BIAS.

biased statistic see BIASED ESTIMATOR.

bias–variance tradeoff the situation in which increasing the complexity of a model to better account for the observed relationships among a set of variables reduces the precision of any estimated values subsequently derived from that model. That is, the model becomes so specific to the particular sample from which it was derived that it no longer is an accurate representation of the larger population of interest. For example, a REGRESSION EQUATION for predicting a person's income may include two variables (education level and career field) that only partially account for variance in salary but nonetheless are applicable to a broad group of individuals beyond those studied. Adding further variables to the equation (e.g., area of residence, parents' education levels, prior experience, age, sex, ethnicity) may ensure that all variance is fully accounted for, but only in the limited set of individuals studied. Researchers therefore tend to seek a balance, opting for either greater intricacy or greater certainty as circumstances warrant.

BIC abbreviation for BAYESIAN INFORMATION CRITERION.

bimodal distribution a set of scores with two peaks or MODES around which values tend to cluster, such that the frequencies at first increase and then decrease around each peak, as in the following hypothetical depiction.

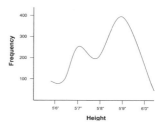

As shown, when graphing the heights of a sample of adolescents one would obtain a bimodal distribution if most people were either 5'7" or 5'9" tall. See also MULTIMODAL DISTRIBUTION; UNIMODAL DISTRIBUTION.

binary trial a single experiment in which there are only two possible outcomes. For example, consider a behavioral researcher observing aggression in a group of schoolchildren during recess. If he or she makes a record every 1 minute, then each such period may be considered a binary trial, with *aggression present* or *aggression absent* as its only two possible outcomes.

binary variable see DICHOTOMOUS VARIABLE.

binomial *n.* an algebraic expression consisting of two terms, such as $(x + y)^2$ or $2x + 4y$. See BINOMIAL EXPANSION; BINOMIAL THEOREM. See also POLYNOMIAL.

binomial confidence interval a CONFIDENCE INTERVAL for estimates of the proportion of a population that exhibits a particular characteristic or outcome, as determined from a sample of that population. A BINOMIAL DISTRIBUTION is assumed. For example, one could sample the pass rate for students in several different states on a nationally administered mathematics exam and then use the information to compute a binomial confidence interval indicating a range of values for the proportion of all U.S. students who will pass the exam.

binomial distribution the PROBABILITY DISTRIBUTION for each possible sequence of outcomes on a variable that has only two possible outcomes, with the likeliness of obtaining each outcome remaining constant. For example, a binomial distribution of the results of trying to predict the outcomes of 10 coin tosses would display the probability of observing each possible set of results, including one success and nine failures, two successes and eight failures, and so forth. This distribution is often denoted by $b(n,\theta)$.

binomial expansion the EXPANSION of an algebraic expression consisting of two terms into a larger series of sums. For example, a possible binomial expansion of $(x + y)^2$ is $(x + y)(x + y)$ or $x^2 + xy + yx + y^2$.

binomial probability within a series of independent observations, the probability of observing a particular combination of outcomes for a variable that can assume only one of two values (e.g., 0 or 1; pass or fail) where there is a fixed likeliness of each value occurring. For example, consider a group of 10 individuals selected from a population of persons aged 40–45, with each selection unrelated to any other selection. A binomial probability could be calculated to determine the likeliness that, for example, seven of those individuals are married while three are not, given known information on the probability of persons of that age being married.

binomial sign test see SIGN TEST.

binomial test a statistical procedure to determine whether an observed data pattern for a variable that can have only one of two values (often represented as 0 and 1) matches a theoretical or expected pattern. In other words, it tests whether the categorical proportions in the obtained data differ significantly from their proportions in the population from which they are believed to derive. See also BINOMIAL PROBABILITY.

binomial theorem the mathematical rule that allows one to reformulate an algebraic expression of two terms—for example, $(x + y)^2$ or $(x + y)^3$—as a longer series of sums. See BINOMIAL EXPANSION.

binomial variable a variable for which there are only two outcomes, typically designated 0 and 1, with each possible outcome having a specified likeliness of being observed. Flipping a coin is an example, as it may land on either heads or tails. See also BINOMIAL DISTRIBUTION.

biographical method the systematic use of personal histories—gathered through such means as interviews, focus groups, observations, and individual reflections and other narratives—in psychological research and analysis. This method emphasizes the placement of the individual within the context of social connections, historical events, and life experiences.

biostatistics *n.* the branch of statistics concerned with collecting and analyzing data that pertain to biological processes or health characteristics, especially in medicine and epidemiology. Also called **biometrics; biometry.** —**biostatistical** *adj.* —**biostatistician** *n.*

biplot *n.* a multivariate graphic that simultaneously displays information about variables and participants. Data about two or more variables usually are denoted by arrows or vectors, and specific measurements for individual cases usually are denoted by dots. The example (opposite) shows the relationship among five task variables: the Boston Naming Test, various letter and category fluency tests, an adapted Simon task, the Stoop Color–Word Interference Test, and the Sustained Attention to Response Task. The dimensions indicate the per-

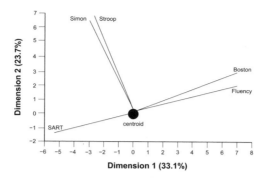

biplot

centage of variance in aspects of lexical access and executive control explained by each. Biplots often are used in PRINCIPAL COMPONENTS ANALYSIS.

bipolar factor in FACTOR ANALYSIS, a latent variable whose values (FACTOR LOADINGS) range from positive to negative with a neutral point at a relatively central position within the range.

bipolar rating scale a set of response options whose lower- and upper-end terms are opposites. For example, a bipolar rating scale for motivation might include response options that range from *very strong* to *very weak*. Also called **bipolar scale**. Compare UNIPOLAR RATING SCALE. See also SEMANTIC DIFFERENTIAL.

birth cohort see COHORT.

birth-cohort study a LONGITUDINAL DESIGN examining groups of individuals who were born around the same time (e.g., in the same year).

biserial correlation coefficient (symbol: r_b, r_{bis}) a measure of the strength of the association between a variable whose values may span a given range (e.g., grade point average) and a variable with only two discrete values (e.g., 0 or 1; pass or fail). It is distinct from the POINT BISERIAL CORRELATION COEFFICIENT in assuming that there is a NORMAL DISTRIBUTION underlying most characteristics. Also called **biserial r**.

bivariate *adj.* characterized by two variables or attributes. For example, a set of height and weight measurements for each participant in a study would be bivariate data. Compare MULTIVARIATE; UNIVARIATE.

bivariate distribution a distribution showing each possible combination of values for two RANDOM VARIABLES according to their probability of occurrence. For example, a bivariate distribution may show the probability of obtaining specific pairs of heights and weights among college students. Also called **bivariate probability distribution**.

bivariate frequency distribution a distribution showing each possible combination of two CATEGORICAL VARIABLES according to their observed frequency. For example, a researcher may use a bivariate frequency distribution to display how many male and female students at a university are majoring in particular fields of study.

bivariate method any approach to data analysis that relies on the simultaneous examination of two variables. CORRELATION ANALYSIS is an example of a bivariate method.

bivariate normality a joint quality of two variables, whereby at each level of the first variable values of the second follow a NORMAL DISTRIBUTION, and vice versa. Bivariate normality is an important assumption in certain statistical procedures, such as CORRELATION ANALYSIS.

bivariate outlier a data point whose combination of values on two variables is extreme or unusual relative to the other combinations in a data set. For example, a student who obtains perfect scores of 100 points on two different math tests would be a bivariate outlier if most other students had combination scores between 75 and 90 points.

bivariate probability distribution see BIVARIATE DISTRIBUTION.

black box a system in which both the input and output are observable but the processes that occur between them are unknown or not observable. For example, in the relationship between leadership ability (input) and on-the-job performance as a project manager (output), the role of the organizational climate could be considered a black box if it is not understood.

blind *adj.* denoting a research procedure in which information about particular aspects or protocols of a study is unknown to participants, investigators, or both. A **single blind** (or **single masked**) procedure is one in which the study participants do not know the experimental conditions or groups to which they have been assigned; a **double blind** (or **double masked**) procedure is one in which neither the study participants nor the researchers who interact with them know which people have been assigned to which groups; and a **triple blind** (or **triple masked**) procedure is one in which the study participants, researchers, and individuals evaluating the data are all unaware of the specific study conditions to which people were assigned. Blinding is undertaken to prevent conscious or unconscious BIAS by eliminating knowledge that could skew results.

blind analysis an evaluation of data in which the analyst is not aware of partic-

ular aspects of the study from which the data derive.

blind review an evaluation of a manuscript to assess its suitability for publication or of a grant proposal to assess its suitability for funding by a person who does not know the identity of the author or proposer.

block *n.* **1.** a group or subset of study participants who share a certain characteristic and are treated as a unit in an experimental design. **2.** a set of variables entered as a single entity into a REGRESSION ANALYSIS or similar statistical procedure.

block design a type of research study in which participants are divided into relatively homogeneous subsets (blocks) from which they are assigned to the experimental or treatment conditions. For example, in a simple block design to evaluate the efficacy of several antidepressants, participants with similar pretest depression scores might be grouped into homogeneous blocks and then assigned to receive different medications. The purpose of a block design is to ensure that a characteristic of the study participants that is related to the target outcome (i.e., a COVARIATE) is distributed equally across treatment conditions. See COMPLETE BLOCK DESIGN; INCOMPLETE BLOCK DESIGN; RANDOMIZED BLOCK DESIGN.

block diagram a graphical representation of a system in which blocks represent key parts and connecting lines indicate relationships between parts. For example, a block diagram could be used to display the decision rules one might follow when conducting statistical tests to compare data from groups of study participants.

blocking *n.* the process of grouping research participants into relatively homogeneous subsets on the basis of a particular characteristic. Such blocking helps adjust for preexisting patterns of variation between experimental units. See BLOCK DESIGN.

blocking factor in a BLOCK DESIGN, an attribute or variable used as a basis for subdividing study participants or other sampling units into homogeneous subsets.

block randomization a method for assigning study participants to experimental conditions in which individuals are arbitrarily divided into subsets or blocks and then some random process is used to place individuals from those blocks into the different conditions. For example, a researcher might divide participants into blocks of 10 and then randomly assign half of the people in each to the CONTROL GROUP and half to the EXPERIMENTAL GROUP. Block randomization is distinct from BLOCKING in that the block does not have any significance other than as an assignment unit.

block sampling a technique, mainly used as part of a multistage procedure, for selecting units for study. A population is divided into groups (blocks) that each have approximately the same number of targets (e.g., adults to be interviewed), a random subset of those blocks is chosen, and a random subset of targets within each selected block is identified. This type of sampling helps to ensure that characteristics of the initial population are well represented in the final sample.

BLUE acronym for BEST LINEAR UNBIASED ESTIMATOR.

BMA abbreviation for BAYESIAN MODEL AVERAGING.

Bonferroni inequality a general rule of probability used when conducting MULTIPLE COMPARISONS on the same data set. It states that the probability of at least one comparison resulting in a TYPE I ERROR (i.e., incorrectly rejecting the NULL HYPOTHESIS) cannot exceed the sum of the individual probabilities from each separate comparison. [Carl

Emilio **Bonferroni** (1892–1960), Italian mathematician]

Bonferroni t test see DUNN–BONFERRONI PROCEDURE. [Carl Emilio **Bonferroni**]

Boole's inequality a rule in probability theory stating that the probability of one event from a fixed set of events occurring is at most equal to the sum of the probabilities of each individual event. [George **Boole** (1815–1864), British mathematician and logician]

bootstrapping *n.* a statistical technique to estimate the variance of a PARAMETER when standard assumptions about the shape of the data set are not met. For example, bootstrapping may be used to estimate the variance of a set of scores that do not follow a NORMAL DISTRIBUTION. In this procedure, a subset of values is taken from the data set, a quantity (e.g., the mean) calculated, and the values reinserted into the data; this sequence is repeated a given number of times. From the resulting set of calculated values (e.g., the set of means), the summary value of interest is calculated (e.g., the standard deviation of the mean). See also JACKKNIFE.

bottom-up clustering (**bottom-up hierarchical clustering**) see AGGLOMERATIVE CLUSTERING.

box-and-whisker plot a graphical display of the central value, variance, and extreme values in a data set. A rectangle (**box**) is drawn along the vertical *y*-axis of the plot, which shows the range of data values. The length of the box indicates the middle 50% of scores and its two ends indicate the upper and lower HINGES. Lines (**whiskers**) extending outward from the box denote variation in the upper and lower 25% of scores, while a separate line within the box indicates the score that falls in the very middle of the set (i.e., the MEDIAN). Stars or other single points indicate extreme scores. Consider the following example (overleaf).

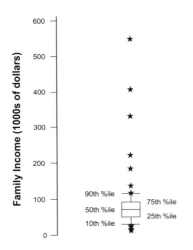

A box-and-whisker plot is useful in EX-PLORATORY DATA ANALYSIS for indicating whether a distribution is skewed and whether the data set includes any OUT-LIERS; it can also be used to compare data sets when large numbers of observations are involved. Also called **box-and-whisker diagram**; **box-and-whisker display**; **boxplot**.

Box–Cox transformation a TRANS-FORMATION that enables the relationship between one or more predictor variables and an outcome variable to be described by a summative formula and thus to be plotted by a straight line when graphed. Based on MAXIMUM LIKELIHOOD estimation, the technique transforms the outcome variable to obtain LINEAR-ITY and approximate NORMALITY in a data set. Compare BOX–TIDWELL TRANS-FORMATION. [George E. P. **Box** (1919–   ) and David Roxbee **Cox** (1924–   ), British statisticians]

Box–Jenkins model see AUTOREGRES-SIVE INTEGRATED MOVING-AVERAGE MODEL. [George E. P. **Box**; Gwilym M. **Jenkins** (1933–1982), British statistician]

Box–Ljung test see LJUNG–BOX TEST.

Box–Müller transformation a TRANS-FORMATION in which scores obtained through a process that generates values showing a UNIFORM DISTRIBUTION are changed to conform to a NORMAL DIS-TRIBUTION. The Box–Müller transformation commonly is used in the computer generation of data. [George E. P. **Box**; Mervin E. **Müller**, computer scientist]

Box–Pierce test a method for evaluating the assumption that scores in a TIME SERIES are unrelated. More specifically, it uses an AUTOREGRESSIVE INTEGRATED MOVING-AVERAGE MODEL to determine whether there is any AUTOCORRELATION among the RESIDUALS of the observations. See also LJUNG–BOX TEST. [George E. P. **Box**; David A. **Pierce**]

box-score method a method of summarizing results from multiple studies of the same general research question that considers both statistically meaningful and nonmeaningful results but ignores the magnitude of the research findings (e.g., the size of a treatment effect). META-ANALYSIS generally is preferred over the box-score method.

Box's test a statistical procedure to evaluate the similarity of two or more SQUARE MATRICES showing the extent to which variance in each variable from a set is related to variance in all other variables in the set. In other words, it is a method to test the hypothesis that COVARIANCE MATRICES are equal. Typically used in MULTIVARIATE ANALYSES OF VARIANCE and similar to the BART-LETT TEST FOR EQUALITY OF VARIANCE, Box's test is not appropriate for NONLIN-EAR data and has limited applicability to data that do not follow a NORMAL DIS-TRIBUTION. Also called **Box's M test**; **Box's test for equality of covariance matrices**. [George E. P. **Box**]

Box–Tidwell transformation a TRANSFORMATION used to modify a set of PREDICTOR VARIABLES so that the relationship between those predictors and the outcome variable resembles a straight line. It is similar to the BOX–COX TRANS-FORMATION for correcting nonlinearity but instead is applied to the independent variables (predictors) involved. [George E. P. **Box**; Paul W. **Tidwell**]

bracketing *n.* in estimation problems, the specification of a range or interval known to contain a target value. For example, the probability of an event may be expressed as $p < .05$ or as $.01 < p < .05$.

Bradley–Terry model a model used to create a scale of preferences from data obtained from PAIRWISE COMPARISONS of items. It is widely used to estimate the probability of certain items being preferred over others. For example, the Bradley–Terry model might be applied in determining whether a depressed individual will opt to receive one treatment (A) rather than another treatment (B). [Ralph A. **Bradley** (1923–2001), Canadian-born U.S. statistician; Milton E. **Terry**, U.S. statistician]

breakdown point the smallest number or proportion of extreme observations (OUTLIERS) that can be present in a data set before an ESTIMATOR (e.g., the sample mean) will assume arbitrarily large values.

Breslow–Day test a test for the homogeneity of ODDS RATIOS across different levels of a variable (e.g., participant incomes) within a data set. [Norman E. **Breslow** (1941–), U.S. biostatistician; Nicholas E. **Day** (1939–), British biostatistician and epidemiologist]

Breslow test a method used in SURVIVAL ANALYSIS to compare the outcomes of different groups of individuals. More specifically, it evaluates the equality of two or more SURVIVAL FUNCTIONS depicting mortality or failure across time. Also called **Gehan's generalized Wilcoxon test**. [Norman E. **Breslow**]

Brown–Forsythe test a statistical method for determining whether there is HOMOGENEITY OF VARIANCE across two or more populations. The test, which uses the absolute values of the deviations of scores from the MEDIAN to calculate variance, is a helpful preliminary step in determining whether the required ASSUMPTIONS have been met for certain statistical procedures, such as ANALYSIS OF VARIANCE. [Morton B. **Brown**, Canadian-born U.S. statistician; Alan B. **Forsythe**, U.S. statistician]

Brown–Spearman formula see SPEARMAN–BROWN PROPHECY FORMULA.

BRR abbreviation for BALANCED REPEATED REPLICATION.

brushing *n.* an interactive data-analysis technique in which a computer user manipulates several multidimensional SCATTERPLOTS in real time, using a mouse or other device to continuously change display features and immediately view the results.

bubble plot a graphical representation of data that is similar to a SCATTERPLOT but includes an additional third variable whose values are represented by differently sized circles. For example, a researcher might use a bubble plot to show the relationship between income, years of education, and age within a particular profession. The first two variables would be arrayed along the horizontal x-axis and vertical y-axis, respectively, with circles placed in the graph to indicate points of intersecting values; the radius of each circle would correspond to values of age, with larger circles indicating greater age (see example overleaf).

bump hunting an examination of the distribution of values in a data set to identify any SPIKES or MODES; in graphic terms, it is a search for any significant "bumps" on an otherwise smooth curve. Bump hunting is useful for finding portions of data that are different enough to potentially represent distinct subgroups of cases.

burn-in *n.* in the MARKOV CHAIN MONTE CARLO METHOD, an initial series of sampling runs whose values are discarded and not incorporated into subsequent

B

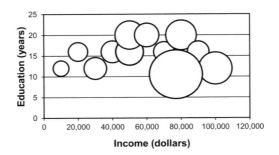

bubble plot

calculations and analysis. Researchers may run a chain for several hundred (or several thousand) steps during a burn-in, as these initial points are not likely to represent the target distribution.

Burt matrix a matrix showing all two-way CROSS-TABULATIONS between a set of CATEGORICAL VARIABLES. Used in multiple CORRESPONDENCE ANALYSIS, a Burt matrix is created by arranging the data in rows and columns, obtaining the TRANSPOSE of this matrix, and multiplying the latter by the former. Also called **Burt table**. [Ronald S. **Burt** (1949–), U.S. sociologist]

Cc

C symbol for COEFFICIENT OF CONTINGENCY.

calibration *n.* the process of assigning values to a measuring device (instrument, test, or scale) relative to a reference standard. For example, it would be useful to compare the scores on a new test of intelligence with those from an older, well-accepted test to ensure that the new test scores provide comparable ratings or values. To do so, a researcher might select a group of people (the **calibration sample**), administer each individual both the old and new tests, and then assess the results.

caliper matching see MATCHING.

canonical *adj.* in data analysis, describing procedures that utilize linear combinations of measured variables rather than the actual individual variables.

canonical analysis any of a class of statistical procedures that assess the degree of relationship between sets of variables via interpretation of a limited number of linear combinations of specific values of those variables. The overall objective of such procedures is to reduce the DIMENSIONALITY of the data under investigation. Examples include CANONICAL CORRELATION ANALYSIS, DISCRIMINANT ANALYSIS, MULTIPLE REGRESSION, and MULTIVARIATE ANALYSIS OF VARIANCE, among others.

canonical correlation analysis a method of data analysis that provides a measure of the strength of the relationship between a linear combination of predictor variables and a linear combination of outcome measures. Essentially, it extends a basic CORRELATION ANALYSIS, which relates only one variable with another variable, and it extends MULTIPLE REGRESSION, which relates several INDEPENDENT VARIABLES with only one DEPENDENT VARIABLE. For example, a researcher might use a canonical correlation analysis to investigate whether several measures of attitude toward learning (e.g., confidence, anxiety, interest, enjoyment) are related to several measures of achievement (e.g., grade point average, the number of math classes taken, the number of memberships in honor societies).

canonical correlation coefficient (symbol: R_c) an index of the magnitude of the linear relationship between a linear combination of one set of variables and a linear combination of a different set of variables, with each linear combination made in such a way as to maximize the strength of the relationship between the two variable sets. It ranges in value from –1 to +1.

canonical discriminant analysis see DISCRIMINANT ANALYSIS.

canonical discriminant function see DISCRIMINANT FUNCTION.

canonical loading see DISCRIMINANT LOADING.

canonical variate the result of a weighted, linear combination of a set of variables, often used as a dependent or independent variable in a CANONICAL CORRELATION ANALYSIS.

capitalization on chance drawing a conclusion from data wholly or partly biased in a particular direction by chance. A common example of capitalization on chance is the presentation of all the significant results in a study without considering the number of results examined.

capture–tag–recapture sampling a method of SAMPLING that is used to estimate population size. For example, in order to estimate the number of fish in a lake, a random sample of fish (e.g., 100) would be drawn and tagged, then returned to the lake. The lake would be resampled, and the results (i.e., the fraction of tagged fish in the new sample) would be used to estimate the total number of fish in the lake. Also called **capture–recapture sampling**; **mark-and-recapture sampling**.

cardinal *adj.* describing a number that indicates a count of a set of items, such as two dogs or three circles, but does not indicate order within the set. A child's understanding of the concept of cardinal numbers is an important area of study in developmental psychology. Compare NOMINAL; ORDINAL.

carryover effect the effect on the current performance of a research participant of the experimental conditions that preceded the current conditions; where such an effect is significant, it may be difficult to determine the specific influence of the variable under study. For example, in a CROSSOVER DESIGN in which a particular drug is administered to animals in the first experimental condition, a carryover effect would be evident if the drug continued to exert an influence on the animals' performance during a subsequent experimental condition. Also called **holdover effect**. See WASH-OUT PERIOD.

CART analysis classification and regression tree analysis: a method of classifying data into successively smaller and more homogeneous subgroups according to a set of PREDICTOR VARIABLES. CART analysis is similar to but distinct from REGRESSION ANALYSIS in its homogeneity of case subsets. The results of a CART analysis may be displayed in a diagram resembling a tree—subsets of data, based on values of the outcome variable, are shown to branch off from higher level subsets of data.

Cartesian coordinate system a system for locating a point in an *n*-dimensional space on a graph by indicating the distance of the point from a common origin along each of *n* axes. The most common application of the Cartesian system is one based on two dimensions, represented by two perpendicular lines that intersect at a specific spot called the **origin**. In such a two-dimensional Cartesian coordinate system, the horizontal line is often referred to as the X-AXIS and the vertical line as the Y-AXIS. For example, the coordinate (3, 4) represents an *x* value of 3 and a *y* value of 4 on the graph; thus, from the origin one would count three units over on the *x*-axis and four units up on the *y*-axis to locate the coordinate point, as shown in the following illustration.

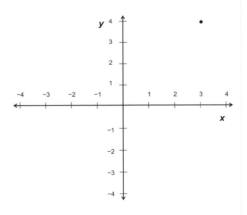

[René **Descartes** (1596–1650), French philosopher, mathematician, and scientist]

Cartesian product a set of all possible pairings of units in one set with units in another set. As an example, let A be a set of three colors (e.g., blue, green, yellow), and let B be a set of two shapes (e.g., square, circle). The Cartesian product of A × B is the set of all possible pairings: blue square, blue circle, green square, green circle, yellow square, and yellow circle. That is, the Cartesian product of A × B is 3 × 2 = 6. [René **Descartes**]

case *n.* a unit or observation to be analyzed, such as a nonhuman animal, a person, a group, an institution, an object, or any other entity from which a researcher gathers data.

case-control study a type of study in which a group of individuals diagnosed with a disease or other condition is compared to a group of individuals without the disease diagnosis, specifically with regard to the proportion of people in each group who were exposed to a certain risk factor. Also called **case-control design**; **case-referent study**.

case study an in-depth investigation of a single individual, family, event, or other entity. Multiple types of data (psychological, physiological, biographical, environmental) are assembled, for example, to understand an individual's background, relationships, and behavior. Although case studies allow for intensive analysis of an issue, they are limited in the extent to which their findings may be generalized.

casewise deletion see LISTWISE DELETION.

catch trial a trial within an experiment in which a stimulus is not present but the participants' responses nonetheless are recorded. For example, in an experiment in which participants identify auditory signals, catch trials are those in which no signal is given. The use of a catch trial may help to estimate the level at which a participant is guessing when no stimulus is present.

categorical *adj.* referring to a characteristic that is used to classify units, usually individuals or experimental conditions, for the purposes of study. For example, participants may be classified as males or females in a particular study; in this case, sex is categorical.

categorical data information that consists of counts or observations in specific categories rather than measurements. Categorical data that have a meaningful order are referred to more specifically as ORDINAL DATA, whereas categorical data without a meaningful order are known as NOMINAL DATA.

categorical data analysis any of several statistical procedures used to model variables that indicate counts or observations in specific categories, often as a function of one or more predictor variables. For example, counts of survival status (e.g., life vs. death) may be compared by treatment condition (e.g., treatment vs. no treatment). Techniques commonly used in categorical data analysis include the CHI-SQUARE TEST, LOGISTIC REGRESSION, and PROBIT ANALYSIS.

categorical scale a sequence of numbers that identify items as belonging to mutually exclusive categories. For example, a categorical scale for the political party affiliation of a group of Americans might use 1 to denote Republican, 2 to denote Democrat, and 3 to denote Independent. When the number sequence has a meaningful order a categorical scale is more precisely called an ORDINAL SCALE; when it is devoid of such meaningful order it is known as a NOMINAL SCALE.

categorical variable a variable that is defined by a set of two or more categories. Examples include a person's sex, marital status, or rankings of particular stimuli (such as the relative loudness of different sounds). Specialized methods of CATEGORICAL DATA ANALYSIS are available for assessing information obtained from the measurement of categorical variables.

Cattell's scree test see SCREE PLOT. [Raymond **Cattell** (1905–1998), British-born U.S. psychologist]

Cauchy–Schwarz inequality a statement asserting that the ABSOLUTE VALUE of the product of two numbers can equal but not exceed the product of their individual absolute values. For example, consider the numbers –2 and +3, whose product is –6, the absolute value of which is +6; similarly, the pair of +2 and –3 also yields a product of –6, which also has an absolute value of +6. In either case, the absolute values of the individual numbers are 2 and 3, which yields the same product of 6. The Cauchy–Schwarz inequality is fundamental in many areas of statistical theory, including probability theory. [Augustin-Louis **Cauchy** (1789–1857), French mathematician; Hermann Amandus **Schwarz** (1843–1921), German mathematician]

causal analysis an attempt to draw dependable inferences about cause-and-effect relationships from research data. Encompassing a variety of methods (e.g., PATH ANALYSIS, STRUCTURAL EQUATION MODELING), such analyses differ in the degree to which they are statistically complex and the degree to which causal inferences from them are, in fact, justified.

causal diagram see PATH DIAGRAM.

causal hypothesis a HYPOTHESIS about how change in one variable leads to a subsequent change in another variable. A causal hypothesis may be used, for instance, to formally state how the application of a treatment will subsequently affect behavior or performance.

causal indicator in STRUCTURAL EQUATION MODELING, a measure used to represent a factor that is assumed to be the cause of a dependent LATENT VARIABLE. Compare EFFECT INDICATOR.

causal inference the reasoned process of concluding that change in one variable produced change in another variable. See CAUSAL ANALYSIS.

causal modeling any procedure used to test for cause-and-effect relationships (as opposed to mere correlation) between multiple variables. STRUCTURAL EQUATION MODELING is the best known example. For a causal model to be a useful evaluative tool, strict conditions concerning the measurement of the variables must be met.

causal variable see INDEPENDENT VARIABLE.

causation *n.* the empirical relation between two events, states, or variables such that change in one (the cause) brings about change in the other (the effect). **—causal** *adj.*

CDF abbreviation for CUMULATIVE DISTRIBUTION FUNCTION.

ceiling effect a situation in which the majority of values obtained for a variable approach the upper limit of the scale used in its measurement. For example, a test whose items are too easy for those taking it would show a ceiling effect because most people would achieve or be close to the highest possible score. In other words, the test scores would exhibit SKEWNESS and have little VARIANCE, thus prohibiting meaningful analysis of the results. Compare FLOOR EFFECT.

cell *n.* a combination of two or more characteristics represented by the intersection of a row and a column in a statistical table. A tabular display resulting from a study of handedness in men and women, for instance, might consist of four cells: left-handed females, left-handed males, right-handed females, and right-handed males. See also EMPTY CELL.

cell frequency a count of observations that have a specific combination of two or more characteristics as displayed in a statistical table. For example, results from a survey in which respondents are asked to report their transportation mode and sex may be described by a two-way CONTINGENCY TABLE, in which cell frequencies provide the number of people who fall into the different possible category combinations (e.g., females who bike, males who bike, females who drive, males who drive, females who take public transit, males who take public transit).

cell mean a mathematical average of the numeric values associated with a specific combination of two or more characteristics as displayed in a statistical table. For example, results from a study of response time under specific combinations of several factors may rely on a comparison of cell means to GROUP DIFFERENCES in response times between experimental conditions.

cell-means model an approach in which a set of observed responses on a DEPENDENT VARIABLE are analyzed at each level or condition of an INDEPENDENT VARIABLE in order to identify differences in their average values. Each such average is obtained by adding a random error term to the typical response value for the larger population from which the observations derive, as estimated from the sample data. For example, a researcher examining the influence of sleep on exam performance might use the cell-means model to determine whether there are any differences in the average exam score obtained by participants who got 6 hours of sleep the previous night, those who got 8 hours, and those who got 10 hours.

censored data a set of data in which some values are unknown because they are not observed or because they fall below the minimum or above the maximum value that can be measured by the scale used. For example, in a study of survival rates of a group of people with a particular disease, censored data would be obtained if the deaths of some participants occurred after the study ended. See also DOUBLY CENSORED DATA.

censored linear regression model see ACCELERATED FAILURE TIME MODEL.

censored observation a score that is missing from a data set, either because the event of interest has not occurred by the end of the study period or because the response falls into an unmeasurable portion of the scale. A response measured by a meter, for instance, may not be recorded because it is too small to be detected or is so large that it exceeds the meter's capability to record. In such a situation, the minimum value is assigned to an undetectable observation, and the maximum value is assigned to an excessive observation.

censored regression see TOBIT ANALYSIS.

censoring *n.* the situation in which some observations are missing from a set of data (see CENSORED DATA). Censoring is common in studies of survival time, in which the research often ends before the event of interest occurs for all study units. See also LEFT CENSORING; RIGHT CENSORING.

census *n.* the complete count of an entire population. A census differs from most experimental studies, which use a SAMPLE from a population in hopes of generalizing from that observed subset to the larger group.

centile a shortened name for PERCENTILE.

centile reference chart a table used to compare a measurement on an individual to values in a population. The PERCENTILE value from the population may be used to judge whether the individual's score is atypical in that context. Thus, a centile reference chart may be used in assessing a child's growth relative to her weight and height (see chart overleaf from the U.S. Centers for Disease Control).

central distribution see NONCENTRAL DISTRIBUTION.

central limit theorem (**CLT**) the statistical principle that the sum of independent values from any distribution will approach a NORMAL DISTRIBUTION as the number of values in the distribution increases. In other words, the larger the sample size, the more closely the SAMPLING DISTRIBUTION approximates a normal distribution. The central limit theorem is used to justify certain data

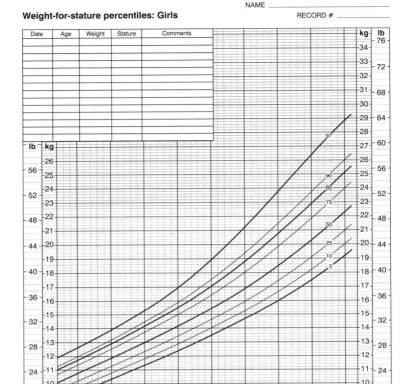

NAME _____

Weight-for-stature percentiles: Girls

RECORD # _____

centile reference chart

analysis methods when the appropriateness of a method relies on an assumption of normality.

central moment a MOMENT that describes the shape of a set of scores with regard to its deviation about the mean. Four common central moments that describe a RANDOM VARIABLE are the MEAN (the first central moment), the VARIANCE (the second central moment), the SKEWNESS (the third central moment), and the KURTOSIS (the fourth central moment). Also called **moment about the mean**.

central tendency the middle or center

point of a set of scores. The central tendency of a sample data set, for instance, may be estimated by a number of different statistics (e.g., MEAN, MEDIAN, MODE). See also MEASURE OF CENTRAL TENDENCY.

central-tendency bias see END-AVERSION BIAS.

central-tendency measure see MEASURE OF CENTRAL TENDENCY.

centroid *n.* **1.** in geometry, the center point of an object or area in multidimensional space. It may be determined by calculating the intersection of all straight lines or planes that divide the area into two equal parts. **2.** the MEAN of multivariate data. It may be obtained by calculating the average of the VECTORS for the set of variables. See also CENTROID METHOD.

centroid factor a single variable identified through its CENTROID value as summarizing responses on multiple other variables. Centroid factors are obtained by the CENTROID METHOD, a data-reduction technique sometimes used in FACTOR ANALYSIS.

centroid method 1. a technique used in FACTOR ANALYSIS to reduce multiple correlated variables to a smaller set of explanatory variables. It is similar to—and indeed was a precursor of—PRINCIPAL COMPONENTS ANALYSIS but involves simpler calculations. Generally, the centroid method is now used only in situations when computers are not available. **2.** an approach to AGGLOMERATIVE CLUSTERING in which CENTROIDS are calculated to determine similarity among separate entities and combine them into higher order groups. Each individual is assigned to the subset closest in centroid value, with the process continuing until the maximum grouping of cases has been obtained.

CERES plot *c*ombined conditional *ex*pectations and *res*iduals plot: a graph that is similar to a PARTIAL RESIDUAL PLOT in displaying relationships among the predictors of a DEPENDENT VARIABLE but distinct in being appropriate for use with nonlinear entities.

CF abbreviation for CUMULATIVE FREQUENCY.

CFA abbreviation for CONFIRMATORY FACTOR ANALYSIS.

CFI abbreviation for Bentler comparative FIT INDEX.

CGF abbreviation for CUMULANT GENERATING FUNCTION.

CHAID abbreviation for CHI-SQUARE AUTOMATIC INTERACTION DETECTOR.

chain graph a graph in which the directional and nondirectional relationships among variables in a data set are indicated by arrows and lines, respectively. Consider the following generic example.

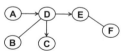

chain-of-events data data regarding a series of events that have occurred to a group of individuals in the same order but not necessarily at the same times.

chain path model a rare synonym of MARKOV CHAIN.

chance difference a difference between two samples that arises from the nature of sampling itself, rather than from any intervention by a researcher. For example, scores obtained from two groups of research participants might vary because of personal factors affecting some individuals (e.g., financial worries) and not because of the conditions of the study.

chance variation see RANDOM VARIATION.

change in R^2 a change in the COEFFICIENT OF MULTIPLE DETERMINATION (R^2) from one model to another. In procedures such as HIERARCHICAL REGRESSION and STEPWISE REGRESSION, in which predictor variables are individually added to or removed from a set, a significant change in R^2 indicates that the predictor of interest has a meaningful role in the explanation of the response variable.

change-point problem in the observation of TIME-SERIES data, the difficulty in judging when exactly a meaningful change in the pattern of data occurs, given a certain degree of indeterminacy or randomness in the behavior of the variable (see STOCHASTIC PROCESS).

change score see DIFFERENCE SCORE.

changing-criterion design an experimental approach in which an initial baseline phase is followed by implementation of a treatment delivered in a series of phases. Each phase has its own criterion rate for the target behavior, and once responding becomes stable an incremental shift in the criterion occurs to implement another phase. For example, a researcher studying the effectiveness of money in reducing caffeine consumption may use a changing-criterion design with four treatment phases, each gradually decreasing the amount below which participants must maintain their caffeine intake. The changing-criterion design is distinguished from other approaches (e.g., the A-B-A DESIGN) in that it does not require the withdrawal of an intervention, an extended baseline, or treatment implementation across multiple behaviors or treatments.

characteristic *n.* a PARAMETER that describes a population distribution, such as its mean or STANDARD DEVIATION.

characteristic function a formula that defines the PROBABILITY DISTRIBUTION of values on a random variable.

characteristic root see EIGENVALUE.

characteristic value see EIGENVALUE.

characteristic vector see EIGENVECTOR.

chart *n.* a graphic or tabular display of data. See also GRAPH; TABLE.

Chebyshev's inequality a theorem stating that in any sample or distribution the great majority of values are close to the mean; the probability that a random variable will take on a value within k STANDARD DEVIATIONS of the mean is at least $1 - 1/k^2$. In simpler terms, this implies that at least 75% of the measurements of any distribution will fall in the range from -2 to $+2$ standard deviations from the mean. The theorem has great utility because it can be applied to distributions that are completely unknown except for mean and variance. [Pafnuty **Chebyshev** (or **Tchebyshev**; 1821–1894), Russian mathematician]

checklist *n.* a list of items that are to be observed, recorded, corrected, or otherwise considered in some manner. See also BEHAVIOR CHECKLIST.

Chernoff faces a representation of data in the form of stylized faces, designed to take advantage of the ability of observers to discern subtle changes in facial expressions.

In the example above, features such as head and eye eccentricity, eyebrow slant, and mouth size represent different values of the variables of interest. [Herman **Chernoff**, 20th-century U.S. statistician]

chi-square (symbol: χ^2) *n.* a statistic that is the sum of the squared differences between the observed scores in a data set and the EXPECTED VALUE. That is, to obtain the chi-square one finds the difference between each observed score and the expected score, squares that difference, and divides by the expected score; finally one adds the resulting values for each score in the set. The smaller the chi-square, the more likely it is that the model from which the expected score is obtained provides a legitimate representation of the phenomenon being measured. See CHI-SQUARE DISTRIBUTION; CHI-SQUARE TEST.

chi-square automatic interaction detector (**CHAID**) an EXPLORATORY DATA ANALYSIS technique in which the relationships between a response variable and a set of potential predictor variables are examined to identify interactions or patterns. In this process, values of the response variable are split into successively smaller subsets according to values of the predictor variables, such that the resulting subsets are relatively homogeneous with regard to the response variable. The response and the predictor variables may be CATEGORICAL, continuous, or any combination thereof.

chi-square distance a measure of the difference between two or more groups with regard to their respective average values on a set of variables. It is similar to EUCLIDEAN DISTANCE in purpose but used with CATEGORICAL DATA.

chi-square distribution (χ^2 **distribution**) a distribution of the sums of independent squared differences between the observed scores in a data set and the expected score for the set. If a random sample is repeatedly drawn from a normal population and measured on some variable and the obtained scores transformed via STANDARDIZATION, multiplied by themselves, and then added, the result will be a chi-square distribution with DEGREES OF FREEDOM equal to the size of the samples drawn. See CHI-SQUARE TEST.

chi-square goodness-of-fit test a statistical method of assessing how well a mathematical model or theoretical expectation fits a set of observed data. The test is used to evaluate hypotheses about the proportions of individuals within different categories of a given NOMINAL variable, such as whether there are different percentages of males and females enrolled in various college majors. The smaller the statistic obtained from this test, the smaller the difference between the proposed model and the obtained data and thus the better the model fit.

chi-square probability plot a graph of the frequency with which particular CHI-SQUARE values are obtained in a data set as compared to the frequency expected according to theory. See PROBABILITY PLOT.

chi-square test any of various procedures that use a CHI-SQUARE DISTRIBUTION to evaluate whether there is a relationship between variables or the degree to which a theory fits a set of observed data. Examples include the CHI-SQUARE GOODNESS-OF-FIT TEST, the CHI-SQUARE TEST FOR HOMOGENEITY, the CHI-SQUARE TEST FOR INDEPENDENCE, the CHI-SQUARE TEST FOR TREND, and the CHI-SQUARE TEST FOR VARIANCE. When unqualified, however, this term usually refers to the test for independence. Also called **chi-square procedure**.

chi-square test for homogeneity a statistical method to evaluate an assumption that some feature of interest is equal between two or more groups (see HOMOGENEITY). The test is used to evaluate whether the frequencies within two or more categories of a given NOMINAL variable are equivalent in different populations, such as whether the same number of fifth graders and sixth graders watch particular cartoons.

chi-square test for independence a statistical method to evaluate whether there is a relationship between two variables whose values are categories. For example, it may be used to test whether sex (male vs. female) is independent of— that is, not related to or associated with—having a household pet (yes vs. no). It compares observed data to the data that would be expected in each cell of a CONTINGENCY TABLE if the two variables were entirely independent. This discrepancy between observed and expected counts is then used to compute the CHI-SQUARE statistic. Overall, larger values of the statistic relative to the number of participants in the study (degrees of freedom) are more likely to be statistically significant. Also called **chi-square test of association**.

chi-square test for trend a statistical method to evaluate change over time in a CATEGORICAL VARIABLE or to determine whether two or more trends in categorical data differ from each other. For example, it may be used to test whether there is a difference in incidences of cancer severity (low, medium, or high) as people age.

chi-square test for variance a statistical method to evaluate a hypothesis about the DISPERSION in a set of scores. For example, it may be used to evaluate whether the STANDARD DEVIATION in recent test scores for a classroom of students is the same as that for the school as a whole.

chi-square test of association see CHI-SQUARE TEST FOR INDEPENDENCE.

choice reaction a response that is dependent on the detection of a stimulus or the differentiation of its different levels. For example, study participants might be measured as to how long it takes them to push a certain computer key after seeing a picture appear on the monitor.

Cholesky factorization the re-expression of a SQUARE MATRIX as the product of two related matrices. More specifically, it is the re-expression of a POSITIVE-DEFINITE symmetric matrix as the product of a lower TRIANGULAR MATRIX and its TRANSPOSE. The process by which this is accomplished is called **Cholesky decomposition** and is one of several numerically stable methods of solving linear equations. [André-Louis **Cholesky** (1875–1918), French mathematician]

Chow test a statistical procedure used to evaluate the equality of the coefficients in two separate REGRESSION EQUATIONS developed to calculate a response variable from one or more predictor variables. [Gregory **Chow** (1929–), Chinese-born U.S. economist]

chronograph *n.* an instrument that records time sequences graphically. —**chronographic** *adj.*

chronometer *n.* a precise clock that runs continuously and is designed to maintain its accuracy under all conditions of temperature, pressure, and the like.

CI abbreviation for CONFIDENCE INTERVAL.

circumplex *n.* a circular depiction of the similarities among multiple variables. For example, a researcher studying emotions might focus on certain core affects and create a circumplex representation of them, with variables having opposite values or characteristics (i.e., tranquility–frenzy; sadness–enthusiasm;

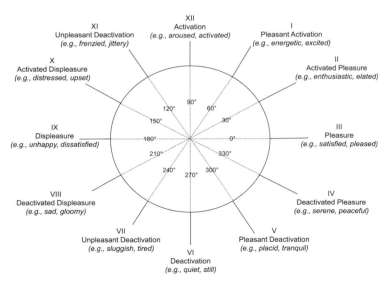

circumplex

sluggishness–excitement) displayed at opposite points on the circumplex.

citation analysis a form of research that examines the history, frequency, and distribution of citations of particular writers or particular books, articles, or other sources. It now mostly involves the automated search of online or electronic databases.

city-block distance an index of the degree of similarity between sets of measurements on different variables: It is calculated as the sum of the ABSOLUTE DIFFERENCES between two values of one variable and the corresponding values of a second variable. City-block distance conceptualizes entities as being arranged in a rectangular grid, such that calculations of distance resemble the approach used by a person when traversing a city—walking horizontally down some streets and vertically up others until arriving at his or her destination. It generally is insensitive to extreme data points (OUTLIERS) and contrasts with the linear EUCLIDEAN DISTANCE approach. Also called **city-block metric; Manhattan distance**.

class *n.* a group, category, or division.

classical inference see FREQUENTIST INFERENCE.

classical probability an approach to the understanding of PROBABILITY based on the assumptions that any random process has a given set of possible outcomes and that each possible outcome is equally likely to occur. An example often used is rolling a die, in which there are six possible outcomes and each outcome is assumed to be equally likely.

classical scaling traditional MULTIDIMENSIONAL SCALING, in which dissimilarities among stimuli are identified via distances between data points. See also NONMETRIC SCALING.

classical statistics a traditional approach to statistics based on FREQUENTIST INFERENCE and CLASSICAL PROBABIL-

ITY. It is often contrasted with BAYESIAN methods.

classical test theory (**CTT**) the theory that an observed score (e.g., a test result) that is held to represent an underlying attribute (e.g., intelligence) may be divided into two quantities—the true value of the underlying attribute and the error inherent to the process of obtaining the observed score. CTT may be represented mathematically as $X_p = T_p + e_p$, where X_p is the observed score for respondent p, T_p is the respondent's TRUE SCORE for the construct or characteristic being measured, and e_p is RANDOM ERROR that dilutes the expression of respondent p's true score. The theory serves as the basis for models of test RELIABILITY and assumes that individuals possess stable characteristics or traits that persist through time. See also GENERALIZABILITY THEORY. Compare ITEM RESPONSE THEORY.

classification *n.* the process of grouping individuals or units into categories based on one or more characteristics. It usually involves a qualitative description of the unit, in which the categories represent types or kinds and not frequency, amount, or degree.

classification and regression tree analysis see CART ANALYSIS.

classification rule a mathematical formula for placing units into groups (e.g., within DISCRIMINANT ANALYSIS) so as to maximize the similarities among group members with regard to a set of characteristics. Also called **allocation rule**.

classification table a table showing the number or percentage of cases correctly categorized by a given model, rule, or algorithm derived for that purpose. Columns represent the model predictions and rows represent the actual classes to which the items in a sample data set belong. For example, a researcher might use a classification table similar to the hypothetical overleaf to

		Predicted attendance category		
Actual attendance	*n*	2-year college	4-year college	No college
2-year college	21	16 (76.2%)	2 (9.5%)	3 (14.3%)
4-year college	45	2 (4.4%)	34 (75.6%)	9 (20.0%)
No college	18	4 (22.2%)	7 (38.9%)	7 (38.9%)

classification table

display the results of a DISCRIMINANT ANALYSIS of college attendance for a group of high school students so as to evaluate the general accuracy of the model used. Also called **classification matrix**; **confusion matrix**.

classification tree a diagram displaying a set of rules for creating successively smaller and increasingly similar subgroups or categories of items from a larger original group. Each node of the classification tree divides into two branches with additional nodes, with the process continuing until there are too few observations in a node to divide them further or until a node is considered homogeneous. For example, consider the classification tree (below) for discriminating children achieving early gain versus no gain in psychotherapy for a variety of disorders. Ellipses are nodes, arrows show branches, and squares illustrate prediction end points. Numbers within the squares give the number of correct predictions divided by the total number of observations classified at that end point. See also CART ANALYSIS.

class interval a range of scores or numerical values that constitute one segment or class of a variable of interest. For example, individual weights can be placed into class intervals such as 100–120 lb, 121–140 lb, 141–160 lb, and so forth. Class intervals often are used in FREQUENCY DISTRIBUTIONS and HISTOGRAMS to present a large data set in a simpler manner that is more easily interpreted.

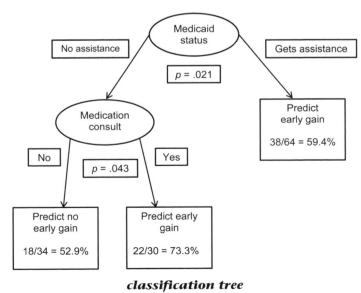

classification tree

class limit the uppermost and lowermost values between which lie a range of values constituting a segment or class of a variable: the upper and lower boundaries of a CLASS INTERVAL.

class size the width of a range of values constituting a segment or class of a variable: the width of a CLASS INTERVAL.

clinical *adj.* in medical diagnosis or treatment, describing a decision based on a clinician's personal opinion and judgment, as opposed to one based on statistical evidence. Compare ACTUARIAL.

clinical sample a sample made up of individuals who have been given a formal diagnosis of a disorder.

clinical significance the extent to which a study result is judged to be meaningful in relation to the diagnosis or treatment of disorders. An example of a clinically significant result would be an outcome indicating that a new intervention strategy is effective in reducing symptoms of depression. See also PRACTICAL SIGNIFICANCE; STATISTICAL SIGNIFICANCE.

clinical test a test or measurement made in a clinical or research context for the purpose of diagnosis or treatment of a disorder.

clinical trial a research study designed to compare a new treatment or drug with an existing standard of care or other control condition (see CONTROL GROUP). Trials generally are designed to answer scientific questions and to find better ways to treat individuals who have a specific disease or disorder. Also called **clinical study; therapeutic trial**. See also RANDOMIZED CLINICAL TRIAL.

clinical utility research see EFFECTIVENESS RESEARCH.

clinical validation the process of acquiring evidence to support the accuracy of a theory by studying multiple cases involving specific procedures for diagnosis or treatment.

closed interval a range of values that includes both its endpoints. For example, the closed interval [0,3] consists of all values not smaller than 0 and not larger than 3. Compare OPEN INTERVAL.

closed question see FIXED-ALTERNATIVE QUESTION.

CLT abbreviation for CENTRAL LIMIT THEOREM.

cluster analysis a method of multivariate data analysis in which individuals or units are placed into distinct subgroups based on their strong similarity with regard to specific attributes. For example, one might use cluster analysis to form groups of individual children on the basis of their levels of anxiety, aggression, delinquency, and cognitive difficulties so as to identify useful typologies that could increase understanding of co-occurring mental disorders and lead to more appropriate treatments for specific individuals. There are several different forms of cluster analysis—including HIERARCHICAL CLUSTERING, K-MEANS CLUSTERING, and LATENT CLASS ANALYSIS—and each is appropriate for use with different types of data. Results of a cluster analysis often are presented in a DENDROGRAM. Also called **clustering**.

cluster centroid the central or typical value in a set of values relating to multiple variables. For example, in a data set that contains patient ages and sex, the cluster centroid would be an individual of the average age and the most common sex for that group. See also CENTROID METHOD.

clustered data a set of observations or scores that can be grouped into multiple subsets (clusters), such that the items in each subset are similar to one another with respect to certain attributes and the distinctions between subsets help explain the overall variation among the values as a whole. See CLUSTER ANALYSIS.

clustering *n.* see CLUSTER ANALYSIS.

cluster randomization a process in which preexisting groups are assigned randomly to specific experimental conditions, as occurs in GROUP EXPERIMENTS, GROUP-RANDOMIZED TRIALS, and other designs in which collective entities form the UNIT OF ANALYSIS. When such a process is applied to single individuals it is called RANDOM ASSIGNMENT.

cluster-randomized trial see GROUP-RANDOMIZED TRIAL.

cluster sampling a tiered method of obtaining units for a study. A population is first subdivided into smaller groups or clusters (often administrative or geographical), and a random sample of these clusters is drawn. The process is then repeated for each sampled cluster until the required level is reached. An example would be sampling voters in a large jurisdiction (e.g., a state) by randomly choosing subgroups (e.g., counties) and then further subgroups (e.g., towns and cities) until individual participants are obtained for a study. See also ADAPTIVE CLUSTER SAMPLING.

cluster seeds a procedure for dividing data into subgroups (clusters). A seed point is identified for each cluster and all objects or individuals within a prescribed distance of that point are included in that cluster. The number of seed points can be established at the beginning of the process and the clustering repeated several times with different starting seed points.

cluster-specific model a representation of a variable or the relationships among a set of variables that is specific to a subset (cluster) of the data obtained for analysis.

Co abbreviation for COMPARISON STIMULUS.

coarse data data that are imprecise in some way, such as reaction times that

have been rounded to the nearest integer or survival times that are missing observations for some units.

Cochran C test a statistical procedure for determining whether HOMOGENEITY OF VARIANCE exists among data obtained from two or more different groups. It is a less popular alternative to the LEVENE TEST FOR EQUALITY OF VARIANCE and the BARTLETT TEST FOR EQUALITY OF VARIANCE. [William Gemmell **Cochran** (1909–1980), Scottish-born U.S. statistician]

Cochran–Mantel–Haenszel test see MANTEL–HAENSZEL TEST.

Cochran Q test a NONPARAMETRIC statistical procedure applied when each experimental unit (e.g., an individual participant) is observed under multiple conditions and the data can have only one of two outcomes (e.g., yes or no, pass or fail). The Q test is used to evaluate the equality of the outcomes under the different conditions. [William Gemmell **Cochran**]

codebook *n.* a source of information relating to a set of variables used in a study, such as the names given to variables, how they were defined, and their possible response options.

coding *n.* the replacement of data values with labels or other markers (i.e., a **code**) so as to conceal the identities of participants or facilitate subsequent analysis.

coefficient *n.* a quantity or value that serves as a measure of some property. For example, the CORRELATION COEFFICIENT is a measure of linear relatedness and a REGRESSION COEFFICIENT is a measure of the relationship between a predictor and a response variable.

coefficient alpha see CRONBACH'S ALPHA.

coefficient of agreement a numerical index that reflects the degree of agreement among a set of raters, judges, or instruments as to which of several categories a case belongs. Coefficients of agreement, such as COHEN'S KAPPA, are often corrected for chance agreement. Also called **agreement coefficient**.

coefficient of alienation (symbol: k) a numerical index that reflects the amount of unexplained variance between two variables. It is a measure of the lack of relationship between the two variables. Also called **alienation coefficient**.

coefficient of association any of various quantities that index the relationship between two variables. For example, the Pearson PRODUCT-MOMENT CORRELATION COEFFICIENT might be used to measure a relationship involving linear associations, whereas the SPEARMAN CORRELATION COEFFICIENT might be used for one involving nonlinear associations.

coefficient of concentration see GINI COEFFICIENT.

coefficient of concordance (symbol: W) a numerical index that reflects the degree to which the rankings of k conditions or objects by m raters are in agreement. Its value ranges from 0 (no agreement) to 1 (perfect agreement). Also called **Kendall's coefficient of concordance**; **Kendall's W**.

coefficient of contingency (symbol: C) a measure of the degree of association between two variables whose values are unordered categories. Its value ranges from 0 to 1, with 0 indicating that the two NOMINAL VARIABLES are independent of each other. Examples include CRAMÉR'S V and YULE'S Q. Also called **contingency coefficient**.

coefficient of determination (symbol: r^2) a numerical index that reflects the proportion of variation in an outcome or response variable that is accounted for by its relationship with a predictor variable. More specifically, it is a measure of the percentage of variance in a DEPENDENT VARIABLE that is accounted for by its linear relationship with a single INDEPENDENT VARIABLE.

Obtained by multiplying the value of the CORRELATION COEFFICIENT (r) by itself, the coefficient of determination ranges in value from 0 to 1. Low values indicate the outcome is relatively unrelated to the predictor, whereas values closer to 1 indicate that the two variables are highly related. For example, if $r = .30$, then the squared correlation coefficient is $.30^2 = .09$ and interpreted to mean 9% of the variance between the two variables is common or overlapping. Also called **determination coefficient**; **squared correlation coefficient**. See also COEFFICIENT OF MULTIPLE DETERMINATION.

coefficient of dispersion a measure of the spread in a set of scores. It is calculated as a ratio of the average distance that a score in the set lies from the score at the middle of the set, relative to that middle score. In other words, it is a ratio of the mean deviation about the MEDIAN relative to the median.

coefficient of equivalence a measure of RELIABILITY for parallel test forms: It quantifies the degree of association between two tests that assess the same material using different items. The two tests are given to the same group of respondents and the correlation between scores on each version is calculated.

coefficient of multiple determination (symbol: R^2) a numerical index that reflects the degree to which variation in a response or outcome variable (e.g., workers' incomes) is accounted for by its relationship with two or more predictor variables (e.g., age, gender, years of education). More specifically, it is a measure of the percentage of variance in a DEPENDENT VARIABLE that is accounted for by its relationship with a weighted linear combination of a set of INDEPENDENT VARIABLES. Obtained by multiplying the value of the MULTIPLE CORRELATION COEFFICIENT (R) by itself, the coefficient of multiple determination ranges in value from 0 to 1. Low values indicate that the outcome is relatively unrelated to the predictors, whereas values closer to 1 indicate that the outcome and the predictors are highly related. For example, if $R = .40$, then the coefficient of multiple determination is $.40^2 = .16$ and interpreted to mean 16% of the variance in outcome is explainable by the set of predictors. Also called **multiple correlation coefficient squared**; **squared multiple correlation coefficient**. See also CO-EFFICIENT OF DETERMINATION.

coefficient of reliability see RELIABILITY COEFFICIENT.

coefficient of reproducibility a measure of the extent to which a set of observed responses on a GUTTMAN SCALE match the pattern of responses expected according to a theory. Its value ranges from 0 to 1, with larger values indicating greater GOODNESS OF FIT.

coefficient of stability see STABILITY COEFFICIENT.

coefficient of variation a measure of variability in a set or distribution of values. It is determined by dividing the distribution's STANDARD DEVIATION by its MEAN. Also called **variation coefficient**.

Cohen's d a measure of EFFECT SIZE based on the standardized difference between two means: It indicates the number of STANDARD DEVIATION units by which the means of two data sets differ. For example, a mentoring intervention associated with a Cohen's d of +0.25 indicates an increase of 0.25 standard deviation units for the average child who received mentoring relative to the average child who did not receive mentoring. The metric is used to represent effect sizes in META-ANALYSIS as well as in the determination of POWER, with values of 0.20, 0.50, and 0.80 representing small, medium, and large effect sizes, respectively. See also GLASS'S D. [Jacob **Cohen** (1923–1998), U.S. psychologist and statistician]

Cohen's kappa (symbol: κ) a numerical index that reflects the degree of agreement between two raters or rating systems classifying data into mutually exclusive categories, corrected for the level of agreement expected by chance alone. Values range from 0 (no agreement) to 1 (perfect agreement), with kappas below .40 generally considered poor, .40 to .75 considered fair to good, and more than .75 considered excellent. In accounting for chance, Cohen's kappa avoids overestimating the true level of agreement as might occur through simply determining the number of times that two raters agree relative to the total number of ratings. [Jacob **Cohen**]

cohort *n.* a group of individuals who share a similar characteristic or experience. The term usually refers to an **age cohort** or **birth cohort**, that is, a group of individuals who are born in the same year and thus of similar age.

cohort analysis a statistical procedure to assess the effects attributed to members of a group sharing a particular characteristic, experience, or event. In other words, it is the evaluation of data obtained from studies involving COHORTS, as may be the case in LONGITUDINAL DESIGNS, for example.

cohort effect any outcome associated with being a member of a group possessing a common characteristic (such as individuals who are born in the same year) and therefore influenced by common historical events and practices. Cohort effects may be difficult to separate from AGE EFFECTS and PERIOD EFFECTS in research.

cohort sampling a method of sampling data in which one or more groups sharing a similar characteristic, such as year of birth, are identified and observed.

cohort-sequential design an experimental design in which multiple measures are taken over a period of time from two or more groups of different ages (COHORTS). If, for instance, individuals ranging in age from 5 to 10 years are sampled and then the members of each age group are studied for a 5-year period, the resulting data would span 15 years of development. Such studies essentially are a combination of a LONGITUDINAL DESIGN and a CROSS-SECTIONAL DESIGN. Also called **accelerated longitudinal design**.

cohort study see LONGITUDINAL DESIGN.

cold-deck imputation one of several methods of inserting values for missing data (see IMPUTATION) in which missing observations are replaced by values from a source unrelated to the data set under consideration. Suppose, for example, that a patient questionnaire was administered in a hospital and that five people failed to respond to an item. Substituting responses from a similar item on a survey conducted previously would be an example of cold-deck imputation. Compare HOT-DECK IMPUTATION.

collaborative evaluation see PARTICIPATORY EVALUATION.

collapsing n. the process of combining multiple response options or categories to form a smaller number of responses or categories. For example, a researcher could collect demographic data for students at a particular college by each year of matriculation (i.e., freshman, sophomore, junior, and senior) and then collapse the information from four to two categories (e.g., lower division and upper division).

collinearity n. in REGRESSION ANALYSIS, the situation in which two INDEPENDENT VARIABLES are so highly associated that one can be closely or perfectly predicted by the other. For example, collinearity likely is present if a researcher examines how height and age contribute to children's weight, since the two predictors are highly interrelated (i.e., as children grow older they

get taller). Collinearity leads to difficulties in interpreting the unique influences of the independent variables and requires the use of PARTIALING procedures to distinguish their separate effects. See also MULTICOLLINEARITY.

column marginal a summary of the values across each vertical set of cells in a table. For a table containing frequency counts it is a sum of the number of counts in each column, whereas for other types of tables it is the average value of all data observations within a given column. Compare ROW MARGINAL.

column sum of squares 1. in an ANALYSIS OF VARIANCE involving two independent variables, the amount of variance among individuals that is associated with either variable, as derived from the values given in the relevant column of the data table. It is obtained by determining the average of all observations in the column, calculating how much each score deviates from that average, multiplying the resulting value by itself, and adding it to the similarly obtained values for all other individuals in the column. The calculated quantities for each column are then used to compute the BETWEEN-GROUPS SUM OF SQUARES, which in turn is used to compute an F RATIO. See also TOTAL SUM OF SQUARES. Compare ROW SUM OF SQUARES. **2.** in EXPLORATORY FACTOR ANALYSIS, the variance accounted for by each factor across variables. It is determined by raising the FACTOR LOADINGS for each column in a factor loading matrix to the second power and then totaling the values.

column vector a data matrix with a single column of values. In other words, it has the dimensions $r \times 1$, where r refers to the number of rows and 1 denotes the single column. Compare ROW VECTOR.

combination n. the selection of r objects from among n objects without regard to the order in which the objects are selected. The number of combinations of *n* objects taken *r* at a time is often denoted as $_nC_r$. A combination is similar to a PERMUTATION but distinguished by the irrelevance of order.

commensurate variable a variable that has a similar scale and degree of variation in responses when compared to another variable. For example, the monthly expenditures and the monthly contributions to savings for households in a particular geographic area are commensurate variables.

commonality analysis in MULTIPLE REGRESSION analysis, a technique by which the known variance in an outcome or response variable is separated out into the parts that can be uniquely attributed to each individual predictor variable and the parts that are common to any two or more variables.

common factor see SPECIFIC FACTOR.

common metric a unit or scale of measurement that is applied to data from different sources. In a META-ANALYSIS, for instance, the results from multiple studies may need to be placed on a common metric so that they may be meaningfully compared.

communality *n.* in FACTOR ANALYSIS, the proportion of variance in one variable that is accounted for by an underlying element common to all of the variables in a set. It is given by the COMMUNALITY COEFFICIENT. Compare UNIQUENESS.

communality coefficient (symbol: h^2) an index of the COMMUNALITY in a variable. It is the sum of squared FACTOR LOADINGS of that variable over all of the common factors (underlying dimensions) in the analysis. The communality coefficient is scaled so that, if the factors completely account for all the variance in the variable, the coefficient is 1.

community control see NEIGHBOR-HOOD CONTROL.

community intervention study research that considers a community as the unit of study, such that whole communities are identified and undergo an intervention or treatment. For example, an investigator interested in the contribution of microbial water contaminants to risks of illness might compare a neighborhood for which a water utility recently changed filtration procedures to one for which the utility still employs the standard filtration procedures.

comparability research a study carried out to evaluate the EQUIVALENCE of different test versions or testing methods. A common example involves comparing participant performance on a paper-and-pencil exam versus a computer-administered exam.

comparable-forms reliability see ALTERNATE-FORMS RELIABILITY.

comparable groups two or more representative SAMPLES drawn from the same POPULATION for the purpose of observation or experiment.

comparable form see ALTERNATE FORM.

comparative method an experimental research method of analyzing and comparing the behavior of different species of animals, different cultures of humans, and different age groups of humans and other animals so as to identify similarities and dissimilarities and obtain an understanding of a phenomenon of interest. For example, macaques are often used as a model for understanding human mother–infant relationships. However, male macaques rarely become interested in or involved with care of the young, so comparative study of other species is needed to understand when and how male care of young develops. Also called **comparative analysis**.

comparative rating scale a type of rating instrument in which the items are not evaluated independently but rather through comparison with other stimuli.

For instance, a respondent may be asked to rank a set of given options in relation to one another, assigning the value 1 to the option that is most important to him or her, 2 to the second most important, and so on. Compare ABSOLUTE RATING SCALE.

comparative trial see CONTROLLED TRIAL.

comparison *n.* any appraisal of two or more groups in order to identify differences, such as that between the mean of a variable in one population and its mean in another. Comparisons may be planned in advance, as in A PRIORI COMPARISONS, or decided upon after data analysis has already begun, as in POST HOC COMPARISONS. Also called **contrast**.

comparison group see CONTROL GROUP.

comparison stimulus (Co) in psychophysical testing, one of a set of stimuli to be compared with a standard stimulus.

comparison-wise error rate see TESTWISE ERROR RATE.

competing risks in SURVIVAL ANALYSIS, the set of multiple outcomes that indicate a target event (failure) has occurred. For instance, a school district might identify such competing risks for student dropout as lack of interest, needing to work to support the family, and moving away. Consequently, administrators might develop a **competing-risks model**, or statistical representation of the relationships among these concepts, in order to understand when dropout is likely to occur and what specific combination of factors will be involved for different students.

complementary events a situation in which there are only two possible outcomes and observation of one outcome necessarily indicates that the other did not occur.

complete block design a study in which participants are first divided into blocks (relatively homogeneous subsets) according to some characteristic (e.g., age) that is not a focus of interest and are then assigned to the different treatments or conditions in such a manner that each treatment appears once in each block. Thus, the number of participants in each block must equal the number of experimental conditions. For example, the following arrangement of four treatments (A, B, C, D) and 16 individuals (from four age groups) is a complete block design:

Block #	Treatment			
1 (children)	A	B	C	D
2 (adolescents)	B	C	D	A
3 (young adults)	C	D	A	B
4 (older adults)	D	A	B	C

By ensuring that the "nuisance" characteristic (here, age) is equally represented across all conditions, complete block designs reduce or eliminate its contribution to experimental error. Compare INCOMPLETE BLOCK DESIGN. See also BLOCK DESIGN; RANDOMIZED BLOCK DESIGN.

complete-case analysis see LISTWISE DELETION.

complete counterbalancing a process of arranging a series of experimental conditions or treatments in such a way that every possible sequence of conditions is given at least once during the study. For instance, the following arrangement of sequences of three treatments (A, B, C), each assigned to a different subgroup of participants, demonstrates complete counterbalancing: A-B-C, A-C-B, B-C-A, B-A-C, C-A-B, and C-B-A. Compare INCOMPLETE COUNTERBALANCING.

complete factorial design a research study involving two or more INDEPENDENT VARIABLES in which every possible combination of the levels of each variable is represented. For instance, in a study of two drug treatments, one (A) having two dosages and the other (B) having three dosages, a complete factorial design would pair the dosages administered to different individuals or groups of participants as follows: A_1 with B_1, A_1 with B_2, A_1 with B_3, A_2 with B_1, A_2 with B_2, and A_2 with B_3. Compare FRACTIONAL FACTORIAL DESIGN.

complete-linkage clustering in HIERARCHICAL CLUSTERING, a method in which the distance between two clusters of items (e.g., people, objects) is computed as the greatest distance between any two objects in the different clusters. Also called **farthest neighbor**. Compare AVERAGE-LINKAGE CLUSTERING; SINGLE-LINKAGE CLUSTERING.

complete null hypothesis a statement regarding the outcome of an experiment that totally (rather than partially) contradicts the ALTERNATIVE HYPOTHESIS.

complex comparison an evaluation that involves comparing some combination of two or more groups against one or more other groups. For example, a researcher investigating the influence of a new teaching style on test scores might examine whether the average score across two classrooms of students differs from that of a third classroom. Compare SIMPLE COMPARISON.

component bar graph a BAR GRAPH in which stacked columns are used to represent two or more aspects of a data set involving categorical variables. For example, a researcher who observed the frequencies of males and females by matriculation year at a particular college might present the results in a component bar graph (see below). The categories of matriculation (freshmen, sophomores, juniors, seniors) would be shown along the x-axis, and the number of males and females would be given by differently colored or patterned bars rising above each category. Also called **sectional bar graph; segmented bar graph; stacked bar graph**.

componential analysis 1. any analysis of data in which a process or system is separated into a series of subprocesses or components. **2.** a set of information-processing and mathematical techniques that enables an investigator to decompose an individual's performance on a cognitive task into the underlying elementary cognitive processes.

component-plus-residual plot see PARTIAL RESIDUAL PLOT.

composite hypothesis a statistical hypothesis that is not specific about all relevant features of a population or that does not give a single value for a characteristic of a population but allows for a range of acceptable values. For example, a statement that the average age of employees in academia exceeds 50 is a composite hypothesis, as there are a variety of ages above that number that the aver-

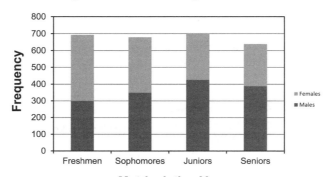

Matriculation Year
component bar graph

age could assume to validate the statement. Alternatively, a composite hypothesis could give a specific value for one characteristic (e.g., the mean) but not others (e.g., the VARIANCE). Compare SIMPLE HYPOTHESIS.

composite reliability 1. the aggregate reliability of two or more similar items, such as judges' ratings. **2.** in STRUCTURAL EQUATION MODELING, the extent to which the set of constructs represented in the model relate to a given latent variable. CRONBACH'S ALPHA is an index of such reliability.

composite score a single value obtained by combining the scores on two or more component measures. For example, a teacher may average the scores from separate tests throughout a semester to calculate a final exam grade for a student.

composite variable a variable constructed from the weighted or averaged combination of two or more component variables. For example, a figure skater's overall skill during a performance might be determined by judges' evaluations of his or her technical merit, program complexity, and presentation.

compositional variable a variable describing one or more substrata of a larger group. An example would be mathematics scores of boys in a class of both boys and girls.

compound bar graph a BAR GRAPH used to display two or more related sets of data simultaneously, typically scores on a variable or variables that fall into different categories. For example, it might be used to show the number of males and females enrolled in each major at a particular college (see below). The different majors would be given along the horizontal X-AXIS and two columns would rise above each—one for males and one for females—to the appropriate height as given by the frequencies along the vertical Y-AXIS. See also COMPONENT BAR GRAPH; DUAL BAR GRAPH.

compound event an event that is the intersection of two or more simpler events. For example, being a man with schizophrenia is the intersection of the event classes being male and having schizophrenia.

compound probability the likeliness that two unrelated (independent) events will occur together, either simultaneously or in succession. For example, one could calculate the compound probability of rolling a 6 twice in a row on a die, of rolling a 6 on the first turn and a 2 on the second, and so forth.

compound symmetry a quality of data in which the values within each sample or subsample have the same degree of variability (i.e., have HOMOGENEITY OF VARIANCE) and the corresponding

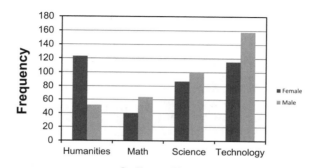

College Major

compound bar graph

55

pairs of values across the different groups have the same COVARIANCE.

comprehensive process analysis a method for the study of qualitative data relating to a process, such as change that occurs during psychotherapy. Important moments that occurred during the process are identified and then described in sequence to help inform existing theories.

computational formula the equation used to calculate values for a statistical concept. This contrasts with the DEFINITIONAL FORMULA, which is the formal verbal definition of the concept.

computational table a matrix that shows the different steps and incremental results involved in performing a calculation.

concealed measure see UNOBTRUSIVE MEASURE.

conceptual formula see DEFINITIONAL FORMULA.

conceptual replication see REPLICATION.

concomitance *n.* a co-occurrence between a response or outcome variable and a variable other than a predictor of interest. —**concomitant** *adj.*

concomitant variable see COVARIATE.

concomitant variation variation of two phenomena at the same time, in which the variables may be causally related or both may be influenced by a third variable.

concordance *n.* the state or condition of being in harmony or agreement. In TWIN STUDIES, for example, it is the presence of a given trait or disorder in both members of the pair. Compare DISCORDANCE. —**concordant** *adj.*

concordance coefficient see COEFFICIENT OF CONCORDANCE.

concurrent validity the extent to which one measurement is backed up by a related measurement obtained at about the same point in time. In testing, the VALIDITY of results obtained from one test (e.g., self-report of job performance) can often be assessed by comparison with a separate but related measurement (e.g., supervisor rating of job performance) collected at the same point in time. See also CRITERION VALIDITY.

condition *n.* a category or level of a variable whose values are manipulated by a researcher. Study participants are then assigned to receive or be exposed to one or more of the different conditions.

conditional distribution a set of scores on one variable expressed as a function of one or more other variables; such a distribution gives the score on one variable given each value of a second variable.

conditional event an outcome that may occur given that another event has occurred.

conditional expectation the long-run average value of a RANDOM VARIABLE as a function of one or more other variables.

conditional independence the situation in which two or more variables are unrelated to one another only when each is a function of one or more others.

conditional likelihood see CONDITIONAL PROBABILITY.

conditional model a model representing a pattern of relationships among a set of variables that is dependent on given levels or categories of one or more other variables. Compare UNCONDITIONAL MODEL.

conditional odds a ratio of the likeliness of an event's occurrence to the likeliness of nonoccurrence, where the outcome is dependent on values of one or more other variables. See ODDS.

conditional probability the likeliness that an event will occur given that another event is known to have occurred. Conditional probability plays an important role in statistical theory. The probability of observing a particular outcome given that another outcome is known to have occurred can be derived from a CONTINGENCY TABLE. Also called **conditional likelihood**.

conditional variance a measure of the fluctuations among the individual observations in a TIME SERIES. The value at each point in the sequence thus is a function of one or more previous points. Compare UNCONDITIONAL VARIANCE.

confederate *n*. in an experimental situation, an aide of the experimenter who poses as a participant but whose behavior is rehearsed prior to the experiment.

confidence band a series of connected CONFIDENCE INTERVALS around a REGRESSION LINE, as shown in the hypothetical example below. A confidence band may be simultaneous (e.g., coverage rate of entire band is .95) or nonsimultaneous (e.g., pointwise coverage rate is .95). In either case it is a representation of the uncertainty in estimating a function value (e.g., salary) for a population based on data (e.g., job satisfaction) from a sample of that population.

confidence interval (**CI**) a range of values for a population PARAMETER that is estimated from a sample with a preset, fixed probability (known as the CONFIDENCE LEVEL) that the range will contain the true value of the parameter. The width of the confidence interval provides information about the precision of the estimate, such that a wider interval indicates relatively low precision and a narrower interval indicates relatively high precision. For example, a confidence interval for the population mean could be calculated with data obtained from a sample and would provide an estimated range of values within which the actual population mean is believed to lie. A confidence interval often is reported in addition to the POINT ESTIMATE of a population parameter.

confidence level a value expressing the frequency with which a given CONFIDENCE INTERVAL contains the true value of the parameter being estimated. For example, a 95% confidence level associated with a confidence interval for estimating a population mean indicates that in 95% of all estimates based on a random sample of a given size the confidence interval will contain the true value of the population mean. The par-

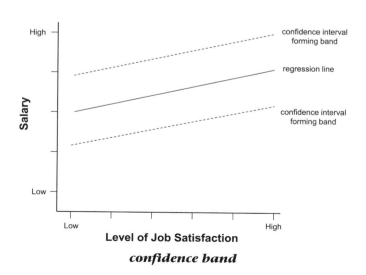

confidence interval forming band

regression line

confidence interval forming band

High

Salary

Low

Low   Level of Job Satisfaction   High

confidence band

ticular confidence level used is up to the researcher but generally is 95% or 99%.

confidence limit either of the values at the upper and lower ends of a CONFIDENCE INTERVAL, which provide an estimated range for the value of a population PARAMETER. Also called **confidence bound**.

confidentiality *n.* a principle of ethics requiring mental health care or medical care providers to limit the disclosure of a patient's identity, his or her condition or treatment, and any data entrusted to professionals during assessment, diagnosis, and treatment. Similar protection is given to research participants and survey respondents against unauthorized access to information they reveal in confidence. See INFORMED CONSENT. —**confidential** *adj.*

configurational frequency analysis a nonparametric method of comparing observed counts within the categories of a variable with the frequencies that are theoretically expected. It is an alternative to similar methods (e.g., CHI-SQUARE TESTS) that require a minimum expected count within each category in order for the results to be valid.

confirmation bias the tendency to gather evidence that confirms preexisting expectations, typically by emphasizing or pursuing supporting evidence while dismissing or failing to seek contradictory evidence.

confirmatory data analysis a statistical analysis designed to address one or more specific research questions, generally with the aim of confirming preconceived hypotheses. Compare EXPLORATORY DATA ANALYSIS.

confirmatory factor analysis (**CFA**) any method of testing A PRIORI hypotheses to the effect that the relationships among a set of observed variables are due to a particular set of unobserved variables. Unlike EXPLORATORY FACTOR ANALYSIS, in which all measured (mani-

fest) variables are examined in relation to all underlying (latent) variables, confirmatory factor analysis imposes explicit theoretical restrictions so that observed measures relate with some (often just one) latent factors but not others.

confirmatory research research conducted with the aim of testing one or more preexisting hypotheses. Compare EXPLORATORY RESEARCH.

confound *n.* in an experiment, an independent variable that is conceptually distinct but empirically inseparable from one or more other independent variables. **Confounding** makes it impossible to differentiate that variable's effects in isolation from its effects in conjunction with other variables. For example, in a study of high-school student achievement, the type of school (e.g., private vs. public) a student attended prior to high school and his or her prior academic achievements in that context are confounds. Also called **confounder**; **confounding factor**; **confounding variable**.

confounded comparison a comparison of values obtained by different experimental groups on an outcome or dependent variable when two or more predictor or independent variables vary simultaneously across the groups. In such cases it is impossible to differentiate the effects of the independent variables. For example, consider a researcher studying how material presentation format (lecture vs. computer) and teacher sex (male vs. female) affect student learning. If the investigator were to examine data for only two groups of students (those who had a male teacher and lecture presentation format vs. those who had a female teacher and computer presentation format), he or she would have created a confounded comparison. Compare UNCONFOUNDED COMPARISON.

confounded effects the indivisible effects of two or more predictor or independent variables on a single response or dependent variable. That is, the unique influence of one predictor cannot be separated out from that of the others. For example, assume a researcher is examining the effectiveness of a hunger-reduction pill for weight loss. If some of the participants receiving the pill discover they are part of the treatment group and concurrently adopt better eating habits and increase their exercise levels, these additional healthy activities will also affect weight loss. Since those in the control group (receiving a PLACEBO sugar pill) are not engaging in these same supplemental activities, effects of eating habits, exercise levels, and the actual treatment will have become confounded.

confounding factor see CONFOUND.

confounding variable see CONFOUND.

confusion matrix see CLASSIFICATION TABLE.

congruence coefficient in FACTOR ANALYSIS, an index of the degree of similarity between two underlying or LATENT VARIABLES that are postulated to account for the data pattern among observed or MANIFEST VARIABLES. It ranges from –1 to +1 in value.

congruent validity see CONVERGENT VALIDITY.

conjoint analysis a method of assessing behavioral choices in which participants are compared on pairs of attributes that have been selected by the researcher as potential explanations or predictors of such choices. For example, an investigator looking at vacation preferences might choose to examine such attributes as warm versus cold climates, hotels versus bed-and-breakfast accommodations, destinations in the United States versus destinations in Europe, and so forth. Conjoint analysis is used particularly in studies of consumer decision making.

conjoint measurement a method for

measuring the joint effect of two or more predictor or INDEPENDENT VARIABLES on the ordering of an outcome or DEPENDENT VARIABLE. It is used with NONMETRIC data, notably in ITEM RESPONSE THEORY.

consensual drift the tendency for two or more observers who are working together to depart gradually from accuracy or an agreed standard, such that they are making errors in the same direction and to the same extent. See OBSERVER DRIFT.

consensual validity the degree to which self-reports made by an individual coincide with scores or ratings made by other people who know that individual (e.g., family members, work colleagues). See VALIDITY.

consent *n.* see INFORMED CONSENT.

consequential validity the extent to which a research project has wider social benefits, such that results from the project influence decisions that affect people's lives. Many researchers question whether this is truly a form of VALIDITY.

consequent variable a variable that is correlated with a primary outcome or DEPENDENT VARIABLE and whose value is predicted by that outcome variable. For example, in studies examining the influence of teaching style on student academic achievement, student motivation may be a consequent variable of achievement. Compare ANTECEDENT VARIABLE.

conservative *adj.* describing statistical methods that have a reduced likelihood of error, particularly of incorrectly rejecting the NULL HYPOTHESIS, but that are less capable of detecting significant relationships among variables. In other words, conservative approaches have less POWER and thus tend to underestimate associations or effects.

consistency check a method often built into an experimental or statistical procedure to verify that data are accurate or that computations have been done correctly. For example, question-naire items with slightly different wording but identical meaning should be answered by individuals in the same way, and respondents claiming to have a high educational degree should be of a certain age.

consistent estimator an ESTIMATOR calculated from sample data whose value becomes more and more representative of the true quantity in the larger population as the sample size increases. That is, a consistent estimator is one for which larger samples result in a reduction of BIAS. An example is the MEAN: As the size of the sample from which it is calculated increases, the obtained value more closely approximates the actual value in the population it is intended to represent.

constant *n.* in mathematics, a fixed quantity that remains unchanged during a specified operation or series of operations. For example, the element *a* in the REGRESSION EQUATION

$$y = a + bx + e$$

is a constant. Compare VARIABLE.

constant comparative analysis a procedure for evaluating QUALITATIVE DATA in which the information is coded and compared across categories, patterns are identified, and these patterns are refined as new data are obtained. For example, a researcher might use constant comparative analysis to assess responses to interview questions, creating categories of answers according to the perspectives expressed, examining their different items, and integrating categories or revising their properties before formulating a theory. Also called **constant-comparison method**.

constant error a SYSTEMATIC ERROR in some particular direction. Constant error is computed as the average positive or negative difference between the observed and actual values along a dimension of interest. For example, if a weight

of 1 kg is judged on average to be 1.5 kg, and a weight of 2 kg is judged to be 2.5 kg, the constant error is 500 g. See also ABSOLUTE ERROR; RANDOM ERROR.

construct *n.* a concept or theoretical entity. It may be derived from empirically verifiable and measurable events or processes—an **empirical construct**—or via processes inferred from data of this kind but not themselves directly observable—a **hypothetical construct**.

construct validity the degree to which a test or instrument is capable of measuring a concept, trait, or other theoretical entity. For example, if a researcher develops a new questionnaire to evaluate respondents' levels of aggression, the construct validity of the instrument would be the extent to which it actually assesses aggression as opposed to assertiveness, social dominance, and so forth. A variety of factors can threaten the basic construct validity of an experiment, including (a) mismatch between the construct and its OPERATIONAL DEFINITION; (b) use of a single method to collect information on all variables in the study, thereby potentially introducing bias; (c) failure to distinguish between constructs and levels of constructs, so that observations made on only a few levels or conditions are extended by inference to other levels; and (d) various EXPERIMENTER EFFECTS and other participant reactions to aspects of the experimental situation. There are two main forms of construct VALIDITY in the social sciences: CONVERGENT VALIDITY and DISCRIMINANT VALIDITY. See also MULTITRAIT–MULTIMETHOD MATRIX.

contaminated normal distribution a distribution that appears to be a NORMAL DISTRIBUTION but is in fact characterized by multiple such distributions, each of which has different parameters (e.g., different STANDARD DEVIATIONS).

contamination *n.* in testing and experimentation, the situation in which prior knowledge, expectations, or other factors relating to the variable under study are permitted to influence the collection and interpretation of data about that variable.

content analysis a procedure for assigning codes to identify themes in written or spoken records. A content analysis of a speech, for example, may involve a count of the number of times a particular behavior occurs or the number of times a particular idea is mentioned.

content-referenced test see CRITERION-REFERENCED TEST.

content validity the extent to which a test measures a representative sample of the subject matter or behavior under investigation. For example, if a test is designed to survey arithmetic skills at a third-grade level, content validity indicates how well it represents the range of arithmetic operations possible at that level. Although researchers traditionally relied upon their own subjective impressions or the judgments of experts as the primary means of determining content validity, modern approaches involve the use of EXPLORATORY FACTOR ANALYSIS and other multivariate statistical procedures.

contextual analysis any method of evaluating data that takes into account the characteristics of the environment in which the information was collected and their influence upon study units.

contextual effect the influence on an outcome or response variable of the environment in which data are collected. For example, a study participant may behave differently in a laboratory than in a public setting.

contextual variable any variable that describes the environment in which data are collected, such as its location or the degree of social interaction.

contingency *n.* **1.** the degree to which one CATEGORICAL VARIABLE is associated with another such variable, as represented by the frequencies recorded in a

CONTINGENCY TABLE. **2.** more generally, the extent to which one event or outcome is dependent on another.

contingency analysis an approach to measuring the association between two variables whose values are represented by unordered categories. For example, a researcher may use contingency analysis to determine whether children who are undergoing a painful medical procedure become less distressed when nurses reassure them or whether nurses reassure children more when they are distressed. See COEFFICIENT OF CONTINGENCY.

contingency coefficient see COEFFICIENT OF CONTINGENCY.

contingency table a two-dimensional table in which frequency values for categories of one variable are presented in the rows and values for categories of a second variable are presented in the columns: Values that appear in the various CELLS then represent the number or percentage of cases that fall into the two categories that intersect at this point. For example, the sex and geographical locations of a sample of individuals applying for a particular job may be displayed in a contingency table.

Location	Sex		
	Female	Male	Total
Los Angeles	19	14	33
New York	19	15	34
Seattle	15	10	25
Tampa	13	12	25
Washington, DC	17	16	33
Total	83	67	150

Thus, the number of women from Los Angeles are given, the number of men from Los Angeles are given, the number of women from New York City are given, the number of men from New York City are given, and so on. Also called **cross-classification table**.

contingent probability the probability, expressed as a number between 0 and 1, that one event or category will occur if another one does. An example would be the probability that the child of a drug user will become a drug user himself or herself. Unusually high or low contingent probabilities (compared to the general population) may, but do not necessarily, imply a causal relationship between the two events.

continuity correction see CORRECTION FOR CONTINUITY.

continuous *adj.* describing a variable, score, or distribution that can take on any numerical values within its range. Compare DISCONTINUOUS; DISCRETE. See also CONTINUOUS VARIABLE.

continuous distribution a DISTRIBUTION in which values can occur anywhere along an unbroken continuum. An example would be any distribution showing variation in human height or weight. A continuous distribution can be plotted as a single smooth line, and it may be used to display the likelihood of specific values occurring (a **continuous probability distribution**) or the actual number of times they have been observed to occur, such as in a research sample (a **continuous frequency distribution**). Compare DISCRETE DISTRIBUTION. See also CONTINUOUS VARIABLE.

continuous function a function—$f(x)$—in which an infinitely small change in input has an infinitely small change on output. When depicted graphically, the values of a continuous function form a smooth, unbroken curve. Compare DISCONTINUOUS FUNCTION.

continuous random variable a variable that may assume any of an infinite range of values according to a particular PROBABILITY DISTRIBUTION. Height and weight are examples. Compare DISCRETE RANDOM VARIABLE.

continuous rating scale a scale on which ratings are assigned along a continuum (e.g., a line) rather than according to categories. Such ratings are made by making a mark on the scale to indicate the exact "placement" of the rating or by assigning a precise numerical value. Also called **continuous scale**.

continuous-time survival model in SURVIVAL ANALYSIS, a method for predicting time until the occurrence of an event in which time is treated as a CONTINUOUS VARIABLE. For example, the time a recovering alcoholic can expect to go without a drink could be expressed as a continuous-time survival model. Compare DISCRETE-TIME SURVIVAL MODEL.

continuous variable a variable that may in theory have an infinite number of possible values. For example, time is a continuous variable because accurate instruments will enable it to be measured to any subdivision of a unit (e.g., 1.76 seconds). By contrast, number of children is not a continuous variable as it is not possible to have 1.76 children. In practice, a continuous variable may be restricted to an artificial range by instrumentation constraints, practical limitations, or other reasons. For example, a researcher assessing the influence of a new technique on student study time may only be able to observe a group of individuals for 1 hour per day, such that the range of time in the data he or she collects may span 0 minutes to 60 minutes, even though some people will in actuality have exceeded that upper figure. Compare DISCONTINUOUS VARIABLE.

contour plot a two-dimensional display of a three-dimensional relationship. The x-axis and y-axis of a CARTESIAN COORDINATE SYSTEM are used to depict the values of two of the variables while the values of the third variable are represented by raised or shaded lines, similar to how elevations are shown on a topographical map. For example, the graphic opposite is a hypothetical contour plot of age and conservative attitudes in a sample and their DENSITY ESTIMATION values in the larger population of interest.

contrast *n.* see COMPARISON.

contrast analysis comparisons between two or more groups that address specific questions about the precise patterns of difference between the MEANS of these groups. Where several groups are being compared, CONTRAST CODING can be used to assign weights to the different means.

contrast coding in ANALYSIS OF VARIANCE and MULTIPLE REGRESSION, a method of assigning weights to values so that specific comparisons of interest can be made. To ensure the statistical independence of the particular quantities being evaluated, the process requires that the weights in each comparison sum to 0. For example, consider a researcher investigating four different methods for teaching course content. If he or she wanted to compare the average performance of the first group to the average performance of the remaining three groups, the investigator would apply contrast weights of +3, −1, −1, and −1 to the respective group means. If, however, he or she wanted to compare the average performance of the first group to the average performance of the fourth group, the investigator instead would apply contrast weights of +1, 0, 0, and −1 to the respective group means. Also called **orthogonal coding**. Compare DUMMY VARIABLE CODING; EFFECT CODING.

contrast weight in CONTRAST CODING, the WEIGHT assigned to each value in a set of values to be compared.

control *n.* **1.** the regulation of all extraneous conditions and variables in an experiment so that any change in the DEPENDENT VARIABLE can be attributed solely to manipulation of the INDEPENDENT VARIABLE and not to any other factors. **2.** see STATISTICAL CONTROL.

control condition in an experiment or research design, a condition that does not involve exposure to the treatment or intervention under study. For example, in an investigation of a new drug, participants in a control condition may receive a pill containing some inert substance, whereas those in the EXPERIMENTAL CONDITION receive the actual drug of interest.

control experiment a follow-up experiment designed to check that the findings of an initial study were in fact caused by the factor under investigation and not by some other variable. For example, consider a case in which initial research appeared to demonstrate the beneficial effect of a new treatment for depression. To confirm these results a control experiment might be devised in which a similar group of individuals was tracked to find the number of individuals whose depression was alleviated without use of the treatment.

control group a comparison group in a study whose members receive either no intervention at all or some established intervention. The responses of those in the control group are compared with the responses of participants in one or more EXPERIMENTAL GROUPS that are given the new treatment being evaluated. See also NO-TREATMENT CONTROL GROUP.

controlled observation an observation made under standard and systematic conditions rather than casual or incidental conditions.

controlled sampling a method of choosing cases for research in which cer-

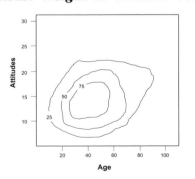

contour plot

tain characteristics are considered undesirable and the probability of their being selected is therefore minimized. For example, an educational researcher may need to adjust his or her sampling technique if certain subsets of students are costly to find or if their obtained data may exert undue influence on study results or otherwise present logistical difficulties.

controlled trial a study in which patients with a particular condition, disease, or illness are assigned either to a treatment group, which receives the new intervention under investigation, or to a CONTROL GROUP, which receives either no intervention or some standard intervention already in use. If individuals are allocated to the different groups at random, then the design is a RANDOMIZED CLINICAL TRIAL. Also called **comparative trial**.

controlled variable 1. see CONTROL VARIABLE. **2.** an infrequent synonym of INDEPENDENT VARIABLE, the variable in a study whose values are manipulated by the researcher.

control procedure a procedure applied before commencing a study in order to equate participants with regard to some variable that is not of research interest but nonetheless may influence the outcome. MATCHING is an example of a control procedure.

control series a series of CONTROL EXPERIMENTS devised to eliminate any alternative explanation of the findings obtained from a test.

control treatment an existing or standard intervention administered to members of a CONTROL GROUP in a study.

control variable a variable that is considered to have an effect on the response measure in a study but which itself is not of particular interest to the researcher. To remove its effects a control variable may be held at a constant level during the study or managed by statistical means (e.g., a PARTIAL CORRELATION). Also called **controlled variable**.

convenience sampling any process for selecting a sample of individuals or cases that is neither random nor systematic but rather governed by chance or ready availability. Interviewing the first 50 people to exit a store is an example of convenience sampling. Data obtained from convenience sampling do not generalize to the larger population; there may be significant SAMPLING BIAS, and SAMPLING ERROR cannot be estimated. Also called **accidental sampling**; **opportunity sampling**.

convergent validity the extent to which responses on a test or instrument exhibit a strong relationship with responses on conceptually similar tests or instruments. This is one of two aspects of CONSTRUCT VALIDITY, the other being DISCRIMINANT VALIDITY. Also called **congruent validity**.

conversation analysis a specialty within DISCOURSE ANALYSIS that focuses upon casual discussions as well as other more formal extended verbal exchanges between two or more speakers.

Cook's distance (Cook's D) in an analysis of the relationship between a response variable and one or more predictor variables, a measure of the difference that is made to the result when a single observation is dropped from the analysis. Cook's D thus indicates the degree of influence of a particular data value. An observation typically is considered influential if it has a Cook's D larger than $4/(n - k - 1)$, where n is the sample size and k is the number of terms in the model. [R. Denis **Cook** (1944–), U.S. statistician]

cooperative study see MULTISITE STUDY.

coordinate axis see AXIS.

coordinate system see CARTESIAN COORDINATE SYSTEM.

corrected moment see UNCORRECTED MOMENT.

correction *n.* a quantity that is added, subtracted, or otherwise introduced to remove inaccuracy from a measure, calculation, or analysis. Corrections are made, for example, when the ASSUMPTIONS about data that accompany a statistical procedure do not correspond to the actual data being analyzed.

correction for attenuation in analyses estimating the relationship between two variables, an adjustment for error introduced during the process of obtaining the measures, where such error serves to underestimate the measured effect.

correction for continuity a procedure that is applied to adjust for the fact that a statistical method is based on an assumption that the data have a CONTINUOUS DISTRIBUTION when, in fact, they have a DISCRETE DISTRIBUTION. YATES'S CORRECTION FOR CONTINUITY is an example. Also called **continuity correction**.

correction for guessing a scoring rule for MULTIPLE-CHOICE TESTS such that the EXPECTED VALUE of getting an item correct under the assumption of no knowledge is 0 rather than $1/n$, where n is the number of alternatives. Thus, if a test taker incorrectly answered four questions, a further $4/n$ would be deleted from his or her score. By thus penalizing inaccurate responses, the correction discourages a test taker from guessing and provides a better estimate of that person's true ability. See also FORMULA SCORING.

correction for range restriction in estimations of the relationship between two variables, an adjustment for error arising from the use of a sample that is not representative of the larger population of interest. For example, consider a researcher who is investigating how cognitive ability and absenteeism are related in the general U.S. workforce. If his or her available sample is taken from organizations that require individuals to have obtained at least a bachelor's degree in order to be employed, then a correction for range restriction would be appropriate. See RESTRICTION OF RANGE.

correlate *n.* a variable that is related to another variable. See CORRELATION.

correlated groups see DEPENDENT SAMPLES.

correlated-groups design see WITHIN-SUBJECTS DESIGN.

correlated-groups t test see DEPENDENT-SAMPLES T TEST.

correlated samples see DEPENDENT SAMPLES.

correlated-samples design see WITHIN-SUBJECTS DESIGN.

correlated-samples t test see DEPENDENT-SAMPLES T TEST.

correlation *n.* the degree of a relationship (usually linear) between two variables, which may be quantified as a CORRELATION COEFFICIENT.

correlation analysis any of various statistical procedures for identifying relationships among variables and determining their strength or degree. CANONICAL ANALYSIS and FACTOR ANALYSIS are examples. Correlation analyses make no inferences about causality (compare CAUSAL ANALYSIS). Also called **association analysis**.

correlational fallacy the fallacy that association implies causation: the practice of drawing conclusions about cause and effect based solely on observations of a relationship between variables. For example, assume a researcher found that dieters tend to weigh more than other people. If the investigator then were to conclude that the diet is responsible for the additional weight, then he or she has committed a correlational fallacy.

correlational research a type of study in which relationships between variables are simply observed without any control over the setting in which those relationships occur or any manipulation by the researcher. FIELD RESEARCH often takes this form. For example, consider a researcher assessing teaching style. He or she could use a correlational approach by attending classes on a college campus that are each taught in a different way (e.g., lecture, interactive, computer aided) and noting any differences in student learning that arise. Also called **correlational design**; **correlational method**; **correlational study**. Compare EXPERIMENTAL RESEARCH.

correlation coefficient a numerical index reflecting the degree of linear relationship between two variables. It is scaled so that the value of +1 indicates a perfect positive relationship (such that high scores on variable x are associated with high scores on variable y), –1 indicates a perfect negative relationship (such that high scores on variable x are associated with low scores on variable y, or vice versa), and 0 indicates no relationship. The most commonly used type of correlation coefficient is the Pearson PRODUCT-MOMENT CORRELATION COEFFICIENT.

correlation matrix a symmetrical SQUARE MATRIX displaying the degree of association between all possible pairs of variables contained in a set. A CORRELATION COEFFICIENT between the ith and jth variables in a set of variables is displayed in the intersection of the ith row and the jth column of the matrix. Consider the hypothetical example below depicting correlations among anhedonia, hopelessness, low self-esteem, and suicidal ideation in a sample of college students.

correlation ratio (symbol: η) a measure of the strength or degree of relationship between two variables whose association is nonlinear (i.e., it cannot be depicted graphically by a straight line). Often referred to as **eta**, the correlation ratio is the nonlinear equivalent of the CORRELATION COEFFICIENT.

correlogram *n.* see AUTOCORRELATION.

correspondence analysis a statistical technique in which information from a two-way CONTINGENCY TABLE is transformed into a graphical display. This can then be analyzed to understand the associations between the various categories of the different variables involved.

cotwin control see TWIN CONTROL.

count data information about the frequency of an attribute or event. An example would be the number of times a third-grader acts out in class during a 30-minute observation period.

counterbalancing *n.* arranging a series of experimental conditions or treatments in such a way as to minimize the influence of extraneous factors, such as practice or fatigue, on experimental results. In other words, counterbalancing is an attempt to reduce or avoid CARRYOVER EFFECTS and ORDER EFFECTS. A simple form of counterbalancing would be to administer experimental condi-

Variable	1	2	3	4
1. Anhedonia	—			
2. Hopelessness	.82	—		
3. Low self-esteem	.77	.31	—	
4. Suicidal ideation	.23	.90	.54	—

correlation matrix

tions in the order A-B to half of the participants and in the order B-A to the other half; a LATIN SQUARE would be a more complex form.

counterfactual *n.* an alternative outcome: a consideration of what would have been observed had something taken place that in fact did not. Counterfactuals are used primarily in RUBIN'S CAUSAL MODEL. For example, consider a researcher seeking to determine the effect of a new depression treatment as compared to an existing standard treatment. According to Rubin's model, the investigator would need to determine the average difference for all participants between (a) the outcome after administering the new treatment and (b) the outcome after administering the alternative treatment. Because the same participants cannot simultaneously be given the new and old treatments, the situation arises in which certain experimental outcomes cannot be observed and become counterfactuals that instead must be estimated.

counternull value the magnitude of an effect (such as a difference in averages between two groups or a measure of the strength of the relationship between two variables) that carries with it a level of statistical support that is equivalent to the statistical support attributed to the value specified under a competing hypothesis (i.e., the NULL HYPOTHESIS). The counternull value helps eliminate two common errors: (a) equating failure to reject a null hypothesis with the estimation of the effect size as equal to zero and (b) equating rejection of a null hypothesis on the basis of a significance test with having demonstrated a scientifically important effect.

counting process a type of STOCHASTIC PROCESS used to describe or analyze data that represent an ordered series of the times to multiple events, such as a study of the time to the first event, time to the second event, and so on.

covariance *n.* a scale-dependent measure of the relationship between two variables such that corresponding pairs of values of the variables are studied with regard to their relative distance from their respective means. A positive covariance results when values of one variable that lie above the mean of that variable tend to be paired with values of the second variable that also lie above the mean of that variable. A negative covariance results when values of one variable that lie above the mean tend to be paired with values of the second variable that lie below the mean. A covariance is equal to 0 when two variables are independent, or unrelated to one another.

covariance analysis see ANALYSIS OF COVARIANCE.

covariance matrix a SQUARE MATRIX that represents how variance in each variable in a set is related to variance in all other variables in the set. Consider the following hypothetical example for five variables pertaining to perceived health. The covariances between pairs of variables are located at the intersection of the row and column that correspond to the two variables. The quantities along

Variable	1	2	3	4	5
1. Ill enough to see doctor in past year	.24	—			
2. Hospitalized or disabled last year	.06	.14	—		
3. Hospitalized or disabled prior 4 years	.03	−.03	.16	—	
4. Self-rated health	−.09	−.08	.00	.65	—
5. Health satisfaction	−.18	−.13	−.02	.62	.91

covariance matrix

the diagonal of the matrix are variances rather than covariances. Also called **dispersion matrix**; **variance–covariance matrix**.

covariance model a mathematical specification of the pattern of relationships among a set of quantitative variables that expresses how variance in each variable may be related to variance in each of the other variables.

covariance structure analysis see ANALYSIS OF COVARIANCE STRUCTURES.

covariate *n.* a variable that exhibits COVARIATION with a measured outcome or DEPENDENT VARIABLE: It is often included in an analysis so that its effect may be taken into account when interpreting the effects of the INDEPENDENT VARIABLES of interest. For example, covariates are used in ANALYSES OF COVARIANCE to statistically adjust groups so that they are equivalent with regard to these variables; they may also be used in MULTIPLE REGRESSION to minimize error that may arise from omitting any noncentral but potentially influential variables. Also called **concomitant variable**.

covariation *n.* a relationship between two quantitative variables such that as one variable tends to increase (or decrease) in value, the corresponding values of the other variable tend to also increase (or decrease). For example, if a person's weight consistently rises as he or she grows older, then the two variables would be exhibiting covariation.

cover story a plausible but false statement about the purpose of a research study that is given to participants to avoid disclosing to them the true hypothesis being investigated. Such deception may be practiced when the participants' behavior in the study is apt to be affected by knowledge of the experiment's true purpose. For ethical reasons, the deception should not flagrantly violate the participants' right to know what they will be getting into by taking part

in the investigation. See DECEPTION RESEARCH.

COVRATIO a numerical value corresponding to a unit (e.g., individual, animal) that indicates the effect of removing the unit from a REGRESSION ANALYSIS. More technically, it is a ratio of the DETERMINANTS of COVARIANCE MATRICES with and without a given observation. Values less than 1 indicate that removal of the unit has little influence on the precision of the estimates obtained from the analysis.

Cox–Mantel test see LOG-RANK TEST. [David **Cox** (1924–), British statistician; Nathan **Mantel** (1919–2002), U.S. biostatistician]

Cox regression analysis a statistical technique used to build multivariate models that relate one or more continuous or categorical variables to SURVIVAL TIMES, without requiring researchers to specify in advance the form or nature of such relationships. For example, one might use Cox regression to determine how likely it is that alcoholics who are abstinent at three months and at six months will relapse. A key methodological concept in Cox regression analysis is the hazard, that is, the immediate potential or "risk" of event occurrence. It is computed from the baseline hazard rate, which estimates the overall risk of event occurrence as a function of time; various coefficients, which describe the relationship between each predictor variable and the rate of event occurrence; and each individual's values on the predictor variables. There are two types of Cox regression: the simpler **standard Cox regression model** (or [**Cox's**] **proportional hazards model**) and a more complex generalization known as the **extended Cox regression model** (or **time-dependent Cox regression model**). The standard model requires that the PROPORTIONAL HAZARDS ASSUMPTION be met and thus is used when the risk of event occurrence for the reference and comparison groups remains constant relative to one another over all time points. The extended model is used when the effect of particular variables on the occurrence of the event of interest changes over time, such that one group has a higher risk of event occurrence at early time points but a lower risk at later time points. [David **Cox**]

Cox–Snell residual the discrepancy between observed and predicted values for a variable defined as the time to a particular event (e.g., time to death). Used in COX REGRESSION ANALYSIS, such RESIDUALS provide a means for evaluating how a theory about changes in SURVIVAL TIMES fits an observed set of data. [David **Cox**; E. Joyce **Snell**]

Cox's proportional hazards model see COX REGRESSION ANALYSIS. [David **Cox**]

Cox–Stuart test for trend a statistical procedure for evaluating whether a sequence of independent scores follows a systematic pattern, for example, whether earlier observations have an overall tendency to be larger or smaller than later observations. [David **Cox**; Alan **Stuart** (1922–1998), British statistician]

Cramér–Rao lower bound a lower limit on the extent to which estimated values of a population parameter may vary, given that the ESTIMATOR is unbiased. For example, suppose a researcher examines a sample to derive possible estimates of the incidence of a rare disorder in the larger population. He or she could obtain a Cramér–Rao lower bound and compare it to the variance of the estimates obtained using a particular UNBIASED ESTIMATOR. Such a comparison indicates whether the estimator in question is efficient, that is, whether given alternative estimators it is the one with the lowest degree of variance. Also called **minimum variance bound**. [Harald **Cramér** (1893–1985), Swedish mathematician; Calyampudi R. **Rao** (1920–), Indian-born U.S. statistician]

Cramér's V (symbol: V; ϕ_c) a measure of the degree of association between two variables that have two or more unordered response categories. More specifically, it is an omnibus EFFECT SIZE that quantifies the overall association among the rows and columns in a CONTINGENCY TABLE. Also called **Cramér's phi**. [Harald **Cramér**]

Cramér–von Mises goodness-of-fit test a statistical procedure to evaluate how well the distribution of an observed set of scores matches a theoretical distribution (e.g., a NORMAL DISTRIBUTION). It examines the discrepancies between obtained scores and their corresponding expected scores to derive a single statistic (W^2), the larger the value of which the poorer the model fit. [Harald **Cramér**; Richard E. **von Mises** (1883–1953), Russian-born U.S. mathematician and engineer]

credible interval in BAYESIAN methods, a range within which a particular value of a population characteristic has a specified probability of falling. It is the Bayesian equivalent of the CONFIDENCE INTERVAL used in FREQUENTIST approaches. Also called **Bayesian confidence interval**; **credible region**.

criterion *n.* a standard against which a judgment, evaluation, or comparison can be made. For example, a well-validated test of creativity might be used as the criterion to develop new tests of creativity.

criterion analysis a method of analyzing responses to a test in which it is assumed that some unobserved variable underlies the target behavior or concept of interest and accounts for the pattern of relationships (CORRELATIONS) among the test items.

criterion contamination a situation in which a response measure (the criterion) is influenced by factors that are not related to the concept being measured. Evidence of this may be observed through correlations of the response measure with variables that are conceptually distinct from that measure. For example, performance discrepancies (in dollars sold) among insurance agents may arise not from any actual differences in ability but rather from socioeconomic differences in territories assigned to the salespeople.

criterion cutoff see CUTOFF SCORE.

criterion group a group tested for traits its members are already known to possess, usually for the purpose of demonstrating that responses to a test represent the traits they were intended to represent. For example, a group of children with diagnosed visual disabilities may be given a visual test to assess its validity as a means of evaluating the presence of visual disabilities.

criterion index an index that measures a specific quality on which a set of scores may be evaluated. Examples include indices of RELIABILITY and VALIDITY.

criterion-referenced test an exam from which decisions are made about an individual's absolute level of accomplishment (i.e., mastery or nonmastery) of the material covered in that exam according to some standard reference point. For example, if a student obtains a score of 70% on a reading exam and a passing score is 65%, then he or she has done well. Also called **content-referenced test**. See also DOMAIN-REFERENCED TEST; NORM-REFERENCED TEST.

criterion scaling a method of changing the values of a predictor and a response variable to make the relationship between the two variables more closely resemble a straight line. In criterion scaling, one calculates the averages of the response variable for subsets of individuals who have similar values on the predictor variable, replaces the predictor values with these subset averages, and then uses the substituted averages to predict the response variable.

criterion score 1. a score on a variable that serves as a standard against which other scores may be judged in a CRITERION-REFERENCED TEST. **2.** in REGRESSION ANALYSIS, a predicted score on an attribute or variable.

criterion validity an index of how well a test correlates with an established standard of comparison (i.e., a CRITERION). Criterion validity is divided into three types: PREDICTIVE VALIDITY, CONCURRENT VALIDITY, and RETROSPECTIVE VALIDITY. For example, if a measure of criminal behavior is valid, then it should be possible to use it to predict whether an individual (a) will be arrested in the future for a criminal violation, (b) is currently breaking the law, and (c) has a previous criminal record. Also called **criterion-referenced validity**; **criterion-related validity**.

criterion variable see DEPENDENT VARIABLE.

critical difference in comparisons of means or other statistics obtained from two or more samples, the minimum difference that is deemed necessary to judge a test result as having STATISTICAL SIGNIFICANCE. The critical difference will vary according to the procedure used.

critical experiment see CRUCIAL EXPERIMENT.

critical ratio the result of dividing a particular quantity resulting from a statistical test by a measure of the error related to the test result. For example, a calculated sample mean may be divided by its corresponding STANDARD ERROR to derive a critical ratio, which may then be used to evaluate the STATISTICAL SIGNIFICANCE of that mean. Thus, if one obtains a critical ratio of 2.0, the observed mean difference is twice as large as that expected on the basis of sampling error.

critical region a range of values that may be obtained from a statistical procedure that would lead to rejecting a specific claim about a population. More specifically, it is the portion of a PROBA-BILITY DISTRIBUTION containing the values for a test statistic that would result in rejection of a NULL HYPOTHESIS in favor of its corresponding ALTERNATIVE HYPOTHESIS. Also called **rejection region**. Compare ACCEPTANCE REGION.

critical value a value used to make decisions about whether a test result is statistically meaningful. For example, to evaluate the result of a T TEST to determine whether a sample mean is significantly different from the hypothesized population mean, a researcher would compare the obtained test statistic to the values from a T DISTRIBUTION at a given PROBABILITY LEVEL. If the statistic exceeds the critical value within that distribution, the NULL HYPOTHESIS is rejected and the result is considered significant. Also called **rejection value**. See also CRITICAL REGION.

Cronbach's alpha a measure of the average strength of association between all possible pairs of items contained within a set of items. It is a commonly used index of the INTERNAL CONSISTENCY of a test and ranges in value from 0, indicating no internal consistency, to 1, indicating perfect internal consistency. Also called **alpha coefficient**; **coefficient alpha**. [Lee J. **Cronbach** (1916–2001), U.S. psychologist]

cross-case analysis an examination to identify similarities and differences between units of study, such as organizations or people. Such an analysis generally follows an initial case-specific analysis in which each unit is examined individually to identify its unique characteristics.

cross-classification *n.* the placing of observations or individuals into classes based on the features of two or more variables. This is usually carried out by means of a CONTINGENCY TABLE.

cross-classification table see CONTINGENCY TABLE.

cross-correlation *n.* a measure of the degree of association between corresponding values from a series of values for two or more variables.

cross-cultural research the systematic study of human psychological processes and behavior across multiple cultures, involving the observation of similarities and differences in values, practices, and so forth between different societies. Cross-cultural research offers many potential advantages, informing theories that accommodate both individual and social sources of variation, but also involves numerous risks, notable among them the production of cultural knowledge that is incorrect because of flawed methodology. Indeed, there are a host of methodological concerns that go beyond monocultural studies, including issues concerning translation, measurement, equivalence, sampling, data analytic techniques, and data reporting. Also called **cross-cultural method**; **cross-cultural study**.

cross-cultural testing the assessment of individuals from different cultural backgrounds. The use of instruments that are free of bias is essential to valid cross-cultural testing, as it provides for the measurement equivalency necessary to ensure outcomes have the same meaning across diverse populations of interest. For example, scores on a coping questionnaire that possesses bias may be a legitimate measure of coping if they are compared within a single cultural group, whereas cross-cultural differences identified on the basis of this questionnaire may be influenced by other factors, such as translation issues, item inappropriateness, or differential response styles. See also CULTURE-FAIR TEST.

crossed-factor design a study that involves two or more conditions or treatments in which each level of one condition or treatment is combined with each level of every other condition or treatment. For instance, a pharmaceutical treatment (Drug A vs. Drug B) may be combined with a biofeedback treatment (biofeedback vs. no biofeedback) so that each drug is combined with each type of biofeedback to form four possible interventions or treatment plans. The individual conditions being manipulated are known as **crossed factors** or **crossed treatments**. Also called **crossed design**.

cross-fostering *n.* a technique in which very young animals are placed with a nonbiological parent for the purpose of studying environmental and genetic effects on development. For example, this technique has been used to study the role of genetic factors in the origins of disorders. Such a study may involve either (a) having the offspring of biological parents who do not show the disorder reared by adoptive parents who do show the disorder or (b) having offspring of parents who show the disorder reared by parents who do not.

cross-lagged panel design a study of the relationships between two or more variables across time in which one variable measured at an earlier point in time is examined with regard to a second variable measured at a later point in time, and vice versa. For example, suppose an organizational researcher measures job satisfaction and job performance at the beginning of one fiscal year and at the beginning of a second fiscal year. Examining the correlations between satisfaction and performance at the different times provides information about their possible causal association: If the correlation between high performance at Time 1 and satisfaction at Time 2 is significantly stronger than the correlation between satisfaction at Time 1 and performance at Time 2, it is potentially the case that those who perform better are the ones who subsequently are more satisfied with their jobs.

cross-lagged regression a type of RE-GRESSION ANALYSIS used to model the relationship between two or more variables observed at two or more points in time. Measures on one variable at one time point are used to predict values on a second variable at a later time point, and conversely measures on the second variable at the earlier time point are used to predict the values on the first variable at the later time point.

cross-level inference in studies involving NESTING, such as students nested within schools, a conclusion drawn about the relationship between variables at one level of the data (e.g., student level) based on an analysis performed at the other level of the data (e.g., school level). Cross-level inferences are often problematic as the nature of the relationships involved can change depending on the level at which they are studied.

crossover design a study in which different treatments are applied to the same individuals but in different sequences. In the most basic crossover design, a **two-by-two** or **two-period crossover design**, a group of participants receives Treatment A followed by Treatment B while a second group receives Treatment B followed by Treatment A. For example, a researcher could use such a design to assess the effect of attending a day service on stroke survivors, randomly assigning participants to one of two groups, the first of which would attend the service for six months and then not attend for six months, and the second of which would not attend the service for six months and then would attend for six months. As with WITHIN-SUBJECTS DESIGNS, the benefit of this design is the reduction in ERROR VARIANCE. Also called **crossover study**; **crossover trial**. Compare PARALLEL-GROUPS DESIGN. See also GRAECO-LATIN SQUARE; LATIN SQUARE.

crossover interaction see DISORDINAL INTERACTION.

cross-product *n.* the set of values obtained by multiplying each value of one variable (x) by each value of a second variable (y).

cross-product ratio an ODDS RATIO computed from the values in a two-by-two CONTINGENCY TABLE. For example, consider a researcher examining the occurrence of depression in stroke survivors. He or she could calculate a cross-product ratio to determine the relative risk of depression occurring in such individuals as follows: (1) Multiply the number (or percentage) of people who have had a stroke and have been diagnosed with depression by the number of people who have not had a stroke and who have not been diagnosed with depression; (2) multiply the number of people who have had a stroke and who have not been diagnosed with depression by the number of people who have not had a stroke and who have been diagnosed with depression; and (3) divide the value obtained in Step 1 by the value obtained in Step 2.

cross-sectional analysis the examination of data that have been collected at a single point in time. For example, a researcher might conduct a cross-sectional analysis after measuring the income of people in different professions at the end of a particular year. Compare TIME-SERIES ANALYSIS.

cross-sectional design a research design in which individuals, typically of different ages or developmental levels, are compared at a single point in time. An example is a study that involves a direct comparison of 5-year-olds with 8-year-olds. Given its snapshot nature, however, it is difficult to determine causal relationships using a cross-sectional design. Moreover, a cross-sectional study is not suitable for measuring changes over time, for which a LONGITUDINAL DESIGN is required. See also CROSS-SECTIONAL ANALYSIS.

cross-sectional sampling a sampling method in which scores are obtained at a single point in time. For example, cross-sectional sampling may involve collecting data from individuals of various ages or developmental levels so as to study behavioral or other differences among them.

cross-sequential design a study in which two or more groups of individuals of different ages are directly compared over a period of time. It is thus a combination of a CROSS-SECTIONAL DESIGN and a LONGITUDINAL DESIGN. For example, an investigator using a cross-sequential design to evaluate children's mathematical skills might measure a group of 5-year-olds and a group of 10-year-olds at the beginning of the research and then subsequently reassess the same children every six months for the next five years. Also called **cross-sequential study**.

cross-tabulation *n.* the number, proportion, or percentage of cases that have specific combinations of values on two variables that each have multiple categories. Such information may be presented visually in a **cross-tabulation table**. For example, a cross-tabulation table could be used to show the number of study participants according to both their sex and marital status.

cross-validated multiple correlation (symbol: $R^2_{yy'}$) the degree of association between the results obtained from two different portions of the same data sample during a CROSS-VALIDATION test. The correlation expresses the relationship between the actual scores in the CROSS-VALIDATION SAMPLE and the predicted scores in the DERIVATION SAMPLE.

cross-validation *n.* a procedure used to assess the utility or stability of a statistical model. A data set is randomly divided into two subsets, the first of which (the DERIVATION SAMPLE) is used to develop the model and the second of which (the CROSS-VALIDATION SAMPLE) is used to test it. In regression analysis, for example, the first subset would be

C

analyzed in order to develop a REGRESSION EQUATION, which would then be applied to the remaining subset to see how well it predicts the scores that were actually observed.

cross-validation sample in CROSS-VALIDATION, the subset of data that is used to test the model or procedure developed using the DERIVATION SAMPLE. Also called **holdout sample**.

crucial experiment an experiment constructed such that its result will aid in determining which of two opposing theories has made the correct prediction, thus refuting the other. Also called **critical experiment**.

CTT abbreviation for CLASSICAL TEST THEORY.

cubic spline a SPLINE FUNCTION used to join various third-degree POLYNOMIAL segments in order to produce a smoothed representation of the overall shape of a distribution.

culturally loaded item in testing and assessment, a question that is more relevant to the background and experience of the individual who wrote the question than to the individual who is trying to answer the question, such that the response may not be a fair indication of the responder's knowledge. For example, if a question included content about a particular religious tradition it might be perceived as being a culturally loaded item if the test taker were an atheist or of a completely different religion.

cultural test bias partiality of a test in favor of individuals from certain backgrounds at the expense of individuals from other backgrounds. The partiality may be in the content of the items, in the format of the items, or in the very act of taking a test itself. For example, suppose a verbal comprehension exam was delivered on a computer and incorporated passages, pictures, and questions drawn from American literature. The exam is likely to favor individuals who grew up in American families that could afford to have computers and a variety of books at home. In contrast, poorer individuals who emigrated to America and were without computers or many books in the home might find that the exam had some degree of cultural test bias. See also CULTURALLY LOADED ITEM; TEST BIAS.

culture-fair test a test based on common human experience and considered to be relatively unbiased with respect to special background influences. Unlike some standardized intelligence assessments, which may reflect predominantly middle-class experience, a culture-fair test is designed to apply across social lines and to permit equitable comparisons among people from different backgrounds. Nonverbal, nonacademic items are used, such as matching identical forms, selecting a design that completes a given series, or drawing human figures. Studies have shown, however, that any assessment reflects certain socioethnic norms in some degree and hence may tend to favor people with certain backgrounds rather than others. For example, an item that included the phrase "bad rap" could be unclear, as the phrase could refer to unjust criticism or to rap music that was either not very good or rather good, depending on an individual's common use of the word "bad." See also CROSS-CULTURAL TESTING.

cumulant *n.* one of a set of values that describes the basic nature of a DISTRIBUTION. A cumulant is similar to and a logarithmic function of a MOMENT of a distribution, especially for the first few values. The first cumulant (like the first moment) is concerned with the MEAN or average of a set of numbers, the second cumulant (like the second moment) refers to the VARIANCE or degree of spread in a set of numbers, and the third cumulant (like the third moment) indicates the SKEWNESS or degree of lopsidedness in set of numbers. Cumulants and moments may differ beyond these initial values, and statistical methods generally are concerned only with the first three cumulants or moments of a distribution, as well as the fourth moment, KURTOSIS.

cumulant generating function (**CGF**) a formula for obtaining values that describe the basic nature of a DISTRIBUTION. A cumulant generating function is generally the logarithm of a MOMENT GENERATING FUNCTION, producing values related to the MEAN, VARIANCE, and SKEWNESS of a set of variables.

cumulative distribution function (**CDF**) a formula that gives the PROBABILITY, from 0 to 1, that a variable will have a score less than or equal to a specific value. When this is plotted on a graph, the vertical y-axis will indicate the probability value from 0 to 1 for each possible score of the variable listed along the horizontal x-axis. This type of graph usually shows a pattern with a curve that rises from the lower left up to a peak at the upper right, where for the last score the probability that a variable will have a value equal to or less than the highest possible score is 1. Also called **distribution function**.

cumulative frequency (**CF**) a running total of how often specific values occur. Cumulative frequencies are used in DESCRIPTIVE STATISTICS when listing the number of participants who fall into each of several categories of a variable that can be ordered from low to high. For example, if test scores in a particular classroom are 1 F, 2 Ds, 4 Cs, 3 Bs, and 2 As, the cumulative frequency is obtained by successively adding the number of students at each score from an F to an A. Thus, the cumulative frequency values from the lowest to the highest would be 1, 3, 7, 10, and 12 for F, D, C, B, and A, respectively. See also CUMULATIVE FREQUENCY DISTRIBUTION.

cumulative frequency distribution a table with three columns where the first column (labeled X) lists the possible values for a variable, the second column (labeled f, for frequency) lists the number of scores that occur at each of the possible values given in the first column, and the third column (labeled CF, for CUMULATIVE FREQUENCY) gives the running total of each of the values in the second column. For example, a teacher administers a test and the students' scores are 1 F, 2 Ds, 4 Cs, 3 Bs, and 2 As. In a cumulative frequency distribution, the first column (X) represents exam scores, with F, D, C, B, and A listed from the bottom to the top. In the second column (f) are the values of 1, 2, 4, 3, and 2 to indicate 1 F, 2 Ds, 4 Cs, 3 Bs, and 2 As. In the final column (CF) are running totals of the second column from the bottom up, listing 1, 3, 7, 10, and 12 to indicate the summed total of scores at each of the grades, with the total number of scores listed at the top (i.e., there are 12 total scores in this cumulative frequency distribution).

Score (X)	Frequency (f)	Cumulative frequency (CF)
A	2	12
B	3	10
C	4	7
D	2	3
F	1	1

This type of table is useful in DESCRIPTIVE STATISTICS to depict the number of scores at or below each score level, and to provide an organized display of data that could also be graphed in a CUMULATIVE FREQUENCY POLYGON. Also called **cumulative distribution**; **cumulative frequency table**.

cumulative frequency polygon a graphical representation of a CUMULATIVE FREQUENCY DISTRIBUTION, with points along the vertical y-axis depicting the number of scores falling at or below the particular values given along the horizontal x-axis. The resulting points

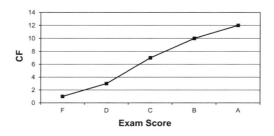

cumulative frequency polygon

are connected with straight lines, revealing a pattern that tends to increase or remain constant as one moves from the lower left to the upper right portion of the graph (see example above). Also called **cumulative frequency curve**; **cumulative frequency diagram**; **cumulative frequency graph**.

cumulative hazard function in a SURVIVAL ANALYSIS, a mathematical description of the accumulating number of failures or deaths over time: It can be interpreted as giving the probability of death or failure at a specific time, given survival until that time. For example, a cumulative hazard function might be used in a research project to examine the running pattern of deaths due to cancer over a five-year period. It is an extension of a HAZARD FUNCTION beyond a specific individual or single occurrence.

cumulative odds ratio a WEIGHTED AVERAGE of a set of values formed by calculating the probability of an event occurring in one group over the probability of the event not occurring in the same group, then dividing this by the probability of the same event occuring in a second group over the probability of the event not occurring in this group. For example, a medical researcher may examine the probability of cancer occurrence in a treatment group versus a control group every month for six months. The researcher then finds the average of these values, after weighting them for the number of individuals involved in each of the monthly calculations. A cu-

mulative odds ratio is an extension of the single ODDS RATIO, which is the value formed at just one time point.

cumulative outcome analysis a procedure for assessing the PROPORTION of occurrence of an event, usually across time. This procedure can be performed as part of SURVIVAL ANALYSIS, which studies the rate of survival or success (or conversely the rate of death or failure) over a period of time. For example, a researcher may want to assess patients who remain alive at one-year intervals across a five-year period, based on an initial sample of 100 patients. Before the start of the study, the proportion is equal to 1.0, as all of the patients that will be in the study are now alive. At the end of the first year, if 85 patients are still alive, the proportion would be 85/100 or .85. At the end of the second year, if 62 patients are still alive, the proportion would be 62/85 = .73; and so on. Cumulative outcome analysis may also be used in examining LIFE TABLES.

cumulative percentage a running total of the PERCENTAGE values occurring across a set of responses. The total will either remain the same or increase, reaching the highest value of 100% after totaling all of the previous percentages. For example, if the percentage of freshmen, sophomores, juniors, and seniors among all of the students at a college were 40%, 25%, 20%, and 15%, respectively, the cumulative percentage values would be 40%, 65%, 85%, and 100% when summing from the percentage of freshman up to the percentage of seniors.

cumulative probability a running total of the chance of a score occurring at or below a certain point, where the largest running total is a value of 1.0. For example, a college teacher may want to know the cumulative probability values showing the chance that a grade selected from the entire set of grades on a recently given test would be an F, D, C, B, or A. If there were 8.3% Fs, 16.7% Ds, 33.3% Cs, 25% Bs, and 16.7% As, the cumulative probability values would be .083, .250, .583, .833, and 1.000, respectively, when totaling from the F to the A values.

cumulative probability distribution a graphical representation of a set of data that displays along the vertical y-axis the chance that a case picked at random from that set will have a value less than or equal to the corresponding value on the horizontal x-axis. When the variable of interest has DISCRETE or CATEGORICAL whole-integer values, as with the number of students in a class, the cumulative probability distribution also may be called a **cumulative probability function**.

cumulative record a continuous tally or graph to which new data are added. In conditioning, for example, a cumulative record is a graph showing the running total of the number of responses over a continuous period of time.

cumulative relative frequency a running sum of the PROPORTION of times specific scores occur compared to the total number of individual score occurrences in a set of data. For example, a teacher may find that there was just one score of F out of a total of 12 scores, such that the first cumulative relative frequency distribution value was .083 (i.e., 1/12). If there were two scores of D added to the one score of F, the second value would be .250 (i.e., 1/12 + 2/12 = 3/12); and so on up through the values to a score of A, which would equal 1.0 as all of the scores would be taken into account at that point (i.e., 12/12 = 1.0). A collection or table of cumulative relative frequencies is called a **cumulative relative frequency distribution**.

Score (X)	Frequency (f)	Cumulative relative frequency
A	2	1.000
B	3	.833
C	4	.583
D	2	.250
F	1	.083

This can be graphed as the intersection of the running proportion on the vertical y-axis and the individual score options along the horizontal x-axis; the plotted pattern is often called a **cumulative relative frequency curve**, **cumulative relative frequency diagram**, or **cumulative relative frequency graph**. For the exam score example, propor-

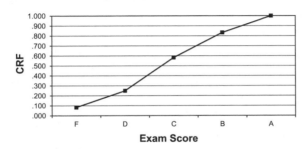

cumulative relative frequency graph

tions from 0 to 1.0 would be listed vertically and the grades F, D, C, B, and A would be listed horizontally. When plotted, the running total of the proportions of each score that occurred would have a height of .083 for the score of F, on up to a height of 1.0 for a score of A. Also called **cumulative proportion**.

cumulative scale see GUTTMAN SCALE.

cumulative sum chart (CuSum chart) a graph of a group of values that are calculated by setting an initial value of 0 and obtaining each subsequent value by adding the previous value to the difference between the current score and the mean of all of the scores. For example, if there were three IQ scores of 92, 103, and 105, the mean is equal to $(92 + 103 + 105)/3 = 100$. Then, the initial value of the cumulative sum chart would be set to equal 0, and the next value would equal $0 + (92 - 100) = -8$. The next value would equal $-8 + (103 - 100) = -5$; and the last value would equal $-5 + (105 - 100) = 0$.

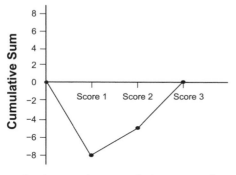

As shown, the cumulative sum values are given along the vertical y-axis and the IQ scores are given along the horizontal x-axis.

cumulative test a type of test that assesses all of the information taught up to the point that it is taken. For example, cumulative tests in school include an integration of all of the material that a teacher covered over the entire term, rather than just the most recent information that was taught.

cure rate model a representation of the PROPORTION of individuals who have survived an illness after treatment, which includes those who have survived up to a certain point but have not been cured. This proportion is important in SURVIVAL ANALYSES of complex illnesses, such as cancer. For example, it might be useful to construct a cure rate model that estimates the number of patients who survive cancer and appear to no longer have the disease as well as the number who still have cancer but might be expected to still be alive at specific times after treatment.

curse of dimensionality the problem that the volume of a mathematical space increases exponentially with every new facet that is added, such that it becomes increasingly difficult or even intractable to study spaces as the number of the variables increases.

curve fitting any of various statistical techniques for obtaining a function that graphically represents a given set of data as closely as possible, with minimal error. A simple example of curve fitting occurs in LINEAR REGRESSION, where a straight line function is said to provide the closest approximation to the expected values of the outcome with a specific predictor and have the fewest discrepancies between the predicted values and the actual, observed values.

curvilinear *adj.* describing an association between variables that does not consistently follow an increasing or decreasing pattern but rather changes direction after a certain point (i.e., involves a curve in the set of data points). For example, the relationship between anxiety and achievement often has a curvilinear pattern of increasing achievement with increasing anxiety (i.e., motivation to study) up to a certain point when there is so much anxiety that achievement tends to decrease. Thus, individuals who are not at all anxious and those who are extremely anxious would both be expected to have poor performance, whereas moderately anxious individuals would be expected to have reasonably high performance. See also NONLINEAR.

curvilinear regression see NONLINEAR REGRESSION.

CuSum chart abbreviation for CUMULATIVE SUM CHART.

cutoff score a value or criterion that is held to mark the lowest point at which a certain status or category is attained. For example, the cutoff score for passing a course is often 60%. Similarly, the cutoff score for being considered overweight is a body mass index of 25 to 29. Also called **cutoff point; criterion cutoff**.

Cuzick's trend test an extension of the WILCOXON RANK-SUM TEST: a nonparametric procedure used with ORDINAL DATA for estimating the pattern of relationship between rankings across three or more independent random samples. For example, Cuzick's trend test could assess the similarity of sets of standardized achievement test scores for applicants to private, Ivy League, and state colleges. [Jack **Cuzick**, U.S. epidemiologist and statistician]

cycle *n.* a distinct pattern within a TIME SERIES of data for a specific variable. The pattern can be evenly spaced (e.g., as with seven-day weekly sales figures) or irregular (e.g., as with shifts in sales due to weather changes or economic factors).

cycle plot a graph that highlights regular patterns in TIME-SERIES data by displaying a separate line for each phase (e.g., week, month) for every major point (e.g., day of the week) along the series. For example, a professor may want to examine the number of student e-mails he or she receives each week over a 14-week semester by charting the 14 points for specific numbers of e-mails received on Sundays in the first line of the graph, followed by the 14 points for the number of e-mails received on Mondays in the second line, and so forth. When finished, the graph displays the number of e-mails on the vertical *y*-axis and the days of the week on the horizontal *x*-axis, with the specific patterns over the 14-week semester for each day clearly visible (see below).

In this way, it would be more obvious on what days of the week and during which weeks of the semester (e.g., just before exams, after holidays) more time would need to be designated for attending to student questions and feedback. A cycle plot is thus more revealing than a standard time series graph that, for

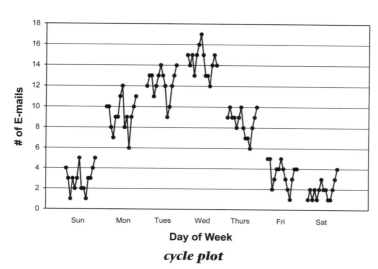

cycle plot

this example, would list all of the days of the week over each of the 14 weeks (i.e., $7 \times 14 = 98$ points) along the x-axis, with the latter making it difficult to perceive daily or weekly patterns as clearly.

cyclic component the portion of a plot of TIME-SERIES data that shows a noticeable, distinct pattern, presumably due to some identifiable factor. For example, it could be important to identify the cyclic component in car sales due to long-term fluctuations in the economy, in addition to taking into account a seasonal pattern showing more predictable increases at the end of the year and during holidays.

cyclic data a set of information, especially a TIME SERIES, in which a recurring distinct pattern is identifiable. For example, a psychiatrist may note that patients tend to require more visits or medication during regular time periods around holidays or the anniversary of the death of a loved one.

cyclic variation a change in the pattern of data across a TIME SERIES that is recurring and identifiable. For example, sales, doctor visits, and student e-mails may show regular patterns over time that are useful to identify. See also CYCLIC COMPONENT.

Dd

d 1. see COHEN'S D. **2.** see GLASS'S D.

d′ symbol for D PRIME.

D 1. symbol for DIFFERENCE SCORE. **2.** see COOK'S DISTANCE.

D² symbol for MAHALANOBIS DISTANCE.

DAG abbreviation for DIRECTED ACYCLIC GRAPH.

D'Agostino test 1. a statistical assessment of the degree of SKEWNESS (lopsidedness) in a distribution. Its full name is the **D'Agostino test for skewness. 2.** (symbol: K^2) a statistical assessment of the degree to which a distribution departs from a NORMAL DISTRIBUTION, in which skewness and KURTOSIS are expected to be zero. Its full name is the **D'Agostino–Pearson omnibus test for normality.** [Ralph B. **D'Agostino** (1940–), U.S. biostatistician]

damped regression see RIDGE REGRESSION.

Daniell weights values that can be used to adjust the beginning, end, and middle of a MOVING AVERAGE form of TIME SERIES, allowing a clearer view of the nature of the trends in the data that are distinct from RANDOM ERROR.

Darling test an assessment, more formally known as the **Anderson–Darling test**, of whether a sample of data came from a particular probability distribution. It is considered a very powerful test of whether data differ from a NORMAL DISTRIBUTION. [Donald A. **Darling** (1915–), U.S. mathematician]

data *pl. n.* (*sing.* **datum**) observations or measurements, usually quantified and obtained in the course of research. For example, a researcher may be interested in collecting data on health-related be-

haviors such as frequency and amount of exercise, number of calories consumed per day, number of cigarettes smoked per day, number of alcoholic drinks per day, and so forth.

data analysis the process of applying graphical, statistical, or quantitative techniques to a set of observations or measurements in order to summarize it or to find general patterns. For example, a very basic data analysis would involve calculating DESCRIPTIVE STATISTICS (e.g., MEAN, MEDIAN, MODE, STANDARD DEVIATION) and possibly graphing the observations with a HISTOGRAM or BAR GRAPH.

data augmentation (DA) the use of algorithms to simulate data so as to estimate functions that are difficult to calculate directly from the existing data. Data augmentation has been used in MARKOV CHAIN MONTE CARLO METHODS and other approaches.

database *n.* a large, structured collection of information stored in retrievable form on a computer. For example, most researchers keep a record of information collected from their studies on a computer to allow for easy access, manipulation, and analysis in testing relevant HYPOTHESES.

data capture the automatic collection of data, often via scanning or computer devices that record information quickly and unobtrusively. For example, information is retained about a person's online purchases with a particular credit card, which in turn may be used by a company to help determine that person's preferences and make suggestions about other items he or she might be interested in purchasing.

data coding the process of putting information into understandable, usually QUANTITATIVE or QUALITATIVE, forms to allow analyses that can summarize the main themes that emerge or test relevant HYPOTHESES. For example, a researcher may collect information on a 20-item survey that contains questions on a number of areas of substance use. Based on this information, several quantitative variables can be formed assessing, for example, the amount of alcohol use, the frequency of alcohol use, the amount of hard drug use, and the frequency of hard drug use.

data collection a systematic gathering of information for research or practical purposes. Examples include mail surveys, interviews, laboratory experiments, and psychological testing.

data dredging the inappropriate practice of searching through large files of information to try to confirm a preconceived HYPOTHESIS or belief without an adequate design that controls for possible CONFOUNDS or alternate hypotheses. Data dredging may involve selecting which parts of a large data set to retain in order to get specific, desired results. An extreme example might occur if a marketing researcher found that 91 out of 100 people surveyed were opposed to a certain product and then chose to only focus on the last 10 people in order to state that 9 out of 10 people prefer this product, when in fact there were only 9 out of 100 who preferred the product. See DATA SNOOPING.

data matrix (symbol: **X**) an arrangement of data in a MATRIX, usually with one row for each participant and one column for each piece of information gathered from the participants. A data matrix may be used in analyses to test HYPOTHESES and examine patterns.

data mining the automated (computerized) examination of a large set of observations or measurements, particularly as collected in a complex database, in order to discover patterns, correla-

tions, and other regularities that can be used for predictive purposes. Although a relatively new discipline, data mining has become a widely utilized technique within commercial and scientific research. For example, retailers often use data mining to predict the future buying trends of customers or design targeted marketing strategies, while clinicians may use it to determine variables predicting hospitalization in psychological disorders. Data mining incorporates methods from statistics, logic, and artificial intelligence.

data point a specific piece of information derived from a larger set of data. A data point is often formed by the intersection of two other pieces of information, as in the intersection of a person's score on one variable with his or her score on a second variable in a SCATTERPLOT. For example, 10 people could be asked their average number of hours of sleep per night and the number of colds they tend to have in a year. Then, the number of sleep hours could be recorded along the horizontal x-axis and the number of colds per year recorded along the vertical y-axis, resulting in 10 separate data points falling, most likely, in a negative pattern from the upper left portion to the bottom right portion of the scatterplot (i.e., the more hours of sleep, the fewer colds).

data pooling combining the information from two or more studies or substudies, for example, by averaging STANDARD DEVIATIONS or VARIANCES across groups to form a single value for use in a T TEST or ANALYSIS OF VARIANCE. Although it can be helpful to synthesize information in this way, data pooling can sometimes lead to misleading conclusions, as in SIMPSON'S PARADOX.

data record a set of information, often relating to a single participant, that is stored in a larger file or DATABASE. For example, a researcher may want to focus on the specific information or data record gathered from the 10th participant, which would most likely be found in the 10th row of the larger file.

data reduction the process of reducing a set of measurements or variables into a smaller, more manageable, more reliable, or better theoretically justified set or form. For example, a researcher may conduct a FACTOR ANALYSIS on a set of 50 items on well-being and satisfaction to determine whether the information could be summarized more efficiently on UNDERLYING DIMENSIONS of relationship satisfaction, degree of meaning in life, job satisfaction, and general health.

data screening a procedure in which one subjects a large set of information to preliminary review for any of a variety of reasons: to check for accuracy, to identify unusual patterns (e.g., OUTLIERS that are very different from the information from most participants) or any missing information, to determine whether the information would meet a statistical ASSUMPTION (e.g., of normality), to reduce the data to more manageable dimensions, and so forth.

data set a collection of individual but related observations or measurements considered as a single entity. For example, the entire range of scores obtained from a class of students taking a particular test would constitute a data set.

data snooping 1. looking for unpredicted, post hoc effects in a body of data. **2.** examining data before an experiment has been completed, which can sometimes result in erroneous or misleading conclusions. See also DATA DREDGING.

debriefing *n.* the process of giving participants in a completed research project a fuller explanation of the study in which they participated than was possible before or during the research.

deceleration *n.* a decrease in speed of movement or rate of change. For example, a medical researcher may be interested in the deceleration of an illness or

symptom as evidence that a treatment is working effectively. Compare ACCELERATION.

deception by commission see ACTIVE DECEPTION.

deception by omission see PASSIVE DECEPTION.

deception research any study in which participants are deliberately misled or not informed about the purpose of the investigation in order to avoid the possibility that responses may be given to meet the perceived expectations of researchers. For example, a social psychologist may use a **deception experiment** in which participants are randomly assigned to either of two scenarios that each describe job applicants in identical terms except that one is said to be a male and the other is said to be female. The researcher may then assess any gender bias in the participants by asking how likely the applicant is to be hired, instead of directly asking participants about their attitudes toward gender. See ACTIVE DECEPTION; DOUBLE DECEPTION; PASSIVE DECEPTION.

decile *n.* one of a series of values that divide a statistical distribution into 10 equal-sized parts. Thus, the first decile is the value below which lie 10% of cases, the second decile is the value below which lie 20% of cases, and so on.

decision error a conclusion that a study obtained positive results when in fact the research did not do so in 95% of similar studies or a conclusion that a study was not effective when it actually produced effective results in most other reported research. The former conclusion of a false positive is referred to as a TYPE I ERROR, whereas the latter conclusion of a false negative is called a TYPE II ERROR.

decision function a procedure or set of procedures that determines the conclusions to be drawn or actions to be taken on the basis of certain observed data. Also called **decision rule**.

decision rule 1. in HYPOTHESIS TESTING, a formal statement of the set of values of the test statistic that will lead to rejection of the NULL HYPOTHESIS that there is no significant effect in the study being examined. For example, a common decision rule is to reject the null hypothesis when the value of a Z TEST statistic exceeds 1.96. **2.** see DECISION FUNCTION.

decision table a table that sets out the key conditions and actions involved in coming to a conclusion. In statistics, a widely used decision table sets out the conditions of there being either a true NULL HYPOTHESIS or a false null hypothesis, the actions of rejecting the null hypothesis or retaining the null hypothesis, and the corresponding PROBABILITY associated with each action. If the null hypothesis is true and it is rejected, a TYPE I ERROR has occurred with a probability equal to ALPHA (α; often .05); if it is retained, a correct decision has been made with a probability equal to $1 - \alpha$ (in this case, .95). If the null hypothesis is false and it is retained, a TYPE II ERROR will occur with the probability equal to a value designated as BETA (β); if it is rejected, a correct decision has been made with a probability equal to $1 - \beta$, which is labeled as POWER.

decision theory a broad class of presumptions in the quantitative, social, and behavioral sciences that aim to explain the process and identify optimal ways of arriving at conclusions in such a way that prespecified criteria are met.

decision tree a diagram that uses a tree-like structure of branches and nodes to delineate conditions, action choices, and the further conditions these choices give rise to. A decision tree starts small and grows in size and complexity as it advances from left to right. For example, to decide which statistical analysis to conduct in a given case, a diagram could begin at the left with a single node asking what the focus of the analysis is to be.

A branch going off to the upper right could specify a node with the focus of obtaining mean differences between groups, and another branch going off to the lower right could specify a node for examining relationships among vari-

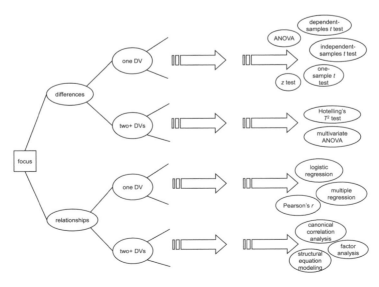

decision tree

ables. Off of each of those branches would be additional branches indicating the number of DEPENDENT VARIABLES, with still further branches leading eventually to nodes for different types of tests, depending on further conditions (e.g., population information, number and nature of samples). Similarly, branches off of the relationships among variables node could eventually lead to choices of different analytic techniques, depending on the number, nature, and focus of the variables. A generic depiction of such a decision tree is given on the previous page.

decoding *n.* the process of translating coded information back into its source terms or symbols. Decoding is used in information processing, communication, and computer science, for example. See CODING. **—decode** *vb.*

decomposable model a system or representation that can be broken down into meaningful subsets. Decomposable models are used in many areas, including BAYESIAN methods, MARKOV CHAINS, GRAPHIC MODELS, and STRUCTURAL EQUATION MODELING. For example, a full structural equation model with predictions from one or more INDEPENDENT VARIABLES, one or more MEDIATORS, and one or more DEPENDENT VARIABLES can be broken down into a direct effects portion with predictions from the independent variable(s) to the dependent variable(s) but not involving the intervening variables; and a mediational model with predictions from the independent to the intervening variables, and in turn from the intervening to the dependent variables.

decomposition *n.* in statistics, the breaking down of total effects or parameters into their different aspects. For example, in an ANALYSIS OF VARIANCE one may break down the total variance into the portion that concerns how the means vary between groups (BETWEEN-GROUPS MEAN SQUARE) and the portion that concerns how much random variance there is within each group (WITHIN-GROUPS MEAN SQUARE). If the between-group variance is significantly larger than the within-group variance, there is some evidence for a difference in means across groups. Likewise, in STRUCTURAL EQUATION MODELING, one may break down the total effects into the additive direct effects of independent and intervening variables on a dependent variable and the indirect effect of an independent variable on a dependent variable through the intervening variable.

deduction *n.* **1.** a conclusion derived from formal premises by a valid process of reasoning. **2.** the process of inferential reasoning itself. Compare INDUCTION. **—deductive** *adj.*

defender's fallacy the error of not taking into account CONDITIONAL PROBABILITY when drawing a conclusion about the possibility of an event occurring. For example, suppose that at the scene of a crime a specific blood type was found that has only a 1 in 10,000 chance of occurring, and that the defendant is found to have this blood type. The lawyer for the defendant could argue that as the population of the city was 8,000,000, there were 800 individuals with the same blood type who could be guilty of the crime. The lawyer would be committing the defender's fallacy, as he or she has not taken into account the fact that there was not any other evidence that the other 799 individuals in the city with that blood type had anything to do with the crime, whereas there was other evidence (e.g., from witnesses) that the defendant was at the scene of the crime. The defender's fallacy contrasts with the **prosecutor's fallacy**, which would occur if the prosecuting lawyer claimed that as there was only a 1 in 10,000 chance of having this blood type the defendant must certainly be guilty, without taking into account additional evidence of others who have this blood type and who may have been at or near the crime scene.

definitional formula the formal verbal definition of a statistical concept. For example, the definitional formula of VARIANCE states that it is the mean squared difference between a score and the mean of all of the scores. This contrasts with the COMPUTATIONAL FORMULA, which is the equation used to calculate values for the concept. Also called **conceptual formula**; **definition formula**.

definitional validity the extent to which the methods or approaches used by a researcher are consistent with the significance claimed (explicitly or implicitly) for the research. See also EXTERNAL VALIDITY; INTERNAL VALIDITY; EMPIRICAL VALIDITY; FACE VALIDITY.

degrees of freedom (symbol: df) the number of elements that are allowed to vary in a statistical calculation, or the number of scores minus the number of mathematical restrictions. If the MEAN of a set of scores is fixed, then the number of degrees of freedom is one less than the number of scores. For example, if four individuals have a mean IQ of 100, then there are three degrees of freedom, because knowing three of the IQs determines the fourth IQ.

dehoaxing *n.* DEBRIEFING participants who have been involved in DECEPTION RESEARCH to inform them that they were misled as part of the study. This may involve **desensitizing** participants, so that their self-image is not harmed by having participated in a deceptive study.

deletion residual in a statistical procedure, the difference that results from deleting data based on one of the participants in a sample. If this difference is large, there is some evidence that the removed participant was an OUTLIER, who was very different from the remaining participants. Also called **likelihood residual**. See REGRESSION DIAGNOSTICS.

deliberate sampling any method of selecting individuals to participate in research on the basis of a specific plan, rather than randomly. This includes simple nonrandom techniques, such as JUDGMENT SAMPLING and CONVENIENCE SAMPLING. In more sophisticated methods, such as QUOTA SAMPLING and STRATIFIED SAMPLING, various steps are taken with the aim of creating a sample that is representative of the larger population.

delta (symbol: Δ) *n.* **1.** a measure of the change in a PARAMETER. For example, ΔR^2 indicates how much of the change in R^2 (the COEFFICIENT OF MULTIPLE DETERMINATION) was caused or explained by a given step (e.g., adding a specific variable to an analysis). **2.** see GLASS'S D.

delta method a procedure used to arrive at the approximate PROBABILITY DISTRIBUTION of a variable that is expected to have a NORMAL DISTRIBUTION. For example, the delta method would allow a researcher to find the probability of having a low, medium, or large income if income was expected to be normally distributed in the population of interest. The delta method is based on the CENTRAL LIMIT THEOREM. Also called **delta technique**.

demand characteristics in an experiment or research project, cues that may influence or bias participants' behavior, for example, by suggesting the outcome or response that the experimenter expects or desires. Such cues can distort the findings of a study. See also EXPERIMENTER EFFECT.

Deming–Stephan algorithm a procedure for deriving a LOG-LINEAR ANALYSIS or model from a CONTINGENCY TABLE of frequencies for two CATEGORICAL VARIABLES. For example, this procedure might be used to examine whether gender and college major are independent (the NULL HYPOTHESIS expectation) or related (the ALTERNATIVE HYPOTHESIS expectation) in a sample of data from college students. [W. Edwards **Deming** (1900–1993) and Frederick F. **Stephan**, U.S. statisticians]

Demmler–Reinsch spline see REINSCH SPLINE.

dendrogram *n.* a type of treelike diagram used in AGGLOMERATIVE CLUSTERING and DIVISIVE CLUSTERING. It lists all of the participants at one end and then directs branches out from those participants who are similar and connects them with a node that represents a cluster, as in the generic illustration below.

A dendrogram could be used, for example, to cluster individuals into various risk categories depending on their number of sexual partners, their frequency of unprotected sex, and the perceived risk of their partners. Individuals who had few sexual partners with little or no unprotected sex and who perceived little or no partner risk of HIV infection would be branched into a cluster that could be labeled low risk, whereas individuals with high values on these three variables would branch into a high-risk cluster, with other individuals presumably clustering into a medium-risk group.

density curve see PROBABILITY CURVE.

density estimation an estimate as to the incidence of a specific occurrence in a POPULATION based on data from a random SAMPLE of that population. For example, a researcher could make a density estimation about the occurrence of an illness in the population at large based on the incidence found in a random sample of individuals who have the illness.

density function see PROBABILITY DENSITY FUNCTION.

dependence *n.* **1.** the state of having some reliance on or ASSOCIATION with another entity or event, as when one variable is formed from another variable in an analysis. For example, dependence would be seen if a researcher included IQ, formed from mental age over actual age, in an analysis that already has age as a variable. **2.** see STATISTICAL DEPENDENCE.

dependent events in probability theory, EVENTS that have a relationship such that the outcome of one affects the outcome of the other. For example, overeating and being overweight are dependent events, whereas shoe size and political party preference are most likely not. Compare INDEPENDENT EVENTS.

dependent groups see DEPENDENT SAMPLES.

dependent-groups analysis of variance see WITHIN-SUBJECTS ANALYSIS OF VARIANCE.

dependent-groups design see WITHIN-SUBJECTS DESIGN.

dependent samples sets of data that are related owing to their having been collected from the same group on two or more occasions (as with a pre- and post-test), or from two or more sets of individuals who are related or otherwise closely associated (e.g., parents and their children). Also called **correlated samples**;

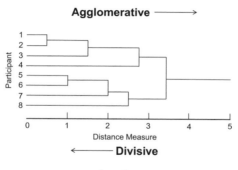

dendrogram

dependent groups; related samples. Compare INDEPENDENT SAMPLES.

dependent-samples analysis of variance see WITHIN-SUBJECTS ANALYSIS OF VARIANCE.

dependent-samples design see WITHIN-SUBJECTS DESIGN.

dependent-samples t test a T TEST used to analyze data from two or more sets of associated individuals or from one set of individuals measured on different occasions (e.g., pre- and posttreatment). Also called **correlated-groups t test; correlated-samples t test; related-samples t test; repeated measures t test**. See WITHIN-SUBJECTS DESIGN. Compare INDEPENDENT-SAMPLES T TEST.

dependent variable (**DV**) the outcome that is observed to occur or change after the occurrence or variation of the INDEPENDENT VARIABLE in an experiment, or the effect that one wants to predict or explain in CORRELATIONAL RESEARCH. Dependent variables may or may not be related causally to the independent variable. Also called **criterion variable; effect variable; outcome variable; response variable**.

derivation sample a portion of an initial data set used to explore a model, test, or analysis so as to assess the VALIDITY of its initial results. For example, a researcher may want to explore the factor structure of a new test in an initial derivation sample and then verify the findings afterward using CONFIRMATORY DATA ANALYSIS on a separate CROSS-VALIDATION SAMPLE. Likewise, a researcher may want to use a derivation sample to examine the predictions provided by a REGRESSION EQUATION.

derivation study research that uses a DERIVATION SAMPLE to explore a new model or area of interest, before using VALIDATION research to verify these findings.

derivative *n.* in calculus, a measure of the change in a variable that results from

change in another variable. Compare INTEGRAL.

derived score a score derived from initial RAW DATA to make it more interpretable. For example, a score on a standardized test, such as the Scholastic Assessment Test or the Graduate Record Examinations, is often converted from an initial value to a derived score with a MEAN of 500 and a STANDARD DEVIATION of 100.

descriptive average an approximate estimate of the center point of a set of values, indicating where information "piles up," which is sometimes made on the basis of imprecise or partial data. For example, a teacher could provide a descriptive average (e.g., 75%) that indicates how most people performed on an exam.

descriptive discriminant analysis a statistical procedure that distinguishes between two or more groups of a categorical outcome on the basis of several initial explanatory or PREDICTOR VARIABLES. The focus is on a set of standardized weights linking each initial variable to the grouping variable; high weights (in absolute value) indicate variables that tend to differ across the groups. For example, a researcher may want to study what differentiates those who survive cancer from those who do not by using a set of background variables, such as age, weight, frequency of saturated fat in the diet, and family history of cancer. The descriptive discriminant analysis may reveal negative standardized weights in the moderate to high range, suggesting that within the sample examined more family history of cancer, older age, higher weight, and more saturated fat in the diet are significantly linked with a lower chance of surviving cancer. Compare PREDICTIVE DISCRIMINANT ANALYSIS.

descriptive hypothesis a HYPOTHESIS that states an expected outcome but does not offer any causal explanations.

For example, a teacher may form a descriptive hypothesis that students will understand at least 70% of the course material, without delving into the specific reasons for such understanding.

descriptive measure a variable that measures something essential about a data SAMPLE, without making an inference as to the population PARAMETER for that variable. For example, a teacher may provide a descriptive measure to a specific class that the average grade on an exam was 75%, without inferring that all students outside of the class also would understand 75% of the exam material.

descriptive research an empirical investigation designed to test prespecified hypotheses or to provide an overview of existing conditions and, sometimes, relationships, without manipulating variables or seeking to establish cause and effect. For example, a survey undertaken to ascertain the political party preferences of a group of voters would be a descriptive study because it is intended simply to identify attitudes rather than systematically infer or analyze influencing factors.

descriptive statistics procedures for depicting the main aspects of sample data, without necessarily inferring to a larger population. Descriptive statistics usually include the MEAN, MEDIAN, and MODE to indicate CENTRAL TENDENCY, as well as the RANGE and STANDARD DEVIATION that reveal how widely spread the scores are within the sample. Descriptive statistics could also include charts and graphs such as a FREQUENCY DISTRIBUTION or HISTOGRAM, among others. Compare INFERENTIAL STATISTICS.

descriptive survey a questionnaire designed to assess a specific sample on a given set of items without implying or inferring any causal link between variables.

deseasonalization *n.* the process of removing short-term cyclical variations in a TIME SERIES to reveal the underlying trend. For example, a marketing researcher may want to investigate whether a particular advertising strategy increased sales, after removing the fluctuations in the data that have to do with the time of year (e.g., holiday sales, summer spending). Compare DETRENDING.

desensitizing *n.* see DEHOAXING.

design *n.* the format of a research study, describing how it will be conducted and the data collected. For example, an EXPERIMENTAL DESIGN involves an INDEPENDENT VARIABLE and at least two groups, a treatment or EXPERIMENTAL GROUP and a CONTROL GROUP, to which participants are randomly assigned and then assessed on the DEPENDENT VARIABLE. A variety of other design types exist, including CORRELATIONAL RESEARCH, QUASI-EXPERIMENTAL DESIGNS, LONGITUDINAL DESIGNS, NATURAL EXPERIMENTS, and OBSERVATIONAL STUDIES, among others.

designatory scale a system in which a number is assigned without that number having an actual quantitative value. For example, social security numbers use a designatory scale to uniquely identify each person, but a larger social security number does not indicate anything different than a smaller social security number.

design effect an adjustment, used in GROUP-RANDOMIZED TRIALS or HIERARCHICAL LINEAR MODELS, for the dependence in the data when groups of similar individuals (e.g., those in particular classrooms or hospitals) are randomly assigned to treatment conditions. The formula for the design effect takes into account the number of individuals in each cluster or group and the degree of dependence among scores (the INTRACLASS CORRELATION). STANDARD ERRORS are adjusted with the design effect to correct the negative BIAS that occurs when using dependent data.

design matrix a grid of data whose elements denote the presence or absence of each participant (row) in a treatment (column) of an experimental study.

determinant *n.* a value that represents the generalized variance in a MATRIX of numbers, with large values indicating that the matrix numbers are very dissimilar and thus have more varied information. A determinant can be calculated by multiplying the EIGENVALUES of a matrix by one another. For example, a 2×2 CORRELATION MATRIX with two OR-THOGONAL (i.e., unrelated) variables would have eigenvalues of 1 and 1, which would yield a determinant of 1×1, or 1. In contrast, a correlation matrix with two collinear or completely related variables would have eigenvalues of 1 and 0, yielding a determinant of 0. Thus, the determinant of an orthogonal set of variables is very high (i.e., 1), as the two variables provide very different information. In contrast, the determinant of the correlation matrix with completely collinear variables would be as low as possible (i.e., 0), as the two variables are redundant. Also called **generalized variance**.

determination coefficient see COEF-FICIENT OF DETERMINATION.

deterministic model a mathematical function in which the outcome can be exactly established. In other words, the model explains all of the variance in a DEPENDENT VARIABLE and no ERROR TERM is needed. This contrasts with a STOCHASTIC MODEL, from which a range of possible values may result.

deterministic process see STOCHAS-TIC PROCESS.

detrended normal plot a graph in which the vertical *y*-axis represents deviations from normal and the horizontal *x*-axis indicates the range of values for an observation. When observations are normally distributed, the points of a detrended normal plot will fall on a straight horizontal line at zero, indicat-ing no difference from normal. See also NORMAL PROBABILITY PLOT.

detrending *n.* the practice of removing a specific existing pattern from data, often collected in a TIME SERIES, in order to reveal other expected patterns or sequences in the data. DESEASONALIZ-ATION is a similar process but removes the effect of seasonal shifts in the data.

developmental survey an assessment of information across time on a set of individuals. For example, a researcher may wish to assess the lifestyle habits and attitudes of adolescents over a 10-year period.

deviance *n.* in statistics, a measure of the GOODNESS OF FIT between a smaller HIERARCHICAL MODEL and a fuller model that has all of the same parameters plus more. The difference or deviance between these models follows a CHI-SQUARE DISTRIBUTION, with the DE-GREES OF FREEDOM equal to the number of parameters that are added by the fuller model. If the deviance reveals a SIGNIFICANT DIFFERENCE, then the larger model is needed. If the deviance is not significant, then the smaller, more parsimonious model is retained as more appropriate.

deviance information criterion (**DIC**) an index that reveals the DEVI-ANCE between HIERARCHICAL MODELS, where one model has a larger number of parameters than the other. It is similar to AKAIKE'S INFORMATION CRITERION and the BAYESIAN INFORMATION CRITERION but usually easier to calculate. In all three indices or criteria, a smaller value indicates a more acceptable model.

deviance residual an index of the contribution made by a single observation to the DEVIANCE between two models.

deviant case analysis a procedure used first to understand why specific observations or data points differ from what is expected in a specific model and then to adjust the model to accommodate most of the data. Also called **negative case analysis**.

deviate *n.* in statistics, the extent to which a score differs from a specified value, such as the MEAN. Thus, a negative deviate from the mean indicates how much lower than average the score is, while a positive deviate from the mean indicates how much higher than average the score is.

deviation *n.* a significant departure or difference. This conceptually broad term has a variety of applications in psychology and related fields but in statistics refers to the arithmetic difference between one of a set of values and some fixed amount, generally the MEAN of the set or the value predicted by a model. See STANDARD DEVIATION.

deviational formula an equation that computes the average difference of each score in a set of data from the MEAN score. In other words, it is the equation to calculate STANDARD DEVIATION, which is equal to the square root of the VARIANCE.

deviation score the difference between an observation or value x and the MEAN value (i.e., x – mean) in a set of data. The sum of the deviation scores for a given data set will equal zero, as approximately half of the values will be less than the mean and half will be greater than the mean. Also called **deviation value**.

df symbol for DEGREES OF FREEDOM.

DFBETAS in REGRESSION ANALYSIS, *dif*ferences in *beta* values: an index that describes the influence of the ith case upon the estimates of REGRESSION COEFFICIENTS. It is one of several indices that are useful in diagnosing problems in regression analysis, showing how much a coefficient would change if a single given case (e.g., an OUTLIER) were dropped from the data. One rule of thumb is to delete a case if its DFBETAS value is greater than $2/\sqrt{n}$, where n is the number of observations or cases in the sample.

DFFITS in REGRESSION ANALYSIS, *dif*ference in *fits*: an index of the influence that a particular case (i) has upon the fitted value $\hat{y}_i$. It is one of several indices that are useful in diagnosing problems in regression analysis, and shows how much a predicted y ($\hat{y}$) changes when a particular case is excluded from the calculation of the weights in the regression equation. One rule of thumb is to delete a case if its DFFITS absolute value is greater than $2/\sqrt{(p/n)}$, where n is the number of observations or cases in the sample and p is the number of predictor variables plus 1.

diachronic *adj.* see SYNCHRONIC.

diagnostics *pl. n.* procedures for evaluating how much a model differs from expected patterns and ASSUMPTIONS. For example, diagnostics may reveal how much a set of data departs from assumptions of NORMALITY, LINEARITY, and HOMOGENEITY OF VARIANCE, possibly showing skewed, curvilinear, and unequal variances across levels of another variable, respectively. See also REGRESSION DIAGNOSTICS.

diagnostic test any examination or assessment measure that may help reveal the nature and source of an individual's physical, mental, or behavioral problems or anomalies. In medical research, for example, a diagnostic test would be expected to show SENSITIVITY (i.e., correctly identifying individuals with a certain illness) and SPECIFICITY (i.e., correctly identifying those who do not have a specific illness).

diagonal matrix a SQUARE MATRIX in which all of the values in the lower and upper triangular sections are equal to zero. Probably the most common diagonal matrix is the IDENTITY MATRIX, which has values of one on the main diagonal (upper left to lower right) and values of zero elsewhere.

diagonals model a statistical representation that draws on those values that appear on the main diagonal (upper left to lower right) in a SQUARE MATRIX. This kind of representation is useful if data are believed to be ORTHOGONAL or independent, such that the values in the lower and upper triangular portions of a matrix are not needed as they are close to zero. Also called **independent diagonals model**.

diary method a technique for compiling detailed data about an individual who is being observed or studied by having the individual record his or her daily behavior and activities. Also called **diary survey**.

DIC abbreviation for DEVIANCE INFORMATION CRITERION.

dichotomized variable an item or score that initially had a set of continuous values (e.g., age) but was then separated into two possible values (e.g., younger and older). It may be useful to create a dichotomized variable when there are TRUNCATED DATA.

dichotomous data items or scores that have two categories. For example, gender (male or female) and success (pass or fail) are instances of dichotomous data.

dichotomous events EVENTS in which there are only two possible outcomes, which are independent and mutually exclusive of one another. For example, health science researchers may study whether patients have a disease or do not have a disease, and also whether patients survive an illness or do not survive. Both disease status and survival status are dichotomous events with just two independent and mutually exclusive outcomes (i.e., one cannot fall into both categories).

dichotomous items measures that have only two independent and mutually exclusive possible responses. For example, true–false questions are dichotomous items because there are just two

possible answers, each of which is completely separate from the other. The answers themselves are referred to as **dichotomous responses**.

dichotomous variable a variable that can have only two values (typically, 0 or 1) to designate membership in one of two possible categories, such as female versus male or Republican versus Democrat. Also called **binary variable**.

dichotomy *n.* in statistics, the division of scores into two categories (e.g., above vs. below the median). See also DICHOTOMOUS EVENTS; DICHOTOMOUS ITEMS; DICHOTOMOUS VARIABLE.

Dickey–Fuller test see UNIT ROOT TEST. [David Alan **Dickey** and Wayne Arthur **Fuller** (1931–), U.S. statisticians]

DIF abbreviation for DIFFERENTIAL ITEM FUNCTIONING.

difference between means in research involving two or more groups, the difference between the mean score on a DEPENDENT VARIABLE in one group and the mean score on the same variable in another group. The mean is not expected to be the same across the groups, particularly when the study involves an EXPERIMENTAL GROUP and a CONTROL GROUP. In such cases, tests are used to confirm that the difference between means has STATISTICAL SIGNIFICANCE.

difference score (symbol: D) an index of dissimilarity or change between observations from the same individual across time, based on the measurement of a construct or attribute on two or more separate occasions. For example, it would be helpful to calculate a difference score for a person's weight at the beginning of a diet and exercise program and the final weight six months later. Also called **change score**; **gain score**.

differences vs. totals plot a graph used to analyze results from a 2 × 2 CROSSOVER DESIGN. The difference between the scores from one treatment to the second is tracked along the vertical

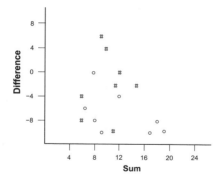

differences vs. totals plot

y-axis, and the sum of the two treatment scores is tracked along the horizontal *x*-axis, with the order of treatments indicated by separate symbols on the graph. Consider the hypothetical example above.

If there appears to be a clear difference between sums along the *x*-axis in the two different ordered treatment pairs, there is some evidence for a CARRYOVER EFFECT, which would not allow straightforward conclusions. In contrast, if there are not clear differences along the *x*-axis and there are more obvious differences along the *y*-axis, this would be evidence for a TREATMENT EFFECT, which would be desirable.

differencing *n.* a type of adjustment used to achieve STATIONARITY when adjacent scores are correlated in a TIME SERIES. Differencing helps remove the AUTOCORRELATION so that other trends in the data may be examined more clearly. See also DESEASONALIZATION; DETRENDING.

differential *n.* in psychometric testing, any lack of similarity in responding to an item observed between two categories of respondent. In ITEM RESPONSE THEORY the term is used to indicate that items are responded to differently by individuals with similar abilities but different characteristics (e.g., different gender or ethnicity). See DIFFERENTIAL ITEM FUNCTIONING.

differential carryover effect in a 2 × 2 CROSSOVER DESIGN in which all participants get both treatments at different times, an apparent difference in outcomes across the groups who had different orderings of the treatments. Differential carryover effects limit the extent of causal conclusions. See CARRYOVER EFFECT; DIFFERENCES VS. TOTALS PLOT.

differential item functioning (**DIF**) the circumstance in which two individuals of similar ability do not have the same probability of answering a question in a particular way. This often is examined to assess whether men and women or individuals of different ethnicity are likely to provide disparate answers on a test. If so, the fairness of the test can be called into question.

differential mortality the differences in the death rate between various subgroups of a population, such as those defined by sex, age, income bracket, lifestyle, and so forth.

differential prediction the situation in which a REGRESSION EQUATION calculated from the total data in a SAMPLE yields systematically different results for individual subgroups in the sample. For example, an overall regression equation that is useful for an entire group comprising both males and females may underestimate or overestimate scores when it is applied separately to the males or to the females of that group.

differential scoring a method of forming a COMPOSITE VARIABLE in which the individual items that contribute to the composite are given different WEIGHTS. For example, a composite based on a clinical diagnostic test could use differential scoring by applying FACTOR SCORES or REGRESSION COEFFICIENTS to individual items, such as family history, degree of symptoms, and patient age, so as to take into account how much each of these variables is linked to a diagnostic outcome.

differential validity 1. the accuracy of a battery of tests in discriminating between a person's subsequent success in two or more different criterion tasks. **2.** differences in VALIDITY COEFFICIENTS across groups. For example, the correlation between test scores and job performance may differ for males and females.

difficulty scale an index of the complexity of a test item. It is related to an ABILITY SCALE, which refers to the level of competence required to complete items successfully.

difficulty value the complexity of a test item as measured by the percentage of participants or students in a designated class, age level, or experimental group who respond to the item correctly. See DIFFICULTY SCALE.

diffuse comparison a procedure often used in META-ANALYSIS to assess whether SIGNIFICANCE LEVELS or EFFECT SIZES are different across studies. Values are standardized across studies and compared to the mean over all of the studies. If the resulting **diffuse comparison score** (usually obtained via a CHI-SQUARE TEST) is significantly different from zero, a meta-analyst could conclude that the significance levels or effect sizes showed HETEROGENEITY across studies and could not be seen as producing a similar value.

diffusion of treatments a situation in which research participants adopt a different intervention from the one they were assigned because they believe the different intervention is more effective. When diffusion of treatments occurs, the INTERNAL VALIDITY of a study is called into question, as it would be difficult to attribute a specific outcome to a specific intervention. For example, participants in a weight-reduction program may be assigned to a low-carbohydrate intervention, a low-fat intervention, a low-calorie intervention, or a control group that only receives educational material on losing weight. If some participants in the control condition found out that those in one of the other conditions were losing more weight and they adopted that intervention, there would be diffusion of treatments.

diffusion process a specific type of STOCHASTIC PROCESS in a MARKOV CHAIN.

Diggle–Kenward model for dropouts a procedure for assessing the nature of missing values and estimating scores for individuals who did not remain in a LONGITUDINAL DESIGN, based on their scores while in the study. [Peter J. **Diggle** (1950–), Australian-born British statistician; Michael G. **Kenward**, British biostatistician]

digital data information that is represented by a series of numerical values, usually so that it can be stored in a computer. Digital data may also be information from sound or light waves that is recorded as signals or numbers (e.g., a digital recording of music or a movie).

digit preference the practice of rounding a number to a preferred value instead of keeping the original value. For example, health researchers may prefer to round the weight of study participants to end in a .0 or .5 to accommodate those scales that do not provide more accurate information on weight. For example, 140.0 to 140.4 pounds in actual body weight may register as 140.0 on a scale, whereas a weight of 145.5 to 145.9 may register as 145.5. Thus, the scale and researchers using it can be said to have a digit preference for weight recorded in decimals ending in 0 or 5.

digram-balanced *adj.* describing an experimental design in which treatments are arranged so as to avoid a SE-QUENCE EFFECT. For example, a research study that had four possible treatment conditions (A, B, C, D) that were all assigned to each participant would be digram-balanced if different individuals received the treatments in varying orders: ABCD, DCBA, ACBD, DBCA. In such a case, the research design itself is known as a BALANCED LATIN SQUARE. Also called **diagram-balanced**. See also COUNTER-BALANCING; GRAECO-LATIN SQUARE.

digraph *n.* a shortened name for DI-RECTED GRAPH.

dimension *n.* in statistics, a factor or component that is applied in measuring a set of variables. For example, some intelligence scales are considered to have two important dimensions consisting of verbal and nonverbal intelligence.

dimensionality *n.* the number of DIMENSIONS applied in measuring a construct. In FACTOR ANALYSIS and PRINCIPAL COMPONENTS ANALYSIS, it is important to assess the dimensionality of a set of items on a scale in order to form cohesive subscales that each describe a similar set of items.

dip test of unimodality a statistical procedure to assess whether there is more than one peak or MODE in a set of data. For example, a dip test of unimodality for a bell-shaped NORMAL DISTRIBUTION would be nonsignificant, as such a distribution has only one peak.

direct correlation see POSITIVE CORRELATION.

directed acyclic graph (DAG) a DI-RECTED GRAPH in which there is no way of moving through all of the points (nodes) in a sequence that returns to the

starting point. The following is a generic example.

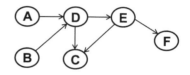

It may be used to represent data from any of various statistical methods—such as STRUCTURAL EQUATION MODELING, PATH ANALYSIS, and REGRESSION ANALYSIS—in which one variable predicts one or more other variables but the reverse is not true; that is, prediction is not allowed in both directions (e.g., if x predicts y, then y cannot also predict x). Also called **acyclic digraph**.

directed graph any display in which points (nodes) of information are connected by lines (edges) showing direction (i.e., the edges have arrows or the nodes are numbered). Consider the following generic example.

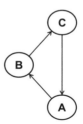

Such graphs are used to represent a directional process (e.g., Point A predicts Point B and Point B predicts Point C). Also called **digraph**. Compare UNDI-RECTED GRAPH.

directional hypothesis a scientific prediction stating (a) that an effect will occur and (b) whether that effect will specifically increase or specifically decrease, depending on changes to the IN-DEPENDENT VARIABLE. For example, a directional hypothesis could predict that depression scores will decrease following a six-week intervention, or conversely that well-being will increase following a six-week intervention. Also called **directional alternative hypothesis; one-tailed hypothesis**. Compare NONDIRECTIONAL HYPOTHESIS.

directionality problem in CORRELATIONAL RESEARCH, the situation in which it is known that two variables are related although it is not known which is the cause and which is the effect.

directional test a statistical test of a DIRECTIONAL HYPOTHESIS. Also called **directional alternative hypothesis test; directional hypothesis test; one-tailed test**. Compare NONDIRECTIONAL TEST.

directly proportional describing a correlation between two variables in which each increases or decreases with the other. This contrasts with an **inversely proportional** relation, in which one variable increases as the other decreases. An example of a directly proportional relationship is weight and amount of calorie intake, while an example of an inversely proportional relationship is amount of alcoholic drinks in a two-hour period and visual perception while driving. Directly proportional relationships may be indexed by POSITIVE CORRELATIONS.

direct model a representation in which interest centers on how one or more variables specifically correlate with one or more other variables, without the inclusion of a MEDIATOR or intervening variable. For example, a researcher may hypothesize that an individual's health background relates to his or her coping style, which in turn may be related to the individual's sense of well-being. A direct model of this research would focus on how health background relates to well-being without considering the mediator of coping style.

direct observation a method of collecting data in which a researcher simply views or listens to the subjects of the research, without asking specific questions or manipulating any variables. The method of direct observation is useful in EVALUATION RESEARCH or FIELD RESEARCH. See also NATURALISTIC OBSERVATION.

direct observation coding system in FIELD RESEARCH, a method of providing descriptors and quantifying results so that the specific information to be recorded and later analyzed is explicitly identified.

direct relationship 1. an association between two variables such that they rise and fall in value together. For example, the number of hours studied and the level of test performance form a direct relationship in that as the number of study hours increases, the level of performance also increases, and vice versa. **2.** in STRUCTURAL EQUATION MODELING, a correlation or prediction between two variables that does not involve a MEDIATOR or intervening variable. Also called **positive relationship**. Compare INDIRECT RELATIONSHIP.

direct replication the process of repeating a study with different data under similar conditions, or of conducting several different studies with the same data. Direct replication is useful for establishing that the findings of the original study are reliable (see RELIABILITY). In contrast, SYSTEMATIC REPLICATION uses a different data set and also adjusts the conditions in specific ways.

Dirichlet distribution a group of PROBABILITY CURVES or patterns that encompass MULTIVARIATE extensions of a beta probability pattern, such that the marginals of a Dirichlet distribution are BETA DISTRIBUTIONS. A Dirichlet distribution may be used in BAYESIAN statistics when estimating a PRIOR DISTRIBUTION. [Johan Peter Gustav Lejeune **Dirichlet** (1805–1859), German mathematician]

dirty data a set of observations or measurements that contains errors. For example, information may have been inaccurately reported by a participant or may have been incorrectly entered into computer records.

disaggregation *n.* the process of breaking down data into smaller units or sets of observations. For example, faculty salary data initially may show a significant difference between men and women. After disaggregating the data into separate levels (e.g., assistant, associate, full professor), however, one may find that there are no significant differences in salary among men and women at the assistant professor level but that there are differences at the full professor level. Thus, disaggregating the data reveals a finer-tuned pattern, suggesting that long-term faculty differential compensation practices applied in the past have been maintained over time. Compare AGGREGATION.

disattenuated correlation a CORRELATION COEFFICIENT that removes the effects of MEASUREMENT ERROR, on the principle that the obtained correlation between x and y is limited by the RELIABILITY of each of the variables; an unreliable measure (e.g., x) cannot predict another unreliable measure (e.g., y). It is formed by dividing a correlation between x and y by the square root of the product of the respective reliabilities for x and y. For example, assume the correlation between x and y was .30, the reliability of x was .70, and the reliability of y was .60. The disattenuated or corrected correlation would be

$$.30 / \sqrt{(.70 \times .60)} = .46.$$

Thus, removing the effect of unreliability in both x and y would result in a medium-size correlation of .30 becoming closer to a large (i.e., .50) correlation of .46. Compare ATTENUATION.

disclosure of deceptions in DECEPTION RESEARCH, a participant's revelation of the true nature of the study, even though he or she was asked not to give others any information about it.

discontinuous *adj.* intermittent or disconnected. For example, a sequence of ORDINAL numbers is discontinuous because it does not have a smooth flow from one value to the next. See also DISCRETE. Compare CONTINUOUS.

discontinuous function a graph in which there is a sudden break or disconnection in the flow of points that are plotted. Compare CONTINUOUS FUNCTION.

discontinuous variable a variable that has distinct, DISCRETE values but no precise numerical flow. For example, gender can be thought of as a discontinuous variable with two possible values, male or female. In contrast, a CONTINUOUS VARIABLE involves numerically precise information, such as height, weight, and miles per hour. Also called **discrete variable**.

discordance *n.* the state or condition of being at variance. For example, in TWIN STUDIES discordance refers to dissimilarity between a pair of twins with respect to a particular trait or disease. Compare CONCORDANCE. —**discordant** *adj.*

discordant sibling study research that involves family members who differ on specific characteristics or traits. For example, researchers may collect data on families that have children with differing gender, eye color, or blood types.

discourse analysis a method of studying verbal communications that extends beyond the single sentence to encompass conversations, narratives, and written arguments. Discourse analysis is particularly concerned with the ways in which a sequence of two or more sentences can produce meanings that are different from or additional to any found in the sentences considered separately. An important source of such meanings is the "frame" or format of the discourse (news item, fairytale, joke, etc.) and a recognition of the various norms that this implies. The norms and expectations that govern conversation are a major concern of discourse analysis, as is the structure of conversational language generally.

discovery research studies that focus on uncovering new treatments or interventions, such as pharmaceutical studies in which investigators are interested in finding new drugs to treat a particular illness.

discrete *adj.* separate or distinct; often referring to CATEGORICAL or ORDINAL data that have names or ranks as values. In contrast, CONTINUOUS data have a potentially infinite flow of precise numerical information. See also DISCONTINUOUS.

discrete distribution a delineation of separate, distinct values. For example, the number of children in a family can be displayed in a discrete distribution with values of 0, 1, 2, 3, and 4. Compare CONTINUOUS DISTRIBUTION.

discrete measure a measure of a DISCONTINUOUS value, for example, the grade level of a student.

discrete random variable a variable having distinct values that follow a known pattern or probability. For example, the outcome of rolling two dice is a discrete RANDOM VARIABLE: The value could be 2, 3, 4, and so forth up to 12, with a symmetric probability curve that peaks at the value 7, which is most likely to occur as it has the most combinations available to produce it (i.e., with the two dice having a 1 and 6, or a 6 and 1, or a 2 and a 5, or a 5 and a 2, or a 3 and a 4, or a 4 and a 3). Compare CONTINUOUS RANDOM VARIABLE.

discrete-time Markov chain see MARKOV CHAIN.

discrete-time stochastic process see STOCHASTIC PROCESS.

discrete-time survival model a model that depicts the probability of an event occurring at a certain point, given events at all previously countable points. For example, the number of years a cancer patient can expect to live after a diag-

nosis could be expressed as a discrete-time survival model that would show the probability of living six years post-diagnosis, given that the cancer patient has survived for five years. Compare CONTINUOUS-TIME SURVIVAL MODEL.

discrete variable see DISCONTINUOUS VARIABLE. See also DISCRETE RANDOM VARIABLE.

discriminability *n.* the quality that enables an object, variable, or person to be readily distinguished from something or someone else.

discriminal dispersion in an experiment involving the differentiation of stimuli, the distribution of responses around a given MEAN.

discriminant analysis a MULTIVARIATE method of data analysis that uses a linear combination of values from a set of quantitative variables to predict differences among a set of predefined categories or groups of another variable. For example, a researcher might use a discriminant analysis to determine whether several measures of personality can differentiate those who pursue different majors in college. When the outcome variable has only two categories (i.e., is a DICHOTOMOUS VARIABLE), discriminant analysis results are similar to those achieved with MULTIPLE REGRESSION as far as the overall significance between the set of predictors and the grouping variable, and the magnitude and importance of each of the predictors. If there are more than two outcome categories, MULTIPLE DISCRIMINANT ANALYSIS is used. Also called **canonical discriminant analysis**. See also DESCRIPTIVE DISCRIMINANT ANALYSIS; PREDICTIVE DISCRIMINANT ANALYSIS.

discriminant function 1. any of a range of statistical techniques used to situate an item that could belong to any of two or more variables in the correct set, with minimal probability of error. **2.** in DISCRIMINANT ANALYSIS more specifically, a linear combination of predictor variables that is used to categorize items into distinct groups. The first discriminant function denotes the linear combination that best distinguishes among the discrete groups, the second discriminant function is the linear combination that is the next best in distinguishing among the groups, and so forth. Also called **canonical discriminant function**.

discriminant loading a correlation between a variable and an underlying dimension found when trying to predict a categorical outcome from a set of predictor variables. It may range from –1 to +1, where values near either extreme indicate a variable that is able to clearly differentiate among the categories of the outcome. A discriminant loading is analogous to a standardized weight in a MULTIPLE REGRESSION analysis when the outcome is dichotomous (i.e., has only two possible categories, such as pass or fail). Also called **canonical loading**.

discriminant validity the degree to which a test or measure diverges from (i.e., does not correlate with) another measure whose underlying construct is conceptually unrelated to it. This is one of two aspects of CONSTRUCT VALIDITY, the other being CONVERGENT VALIDITY. Also called **divergent validity**.

discriminating power 1. a measure of the ability of a test to distinguish between two or more groups being assessed. **2.** in DISCRIMINANT ANALYSIS, the degree of accuracy with which a set of predictor variables differentiates outcomes into categories.

discrimination index see INDEX OF DISCRIMINATION.

discrimination information the amount of additional evidence required to substantiate a true ALTERNATIVE HYPOTHESIS over that required to substantiate a NULL HYPOTHESIS. This is sometimes referred to as KULLBACK–LEIBLER INFOR-

MATION when comparing PROBABILITY DISTRIBUTIONS.

discrimination parameter in ITEM RESPONSE THEORY, the STANDARD DEVIATION of the MEASUREMENT ERROR of an item in a test, which indicates how well that item distinguishes among test takers on the attribute being measured.

discrimination range the range of item DIFFICULTY VALUES, usually between .40 and .60, that indicates an appropriate proportion of people are getting an item correct, such that the item is moderately differentiating among individuals. If the item difficulty values are too high, most people get the item wrong and it thus is not particularly differential. Conversely, a very low value indicates that too many people get the item correct, which also is not useful in distinguishing among test takers.

discrimination value an index of how much a term or variable helps in differentiating among two groups, distributions, or situations.

discursive *adj.* referring or relating to the use of analytical reasoning as opposed to intuition.

discursive psychology the study of social interactions and interpersonal relationships with a focus on understanding the ways in which individuals construct events via written, spoken, or symbolic communication.

dishabituation *n.* the reappearance or enhancement of a habituated response (i.e., one that has been weakened following repeated exposure to the evoking stimulus) due to the presentation of a new stimulus. Dishabituation can be interpreted as a signal that a given stimulus can be discriminated from another habituated stimulus and is a useful method for investigating perception in nonverbal individuals or animals. Compare HABITUATION.

disjoint sets in SET THEORY, two sets that have no elements in common. The intersection of the groups is empty, and they are mutually exclusive. An example of disjoint sets would be the set of all males and the set of all females.

dismantling study research that examines whether individual components of a larger protocol can be just as effective and with less effort and expense. For example, a condition traditionally treated by several months of therapy in addition to medications could be investigated via a dismantling study to assess whether just the therapy, just the medication, or perhaps a reduced time in therapy plus some medication would be equally as effective as the full intervention.

disordinal interaction in a FACTORIAL ANALYSIS OF VARIANCE, an INTERACTION EFFECT in which the direction of influence of one of the INDEPENDENT VARIABLES differs depending on the level of a second independent variable. A disordinal interaction is indicated by a pattern of crossed lines when plotting the two MAIN EFFECTS from the analysis. For example, if a researcher found that a particular treatment for dementia improved functioning in individuals with mild and moderate degrees of the disease but hindered functioning in those with a severe degree, then a disordinal interaction would be present. Also called **crossover interaction**. Compare ORDINAL INTERACTION.

dispersion *n.* the degree to which a set of scores deviate from the mean. Also called **spread**. See also RANGE; STANDARD DEVIATION; VARIANCE.

dispersion matrix see COVARIANCE MATRIX.

dispersion measure an index of variability, or how dispersed a set of values is for a given variable. Common measures of dispersion include the RANGE, which is the highest minus the lowest score, and the STANDARD DEVIATION, which is the average distance of scores from the MEAN. The larger the dispersion measure, the more spread out the scores.

dispersion parameter an index of the SKEWNESS (lopsidedness) or KURTOSIS (peakedness) of a distribution. The NORMAL DISTRIBUTION thus does not need a dispersion parameter because skewness and kurtosis are not present (i.e., equal zero) in such a distribution. Also called **scale parameter**.

dispersion test an assessment of whether two samples have a similar spread of values on a variable of interest. This is useful in determining whether there is evidence for HOMOGENEITY OF VARIANCE, which allows for pooling or averaging variances across samples.

display *n.* the presentation of stimuli to any of the senses.

dissimilarity coefficient an index of difference or distance between two objects, variables, or samples. It may be based on CORRELATION, with lower values indicating more difference or distance, or VARIANCE, with higher values indicating greater difference or distance. A dissimilarity coefficient often is used to assess the difference between variables or entities in multivariate procedures such as CLUSTER ANALYSIS, CORRESPONDENCE ANALYSIS, MULTIDIMENSIONAL SCALING, and PRINCIPAL COMPONENTS ANALYSIS. Also called **distance measure**. Compare SIMILARITY COEFFICIENT.

dissimilarity matrix a MATRIX used to indicate the distance or difference between pairs of objects, variables, or samples. Also called **distance matrix**. See also DISSIMILARITY COEFFICIENT. Compare SIMILARITY MATRIX.

distal cause see ULTIMATE CAUSE.

distal control a CONTROL GROUP for an experiment or research project that is kept physically distant from the EXPERIMENTAL GROUP. A distal control group may permit a better experimental comparison in that there is less chance of contamination or DIFFUSION OF TREATMENT. On the other hand, a distal control group may not be as closely matched to the experimental group as a NEIGHBORHOOD CONTROL group or as central to the nature of the study. Because of these factors a design may use both a local and a distal control group.

distance *n.* the disparity between two values or entities. In statistics, the term often refers to the difference or DEVIATION between a RAW SCORE and a mean score. It may also refer to MAHALANOBIS DISTANCE, which provides an indication of dissimilarity between two vectors or data sets.

distance function a FUNCTION describing how disparate two points, variables, or other entities are from one another. A distance function is often used in multivariate methods such as CLUSTER ANALYSIS.

distance matrix see DISSIMILARITY MATRIX.

distance measure see DISSIMILARITY COEFFICIENT.

distractor *n.* a stimulus or an aspect of a stimulus that is irrelevant to the task or activity being performed, used to divert attention, prevent the occurrence of some unwanted response, or interfere with some behavior. For example, in memory studies, the participant might be given some arithmetic problems to solve as a distractor task between the study and recall phases of an experiment in order to minimize rehearsal of the material to be remembered.

distributed-lag model a model in which past values of an independent variable have an ongoing effect on current values of a dependent variable.

distribution *n.* the relation between the values that a variable may take and the relative number of cases taking on each value. A distribution may be simply an empirical description of that relationship or a mathematical (probabilistic) specification of the relationship. For example, it would be helpful to examine the distribution of scores for a college exam to view the frequency of students who achieved various percentages correct on an exam. In a NORMAL DISTRIBUTION most of the scores would fall in the middle (i.e., about 70% correct or a score of C), with fewer students achieving a D (i.e., 60–69% correct) or a B (i.e., 80–89% correct) and even fewer earning 59% or less (i.e., an F) or 90% to 100% (e.g., an A score). See also FREQUENCY DISTRIBUTION; PROBABILITY DISTRIBUTION.

distribution curve a graph depicting the possible values of a variable along the horizontal x-axis and the frequency of occurrences for each value along the vertical y-axis. The normal BELL CURVE is a common example of a distribution curve.

distribution-dependent test see PARAMETRIC TEST.

distribution-free statistics see NONPARAMETRIC STATISTICS.

distribution-free test see NONPARAMETRIC TEST.

distribution function see CUMULATIVE DISTRIBUTION FUNCTION.

disturbance term see ERROR TERM.

divergent validity see DISCRIMINANT VALIDITY.

diversity index a quantification of the variety among a species or population, used in fields such as biology and demography. The measure usually ranges from 0 to 1, with values closer to 0 most often indicating more HOMOGENEITY or similarity (i.e., less diversity) and values closer to 1 most often indicating high HETEROGENEITY.

divisive clustering a form of CLUSTER ANALYSIS that starts with all entities, persons, or variables in a single data set and then divides them into progressively smaller groups that have similar characteristics within groups and different characteristics across groups until each entity is in its own single cluster. Divisive clustering can be contrasted with AGGLOMERATIVE CLUSTERING, a type of HIERARCHICAL CLUSTERING in which each entity starts out in its own group and then groups are collapsed together if there is high similarity between them. Also called **top-down (hierarchical) clustering**.

domain *n*. in SET THEORY, the set of elements over which a function is defined.

domain-referenced test an assessment that covers a specific area of study such that a score will reveal how much of this area has been mastered. This is similar to a CRITERION-REFERENCED TEST, in which a content area is mapped and scores reflect whether a particular standard or criterion has been achieved. These kinds of tests are contrasted with NORM-REFERENCED TESTS, in which scores indicate how well a test taker performed on the items relative to others who took the test. Thus, if an individual got 90% of the items correct in a domain-referenced or criterion-referenced test, this would be a high score indicative of his or her deep knowledge and understanding of the content covered in the test.

domain sampling the process of selecting the content of a test from a specific content area. For example, most teacher-made tests use domain sampling to create items from the material covered during a particular set of lectures.

dominance matrix a SQUARE MATRIX that maps the performance of a set of entities by listing a 1 if a row entity exceeds or wins over the column entity and a 0 otherwise. For example, a dominance matrix might be used to rank college basketball teams according to which college won over which other colleges. Rankings could be formed by adding up the row values in the dominance matrix to see which college team had the most wins. An examination of the body of the matrix could yield information on which teams appeared to dominate over teams that had won over other teams (i.e., demonstrating two-step dominance). Dominance matrices frequently are used in GAME THEORY research.

dominance statistic an index that quantifies the number of cases in one group that outscore cases in another group.

Doolittle method a procedure for factoring (decomposing) a SQUARE MATRIX into the product of two other matrices: a lower TRIANGULAR MATRIX with values of 1 along the diagonal and an upper triangular matrix. This procedure is similar to the CHOLESKY FACTORIZATION method, which yields a lower triangular matrix multiplied by its TRANSPOSE.

D-optimal design a research design in which only those conditions that create the least COVARIANCE among the parameters are included, such that a full design of all variable levels is not implemented. To identify a D-optimal design, the number of levels and their arrangements are modified to determine how RELIABILITY changes with different kinds of designs. If two designs produce essentially the same reliability, the researcher can choose the one that is logistically easier or is less costly to conduct. Alternatively, for a fixed cost a researcher can identify the design that maximizes reliability. See also A-OPTIMAL DESIGN; E-OPTIMAL DESIGN.

Doran estimator a procedure to fill in missing data for a TIME-SERIES ANALYSIS that is useful when there are more data missing at the beginning of a series than at the end. For example, assume a particular company only provides quarterly sales data during the first half of the year and both quarterly and monthly sales data in the latter half of the year. One could use the Doran estimator to guess the missing monthly sales values by using only the quarterly sales information. [Howard E. **Doran**, U.S. econometrician]

dose-ranging trial a clinical trial in which patients are randomly assigned to treatment groups to receive one of several different dosages of a drug. A dose-ranging trial provides information on how much medicine is needed for it to be effective. Also called **dose-ranging study**.

dot plot see SCATTERPLOT.

double bar graph see DUAL BAR GRAPH.

double-barreled question an item on a survey that simultaneously asks about two kinds of information instead of just one, thus making the responses difficult to interpret. An example of a double-barreled question is "How often do you use a condom after drinking alcohol?" If a respondent said very often, a researcher does not know whether this refers to the frequency of condom use, the frequency of drinking alcohol, or both. It would be best to ask two separate questions to obtain this information (e.g., "How often do you use a condom?" and "How often do you drink alcohol?"), with each question having its own set of response choices (e.g., "Never" up to "Quite Often").

double blind see BLIND.

double-blind crossover trial a type of clinical trial in which participants receive two different treatments and neither the researchers nor the participants are aware of which treatments are administered to which individuals at what time. Participants are randomly assigned to a particular order of treatments (Treatment A followed by Treatment B, or Treatment B followed by Treatment A); between treatments they go through a brief WASH-OUT PERIOD to eliminate the effect of the initial treatment before the second treatment is administered. This kind of design should neutralize potential bias from researchers or partici-

pants, and it uses half of the participants needed for a double BLIND between-groups study in which separate groups are randomly assigned to different treatments. A possible problem with the crossover facet of the design is that the effects of an initial treatment may not fully be gone by the time the second treatment is administered, thus causing potential bias in the interpretation of which treatment is causing the most effective outcome. See also CROSSOVER DESIGN.

double bootstrapping a procedure in which samples are randomly drawn, with replacement, from an initial data set and their PARAMETERS and STANDARD ERRORS estimated and averaged across the set of samples. This is then followed by another random sampling of the data, again with replacement, after which parameter estimates and standard errors are obtained a second time. Double bootstrapping usually is less biased than using a single set of BOOTSTRAPPING samples; additional procedures often are applied between the two bootstrapping procedures in order to further reduce BIAS.

double cross-validation a procedure in which a sample is split into two portions or subsamples and a statistical model (e.g., a MULTIPLE REGRESSION EQUATION) is estimated from the first portion and verified with the second portion. The process is then reversed: An estimate of the model is obtained using the second subsample and verified using the first subsample. If results from both validations are similar, there is strong evidence that the model is robust and generalizable across samples that are similar to those used in the two sets of analyses. See CROSS-VALIDATION.

double deception in DECEPTION RESEARCH, an apparent debriefing after the experiment, which is itself a further ploy.

double-dummy technique a research design used when two treatments are dissimilar enough for participants to know which treatment they are receiving just by its form (e.g., a comparison of tablet and capsule medication types). In the double-dummy technique, each participant is randomly assigned to at least one inactive PLACEBO (i.e., dummy) condition plus a regular treatment. Thus, with a double-dummy technique participants are randomly assigned to one of the following three conditions: (1) Treatment A (e.g., active tablet) plus Placebo B (e.g., inactive capsule); (2) Placebo A (inactive tablet) plus Treatment B (active capsule); or (3) Placebo A plus Placebo B, which serves as a CONTROL.

double exponential distribution a graphed curve that rises very quickly to a peak and then falls very quickly to the horizontal axis, forming a symmetrical shape with the appearance of a witch's hat. The pattern is similar to a normal BELL CURVE except that it is not as full at the peak and tails. Also called **Laplace distribution**.

double masked see BLIND.

double sampling a research process in which data can be sampled a second time if the results from a first statistical test just missed significance due to low POWER. Because this process can result in a higher TYPE I ERROR rate, it should be used only when needed to conserve costs and maximize power.

doubly censored data data in which exact measurements are not known for events at both ends of a distribution. For example, assume a health researcher examined the time at which a group of individuals quit smoking cigarettes. Further, consider that there was a subgroup who had already quit smoking at the time of the initial assessment, as well as a subgroup who had not yet quit smoking at the end of the final assessment. Thus, the exact quit dates for those who quit before the study began would not be known, and for purposes of analysis the initial start date of the study would have to be substituted instead. Similarly, the quit date for those who had not yet quit smoking by the conclusion of the study also would not be known, and the end date of the study would have to be substituted instead. Thus, both ends of the distribution of quit dates would be censored. See CENSORED DATA.

doubly multivariate describing a design in which two sets of multiple variables are assessed. For example, assume a researcher evaluates several reading performance outcomes (e.g., number of books read, difficulty level of the books, vocabulary level) for a set of grade-school students. Further, imagine the researcher assesses the students at the beginning, middle, and end of the school year. In assessing multiple reading outcomes at multiple time points, the researcher would be using a doubly multivariate design.

doubly stochastic 1. describing a SQUARE MATRIX of nonnegative numbers in which all of the rows sum to 1 and all of the columns sum to 1. **2.** describing a model in which observations of a RANDOM VARIABLE are modeled in two stages, in the second of which one or more of the parameters used in the first stage are themselves treated as random (STOCHASTIC) variables. Doubly stochastic models are used to model processes with a random probability pattern, such as TIME SERIES.

d prime (symbol: d') a measure of an individual's ability to detect signals; more specifically, a measure of sensitivity or discriminability derived from SIGNAL DETECTION THEORY that is unaffected by response biases. It is the difference (in standard deviation units) between the means of the noise and signal + noise distributions. A value of $d' = 3$ is close to perfect performance; a value of $d' = 0$ is chance ("guessing") performance.

drift *n*. **1.** a reduction in variation in genetic traits that can occur when sampling from continually smaller groups, such that some traits ultimately become excluded from possibility. **2.** a reduction in the reliability of technical instruments or the accuracy of observers over time. See INSTRUMENT DRIFT; OBSERVER DRIFT.

drunkard's walk any process in which a person or thing proceeds by random steps but still arrives at a specified point or goal, much as an intoxicated person may choose randomly among various streets along the way and still arrive home. It is a type of RANDOM WALK, that is, a series of haphazard events. For example, a student who did not study for an exam could be said to follow a random walk by unsystematically guessing the answers for each question. If the student, however, happened to pass the exam despite randomly guessing at each juncture, the process would be a drunkard's walk.

DS abbreviation for DUAL SCALING.

D study decision research performed upon variance components identified in an initial G STUDY. A D study seeks to determine the number of conditions that need to be considered to maintain a reasonable level of RELIABILITY for relative (norm-referenced) or absolute (criterion-referenced) decisions about a measure. For example, a D study could be conducted to analyze how many different conditions would need to be tested before stating that a specific measure (e.g.,

of intelligence) was dependable across a variety of situations (e.g., geographical areas, age groups, content areas).

dual bar graph a BAR GRAPH that depicts the frequencies for two CATEGORICAL VARIABLES. One categorical variable is represented by a series of possible responses (e.g., pizza choice: cheese, vegetable, or meat) listed across the horizontal *x*-axis and the other categorical variable (e.g., gender: male or female) is depicted by drawing separate rectangles that represent the frequency or percentage, shown along the vertical *y*-axis, associated with each of the responses on the first variable.

Thus, if 30% of men prefer cheese pizza, 20% prefer vegetable pizza, and 50% prefer meat pizza, three rectangles that extend to 30, 20, and 50, respectively, on the vertical axis would be shown for men. Similarly, the percentages for women would be depicted by a second set of rectangular lines above the three pizza choices, as shown in the illustration below. Also called **double bar graph**.

dual scaling (**DS**) a method of assessing relationships and patterns, whether linear or nonlinear, among CATEGORICAL DATA that involves assigning scale values to the elements of the data set. For example, DS may be useful when assessing the relationship between achievement motivation and performance. When achievement motivation is low or high, performance is expected to be low;

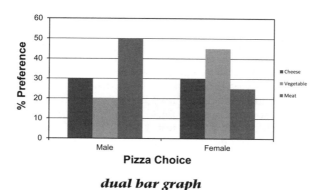

dual bar graph

however, when achievement motivation is moderate, performance is expected to be high. This nonlinear relationship between the two variables can be analyzed more effectively with DS than with conventional statistical methods (e.g., correlation, regression), as the latter require assumptions of LINEARITY and would reveal no apparent association between the variables. Also called **optimal scaling**.

Duhem–Quine thesis the proposition that an individual hypothesis cannot be empirically tested in isolation, because any test involves assuming the truth of a larger body of principles to which the hypothesis belongs. [Pierre **Duhem** (1861–1916), French physicist and mathematician; Willard Van Orman **Quine** (1908–2000), U.S. philosopher and logician]

dummy variable in REGRESSION ANALYSIS, a numerical variable that is created to represent a QUALITATIVE fact, which is done by giving a variable a value of 1 or 0 to indicate the presence or absence of a CATEGORICAL trait. A dummy variable usually represents a DICHOTOMOUS VARIABLE, that is, one that can have only two categories. For example, gender could be coded as a 1 to represent female and a 0 to represent male. When a measure has more than two categories, a researcher creates $k - 1$ dummy variables to represent the total number of different categories, k, with one of the categories indicated by 0. Thus, to code a political party as either Democrat, Republican, or Independent/Other, the first dummy variable would be labeled "Democrat" and allot a 1 to each person who is a Democrat and a 0 to each person who is not. The second dummy variable would be labeled "Republican" and allot a 1 to each person who is a Republican and a 0 to each person who is not. Those who are Independent/Other in political party affiliation would not need a separate variable as they would be denoted by 0 on each of the two other dummy variables. Also called **indicator variable**.

dummy variable coding a method of assigning numerical values to a CATEGORICAL VARIABLE in such a way that the variable reflects class membership. The values of 0 and 1 often are used, with 0 typically representing nonmembership and 1 typically representing membership. Compare CONTRAST CODING; EFFECT CODING.

Duncan's multiple range test (**Duncan's MRT**) a MULTIPLE COMPARISONS test used to follow up on an ANALYSIS OF VARIANCE that yields significant results. After obtaining a significant F RATIO, a researcher could conclude that at least one pair of samples is significantly different on the DEPENDENT VARIABLE and then conduct a Duncan multiple range test on pairs of samples in order to identify that specific pair. The overall TYPE I ERROR rate would be protected, which would not be the case if separate T TESTS were conducted on all possible pairs. Other types of procedures for following up a significant analysis of variance include the SCHEFFÉ TEST and TUKEY'S HONESTLY SIGNIFICANT DIFFERENCE TEST, among others. [David B. **Duncan** (1917–2006), U.S. biostatistician]

Dunn–Bonferroni procedure a statistical method for assessing whether multiple pairs of samples are significantly different from each other, while protecting the overall TYPE I ERROR rate by dividing the alpha or SIGNIFICANCE LEVEL by the number of comparisons made. For example, if a researcher wants to investigate whether three samples are significantly different using an alpha of .05, three T TESTS could be conducted (i.e., between groups 1 and 2, 2 and 3, and 1 and 3) using an alpha level of $.05/3 = .0167$ for each comparison; this approach would hold the overall Type I error rate at .05. Also called **Bonferroni t test**; **Dunn's multiple comparison test**. See also BONFERRONI INEQUALITY.

[O. J. **Dunn**; Carlo Emilio **Bonferroni** (1892–1960), Italian mathematician]

Dunnett's multiple comparison test a statistical method for assessing whether a CONTROL GROUP is significantly different from each of several treatment groups. It is similar to the DUNN–BONFERRONI PROCEDURE but not as stringent in that it does not require the SIGNIFICANCE LEVEL per comparison to be as small. The index of difference that is obtained from this test is called **Dunnett's t**. [Charles W. **Dunnett** (1921–2007), Canadian statistician]

Dunn–Šidák procedure a statistical technique that uses MULTIPLE COMPARISONS to assess whether three or more samples are significantly different. More powerful (requiring a less stringent SIGNIFICANCE LEVEL) than the DUNN–BONFERRONI PROCEDURE, it assumes that each of the comparison tests is independent of all the others. Also called **Dunn–Šidák method**; **Dunn–Šidák test**. [O. J. **Dunn**; Zbyněk **Šidák**]

Dunn's multiple comparison test see DUNN–BONFERRONI PROCEDURE.

duration analysis see SURVIVAL ANALYSIS.

duration recording the process of tracking and measuring the amount of time an individual engages in a specific behavior (e.g., completing homework assignments, interacting socially).

Durbin–Watson test a method for assessing AUTOCORRELATION in a TIME SERIES (i.e., of determining the degree of association between values separated by a given time lag). It is properly called the **Durbin–Watson d test** so as to distinguish it from the **Durbin–Watson h test**, a further refined method for producing an unbiased estimate of autocorrelation that is appropriate for use with large samples. [James **Durbin** (1923–2012), British statistician; Geoffrey **Watson** (1921–1998), Australian statistician]

DV abbreviation for DEPENDENT VARIABLE.

Ee

e 1. abbreviation for EXPONENT. **2.** in measurement theory, abbreviation for ERROR.

E symbol for EXPECTED VALUE.

Eberhardt's statistic an index of randomness in a spatial distribution. If it is significant, a researcher may conclude that the results are not due to randomness but rather have a meaningful pattern.

ECM algorithm abbreviation for EXPECTATION-CONDITIONAL MAXIMIZATION ALGORITHM.

ECME algorithm abbreviation for EXPECTATION-CONDITIONAL MAXIMIZATION EITHER ALGORITHM.

ecological assessment the gathering of observations in various environments to examine whether individuals or entities behave differently depending on the surroundings. For example, a teacher at a child-development center may investigate whether children demonstrate more or less problem behavior in various settings at the center. Findings from the ecological assessment may offer ideas on how to intervene to improve the overall behavior of the children in multiple settings.

ecological correlation a correlation that is calculated between group means instead of between individual scores, thereby showing the relationship between variables at the group level. For example, a university administrator may want to assess the relationship between faculty salary and productivity as measured by the number of publications. An ecological correlation would find the average salary and average number of publications for each department at the university and then find the association between these sets of means. This would provide information at a departmental, instead of an individual, level.

ecological fallacy a mistaken conclusion drawn about individuals based on findings from groups to which they belong. For example, if a university administrator found that the ECOLOGICAL CORRELATION between faculty salary and number of publications at the departmental level was strong and positive (e.g., $r = .60$), it would be an ecological fallacy to assume that for any particular faculty member the correlation would be the same.

ecological inference an assumption about individuals or subsets of individuals on the basis of aggregate data about the larger group. For example, a researcher may wish to make an ecological inference about the education of women from ethnic minorities on the basis of data from a report that provides information by gender or ethnicity but not both together. Various strategies have been suggested for making valid ecological inferences from summary statistics (i.e., inferences that do not commit the ECOLOGICAL FALLACY).

ecological momentary assessment (**EMA**) the process of examining the behavior of individuals at random, multiple time points to get a clearer picture of how they behave in various real-world settings. For example, a researcher may conduct an EMA on individuals who are trying to quit smoking by contacting them randomly throughout a week to inquire about urges to smoke, mood, other people who are interacting with them, and other relevant circumstances that may be occurring at these times.

ecological validity the degree to which results obtained from research or experiments are representative of conditions in the wider world. For example, psychological research carried out exclusively among university students might have a low ecological validity when applied to the population as a whole. Ecological validity may be threatened by EXPERIMENTER BIAS or by naive sampling strategies that produce an unrepresentative selection of participants. See also GENERALIZABILITY.

EDA abbreviation for EXPLORATORY DATA ANALYSIS.

Edgeworth expansion a method of reframing the functional specification of a distribution so that it has properties similar to a more common pattern, such as the NORMAL DISTRIBUTION. [Francis Ysidro **Edgeworth** (1845–1926), Irish economist]

EFA abbreviation for EXPLORATORY FACTOR ANALYSIS.

effect *n.* **1.** in ANALYSIS OF VARIANCE, a statistically significant relationship between variables, such that one variable is held to be an outcome of another (or some combination of others). See MAIN EFFECT; INTERACTION EFFECT. **2.** short for EFFECT SIZE.

effect coding in REGRESSION ANALYSIS, a procedure in which values of 1 or –1 are assigned to represent the categories of a DICHOTOMOUS VARIABLE (or 1, 0, and –1 for a trichotomous variable). The results obtained for the group indicated by values of 1 are then interpreted relative to the larger group comprising all participants. For example, a researcher could assign values of 1 to individuals in an EXPERIMENTAL GROUP and values of –1 to those in a CONTROL GROUP. He or she could conclude that there is a treatment effect if the experimental group has a mean different from the GRAND MEAN across all of the individuals. Compare CONTRAST CODING; DUMMY VARIABLE CODING.

effect coefficient a value indicating the overall influence of one variable upon another, often used in statistical methods such as PATH ANALYSIS or HIERARCHICAL LINEAR MODELING.

effect indicator in STRUCTURAL EQUATION MODELING, a measure used to represent an occurrence that is assumed to be the effect of a LATENT VARIABLE. Compare CAUSAL INDICATOR.

effectiveness research reviewing past studies or conducting new studies in order to evaluate how well current and new treatments work, with the aim of improving the care and treatment of patients. The term is often used synonymously with **clinical utility research**, although some have suggested clinical utility research is a broader term that encompasses studies of additional health-related topics, such as access to care. Compare EFFICACY RESEARCH.

effective range a measure of the distance between the highest score and the lowest score in a set of values that does not take into account any extreme OUTLIER scores. For example, assume an individual kept track of how much he or she exercised over a 12-week period with the number of hours per week as 3, 2, 0, 3, 2, 3, 2.5, 3, 2, 3, 2.5, and 3. The actual range of scores would be the largest number of exercise hours minus the lowest number: 3 – 0 = 3 hours a week. However, the one score of zero is an outlier that may have occurred when this person was sick with the flu and could not exercise. In that case, one would ignore the outlier score and recompute the effective range: 3 – 2 = 1 hour a week.

effective sample size 1. the number of participants needed for a study to be as valid as if participants were randomly sampled from the population, when such random collection of data is not possible (e.g., as with households or classrooms). **2.** in POWER ANALYSIS, the number of units required in a sample in

E

order to achieve a particular level of statistical POWER.

effect modifier a variable that changes the way two other variables are related. See MODERATOR.

effects analysis an assessment of whether an intervention worked or not, particularly when there are more than two groups involved.

effect size any of various measures of the magnitude or meaningfulness of a relationship between two variables. For example, COHEN'S D shows the number of STANDARD DEVIATION units between two means. Often, effect sizes are interpreted as indicating the practical significance of a research finding. Additionally, in META-ANALYSES, they allow for the computation of summary statistics that apply to all the studies considered as a whole. See also STATISTICAL SIGNIFICANCE.

effect-size correlation (symbol: $r_{effect\ size}$) an index of the association between an INDEPENDENT VARIABLE and scores on the DEPENDENT VARIABLE without removing any other sources of variation in the data. An effect-size correlation has values from –1 to +1, with absolute values of .1, .3, and .5 representing small, medium, and large relationships, respectively.

effect variable see DEPENDENT VARIABLE.

efficacy research an empirical study, such as a RANDOMIZED CLINICAL TRIAL, that examines whether a specific treatment or approach works when compared to outcomes in a PLACEBO CONTROL GROUP. Efficacy research is sometimes contrasted with EFFECTIVENESS RESEARCH, which uses NATURALISTIC OBSERVATION to assess whether an approach or treatment is working.

efficacy subset analysis see TREATMENT-RECEIVED ANALYSIS.

efficiency *n.* the degree to which an ESTIMATOR uses all the information in a sample to estimate a particular parameter. It is a measure of the optimality of an estimator when comparing various statistical procedures or experimental designs. —**efficient** *adj.*

efficient estimator an unbiased ESTIMATOR that achieves minimum variance for all possible values of a parameter. An efficient estimator is sometimes referred to as a **minimum variance unbiased estimator** (**MVUE**). The sample MEAN, for example, is an efficient estimator of the population mean.

eigenvalue (symbol: λ) *n.* a numerical index, commonly used in FACTOR ANALYSIS and PRINCIPAL COMPONENTS ANALYSIS, that indicates the portion of the total variance among several correlated variables that is accounted for by a more basic, underlying variable or construct. An eigenvalue may be computed as the sum of the squared FACTOR LOADINGS for all the variables. Eigenvalues are of central importance in linear algebra (i.e., matrix algebra). Also called **characteristic root**; **characteristic value**; **latent root**.

eigenvector *n.* in linear algebra, any vector in a *p*-dimensional space that is associated with a given TRANSFORMATION and is left invariant (except for stretching or shrinking) by that transformation. Eigenvectors are of basic importance in MULTIVARIATE statistics; their values are applied to variables to form a LINEAR COMBINATION that synthesizes much of the variance in a set of variables. Also called **characteristic vector**; **latent vector**.

elaborative validity the extent to which a measure reveals useful information about situations similar to those in which it has been used. For example, a measure of depression may be said to have elaborative validity if it also is related to the extent of a person's hopelessness or suicidal ideation.

element *n.* a member of a set, class, or group. For example, in the set of all PhD-conferring American universities, any one of those American universities that confer the PhD is an element of the set. See also SET THEORY.

elementary event in probability theory, the fundamental outcome of an experiment of chance. For example, in selecting an individual from a list of eligible job candidates, the individuals who might be drawn from the list are the elementary events of the experiment. Also called **simple event**.

elliptically symmetric distribution a DISTRIBUTION in which KURTOSIS is permitted as long as it is equal across variables. The NORMAL DISTRIBUTION is a type of elliptically symmetric distribution, as kurtosis values are equal to zero for all variables.

EMA abbreviation for ECOLOGICAL MOMENTARY ASSESSMENT.

EM algorithm expectation-maximization algorithm: a statistical procedure used to find PARAMETER estimates in models that incorporate LATENT VARIABLES.

emics *n.* see ETICS.

emotional bias the tendency to ignore reason when experiencing strong positive or negative feelings, thus impairing one's ability to accurately understand and evaluate facts and to act accordingly.

empirical *adj.* **1.** derived from or denoting experimentation or systematic observations as the basis for conclusion or determination, as opposed to speculative, theoretical, or exclusively reason-based approaches. Many forms of research attempt to gain **empirical evidence** in favor of a hypothesis by manipulating an INDEPENDENT VARIABLE and assessing the effect on an outcome or DEPENDENT VARIABLE. **2.** based on experience.

empirical Bayes estimation a variation of BAYESIAN INFERENCE in which the probability of the hypothesis being correct is estimated from the observed data. This contrasts with conventional Bayesian methods, in which the probable truth of the hypothesis (the PRIOR DISTRIBUTION) is estimated before seeing the data. Also called **empirical Bayes method**; **empirical Bayes procedure**.

empirical classification the process of grouping entities into categories based on shared characteristics using statistical methods, such as CLUSTER ANALYSIS or MULTIDIMENSIONAL SCALING. For example, a researcher could suggest an empirical classification of sexual risk categories by clustering individuals based on their frequency of unprotected sex, their number of sexual partners, and the perceived risk of their sexual partners. It would be expected that the lowest risk category in the empirical classification would be people who have no or low frequency of unprotected sex, one or few sexual partners, and no or low perceived risk of their sexual partners.

empirical construct see CONSTRUCT.

empirical curve a line on a graph that connects points formed from the values of relevant variables.

empirical distribution the cumulative pattern of frequencies observed for a variable in a sample. Compare THEORETICAL DISTRIBUTION.

empirical law a law that is based on facts, experimental evidence, or systematic observations and expresses a general relationship between variables, as opposed to a law based only on theory.

empirically derived test a test developed using procedures that maximize CONTENT VALIDITY, CRITERION VALIDITY, or CONSTRUCT VALIDITY or a combination of these.

empirically keyed test an assessment in which answers are scored in such a way as to establish differences in responses among groups already known to differ. For example, on a test measuring problem solving, the correct alternative among the response choices would be the one preferred by members of a CRITERION GROUP who were administered the test previously.

empirical method any procedure for conducting an investigation that relies upon experimentation and systematic observation rather than theoretical speculation. The term is sometimes used as a vague synonym for SCIENTIFIC METHOD.

empirical probability the number of times a specific event occurs over the total number of trials in a process. For example, the THEORETICAL PROBABILITY of getting a head when flipping a coin is equal to .5 or ½, whereas the actual empirical probability obtained in an experiment may be different. Also called **experimental probability**.

empirical question a problem that can be solved by conducting an experiment or investigation, rather than by logic or theory. For example, "How many people own a white car?" is an empirical question. Determining its answer would require collecting a rather large, random sample that is representative of the population of car owners and asking each person in the sample the color of his or her car.

empirical test the test of a hypothesis by means of experiments or other systematic observations.

empirical validity the degree to which the accuracy of a test, model, or other construct can be demonstrated through experimentation and systematic observation (i.e., the accumulation of supporting research evidence) rather than theory alone.

empiricism *n.* **1.** an approach to EPISTEMOLOGY holding that all knowledge of matters of fact either arises from experience or requires experience for its validation. In particular, empiricism denies the possibility of innate ideas, arguing

that the mind at birth is like a blank sheet of paper. **2.** the view that experimentation and systematic observation is the most important, if not the only, foundation of scientific knowledge and the means by which individuals evaluate truth claims or the adequacy of theories and models. **3.** in philosophy, the position that all linguistic expressions that are not tautologous must be empirically verifiable if they are to be deemed valid or meaningful. This principle was essential to the philosophy of LOGICAL POSITIVISM. **—empiricist** *adj., n.*

empowerment evaluation see PARTICIPATORY EVALUATION.

empty cell a category of a specified variable or CROSS-TABULATION of variables in which there is no membership. For example, a marketing researcher might be interested in color preferences (pink, blue) for baby clothes by gender (girl, boy). He or she could collect data from a random sample of 100 people in a baby clothes department and then create a CONTINGENCY TABLE of the findings. For example, 40 people may prefer pink clothes for girl babies, 10 may prefer blue clothes for girl babies, 50 may prefer blue clothes for boy babies, and none prefer pink clothes for boy babies. The CELL representing the intersection of "pink" and "boy" is an empty cell because there is no one who endorses that combination of categories.

empty set in SET THEORY, a collection of entities with no ELEMENTS or members. Also called **null set**.

end-aversion bias the tendency for individuals to avoid the extreme choices on a scale and instead select a choice in the middle of the scale, closer to neutral. Such an approach results in a narrower range of responses that most likely will not be an accurate representation of the variable being measured. For example, a supervisor assessing employees would show end-aversion bias if his or her ratings generally were around 4 on a 7-point scale. Also called **central-tendency bias**; **end-of-scale bias**.

endogenous parameter a variable or value that is predicted from or dependent on another variable or value. For example, if the well-being of cancer patients depends on coping style, the outcome of well-being would be an endogenous parameter. Endogenous parameters are of particular importance in STRUCTURAL EQUATION MODELING and PATH ANALYSIS. Compare EXOGENOUS PARAMETER.

endogenous research research that is based on information inherent in a specific area or system, without taking into account outside, independent information.

endogenous variable a DEPENDENT VARIABLE whose values are determined, caused, or explained by factors within the model or system under study. Compare EXOGENOUS VARIABLE.

entropy *n.* an indication of the degree of disorder, disequilibrium, or change of a closed system. For example, an entropy measure may be used to indicate the quality of classification in a CLUSTER ANALYSIS. Clusters with high similarity would have low entropy, whereas clusters with more DISPERSION would have higher entropy.

entropy group in CLUSTER ANALYSIS, a cluster comprising OUTLIERS that are not readily placed in one of the main clusters.

envelope *n.* in a SCATTERPLOT, a pair of lines used to encompass most of the points and portray the main pattern.

E-optimal design an experimental design that uses one or more EIGENVALUES to reduce variance and bias, thereby increasing the amount of information related to parameter estimates in an experiment. See also A-OPTIMAL DESIGN; D-OPTIMAL DESIGN.

Epanechnikov kernel a formula used to estimate the PROBABILITY DENSITY FUNCTION for a RANDOM VARIABLE, depicting the possible values it may take and usually following an inverted U or curvilinear pattern. [V. A. **Epanechnikov**, Russian statistician]

epidemiological sampling any of several methods for enlisting a relevant and sufficient sample of participants for a study to understand a health risk in the population.

epistemological reflexivity an awareness of how one's own theoretical assumptions or situational conditions could affect a research scenario. It is a recognition that research is not conducted in a vacuum but rather is affected by the outlook of the researcher and the context in which he or she is operating.

epistemology *n.* the branch of philosophy concerned with the nature, origin, and limitations of knowledge. It is also concerned with the justification of truth claims. —**epistemological** *adj.*

EPSEM abbreviation for EQUAL PROBABILITY OF SELECTION METHOD.

epsilon (symbol: ε) *n.* a small value, particularly a small degree of RANDOM ERROR in a measure or a REGRESSION EQUATION.

epsilon squared (symbol: ε^2) in ANALYSIS OF VARIANCE or MULTIPLE REGRESSION analysis, a measure of the proportion of shared variance between a grouping variable and an outcome that has been adjusted for the sample size and number of variables. See also ADJUSTED R^2.

equal intervals 1. the requirement for an INTERVAL SCALE to have an equal distance between numbers or units over all parts of the scale. On a Celsius temperature scale, for example, there would be an equal distance between, for example, 20° and 23° and between 10° and 7°. **2.** in developing scales for qualitative characteristics such as attitudes, the assumption that anchor values should be equally distant from one another, so that, for example, the difference between *agree* and *strongly agree* is the same as that between *agree* and *strongly disagree*.

equality constraint a restriction requiring that two or more PARAMETERS have the same value. This is sometimes used in procedures such as CONFIRMATORY FACTOR ANALYSIS, for example, when testing whether a FACTOR LOADING is the same across different measures of the same construct. Compare INEQUALITY CONSTRAINT.

equality of variance see HOMOGENEITY OF VARIANCE.

equal probability of selection method (EPSEM) a procedure for randomly choosing from a larger population, such that each person or entity has an equal chance of being chosen. See RANDOM SAMPLING.

equal probability sampling see UNEQUAL PROBABILITY SAMPLING.

equal weighting see WEIGHTING.

equated score the score distribution from Measure B transformed to match the distribution of Measure A in one or more features. See TRANSFORMATION.

equation *n.* a formal, usually brief, statement showing that two expressions are the same or equal. In mathematics or statistics, an equation is often a statement with y on the left of an equal sign and an expression for delineating or modeling y on the right side. For example, a commonly used equation for a straight line is $y = mx + b$, where m stands for the slope of the line, x stands for different values along the X-AXIS, and b stands for the point where the line crosses the Y-AXIS.

equipercentile method a procedure for showing how two measures are similar, such that a shared value of x on the two measurements implies that the probability of a person drawn at random having a score greater than x is the same for both measures.

equiprobable *adj.* describing two or more different events that have the same probability of occurring. For example, when flipping a fair coin, the occurrence of a head or a tail is equiprobable.

equivalence *n.* a relationship between two or more items, scales, variables, or stimuli that permits one to replace another. See also EQUIVALENCE COEFFICIENT; MEASUREMENT EQUIVALENCE.

equivalence coefficient a numerical index of the similarity of two different assessments of the same measure, often used as an indication of ALTERNATE-FORMS RELIABILITY for slightly different forms of the same test given on two different occasions. For example, there is often a need to calculate an equivalence coefficient for standardized tests administered to a group of persons more than once, to ensure that each form of the test is measuring the same construct, such as verbal or quantitative ability.

equivalence paradox the situation in which two different procedures produce very similar outcomes, despite having different initial assumptions or features. In statistics, the term refers to the fact that PRINCIPAL COMPONENTS ANALYSIS and FACTOR ANALYSIS often produce a similar pattern of dimensions and loadings, although they each have a different premise. Whereas principal components analysis mathematically redistributes all of the variance in the items to form dimensions or components, factor analysis more realistically separates out unique variance in the items before forming dimensions or factors using only the variance that is shared across the variables.

equivalent form see ALTERNATE FORM.

equivalent-forms reliability see ALTERNATE-FORMS RELIABILITY.

equivalent-groups design a study in which the groups of participants are assumed to be the same on all possible variables at the beginning of a study, such that at the end of the study any differences on the response measure can be attributed to the experimental manipulation. Although the best way to achieve an equivalent-groups design is by randomly selecting a large and relevant sample from the population and then randomly assigning participants to either an EXPERIMENTAL GROUP or a CONTROL GROUP, sometimes this is not possible. In such situations, researchers can instead use MATCHING, with the expectation that the resulting two participant groups then would be approximately equivalent (i.e., come from the same population) at the start of the study.

For example, a reading researcher may want to implement a reading intervention in one school and a control or PLACEBO condition in another similar school. Before analyzing results between the two schools, the researcher could administer an intelligence test to students at both schools. Then, the researcher could create similar sets by matching students with the same or highly similar scores across the schools and conducting the study with just those students. See also MATCHED-PAIRS DESIGN. Compare NONEQUIVALENT-GROUPS DESIGN.

erf abbreviation for ERROR FUNCTION.

ergodicity *n.* a principle stating that the average value of a variable over a set of individuals in a defined space or time, such as a SAMPLE, will be the same as the average across a long TIME SERIES of points for a single individual. For example, if ergodicity held for a measure of satisfaction in an organization, the average satisfaction score of all employees in the organization would be the same as the average satisfaction score across a one-year period for one employee. In reality, ergodicity does not always hold, thus giving rise to different streams of NOMOTHETIC and IDIOGRAPHIC research, which focus on the group or the individual, respectively.

error *n.* **1.** a deviation from true or accurate information (e.g., a wrong response, a mistaken belief). **2.** in experimentation, any change in a DEPENDENT VARIABLE not attributable to the manipulation of an INDEPENDENT VARIABLE. **3.** in statistics, a deviation of an observed score from a true score, where true score is often defined by the mean of the particular group or condition in which the score being assessed for error occurs, or from the score predicted by a model. Errors generally are categorized as SYSTEMATIC ERROR or RANDOM ERROR. See also RESIDUAL.

error bar an area on a graph used to depict how much uncertainty or slippage there is around an estimated PARAMETER value, such as the mean. An error bar usually is given as one STANDARD DEVIATION above and below a point, but it also can be a STANDARD ERROR (i.e., the standard deviation divided by the square root of the SAMPLE SIZE).

error distribution the pattern describing how scores can vary randomly around a particular value, such as the mean. It is often a NORMAL DISTRIBUTION with a mean of 0 and a STANDARD DEVIATION of 1.

error function (**erf**) a roughly "S" or half-mountain-shaped pattern on a graph with values of a particular variable (x) given along the horizontal axis and values from –1 to +1 given on the vertical axis. Such a pattern indicates there would be a high level of accuracy if using the mean to estimate a value for x, and conversely a large likelihood of error or inaccuracy if using more extreme values.

error mean square see MEAN SQUARED ERROR.

error of expectation an error arising because of a preconceived idea of the nature of the stimulus to be presented or the timing of the presentation.

error of measurement see MEASUREMENT ERROR.

error of the first kind see TYPE I ERROR.

error of the second kind see TYPE II ERROR.

error rate the frequency with which errors are made. Examples include the proportion of an experimenter's data recordings that are wrong or the number of TYPE I ERRORS that occur during SIGNIFICANCE TESTING.

error-rate estimation the process of predicting how often an error, especially one of classification, will be made for a specific variable. For example, medical researchers may use error-rate estimation to predict how often they may incorrectly diagnose a patient as having a specific disease. This term is often used when conducting a DISCRIMINANT ANALYSIS to assess how often cases will be put into the wrong category on the basis of the predictor scores.

error rate family-wise see FAMILY-WISE ERROR RATE.

error rate per comparison see TESTWISE ERROR RATE.

error score in CLASSICAL TEST THEORY, the difference between a person's observed measurement or score and his or her expected measurement or score. Also called **residual score**.

errors-in-variables problem the commonly occurring situation in which PREDICTOR VARIABLES in a REGRESSION ANALYSIS are not perfectly reliable. A LEAST SQUARES REGRESSION approach will have bias in the parameter estimates when there is MEASUREMENT ERROR in the predictors. The problem has given rise to ATTENUATION procedures that correct for unreliability of the estimates.

error sum of squares the difference between a score and the mean score, multiplied by this same difference. It is part of the denominator of the F RATIO in an ANALYSIS OF VARIANCE and represents the amount of variation in the DEPENDENT VARIABLE that cannot be explained by the INDEPENDENT VARIABLES. Also called **residual sum of squares**; **sum of squared errors (SSE)**.

error term the element of a statistical equation that indicates the amount of change in the DEPENDENT VARIABLE that is unexplained by change in the INDEPENDENT VARIABLES. Also called **disturbance term**; **residual term**.

error variance the element of variability in a score that is produced by extraneous factors, such as measurement imprecision, and is not attributable to the INDEPENDENT VARIABLE or other controlled experimental manipulations. Error variance usually indicates how much random fluctuation is expected within scores and often forms part of the denominator of test statistics, such as the F RATIO in an ANALYSIS OF VARIANCE. Also called **residual error**; **residual variance**; **unexplained** (or **unpredicted**) **variance**.

ESM abbreviation for EXPERIENCE-SAMPLING METHOD.

essay test an examination in which examinees answer questions by writing sentences, paragraphs, or pages. The reliability of grading such assessments is usually lower than that of OBJECTIVE TESTS.

estimable function a function of the parameters of a model that can be uniquely approximated from the data. The estimable function is important in GENERAL LINEAR MODEL applications.

estimate 1. *n.* a best guess of the value of a parameter of a DISTRIBUTION on the basis of a set of empirical observations. **2.** *vb.* to assign a value to a parameter in this way.

estimating function a mathematical equation used to approximate values and properties (e.g., bias, consistency, efficiency) for a specific parameter (e.g., regression coefficient) by using information from the sample data and the parameter of interest. This approach is particularly suitable when a LIKELIHOOD FUNCTION is not easily known.

estimation *n.* in statistics, the process of approximating a population PARAMETER from sample data while allowing for some degree of uncertainty by giving a range of values within which the parameter will most likely fall. Estimation usually requires a large random sample, from which one can calculate POINT ESTIMATE values, such as the mean and STANDARD DEVIATION, in the larger population of interest. The process of estimation also involves building a CONFIDENCE INTERVAL around the obtained sample value, plus and minus some MARGIN OF ERROR. Thus, if one calculates the mean of scores on an achievement test to be 65, this value is a point estimate of the average test score in the population. A 95% confidence interval might yield an interval of 60 to 70, which is likely to capture the true mean score for the population.

estimation theory a system developed to approximate population PARAMETERS from sample data. Ideally, it involves large, random samples and other methods that minimize the amount of bias or error between the true population value, which usually is unknown, and the sample-based estimate.

estimator *n.* a quantity calculated from the values in a sample according to some rule and used to give an approximation of the value in a population. For example, the sample mean or average is an estimator for the population mean; the value of the population mean is the estimate. See EFFICIENT ESTIMATOR.

eta (symbol: η) *n.* **1.** in STRUCTURAL EQUATION MODELING, denoting a LATENT VARIABLE. **2.** see CORRELATION RATIO.

eta squared (symbol: η^2) a measure of the amount of variance in a DEPENDENT VARIABLE that can be explained by one or more INDEPENDENT VARIABLES, as calculated in a variety of statistical proce-

dures. In an ANALYSIS OF VARIANCE, for example, eta squared is calculated as the SUM OF SQUARES for the treatment (i.e., sum of squared differences between a group mean and the GRAND MEAN) divided by the TOTAL SUM OF SQUARES. Eta squared is often used as an EFFECT SIZE measure.

ethics *n.* the principles of morally right conduct accepted by a person or a group or considered appropriate to a specific field. In psychological research, for example, proper ethics requires that participants be treated fairly and without harm and that investigators report results and findings honestly. See RESEARCH ETHICS. **—ethical** *adj.*

ethics committee a designated group (often an INSTITUTIONAL REVIEW BOARD) that oversees the conduct of research to ensure that participants are treated fairly and without harm.

ethnic bias 1. discrimination against individuals based on their ethnic group, often resulting in inequities in such areas as education, employment, health care, and housing. **2.** in testing and measurement, contamination or deficiency in an instrument that differentially affects the scores of those from different ethnic groups. Ideally, researchers strive to create CULTURE-FAIR TESTS.

ethnic research the body of studies that investigates the backgrounds of people from different races and cultures.

ethnography *n.* the descriptive study of cultures or societies based on direct observation (see FIELD RESEARCH) and (ideally) some degree of participation. Compare ETHNOLOGY. **—ethnographer** *n.* **—ethnographic** *adj.*

ethnology *n.* the comparative, analytical, or historical study of human cultures or societies. Compare ETHNOGRAPHY. See also ETICS. **—ethnological** *adj.* **—ethnologist** *n.*

ethology *n.* the comparative study of the behavior of animals, typically in

E

their natural habitat but also involving experiments both in the field and in captivity. Ethology was developed by behavioral biologists in Europe and is often associated with connotations of innate or species-specific behavior patterns. The term increasingly is used to describe research involving observation and detailed descriptions of human behavior as well. **—ethological** *adj.* **—ethologist** *n.*

etics *n.* the study of behaviors or situations that are held to be generalizable across a wide range of cultures and backgrounds. This contrasts with **emics**, which refers to investigation of behaviors and situations specific to a particular culture. For example, an etics-focused researcher might evaluate which facial expressions are fairly universal across different countries and age groups, whereas an emics-focused researcher would investigate those expressions that are unique to a cultural group.

Euclidean distance a simple measure of the distance between two points, as quantified by a ruler or other numerical gauge. Also called **Euclidean metric**.

Euclidean space in statistics and mathematics, a three-dimensional area or plot. Algebra, geometry, and calculus may be used to extend Euclidean spaces beyond three dimensions.

Euler diagram a pictorial image of how entities or situations intersect or overlap. While a VENN DIAGRAM depicts all areas of intersection, a Euler diagram does not necessarily include all areas. For example, a researcher might create a Venn diagram in which a large circle represents a population, a circle inside that represents a sample or subset of the population, and additional overlapping circles inside the previous one indicate additional subsets. If the image were to leave out some of the inner circles, such as the ones representing different kinds of random samples, it would be consid-

ered a Euler diagram. The following is a generic depiction of a Euler diagram.

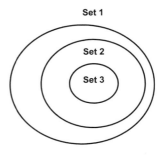

[Leonhard **Euler** (1707–1783), Swiss-born Russian mathematician]

evaluation apprehension uneasiness or worry about being judged by others, especially feelings of worry experienced by participants in an experiment as a result of their desire to be evaluated favorably by the experimenter. Participants experiencing evaluation apprehension may inhibit reactions (e.g., the display of aggression) that they believe will lead the experimenter to regard them as psychologically unhealthy.

evaluation research the use of scientific principles and methods to assess the influence or effectiveness of social interventions and programs, including those related to mental health, education, and safety (e.g., crime prevention, automobile accident prevention). Evaluation research is thus a type of APPLIED RESEARCH. See also ASSESSMENT RESEARCH.

event *n.* in probability theory, any of the namable things that can be said to result from a single trial of an experiment of chance. For example, in the roll of a single die, the events could include (among others) any of the six individual numbers, any even number, and any odd number.

event history analysis see SURVIVAL ANALYSIS.

event history data information collected over a time period, often using diaries or other recording methods that can accurately map what occurred at various points in time. Event history data often are used in psychology, sociology, health sciences, education, and engineering.

event record a log containing the details of a particular situation or occurrence as assessed over a period of time. For example, an event record may collect information over numerous time points throughout a week on the mood of a patient who is enrolled in a study to reduce depression.

event sampling a strategy commonly used in DIRECT OBSERVATION that involves noting and recording the occurrence of a carefully specified behavior whenever it is seen. For example, a researcher may record each episode of apnea that occurs within a 9-hour period overnight while a person sleeps.

event space a subset of the set of all possible outcomes in a situation (the SAMPLE SPACE). For example, the sample space of working days for a particular organization might comprise Sunday, Monday, Tuesday, Wednesday, Thursday, Friday, and Saturday for all employees, but the event space for working days might include only Monday through Friday for some employees.

events paradigm a research design or therapeutic approach based on the interpretation of EVENT HISTORY DATA.

exact identification see JUST-IDENTIFIED MODEL.

exact replication see REPLICATION.

exact test any statistical test in which the probability of finding a result as extreme or more extreme than the one obtained, given the NULL HYPOTHESIS, can be calculated precisely rather than approximated. The FISHER EXACT TEST is an example.

exchangeability *n.* the ability to be used in different circumstances or situations. For example, in measurement and statistics, items that are equally appropriate on different versions of a test and methods or parameters that work well under different conditions show exchangeability.

exclusive *adj.* completely separate and incompatible. For example, gender has two exclusive categories of male and female. See also MUTUALLY EXCLUSIVE EVENTS.

exclusive union in probability studies, the combination of two or more events that have no overlap. For example, the set of all hearts and spades in a deck of cards forms an exclusive union of two separate events, as a card cannot be both a heart and a spade at the same time. In probability, the chance of two separate events occurring together (i.e., an exclusive union) is equal to the probability of the first event plus the probability of the second event.

exhaustive *adj.* complete or all encompassing. For example, a set of 13 hearts, 13 spades, 13 diamonds, 13 clubs, and two jokers forms an exhaustive set of all possible playing cards that could be drawn.

exogenous parameter a PARAMETER that occurs outside of and is not explained by a system or model but nevertheless has an effect on variables within that system. For example, poor socioeconomic status is sometimes seen as leading to lower levels of education, which in turn could lead to lower income levels. Thus, in a study of the effect of education on income level socioeconomic status might be considered an exogenous parameter: It predicts a mediator (education), which then predicts an endogenous or DEPENDENT VARIABLE (income). Compare ENDOGENOUS PARAMETER.

exogenous variable an INDEPENDENT VARIABLE whose value is determined by factors outside the model or system under study. Also called **exogenous factor**. Compare ENDOGENOUS VARIABLE.

exp abbreviation for EXPONENTIAL FUNCTION.

expansion *n.* a description of a mathematical or statistical function via a series of sums. The Taylor expansion (see TAYLOR SERIES) is an example.

expansion factor the amount by which scores can change over time or with differences in testing conditions. It is often important to consider an expansion factor in ITEM RESPONSE THEORY when predicting a pattern of scores.

expectancy *n.* see EXPECTATION. —**expectant** *adj.*

expectancy chart a table or graph that provides estimates of the future outcome for a specific variable. For example, industrial and organizational psychologists may use expectancy charts based on test scores to determine the likelihood of an individual's success in a job, and insurance companies may use expectancy charts to predict how long a person will live based on such factors as health, current age, financial resources, and occupation.

expectancy control design an experimental design in which the EXPERIMENTER EXPECTANCY EFFECT operates separately from the INDEPENDENT VARIABLE of primary substantive interest.

expectancy effect see EXPERIMENTER EXPECTANCY EFFECT.

expectation *n.* the long-term average of a RANDOM VARIABLE. For example, the expectation is that the mean for a specific random variable obtained with an extremely large sample will equal the mean of the population of interest. Also called **expectancy**. See EXPECTED VALUE.

expectation algebra the set of mathematical rules that inform how to find the long-term average of a RANDOM VARIABLE. For example, one of the rules of expectation algebra is that the long-term average of the sum of two variables is equal to the long-term average of the

first variable plus the long-term average of the second variable.

expectation-conditional maximization algorithm (**ECM algorithm**) a procedure for finding MAXIMUM LIKELIHOOD estimates of PARAMETERS in statistical models. Its computations are easier than those of traditional MAXIMUM LIKELIHOOD–EXPECTATION MAXIMIZATION ESTIMATION methods.

expectation-conditional maximization either algorithm (**ECME algorithm**) an iterative procedure for finding MAXIMUM LIKELIHOOD estimates of PARAMETERS in statistical models that alternates between performing an expectation step and a maximization step. It is an improved extension of the EXPECTATION-CONDITIONAL MAXIMIZATION ALGORITHM that is easier and faster to compute.

expectation surface the space or plane that contains a series of points that are the likely values of an outcome given a set of predictor or explanatory variables or parameters.

expected frequency a frequency predicted from a theoretical model, as opposed to an OBSERVED FREQUENCY. Expected frequencies are chiefly used in the CHI-SQUARE TEST. For example, suppose a researcher wishes to compare ethnic distribution of a sample of 100 participants with the ethnic distribution of the entire United States. Based on data from the 2010 U.S. Census, the expected frequency values for ethnic distribution of the sample would be as follows: 63.7 White, 16.3 Hispanic/Latino/Spanish, 12.6 Black/African American, 4.8 Asian, 0.9 Alaskan/Native American, 0.2 Hawaiian/Pacific Island, and 1.5 Other/Mixed. The researcher would compare the observed frequency from the sample of 100 to these expected frequencies and calculate a CHI-SQUARE GOODNESS-OF-FIT TEST. If the chi-square is significantly larger than the CRITICAL VALUE obtained from a statistical chart on 6 DEGREES OF FREEDOM, where the degrees of freedom equal the number of categories minus one, there is evidence that the sample distribution does not match that of the 2010 census. If the calculated chi-square value is smaller than the one obtained from the statistical chart (i.e., the P VALUE is greater than .05), then the researcher cannot reject the hypothesis that there is a good fit between the fitted frequency values in the U.S. population and the sample ethnic distribution observed frequency values. Also called **fitted frequency**.

expected t value the number that would occur due to chance alone when examining the number of estimated STANDARD DEVIATION units a SAMPLE MEAN is from another sample or population mean. Under the NULL HYPOTHESIS, the expected t value is zero, indicating no difference between means. See T TEST.

expected value the value of a random variable or one of its functions as derived by mathematical calculation rather than observation. It is symbolized by $E(x)$, with x varying according to the specific item of interest that is being calculated. Usually, the expected value is a mean or weighted average.

experience-sampling method (ESM) a procedure for assessing research participants' thoughts and feelings at specific, predetermined points in time. For example, researchers conducting a weight reduction program may check in with participants at various times to assess their dietary intake of healthy food and any urges to eat unhealthy food. The experience-sampling method is believed to provide more reliable input on the inner state of participants than may be obtained via after-the-fact feedback.

experiment *n.* a series of observations conducted under controlled conditions to study a relationship with the purpose of drawing causal inferences about that relationship. An experiment involves the manipulation of an INDEPENDENT VARIABLE, the measurement of a DEPENDENT VARIABLE, and the exposure of various participants to one or more of the conditions being studied. RANDOM SELECTION of participants and their RANDOM ASSIGNMENT to conditions also are necessary in experiments. **—experimental** *adj.*

experimental attrition see ATTRITION.

experimental condition a level of the INDEPENDENT VARIABLE that is manipulated by the researcher in order to assess the effect on a DEPENDENT VARIABLE. Participants in an experimental condition receive some form of TREATMENT or experience whereas those in a CONTROL CONDITION do not. For example, patients in an experimental condition may receive a new drug, whereas those in a control condition may receive a pill that looks like the new drug but is only a PLACEBO containing some inert substance.

experimental control see CONTROL.

experimental design an outline or plan of the procedures to be followed in scientific experimentation in order to reach valid conclusions, with consideration of such factors as participant selection, variable manipulation, data collection and analysis, and minimization of external influences.

experimental error the various kinds of ERROR that can occur in a controlled study. An experimental error may be a SYSTEMATIC ERROR, referring to a problem that can be identified, reproduced, and potentially corrected; or a RANDOM ERROR, referring to chance fluctuations that cannot easily be corrected. For example, a researcher may be conducting a study to assess the effectiveness of a new treatment. If the treatment dose is slightly off due to faulty measurements or ingredients, this is a systematic error that could be corrected. If participants react somewhat differently to the treatment, some more positively and some more negatively, this is a random error that is not easily eradicated but that may be somewhat reduced (e.g., by randomly assigning a large set of individuals to EXPERIMENTAL GROUPS VS. CONTROL GROUPS).

experimental ethics see RESEARCH ETHICS.

experimental group a group of participants in a research study who are exposed to a particular manipulation of the INDEPENDENT VARIABLE (i.e., a particular treatment or TREATMENT LEVEL). The responses of the experimental group are compared to the responses of a CONTROL GROUP, other experimental groups, or both. Also called **treatment group**.

experimental hypothesis a premise that describes what a researcher in a scientific study hopes to demonstrate if certain conditions are met, such as RANDOM SELECTION of participants, RANDOM ASSIGNMENT to EXPERIMENTAL GROUPS or CONTROL GROUPS, and manipulation of an INDEPENDENT VARIABLE.

experimental manipulation in an experiment, the manipulation of one or more INDEPENDENT VARIABLES in order to investigate their effect on a DEPENDENT VARIABLE. An example would be the assignment of a specific treatment or PLACEBO to participants in a research study in order to control possible CONFOUNDS and assess the effect of the treatment.

experimental method a system of scientific investigation, usually based on a design to be carried out under controlled conditions, that is intended to test a hypothesis and establish a causal relationship between independent and dependent variables.

experimental probability see EMPIRICAL PROBABILITY.

experimental psychology the scientific study of behavior, motives, or cognition in a laboratory or other controlled setting in order to predict, explain, or influence behavior or other psychological phenomena. Experimental psychology aims at establishing quantified relationships and explanatory theory through the analysis of responses under various controlled conditions and the synthesis of adequate theoretical accounts from the results of these observations.

experimental realism the extent to which a controlled study is meaningful and engaging to participants, eliciting responses that are spontaneous and natural. See also MUNDANE REALISM.

experimental replication see REPLICATION.

experimental research research utilizing randomized assignment of participants to conditions and systematic manipulation of variables with the objective of drawing causal inference. It is generally conducted within a laboratory or other controlled environment, which in reducing the potential influence of extraneous factors increases INTERNAL VALIDITY but decreases EXTERNAL VALIDITY. Compare CORRELATIONAL RESEARCH; FIELD RESEARCH; QUASI-EXPERIMENTAL RESEARCH.

experimental series the trials administered to an EXPERIMENTAL GROUP in a controlled research study, as opposed to those administered to the CONTROL GROUP.

experimental treatment 1. in research, the conditions applied to one or more groups that are expected to cause change in some outcome or DEPENDENT VARIABLE. **2.** an intervention or regimen that has shown some promise as a cure or ameliorative for a disease or condition but is still being evaluated for efficacy, safety, and acceptability.

experimental unit the unit to which an experimental manipulation is applied. For example, if an intervention is applied to a classroom of students, the classroom (not the individual students) is the experimental unit. In QUASI-EXPERIMENTAL RESEARCH and other nonexperimental contexts, the term UNIT OF ANALYSIS is used instead.

experimental variable an INDEPENDENT VARIABLE that is manipulated by the researcher to determine its relationship to or influence upon some outcome or DEPENDENT VARIABLE.

experimentation *n.* the carrying out of EXPERIMENTS.

experimentee *n.* a research participant, that is, a person who is studied under controlled conditions by the researcher or EXPERIMENTER.

experimenter *n.* in a controlled study, the researcher who devises tasks for the EXPERIMENTEE to perform, determines the conditions under which the performance will take place, and monitors and interprets the results.

experimenter bias any systematic errors in the research process or the interpretation of its results that are attributable to a researcher's preconceived beliefs, expectancies, or desires about results. For example, a researcher may inadvertently cue participants to behave or respond in a particular way. See EXPERIMENTER EFFECT.

experimenter biosocial effect in a controlled study, an unintended effect on participants' responses that is associated with individual differences among the biological characteristics of the researcher (e.g., gender, age). Compare EXPERIMENTER PSYCHOSOCIAL EFFECT.

experimenter drift a gradual and unconscious change in the way a researcher conducts or interprets a controlled study, leading to SYSTEMATIC ERROR in the results.

experimenter effect any influence a researcher may have on the results of his or her research, derived from either interaction with participants or unintentional errors of observation, measurement, analysis, or interpretation. In the former, the experimenter's personal characteristics (e.g., age, sex, race), attitudes, and expectations directly affect the behavior of participants. In the latter, the experimenter's procedural errors (often arising from his or her expectations about results) have no effect on participant responses but indirectly distort the research findings.

experimenter expectancy effect a type of EXPERIMENTER EFFECT in which a researcher's expectations about the findings of his or her research are inadvertently conveyed to participants and influence their responses. This distortion of results arises from participants' reactions to subtle cues (DEMAND CHARACTERISTICS) unintentionally given by the researcher—for example, through body movements, gestures, or facial expressions—and may threaten the ECOLOGICAL VALIDITY of the research. The term is often used synonymously with ROSENTHAL EFFECT.

experimenter intentional effect the EXPERIMENTER EFFECT that occurs when a researcher deliberately tries to manipulate the result in order to test whether certain behaviors or characteristics of a researcher can alter the outcome. The experimenter intentional effect may be a positive source of information on factors that can influence an outcome, or it may be a form of EXPERIMENTER BIAS that threatens the INTERNAL VALIDITY of a study.

experimenter interpreter effect a SYSTEMATIC ERROR that results when a researcher's interpretation of the observed data is biased (e.g., by the researcher's expectation).

experimenter modeling effect a SYSTEMATIC ERROR that results in participants responding to a task in a way that is too similar to the way in which the researcher would respond to the task.

experimenter observer effect a SYS-TEMATIC ERROR by an investigator in the perception or recording of data. This is often predictable from a knowledge of the investigator's expectation.

experimenter psychosocial effect in a controlled study, an unintended effect on participants' responses associated with individual differences among the psychological characteristics of the researcher. Compare EXPERIMENTER BIO-SOCIAL EFFECT.

experiment of nature see NATURAL EXPERIMENT.

experiment-wise alpha level the SIGNIFICANCE LEVEL (i.e., the acceptable risk of making a TYPE I ERROR) that is set by a researcher for a set of multiple comparisons and statistical tests. It is often set at the conventional level of .05; by setting the alpha for individual tests (the TESTWISE ALPHA LEVEL) at a lower rate (e.g., .01) it can be ensured that the whole set of tests does not produce error greater than the desired experiment-wise level. When conducting a one-way or one-factor ANALYSIS OF VARIANCE, experiment-wise alpha usually is the same as the FAMILY-WISE ALPHA LEVEL; in an analysis of variance involving two or more factors, family-wise alpha refers to the probability of Type I error for each test of a specific factor.

experiment-wise error rate in a test involving MULTIPLE COMPARISONS, the probability of making at least one TYPE I ERROR over an entire research study. The experiment-wise error rate differs from the TESTWISE ERROR RATE, which is the probability of making a Type I error when performing a specific test or comparison.

expert-choice sampling selecting participants for a study by using the opinions of an authority in the area of interest. Expert-choice sampling is a type of PURPOSIVE SAMPLING that intentionally seeks specific kinds of partici-

pants based on relevant criteria for a study.

explained sum of squares see RE-GRESSION SUM OF SQUARES.

explained variance the proportion of the variance in a DEPENDENT VARIABLE that can be determined or explained by one or more other variables. In ANALYSIS OF VARIANCE procedures the explained variance usually is given by ETA SQUARED or OMEGA SQUARED, whereas in prediction methods, such as MULTIPLE REGRESSION, it usually is given by the COEFFICIENT OF MULTIPLE DETERMINATION. Explained variance also is applied in procedures such as PRINCIPAL COMPONENTS ANALYSIS or FACTOR ANALYSIS to describe the proportion of the variance in a measure that can be understood or predicted from a component or FACTOR. Compare ERROR VARIANCE.

explanatory analysis an analysis that sets out to understand the causes of a particular phenomenon, often involving the specification and testing of MEDIATORS to assess how INDEPENDENT VARIABLES and DEPENDENT VARIABLES are causally related.

explanatory research a study conducted to assess why a particular finding occurred. For example, one might conduct explanatory research to determine why individuals who have been abused as children tend to be at higher risk for negative outcomes as adults. Compare PREDICTIVE RESEARCH.

explanatory trial a CLINICAL TRIAL conducted to understand the causal factors that make a particular treatment effective in bringing about a specific outcome. Explanatory trials contrast with **pragmatic trials**, which are designed to find an effective treatment without necessarily trying to understand why it is effective.

explanatory variable see INDEPENDENT VARIABLE.

explicative research a study conducted to understand the relationships or correlations among variables.

exploratory data analysis (EDA) the analysis of data to generate new research questions or insights rather than to address specific preplanned research questions. Compare CONFIRMATORY DATA ANALYSIS.

exploratory factor analysis (EFA) a method for finding a small set of underlying dimensions from a large set of related measures. The observed data are freely explored in order to discover the underlying (latent) variables that explain the interrelationships among a larger set of observable (manifest) variables. For example, exploratory factor analysis has been conducted to assess whether there are one, two, or more dimensions underlying items used to assess intelligence. The analysis does not yield a unique solution: Although points are fixed in a multidimensional space of underlying factors, the axes according to which one should interpret the factors are not fixed and are infinite in number. These axes may be either ORTHOGONAL (producing uncorrelated factors) or OBLIQUE (producing correlated factors). Compare CONFIRMATORY FACTOR ANALYSIS.

exploratory research a study that is conducted when not much is known about a particular phenomenon. In exploratory research one typically seeks to identify multiple possible links between variables. In contrast, in CONFIRMATORY RESEARCH one tests whether a specific prediction holds under specific circumstances.

exploratory survey an initial study used to test whether a research area is worth pursuing through more formal EXPERIMENTAL RESEARCH. An explanatory survey is similar to but less formal than a PILOT STUDY, which is conducted to provide a preliminary run of a specific study on a smaller scale.

exponent *n.* a number shown as a super-

script of another number to indicate how many times the base number is to be multiplied by itself. For example, the base number 2 with an exponent of 3 (e.g., 2^3) denotes the number formed by multiplying 2 by itself three times (i.e., $2 \times 2 \times 2 = 8$).

exponential *adj.* having an increase or decrease that is proportional to the current value of a function. For example, **exponential growth** of applications to a school would occur if the number of applications received each year doubled, so that after four years applications had increased by a factor of 16.

exponential curve a graph of a rapidly growing FUNCTION in which the increase is proportional to the size of an x variable and the SLOPE is equal to the value of the y variable.

exponential distribution a theoretical distribution of survival times, used in parametric SURVIVAL ANALYSIS when the HAZARD RATE is thought to be constant over time. It is a specific type of GAMMA DISTRIBUTION.

exponential family a set of PROBABILITY DISTRIBUTIONS that include exponential terms and that have similar characteristics. The NORMAL DISTRIBUTION is a commonly known example.

exponential function (exp) a mathematical expression of the type $y = a^x$, where a is a constant. A particular type has the form $y = e^x$, where e is a fundamental mathematical constant that is the base of natural logarithms (with the value 2.718...). Often, functions of this type (e.g., e^{x+a}) are written as $\exp(x + a)$.

exponential notation a shorthand way of depicting a number with many zero values. For numbers with many zeros to the left of a decimal, exponential notation lists the number and multiplies it by 10 raised to the number of zeros; for numbers with many zeros to the right of a decimal, exponential notation lists the number and multiplies it by 10 raised to the negative of the number of zeros. For example, 5,000,000 written in exponential notation is 5×10^6, and 0.0000005 written in exponential notation is 5×10^{-6}.

exponential smoothing a method of weighting TIME-SERIES data using exponentially decreasing weights for older events. This reduces random fluctuations in the data so that one is better able to see the underlying trends in the series and gives recent data relatively greater importance in forecasting. Exponential smoothing is widely used with financial and economic data.

exponential trend a pattern in which data values increase over time proportional to a specific value. For example, housing costs that increase annually by a factor of 1.04 could be said to manifest an exponential trend, such that one could use the trend to predict the future value of any given house based on its original cost. Thus, a house that cost $100,000 to purchase originally would cost an estimated $148,000 to purchase 10 years later, as determined by multiplying the original house cost by 1.04, multiplying the resulting value by 1.04, and then repeating the second multiplication step 10 times.

ex post facto data information about past occurrences. For example, a health researcher could collect ex post facto data on the number of hours per week a person believes he or she exercised over the past month.

ex post facto design research that examines past occurrences in order to understand a current state. Although this type of design involves both a DEPENDENT VARIABLE and an INDEPENDENT VARIABLE, the investigator cannot manipulate the latter. For example, a researcher who is interested in determining the effectiveness of a particular television advertisement on consumer behavior may recruit a group of participants who saw the advertisement and a group of participants who did not, yet the researcher has no control over which specific people actually view the advertisement. Also called **ex post facto study**.

ex post facto hypothesis a HYPOTHESIS about what caused or brought about a condition that is made only after one has examined information already collected about that condition.

extended Cox regression model see COX REGRESSION ANALYSIS.

external reliability the extent to which a measure is consistent when assessed over time or across different individuals. External reliability calculated across time is referred to more specifically as RETEST RELIABILITY; external reliability calculated across individuals is referred to more specifically as INTERRATER RELIABILITY.

external validity the extent to which the results of research or testing can be generalized beyond the sample that generated the results to other individuals, situations, and time periods. For example, if research has been conducted only with male participants, it cannot be assumed that similar results will apply to female participants. The more specialized the sample, the less likely will it be that the results are highly generalizable. Compare INTERNAL VALIDITY.

extraneous variable a measure that is not under investigation in an experiment but may potentially affect the outcome or DEPENDENT VARIABLE and thus influence results. Such potential influence often requires that an extraneous variable be controlled during research. See also CONFOUND.

extraneous variance variation in scores that is caused by CONFOUNDS, HIDDEN VARIABLES, or other factors that are not under investigation in a study.

extrapolation *n.* the process of estimating or projecting unknown score values on the basis of the known scores obtained from a given sample. For example, a researcher might estimate how well students will do on an achievement test on the basis of their current performance, or estimate how well a similar group of students might perform on the same achievement test.

extreme-value distribution a limited DISTRIBUTION of the greatest or least values of a large set of random variables that form an approximately straight line from the lower left to the upper right of a graph. The GUMBEL DISTRIBUTION is an example.

eyeballing *n.* slang for a preliminary casual look at research results, usually prior to a more formal analysis of the data. Also called **eyeball test**.

E

Ff

f 1. in an ANALYSIS OF VARIANCE or an ANALYSIS OF COVARIANCE, an EFFECT SIZE index that represents the STANDARD DEVIATION of a set of group means divided by the average standard deviation of scores across the set of groups. Its value ranges from 0 to infinity, with small, medium, and large effect size values suggested as .10, .25, and .40, respectively. **2.** in a table or distribution, symbol for FREQUENCY.

F symbol for F RATIO.

FA abbreviation for FACTOR ANALYSIS.

facet *n.* **1.** any component of an entity that itself may be assessed as an independent entity. For example, cooperation and trust might be considered facets of agreeableness in personality assessment. **2.** in GENERALIZABILITY THEORY, an aspect of data that causes scores to vary. For example, fluctuation in a set of scores due to using different raters, different time points, or different items for a particular test could be considered a facet. **3.** in FACTOR ANALYSIS, a primary or FIRST-ORDER FACTOR associated with one or more SECOND-ORDER FACTORS.

face validity the apparent soundness of a test or measure. The face validity of an instrument is the extent to which the items or content of the test appear to be appropriate for measuring something, regardless of whether they actually are. A test with face validity, however, may lack EMPIRICAL VALIDITY.

factor *n.* **1.** anything that contributes to a result or has a causal relationship to a phenomenon, event, or action. **2.** an underlying influence that accounts in part for variations in individual behavior. **3.** in ANALYSIS OF VARIANCE and other statistical procedures, an independent variable. **4.** in FACTOR ANALYSIS, an underlying, unobservable LATENT VARIABLE thought (together with other factors) to be responsible for the interrelations among a set of variables. **5.** in mathematics, a number that divides without remainder into another number.

factor analysis (**FA**) a broad family of mathematical procedures for reducing a set of intercorrelations among MANIFEST VARIABLES to a smaller set of unobserved LATENT VARIABLES or factors. For example, a number of tests of mechanical ability might be intercorrelated to enable factor analysis to reduce them to a few factors, such as fine motor coordination, speed, and attention. This technique is often used to examine the common influences believed to give rise to a set of observed measures (measurement structure) or to reduce a larger set of measures to a smaller set of linear composites for use in subsequent analysis (data reduction). See CONFIRMATORY FACTOR ANALYSIS; EXPLORATORY FACTOR ANALYSIS; PRINCIPAL COMPONENTS ANALYSIS.

factorial 1. *adj.* describing a design for an ANALYSIS OF VARIANCE in which the effect of multiple INDEPENDENT VARIABLES, each having two or more categories of response, is assessed. For example, a researcher may wish to examine the effect by gender (male vs. female) of a new drug treatment (drug vs. no drug). **2.** *n.* the value obtained when multiplying a given integer by each of the positive integers preceding it in value. Factorials are indicated by a number followed by an exclamation point. For example, 4! (4 factorial) denotes $1 \times 2 \times 3 \times 4$, which equals 24.

factorial analysis of covariance a statistical procedure to understand the effect on a DEPENDENT VARIABLE of two or more INDEPENDENT VARIABLES that are CATEGORICAL in nature, plus one or more additional correlated variables that are QUANTITATIVE in nature. For example, a researcher may use a factorial analysis of covariance to understand reading performance by examining the effect of phoneme training (i.e., yes vs. no) and gender (male vs. female), after taking into account the intelligence scores of the research participants. The factorial analysis thus provides a test of whether there are treatment condition and gender differences, as well as whether there is an interaction after controlling for pre-existing intelligence differences among the participants.

factorial analysis of variance a statistical procedure to understand the effect on a DEPENDENT VARIABLE that is QUANTITATIVE in nature of two or more INDEPENDENT VARIABLES that are CATEGORICAL in nature. For example, a health researcher may use a factorial analysis of variance to examine the effects of diet (e.g., high vs. low carbohydrates) and exercise (e.g., 3 hours per week vs. 1 hour per week) on weight.

factorial design an experimental study in which two or more CATEGORICAL VARIABLES are simultaneously manipulated or observed in order to study their joint influence (INTERACTION EFFECT) and separate influences (MAIN EFFECTS) on a separate DEPENDENT VARIABLE. For example, a researcher could use a factorial design to investigate treatment type (e.g., new exercise procedure vs. traditional procedure) and age (< 40 vs. > 40). The primary advantages of factorial designs are that they allow for the evaluation of interrelationships and that they are more efficient than conducting multiple studies with one variable at a time. See also FRACTIONAL FACTORIAL DESIGN; TWO-BY-TWO FACTORIAL DESIGN.

factorial invariance the situation in which the pattern of FACTOR LOADINGS on a LATENT VARIABLE in a FACTOR ANALYSIS remains identical from sample to sample. For example, if the same factor loading values were obtained for a measure of general intelligence whether a researcher tested men or women, the general intelligence test would be said to demonstrate factorial invariance by gender. In other contexts, factorial invariance is referred to more broadly as MEASUREMENT INVARIANCE.

factorial replication the appearance of the same underlying LATENT VARIABLE (factor) across repeated analyses. For example, a researcher might investigate factorial replication for a new version of an intelligence test by assessing whether the FACTOR LOADINGS showing how strongly items relate to the underlying intelligence dimension were the same on two random samples of participants.

factorial table a CROSS-TABULATION that shows the extent to which two INDEPENDENT VARIABLES affect a DEPENDENT VARIABLE. For example, in an ANALYSIS OF VARIANCE, a factorial table might be used to display the findings from a design that investigated how much teaching style (lecture vs. hands on) and gender (male vs. female) relate to student performance in a statistics class. The factorial table would show the mean performance for women in a lecture class, women in a hands-on class, men in a lecture class, and men in a hands-on class.

factorial validity confirmation that the underlying structure of dimensions and loadings are as expected when conducting a FACTOR ANALYSIS on a set of items. For example, a test of well-being would be said to have factorial validity if the items measuring satisfaction loaded positively and the items measuring meaninglessness loaded negatively, with similar values across several random sam-

F

F

ples of individuals. Also called **structural validity**.

factoring *n.* **1.** in FACTOR ANALYSIS, the process of extracting dimensions or underlying LATENT VARIABLES (factors). **2.** in mathematics, the subdivision of a target number into a series of numbers whose product is the target number.

factor loading in FACTOR ANALYSIS, the correlation between a MANIFEST VARIABLE and a LATENT VARIABLE (factor). The factor loading reflects the degree to which a manifest variable is said to be "made up of" the factor being examined.

factor method any means by which LATENT VARIABLES (factors) are extracted or identified in FACTOR ANALYSIS. Widely used factor methods include PRINCIPAL COMPONENTS ANALYSIS, which seeks to find a set of LINEAR COMBINATIONS called components that help explain the correlations among variables; and PRINCIPAL-AXIS FACTOR ANALYSIS, in which underlying dimensions or factors are sought to explain the correlations among variables after separating out COMMUNALITY and putting aside the ERROR VARIANCE in a set of variables.

factor pattern matrix in FACTOR ANALYSIS, a matrix of regression-like WEIGHTS that indicate the composition of the MANIFEST VARIABLE in terms of the underlying LATENT VARIABLES or factors. Consider the example below.

It provides information about the unique relation of a measured item to the factor in question (Factor 1), controlling for other factors (Factor 2). See also FACTOR STRUCTURE MATRIX.

factor reflection changing the signs of a set of FACTOR LOADINGS from positive to negative, or vice versa. For example, researchers studying a newly revised scale to measure happiness might use factor reflection to change a negative sign on the factor loadings for positive items as well as to change a positive sign for sadness items. The resulting pattern of loadings thus shows positively focused items as having a positive sign and sadness-focused items as having a negative sign, such that the entire scale could accurately be said to measure the positive state of happiness.

factor rotation in FACTOR ANALYSIS, the repositioning of LATENT VARIABLES (factors) to a new, more interpretable configuration by a set of mathematically specifiable TRANSFORMATIONS. Factors initially are extracted to meet a mathematical criterion of maximal variance explanation, which often does not result in a scientifically meaningful representation of the data. Indeed, for any one

Item	1	2
1. I am emotionally stable.	−.19	−.58
2. Others consider me to be emotionally stable.	−.61	−.19
3. I have a positive self-evaluation.	.19	.89
4. Others evaluate me positively.	.90	.21
5. I have an internal locus of control.	.16	.55
6. Others describe me as having an internal locus of control.	.61	.10
7. I am self-efficacious.	.19	.85
8. Others describe me as self-efficacious.	.88	.27
9. My self-esteem is high.	.17	.85
10. Others believe my self-esteem is high.	.85	.20

factor pattern matrix

factor solution that fits the data to a specific degree there will exist an infinite number of equally good mathematical solutions, each represented by a different FACTOR STRUCTURE MATRIX. Thus, rotation is required to obtain a solution that is both mathematically viable and logically sound. See OBLIQUE ROTATION; ORTHOGONAL ROTATION.

factor score an estimate of the quantitative value that an individual would have on a LATENT VARIABLE were it possible to measure this directly; the latent variable or factor is determined through FACTOR ANALYSIS.

factor structure in FACTOR ANALYSIS, the pattern of FACTOR LOADINGS that shows how a set of items correlate with underlying latent variables. See FACTOR STRUCTURE MATRIX.

factor structure matrix in FACTOR ANALYSIS, a matrix of FACTOR LOADINGS showing the correlations between items and underlying LATENT VARIABLES (factors). This is in distinction to a FACTOR PATTERN MATRIX, which gives the correlations with a factor while taking into account other factors. When examining ORTHOGONAL or uncorrelated factors, the factor pattern matrix and factor structure matrix are the same, whereas they are different when examining correlated factors in an OBLIQUE SOLUTION.

factor theory in CLASSICAL TEST THEORY, the supposition that a set of correlated variables can be reduced to a smaller set of underlying dimensions or FACTORS. It follows that each person's observed score can be represented by a FACTOR LOADING times a factor plus ERROR VARIANCE.

fail-safe N a value often used in META-ANALYSIS to indicate the number of nonsignificant studies that would be needed to render a significant EFFECT SIZE no longer significant. For example, if a researcher conducted a meta-analysis and estimated a significant effect size, the fail-safe N could be calculated to show the number of additional studies that would need to be added (e.g., from unpublished FILE-DRAWER ANALYSIS) in order to make the effect size nonsignificant. The larger the value of fail-safe N, the higher the credibility of the estimated meta-analytic effect size.

failure time see SURVIVAL TIME.

fairness n. the equitable treatment of test takers in order to eliminate systematic variance in outcome scores among people with different racial or cultural experiences and other background influences. Fundamentally a sociocultural (rather than a technical) issue, fairness is a broad area encompassing quality management in test design, administration, and scoring; adequate coverage of relevant content; sufficient work to establish CONSTRUCT VALIDITY; equal learning opportunities and access to testing; and items measuring only the skill or ability under investigation without being unduly influenced by construct-irrelevant variance introduced through test-taker background factors. See also CULTURE-FAIR TEST.

faithful-subject role the behavior adopted by a participant in a research study who tries to respond accurately and does not try to provide what he or she perceives as the researcher's desired response. Compare APPREHENSIVE-SUBJECT ROLE; GOOD-SUBJECT ROLE; NEGATIVISTIC-SUBJECT ROLE.

false negative a case that is incorrectly excluded from a group by the test used to determine inclusion. In diagnostics, for example, a false negative is an individual who, in reality, has a particular condition but whom the diagnostic instrument indicates does not have the condition. In INFERENTIAL STATISTICS, a false negative is also referred to as a TYPE II ERROR; this is the error that occurs when a study's findings indicate there is not a significant treatment effect when in fact there is such an effect. Compare FALSE POSITIVE.

false positive a case that is incorrectly included in a group by the test used to determine inclusion. In diagnostics, for example, a false positive is an individual who, in reality, does not have a particular condition but whom the diagnostic instrument indicates does have the condition. In INFERENTIAL STATISTICS, a false positive is also called a TYPE I ERROR; this is the error that occurs when a research study is thought to have significant findings when in fact it does not. Compare FALSE NEGATIVE.

falsifiability *n.* the condition of admitting falsification: the logical possibility that an assertion, hypothesis, or theory can be shown not to be true by an observation or experiment. The most important properties that make a statement falsifiable in this way are (a) that it makes a prediction about an outcome or a universal claim of the type "All *X*s have property *Y*" and (b) that what is predicted or claimed is observable. Falsifiability is an essential characteristic of any genuinely scientific hypothesis. See also FALSIFICATIONISM. **—falsifiable** *adj.*

falsificationism *n.* the position that (a) the disproving, rather than proving, of hypotheses is the basic procedure of scientific investigation and the chief means by which scientific knowledge is advanced; and (b) FALSIFIABILITY is the property that distinguishes scientific claims from truth claims of other kinds, such as those of metaphysics or political ideology. **—falsificationist** *adj.*

family *n.* a collection of mathematically or statistically related entities. For example, a set of statistical tests conducted when there are more than two groups for an INDEPENDENT VARIABLE within an ANALYSIS OF VARIANCE constitutes a family of tests. See also FAMILY-WISE ALPHA LEVEL; FAMILY-WISE ERROR RATE. **—familial** *adj.*

family-based association study research assessing the connection between genes and disease by examining the pattern of alleles (i.e., alternate forms of genes on paired chromosomes) that are transmitted and those that are not transmitted to a child from both parents. See also FAMILY STUDY.

family study research conducted among siblings, parents, or children to assess evidence for genetic links for characteristics or outcomes, often related to health or disease. For example, a family study might be conducted to assess whether individuals from the same family who share a similar genetic structure also have similar responses to a health-promotion intervention such as diet, exercise, or medication. See also FAMILY-BASED ASSOCIATION STUDY.

family-wise alpha level a set value of the probability of making a TYPE I ERROR when carrying out a set of hypothesis tests (e.g., when conducting MULTIPLE COMPARISONS within a data set). In many studies, family-wise alpha is kept at .05, such that there is only a 5% total chance of rejecting a NULL HYPOTHESIS when it should be retained over a set of tests. See also FAMILY-WISE ERROR RATE.

family-wise error rate the probability of making a TYPE I ERROR when conducting MULTIPLE COMPARISONS among groups within a data set. Although similar to the FAMILY-WISE ALPHA LEVEL, which is a predetermined probability value to keep the amount of FALSE-POSITIVE errors at a manageable level, the family-wise error rate is assessed after a set of hypothesis tests have been conducted. Researchers often like to keep this value at .05. See also TESTWISE ERROR RATE.

fan-spread hypothesis a prediction that differences between groups in QUASI-EXPERIMENTAL RESEARCH will be proportional to the means and STANDARD DEVIATIONS of the individual groups over time. In other words, when the gap between two groups' mean scores increases or decreases over time, the variation of individual scores within each group also increases or decreases. The fan-spread hypothesis recognizes that changes over time may get smaller as individuals reach an ultimate goal. For example, students in a program to increase learning would not be expected to keep a constant rate of improvement but rather to improve faster than a comparison group of students.

farthest neighbor see COMPLETE-LINKAGE CLUSTERING.

fatigue effect a decline in performance on a prolonged or demanding research task that is generally attributed to the participant becoming tired or bored with the task. The fatigue effect is an important consideration when administering a lengthy survey or test in which participants' performance may worsen simply due to the challenges of an extended task.

FDA abbreviation for FUNCTIONAL DATA ANALYSIS.

F distribution a theoretical PROBABILITY DISTRIBUTION widely used in the ANALYSIS OF VARIANCE, MULTIPLE REGRESSION, and other statistical tests of hypotheses about population variances. It is the ratio of the variances of two independent random variables each divided by its DEGREES OF FREEDOM. In an analysis of variance, for example, the *F* distribution is used to test the hypothesis that the variance between groups is significantly greater than the variance within groups, thus demonstrating evidence of some differences among the means. Also called **Fisher distribution**; **Fisher's F distribution**; **Fisher–Snedecor distribution**; **Snedecor's F distribution**. See F RATIO; F TEST.

F distribution table a table of values listing the DEGREES OF FREEDOM for the BETWEEN-GROUPS SUM OF SQUARES along one side and the degrees of freedom for the WITHIN-GROUPS SUM OF SQUARES along another right-angle side, with values in the middle corresponding to the

CRITICAL VALUE of the F RATIO needed to reject the NULL HYPOTHESIS. See F TEST.

feasibility study see PILOT STUDY.

fidelity *n.* the degree of accuracy of a measuring instrument or STATISTICAL MODEL. For example, a representation derived from STRUCTURAL EQUATION MODELING that depicts a pattern of relationships between health attitudes and behaviors could be said to have fidelity if it accurately explains the VARIATION and COVARIATION in the data.

field *n.* somewhere other than a laboratory, library, or academic setting in which experimental or NONEXPERIMENTAL work is carried out or data collected.

field experiment a study that is conducted outside the laboratory in a "real-world" setting. Participants are exposed to one of two or more levels of an INDEPENDENT VARIABLE and observed for their reactions; they are likely to be unaware of the research. Such research often is conducted without RANDOM SELECTION or RANDOM ASSIGNMENT of participants to conditions and no deliberate experimental manipulation of the independent variable by the researcher. See FIELD RESEARCH; QUASI-EXPERIMENTAL RESEARCH.

field notes notes on observations made in natural settings (i.e., the field) rather than in laboratories. Field notes comprise the data for subsequent analysis in FIELD EXPERIMENTS and FIELD RESEARCH.

field research studies conducted outside the laboratory, in a "real-world" setting, which typically involve observing or interacting with participants in their typical environments over an extended period of time. Field research has the advantages of ECOLOGICAL VALIDITY and the opportunity to understand how and why behavior occurs in a natural social environment; it has the disadvantages of loss of environmental control and ability to do precise experimental manipulations. Thus, field research is often said to have more EXTERNAL VALIDITY and less INTERNAL VALIDITY than laboratory-based research. See also FIELD EXPERIMENT.

field survey an assessment that involves collecting information on a specific topic in a relevant group of individuals or entities, usually in their natural environment. For example, a field survey could be conducted on a sample of students from underrepresented groups to assess their attitudes, experience, and performance regarding quantitative methods before providing an intervention to increase quantitative reasoning. See also FIELD RESEARCH.

figure *n.* a graph, drawing, or other depiction used to convey the essential findings from a research study. Common figures used in psychological research include BAR GRAPHS, which show the frequency of endorsement for several categories (e.g., the number of individuals who have various diseases), and VENN DIAGRAMS, which use overlapping circles to show how much shared variance there is between two or more variables.

file-drawer analysis a statistical procedure for addressing the FILE-DRAWER PROBLEM by computing the number of unretrieved studies, averaging an EFFECT SIZE of .00, that would have to exist in file drawers before the overall results of a META-ANALYSIS would become nonsignificant at $p \geq .05$, that is, would exceed an acceptable probability level (.05) of occurring by chance. A small computed value indicates a finding may have SPURIOUS PRECISION, such that it may just be due to chance. Conversely, a large value suggests that the finding is rather robust, as it would take a large number of nonsignificant findings to provide enough evidence to refute the results.

file-drawer problem the fact that a large proportion of all studies actually conducted are not available for review because they remain unpublished in "file drawers," having failed to obtain positive results. Thus, the results of a meta-analysis may not yield reliable EFFECT SIZE estimates since only studies that have been published or otherwise are widely available to researchers can be included in the analysis. See FILE-DRAWER ANALYSIS.

filler material information added to a test, questionnaire, or survey that is not related to the actual research, in order to keep individuals from discerning the true nature of the study. The filler material usually is not analyzed as part of the statistical findings.

filter *n.* any analytical procedure used in TIME-SERIES ANALYSIS to remove fluctuations from the data and separate out its trend and cyclical components. A MOVING AVERAGE is an example of a filter.

filter coefficient a value needed to estimate a process, as is common in SIGNAL DETECTION THEORY and APPLIED STATISTICS. Processes that have fewer filter coefficients generally are easier to estimate.

filter question a preliminary inquiry to assess whether a specific condition exists that would require further assessment. For example, a health researcher could use a filter question to determine if participants have ever experienced a specific health concern, such as high blood pressure. If the participant answers yes then the researcher could ask a subsequent set of questions to elicit more information, such as the weight, diet, exercise levels, and family history relating to high blood pressure of these participants.

finite mixture distribution a data set that is believed to describe several fairly distinct and limited clusters or subgroups of individuals, even if the actual clusters are not completely observable. For example, a health researcher may collect data from a sample of people to assess their frequency of unprotected sex, their number of sexual partners, and the perceived risk of sexual partners. The ultimate goal of the research could be to uncover, through a procedure such as CLUSTER ANALYSIS or LATENT CLASS ANALYSIS, several distinct clusters of individuals at varying risk for HIV, such as a low-risk group, whose members have varying frequency of unprotected sex and a monogamous sexual relationship of low perceived sexual risk; a moderate-risk group, whose members have moderate frequency of unprotected sex and several sexual partners of varying perceived partner risk; and a high-risk group, whose members have high values for all three variables. From this analysis, the researcher may conclude that the sample contained a finite mixture distribution of three clusters of sexual risk, where each cluster most likely has different MEAN and VARIANCE values.

finite population a limited universe of individuals or entities from which a researcher may wish to sample for a study. For example, an educational psychologist may consider the finite population of elementary-school-age children in a limited geographical area (e.g., city, county, state) to recruit participants for a study of learning and attention deficit disorders.

finite population correction an adjustment made to a PARAMETER estimate, often a VARIANCE, when sampling from a limited subset of a larger defined POPULATION. For example, using $N - 1$ in the denominator of a variance calculation, instead of just N, could be seen as a finite population correction when estimating the variance of intelligence in a sample of students drawn from a FINITE POPULATION.

first moment see MOMENT.

first-order autoregressive model a statistical process, often examined using TIME-SERIES ANALYSIS, in which each score is believed to be related to the immediately previous score plus some RANDOM ERROR. See also AUTOREGRESSIVE MODEL.

first-order factor in FACTOR ANALYSIS, any of the LATENT VARIABLES (factors) that are derived from the CORRELATION (or covariance) among the MANIFEST VARIABLES, as opposed to SECOND-ORDER FACTORS, which are determined from the correlation (or covariance) among the factors. Also called **primary factor**.

first-order interaction an effect in which the pattern of values on one variable changes depending on the combination of values on two other variables. For example, an analysis could reveal that although gender and teaching style may each have some effect on performance, the specific degree or amount of the performance effect changes depending on the particular combination of gender and teaching method. Thus, male students may show moderately high performance regardless of teaching style, whereas female students may show high performance with a hands-on teaching style and low to moderate performance with a lecture teaching style. See also HIGHER ORDER INTERACTION.

first-order Markov model a statistical model in which each value in a MARKOV CHAIN is described in terms of its relation to the immediately previous value. A **second-order Markov model** would be required to describe the current value in the chain in relation to the two previous stages, and so on.

first-order partial correlation the association between two variables, x and y, after controlling for or taking into account the effect of one other variable, z. In other words, a first-order partial correlation is the relationship between the RESIDUAL from x and the residual from y after predicting each of x and y with another variable, z. The actual quantitative value describing the relationship is called the **first-order partial correlation coefficient**. Also called **first-order partial**. See also PARTIAL CORRELATION.

first passage time the amount of time that elapses until the occurrence of a random process in an entity or individual. For example, a medical researcher may be interested in the first passage time for a specific disease in a specific patient.

first quartile see QUARTILE.

Fisher–Behrens problem see BEHRENS–FISHER PROBLEM.

Fisher distribution see F DISTRIBUTION. [Sir Ronald Aylmer **Fisher** (1890–1962), British statistician and geneticist]

Fisher exact test a statistical procedure to determine whether two CATEGORICAL variables are related. Appropriate for small samples (a CHI-SQUARE TEST FOR INDEPENDENCE is used with large samples), it examines the associations between the rows and columns of data in a fourfold (2×2) CONTINGENCY TABLE. For example, the Fisher exact test could be used to assess whether there is a relationship between gender (male or female) and pizza topping preference (cheese or multitopping) in a group of 20 individuals. The test yields an exact p value rather than a range of p values (e.g., $p < .05$). Also called **Fisher–Irwin test**; **Fisher–Yates test**. [Sir Ronald Aylmer **Fisher**; Joseph Oscar **Irwin** (1898–1982), British statistician; Frank **Yates** (1902–1994), British statistician]

Fisher–Freeman–Halton test an extension of the FISHER EXACT TEST used to assess whether two variables, each having two or more categories, are related in a relatively small data sample. For example, the Fisher–Freeman–Halton test could be used to assess whether gender and pizza topping preference are related when the latter has several choices (e.g., cheese, vegetable, meat, everything). [Sir Ronald Aylmer **Fisher**; G. H. **Freeman**;

John H. **Halton**, British-born U.S. computer scientist]

Fisher F test see F TEST. [Sir Ronald Aylmer **Fisher**]

Fisher g test a statistical procedure for analyzing whether there is any difference between the patterns of observed and expected CATEGORICAL DATA. The Fisher g test is a LIKELIHOOD-RATIO TEST that is approximately distributed as a CHI-SQUARE and can be used in the same situations. [Sir Ronald Aylmer **Fisher**]

Fisher–Hayter multiple comparison test a statistical procedure for assessing whether pairs of means are significantly different that is used after a significant F TEST. The Fisher–Hayter multiple comparison test is a modification of the FISHER LEAST SIGNIFICANT DIFFERENCE TEST that controls for FAMILY-WISE ERROR RATE; it is relatively easy to calculate. See POST HOC COMPARISON. [Sir Ronald Aylmer **Fisher**; Anthony J. **Hayter**, British-born U.S. statistician]

Fisher least significant difference test (Fisher LSD test; LSD test) a statistical procedure to compare pairs of means, conducted after an F TEST has revealed that at least one pair of means is significantly different. The test calculates the smallest value that would be statistically different from chance when subtracting one mean from another mean. If the absolute value of the actual difference between a pair of means is larger than this **least significant difference (LSD)**, a researcher can reject a NULL HYPOTHESIS that the means are equal and conclude that they are significantly different. Also called **protected t test**. [Sir Ronald Aylmer **Fisher**]

Fisher scoring method a procedure for finding a MAXIMUM LIKELIHOOD solution when estimating PARAMETERS, such that the resulting estimates are selected to make the sample data have the highest probability of being drawn from a population with the given estimates. [Sir Ronald Aylmer **Fisher**]

Fisher's F distribution see F DISTRIBUTION. [Sir Ronald Aylmer **Fisher**]

Fisher's information a variance or covariance, often of MAXIMUM LIKELIHOOD estimates. When the variances and covariances are organized together in a SQUARE MATRIX the resulting display is called **Fisher's information matrix**. [Sir Ronald Aylmer **Fisher**]

Fisher's least significant difference see FISHER LEAST SIGNIFICANT DIFFERENCE TEST.

Fisher's linear discriminant function an additive combination of continuous variables that helps explain a CATEGORICAL outcome. For example, an organizational psychologist could examine whether measures of perceived career influence, work respect, and institutional climate distinguish among three different departments within the institution. A Fisher's linear discriminant function analysis would reveal two linear discriminant functions in which the discriminant coefficients associated with each predictor variable for each function indicate how strongly that variable relates to the set of departments. See DISCRIMINANT FUNCTION. [Sir Ronald Aylmer **Fisher**]

Fisher–Snedecor distribution see F DISTRIBUTION. [Sir Ronald Aylmer **Fisher**; George W. **Snedecor** (1881–1974), U.S. statistician]

Fisher's randomization procedure a statistical test that compares the actual difference between sample means for two distinct groups, with a set of mean differences obtained by randomly splitting the combined data from the two groups into all possible rearrangements of two arbitrary groups. The proportion of mean differences from the various sets of randomly split data is viewed as a P VALUE, such that if the proportion is less than, say, .05, it indicates that there is a less than 5% chance of finding means as different or more so than the two sample means if the NULL HYPOTHESIS is true (i.e., assuming the means are equal). Thus, the null hypothesis can be rejected and a researcher can conclude that there is evidence that the two means differ more than would occur by chance. [Sir Ronald Aylmer **Fisher**]

Fisher's r to z transformation a statistical procedure that converts a Pearson PRODUCT-MOMENT CORRELATION COEFFICIENT to a standardized z SCORE in order to assess whether the correlation is statistically different from zero. The test is useful in providing a normally distributed statistic (called the **Fisher transformed value** or **Fisher's z**) that can be used in HYPOTHESIS TESTING or in forming a CONFIDENCE INTERVAL. Also called **Fisher transformation**; **Fisher z transformation**; **z transformation**. [Sir Ronald Aylmer **Fisher**]

Fisher–Yates test see FISHER EXACT TEST. [Sir Ronald Aylmer **Fisher**; Frank **Yates** (1902–1994), British statistician]

fishing *n.* an informal term for searching unsystematically through a data set in order to look for any noticeable patterns of relationship among variables. More formal procedures called DATA MINING have been developed using statistical and computer-science methods to discern recognizable patterns in huge data sets. Fishing should not substitute for more rigorous methods based on sound EXPERIMENTAL DESIGN. See also DATA DREDGING; DATA SNOOPING.

fit *n.* the degree to which values predicted by a model correspond with empirically observed values. For example, in STRUCTURAL EQUATION MODELING, a researcher may want to see how well his or her hypothesized model of the relationships among a set of variables actually fits the VARIATION and COVARIATION in the data.

fit index a quantitative measure of how well a statistical model corresponds to the VARIATION and COVARIATION in a set of data. For example, in STRUCTURAL EQUATION MODELING, a well-recognized

F

F

fit index is the **Bentler comparative fit index** (**CFI**), which indicates how well a proposed model fits the data compared to a null model that just posits variances for the variables and no relationships among the variables. An index value greater than .90 (or preferably .95) indicates a model that explains the pattern of relationships in the data reasonably well. If the fit of a model is poor, then the model needs to be respecified and then reanalyzed. See GOODNESS OF FIT. See also BENTLER–BONETT INDEX.

fitted distribution a known statistical pattern of data (e.g., a NORMAL DISTRIBUTION) that is compared to sample data. To assess whether a fitted distribution is a good match for the data, one (a) plots the sample data with a HISTOGRAM or BAR GRAPH; (b) compares the sample graph with the known statistical pattern (e.g., using a program designed for that purpose); and (c) assesses how closely the sample data and statistical pattern match using a GOODNESS-OF-FIT statistic (e.g., CHI-SQUARE). If the fitted distribution describes the sample data fairly closely, the goodness-of-fit statistic should be small and nonsignificant, indicating there is little difference between the statistical pattern (e.g., normal distribution) and the sample data pattern (depicted in the initial histogram).

fitted frequency see EXPECTED FREQUENCY.

fitted residual the value obtained when subtracting an expected or predicted value from the original data value. For example, in LINEAR REGRESSION the fitted residual equals $y - y'$, where y' is the predicted value formed from filling actual x values into the regression equation; and $y' = a + bx$, where a equals the Y-INTERCEPT, b equals the unstandardized REGRESSION COEFFICIENT, and x is a predictor variable.

fitted value the predicted value of a particular score where a statistical model is compared to actual data. For example,

in LINEAR REGRESSION the fitted value is y', where $y' = a + bx$, in which a equals the Y-INTERCEPT, b equals the unstandardized REGRESSION COEFFICIENT, and x is a predictor variable. Note that subtracting a fitted value from an actual y score in linear regression will equal a FITTED RESIDUAL, which will be close to zero if the linear regression model is a good match to the data.

five-number summary in EXPLORATORY DATA ANALYSIS, the characterization of a data set through the use of five summary statistics: the two extreme scores, the upper and lower QUARTILES, and the MEDIAN or middle quartile. For example, suppose the scores on a test are 100, 93, 90, 82, 76, 72, 64, 61, 60, and 47. The five-number summary from highest to lowest numbers would be 100, 90, 74, 61, and 47—that is, 100 is the highest extreme score, 90 is the highest quartile (the midpoint in the top half of the data), 74 is the middle point, 61 is the lowest quartile (the midpoint in the bottom half of the data), and 47 is the lowest extreme score. These values provide the basic highlights of a set of data and can be used to create a BOX-AND-WHISKER PLOT.

fixed-alternative question a test or survey item in which several possible responses are given and participants are asked to pick the correct response or the one that most closely matches their preference. An example of a fixed-alternative question is "Which of the following most closely corresponds to your age: 12 or younger, 13 to 19, 20 to 39, 40 to 59, 60 to 79, or 80 or older?" A fixed-alternative question is sometimes referred to as a **closed question**, although this can also refer to any inquiry requesting a short definite answer (e.g., "How old are you?"). Also called **fixed-choice question**; **forced-choice question**; **multiple-choice question**. Compare FREE-RESPONSE QUESTION.

fixed effect an INDEPENDENT VARIABLE whose levels are specified by the researcher rather than randomly chosen within some level of permissible values. For example, a health researcher who specifically chose to examine the effect on weight loss of no exercise, one hour of exercise, or three hours of exercise per week would be treating time spent exercising as a fixed effect. In other words, all levels of interest are included in the design and thus anyone wanting to replicate the study would have to use the same levels of exercise as in the original. As a rule, one should not generalize results of fixed-effect studies beyond the specific levels or conditions used in the experiment (see FIXED-EFFECTS FALLACY). Also called **fixed factor**. See FIXED-EFFECTS MODEL; RANDOM-EFFECTS MODEL. Compare RANDOM EFFECT.

fixed-effects analysis of variance a statistical procedure to determine whether means for an outcome or DEPENDENT VARIABLE differ across a specific set of conditions (i.e., levels of the INDEPENDENT VARIABLE) that have been selected by a researcher. This is contrasted with a RANDOM-EFFECTS ANALYSIS OF VARIANCE, in which the conditions have been randomly selected from a wide range of possible choices before any mean differences are examined.

fixed-effects fallacy a situation in which researchers inappropriately generalize beyond the specific conditions they tested in an analysis, treating a study design as if it were based on randomly selected conditions that would more appropriately allow generalization. For example, a fixed-effects fallacy occurs when a researcher uses a FIXED-EFFECTS ANALYSIS OF VARIANCE but states his or her results as if he or she had used a RANDOM-EFFECTS ANALYSIS OF VARIANCE, in which the conditions examined were selected from a large population of possible condition options.

fixed-effects model any statistical procedure or experimental design that uses independent variables whose levels are specifically selected by the researcher

for study rather than randomly chosen from a wide range of possible values. For example, a researcher may wish to investigate the effects of the available dosages of a certain drug on symptom alleviation. Fixed-effects models generally are intended to make inferences solely about the specific levels of the independent variables actually used in the experiment. Compare MIXED-EFFECTS MODEL; RANDOM-EFFECTS MODEL.

fixed factor see FIXED EFFECT.

fixed parameter a specific value assigned (as opposed to estimated) by a researcher when testing a statistical model. For example, in STRUCTURAL EQUATION MODELING, researchers may use a fixed parameter of 1.0 for one of the FACTOR LOADINGS or variances of each LATENT VARIABLE in a model. Compare FREE PARAMETER.

fixed population a specific range of individuals or entities that constitute the larger base of interest to a researcher. See POPULATION.

fixed variable a variable whose value is specified by a researcher or otherwise predetermined and not the result of chance. Compare RANDOM VARIABLE.

floor effect the situation in which a large proportion of participants perform very poorly on a task or other evaluative measure, thus skewing the distribution of scores and making it impossible to differentiate among the many individuals at that low level. For example, a test whose items are too difficult for those taking it would show a floor effect because most people would obtain or be close to the lowest possible score of 0. Also called **basement effect**. Compare CEILING EFFECT.

flowchart *n.* a diagram representing the ordered steps to follow when conducting a procedure, such as constructing a computer program or performing a specific research study. The illustration overleaf gives a basic example.

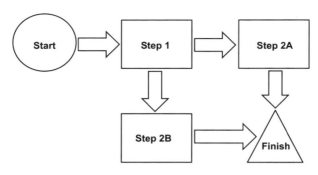

flowchart

Flowcharts also are used in PATH ANALYSIS and STRUCTURAL EQUATION MODELING to illustrate the causal links among the variables being studied.

fluctuation *n.* **1.** variation in size or value. **2.** in TIME-SERIES ANALYSES, an irregularity that is not related to any trend and is thus often removed via SMOOTHING.

F_{max} distribution in an ANALYSIS OF VARIANCE, a pattern of values used for assessing whether variances are homogeneous across the groups being studied. See F_{MAX} STATISTIC.

F_{max} statistic in an ANALYSIS OF VARIANCE, a value formed from the ratio of the largest variance over the smallest variance from the set of groups being assessed. The F_{max} statistic is assessed for significance by looking up the CRITICAL VALUE in a statistical table for the relevant number of groups and DEGREES OF FREEDOM. If the calculated F_{max} statistic is larger than the critical ratio, then there is evidence of HETEROGENEITY OF VARIANCE, which violates one of the assumptions of the analysis and renders its results invalid. Otherwise, a researcher can assume that there is not enough evidence for heterogeneity and the assumption of HOMOGENEITY OF VARIANCE can be reasonably maintained.

F_{max} test the procedure used to obtain an F_{MAX} STATISTIC and evaluate it for significance. Also called **Hartley F_{max} test**; **Hartley F_{max} test for homogeneity of variance**; **Hartley test**; **Hartley test for homogeneity of variance**.

focused comparison in research, the practice of putting the same set of carefully chosen, strictly relevant questions to each participant in an experiment (or to the same participant on multiple occasions in a WITHIN-SUBJECTS DESIGN). This allows for systematic comparison of the answers given and produces more generalizable and replicable findings than does asking questions that vary from case to case.

focus group a small set of people, typically 8 to 12 in number, who share common characteristics (e.g., working parents with 5- to 8-year-old children) that are relevant to the research question and who are selected to discuss a topic of which they have personal experience (e.g., their children's reading abilities and school performance). A leader conducts the discussion and keeps it on target while also encouraging free-flowing, open-ended debate. Originally used in marketing to determine consumer response to particular products, focus groups are now used for determining typical reactions, adaptations, and solutions to any number of issues, events, or topics and are associated particularly with QUALITATIVE RESEARCH.

foldover design a type of FRACTIONAL

F

FACTORIAL DESIGN in which the researcher deliberately removes INTERACTION EFFECTS among the variables. This is achieved by carrying out a second run of tests in which the elements in the DESIGN MATRIX are multiplied by –1. The results from the two runs of test are then combined to eliminate the interaction effects, such that the MAIN EFFECTS become the primary focus. A foldover design may be useful when there are several variables that each have two or more levels, such that it is difficult to analyze the full set of possible conditions.

follow-back study research that collects earlier data in order to understand the causes of an event of interest. For example, a researcher might conduct a follow-back study of deceased hospital patients, gathering additional information regarding cause of death so as to understand the progress of different diseases.

follow-through *n.* an exercise in which researchers provide summaries of their main findings in order to provide practical guidance to policymakers, funding agencies, or professionals in the relevant fields.

follow-up plot (**FU plot**) a type of graph, mainly used in LONGITUDINAL DESIGNS, in which the specific results for specific individuals are displayed over time. Below is a hypothetical example.

follow-up study a long-term research project designed to examine the degree to which effects seen shortly after the imposition of an intervention persist over time. Follow-up studies are also used for the long-term study of participants in a laboratory experiment to examine the degree to which effects of the experimental conditions are lasting.

follow-up test see POST HOC TEST.

forced-choice question see FIXED-ALTERNATIVE QUESTION.

forced distribution a rating system in which raters must make a prescribed number of entries for each level of the rating scale used. For example, in employee evaluation a forced distribution might be used in which it is required that 5% of employees are categorized as poor, 15% as below average, 60% as average, 15% as above average, and 5% as excellent.

forecast *n.* a prediction about a future event based on current status and past history. For example, TIME-SERIES ANALYSES often are used to create statistical forecast models that provide a best guess about what to expect for variables of interest.

foreperiod *n.* in reaction-time experiments, the pause or interval between the "ready" signal and the presentation of the stimulus.

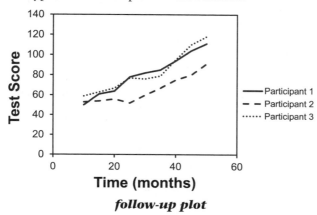

follow-up plot

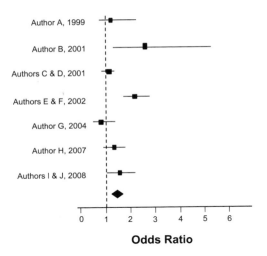

Odds Ratio

forest plot

forest plot a graph, often used in META-ANALYSES, in which the authors or titles of the studies are listed along the left side, and the corresponding EFFECT SIZE for each is given on the right. Consider the example above, in which effect sizes are given as ODDS RATIOS.

The effect sizes for the individual studies are usually indicated by squares in which the size of the square is proportional to the size of the effect for a specific study. At the bottom the overall effect size is given, usually in a diamond shape whose width indicates the outer points of a CONFIDENCE INTERVAL for the overall effect across all of the studies listed.

formal experimentation a strictly controlled study in which the INDEPENDENT VARIABLE is manipulated and one group of individuals or entities is randomly assigned to receive the TREATMENT and another set of individuals or entities is randomly assigned to act as a CONTROL GROUP. Results from formal experimentation can attribute a CAUSAL INFERENCE to the independent variable if those in the treatment group perform better than those in the control group.

formal theory a model or set of rules and assumptions used to understand various behaviors in mathematical terms. Formal theories often are developed and studied in the field of political science and psychology. An example of a formal theory is the so-called "prisoner's dilemma" model, which can be applied to various situations in which participants have to decide between the costs and benefits of cooperating or competing. The model uses a series of rules to determine the outcomes of various behaviors where two suspects separately have the option to confess or refuse to speak about a potential crime. If both refuse to speak, they both get a minor penalty (e.g., 1 month in jail). If both confess, they both get a moderate penalty (e.g., 3 months in jail). If one confesses and the other refuses to speak, the one who confesses goes free and the other gets a severe penalty (e.g., 1 year in jail).

formative evaluation a process intended to improve or guide the development of a program in its early stages through the use of qualitative or quantitative research methodology. Ideally, the individual performing a formative evaluation will repeatedly interact, often informally, with the program personnel from the outset of the work to clarify goals, monitor implementation, and assess staff and resource requirements. See also SUMMATIVE EVALUATION.

formula *n.* a precise statement about how two pieces of information, usually mathematical, are related. The most common type of formula is a mathematical EQUATION in which one variable is a weighted FUNCTION of another variable plus a constant. For example, the formula for a straight line is $y = mx + b$, where y is an outcome plotted on a vertical or y-axis, m is the slope of the line, x is the value of a variable along the horizontal or x-axis, and b is where the straight line crosses the vertical axis.

formula scoring a method of scoring a multiple-choice test that includes a CORRECTION FOR GUESSING. Participants are encouraged to respond to an item if they can rule out at least one response choice, but they are discouraged from responding if they do not have any idea of the correct answer. A participant's score is determined by noting the number of items he or she got right (R) and subtracting the number of wrong items (W) divided by the response choices per item minus 1 ($C - 1$). For example, if a participant had 40 right answers and 10 wrong answers on a 50-item test that has four response choices per question (e.g., A, B, C, or D), that person's formula score (FS) would be

$$FS = R - [W/(C - 1)] = 40 - 10/3 = 36.67.$$

Note that without the correction, the score would have been 40. Thus, the formula score assumes that the participant guessed among three choices after ruling out one of them on each of the 10 items that were missed. This would mean that he or she would get 1/3 correct purely by guessing, hence this amount (.333 of 10 or 3.33) is subtracted from the score of 40 to give the corrected formula score of 36.67.

forward-looking study see PROSPECTIVE RESEARCH.

forward selection a technique used in creating MULTIPLE REGRESSION models in which independent variables from a large set of such variables are added to the REGRESSION EQUATION in the order of their predictive power (i.e., largest to smallest increase in the COEFFICIENT OF MULTIPLE DETERMINATION) until a preset criterion is reached and there is no further significant change in the model's predictive power. Also called **forward inclusion; forward stepwise regression; stepup selection**. See also F-TO-ENTER; F-TO-REMOVE.

fourfold point correlation coefficient see PHI COEFFICIENT.

fourfold table see TWO-BY-TWO TABLE.

fourth moment see MOMENT.

fractal *n.* a geometric shape that can be divided into parts that each resemble the pattern of the whole shape. In other words, a fractal is a shape possessing the quality of **self-similarity**.

fractile *n.* see QUANTILE.

fractional factorial design a type of experimental design in which some conditions are omitted, such that not all levels of one or more of the INDEPENDENT VARIABLES are combined with all other levels of the other variables. A LATIN SQUARE is an example. Fractional factorial designs might be used because of a small overall sample available for study or because of difficulty obtaining participants or assigning them to some conditions. Additionally, there may simply be too many combinations to study (e.g., in a $3 \times 4 \times 2 \times 5$ design, there are 120 combinations of levels). Fractional factorial designs can be used to examine MAIN EFFECTS (and sometimes TWO-WAY INTERACTIONS) but cannot be used to assess any three-way or other HIGHER ORDER INTERACTIONS. Also called **incomplete factorial design**. Compare COMPLETE FACTORIAL DESIGN.

fractional polynomial a transformation of a continuous variable to a quadratic, cubic, or further power when the relationship is believed to be NONLINEAR. For example, if a researcher expects a relationship between achievement motivation and performance that resembles an upside-down U (CURVILINEAR) shape, a fractional polynomial could be formed by squaring the achievement motivation score for each individual in order to predict achievement more accurately as a nonlinear pattern.

frailty model a form of SURVIVAL ANALYSIS that allows for HETEROGENEITY in the sample. It incorporates a RANDOM EFFECT to account for COVARIATES across different subsets of participants in the sample.

F ratio (symbol: F) in an ANALYSIS OF VARIANCE or a MULTIVARIATE ANALYSIS OF VARIANCE, the amount of EXPLAINED VARIANCE divided by the amount of ERROR VARIANCE; that is, the ratio of between-groups variance to within-group variance. Its value determines whether or not to accept the NULL HYPOTHESIS stating that there is no difference between the treatment and control conditions, with a large value indicating the presence of a significant effect. Ideally, a researcher prefers to have rather small variation within each group and maximal variation between the groups in order to demonstrate significant group differences. Also called **F statistic**; **F value**.

freedom from harm one of the basic rights of research participants that is ensured by an INSTITUTIONAL REVIEW BOARD. Freedom from harm states that a research participant should not incur undue risk as a result of taking part in a study. See also FREEDOM TO WITHDRAW; PARTICIPANTS' RIGHTS.

freedom to withdraw one of the basic rights of research participants that is ensured by an INSTITUTIONAL REVIEW BOARD. Freedom to withdraw allows a research participant to drop out of a study at any time without penalty. See also FREEDOM FROM HARM; PARTICIPANTS' RIGHTS.

Freeman–Tukey test a GOODNESS-OF-FIT TEST used with data that have multiple categories of counts or frequencies. [M. F. **Freeman**, U.S. statistician; John Wilder **Tukey** (1915–2000), U.S. statistician]

free parameter a value that is estimated from data, usually in a modeling procedure such as STRUCTURAL EQUATION MODELING. A free parameter contrasts with a FIXED PARAMETER, which is kept at a known, specific value. For example, in CONFIRMATORY FACTOR ANALYSIS, one FACTOR LOADING for each LATENT VARIABLE is usually a fixed parameter of 1.0 and the other loadings are free parameters that are estimated.

free-response question a test or survey item that allows the respondent to respond entirely as he or she pleases, as opposed to a FIXED-ALTERNATIVE QUESTION, in which the respondent must choose from several provided responses.

frequency (symbol: f) *n.* the number of occurrences of a particular phenomenon, particularly a CATEGORICAL VARIABLE such as gender. For example, it is often of interest to find the frequencies or counts of the men and women who are participating in a research study. Also called **absolute frequency**. See also RELATIVE FREQUENCY.

frequency data information that represents the counts or number of occurrences of particular response classes, usually for a CATEGORICAL VARIABLE. For example, a political psychologist may want to record frequency data on the number of men and women, the number of different ethnic groups, and the number of individuals who endorse a Democratic, Republican, or other political party affiliation.

frequency density the number of occurrences of an event divided by the class size for a particular CATEGORICAL VARIABLE of interest.

frequency distribution a tabular representation of the number of times a specific value or datum point occurs. The left column lists the different categories of a CATEGORICAL VARIABLE or scores of a CONTINUOUS VARIABLE, and the right column lists the number of occurrences of each. For example, one could construct a frequency distribution of the variable gender for a sample of 40 women and 60 men, as depicted below.

Gender	Frequency (f)
Female	40
Male	60

When a frequency distribution is plotted on a graph, it is often called a **frequency curve**, **frequency diagram**, or FREQUENCY POLYGON. When represented mathematically via an equation, it is called a **frequency function**. Also called **frequency table**. See also CUMULATIVE FREQUENCY DISTRIBUTION; RELATIVE FREQUENCY DISTRIBUTION.

frequency polygon a graph depicting a statistical distribution, made up of lines connecting the peaks of adjacent intervals. A LINE GRAPH connecting the

midpoints of the bars of a HISTOGRAM is a frequency polygon, as in the hypothetical example below.

frequency test a statistical procedure for assessing data that contain counts or the numbers of occurrences of various categories or classes. A common example of a frequency test is a CHI-SQUARE TEST that compares the pattern of observed counts or frequencies to those that are expected to occur.

frequency-within-interval recording the process of tracking the number of occurrences of an event or behavior across various time periods. It is a commonly used tool when working with clinical populations (e.g., those with autism) on behavioral change.

frequentist *n.* a researcher who approaches issues of PROBABILITY in terms of the frequency (number of occurrences) for a particular parameter over a period of time. This approach is contrasted with that of a BAYESIAN, who examines the data and assesses whether particular values are more credible or believable than others.

frequentist inference an approach to drawing conclusions from statistical samples that is based on the number of times an event is expected to occur in the long run if the conditions for observing the event are held constant. It con-

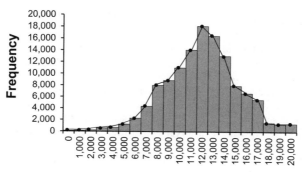

Debt (dollars)

frequency polygon

siders any research study to be one of a very large possible number of replications. Also called **classical inference**. Compare BAYESIAN INFERENCE.

Friedman two-way analysis of variance a NONPARAMETRIC TEST of whether two categorical INDEPENDENT VARIABLES have a consistent relationship with a DEPENDENT VARIABLE that involves ORDINAL DATA. For example, a researcher might use the Friedman two-way analysis of variance to determine whether three different tests produce consistent outcomes when they are used to rank the performance of students undergoing three different training programs. Also called **Friedman rank test**; **Friedman test**. [Milton **Friedman**]

F statistic see F RATIO.

F test any of a class of statistical procedures, such as ANALYSIS OF VARIANCE or MULTIPLE REGRESSION, that rely on the assumption that the calculated statistic—the F RATIO—follows the F DISTRIBUTION when the null hypothesis is true. *F* tests are tests of hypotheses about population variances or of whether REGRESSION COEFFICIENTS are zero. Also called **Fisher's F test**; **variance ratio test**.

F-to-enter *n.* in model-building procedures such as FORWARD SELECTION and forward STEPWISE DISCRIMINANT ANALYSIS, the specific ratio of variances needed to justify adding a variable as a predictor. Generally, an F-to-enter value around 4.0 is sufficient to allow a variable to be included in an analysis. For example, if researchers want to assess which of a set of six variables are the most important in predicting an outcome, they could conduct a STEPWISE REGRESSION. The regression analysis would begin with no variables. Then, the variable with the largest F-to-enter that met the initial criterion (e.g., 4.0) would be added as a predictor. The researchers would then assess whether the

F-to-enter for any of the remaining variables was at least 4.0 and if so would add that variable into the analysis as well. When the researchers found an F-to-enter for a variable less than 4.0, they would stop the process and examine only those variables that had been added to that point. Compare F-TO-REMOVE.

F-to-remove *n.* in model-building procedures such as BACKWARD ELIMINATION, STEPWISE REGRESSION, or backward STEPWISE DISCRIMINANT ANALYSIS, the specific ratio of variances needed to justify keeping a variable as a predictor. Generally, an F-to-remove value around 4.0 is sufficient to allow a variable to be retained in an analysis. For example, if researchers want to assess which of a set of six variables are the most important in predicting an outcome, they could conduct a backward stepwise multiple regression. All six variables initially would be included in the regression analysis, providing an index of the amount of variance explained by the set of six variables. Then, the variable that had the smallest F-to-remove value (i.e., less than 4.0) would be removed from the analysis. The researchers would continue by evaluating each of the remaining five variables and dropping any that had an F-to-remove less than 4.0, such that only the retained variables ultimately are examined in the analysis. Compare F-TO-ENTER.

fugitive literature see GRAY LITERATURE.

full model a statistical representation that includes all of the variables of interest, or all of the main PARAMETERS (e.g., REGRESSION COEFFICIENTS), among a set of variables. For example, in STRUCTURAL EQUATION MODELING, a full model might include estimated regression parameters between a set of INDEPENDENT VARIABLES, MEDIATORS, and DEPENDENT VARIABLES. Where there are as many parameters estimated in a full model as there are DEGREES OF FREEDOM, it is said to be a SATURATED MODEL. Also called **unrestricted model**.

full-normal plot see NORMAL PROBABILITY PLOT.

full rank the quality of a MATRIX in which each of the rows (or columns) are independent of each other, such that they do not provide redundant information. For example, a CORRELATION MATRIX of three variables would be of full rank if each of the three variables was unique, such that no variable completely overlapped with another variable. If, however, the three variables in the matrix were verbal intelligence, nonverbal intelligence, and full scale intelligence (i.e., some combination of verbal and nonverbal intelligence), the matrix would not be of full rank.

fully recursive model a statistical representation in which one variable predicts a second variable and the second variable predicts the first variable. In other words, all the variables in a fully recursive model are reciprocally linked.

function *n*. (symbol: f) a mathematical procedure that relates or transforms one number, quantity, or entity to another according to a defined rule. For example, if $y = 2x + 1$, y is said to be a function of x. This is often written $y = f(x)$. Here y is the dependent variable and x is the independent variable.

functional data analysis (**FDA**) an area of statistics in which mathematical FUNCTIONS are used to study how things change across time. It usually involves the use of derivatives to form curves that model the pattern of change in some phenomenon (e.g., health, achievement).

functional principal components analysis the reduction of data to a smaller set of dimensions or components, where the data are FUNCTIONS or curves rather than simple variables. See PRINCIPAL COMPONENTS ANALYSIS.

functional relationship a mathematical equation that describes how values of one variable are dependent on another variable. The formula for a straight line, $y = mx + b$, describes a functional relationship: The value y can be determined by knowing the SLOPE, m, of a line multiplied by a value, x, plus the point where the line crosses the Y-AXIS, b.

functional variable a variable with quantitative values that form a curve when plotted on a graph.

function coefficient a quantitative value that multiplies a variable and that can change depending on other variables or COVARIATES. A function coefficient differs from other coefficients (e.g., a REGRESSION COEFFICIENT) in that it can vary whereas the others are constant over all entities or participants. A function coefficient is often used in statistical methods such as REGRESSION ANALYSIS and TIME-SERIES ANALYSIS, particularly when the data change over time or space.

fundamental science see BASIC SCIENCE.

funnel plot a graph of EFFECT SIZES along the horizontal X-AXIS and some measure of sample size along the vertical Y-AXIS. It is used to check for the possibility of bias in META-ANALYSIS studies. A funnel plot that has a pyramidal, upside-down cone shape—as in the following example—is thought to indicate low levels of bias.

The funnel shape reflects the fact that most of the studies found approximately

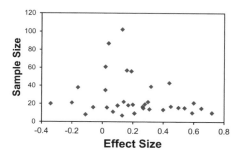

medium-sized effects and used somewhat large sample sizes, with a few small or large effects found with smaller sample sizes. Consider, however, a graph of effect sizes and sample sizes that depicts a growing, slanted mountain shape increasing from lower left to upper right. This positive slanted pattern would indicate a direct and positive relationship (i.e., bias) between effect size and sample sizes. Conversely, if the graph revealed a left-slanted mountain shape, from upper left to lower right, this would indicate a negative relationship (and bias) between effect size and sample size. This negative, inverse pattern would reveal that smaller effects could only be noticed with large sample sizes and larger effects could be seen with smaller sample sizes.

funnel sequence a method of structuring the order of questions in surveys and interviews that starts with general items and gradually narrows the focus to more specific items.

FU plot abbreviation for FOLLOW-UP PLOT.

fuzzy set theory an approach to SET THEORY that allows gradations of membership in a set, instead of only assigning a 0 or a 1 that would indicate nonmembership or absolute membership, respectively. Some phenomena are more readily modeled with fuzzy set theory than conventional binary set theory, particularly when there is incomplete information or varying degrees of the entity being studied. For example, in designation of a mental illness fuzzy set theory may be employed to allow for cases in which individuals could be classified somewhere between an absence or a full diagnosis of a particular condition.

F value see F RATIO.

Gg

G² symbol for LIKELIHOOD-RATIO CHI-SQUARE.

G² test see LIKELIHOOD-RATIO TEST.

gain score see DIFFERENCE SCORE.

Galbraith plot see RADIAL PLOT. [Rex F. **Galbraith**, British statistician]

GAM abbreviation for GENERALIZED ADDITIVE MODEL.

gambler's fallacy a failure to recognize the independence of chance events, leading to the mistaken belief that one can predict the outcome of a chance event on the basis of the outcomes of past chance events. For example, a person might think that the more often a tossed coin comes up heads, the more likely it is to come up tails in subsequent tosses, although each coin toss is independent of the others, and the true probability of the outcome of any toss is still just .5.

game theory a branch of mathematics concerned with the analysis of the behavior of decision makers (called *players*) whose choices affect one another. Game theory is often used in both theoretical modeling and empirical studies of conflict, cooperation, and competition, and it has helped to structure interactive decision-making situations in numerous disciplines, including economics, political science, social psychology, and ethics. A simple game theory example could be a scenario from a reality television show in which the final two players are each asked privately to make a decision to share or keep the entire game prize. The players are told that the outcome will be decided by the following rules: (a) If one player decides to keep the entire prize and the other decides to share, then the first player gets the entire prize. (b) If both players decide to share the prize, then the prize is split. (c) If both players decide to keep the entire prize, then both leave empty-handed. The players must therefore base their decisions on what they think the other will choose to do.

GAMM abbreviation for GENERALIZED ADDITIVE MIXED MODEL.

gamma (symbol: γ) *n.* any of several different statistical indices, most commonly GOODMAN–KRUSKAL'S GAMMA.

gamma distribution a pattern of data that can be depicted on vertical and horizontal axes where information is known about two parameters, scale and shape, both of which are values equal to zero or higher. For example, a **standard gamma distribution** is one in which the shape and location parameters of the continuous probability function are 0 and 1, respectively. Gamma distributions are common in Bayesian statistics and often used to describe waiting times and reaction times.

garbage in, garbage out (**GIGO**) an expression indicating that if the data used in analyses are not reliable or coherent, the results will not prove useful. The phrase was first used in computer science, cautioning users against trusting computer output derived from unreliable input. Although the term is not used much currently, it remains a relevant reminder to researchers to pay attention to how studies are designed and how data are collected, and not to depend on analyses to produce meaningful results where the input data are not themselves meaningful.

GARCH abbreviation for GENERALIZED

AUTOREGRESSIVE CONDITIONAL HETERO-SCEDASTICITY.

Gaussian distribution see NORMAL DISTRIBUTION. [Karl Friedrich **Gauss** (1777–1855), German mathematician]

Gaussian kernel a formula or function used in SMOOTHING out the rectangular bar pattern of data in a HISTOGRAM. It is a particular type of KERNEL DENSITY ESTIMATOR often applied to estimate the shape of the underlying PROBABILITY DENSITY FUNCTION, which is believed to have a more continuous pattern than that found in histograms and other discrete plots. [Karl Friedrich **Gauss**]

Gauss–Markov theorem a fundamental theorem of mathematical statistics that deals with the generation of linear unbiased ESTIMATORS with minimum variance in the GENERAL LINEAR MODEL. [Karl Friedrich **Gauss**; Andrei **Markov** (1856–1922), Russian mathematician]

GCR abbreviation for GREATEST CHARACTERISTIC ROOT.

GEE abbreviation for GENERALIZED ESTIMATING EQUATION.

Gehan's generalized Wilcoxon test see BRESLOW TEST. [Edmund A. **Gehan** (1929–), U.S. biostatistician; Frank **Wilcoxon** (1892–1965), Irish-born U.S. statistician]

gender research the study of issues related to femininity, masculinity, sexuality, and gay, lesbian, and transsexual concerns. Gender research may involve QUALITATIVE studies that use focus groups or interviews to understand behavior as well as QUANTITATIVE analyses that examine potential gender group differences or prediction models. For example, traditional research has assessed whether there are significant group differences between men and women on math and science performance. In more recent times, more complex prediction models are sometimes examined to demonstrate that multiple factors are needed to understand performance, such as cultural norms and expectations.

general effect an overall scientific finding about a relationship between phenomena. For example, a researcher examining the relationship between various teaching styles and academic performance may conclude the existence of a general effect in which better student performance is obtained with an applied, hands-on style. This conclusion might be made on the basis of a single EXPERIMENTAL DESIGN in which students were randomly assigned to teaching conditions, or more likely it may be based on multiple studies with varied conditions (e.g., male or female teacher, elementary or secondary education) and course content (e.g., math, science, language). See also INTERACTION EFFECT; MAIN EFFECT.

generalizability *n.* the extent to which results or findings obtained from a sample are applicable to a broader population. For example, a theoretical model of change would be said to have high generalizability if it applied to numerous behaviors (e.g., smoking, diet, substance use, exercise) and varying populations (e.g., young children, teenagers, middle-age and older adults). A finding that has greater generalizability also is said to have greater EXTERNAL VALIDITY, in that conclusions pertain to situations beyond the original study.

generalizability coefficient a numerical value that indicates how likely a finding is to occur across different conditions, people, and situations. A generalizability coefficient is similar to the RELIABILITY COEFFICIENT used in CLASSICAL TEST THEORY and can take on values ranging from zero to one. See GENERALIZABILITY THEORY.

generalizability model in GENERALIZABILITY THEORY, a statistical model used to predict and test the broader applicability of a specific study's results for a particular phenomenon. For example, a generalizability model could be hypothesized and assessed to determine whether certain findings are relevant not only to the young adults initially evaluated but also to older adults, males and females, and individuals from different ethnic backgrounds.

generalizability theory a framework of principles and assumptions about how to determine the RELIABILITY of a set of data. Researchers investigate the various FACETS of a study (items, raters, settings, etc.) to understand specific sources of error and to determine the conditions under which observations will be consistent and applicable across different contexts (e.g., age groups, geographic regions, socioeconomic status).

generalized additive mixed model (GAMM) a type of statistical procedure used to analyze data with more than one subgroup (e.g., different classrooms of students) when the data within subgroups are correlated. The generalized additive mixed model is an extension of the GENERAL LINEAR MODEL that takes such dependency within subgroups into account. It is also a specialized form of a MIXED-EFFECTS MODEL, as it incorporates both FIXED EFFECTS (e.g., specific choice of teaching strategy) and RANDOM EFFECTS (e.g., a set of student study times randomly chosen from a set of all possible times).

generalized additive model (GAM) a statistical procedure for analyzing data that may not strictly conform to a LINEAR MODEL. A generalized additive model still assumes that there is an ADDITIVE EFFECT of the INDEPENDENT VARIABLES on the DEPENDENT VARIABLE, such that no effect depends on any other and the individual effects add up to the total explained effect. It is an extension of the GENERAL LINEAR MODEL that allows a researcher to posit and assess various nonlinear patterns in a data set and discern which pattern most closely approximates the data. See ADDITIVE MODEL.

generalized autoregressive conditional heteroscedasticity (GARCH) a condition sometimes present in TIME-SERIES data and particularly in AUTO-REGRESSIVE MOVING-AVERAGE MODELS, in which one observation depends on a previous observation (see AUTO-CORRELATION). In other words, the data show differing VARIANCE of one variable at different levels of another variable (i.e., heteroscedasticity). GARCH models are important in econometrics and financial modeling.

generalized distance see MAHALA-NOBIS DISTANCE.

generalized estimating equation (GEE) any of a set of statistical procedures used to analyze correlated data that do not require all of the ASSUMPTIONS of the GENERAL LINEAR MODEL, such that normality and independence are not needed.

generalized eta squared (symbol: η_G^2) in analysis of variance, a measure of effect that takes into account specific features in the design that could alter the size of the effect. Generalized eta squared ranges from 0 to 1 in value, with larger values indicating that a specific factor explains more of the VARIANCE in the DEPENDENT VARIABLE. See also ETA SQUARED.

generalized gamma distribution a PROBABILITY DISTRIBUTION that extends the GAMMA DISTRIBUTION to include a third parameter of rate or location as well as the two parameters of scale and shape. It often is used in SURVIVAL ANALYSIS to model the time until a specific event, such as death or onset of an illness. Various special cases of the generalized gamma distribution include the EXPONENTIAL DISTRIBUTION and LOG-NORMAL DISTRIBUTION.

generalized inverse (g inverse) a MATRIX that serves as a divisor to another matrix when there is not a common denominator matrix or INVERSE MATRIX readily available to provide a direct solution. A generalized inverse also allows the division of matrices that are not square (i.e., do not have the same number of rows as columns). For example, in a MULTIVARIATE ANALYSIS OF VARIANCE, one obtains a ratio by dividing the matrix of between-groups variance by the matrix of within-groups variance. If it is difficult to find the within-groups inverse matrix that would allow this calculation, a generalized inverse could be found instead. Also called **pseudoinverse**.

generalized least squares regression a procedure used to estimate RE-GRESSION COEFFICIENTS and other PA-RAMETERS when ERROR VARIANCES are correlated or show HETEROGENEITY OF VARIANCE, such that a conventional ordinary LEAST SQUARES REGRESSION procedure will produce biased results.

generalized linear mixed model (**GLMM**) a model that takes into account both specifically selected FIXED EFFECTS and a broader range of RANDOM EFFECTS in the data. A generalized linear mixed model is an extension of the more common GENERALIZED LINEAR MODEL (which only involves fixed effects) and provides greater EXTERNAL VALIDITY when generalizing beyond a specific study. Also called **generalized mixed model** (**GMM**). See also MIXED-EFFECTS MODEL.

generalized linear model (**GLM**) a broad class of statistical procedures that allow variables to be related in a prediction or REGRESSION ANALYSIS by taking into account the variance of each. The generalized linear model extends ordinary LEAST SQUARES REGRESSION to include other procedures—such as LOGISTIC REGRESSION and POISSON REGRESSION—that allow for the use of categorical dependent variables having very lopsided distributions, in which most people endorse a particular category (e.g., no heroin use) or fail to endorse a particular category (e.g., heroin use). See also GEN-ERALIZED MULTILEVEL MODEL.

generalized maximum-likelihood ratio test a NONPARAMETRIC statistical analysis used with data that follow a CHI-SQUARE DISTRIBUTION but do not meet conventional ASSUMPTIONS such as NORMALITY and HOMOGENEITY OF VARIANCE. It can be used in more circumstances than the traditional MAXI-MUM LIKELIHOOD ratio test.

generalized mixed model (**GMM**) see GENERALIZED LINEAR MIXED MODEL.

generalized multilevel model a more specific extension of the GENERAL-IZED LINEAR MODEL that incorporates procedures for addressing multiple groups of data, such as classrooms of students.

generalized odds ratio an extension of the proportional hazards model (see COX REGRESSION ANALYSIS) that is used to assess relationships between ORDINAL VARIABLES having more than two categories.

generalized Poisson distribution an extension of the traditional POISSON DISTRIBUTION in which the variance and mean are not required to be equal. For example, the number of deaths from automobile crashes may be a constant low rate in a rural area with a temperate climate. In an urban area having different weather and traffic patterns throughout the year, however, the number of automobile-related deaths may vary widely such that a generalized Poisson distribution may provide a more accurate representation of the process over time.

generalized variance see DETERMI-NANT.

general linear model (**GLM**) a large class of statistical techniques, including REGRESSION ANALYSIS, ANALYSIS OF VARIANCE, and CORRELATION ANALYSIS, that describe the relationship between a DEPENDENT VARIABLE and one or more explanatory or INDEPENDENT VARIABLES. It is a more specific type of GENERALIZED LINEAR MODEL. Most statistical techniques employed in the behavioral sciences can be subsumed under the general linear model.

general norm a standard that is widely accepted, such as a regularly occurring level of performance on an intelligence test or an expected pattern of alcohol use on college campuses.

general systems theory an interdisciplinary conceptual framework focusing on wholeness, pattern, relationship, hierarchical order, integration, and organization. It was designed to move beyond the reductionistic and mechanistic tradition in science (see REDUCTIONISM) and integrate the fragmented approaches and different classes of phenomena studied by contemporary science into an organized whole. In this framework, an entity or phenomenon should be viewed holistically as part of a set of elements interacting with one another; the goal of general systems theory is to identify and understand the principles applicable to all entities in the set. The impact of each element depends on the role played by other elements involved and order arises from interaction among these elements. Also called **systems theory**.

generating function a mathematical method of finding the number of occurrences in a large sequence. It is formed by a power series where the kth variable is raised to the kth power. For example, a generating function may take the form $a_0X^0 + a_1X^1 + a_2X^2 + a_3X^3 \ldots$, where a is a weight and the generating function is a weighted sum. See also MOMENT GENERATING FUNCTION; PROBABILITY GENERATING FUNCTION.

geometric distribution the PROBABILITY DISTRIBUTION of the number of failed trials before the first success in a series of BERNOULLI TRIALS.

geometric mean a measure of CENTRAL TENDENCY calculated for k numbers $x_1 \ldots x_k$ as $(x_1 \times x_2 \times x_3 \ldots x_k)^{1/k}$. A geometric mean is similar to an arithmetic

MEAN except that the latter involves the sum of the quantities divided by the number of quantities, whereas the former is the product of the quantities with the product raised to the power of 1 divided by the number of quantities. Thus, for the numbers 1, 2, and 3 the arithmetic mean is 6/3 = 2, and the geometric mean is the cube root of $(1)(2)(3) = 6^{1/3} = 1.817$. See also HARMONIC MEAN.

geometric progression a series of numbers in which each successive number is the product of the previous number times a constant. For example, the geometric progression 5, 10, 20, and 40 would have 80 as the next number and the constant, called the common ratio, is 2 (i.e., $2 \times 5 = 10$; $2 \times 10 = 20$; $2 \times 20 = 40$; $2 \times 40 = 80$; etc.). Also called **geometric sequence**; **geometric series**.

geostatistics *n.* a set of methods for analyzing data related to the physical environment. In psychology, for example, geostatistics could be used to understand which factors in the environment can bring about or exacerbate behavioral conditions, such as substance abuse, or spread diseases, such as AIDS.

Gibbs sampling a statistical method of randomly generating sets of data that incorporate the patterns of values or PROBABILITY DISTRIBUTIONS from two or more variables. Also called **Gibbs sampler**. [Josiah W. **Gibbs** (1839–1903), U.S. mathematician and physicist]

GIGO abbreviation for GARBAGE IN, GARBAGE OUT.

Gini coefficient a measure of variance in a FREQUENCY DISTRIBUTION, providing a numerical summary of a LORENZ CURVE. It ranges in value from 0, indicating no variance such that all entities are equal, to 1, indicating maximum variance such that every entity is different. Also called **coefficient of concentration**; **Gini concentration**; **Gini index**; **Gini ratio**; **Gini statistic**. [Corrado **Gini** (1884–1965), Italian statistician and sociologist]

G

g inverse abbreviation for GENERALIZED INVERSE.

Glass's d an EFFECT SIZE measure that represents the standardized difference between means (i.e., the difference in average values for two samples divided by the STANDARD DEVIATION of the second sample). It is often used in META-ANALYSIS and other research in which it is important to determine whether an effect persists across studies in order to consolidate a result. Also called **Glass's delta**. See also COHEN'S D; HEDGES'S G. [Gene V. **Glass** (1940–), U.S. statistician]

GLM 1. abbreviation for GENERAL LINEAR MODEL. **2.** abbreviation for GENERALIZED LINEAR MODEL.

GLMM abbreviation for GENERALIZED LINEAR MIXED MODEL.

global maximum the largest possible value in a set of numbers. For example, the global maximum for a CORRELATION COEFFICIENT is 1, whereas the global maximum for a STANDARD DEVIATION or VARIANCE is not finite (i.e., infinity).

global minimum the smallest possible value in a set of numbers. For example, the global minimum for a CORRELATION COEFFICIENT is –1 and for a STANDARD DEVIATION or VARIANCE it is 0.

GLS abbreviation for generalized least squares. See GENERALIZED LEAST SQUARES REGRESSION.

GMM abbreviation for generalized mixed model. See GENERALIZED LINEAR MIXED MODEL.

Gompertz curve a function or curve used to describe a pattern of growth that is slow at the beginning and end but rather rapid or steep in the middle, thus forming a shape resembling a leaning letter S. For example, the adoption of a fashion fad may follow a Gompertz curve: Few people purchase the product initially but there is a subsequent period of highly increased sales that precedes a lessening of interest in the product and ultimately very low sales as the fad dies out. Gompertz curves often are used in SURVIVAL ANALYSIS. Also called **Gompertz distribution**; **Gompertz function**. [Benjamin **Gompertz** (1779–1865), British mathematician]

Goodman–Kruskal's gamma a measure of association between two CATEGORICAL VARIABLES, where 0 represents no relationship and 1 represents perfect association. For example, a marketing researcher may want to assess the relationship between the location of a store and the type of clothes purchased. A Goodman–Kruskal's gamma of .30 or higher would indicate a medium-sized correlation such that clothes distributors desiring to maximize sales should provide specific kinds of clothes at specific locations. Also called **Goodman–Kruskal's tau**. [Leo A. **Goodman** (1928–) and William Henry **Kruskal** (1919–2005), U.S. statisticians]

goodness of fit the degree to which values predicted by a model agree with empirically observed values. For example, a researcher may wish to assess whether a pattern of frequencies from a study is the same as theoretically expected, whether two CATEGORICAL VARIABLES are independent, or whether a REGRESSION EQUATION correctly predicts obtained data. A small, non-significant value from a GOODNESS-OF-FIT TEST indicates a well-fitting model.

goodness-of-fit test any of various statistical procedures that assess how closely data obtained from a sample match an expected population pattern or model. The CHI-SQUARE GOODNESS-OF-FIT TEST is a commonly used example.

good-subject role the behavior displayed by a participant in a research study who is eager to perform as he or she thinks is desired or wanted. The adoption of such a role could bias study results as the true effect of the INDEPENDENT VARIABLE cannot

G

be adequately determined. See DEMAND CHARACTERISTICS. Compare APPREHENSIVE-SUBJECT ROLE; FAITHFUL-SUBJECT ROLE; NEGATIVISTIC-SUBJECT ROLE.

Gower similarity coefficient a measure of proximity used in CLUSTER ANALYSIS to indicate the similarity of different entities or participants. It may assume values from 0 to 1, with the former indicating items that are very distinct and the latter indicating items that are very similar or alike. [John C. **Gower**]

grade-of-membership model a statistical representation or procedure for describing the underlying structure of continuous data. It is an extension of LATENT CLASS ANALYSIS, which is used with discrete CATEGORICAL DATA, to CONTINUOUS VARIABLES by allowing individuals or entities to simultaneously be partial members of several classes or categories.

Graeco-Latin square (**Greco-Latin square**) an experimental design that superimposes one LATIN SQUARE upon another. In this type of FRACTIONAL FACTORIAL DESIGN, two sets of elements are arranged in the same set of cells in such a way that every row and every column contains each element of both sets once and once only, and each cell contains a different ordered pair. The following is a hypothetical example for research comparing three methods of praise (1, 2, and 3) administered for three types of task (A, B, and C) under three conditions of supervision (α, β, and γ).

	Treatment		
	1	2	3
Participant 1	Aα	Bβ	Cγ
Participant 2	Bγ	Cα	Aβ
Participant 3	Cβ	Aγ	Bα

Graeco-Latin squares are used in research to minimize or eliminate the influence of extraneous variables and to balance ORDER EFFECTS.

Gramian matrix a SQUARE MATRIX formed from the inner products of a set of VECTORS. Gramian matrices are important in STRUCTURAL EQUATION MODELING or when working with COVARIANCE structures. Also called **Gram matrix**. [Jørgen Pedersen **Gram** (1850–1916), Danish mathematician]

grand mean a numerical average (MEAN) of a group of averages. For example, if the average test score for one classroom is 75 and the average score for another classroom is 73, the grand mean of the two classrooms is $(75 + 73)/2 = 74$. Similarly, if an ANALYSIS OF VARIANCE reveals average values of 3, 10, and 20 on a response or DEPENDENT VARIABLE for three groups of study participants, the grand mean of scores—that is, the average of all participants' responses regardless of the condition of the INDEPENDENT VARIABLES—is $(3 + 10 + 20)/3 = 11$.

Granger causality the condition that arises when a TIME SERIES, x, is found to predict values of another time series, y. Granger causality involves a process of HYPOTHESIS TESTING to assess whether a value of x at one time point is related to one or more future values of y. [Clive **Granger** (1934–2009), British-born U.S. economist]

graph *n.* a visual representation of the relationship between numbers or quantities, which are plotted on a drawing with reference to axes at right angles (see X-AXIS; Y-AXIS) and linked by lines, dots, or the like. BAR GRAPHS, HISTOGRAMS, and FREQUENCY POLYGONS are commonly used examples.

graphic model a graph depicting the relations of CONDITIONAL INDEPENDENCE between three or more RANDOM VARIABLES. Graphic models are often used in BAYESIAN NETWORKS and MARKOV CHAINS, in which they take the form of DIRECTED ACYCLIC GRAPHS and UNDIRECTED GRAPHS. Also called **graphical model**.

graphic rating scale a series of anchored points (usually from low to high)

Employee overall performance during past year

1	2	3	4	5
poor	below average	average	above average	excellent

graphic rating scale

on a continuum, often used to evaluate the performance or behavior of individuals in a work or learning environment. For example, a graphic rating scale for assessing an employee's overall performance during the past year might take the form of a line with the response options of 1 (*poor*), 2 (*below average*), 3 (*average*), 4 (*above average*), and 5 (*excellent*) listed, as shown above. The supervisor would mark the line to indicate the employee's performance level.

gray literature research findings that are not readily available because they have not been published in archival sources. Examples include dissertations, papers presented at meetings, papers either not submitted or rejected for publication, and technical reports. Gray literature contributes to the FILE-DRAWER PROBLEM in META-ANALYSIS, the situation in which analytic results are biased due to researchers not having access to nonsignificant findings that are not easily found. Also called **fugitive literature**.

greatest characteristic root (GCR) the largest EIGENVALUE of a matrix that describes the variance of the largest LINEAR COMBINATION of variables in that data array, summarizing the association between a set of independent variables and a set of dependent variables. GCRs are used in analyses involving several variables, such as CANONICAL CORRELATION ANALYSIS, MULTIVARIATE ANALYSIS OF VARIANCE, or PRINCIPAL COMPONENTS ANALYSIS. In the multivariate analysis of variance, for example, one of the methods for assessing the results is

to examine the greatest characteristic root of the between-groups matrix and compare it to the greatest characteristic root of the within-groups matrix. Also called **largest characteristic root**; **Roy's greatest characteristic root**; **Roy's greatest root**; **Roy's largest root**.

greatest-characteristic-root test one of several criteria used to assess the significance of between-groups and within-groups differences in a MULTIVARIATE ANALYSIS OF VARIANCE. It involves finding the largest EIGENVALUE of the between-subjects matrix over the within-subjects matrix. Also called **largest-root test**; **Roy's greatest-root test**; **Roy's greatest-characteristic-root test**; **Roy's largest-root test**; **Roy's root test**. See GREATEST CHARACTERISTIC ROOT.

Greco-Latin square see GRAECO-LATIN SQUARE.

grid sampling the process of dividing an area into equal sections, randomly checking each section, and making improvements and changes to some process based on the findings. Grid sampling is often used in agricultural research and was conducted by Sir Ronald Fisher when he devised the often-used ANALYSIS OF VARIANCE and its accompanying F TEST.

grounded theory a set of procedures for the systematic analysis of unstructured QUALITATIVE DATA so as to derive by INDUCTION a supposition that explains the observed phenomena. A researcher typically observes the entity of interest in a natural setting before drawing conclusions about its nature and existence.

group *n.* a collection of participants in a research study whose responses are to be compared to the responses of one or more other collections of research participants. Participants in a particular group all experience the same experimental conditions or receive the same treatment, which differs from the experimental conditions or treatments participants in other groups experience or receive.

group-average clustering see AVERAGE-LINKAGE CLUSTERING.

group class 1. in statistical methods such as ANALYSIS OF VARIANCE, the designation of the response options for a CATEGORICAL VARIABLE as the levels of an INDEPENDENT VARIABLE. For example, if a researcher is studying religious affiliation, he or she may include gender as a variable in the analysis and use its two distinct options (i.e., female and male) as levels for comparison. **2.** the results derived from such groups.

group-comparison design a type of research approach that investigates potential differences across sets of individuals who are often randomly assigned to a CONTROL CONDITION or to one or more specific EXPERIMENTAL CONDITIONS. Data from a group-comparison design are often analyzed with such statistical methods as a T TEST or ANALYSIS OF VARIANCE. Also called **group-difference design**.

group design any of a variety of procedures intended to compare two or more collections of individuals or entities.

group difference any observed variation between groups of participants in an experiment when considering each group as a single entity. See GROUP-COMPARISON DESIGN.

group dimension the perspective gained by viewing results at a larger, combined level instead of at an individual level. For example, educational researchers may be interested in providing a group dimension by depicting results at the classroom level rather than by individual students.

group distribution the scores for a group of individuals. For example, researchers may be interested in providing the group distribution performance scores for separate classrooms or schools.

group-divisible design a research design in which separate groups each contain a unique set of BLOCKS whose members are assigned a unique pair of treatments. The group-divisible design provides a balanced structure for assigning multiple treatments across blocks and across two or more groups.

grouped data information that is grouped into one or more sets in order to analyze, describe, or compare outcomes at a combined level rather than at an individual level. For example, data from a FREQUENCY DISTRIBUTION may be arranged into CLASS INTERVALS. See also GROUP-COMPARISON DESIGN; GROUP-DIVISIBLE DESIGN.

grouped frequency distribution a description of how often a set of specific responses, organized into equal-sized subsets of possible responses, occur in a sample. It is a type of FREQUENCY DISTRIBUTION that is particularly useful when there are a large number of response choices (e.g., 10–20 or more) and researchers wish to present the information more concisely. For example, suppose that a researcher wants to summarize the individuals in a sample in which age ranges from 18 to 85 years. Instead of listing all 68 different ages, the researcher could combine the data into 5-year intervals, which would produce 14 subsets of ages. More specifically, the researcher would create two columns, listing in the left-hand one the 14 age subsets (e.g., 16–20, 21–25, 26–30, … 81–85). In the right column, the re-

G

searcher would list the frequencies of each age subset; that is, how often each age subset was endorsed by the individuals in the sample, thus reducing a large number of scores into smaller, more manageable groups.

group effect a research finding specific to the group of individuals to which a participant belongs. A group effect could appear in an assigned subset, such as a treatment or intervention, or in a naturally occurring subset, such as age level or classroom. For example, a researcher might be interested in a group effect of a specific reading intervention, or in a group effect of book reading for students in the current decade who may be reading less than previous sets of students owing to more common use of the computer and television.

group experiment an experiment in which subsets of individuals serve as the unit of analysis. For example, a researcher could compare the performance of different classrooms rather than of specific individuals.

group interview an interview in which one or more questioners elicit information from two or more respondents in an experimental or real-life situation. The participation and interaction of a number of people, particularly if they are acquainted with each other as members of a club or similar group, is believed to yield more informative responses than are typically obtained by interviewing individuals separately.

group matching see MATCHING.

group-randomized trial a research design in which groups of individuals are randomly assigned to TREATMENT conditions or CONTROL CONDITIONS. In educational or organizational settings, for example, a group-randomized trial could be used to study classrooms or departments, with HIERARCHICAL LINEAR MODELING and similar analyses that take the larger group membership (e.g., classroom or department) into account

being used to evaluate the data. It is similar to a RANDOMIZED CLINICAL TRIAL but distinct in assigning intact clusters of participants to the specific conditions rather than individual participants. Also called **cluster-randomized trial**.

group sequential design a research design in which a treatment is randomly assigned to different groups at varying times, such that every group receives the treatment eventually. A group sequential design is useful when it is important for each participant to have an opportunity to benefit from the treatment but a comparison group nonetheless is required: The portion of the sample that receives the treatment later acts as a CONTROL GROUP initially.

growth curve a graphic representation of progress over time on a specific variable within a specific group (e.g., the development of an organism, as in the hypothetical example opposite).

Data in a growth chart often are evaluated with TIME-SERIES ANALYSIS, LATENT GROWTH CURVE ANALYSIS, or other longitudinal methods.

growth curve analysis a statistical procedure for assessing the level and rate (SLOPE) of change over time on a specific variable in a sample of individuals. See also LATENT GROWTH CURVE ANALYSIS.

growth function the relationship between a DEPENDENT VARIABLE and several levels of an INDEPENDENT VARIABLE defined in units of time (e.g., days, weeks, months, years).

G statistic 1. a value used to assess the presence of spatial clustering or AUTOCORRELATION in a data set. A large G statistic with a small accompanying P VALUE (e.g., < .05) suggests there are subsets of dependence or clustering. **2.** see G^2.

G study generalizability study: research about the widespread applicability of a particular measure or test. A G study assesses several facets or factors (e.g., in-

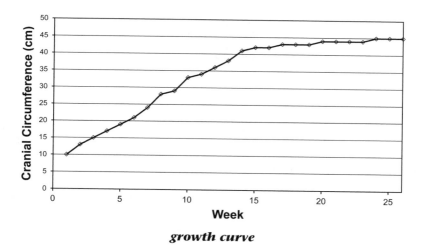

growth curve

strument type, administration occasion) to determine under which conditions the measurement provides reliable information. See also D STUDY.

G test see LIKELIHOOD-RATIO TEST.

Gumbel distribution a statistical pattern often used in SURVIVAL ANALYSIS to describe data having either very large or very small values. It is a type of EXTREME-VALUE DISTRIBUTION. [Emil Julius **Gumbel** (1891–1966), German mathematician]

Guttman scale a type of attitude scale that consists of multiple verbal statements ordered to reflect increasing levels of positive evaluation. Endorsement of a particular statement implies en-

dorsement of all statements less extreme than that statement. For example, Item 1 could state "I believe that education is valuable," Item 2 could state "I believe that people who are educated are more productive," and Item 3 could state "I believe that I would be more productive if I had more education." A person who agreed with the third statement would also agree with the first and second statements. Although generally used to measure attitudes, Guttman scales can also be used to assess other properties of a target of judgment. Also called **cumulative scale**; **scalogram**. [first described in 1944 by Louis **Guttman** (1916–1987), U.S. experimental psychologist]

Hh

h^2 symbol for COMMUNALITY COEFFICIENT.

H_0 symbol for NULL HYPOTHESIS.

H_1 symbol for ALTERNATIVE HYPOTHESIS.

H_a symbol for ALTERNATIVE HYPOTHESIS.

habituation *n.* the weakening of a response to a stimulus, or the diminished effectiveness of a stimulus, following repeated exposure to the stimulus. Compare DISHABITUATION.

half-normal plot a graph in which the ABSOLUTE VALUES obtained for a variable are given along the horizontal *x*-axis and their corresponding probabilities of occurrence under a STANDARDIZED DISTRIBUTION are given along the vertical *y*-axis. For example, a half-normal plot could be used to assess the importance of observed experimental effects: Points that fall close to the mean of zero are considered minor or unimportant, whereas those that are further removed from zero (e.g., two or more standard deviations) are considered significant. Alternatively, when plotting RESIDUALS, points far from zero reveal the existence of OUTLIERS that indicate a poorly fitting regression model. The related full-normal plot (see NORMAL PROBABILITY PLOT) shows both the original positive and negative variable values.

halo effect a rating bias in which a general evaluation (usually positive) of a person, or an evaluation of a person on a specific dimension, influences judgments of that person on other specific dimensions. For example, a person who is generally liked might be judged as more intelligent, competent, and honest than he or she actually is.

hanging rootogram a type of HISTOGRAM in which the horizontal X-AXIS is slightly elevated and the vertical Y-AXIS

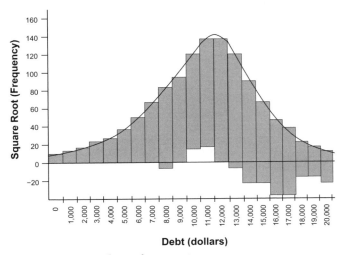

hanging rootogram

depicts the square root of frequencies using bars that "hang" downward from a curve showing the expected NORMAL DISTRIBUTION. Consider the hypothetical example on the previous page.

A hanging rootogram allows researchers to see how well their OBSERVED DISTRIBUTION (e.g., of debt for a group of middle-class families) fits an expected THEORETICAL DISTRIBUTION. If the observed data differ from the expected pattern, the hanging histogram bars will drop below the elevated horizontal axis, thereby indicating places of poor match between the observed and theoretical distributions. Also called **suspended rootogram**. See ROOTOGRAM.

haphazard sampling any method of selecting research participants that is neither random nor systematic and hence likely to be biased. CONVENIENCE SAMPLING is an example. Thus, if researchers decided to solicit participants from an Internet advertisement the process would be biased toward individuals who own a computer and who are more likely to respond to computer-based communications. Depending on the prevalence and likelihood of computer use in various facets of the population, the sample could be biased by gender, ethnicity, geographical location, economic status, or age, among other possible variables.

hard data information that is QUANTITATIVE and specific, usually obtained from rigorous EXPERIMENTAL RESEARCH, systematic measurement, and STATISTICAL ANALYSIS. Hard data are sometimes contrasted with SOFT DATA, which may be more QUALITATIVE and involve anecdotal evidence that is not obtained systematically.

harmonic analysis a form of THEORETICAL STATISTICS used in SIGNAL DETECTION THEORY and neuroscience, which translates signals into frequencies.

harmonic mean a measure of CENTRAL TENDENCY. It is computed for n scores by dividing the scores by the sum of their RECIPROCALS; that is, n divided by the sum of $1/x_1 + 1/x_2 + 1/x_n$. See also GEOMETRIC MEAN; MEAN.

Hartley F_{max} test see F_{MAX} TEST. [Hermann Otto **Hartley** (1912–1980), German-born U.S. statistician]

Hartley test for homogeneity of variance see F_{MAX} TEST. [Hermann Otto **Hartley**]

hat matrix (abbreviation: **H**) in statistical procedures such as LINEAR REGRESSION, a MATRIX used to compare an OBSERVED DISTRIBUTION of values to FITTED VALUES. When there are large discrepancies between the observed and expected (fitted) values, there is evidence for OUTLIERS, indicating that the statistical model may not be appropriate for the data.

Hawthorne effect the effect on the behavior of individuals of knowing that they are being observed or are taking part in research: Participants typically improve their performance simply as a result of knowing that an interest is being shown in them, rather than as a result of any experimental manipulation. The Hawthorne effect is named after the Western Electric Company's Hawthorne Works plant in Cicero, Illinois, where the phenomenon was first observed during a series of studies on worker productivity conducted from 1924 to 1932. These **Hawthorne Studies** began as an investigation of the effects of particular job characteristics—such as illumination conditions, monetary incentives, and rest breaks—on productivity, but it evolved into a much wider consideration of the role of worker attitudes, supervisory style, and group dynamics when initial results showed that performance increased regardless of the levels of the job characteristics employed by the company.

hazard analysis an analysis used to identify the level of risk associated with, say, an engineering process or a new medical or food product. It involves identifying potential hazards, determining their probability, and evaluating the likely severity of their effects. Also called **hazard modeling**.

hazard function a mathematical formula that describes the relationship between the risk of a particular event occurring and time. It is one element of SURVIVAL ANALYSIS.

hazard plot in HAZARD ANALYSIS, a graph used to indicate the rate of failures over successes across specific points in time. For example, in a study of a particular disease, a hazard plot would show the number of individuals who died from the disease divided by the number who survived at various time points during the course of the study.

hazard rate in HAZARD ANALYSIS, a value used to indicate the immediate potential or risk of an event's occurrence at a particular instance in time. It often is used in health studies and will vary depending on the time point of interest. For example, a hazard rate may be used to determine whether an individual who is abstinent from alcohol or drugs at six months is likely to relapse in the near future.

hazard ratio in HAZARD ANALYSIS, a value used to indicate the risk of an event's occurrence in a reference group versus that in a comparison group. For example, a researcher studying rehabilitation among older adults who have broken a bone may compute a hazard ratio for completion of rehabilitation treatment according to cognitive status, with high functioning patients considered the reference group and low functioning patients the comparison group.

hazard regression a statistical procedure used in SURVIVAL ANALYSIS to analyze which variables are useful in predicting the occurrence of an event, such as disease or death.

Hedges's g an EFFECT SIZE measure that represents the standardized difference between means. Hedges's g differs from the more widely used COHEN'S D in that, whereas both use a pooled STANDARD DEVIATION in the denominator, the former uses $n - 1$ and the latter uses n when calculating the standard deviations. Thus, Hedges's g tends to be considered as having less bias than Cohen's d. See also GLASS'S D. [Larry V. **Hedges**, U.S. statistician]

Hellinger distance a value that describes how dissimilar two PROBABILITY DISTRIBUTIONS are. A Hellinger distance of 1 indicates that the two distributions are completely different, whereas a Hellinger distance of 0 indicates the two distributions are probabilistically the same. [Ernst David **Hellinger** (1883–1950), German-born U.S. mathematician]

heterogeneity *n.* the quality of having very different characteristics or values. For example, HETEROGENEITY OF VARIANCE is present in an ANALYSIS OF VARIANCE when the average squared distance of each score from the mean differs for each group in the study (e.g., control group vs. treatment group). Compare HOMOGENEITY.

heterogeneity of regression the situation in which there are different values for the SLOPE between a COVARIATE and DEPENDENT VARIABLE across different groups in an ANALYSIS OF COVARIANCE. Heterogeneity of regression violates one of the basic assumptions of such an analysis, as it indicates that the differences among groups are too substantial for a researcher to average REGRESSION COEFFICIENTS in order to estimate the effect of a covariate on a dependent variable. Compare HOMOGENEITY OF REGRESSION.

heterogeneity of variance the situation in which the variance of a random variable is different at each level or value of another variable. Var($y|x$) is not the same for all values of x; that is, the variance in y is a function of the variable x. Heterogeneity of variance violates one of the basic assumptions of REGRESSION ANALYSIS and other statistical prodedures. Also called **heteroscedasticity**. Compare HOMOGENEITY OF VARIANCE.

heteromethod block in a MULTITRAIT–MULTIMETHOD MATRIX, the block of values representing the correlations between traits (e.g., depression, self-esteem) assessed with different procedures (e.g., paper-and-pencil survey, clinical interview, physiological measure). If the correlations are similar regardless of the type of procedure used to assess the traits, a researcher may conclude he or she is assessing the true value of the traits rather than obtaining scores that are merely ARTIFACTS of the measurement procedure used. See HETERO-TRAIT–HETEROMETHOD COEFFICIENT.

heteroscedasticity *n.* see HETEROGENEITY OF VARIANCE. —**heteroscedastic** *adj.*

heterotrait–heteromethod coefficient in a MULTITRAIT–MULTIMETHOD MODEL, a number that indicates the strength of the association between different characteristics or variables measured with different procedures. See also HETEROMETHOD BLOCK.

heterotrait–monomethod coefficient in a MULTITRAIT–MULTIMETHOD MODEL, a number that indicates the strength of the association between different characteristics or variables measured with the same procedures. See also HETEROMETHOD BLOCK.

heuristic *n.* in the social sciences, a conceptual device, such as a model or working hypothesis, that is intended to explore or limit the possibilities of a question rather than to provide an explanation of the facts. See also CONSTRUCT.

Heywood case any CORRELATION COEFFICIENT, REGRESSION COEFFICIENT, FACTOR LOADING, or similar PARAMETER estimate having a value that is impossible or very rare (e.g., a negative ERROR VARIANCE estimate). Heywood cases may indicate any of the following: a sample that is too small to adequately estimate the parameters; data that do not have a NORMAL DISTRIBUTION or that contain OUTLIERS; a misspecified model that is not appropriate for the data; or a parameter whose true value is so close to a boundary (e.g., 1 or 0) in the population that its estimate exceeded this limit due to sampling fluctuation.

hidden Markov model a statistical representation of a series of time-ordered events in which (a) each event is related to the immediately prior event but not to earlier events and (b) the process that is driving the series is not directly observable (i.e., is a LATENT VARIABLE). For example, consider a study of the number of cigarettes a day that are smoked by individuals in a smoking cessation program. If a hidden Markov model were used to represent the process, this would indicate the presence of unobservable states or events (e.g., peer pressure to smoke; stress or environmental cues to smoke, as in the social context of a bar) that are linked to the number of cigarettes smoked, and that the best prediction of the number of cigarettes that will be smoked the following day is the number smoked on the current day rather than the number smoked on any prior days. See MARKOV CHAIN.

hidden variable an undiscovered causative variable. When a relationship is found between variables x and y, variable x may erroneously be thought to be the cause of y. However, the cause of y may be a hidden variable z that is correlated with variable x. Also called **lurking variable**; **third variable**. See THIRD-VARIABLE PROBLEM.

hierarchical agglomerative clustering see AGGLOMERATIVE CLUSTERING.

hierarchical clustering a multistage procedure in which entities are grouped into ever larger and more heterogeneous clusters or separated into ever smaller and more homogeneous clusters (see CLUSTER ANALYSIS). The most common form of hierarchical clustering is AGGLOMERATIVE CLUSTERING, in which the individual entities are first paired, then these pairs are paired, and so on until ultimately all entities form a single large group or cluster. A second form of hierarchical clustering is DIVISIVE CLUSTERING, in which all entities initially are part of one large group which is split into progressively smaller groups according to dissimilarity until ultimately each entity is in its own group or cluster. The outcome of both types of hierarchical clustering may be represented graphically as a DENDROGRAM.

hierarchical correlation a pattern in which variables or entities that are similar or proximal to one another show a higher degree of association than variables or entities that are further away. Hierarchical correlations may be examined via CLUSTER ANALYSIS. For example, individuals belonging to the same cluster may have similar scores compared to individuals who are part of more distant clusters or groups.

hierarchical design see HIERARCHICALLY NESTED DESIGN.

hierarchical linear model (HLM) a statistical model that acknowledges different levels in the data, such that individuals or entities within each level have correlated scores. The model enables a researcher to test hypotheses about cross-level effects and partition the VARIANCE and COVARIANCE components among levels. For example, hierarchical linear models often are used in educational research since they can account for the fact that students within a classroom will behave similarly, as will classrooms within the same school, and so on up the hierarchy of levels. Also called **multilevel model**.

hierarchically nested design any research design that involves several levels of sampling, such that the entities on the lower levels of the design are nested or subsumed within higher order groups. For example, a hierarchically nested design for an educational study might involve students (A), who are nested within classrooms (B), which are nested within schools (C), which are further nested within school districts (D). Several statistical procedures (e.g., ANALYSIS OF VARIANCE, REGRESSION ANALYSIS, HIERARCHICAL LINEAR MODELS) also incorporate a hierarchical aspect. Also called **hierarchical design; nested design**.

hierarchical model a statistical procedure that takes into account situations in which lower level variables or entities are part of a larger set or sets. For example, a hierarchical FACTOR ANALYSIS model posits that relationships among a subset of lower level primary variables (e.g., verbal, mathematical, and social intelligence) can be explained by a higher order or general factor (e.g., general intelligence). Similarly, a HIERARCHICAL LINEAR MODEL is a particular type of hierarchical model that includes several levels of actual variables as components of a progressively larger overall set. Also called **nested model**.

hierarchical regression a statistical procedure in which hypothesized predictors of a DEPENDENT VARIABLE are included in an analysis in several steps that illuminate the contribution of each set of variables. For example, a researcher interested in predicting career satisfaction could use hierarchical regression to assess the contribution of individual-level variables (e.g., career influence), institutional-level variables (e.g., work climate), and interactional-level variables (e.g., work respect). In this form of MULTIPLE REGRESSION, the investigator would enter the variables into the analysis in a prespecified order, usually one suggested by temporal factors or by a particular theory. After separately adding each of the three variables, hierarchical regression would enable an assessment of whether and how much the COEFFICIENT OF MULTIPLE DETERMINATION increased after each addition. Also called **hierarchical multiple regression; hierarchical regression analysis; sequential regression**. Compare SIMULTANEOUS REGRESSION.

hierarchical sum of squares see TYPE II SUM OF SQUARES.

higher order correlation see PARTIAL CORRELATION.

higher order design any research design that attempts to understand a phenomenon by assessing the separate and joint effects of several factors at once. For example, an experiment could be conducted to assess the effect of a TREATMENT condition versus a CONTROL CONDITION on cognitive functioning while simultaneously assessing the influence of gender; this would allow an assessment of the MAIN EFFECTS for each factor (treatment condition and gender) as well as the interaction between them. Data from such a design involving only one outcome variable could be assessed using a higher order ANALYSIS OF VARIANCE. If one or more COVARIATES were included in the study as additional INDEPENDENT VARIABLES, a higher order ANALYSIS OF COVARIANCE would be used for data analysis, and if several measures of cognitive functioning were assessed a higher order MULTIVARIATE ANALYSIS OF VARIANCE would be adopted.

higher order factor a dimension or variable that incorporates other dimensions or variables that are at a more basic or primary level. For example, a higher order factor of general intelligence could be posited to explain several primary factors of intelligence (e.g., verbal, mathematical, social), which in turn could explain several sets of variables (e.g., vocabulary, comprehension, prob-

lem solving, algebra, relationships, communication).

higher order interaction in an ANALYSIS OF VARIANCE, the joint effect of three or more INDEPENDENT VARIABLES on the DEPENDENT VARIABLE. For example, a researcher could conduct a study to assess the effect of a particular treatment (e.g., treatment vs. no treatment) as well as the effect of age and socioeconomic status on cognitive functioning. This design would allow an examination of the MAIN EFFECTS for treatment, age, and socioeconomic status individually; the TWO-WAY INTERACTIONS between treatment and age, age and socioeconomic status, and treatment and socioeconomic status; and the higher order THREE-WAY INTERACTION between treatment, age, and socioeconomic status.

higher order partial correlation see PARTIAL CORRELATION.

highest posterior density region the area in a CREDIBLE INTERVAL that has the greatest probability of occurrence for a given score.

high-risk design a research design used to study individuals or groups in which there is thought to be a high probability of some disorder. For example, a high-risk design could be used to study families in which one or more individuals have bipolar disorder so as to gauge the likelihood of additional family members subsequently experiencing the disorder.

hill-climbing algorithm a mathematical procedure for arriving at an acceptable, although not necessarily ideal, solution to an optimization problem. A researcher can use a hill-climbing algorithm to make small improvements (i.e., as in inching up a hill) until gradually a better solution is obtained.

hinge *n.* in EXPLORATORY DATA ANALYSIS, either of the scores in a data set that divide the lower 25% of cases (the **lower**

H

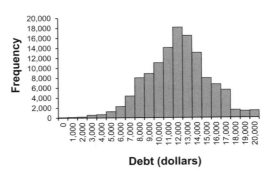

Debt (dollars)

histogram

H

hinge) and the upper 25% of cases (the **upper hinge**) from the remainder of the cases.

histogram *n.* a graphical depiction of continuous data using bars of varying height, similar to a BAR GRAPH but with blocks on the *x*-axis adjoining one another so as to denote their continuous nature.

Consider the example above, showing the average credit card debt of individuals. Bars along the *x*-axis represent amount of debt and are connected to one another, while the heights of the bars represent the number or frequency of individuals with each debt amount.

historical analysis research that examines past events to understand current or future events. For example, researchers could perform a historical analysis of an individual's or a family's substance use experiences to understand the present substance use behavior of that person or group.

historical control group a CONTROL GROUP whose participants are selected to be similar to those in the treatment group on the basis of data collected some time in the past.

historical prospective study a research project that examines LONGITUDINAL DATA obtained in the past to track the incidence of a particular disorder over time and its association with various risk factors. For example, a re-

searcher could examine the health records of, say, smokers and nonsmokers to follow the path of an illness from before its manifestation through to its diagnosis and treatment. It is distinct from PROSPECTIVE RESEARCH generally, which begins with individuals who are apparently healthy in the present and moves forward to investigate whether a specific disorder will occur over time.

historigram *n.* a graph of quantitative TIME-SERIES data, with the value of the variable being examined given on the vertical Y-AXIS and time given on the horizontal X-AXIS. For example, a historigram for a weight reduction program might depict daily weight along the *y*-axis over a six-month time period along the *x*-axis (see overleaf).

If the weight reduction program was effective then the historigram would be expected to slope downward from a high point at the upper left.

history effect the influence of events or circumstances outside an experiment on an outcome variable of interest. QUASI-EXPERIMENTAL RESEARCH often attempts to take history effects into account in order to rule out potential CONFOUNDS to a posited or apparent link between two variables. An example would be the occurrence of an actual earthquake during a field study of the effects of training in earthquake preparedness; this would likely increase news coverage of earthquakes, thereby resulting in greater knowledge dissemination outside of the training program.

history taking the process of compiling background information about a patient or research participant. Information can be obtained from the individual directly and from other sources, such as the patient's family, hospitals or clinics, psychiatrists or psychologists, neurologists, social workers, and others who have direct knowledge of the individual.

HLM abbreviation for HIERARCHICAL LINEAR MODEL.

Hodges–Lehmann estimator an ESTIMATOR used to approximate the median value of a population, when conventional PARAMETRIC STATISTICS are not appropriate as the data do not meet statistical ASSUMPTIONS. It is an example of a ROBUST ESTIMATOR. [Joseph L. **Hodges** (1922–2000) and Erich L. **Lehmann** (1917–2009), U.S. statisticians]

holdout sample see CROSS-VALIDATION SAMPLE.

holdover effect see CARRYOVER EFFECT.

Holland–Rosenbaum test of unidimensionality see ROSENBAUM'S TEST OF UNIDIMENSIONALITY.

homogeneity *n.* equality or near equality between two statistical quantities of interest. The term most often is used in connection with different populations. For example, homogeneity of means would be present in a ONE-WAY ANALYSIS OF VARIANCE if the average values of the population groups being investigated were the same. Compare HETEROGENEITY.

homogeneity of covariance the condition in which multiple groups in an experimental design have the same COVARIANCE MATRIX. A basic assumption in a MULTIVARIATE ANALYSIS OF VARIANCE, it is the multivariate analog of HOMOGENEITY OF VARIANCE.

homogeneity of regression the condition in which the regression slopes between the dependent variable of interest and the covariates are equal for all population groups. It is a basic assumption in an ANALYSIS OF COVARIANCE.

homogeneity of variance the statistical ASSUMPTION of equal variance, meaning that the average squared distance of a score from the mean is the same across all groups sampled in a study. This condition must be fulfilled in statistical methods that use a single term to represent how widely scores vary across groups, as with ANALYSIS OF VARIANCE, MULTIPLE REGRESSION analysis, and other procedures. Also called **equality of variance**; **homoscedasticity**. Compare HETEROGENEITY OF VARIANCE.

homoscedasticity *n.* see HOMOGENEITY OF VARIANCE. **—homoscedastic** *adj.*

honestly significant difference test see TUKEY'S HONESTLY SIGNIFICANT DIFFERENCE TEST.

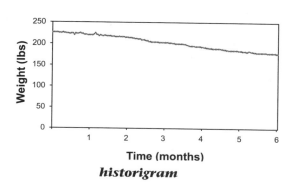

historigram

horizontal axis see X-AXIS.

hot-deck imputation one of several methods of inserting values for missing data (see IMPUTATION) in which missing observations or data points are replaced by values from similar responses in the sample at hand. Suppose that a patient survey was conducted in two hospitals, A and B, and that five people from Hospital A failed to respond to an item of the survey. Sampling five values from the respondents who did respond to that item at Hospital A and substituting these values for the missing observations is an example of a hot-deck imputation. Compare COLD-DECK IMPUTATION.

Hotelling's trace a statistic used in a MULTIVARIATE ANALYSIS OF VARIANCE to evaluate the significance of any MAIN EFFECTS and INTERACTION EFFECTS that have been identified. It is the pooled ratio of the amount of variance in an effect that is attributed to the independent variable (i.e., the EXPLAINED VARIANCE) to the amount of variance that remains unexplained (i.e., the ERROR VARIANCE). Also called **Hotelling–Lawley trace**. See also PILLAI–BARTLETT TRACE; WILKS'S LAMBDA. [Harold **Hotelling** (1895–1973), U.S. mathematician; D. N. **Lawley**]

Hotelling's T^2 test a MULTIVARIATE ANALYSIS OF VARIANCE used to test the significance of the mean difference between two groups in their scores or outcomes on multiple dependent variables. An extension of the univariate T TEST, it is applicable to only two groups, rather than three or more groups. Also called **Hotelling's T^2**; **Hotelling's T-squared test**; **multivariate t test**; **T-squared test**. [Harold **Hotelling**]

hot-hand hypothesis the widespread but groundless belief that a string of successes will breed further success. According to this belief, which is common in professional sports, financial speculation, and the like, the probability that a run of successes will continue becomes greater the longer that the winning streak goes on. This is in defiance of the laws of probability. A gambler's belief that his or her winning streak on a casino slot machine will continue is an example of the hot-hand hypothesis. Also called **streaky hypothesis**.

household interview survey any series of door-to-door or telephone interviews with household residents in which samples are based on geographic boundaries, such as cities and counties. The national census conducted every 10 years by the United States Census Bureau is an example of a household interview survey.

HSD test abbreviation for honestly significant difference test. See TUKEY'S HONESTLY SIGNIFICANT DIFFERENCE TEST.

H spread see INTERQUARTILE RANGE.

hyperbolic distribution a continuous PROBABILITY DISTRIBUTION the logarithm of which is a hyperbola (see example opposite).

The distribution is similar in shape to the NORMAL DISTRIBUTION but decreases more slowly and is generally asymmetric around its MODE.

hyperbolic logarithm see LOGARITHM.

hyperexponential distribution a continuous distribution in which the probability of obtaining a particular value for a RANDOM VARIABLE, x, depends on, or is a FUNCTION of, the proportionally increasing or decreasing values of another random variable, y.

hypergeometric distribution a discrete PROBABILITY DISTRIBUTION of the number of successes (or failures) in a sequence of draws that involve SAMPLING WITHOUT REPLACEMENT; in this situation each trial has two possible outcomes and the outcome of each trial alters the probability of the outcome of the next and succeeding trials. If the sampling is done with replacement a BINOMIAL DISTRIBUTION is obtained instead.

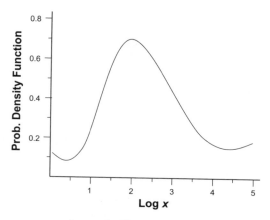

hyperbolic distribution

H

hyperparameter *n.* in BAYESIAN statistics, a numerical constant describing a probability within a population that is itself based upon a distribution of prior probabilities. For example, if p is the probability of success in each of a series of BERNOULLI TRIALS and a BETA DISTRIBUTION with parameters a and b (a, b > 0) is chosen as the PRIOR DISTRIBUTION for the parameter p, then a and b are hyperparameters.

hypothesis *n.* (*pl.* **hypotheses**) an empirically testable proposition about some fact, behavior, relationship, or the like, usually based on theory, that states an expected outcome resulting from specific conditions or assumptions.

hypothesis testing a statistical inference procedure for determining whether or not a given proposition about a population PARAMETER should be rejected on the basis of observed sample data. See also SIGNIFICANCE TESTING.

hypothesis validity in experimental design, the extent to which any results obtained from a study are likely to provide evidence for or against the hypothesis under investigation. If the hypothesis validity of a study is low, even clear results are unlikely to provide either support for, or refutation of, theoretically derived predictions in a decisive and unambiguous manner.

hypothetical construct see CONSTRUCT.

hypothetico-deductive method a method of scientific inquiry in which the credibility or explanatory power of a falsifiable hypothesis is tested by making predictions on the basis of this hypothesis and determining whether or not these predictions are consistent with empirical observations. It is one of the most widely used SCIENTIFIC METHODS for disproving hypotheses and building corroboration for those that remain. Also called **mathematico-deductive method**.

Ii

I_n symbol for WILLIAMS'S AGREEMENT MEASURE.

ICC 1. abbreviation for INTRACLASS CORRELATION coefficient. **2.** abbreviation for ITEM CHARACTERISTIC CURVE.

IDA abbreviation for INITIAL DATA ANALYSIS.

idealized experiment see THOUGHT EXPERIMENT.

identification *n.* in CONFIRMATORY FACTOR ANALYSIS and STRUCTURAL EQUATION MODELING, a situation in which the model contains a sufficient number of both fixed and free PARAMETERS to result in unique estimates from the observed data. A model is said to be identified or identifiable if a unique set of its parameter values can be determined from observations. OVERIDENTIFICATION occurs when there are more knowns than free parameters, and UNDERIDENTIFICATION occurs when it is not possible to estimate all of the model's parameters. See also IDENTIFICATION PROBLEM; OVERIDENTIFIED MODEL; UNDERIDENTIFIED MODEL.

identification problem in CONFIRMATORY FACTOR ANALYSIS and STRUCTURAL EQUATION MODELING, the problem as to whether the PARAMETER estimates obtained are stable given the number of subjects and variables in the observed sample data. The problem arises from the fact that more than one set of parameter values may be associated with the same PROBABILITY DISTRIBUTION of a statistical model. When the identification problem arises, a model is said to be unidentifiable and its parameter values cannot be interpreted. For example, assume that the two parameters b and c in the linear regression model $y = ax + b + c + N(0, \sigma^2)$ are fully interchangeable. In

this case, an infinite number of combinations of their values may yield the same model prediction, such that one cannot determine from a given set of observations which values of the parameters actually generated the data.

identity matrix (symbol: **I**) a SQUARE MATRIX with values of one along its main diagonal and zeros elsewhere. The following is an example.

$$\begin{bmatrix} 1 & 0 & 0 \\ 0 & 1 & 0 \\ 0 & 0 & 1 \end{bmatrix}$$

Identity matrices are used in FACTOR ANALYSIS solutions and matrix algebra. Also called **unit matrix**.

idiographic *adj.* relating to the description and understanding of an individual case, as opposed to the formulation of general laws describing the average case. An **idiographic approach** involves the thorough, intensive study of a single person or case in order to obtain an in-depth understanding of that person or case, as contrasted with a study of the universal aspects of groups of people or cases. In those areas of psychology in which the individual person is the unit of analysis (e.g., in personality, developmental, or clinical psychology), the idiographic approach has appeal because it seeks to characterize a particular individual, emphasizing that individual's characteristic traits and the uniqueness of the individual's behavior and adjustment, rather than to produce a universal set of psychological constructs that might be applicable to a population. Compare NOMOTHETIC.

IID independent and identically distributed: denoting a collection of random variables that have the same PROBABIL-ITY DISTRIBUTION but are statistically un-related to one another. For example, a sequence of random tosses of a fair coin is IID, as is a sequence of colored balls randomly drawn from an urn with re-placement after each draw. IID is a key assumption in the CENTRAL LIMIT THEO-REM and also a standard assumption in probability and statistical theory.

ill-conditioned *adj.* denoting a SQUARE MATRIX in which the ratio of the largest EIGENVALUE to the smallest eigenvalue is much larger than 1, such that small changes to the entries in the matrix result in a significantly large change in its INVERSE MATRIX. An ill-conditioned matrix thus is very sensitive to inconsequential changes (e.g., round-ing errors in computer calculations), thereby making the calculations it yields difficult to interpret. See also COLLIN-EARITY.

illusory correlation 1. the appear-ance of a relationship that in reality does not exist. **2.** an overestimation of the de-gree of relationship (i.e., correlation) be-tween two variables. For example, if an unusual action occurred at the same time that an adolescent was present, the assumption that the action was carried out by the adolescent would be an illu-sory correlation.

impact analysis a quantitative ana-lytic procedure used to assess the net success or failure of a program, usually through controlled experimentation. It is appropriate only if the program's ob-jectives are specifiable and measurable, the program is well implemented for its intended participants, and the outcome measures are reliable and valid. Also called **impact assessment**. See also SUMMATIVE EVALUATION.

implicit measure a measurement of a psychological construct that is obtained while the individual being assessed is unaware that the measurement is taking place, often used to assess attitudes, ste-reotypes, and emotions in social cogni-tion research. Typically, an implicit measure is assessed as a response out-come of an experimental procedure in which the participant is engaged in a cognitive task. For example, a word-stem completion task might be employed to assess emotion implicitly, such that jo_ could be completed to form a positive emotional word (e.g., *joy*) or a neutral word (e.g., *jog*).

importance sampling a MONTE CARLO RESEARCH method for computing expected values of a RANDOM VARIABLE in which samples are generated from a distribution similar to the distribution of interest, which cannot be directly sampled. The method is particularly use-ful for high-dimensional models with many variables or parameters and is fre-quently used in BAYESIAN statistics.

imposed etics the imposition of one's own cultural perspective and bias when studying another culture. See ETICS.

improper prior in BAYESIAN statistics, a PRIOR DISTRIBUTION that does not in-tegrate to one. Although an improper prior in itself is not necessarily problem-atic, especially when the corresponding POSTERIOR DISTRIBUTION is proper, it can sometimes lead to an uninterpret-able and misleading estimate of the BAYES FACTOR.

imputation *n.* a procedure for filling in missing values in a data set before ana-lyzing the resultant completed data set. There are several methods of imputa-tion, including HOT-DECK IMPUTATION, in which missing values are replaced with values drawn randomly from a sim-ilar sample in the same data set; and **re-gression imputation**, in which missing values are replaced with predicted values estimated from a statistical model of the nonmissing values in the data. See also COLD-DECK IMPUTATION; MULTIPLE IM-PUTATION.

incidental stimulus an unintentional or coincidental stimulus that may occur during an experiment or study, which may elicit an unplanned response from the participants or result in the distortion of research findings.

inclusion–exclusion criteria in clinical research, criteria used to determine which individuals are eligible to participate in a particular study. Inclusion criteria might specify, for example, age range, whereas exclusion criteria might specify, for example, the existence of more than one illness or psychological disorder.

incomplete block design an experimental design in which treatments are grouped into sets or "blocks," not all of which include every treatment, and each block is administered to a different group of participants. Incomplete block designs often are employed to avoid administering too many treatment conditions to the same group of participants, which may contribute to undesirable error. For instance, the following arrangement of four treatments (A, B, C, D) is an incomplete block design: Block 1 = A-B-C; Block 2 = A-B-D; Block 3 = A-C-D; and Block 4 = B-C-D. In this particular design, each block contains three treatments, each treatment occurs three times across all blocks, and each pair of treatments occurs together two times across all blocks. An incomplete block design with such properties is called a **balanced incomplete block design**. Compare COMPLETE BLOCK DESIGN. See BLOCK DESIGN.

incomplete counterbalancing an experimental design that controls for ORDER EFFECTS by using a limited number of possible sequences of treatments administered in such a way that each treatment appears equally often in each position. For instance, the following arrangement of sequences of three treatments (A, B, C), each assigned to a different subgroup of participants, demonstrates incomplete counterbalancing: A-B-C to Subgroup 1, B-C-A to Subgroup 2, and C-A-B to Subgroup 3. Compare

COMPLETE COUNTERBALANCING. See also LATIN SQUARE.

incomplete factorial design see FRACTIONAL FACTORIAL DESIGN.

incremental validity the improvement obtained by adding a particular procedure or method to an existing combination of assessment methods. In other words, incremental validity reflects the value of each measure or piece of information to the process and outcome of assessment. The standards for evaluating incremental validity depend on the goal of the assessment, such as whether one wishes to gather unique information, predict a criterion, make a diagnosis, or choose a treatment. For example, teacher observations of the daily frequency of a child's vocal tic may not add critical information in diagnosing a tic disorder but may contribute significantly when the purpose of the assessment is to monitor treatment progress.

independence *n.* **1.** the condition of being unrelated to or free from the influence of something else. For example, a standard assumption in ANALYSIS OF VARIANCE, MULTIPLE REGRESSION, and many other statistical analyses is **independence of observations**, or the fact that the occurrence of one observation does not influence the occurrence of any others. Similarly, variables exhibiting independence have a complete lack of relationship, such that none is influenced by any other and that changes in one have no implication for changes in any other. See also INDEPENDENT EVENTS. **2.** see STATISTICAL INDEPENDENCE. **—independent** *adj., n.*

independence model any statistical representation of a concept or process in which explanatory variables are assumed not to interact and instead to be unaffected by one another.

independent contribution in MULTIPLE REGRESSION, the portion of the variance that can be explained uniquely by a given explanatory variable after

PARTIALING out or holding constant the effects of all other explanatory variables. See also COLLINEARITY.

independent diagonals model see DIAGONALS MODEL.

independent events the situation in which observing one event does not provide any additional information about the occurrence or outcome of another event. For example, the outcome of a coin flip and the Dow Jones Industrial Average are independent events, whereas the temperatures of two consecutive days are not necessarily independent. Formally, two events, A and B, are independent if the probability of event A is the same as the conditional probability of event A given event B, that is, $P(A) = P(A|B)$, or equivalently, $P(B) = P(B|A)$. Compare DEPENDENT EVENTS.

independent groups see INDEPENDENT SAMPLES.

independent-groups analysis of variance see BETWEEN-SUBJECTS ANALYSIS OF VARIANCE.

independent-groups design see BETWEEN-SUBJECTS DESIGN.

independent-measures analysis of variance see BETWEEN-SUBJECTS ANALYSIS OF VARIANCE.

independent-measures design see BETWEEN-SUBJECTS DESIGN.

independent random sampling see SIMPLE RANDOM SAMPLING.

independent random variables RANDOM VARIABLES that exhibit a complete lack of relationship, such that no information about one variable, x, conveys any information about another variable, y. Any events related to these variables are INDEPENDENT EVENTS.

independent samples groups of individuals or sets of data that are unrelated to one other. For example, experimental groups consisting of different and unrelated participants are independent samples, as are the data sets obtained from

these groups. Also called **independent groups**. Compare DEPENDENT SAMPLES.

independent-samples analysis of variance see BETWEEN-SUBJECTS ANALYSIS OF VARIANCE.

independent-samples design see BETWEEN-SUBJECTS DESIGN.

independent-samples t test a T TEST used to analyze data from a BETWEEN-SUBJECTS DESIGN, in which the different groups of individuals or other entities measured are not associated with one another. In the independent-samples t test, one calculates the value of the TEST STATISTIC t from the means, standard deviations, and sizes of the two groups of interest, and compares its value to a T DISTRIBUTION for a given DEGREE OF FREEDOM under the assumptions of normality and INDEPENDENCE of observations, among others. Also called **independent-measures t test; unrelated t test**. Compare DEPENDENT-SAMPLES T TEST.

independent sampling a process for selecting a sample of study participants from a larger potential group of individuals such that the probability of each person being selected for inclusion is not influenced by which people have been chosen already. The resulting samples will be INDEPENDENT SAMPLES.

independent variable (**IV**) the variable in an experiment that is specifically manipulated or is observed to occur before the occurrence of the dependent, or outcome, variable, in order to assess its effect or influence. Independent variables may or may not be causally related to the DEPENDENT VARIABLE. In statistical analyses—such as PATH ANALYSIS, REGRESSION ANALYSIS, and STRUCTURAL EQUATION MODELING—an independent variable is likely to be referred to as a **causal variable, explanatory variable, regressor variable,** or PREDICTOR VARIABLE. See also EXOGENOUS VARIABLE; TREATMENT.

indeterminacy *n.* **1.** the inability to uniquely determine the form or magnitude of a relationship. **2.** the inability to arrive at a unique solution to a problem or mathematical form. **3.** in FACTOR ANALYSIS, the inability to form a unique representation of the factor structure.

index *n.* **1.** a reference point, standard, or indicator. **2.** a variable that is employed to indicate the presence of another phenomenon or event. **3.** a number formed from a combination of other measures to represent another, more general entity. For example, an index of a person's graduate school potential might be formed from his or her undergraduate grade point average and score on an admissions test.

index of determination see COEFFICIENT OF DETERMINATION.

index of discrimination the degree to which a test or test item differentiates between individuals of different performance levels, often given as the percentage difference between high-performing and low-performing individuals who answer a target item correctly. Also called **discrimination index**.

index of dispersion see DISPERSION MEASURE.

index of forecasting efficiency in LINEAR REGRESSION, a measure of the amount of reduction in prediction errors relative to the baseline prediction using the mean of the dependent variable, when prediction errors are measured by the STANDARD ERROR OF ESTIMATE. Formally, the index of forecasting efficiency is defined as $1 - \sqrt{(1 - r^2)}$, where r^2 is the COEFFICIENT OF DETERMINATION. An index value of 0 indicates no reduction in errors beyond the mean prediction, whereas a value of 1 indicates the full, maximum possible reduction.

index of reliability see RELIABILITY COEFFICIENT.

index of validity see VALIDITY COEFFICIENT.

index of variability see DISPERSION MEASURE.

indicator variable 1. see DUMMY VARIABLE. **2.** see MANIFEST VARIABLE.

indifference point the intermediate region between experiential opposites. For example, on the pleasure–pain dimension, it is the degree of stimulation that provokes an indifferent or neutral response.

indifferent stimulus any stimulus that has not yet elicited the reaction being studied.

indirect correlation see NEGATIVE CORRELATION.

indirect measurement a method in which a researcher gathers data about one variable (or a combination of variables) as a means of representing a second variable of interest, which cannot be assessed in a more straightforward manner. See PROXY VARIABLE.

indirect relationship in STRUCTURAL EQUATION MODELING, a correlation between two variables that involves an intervening variable or MEDIATOR. For example, age may affect rate of pay, which in turn may affect job satisfaction: This being so, the correlation between age and job satisfaction would be an indirect relationship. The term is often used incorrectly to denote a NEGATIVE RELATIONSHIP. Compare DIRECT RELATIONSHIP.

individual comparison see COMPARISON.

individual differences traits or other characteristics by which individuals may be distinguished from one another. See also SUBJECT VARIABLE.

individual-differences scaling (**INDSCAL**) a method of studying how personal attributes influence judgments about the similarity among members or items of a category. A form of MULTIDIMENSIONAL SCALING, it assumes that people may differ on both the characteristics they use to define a category and the importance they place on each characteristic. The method not only yields an overall PROXIMITY MATRIX for a group of individuals as a whole but also provides a unique proximity matrix for each individual in the group. Also called **weighted multidimensional scaling**.

individual-difference variable see SUBJECT VARIABLE.

INDSCAL abbreviation for INDIVIDUAL-DIFFERENCES SCALING.

induction *n.* **1.** a general conclusion, principle, or explanation derived by reasoning from particular instances or observations. Compare DEDUCTION. **2.** the process of inductive reasoning itself. **—inductive** *adj.*

inductive statistics see INFERENTIAL STATISTICS.

inequality constraint in parameter ESTIMATION and other optimization problems, a condition requiring that particular items do not have the same value. For example, one may wish to find the values of *a* and *b* that minimize a function $f(a, b) = 3a^4 - 5a^2b + 2b^2 + 10$ under the following inequality constraints: $0 < a < 10$ and $b < 0$. Compare EQUALITY CONSTRAINT.

inference *n.* **1.** a conclusion deduced from an earlier premise or premises according to valid rules or procedures for drawing such a conclusion. Some hold that an inference, as contrasted with a mere conclusion, requires that the person making it actually believes that the inference and the premises from which it is drawn are true. Also called **logical inference**. **2.** in statistical analysis, a conclusion about a population based on logical reasoning from data gathered about a smaller sample (see INFERENTIAL STATISTICS). The most common example of this type of inference is statistical hypothesis testing (see INFERENTIAL TEST). **—inferential** *adj.*

inferential statistics a broad class of statistical techniques that allow INFERENCES about characteristics of a population to be drawn from a sample of data from that population while controlling (at least partially) the extent to which errors of inference may be made. These techniques include approaches for testing hypotheses, estimating the value of parameters, and selecting among a set of competing models. Also called **inductive statistics; interpretive statistics**. Compare DESCRIPTIVE STATISTICS.

inferential test any statistical procedure used to evaluate hypotheses about differences between sample and population distributions. Examples include the CHI-SQUARE GOODNESS-OF-FIT TEST, the F TEST, and the T TEST. Inferential tests more commonly are known as **significance tests** (see SIGNIFICANCE TESTING).

inferential validity the extent to which causal inferences made in a laboratory setting are applicable to the real-life experiences they are meant to represent. See also EXTERNAL VALIDITY.

infinite sequence an ordered list of numbers or items that continues without end. Examples of an infinite sequence are

$$S = \{1, 1/2, 1/4, 1/8, 1/16, \ldots\}$$

and

$$V = \{a, ab, ab^2, ab^3, ab^4, \ldots\}.$$

The sum of the terms of an infinite sequence is called an **infinite series**.

influence analysis a set of techniques that allows one to determine the degree to which specific data points affect the overall result of a statistical procedure. For example, in REGRESSION ANALYSIS it is used to examine which observations have a disproportionate influence on the proposed REGRESSION EQUATION.

information matrix see FISHER'S INFORMATION.

informative prior in BAYESIAN statistics, a type of PRIOR DISTRIBUTION based on large amounts of previously accumulated knowledge about the phenomenon of interest. An informative prior tends to provide more specific information and have a stronger influence upon calculations of an associated POSTERIOR DISTRIBUTION than a NONINFORMATIVE PRIOR.

informed consent a person's voluntary agreement to participate in a procedure on the basis of his or her understanding of its nature, its potential benefits and possible risks, and available alternatives. Informed consent is a fundamental requirement of research with humans and typically involves having participants sign documents prior to the start of a study describing specifically what their involvement would entail and noting that they are free to decline participation or to withdraw from the research at any time. See also INSTITUTIONAL REVIEW BOARD.

initial data analysis (IDA) an examination of the quality of a data set that is undertaken before beginning more complex statistical tests of hypotheses. It often involves calculating DESCRIPTIVE STATISTICS such as the mean and STANDARD DEVIATION, identifying minimum and maximum values, and graphing the data points to determine whether their arrangement follows a known or expected distribution. IDA is important for ensuring that data conform to assumptions of the statistical models that will be used for subsequent formal analysis.

inlier *n.* an incorrect value in a data set. Inliers may arise from SYSTEMATIC ERROR, respondent error, or processing error. For example, a researcher may inadvertently report a value in the wrong unit, such as including a RAW SCORE in a distribution of STANDARDIZED SCORES.

institutional research a study conducted to obtain information about an academic setting. For example, a university may research its faculty, staff, students, finances, technology, campus climate, and other characteristics so as to facilitate better decision making.

institutional review board (IRB) a committee named by an agency or institution to review research proposals originating within that agency for ethical acceptability and compliance with the organization's codes of conduct. IRBs help protect research participants and are mandatory at any U.S. institution receiving federal funds for research.

institutional survey in INSTITUTIONAL RESEARCH, a questionnaire or interview used to collect information about a university and its operations.

instructional variable 1. any INDEPENDENT VARIABLE that is studied in researching the outcomes and effectiveness of learning programs. Examples of instructional variables include the specific activities used, instructor quality, learner workload, and learner motivation. **2.** more generally, any set of directions manipulated in an experiment. For example, a researcher investigating goal-setting may wish to assess how the performance of participants who are instructed simply to do their best differs from that of participants told to try to achieve a specified target level.

instrument *n.* any tool, device, or other means by which researchers assess or gather data about study participants. Examples include tests, INTERVIEWS, QUESTIONNAIRES, SURVEYS, RATING SCALES, and reaction-time apparatus. See also ASSESSMENT INSTRUMENT.

instrumentalism *n.* **1.** in the philosophy of science, the position that theories are not to be considered as either true or false but as instruments of explanation that allow observations of the world to be meaningfully ordered. **2.** a theory of knowledge that emphasizes the pragmatic value, rather than the truth value, of ideas. In this view, the value of an idea, concept, or judgment lies in its ability to explain, predict, and control one's concrete functional interactions with the experienced world. This view is related to PRAGMATISM. **—instrumentalist** adj., n.

instrumental variable in REGRESSION ANALYSIS, STRUCTURAL EQUATION MODELING, or PATH ANALYSIS, a new variable substituted for an INDEPENDENT VARIABLE when the latter is correlated with the ERROR TERM. Often a MEDIATOR, an instrumental variable must be associated with the independent variable it is replacing.

instrumentation n. the creation and use of equipment and devices (including psychological tests) for the measurement of some attribute or the control of experiments (e.g., automation of stimulus presentation and data collection). It is important that a measurement instrument not only be trustworthy and reliable but also properly maintained and consistently administered so as to ensure INTERNAL VALIDITY.

instrumentation effect any change in the DEPENDENT VARIABLE in a study that arises from changes in the measuring instrument used. For example, an experimenter may subtly but unintentionally alter his or her testing method across sessions, such that a pretest and a posttest are administered differently. Instrumentation effects pose a threat to INTERNAL VALIDITY. See also INSTRUMENT DRIFT.

instrument drift changes in an INSTRUMENT, usually gradual and often predictable, that can threaten the validity of conclusions drawn from the data obtained with that instrument. An example would be the stretching of spring scales. Periodic recalibration of the measuring device helps minimize or rectify instrument drift. Also called **instrument decay**. See also OBSERVER DRIFT.

intact group a naturally occurring collection of individuals, rather than one to which participants have been randomly assigned. An example is a classroom of students in a school. Intact groups often are used in studies using a NONEQUIVALENT-GROUPS DESIGN.

integral n. **1.** a whole number (e.g., 2, 9, 11), as opposed to numbers that are fractions (e.g., 1/4, 1.5). **2.** the area underneath a curve plotted on an x-axis and y-axis between two points, a and b. It is one of two main concepts—the other being the DERIVATIVE—applied within calculus to the study of change and area. Also called **antiderivative**.

intention-to-treat analysis in RANDOMIZED CLINICAL TRIALS, a strategy for minimizing BIAS in which a researcher examines data for all patients who met the criteria for initial entry into the trial and were to receive the experimental treatment, regardless of whether or not they actually complete the trial or experience the treatment. For example, many people enrolled in a weight-loss study for whom the new diet being investigated is ineffective may drop out. Since the remaining participants primarily are those actually losing weight, the new diet may seem to be more beneficial than it actually is if the researcher were to examine data only for the individuals who finished the trial.

interaction analysis the identification and examination of an INTERACTION EFFECT among variables using INTERACTION CONTRASTS and other techniques.

interaction contrast the statistical comparison of specific levels of the various INDEPENDENT VARIABLES studied in a FACTORIAL DESIGN. For example, suppose a researcher obtains a significant F RATIO in an ANALYSIS OF VARIANCE and discovers that three methods of instruction (A_1, A_2, A_3) and two types of content (B_1, B_2) jointly influence student academic performance. He or she could then use several different interaction contrasts to examine which specific combinations of methods and content have the greatest influence. Thus, the researcher may evaluate how A_1 and A_2 interact with B_1 and B_2, how A_1 and A_3 interact with B_1 and B_2, and so forth. Interaction contrasts may be undertaken as suggested by ongoing evaluation of study data (see POST HOC COMPARISON) or may be decided upon in advance (see A PRIORI COMPARISON). Also called **interaction comparison**.

interaction effect in a FACTORIAL DESIGN, the joint effect of two or more independent variables on a dependent variable above and beyond the sum of their individual effects: The independent variables combine to have a different (and multiplicative) effect, such that the value of one is contingent upon the value of another. This indicates that the relationship between the independent variables changes as their values change. For example, if a researcher is studying how gender (female vs. male) and dieting (Diet A vs. Diet B) influence weight loss, an interaction effect would occur if women using Diet A lost more weight than men using Diet A. Interaction effects contrast with—and may obscure— MAIN EFFECTS. See also HIGHER ORDER INTERACTION. Compare ADDITIVE EFFECT.

interaction sum of squares the SUM OF SQUARES associated with the INTERACTION EFFECT between two or more variables. In an ANALYSIS OF VARIANCE or MULTIPLE REGRESSION, the total sum of squares can be divided into that for each variable individually, that for the interaction of the variables, and that due to error.

interaction variance in a FACTORIAL DESIGN, the amount of variance in the dependent variable that is explained by an INTERACTION EFFECT between two or more independent variables.

intercept *n.* the point at which either axis of a graph is intersected by a line plotted on the graph. For example, it is the value of y when $x = 0$ in an equation of the form $y = a + bx$, or the value of x where a REGRESSION LINE crosses the y-axis, as shown below. See also X-INTERCEPT; Y-INTERCEPT.

interclass correlation the degree of bivariate relationship between two variables from different measurement classes (i.e., the variables have distinct metrics and variances). For example, one may

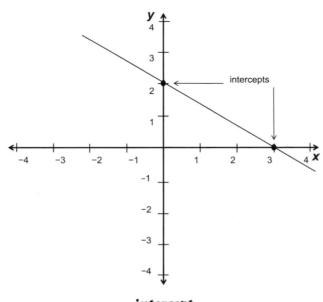

intercept

use an interclass correlation to determine the relation of IQ points (a class of measurement representing aptitude) to grade point averages (a class of measurement representing achievement), or the relation of length (e.g., inches) to weight (e.g., pounds). Currently, the only interclass correlation in common use is the Pearson PRODUCT-MOMENT CORRELATION COEFFICIENT. Compare INTRACLASS CORRELATION.

interclass variance a rare synonym of between-groups variance. See BETWEEN-GROUPS MEAN SQUARE.

intercoder reliability see INTERRATER RELIABILITY.

intercorrelation *n.* the CORRELATION between each variable and every other variable in a group of variables.

interdecile range the difference between the ninth and first DECILES of a distribution (i.e., the number obtained by subtracting the 10th PERCENTILE score from the 90th percentile score). The interdecile range provides a measure of DISPERSION in a data set that is minimally affected by OUTLIERS (extreme values). See also INTERQUARTILE RANGE.

interitem correlation the degree of correlation between each test item in a set, used as a measure of the INTERNAL CONSISTENCY of a test and thus of its RELIABILITY. For example, a participant's responses to each item on a 10-item test could be correlated with his or her responses to every other item on the test to determine the extent to which the items reflect the same construct.

intermediary variable see MEDIATOR.

internal consistency the degree of interrelationship or homogeneity among the items on a test, such that they are consistent with one another and measuring the same thing. Internal consistency is an index of the RELIABILITY of a test. Also called **internal consistency reliability; internal reliability; scale**

homogeneity. See also INTERITEM CORRELATION.

internal validity the degree to which a study or experiment is free from flaws in its internal structure and its results can therefore be taken to represent the true nature of the phenomenon. In other words, internal validity pertains to the soundness of results obtained within the controlled conditions of a particular study, specifically with respect to whether one can draw reasonable conclusions about cause-and-effect relationships among variables. Compare EXTERNAL VALIDITY.

interobserver reliability see INTERRATER RELIABILITY.

interpolation *n.* a strategy for determining an unknown value given knowledge of surrounding data points. For example, if the average score on a test is 70 for a group of beginner students and the average score on the same test is 90 for an advanced group of students, one might use interpolation to estimate an average score of 80 on the test for an intermediate group of students.

interpretive phenomenological analysis (IPA) a QUALITATIVE approach in which a researcher explores how a participant understands his or her personal and social worlds and gives meaning to particular experiences, events, and states. For example, the strategy might be used to understand how a person comes to terms with the death of a spouse. IPA uses STRUCTURED INTERVIEWS to gather verbal and nonverbal information, which is then analyzed to uncover and describe underlying themes.

interpretive statistics see INFERENTIAL STATISTICS.

interquartile range (IQR) an index of the DISPERSION within a data set: the difference between the 75th and 25th PERCENTILE scores (also known as the upper and lower HINGES) within a distri-

I

bution. Also called **H spread**; **mid-spread**.

interrater reliability the extent to which independent evaluators produce similar ratings in judging the same abilities or characteristics in the same target person or object. It often is expressed as a CORRELATION COEFFICIENT. If consistency is high, a researcher can be confident that similarly trained individuals would produce similar scores on targets of the same kind. If consistency is low, there is little confidence the obtained scores could be reproduced with a different set of raters. Also called **intercoder reliability**; **interjudge reliability**; **interobserver reliability**; **interscorer reliability**.

interrupted time-series design a QUASI-EXPERIMENTAL DESIGN in which the effects of an intervention are evaluated by comparing outcome measures obtained at several time intervals before and several time intervals after the intervention was introduced. Unlike traditional TIME-SERIES DESIGNS, which make use of a continuous predictor variable, an interrupted time-series design uses a categorical predictor—the absence or presence of an intervention.

interscorer reliability see INTER-RATER RELIABILITY.

intertrial interval (ITI) the time between successive presentations of the stimulus in a series of experimental trials.

interval *n.* a range of scores or values, such as a CLASS INTERVAL or CONFIDENCE INTERVAL.

interval-censored observation an event of interest whose exact value or timing is not known because it occurred during an interval of time when recording did not take place. Interval-censored observations are common in clinical trials, during which patients are seen only at prescheduled times rather than being continuously monitored. For example, in a study of asthmatic symptoms among mine workers, the onset of a particular symptom in an individual might only be known to have occurred between two health examinations. See CENSORED DATA.

interval data numerical values that indicate magnitude but lack a "natural" zero point. Interval data represent exact quantities of the variables under consideration, and when arranged consecutively they have equal differences among adjacent values (regardless of the specific values selected) that correspond to genuine differences between the physical quantities being measured. Temperature is an example of interval data: The difference between 50 °F and 49 °F is the same as the difference between 40 °F and 39 °F, but a temperature of 0 °F does not indicate that there is no temperature. Compare RATIO DATA. See also INTERVAL SCALE.

interval estimate an estimated range of likely values for a given population PARAMETER. For example, a researcher might use data from a sample to determine that the average score on a particular variable in the larger population falls between 20 and 25. Compare POINT ESTIMATE.

interval recording a process in which a researcher divides a specific observation period into equally sized smaller time periods (intervals) and indicates whether or not a target behavior occurred during each interval. Either PARTIAL-INTERVAL RECORDING or WHOLE-INTERVAL RECORDING may be used. See also TIME SAMPLING.

interval sampling a form of RANDOM SAMPLING in which participants at uniformly separated points are selected for study and the starting point for selection is arbitrary. An example is choosing every 10th name from a list of candidates.

interval scale a scale marked in equal intervals so that the difference between any two consecutive values on the scale is equivalent regardless of the two values selected. Interval scales lack a true, meaningful zero point, which is what distinguishes them from RATIO SCALES. For example, Fahrenheit temperature uses an interval scale: The difference between 50 °F and 49 °F is the same as the difference between 40 °F and 39 °F, but a temperature of 0 °F does not indicate that there is no temperature. See also INTERVAL DATA.

interval variable a variable that is measured using an INTERVAL SCALE. Because values on such a scale are equally spaced, the differences between values of an interval variable are meaningful. Compare ORDINAL VARIABLE.

interval width the difference between the upper REAL LIMIT and the lower real limit of the CLASS INTERVALS used in a FREQUENCY DISTRIBUTION. For example, one might construct a distribution showing the number of students with test scores between 1 and 10 points, 11 and 20 points, 21 and 30 points, and so forth. The corresponding real limits of each class interval are 0.5 and 10.5, 10.5 and 20.5, 20.5 and 30.5, and so on. Subtracting the real lower limit from the real upper limit (e.g., 10.5 – 0.5) yields an interval width of 10.

intervening variable see MEDIATOR.

intervention *n.* in research design, an EXPERIMENTAL MANIPULATION.

intervention research strategies and processes designed to measure the change in a situation or individual after a systematic modification (i.e., diet, therapeutic technique, etc.) has been imposed or to measure the effects of one type of intervention program as compared to those of another program. Experimentation is the most common type of intervention research but CLINICAL TRIALS and qualitative studies may also be used. Also called **intervention study**.

interview *n.* a directed conversation in which a researcher, therapist, clinician, employer, or the like (the **interviewer**) intends to elicit specific information from an individual (the **interviewee**) for purposes of research, diagnosis, treatment, or employment. Conducted face to face or by telephone, interviews may be either standardized, including set questions, or open ended, varying with material introduced in responses by the interviewee. Their RELIABILITY is of particular concern, and interviewers must be careful to minimize or eliminate personal judgment and biases in evaluating responses. See STRUCTURED INTERVIEW; UNSTRUCTURED INTERVIEW.

interviewer effect the influence of the characteristics of an interviewer upon the responses provided by an interviewee. The interviewer's age, gender, and level of experience may affect the manner in which the interviewee responds, as may his or her general demeanor and nonverbal cues. For example, a person might discuss sensitive topics, such as sexual or drinking behavior, more openly and truthfully with an interviewer who is of the same gender.

intraclass contingency table a table that presents the pooled frequency counts on certain CATEGORICAL VARIABLES for pairs of entities where there is no meaningful distinction between the pair. Thus, it is an amalgamation of the separate CONTINGENCY TABLES for the pair members individually. For example, suppose a researcher wishes to examine the occurrence of cancer and heart disease across sibling pairs and genetic twins. Since it is irrelevant which person in each pair is affected by a disease (i.e., what matters is simply that the disease is present in the pair), the researcher might study the relationship between the diseases by creating an intraclass contingency table that shows the overall number of sibling pairs with each disease and the overall number of twin pairs with each disease.

intraclass correlation the degree of homogeneity among unordered members (people, items, etc.) of a group. For example, it may reflect the level of agreement among different judges rating a specific attribute. It is indexed by the **intraclass correlation coefficient** (**ICC**), which ranges from 0 to 1 in value. A larger ICC indicates more homogeneity, and thus that a correspondingly smaller proportion of the total variance in a dependent variable is attributable to INDIVIDUAL DIFFERENCES within the group. Compare INTERCLASS CORRELATION.

intraclass variance within-groups variance: the variability among entities in a group. See WITHIN-GROUPS MEAN SQUARE.

intraindividual differences the variations between two or more traits, behaviors, or characteristics of a single person. For example, certain aptitude tests measure a testee's strengths in mathematical, verbal, and analytic abilities; differences among the three standardized scores represent intraindividual differences. Compare INDIVIDUAL DIFFERENCES.

invariance *n.* the property of being unchanged by a TRANSFORMATION. For example, after adding a constant value to each of a set of scores on a test, the degrees of difference among the scores will demonstrate invariance, being the same for the original and transformed set. —**invariant** *adj.*

inventory *n.* a list of items, often in question form, used in describing and studying behavior, interests, and attitudes.

inverse correlation see NEGATIVE CORRELATION.

inverse distribution function an inverted CUMULATIVE DISTRIBUTION FUNCTION: for any given probability value from 0 to 1, a formula that yields the specific value that a random variable

will assume or below which it will fall. Also called **percent point function**.

inverse factor analysis see Q-TECHNIQUE FACTOR ANALYSIS.

inverse Fisher transformation a statistical procedure applied to convert the PROBABILITY DENSITY FUNCTION of a data set to one that will yield a shape that more closely resembles a NORMAL DISTRIBUTION. See FISHER'S R TO Z TRANSFORMATION. [Sir Ronald Aylmer **Fisher** (1890–1962), British statistician and geneticist]

inverse function a mathematical FUNCTION that reverses the input and output of another function; that is, it uses the results from the original function to calculate the initial values of that function. For example, if $y = x^2$, then its inverse function is $x = \sqrt{y}$.

inverse Gaussian distribution a distribution having positive SKEWNESS that is used to model nonnegative data. Also called **inverse normal distribution**; **Wald distribution**. [Karl Friedrich **Gauss** (1777–1855), German mathematician]

inversely proportional see DIRECTLY PROPORTIONAL.

inverse matrix a SQUARE MATRIX that is the RECIPROCAL of another such matrix, as in the following example.

$$\mathbf{A} \qquad \mathbf{A}^{-1} \text{ (inverse)}$$
$$\begin{bmatrix} 2 & 3 \\ 3 & 4 \end{bmatrix} \quad \begin{bmatrix} -4 & 3 \\ 3 & -2 \end{bmatrix}$$

The product of a square matrix and its inverse matrix is an IDENTITY MATRIX. Inverse matrices are commonly used in FACTOR ANALYSIS and similar multivariate statistical procedures.

inverse normal distribution see INVERSE GAUSSIAN DISTRIBUTION.

inverse prediction see REGRESSION OF X ON Y.

inverse relationship see NEGATIVE RELATIONSHIP.

inverse sine transformation see ARC SINE TRANSFORMATION.

inverse transformation see RECIPROCAL TRANSFORMATION.

inverted U-shaped distribution see U-SHAPED DISTRIBUTION.

invertible matrix see NONSINGULAR MATRIX.

IPA abbreviation for INTERPRETIVE PHENOMENOLOGICAL ANALYSIS.

ipsative method a type of research procedure in which a person's responses (e.g., scores) are compared only to other responses of that person rather than to the responses of other people. It is thus an IDIOGRAPHIC approach rather than a NORMATIVE one.

ipsative scale a scale in which the points distributed to the various different items must sum to a specific total. In such a scale, all participants will have the same total score but the distribution of the points among the various items will differ for each individual. For example, a supervisor using an ipsative scale to indicate an employee's strength in different areas initially might assign 20 points for communication, 30 for timeliness, and 50 for work quality but a few months later assign 30 points for communication, 30 for timeliness, and 40 for quality of work. The total number of points distributed in each case, however, is the same (100). Ipsative scales also may involve ranks: Respondents use the same numbers for ranking but may assign them differently. For example, two individuals indicating their preferences for 10 different restaurants will both use the ranks 1 through 10 but the restaurant chosen as #1 will not be the same for each person, the restaurant chosen as #2 will not be the same, and so on.

IQR abbreviation for INTERQUARTILE RANGE.

IRB abbreviation for INSTITUTIONAL REVIEW BOARD.

IRT abbreviation for ITEM RESPONSE THEORY.

isosensitivity function see RECEIVER-OPERATING CHARACTERISTIC CURVE.

isotonic regression a type of LEAST SQUARES REGRESSION in which the variables in the regression equation are assumed to be MONOTONIC (i.e., the variables all trend in the same direction with no NEGATIVE RELATIONSHIPS between variables).

item analysis a set of procedures used to evaluate the statistical merits of individual items comprising a psychological measure or test. These procedures may be used to select items for a test from a larger pool of initial items or to evaluate items on an established test. A variety of different statistics may be computed in item analyses, including DIFFICULTY VALUES, INDEXES OF DISCRIMINATION, INTERITEM CORRELATIONS, and ITEM DISCRIMINABILITIES.

item characteristic curve (ICC) a plot of the probability that a test item is answered correctly against the examinee's underlying ability on the trait being measured, as in the example overleaf.

The item characteristic curve is the basic building block of ITEM RESPONSE THEORY: The curve is bounded between 0 and 1, is monotonically increasing, and is commonly assumed to take the shape of a LOGISTIC FUNCTION. Each item in a test has its own item characteristic curve.

item difficulty see DIFFICULTY VALUE.

item discriminability a statistical measure of how well an item on a test differentiates among subgroups of test takers, typically those individuals who possess a high degree of some ability versus those who possess a low degree of the ability. Item discriminabilities typically are given as CORRELATION COEFFICIENTS ranging from –1 to +1 in value, with the latter indicating a perfect discriminator. INTERITEM CORRELATIONS also may be used in determining item discriminability. See ITEM ANALYSIS.

item distractor one of the alternatives to the correct answer provided for each item on a MULTIPLE-CHOICE TEST. Well-chosen distractors can differentiate among the different classes of test takers: Those who know the material should select the correct alternative despite the presence of plausible distractors, whereas those with limited knowledge are likely to guess randomly from among the available distractors.

item homogeneity see INTERNAL CONSISTENCY.

item nonresponse see NONRESPONSE.

item reliability see INTERNAL CONSISTENCY.

item response theory (**IRT**) a psychometric theory of measurement based on the concept that the probability that an item will be correctly answered is a function of an underlying trait or ability that is not directly observable, that is, a latent trait (see LATENT TRAIT THEORY).

Item response theory models differ in terms of the number of parameters included in the model. For example, the RASCH MODEL is based on the single parameter of item difficulty, whereas other models additionally examine ITEM DISCRIMINABILITY and the chances of successful guessing. Compare CLASSICAL TEST THEORY.

item scaling the assignment of a test item to a scale position on some dimension, often that of item difficulty.

item selection the selection of test items for inclusion in a test battery based upon the final psychometric properties of the test battery, the ITEM RESPONSE THEORY parameters of the individual items, and the clarity and fairness of the individual items.

item–total correlation the degree to which scores on a single item from a test are related to the total score for the test as a whole, used in determining the INTERNAL CONSISTENCY of the test. Low item–total correlations (i.e., less than 0.2) indicate poor associations of an item with others on the test, such that it is not measuring the same construct and should be discarded.

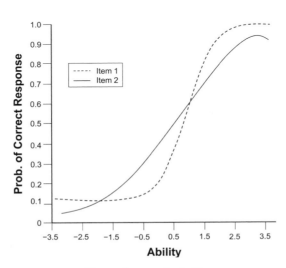

item characteristic curve

item validity the extent to which an individual item in a test or experiment measures what it purports to measure.

item weighting a numerical value assigned to a test item that expresses its percentage of the total score of the test. For example, an essay question may be assigned a value of 40, representing 40 out of 100 possible points. See WEIGHTING.

iterated bootstrapping a BOOTSTRAPPING procedure in which samples are randomly drawn (with replacement) from an observed data set, values for different population characteristics are estimated, and the estimates averaged across the set of samples. Then, the samples created during this initial procedure are themselves sampled and their PARAMETERS estimated and averaged. The resampling and recalculating process continues until a stable parameter estimate is obtained. Iterated bootstrapping usually is less prone to error than using a single set of bootstrapping samples.

iteration *n.* the repetition of a certain computational step until further repetition no longer changes the outcome or until the repetition meets some other predefined criterion.

iterative algorithm a mathematical process of successive approximation in which a sequence of increasingly accurate procedures for solving a class of problems is generated. The outcome of new ALGORITHMS is compared to that of the prior algorithms from which they are derived until certain criteria have been satisfied or a certain condition obtained.

iterative proportional fitting a mathematical procedure in which a series of calculations is repeatedly applied to adjust the values in one data set so that they gradually conform to the constraints in another associated data set. For example, a researcher may have both CELL FREQUENCIES and MARGINAL FREQUENCIES for sales of a product in the previous year but only estimates of marginal frequencies for the current year. He or she might use iterative proportional fitting to adjust the cell frequencies from the previous year to fit the estimated marginals of the current year.

ITI abbreviation for INTERTRIAL INTERVAL.

IV abbreviation for INDEPENDENT VARIABLE.

Jj

jackknife *n*. a statistical procedure used to estimate the variability of a PARAMETER associated with a set of data, such as the STANDARD ERROR or CONFIDENCE INTERVAL. It is particularly appropriate when the VARIANCE or underlying distribution is not known. A number of samples are obtained from the original data by eliminating one or more observations at a time, the parameter in question is calculated for each sample, and the individual parameters are combined to provide an estimate of the overall parameter for the entire data set. A jackknife is similar to BOOTSTRAPPING, except that bootstrapping involves replacing observations after they have been sampled, such that after each observation is chosen it is reinserted into the data for possible selection again.

James–Stein estimator a formula used to approximate a population PARAMETER from sample data. It is an improved version of the ordinary LEAST SQUARES ESTIMATOR, providing a smaller and more accurate measure of the MEAN SQUARED ERROR between actual and predicted scores. [Willard **James**, U.S. mathematician; Charles M. **Stein** (1920–), U.S. statistician]

J curve a pattern on a graph that resembles the letter J: There is an initial drop in value for a short period of time followed by a continuous increase. For example, a high achieving person training for a difficult job might show a J curve for performance (as shown in the diagram below). His or her performance initially might drop below that of other employees while he or she learns difficult skills but rapidly increase to excellence after fully attaining the required job skills. Also called **J-shaped distribution**.

Jeffreys's prior in BAYESIAN statistics, a method used to estimate the PROBABILITY DISTRIBUTION for a PARAMETER of interest, such as the population mean. Jeffreys's prior is based on the square root of the DETERMINANT of FISHER'S INFORMATION, which provides an approximation of the degree of variability that

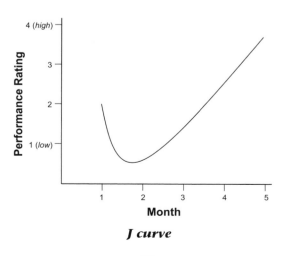

J curve

Not Jittered

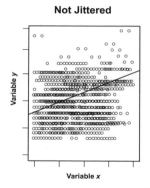

Jittered

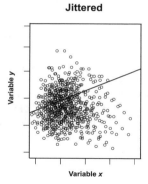

jittering

could be expected for the parameter. See also PRIOR DISTRIBUTION. [Sir Harold **Jeffreys** (1891–1989), British mathematician and geophysicist]

Jensen's inequality a mathematical FUNCTION stating that a convex TRANSFORMATION of a mean value will be equal to or smaller than the mean of a set of convex transformed values. In other words, a transformation that creates a set of smaller values that follow a convex pattern will yield a smaller overall value than will the average of a set of values that have already undergone a convex transformation. [Johan **Jensen** (1859–1925), Danish mathematician]

jittering *n.* deliberately adding a small amount of random noise to each observation in a SCATTERPLOT where variables take on relatively few values, resulting in identical data points that stack on top of each other and thus are hard to interpret. Consider the generic example above. Primarily a data visualization technique, jittering helps sepa-

rate the points and make it easier to discern a pattern or relationship.

joint distribution the pattern of values obtained when estimating the probability of occurrence of two or more RANDOM VARIABLES. For example, the probability values for drawing a heart and a jack in a deck of cards would form the following joint distribution: $(13/52) \times (48/52)$ to obtain a heart but not a jack; $(39/52) \times (48/52)$ to obtain a nonheart and a nonjack; $(39/52) \times (4/52)$ to obtain a nonheart and a jack; and $(13/52) \times (4/52)$ to obtain a heart that is also a jack. This is illustrated below.

A joint distribution for two variables is referred to more specifically as a BIVARIATE DISTRIBUTION, whereas a joint distribution for more than two variables is called a MULTIVARIATE DISTRIBUTION.

joint probability the chance that two events will occur simultaneously. For example, the joint probability of drawing a heart that is a jack from a deck of 52 cards is equal to $(13/52) \times (4/52)$, or

Card suit	Jack	Nonjack
Heart	$1/52 = .02 = 2\%$	$12/52 = .23 = 23\%$
Nonheart	$3/52 = .06 = 6\%$	$36/52 = .69 = 69\%$

joint distribution

1/52. See also JOINT DISTRIBUTION; JOINT PROBABILITY DENSITY FUNCTION.

joint probability density function the statistical formula for calculating the likelihood of the simultaneous occurrence of particular values on two or more continuous variables (e.g., age and income). The joint probability density function thus underlies a JOINT DISTRIBUTION where the variables have a continuous, rather than a discrete or categorical, form. See also PROBABILITY DENSITY FUNCTION.

Jonckheere k-sample test a NONPARAMETRIC method for analyzing whether two or more ordered samples are significantly different. The Jonckheere k-sample test is a MANN–WHITNEY U TEST on multiple samples and is similar to a KRUSKAL–WALLIS ONE-WAY ANALYSIS OF VARIANCE. Also called **Jonckheere–Terpstra k-sample test**; **Jonckheere–Terpstra test**. [A. R. Jonckheere (1920–2005), French-born British statistician and psychologist; T. J. **Terpstra**, Dutch mathematician]

J-shaped distribution see J CURVE.

judgment sampling selecting a group from which to gather data on the basis of personal opinion as to what is representative of the population under study. For example, judgment sampling could involve choosing a number of well-informed people from different social groups and asking them who they believe will be the next U.S. president. The outcome from such a study may well not be consistent with the result of asking a RANDOM SAMPLE from the population. This means that although judgment sampling may be useful in a PILOT STUDY, it generally does not result in warranted inference to any population of interest. See DELIBERATE SAMPLING.

just-identified model a model in which the number of population PARAMETERS estimated is the same as the number of data points in the sample data set (i.e., the DEGREES OF FREEDOM of the model are equal to zero). In nonstatistical terms, a just-identified model is like having funding (e.g., data points) to pay for a major intervention (e.g., to estimate parameters) without having any left (e.g., degrees of freedom) to evaluate whether the intervention was successful (e.g., whether the model fit or not). Also called **exact identification**. Compare OVERIDENTIFIED MODEL; UNDERIDENTIFIED MODEL.

Kk

k 1. symbol for COEFFICIENT OF ALIENATION. **2.** symbol for the number of individuals, groups, or other units in a statistical analysis.

Kaiser–Meyer–Olkin test of sampling adequacy (**KMO test**) a measure of whether the PARTIAL CORRELATIONS among a set of variables are sufficient to conduct a FACTOR ANALYSIS. KMO test values may range from 0 to 1, with values of .50 or higher indicating there is a sufficient degree of relationship among the variables that they reasonably could be analyzed to reveal one or more underlying factors. [Henry F. **Kaiser** (1927–1992), U.S. psychometrician and statistician; Michael **Meyer**, U.S. statistician; Ingram **Olkin** (1924–   ), U.S. statistician]

Kalman filter a statistical method used in TIME-SERIES ANALYSES and other longitudinal procedures that combines estimates from several sources (e.g., actual measures, predicted values) to obtain a more precise indication of a set of values over time. It is similar to a HIDDEN MARKOV MODEL but based on CONTINUOUS rather than DISCRETE measures. For example, a Kalman filter could be applied to assess the amount of drug use across time for one or more individuals, whereas a hidden Markov model would be used to assess the distinct stages of substance use across time. [Rudolf E. **Kalman** (1930–   ), Hungarian-born U.S. electrical engineer and mathematician]

Kaplan–Meier estimator a statistical method used in SURVIVAL ANALYSIS with CENSORED DATA for estimating the percentage of individuals (or other entities) that will remain after a set amount of time. For example, the Kaplan–Meier estimator could be used in health studies to estimate the percentage of patients who are expected to survive a specific illness over varying numbers of years; the graph of values from a Kaplan–Meier estimator presumably would show a decline over time, with fewer and fewer surviving patients. Also called **product-limit estimator**. [Edward L. **Kaplan**, U.S. mathematician; Paul **Meier** (1924–2011), U.S. biostatistician]

kappa *n.* see COHEN'S KAPPA.

Kendall robust line-fit method see THEIL–SEN ESTIMATOR. [Sir Maurice **Kendall** (1907–1983), British statistician]

Kendall's coefficient of concordance see COEFFICIENT OF CONCORDANCE. [Sir Maurice **Kendall**]

Kendall's tau (symbol: τ) a nonparametric measure of the degree of association between two ordinal variables (i.e., rank-ordered data). For example, a researcher could calculate Kendall's tau to assess how much relationship there is between the rankings of students' performance provided by two observers (e.g., a teacher and a teaching assistant). Also called **Kendall's rank correlation coefficient**. [Sir Maurice **Kendall**]

Kendall's W see COEFFICIENT OF CONCORDANCE. [Sir Maurice **Kendall**]

kernel density estimator a method for approximating a smooth, bell-shaped distribution from the choppy representation in a bar graph or histogram. For example, one might apply a kernel density estimator to the possible values when throwing two dice (e.g., one frequency of 2: a 1 and a 1; two frequencies of 3: a 1 and a 2 or a 2 and a 1; three frequencies of 4: a 3 and a 1, a 1 and a 3, and a 2 and a 2; etc.), as they yield a boxy histogram that peaks in the middle at 7 and has low frequencies of one to the far left and far right for 2 and 12, respectively. Also called **kernel estimator**; **Parzen window estimator**.

kernel function a NONPARAMETRIC method used to estimate the distribution for a RANDOM VARIABLE. For example, a kernel function may estimate a rectangular-shaped UNIFORM DISTRIBUTION, indicating approximately the same number of low, medium, and high scores. Such a kernel function would be in contrast to the bell-shaped pattern of a NORMAL DISTRIBUTION, in which most scores pile up in the middle and gradually decline on either side.

kernel regression a NONPARAMETRIC method of forming a smooth pattern when estimating the relationship between two variables. For example, kernel regression could be used to find a relatively smooth (i.e., not choppy) pattern in a SCATTERPLOT depicting the age and height of each child in a classroom. Also called **kernel regression smoothing**; **kernel smoother**.

k-means clustering a type of CLUSTER ANALYSIS that separates a large set of entities into a smaller number of *k* subsets (i.e., clusters) by assigning each entity to the subset closest in mean value. For example, *k*-means clustering might take a group of individuals and separate them into three subsets or clusters depending on the closeness of their IQ scores to the cluster means of, say, 70, 100, and 130, for low, medium, and high IQ, respectively.

KMO test abbreviation for KAISER–MEYER–OLKIN TEST OF SAMPLING ADEQUACY.

known-group validity the demonstration that an instrument can distinguish between several groups known to vary on the dimension being measured. For example, a newly created measure of depression would be said to have known-group validity if it resulted in low scores for high-functioning and happy individuals, and high scores for individuals with depressed affect who demonstrated little activity or motivation. It is a form of CONSTRUCT VALIDITY.

Kolmogorov–Smirnov goodness-of-fit test a NONPARAMETRIC method for comparing the distribution from a sample data set to an expected distribution or the known distribution of a given population. If the test yields a discrepancy (*D*) larger than the CRITICAL VALUE, then the sample data are considered to be significantly different from the reference distribution. Also called **Kolmogorov–Smirnov D test**; **Kolmogorov–Smirnov one-sample test**. Compare KOLMOGOROV–SMIRNOV TWO-SAMPLE TEST. [Andrei Nikolaevich **Kolmogorov** (1903–1987) and Nikolai Vasilevich **Smirnov** (1900–1966), Soviet mathematicians]

Kolmogorov–Smirnov two-sample test a NONPARAMETRIC method for comparing the distributions from two samples to see if they are similar. A significant result from a Kolmogorov–Smirnov two-sample test indicates that the two samples are derived from different distributions. In contrast, the KOLMOGOROV–SMIRNOV GOODNESS-OF-FIT TEST is used when only one sample is available but the larger population distribution is known. [Andrei **Kolmogorov** and Nikolai **Smirnov**]

K-R 20 abbreviation for Kuder–Richardson formula 20. See KUDER–RICHARDSON FORMULAS.

K-R 21 abbreviation for Kuder–Richardson formula 21. See KUDER–RICHARDSON FORMULAS.

kriging *n.* a statistical method that uses INTERPOLATION to estimate an unknown value between two known values while minimizing prediction error. For example, a simple form of kriging could estimate that the unknown point halfway between two known points of 1 and 9 would be a value of 5. [Daniel

Gerhardus **Krige** (1919–), South African geostatistician]

Kronecker product of matrices the SQUARE MATRIX that results from multiplying each of the values in one matrix by each of the values in another matrix: It consists of four blocks corresponding to each of the row values in the first matrix by each of the column values in the second matrix. For example, imagine a matrix **A** with two rows of values 1, 3 and 2, 4, respectively, and a matrix **B** with two rows of values 6, 8 and 5, 7, respectively.

$$
\begin{array}{ccc}
\mathbf{A} & \mathbf{B} & \begin{array}{c}\text{Kronecker product}\\ \text{of } \mathbf{A} \times \mathbf{B}\end{array}\\
\begin{bmatrix}1 & 3\\ 2 & 4\end{bmatrix} & \begin{bmatrix}6 & 8\\ 5 & 7\end{bmatrix} & \begin{bmatrix}6 & 8 & 18 & 24\\ 5 & 7 & 15 & 21\\ 12 & 16 & 24 & 32\\ 10 & 14 & 20 & 28\end{bmatrix}
\end{array}
$$

As shown, the Kronecker product of matrices **A** and **B** is a 4×4 matrix with values of 6, 8, 18, and 24 in the first row; 5, 7, 15, and 21 in the second row; 12, 16, 24, and 32 in the third row; and 10, 14, 20, and 28 in the fourth row. [Leopold **Kronecker** (1823–1891), German mathematician]

Kruskal stress a measure of the distance between predicted and actual dissimilarities in a MULTIDIMENSIONAL SCALING analysis of the perceived similarities between stimuli. See also DISSIMILARITY COEFFICIENT; SIMILARITY COEFFICIENT. [Joseph B. **Kruskal** (1928–2010), U.S. statistician and computer scientist]

Kruskal–Wallis one-way analysis of variance a NONPARAMETRIC TEST for assessing whether the MEDIANS of multiple samples of ranked data are equal. It is an extension of the MANN–WHITNEY U TEST, which is conducted when there are only two independent samples. Also called **Kruskal–Wallis test**. [William Henry **Kruskal** (1919–2005) and Wilson Allen **Wallis** (1912–1998), U.S. statisticians]

Kuder–Richardson formulas two methods, **Kuder–Richardson formula 20 (K-R 20)** and **Kuder–Richardson formula 21 (K-R 21)**, for assessing the INTERNAL CONSISTENCY reliability of a test or subtest made up of binary variables (i.e., DICHOTOMOUS ITEMS). The K-R 21 requires that all of the dichotomous items be equally difficult, whereas the K-R 20 does not. For example, a teacher could use the K-R 21 formula to calculate internal consistency reliability for a test of 20 equally difficult items, but would use the K-R 20 formula for test items differing in difficulty level. [Frederic **Kuder** (1903–2000) and Marion Webster **Richardson** (1896–1965), U.S. psychologists]

Kullback–Leibler information the amount of extra data that is needed to approximate an expected or theoretical distribution from an observed distribution. The Kullback–Leibler information is sometimes referred to as the **Kullback–Leibler deviance** to indicate the discrepancy or deviance between the expected and actual distributions. [Solomon **Kullback** (1907–1994) and Richard **Leibler** (1914–2003), U.S. mathematicians]

kurtosis *n.* the fourth CENTRAL MOMENT of a PROBABILITY DISTRIBUTION. It is a statistical description of the degree of peakedness of that distribution. For example, the ages of a sample of college freshmen would probably show kurtosis, having a high peak at age 18. See LEPTOKURTIC; MESOKURTIC; PLATYKURTIC.

K

Ll

laboratory analogue see ANALOGUE STUDY.

laboratory research scientific study conducted in a laboratory or other such workplace, where the investigator has some degree of direct control over the environment and can manipulate the INDEPENDENT VARIABLES. Although laboratory research generally has greater INTERNAL VALIDITY than FIELD RESEARCH, it tends to be less generalizable to the real world (i.e., has less EXTERNAL VALIDITY). See EXPERIMENTAL RESEARCH.

lack of fit the degree to which the values predicted by a model—typically, one developed in REGRESSION ANALYSIS, STRUCTURAL EQUATION MODELING, or CONFIRMATORY FACTOR ANALYSIS—diverge from the corresponding empirical values. A large, significant value from a GOODNESS-OF-FIT TEST indicates a poorly fitting model.

laddering *n.* a knowledge elicitation technique used in interviews to impose a systematic framework upon questioning so as to reveal complex themes across answers. In laddering, a respondent replies to a series of "why?" probes, thus requiring him or her to expose and explain choices or preferences and justify behavior in terms of goals, values, and personal constructs. Laddering is concerned with establishing links between concepts elicited from the participant (e.g., attitudes and beliefs associated with a particular consumer product) and provides greater scope for probing salient issues while optimizing the often limited time available with respondents.

lagged dependent variable in TIME-SERIES ANALYSIS, an outcome variable exhibiting AUTOCORRELATION in that its value at a given point in time is related to its value at an earlier time point.

lagged independent variable in TIME-SERIES ANALYSIS, an explanatory variable exhibiting AUTOCORRELATION in that its value at a given point in time is related to its value at an earlier time point.

Lagrange multiplier test in REGRESSION ANALYSIS, a procedure used to estimate the improvement in the fit of a model to observed data that is gained by the inclusion of additional variables. For example, a researcher may hypothesize that high-school grade point average and college admission test scores have more influence on grade point average in college than do gender and ethnicity. Thus, he or she could develop a model that includes only those two items as predictor variables and then use a Lagrange multiplier test to determine whether adding gender and ethnicity results in a significantly better fitting model. [Joseph Louis **Lagrange** (1736–1813), Italian-born French mathematician]

lambda 1. (symbol: λ) see EIGENVALUE. **2.** (symbol: Λ) see WILKS'S LAMBDA.

Laplace distribution see DOUBLE EXPONENTIAL DISTRIBUTION. [Pierre Simon **Laplace** (1749–1827), French mathematician]

large-N design a research approach in which groups comprising numerous individuals are studied. Generally, the larger the number of observations or participants in a research study, the greater the statistical POWER in hypothesis testing during data analysis. Compare SMALL-N DESIGN.

large-numbers law see LAW OF LARGE NUMBERS.

large-sample method see ASYMPTOTIC METHOD.

largest characteristic root see GREATEST CHARACTERISTIC ROOT.

largest-root test see GREATEST-CHARACTERISTIC-ROOT TEST.

last observation carried forward (**LOCF**) a strategy for handling missing data in LONGITUDINAL DESIGNS: the value immediately prior is substituted for any missing data points and the completed data set analyzed as usual. Although this approach preserves the sample size, it may involve unwarranted assumptions about the missing data, which in turn may bias study findings.

latent class analysis (**LCA**) a method for finding discrete subgroups of related cases (**latent classes**) from multivariate CATEGORICAL DATA. For example, a health researcher might use latent class analysis to determine into which one of 10 diagnostic categories to place each individual in a group on the basis of the presence or absence of several distinct symptoms. The procedure is analogous to CLUSTER ANALYSIS, in that from a given sample of cases measured on several variables, the researcher attempts to identify a smaller number of underlying dimensions on which to classify them. The use of a categorical LATENT VARIABLE, however, is what distinguishes latent class analysis from more traditional clustering approaches such as FACTOR ANALYSIS, which involve continuous latent variables. Also called **latent class modeling**.

latent construct see LATENT VARIABLE.

latent curve modeling see LATENT GROWTH CURVE ANALYSIS.

latent factor see LATENT VARIABLE.

latent growth curve analysis a type of GROWTH CURVE ANALYSIS in which a researcher attempts to estimate a PA-RAMETER (or set of parameters) underlying the observed rate of change in a directly measured variable. Also called **latent curve modeling**; **latent growth curve modeling**.

latent root see EIGENVALUE.

latent structure analysis any of various statistical procedures that attempt to explain relationships among observed variables in terms of underlying LATENT VARIABLES, whether continuous or categorical. Examples include FACTOR ANALYSIS, LATENT CLASS ANALYSIS, and STRUCTURAL EQUATION MODELING. Also called **latent structure modeling**.

latent trait theory a general psychometric theory contending that observed traits, such as intelligence, are reflections of more basic unobservable traits (i.e., latent traits). Several quantitative models (e.g., ITEM RESPONSE THEORY, FACTOR ANALYSIS) have been developed to allow for the identification and estimation of these latent traits from manifest observations.

latent transition analysis (**LTA**) an extension of LATENT CLASS ANALYSIS that is used to study changes over time in the unobservable categorical dimensions that underlie measured variables. For example, an educational researcher might use LTA to model how the interests (majors) of a class of college students change as they progress from their freshman to senior years using data about the classes each individual has taken. Such an analysis would yield estimates of the probability of pursuing a particular major at a future time given a person's chosen major at a prior time.

latent variable a theoretical entity or construct that is used to explain one or more MANIFEST VARIABLES. Latent variables cannot be directly observed or measured but rather are approximated through various measures presumed to assess part of the given construct. For example, suppose a researcher is interested in student conscientiousness.

Since conscientiousness is a concept that cannot be directly evaluated, he or she might develop a survey containing items pertaining to behavior indicative of conscientiousness, such as consistently attending classes, turning in assignments on time, engaging in school-sponsored fundraising activities, and so forth. Participants' responses could then be analyzed to identify patterns of interrelationships from which the values of the latent variable of conscientiousness are inferred. Also called **latent construct**; **latent factor**; **synthetic variable**. See also FACTOR ANALYSIS; STRUCTURAL EQUATION MODELING.

latent vector see EIGENVECTOR.

Latin square a type of WITHIN-SUBJECTS DESIGN in which treatments, denoted by Latin letters, are administered in sequences that are systematically varied such that each treatment occurs equally often in each position of the sequence (first, second, third, etc.). The number of treatments administered must be the same as the number of groups or individual participants receiving them. For example, consider the following possible Latin square for an experimental design involving four treatments (A, B, C, and D) and four people:

Treatment Order

	1	2	3	4
Participant 1	A	B	C	D
Participant 2	B	C	D	A
Participant 3	C	D	A	B
Participant 4	D	A	B	C

As shown, each treatment appears exactly once in each order position: One person receives treatment A, then B, then C, and then D; a second person receives them in sequence B, C, D, and A; a third person in sequence C, D, A, and B; and a fourth person in sequence D, A, B, and C. It is important to note that although Latin squares control for ORDER EFFECTS they do not control for CARRYOVER EFFECTS or PRACTICE EFFECTS. See also BALANCED LATIN SQUARE; GRAECO-LATIN SQUARE.

law *n.* **1.** a formal statement describing a regularity (e.g., of nature) to which no exceptions are known or anticipated. **2.** in science, mathematics, philosophy, and the social sciences, a theory that is widely accepted as correct and that has no significant rivals in accounting for the relationships of interest or the facts within its domain.

law of large numbers a mathematical principle indicating that as the sample size increases, the theoretical expectations of its statistical properties will be more and more closely realized. For example, as the number of replications of an experiment increases, the average (MEAN) of the observed results will approach the true average (theoretical probability in the population) with increasing accuracy. Or, as the number of trials of a random process increases, the difference between the expected and actual frequencies of a particular outcome will decrease to zero. According to the **strong law of large numbers**, the average of the results obtained from a large number of trials will converge upon the theoretically expected value, becoming closer as more trials are performed. In distinction, the **weak law of large numbers** states that the average is likely to converge upon the expected value as more trials are conducted. Thus, the essential difference between the two laws is that the former insists on convergence whereas the latter expects convergence. Also called **averages law; Bernoulli's theorem; large-numbers law; law of averages**.

law of parsimony the principle that the simplest explanation of an event or observation is the preferred explanation. Simplicity is understood in various ways, including the requirement that an explanation should (a) make the smallest number of unsupported assumptions, (b) postulate the existence of the fewest entities, and (c) invoke the fewest unobservable constructs. Also called **principle of parsimony**. See OC-CAM'S RAZOR.

law of total probability see TOTAL PROBABILITY LAW.

LCA abbreviation for LATENT CLASS ANALYSIS.

leading diagonal see MAIN DIAGONAL.

least significant difference (LSD) see FISHER LEAST SIGNIFICANT DIFFERENCE TEST.

least squares criterion in REGRESSION ANALYSIS and similar statistical procedures, the principle that one should estimate the values of PARAMETERS in a way that will minimize the squared error of predictions from the model. That is, one should strive to build models that minimize the squared differences between actual scores (observed data) and expected scores (those predicted by the model). Also called **least squares principle**. See LEAST SQUARES REGRESSION.

least squares estimator in LEAST SQUARES REGRESSION, the model or procedure that yields the smallest differences between observed data points and their values as predicted by the model. See also LEAST SQUARES CRITERION.

least squares regression a type of REGRESSION ANALYSIS in which the researcher strives to develop a **least-squared-errors solution** or **least squares solution** to describe the relationship between an outcome or DEPENDENT VARIABLE and one or more predictors or INDEPENDENT VARIABLES. That is, one develops a model that is the best fit for the data because it yields the smallest squared differences between the actual observations and their values as predicted by the model. Also called **least squares estimation; ordinary least squares (OLS) regression**. See LEAST SQUARES CRITERION.

left censoring the situation in which a researcher cannot determine the precise time at which a target event occurred for some individuals within a sample because those participants experienced the event prior to the observation period. For example, left censoring might arise in a study of alcohol initiation among high school students because a subset of the sample is likely to have initiated use prior to high school entry. See also RIGHT CENSORING.

leptokurtic *adj.* describing a frequency distribution that is more peaked than the NORMAL DISTRIBUTION.

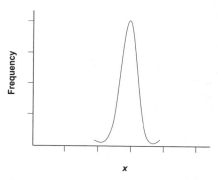

It has more scores in the center and fewer at the two extremes. See also MESOKURTIC; PLATYKURTIC.

level *n.* in an experimental design, the quantity, magnitude, or category of the INDEPENDENT VARIABLE (or variables) being studied. For example, if a researcher is assessing the effect of alcohol on cognition, each specific amount of alcohol included in the study is a level (e.g., 0.0 oz, 0.5 oz, 1.0 oz, 1.5 oz).

level of analysis see UNIT OF ANALYSIS.

level of measurement see MEASUREMENT LEVEL.

level of significance see SIGNIFICANCE LEVEL.

Levene test for equality of variance a method for evaluating whether the VARIANCE in a set of scores is equivalent across two or more groups being

L

studied. Equality of variance is required in ANALYSIS OF VARIANCE and other statistical techniques in order to obtain valid results. See HOMOGENEITY OF VARIANCE. [Howard **Levene** (1914–2003), U.S. statistician and geneticist]

leverage point in REGRESSION ANALYSIS, an observation, value, or score that is extremely different from the average for a given predictor or INDEPENDENT VARIABLE. Leverage points in a data set may distort regression results.

lie scale a set of items within a psychological instrument (particularly a personality assessment) used to indicate whether a respondent has been truthful in answering. For example, an honest participant would respond similarly to the items "I never regret the life decisions I have made" and "I've never done anything I later wished I could take back," which are different ways of presenting the same concept. Conversely, a respondent trying to present himself or herself as positively as possible might answer such related questions inconsistently.

life table a table of the expected or actual death rates in a specific area or for those with specific conditions. For example, a life table could be constructed to show the life expectancies for individuals who are of a certain age, who have a particular illness, who smoke, and so forth. Life tables typically yield such information as the number or proportion of people alive at given points and their probability of continued survival, as well as the number or proportion who died at those same points. They may be expanded to include additional information and often are used in SURVIVAL ANALYSIS for any time-to-event data. Also called **mortality table**.

likelihood *n.* in statistics, the probability of obtaining a particular set of results given a set of assumptions about the DISTRIBUTION of the phenomena in the population and the PARAMETERS of that distribution.

likelihood function a formula that yields the probability of obtaining a particular distribution of values in a sample for each known value of an associated population PARAMETER. In other words, it indicates how likely a particular population is to produce the observed sample data under certain conditions.

likelihood principle a foundational tenet of statistical inference stating that where there is an unknown population PARAMETER, θ, and an observed sample distribution, *x*, all relevant information about the population distribution is contained in the LIKELIHOOD FUNCTION for *x*.

likelihood ratio (**LR**) the ratio of two probabilities, *a/b*, where *a* is the probability of obtaining the data observed if a particular research hypothesis (A; the NULL HYPOTHESIS) is true and *b* is the probability of obtaining the data observed when a different hypothesis (B; the ALTERNATIVE HYPOTHESIS) is true.

likelihood-ratio chi-square (symbol: G^2) a test statistic calculated from LIKELIHOOD RATIOS and used for determining GOODNESS OF FIT in LOGISTIC REGRESSION and other multivariate procedures and for assessing INDEPENDENCE in CONTINGENCY TABLES.

likelihood-ratio test a procedure in which LIKELIHOOD RATIOS are used to evaluate the GOODNESS OF FIT of different statistical models representing relationships among variables or to determine INDEPENDENCE. If the statistic obtained—the LIKELIHOOD-RATIO CHI-SQUARE or G^2—is large and has a small P VALUE (e.g., $p < .05$), there is evidence that the observed data are significantly different from the data predicted by the model (i.e., the model is a poor fit). Similarly, when testing two CATEGORICAL VARIABLES for independence a large G^2 indicates the variables are related (i.e., are not independent). A likelihood-ratio test is considered more appropriate than a CHI-SQUARE TEST when the sample size is small. Also called **G test**; **G² test**. See also LOG-LIKELIHOOD RATIO.

likelihood residual see DELETION RESIDUAL.

Likert scale a type of direct attitude measure that consists of statements reflecting strong positive or negative evaluations of an object. Five-point scales are common and a neutral middle point may or may not be included. For example, an assessment item using a Likert scale response format (i.e., a **Likert-type question**) might include the following statement choices: *strongly disagree, disagree, neither disagree nor agree, agree*, and *strongly agree*. The respondent chooses the option most representative of his or her view (e.g., on whether same-sex marriages should be permitted) and these ratings are summed to provide a total attitude score for a topic of interest. Also called **Likert summated rating procedure**. [Rensis **Likert** (1903–1981), U.S. psychologist]

linear *adj.* describing any relationship between two variables (x and y) that can be expressed in the form $y = a + bx$, where a and b are numerical constants. No COEFFICIENT can be raised to a power greater than 1 or be the denominator of a fraction. When depicted graphically, the relationship is a straight line. Compare NONLINEAR.

linear combination a pattern in which the value of one variable is derived by multiplying the values of several other variables in a set by a constant quantity and then adding the results. For example, the REGRESSION EQUATION $y = a + b_1 x_1 + b_2 x_2 + b_3 x_3$ represents a linear combination: y is obtained by adding the constant (a) and the values of the three x variables, each of which is first multiplied by a unique weight (b).

linear contrast a method of comparing the mean values on a variable for two or more groups using CONTRAST CODING. The mean value for each group is multiplied by a chosen weight with the requirement that the total of the weights used in any comparison equals zero (e.g., weights of +1 and –1).

linear correlation a measure of the degree of association between two variables that are assumed to have a LINEAR RELATIONSHIP, that is, to be related in such a manner that their values form a straight line when plotted on a graph. It provides an index of the degree of constant change in the value of one variable (y) for each unit change in the value of another variable (x).

linear equation an equation that relates elements in a summative fashion and involves no exponential powers greater than 1. For example, $y = a + bx$ is a linear equation and will form a straight line when depicted graphically. Compare NONLINEAR EQUATION.

linear function a mathematical procedure that transforms one number, quantity, or entity to another through summation, without involving any exponential powers greater than 1. For example, $y = 2x + 4x$ is a linear function. In contrast, a **nonlinear function** involves interactions (exponents greater than 1) among the quantities, as in $y = 2x^2 + 4x^2$.

linear interpolation a method of INTERPOLATION (i.e., constructing new data points between two existing data points) that uses a summative formula without any exponential powers greater than 1. Graphically, linear interpolation involves connecting two adjacent known values with a straight line. Compare NONLINEAR INTERPOLATION.

linearity *n.* a relationship in which one variable is associated with another via a summative formula in which all COEFFICIENTS are to the first power. See LINEAR COMBINATION; LINEAR CORRELATION.

linearizing *n.* see LINEAR TRANSFORMATION.

linear model any model for empirical data that attempts to relate the values of an outcome or dependent variable to the explanatory or independent variables through a LINEAR FUNCTION, that is, one that simply sums terms and includes no exponents greater than 1. Most commonly used statistical techniques (ANALYSIS OF VARIANCE, REGRESSION ANALYSIS, etc.) can be represented as linear models. Compare NONLINEAR MODEL.

linear regression a REGRESSION ANALYSIS in which the predictor or independent variables (*x*s) are assumed to be related to the criterion or dependent variable (*y*) in such a manner that increases in an *x* variable result in consistent increases in the *y* variable. In other words, the direction and rate of change of one variable is constant with respect to changes in the other variable. The analysis yields a REGRESSION EQUATION that includes an INTERCEPT and REGRESSION COEFFICIENTS for the predictors. Compare NONLINEAR REGRESSION.

linear relationship an association between two variables that when subjected to REGRESSION ANALYSIS and plotted on a graph forms a straight line. In linear relationships the direction and rate of change in one variable are constant with respect to changes in the other variable. Compare NONLINEAR RELATIONSHIP.

linear scale a scale of measurement that presents actual quantities of the characteristic of interest in EQUAL INTERVALS. For example, a ruler represents a linear scale in inches. Compare LOGARITHMIC SCALE.

linear transformation the TRANS-FORMATION of a set of raw data using an equation that involves addition, subtraction, multiplication, or division with a constant. An example is the transformation of *x* to *y* by means of the equation $y = a + bx$, where *a* and *b* are numerical constants. A plot of such transformed data would form a straight line. Data are often subjected to **linearizing** to determine whether a linear model provides a better fitting or more parsimonious explanation of the variables. Compare NONLINEAR TRANSFORMATION.

line graph a graph in which data points representing a series of individual measurements are shown connected by straight line segments. Consider the example below using data from the U.S. census.

Line graphs often are used to show trends over time, such as population growth. Also called **line chart**.

line of best fit see BEST FIT.

link function in the GENERALIZED LINEAR MODEL, a formula used to obtain expected values for an outcome or dependent variable that is nonlinearly related to a set of predictor or independent variables. Various link functions are used, each appropriate for different types of data and hypothesized outcome DISTRIBUTIONS (e.g., a POISSON DISTRIBUTION).

listwise deletion a strategy for dealing with the problem of missing data in which an entire case record is excluded

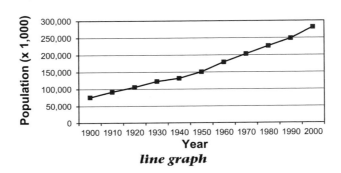

line graph

from statistical analysis if values are found to be missing for any variable of interest. For example, consider a researcher examining the relationships among grade point averages in high school, scores on college admissions tests, and grade point averages in college. If, for whatever reason, a value has not been recorded for one of those variables for certain participants, all of the information for those individuals is removed from the data set and analyses are performed only on the remaining (complete) records. This approach, which assumes data are MISSING COMPLETELY AT RANDOM, reduces the effective sample size and thus is likely to overestimate STANDARD ERRORS and reduce POWER. Also called **casewise deletion**; **complete-case analysis**. Compare PAIRWISE DELETION.

literal replication see REPLICATION.

Ljung–Box test a method used in TIME-SERIES ANALYSIS to evaluate the NULL HYPOTHESIS that any AUTOCORRELATIONS among data values observed across multiple occasions are random. It is a more sophisticated version of the BOX–PIERCE TEST. Also called **Box–Ljung test**; **Ljung–Box Q test**. [Greta M. **Ljung**, U.S. mathematician; George E. P. **Box** (1919–), British statistician]

LLR abbreviation for LOG-LIKELIHOOD RATIO.

ln abbreviation for natural LOGARITHM.

loading *n.* see FACTOR LOADING.

loading matrix see FACTOR STRUCTURE MATRIX.

local effect any outcome from some manipulation in a system or experiment that has a direct but limited influence. For example, a local effect of an analgesic drug is numbing around the injection site. Compare REMOTE EFFECT.

local independence in FACTOR ANALYSIS and other models involving LATENT VARIABLES, the basic assumption that individual observations have no direct influence on one another and that any relationship between them is to be explained by the latent variable underlying them. In ITEM RESPONSE THEORY local independence is the assumption that an examinee's responses to the various items on a test have no influence upon one another, such that an answer to one item will not affect the answer to another. It is assumed that the only factor influencing the respondent's answers is the latent variable that the test is designed to measure.

local maximum the largest value of a FUNCTION within a given range of values. When the function is plotted, the local maximum is the highest point on the graph. Compare LOCAL MINIMUM.

local minimum the smallest value of a FUNCTION within a given range of values. When the function is plotted, the local minimum is the lowest point on the graph. Compare LOCAL MAXIMUM.

local regression (**loess**; **lowess**) a form of REGRESSION ANALYSIS in which a model of the relationship between outcomes and predictors is obtained by fitting different linear or quadratic functions to different segments or intervals of data. Variables are assigned different WEIGHTS in the REGRESSION EQUATIONS to reflect their relative importance at each point and no assumptions are made about the associations among the variables. The overall curve obtained by combining the individual fitted curves for the different data segments shows the general shape of the relationship between the variables. Also called **locally weighted regression**.

LOCF abbreviation for LAST OBSERVATION CARRIED FORWARD.

loess *n.* see LOCAL REGRESSION.

logarithm (**log**) *n.* the number of times that a given value (the **base**) has to be multiplied by itself to produce a specific quantity. For example, the logarithm for the quantity 81 and the base 3 is the number 4 ($3 \times 3 \times 3 \times 3 = 81$). Logarithms are given by the generic formula $y = \log_a x$, thus $4 = \log_3 81$. When the base is the particular value known as the Eulerian number ($e = 2.71828...$), the function is a **natural logarithm** (or **hyperbolic logarithm**) and denoted $y = \log_e x$.

logarithmic distribution a PROBABILITY DISTRIBUTION derived from a logarithmic function. It is used to describe the probability that a random variable (e.g., the number of words understood by a young child) equates to a given value. Logarithmic distributions are skewed, with long right tails, and usually have small MEANS and large VARIANCES: Values are discrete, peak at $x = 1$, and cannot be negative. Also called **log series distribution**.

logarithmic function the function $y = \log_a x$, which gives the relation between a number (x) and its LOGARITHM (y) to the base a. It is equivalent to $x = a^y$.

logarithmic scale a measurement that uses the LOGARITHMS of the values obtained rather than the scale values themselves. Logarithmic scales are useful when the obtained data cover a very large range of values and are more easily described or interpreted when reduced to a smaller, more restricted set of numbers. For example, loudness is assessed on a logarithmic scale, as there is a considerable difference between the loudest and softest sounds that may be detected by the human ear. Compare LINEAR SCALE.

logarithmic transformation the conversion of raw data values into another form via the use of LOGARITHMS. In turning multiplicative relationships into additive ones and eliminating exponential trends, logarithmic transformations allow researchers to analyze data using LINEAR MODELS. Additionally, such transformations may be used to convert raw data into a form that more closely matches the assumptions required in particular statistical analyses, particularly that of NORMALITY.

logical inference see INFERENCE.

logical positivism a philosophical perspective that is committed to the principle of verification, which holds that the meaning and truth of all non-tautological statements is dependent on empirical observation. The positivist view of science is evident in psychology's commitment to empirical scientific methods and focus on testing hypotheses deduced from theory. Logical positivism had waned by the middle of the 20th century. See POSITIVISM. See also POST-POSITIVISM; REDUCTIONISM.

logistic distribution a THEORETICAL DISTRIBUTION of continuous values that describes a set of relationships between variables as defined by a LOGISTIC FUNCTION. Frequently used in studying growth rates, it is similar to the NORMAL DISTRIBUTION in shape but has greater KURTOSIS.

logistic function a basic function of the form $y = c/(1 + a \exp[-bx])$, where y and x are variables, a, b, and c are constants, and exp is the EXPONENTIAL FUNCTION. When graphed, values derived from a logistic function form an S shape called the **logistic curve**. The logistic function is used to describe LONGITUDINAL DATA and growth rates in particular, in which an initial stage of growth is approximately exponential and then, as saturation begins, slows and ultimately ceases altogether.

logistic regression (**LR**) a form of REGRESSION ANALYSIS used when the outcome or DEPENDENT VARIABLE may assume only one of two categorical values (e.g., pass or fail) and the predictors or INDEPENDENT VARIABLES are either categorical or CONTINUOUS. For example, a researcher could use logistic regression to determine the likelihood of graduating from college (yes or no) given such student information as high-

L

school grade point average, college admissions test score, number of advanced placement courses taken in high school, socioeconomic status, and gender. The analysis yields a LOGISTIC REGRESSION EQUATION with an INTERCEPT and REGRESSION COEFFICIENTS that indicate the probability of a specific outcome occurring according to the values of the predictors. Also called **logistic modeling**.

logistic regression equation the formula produced in a LOGISTIC REGRESSION analysis. Given in the form $y = e^{\pi}/(1 - e^{\pi})$, in which e = the natural LOGARITHM and π = the probability of an outcome as determined by $a + b_1x_1 + b_2x_2 + \ldots b_nx_n$ (where a is the INTERCEPT and b is the regression weight of a predictor variable), it is the mathematical expression of the relationship between a binary outcome variable and one or more predictors. A positive regression coefficient indicates that the predictor increases the probability of the outcome, whereas a negative regression coefficient indicates that the predictor decreases the probability of that outcome. A large regression coefficient indicates a predictor that strongly influences the probability of the outcome, whereas a near-zero coefficient indicates a predictor that has little influence on the probability of that outcome.

logistic transformation a TRANSFORMATION in which measurements on a LINEAR SCALE are converted into probabilities between 0 and 1. It is given by the formula $y = e^x/(1 + e^x)$, where x is the scale value and e is the Eulerian number (see LOGARITHM). The inverse of LOGITS, logistic transformations are used in such statistical procedures as LOGISTIC REGRESSION.

logit *n*. a nonlinear probability function. It is given by the formula $\text{logit}(p) = \log(p/[1 - p])$, where p is the probability of an event. In other words, a logit is the logarithm (log) of the ODDS of the occur-

rence of an event. Logits are the inverse of LOGISTIC TRANSFORMATIONS.

logit analysis a statistical procedure similar to LOGISTIC REGRESSION that presents outcome probabilities in terms of LOGITS.

logit model a mathematical model postulating some relation between the LOGIT of observed probabilities in a sample and certain unknown but estimated population PARAMETERS. A logit model often fits the data in cases where a linear model using probabilities does not.

log likelihood the LOGARITHM of a probability value or estimate.

log-likelihood ratio (**LLR**) a ratio whose numerator and denominator comprise LOG LIKELIHOODS. It is used (in the **log-likelihood test**) to evaluate the GOODNESS OF FIT of the NULL HYPOTHESIS and the ALTERNATIVE HYPOTHESIS in explaining sample data. The simpler LIKELIHOOD RATIO indicates how many more times likely the observed values are to occur under one model than under the other, and the LOGARITHMS of those values yield a log-likelihood ratio.

log-linear analysis a method of examining relationships between two or more CATEGORICAL VARIABLES that involves an analysis of the natural LOGARITHMS of frequency counts within a CONTINGENCY TABLE. Log-linear analyses do not distinguish between INDEPENDENT VARIABLES and DEPENDENT VARIABLES but rather attempt to model all significant associations among all variables, including interactions between any combination of the variables, using sets of ODDS and ODDS RATIOS for different category outcomes. Also called **log-linear modeling**.

log-normal distribution a THEORETICAL DISTRIBUTION in which the LOGARITHMS of values on a variable follow the bell-shaped NORMAL DISTRIBUTION.

log odds see LOGIT.

log-rank test a NONPARAMETRIC method

to compare the patterns of survival for two samples that were randomly assigned to a TREATMENT condition and a CONTROL CONDITION. If there is significantly longer survival in the treatment group, such that there are fewer incidences of a problem (e.g., disease, death), then the calculated value of the log-rank test statistic will be larger than its corresponding CRITICAL VALUE and the treatment will be seen as successful. Also called **Cox–Mantel test**; **Mantel–Cox test**.

log series distribution see LOGARITHMIC DISTRIBUTION.

longitudinal data information obtained through multiple measurements of the same individuals over a period of time. For example, a researcher investigating use of coping strategies in college students may evaluate stress levels at the beginning, middle, and end of the fall and spring semesters.

longitudinal design the study of a variable or group of variables in the same cases or participants over a period of time, sometimes of several years. An example of a longitudinal design is a comparative study of the same children in an urban and a suburban school over several years for the purpose of recording their cognitive development in depth. A longitudinal study that evaluates a group of randomly chosen individuals is referred to as a **panel study**, whereas a longitudinal study that evaluates a group of individuals possessing some common characteristic (usually age) is referred to as a **cohort study**. Also called **longitudinal research**; **longitudinal study**. Compare CROSS-SECTIONAL DESIGN.

Lord's paradox an effect in which the relationship between a continuous outcome variable and a CATEGORICAL independent variable (e.g., treatment or control) is reversed when an additional COVARIATE is introduced to the analysis. For example, suppose that a researcher is

studying change in knowledge about a topic following an intervention and obtains results indicating that those who received the treatment had a better outcome (i.e., had higher knowledge scores) than those in the control group. If the researcher decides to adjust for baseline differences, however, by obtaining knowledge scores both before and after the intervention, the pattern of findings could be reversed: Where participants receiving the treatment had substantially more initial knowledge than those in the control group, it might appear that they did not gain from the intervention despite their high scores at the end of the research. [Frederick M. **Lord** (1912–2000), U.S. psychometrician]

Lorenz curve a graphical representation of the inequality between the FREQUENCY DISTRIBUTION for a variable and some comparison distribution. For example, Lorenz curves often are used to illustrate inequities of wealth in a society, as in the following hypothetical illustration.

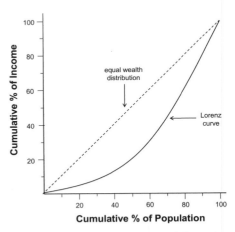

The curve shows the degree of disparity that exists between an arrangement of equal wealth distribution and the actual distribution. See GINI COEFFICIENT. [Max O. **Lorenz** (1876–1959), U.S. economist]

loss function a formula that specifies a

penalty or "cost" associated with obtaining an incorrect value estimate from a statistical model. It provides a quantification of error and DECISION RULES that serve to minimize the risk of drawing inaccurate conclusions.

loss to follow-up the situation in which researchers lose contact with some participants in a study and thus can no longer obtain data for them. Loss to follow-up may occur, for example, in a clinical study of a new drug to treat cancer if some patients unexpectedly move or otherwise become unreachable. A common problem in LONGITUDINAL DESIGNS, loss to follow-up results in missing data that may bias study findings.

lot acceptance sampling see ACCEPTANCE SAMPLING.

lower hinge the point in a distribution of values below which lie one fourth of the data. It is equivalent to the first QUARTILE and lies midway between the MEDIAN and the minimum point of the distribution. Compare UPPER HINGE.

lower quartile see QUARTILE.

lower real limit see REAL LIMIT.

lower-tail probability the probability that a random variable will take a value considerably lower than the mean for that variable (i.e., one appearing at the extreme left on the x-axis in the plot of a PROBABILITY DISTRIBUTION). Lower-tail probabilities are important in certain statistical tests of experimental hypotheses. Compare UPPER-TAIL PROBABILITY.

lower whisker in a BOX-AND-WHISKER PLOT, the line extending from the value at the 25th PERCENTILE to the smallest value within one INTERQUARTILE RANGE of that percentile score. Compare UPPER WHISKER.

lowess *n.* see LOCAL REGRESSION.

LR 1. abbreviation for LIKELIHOOD RATIO. **2.** abbreviation for LOGISTIC REGRESSION.

LSD abbreviation for least significant difference. See FISHER LEAST SIGNIFICANT DIFFERENCE TEST.

LSD test see FISHER LEAST SIGNIFICANT DIFFERENCE TEST.

LTA abbreviation for LATENT TRANSITION ANALYSIS.

lurking variable see HIDDEN VARIABLE.

L

Mm

M symbol for SAMPLE MEAN.

MA abbreviation for MOVING AVERAGE.

MAD 1. abbreviation for MEAN ABSOLUTE DEVIATION. **2.** abbreviation for MEDIAN ABSOLUTE DEVIATION.

magnitude of effect see EFFECT SIZE.

Mahalanobis distance (symbol: D^2) a MULTIVARIATE measure of the degree to which two sets of values differ from one another: the mean distance between two sets of DEVIATION SCORES, relative to the variances and covariances among the respective variables. Larger D^2 values indicate greater distance, and hence less similarity between sets. The Mahalanobis distance is useful for identifying OUTLIERS in a data set and is often applied in CLUSTER ANALYSIS, DISCRIMINANT ANALYSIS, and similar techniques. Also called **generalized distance**. [Prasanta C. Mahalanobis (1893–1972), Indian statistician]

main diagonal the line of values running from the upper left to the lower right of a SQUARE MATRIX.

$$\begin{bmatrix} 1 & .76 & .73 & .67 \\ .76 & 1 & .66 & .67 \\ .73 & .66 & 1 & .71 \\ .67 & .67 & .71 & 1 \end{bmatrix}$$

As shown, the first value in the main diagonal is the number in the first row and the first column of the matrix, the second value is the number in the second row and second column, and so on. Also called **leading diagonal**.

main effect the consistent total effect of a single INDEPENDENT VARIABLE on a DEPENDENT VARIABLE over all other independent variables in an experimental design. It is distinct from, but may be obscured by, an INTERACTION EFFECT between variables.

MA model abbreviation for MOVING-AVERAGE MODEL.

MANCOVA acronym for MULTIVARIATE ANALYSIS OF COVARIANCE.

Manhattan distance see CITY-BLOCK DISTANCE.

manifest variable a variable whose values can be directly observed or measured, as opposed to one whose values must be inferred. In STRUCTURAL EQUATION MODELING and FACTOR ANALYSIS manifest variables are used to study LATENT VARIABLES. Also called **indicator variable**.

manipulated variable see EXPERIMENTAL VARIABLE.

manipulation *n.* in an EXPERIMENTAL DESIGN, the researcher's adjustment of an independent variable such that one or more groups of participants are exposed to specific treatments while one or more other groups experience a CONTROL CONDITION. For example, a health researcher could introduce a manipulation such that a portion of the participants in a study randomly receive a new drug, whereas the remaining participants receive only a PLACEBO. See EXPERIMENTAL VARIABLE.

manipulation check any means by which an experimenter evaluates the efficacy of an EXPERIMENTAL VARIABLE, that is, verifies that a manipulation affected the participants as intended.

Mann–Whitney U test a NONPARAMETRIC TEST of centrality for ORDINAL DATA that contrasts scores from two INDEPENDENT SAMPLES to assess whether there are significant differences between the two sets of rankings. The statistic obtained from this test, U, is calculated by summing the number of ranks in one group that are smaller than each of the ranks in the other group. A Mann–Whitney U test is analogous to a ONE-WAY ANALYSIS OF VARIANCE, except that the former is conducted with ranked data and the latter is conducted with CONTINUOUS data. See also WILCOXON–MANN–WHITNEY TEST. [Henry Berthold **Mann** (1905–2000), Austrian-born U.S. mathematician; Donald Ransom **Whitney** (1915–2001), U.S. statistician]

MANOVA acronym for MULTIVARIATE ANALYSIS OF VARIANCE.

Mantel–Cox test see LOG-RANK TEST. [Nathan **Mantel** (1919–2002), U.S. biostatistician; David **Cox** (1924–), British statistician]

Mantel–Haenszel test a statistical procedure used to determine whether two DICHOTOMOUS VARIABLES are independent of each other across groups that differ on a third variable. For example, a health researcher may want to assess whether smoking status (smoker vs. nonsmoker) and cancer diagnosis (cancer vs. no cancer) are independent in a subsample of men and also in a subsample of women. If smoking and cancer were related in either or both of the subsamples, the **Mantel–Haenszel statistic** obtained from this procedure would be larger than a CRITICAL VALUE. Also called **Cochran–Mantel–Haenszel test**. [William G. **Cochran** (1909–1980), British-born U.S. statistician; Nathan **Mantel**; William M. **Haenszel** (1910–1998), U.S. biostatistician]

MAPE abbreviation for MEAN ABSOLUTE PERCENTAGE ERROR.

MAR abbreviation for MISSING AT RANDOM.

marginal *n.* the sums or averages of any of the rows or columns of data in a matrix. See COLUMN MARGINAL; ROW MARGINAL.

marginal distribution a distribution of scores that shows the effect of one variable of interest after the influence of other variables has been removed from the data. It is obtained by averaging out the different scores resulting from different conditions of the variables that are to be excluded from the analysis. For example, imagine a researcher is conducting a study with two independent variables of treatment (treatment or control) and gender (male or female). In order to understand the MAIN EFFECT of treatment, he or she could examine the marginal distribution of means for the treatment and control groups, respectively, by averaging across the means for men and women. Similarly, to understand the main effect of gender the researcher could examine the marginal distribution of means for the two gender groups by averaging across means for the treatment and control groups, respectively. See also MARGINAL MEAN.

marginal effect a measure of how much an outcome or DEPENDENT VARIABLE changes when an explanatory or INDEPENDENT VARIABLE is modified by one unit. For example, if a researcher is examining grade point average (GPA) and the number of hours studied per week, the marginal effect would show how much GPA would change if study time was increased by one hour.

marginal frequency the sum of any one of the rows or columns in a data matrix. For example, in a table of students classified by sex and area of study, the number of female students, regardless of area of study, would be one marginal frequency, and the number of students enrolled in a specific area of study, regardless of sex, would be another. See also MARGINAL DISTRIBUTION.

marginal homogeneity in a two-way CONTINGENCY TABLE, the situation in which the sum of each row is the same as the sum of the corresponding column. A test of marginal homogeneity often is conducted to assess agreement between

M

two sets of data, such as performance ratings given by two independent figure-skating judges.

marginal mean the average score across two or more groups on one variable, particularly as calculated in an ANALYSIS OF VARIANCE to determine the existence of a MAIN EFFECT. See also MARGINAL DISTRIBUTION.

marginal probability the chance of occurrence of one variable across each level of another variable. For example, a researcher interested in cancer diagnosis and smoking status might list diagnosis (cancer vs. no cancer) in two rows and smoking status (smoker vs. nonsmoker) in two columns. The marginal probabilities for cancer diagnosis would be obtained by summing the individual probabilities across both levels of smoking status, whereas for smoking status the marginal probabilities would be obtained by summing the individual probabilities across both levels of cancer diagnosis. In other words, the marginal probabilities are the total probability values given at the ends of the rows and the bottoms of the columns. See also MARGINAL DISTRIBUTION.

marginal sum of squares see TYPE III SUM OF SQUARES.

margin of error (**MOE**) a statistic expressing the CONFIDENCE INTERVAL associated with a given measurement; it is an allowance for a slight miscalculation or an acceptable deviation. The larger the margin of error for the sample data, the less confidence one has that the results obtained are accurate for the entire population of interest.

mark-and-recapture sampling see CAPTURE–TAG–RECAPTURE SAMPLING.

marker variable technique in FACTOR ANALYSIS, a technique used to control for common method variance (CMV), that is, the systematic error that can arise from using a single method of measurement. In order to account for

any CMV, the researcher introduces a **marker variable** into the study: This is a new variable that is theoretically unrelated to at least one of the main variables of interest. The correlation between the marker variable and the unrelated variable of interest is taken as an estimate of the common method variance in the study.

Markov chain a sequence of steps or events in which the probability of each transition depends only on the immediately preceding step, and not on any earlier step. For example, when a person considers a behavior change such as losing weight he or she experiences certain stages: The individual could move from not thinking about losing weight (precontemplation) to considering a weight loss plan (contemplation), through to maintaining a reasonable weight (maintenance) and conceivably back to not wanting to think about weight loss. This process could be described as a Markov chain. Also called **discrete-time Markov chain**; **Markov process**. Compare RANDOM WALK. [Andrei **Markov** (1856–1922), Russian mathematician]

Markov chain Monte Carlo method (**MCMC method**) a statistical simulation procedure that tries to find a reasonable pattern of probabilities for moving from one designated state to another in a MARKOV CHAIN. It involves sampling from various THEORETICAL DISTRIBUTIONS to see which is the best fit for observed data. For example, a Markov chain Monte Carlo method could be used to find the plausible pattern of probabilities of moving from substance dependence to recovery. See also MONTE CARLO RESEARCH. [Andrei **Markov**]

Markov matrix see TRANSITION MATRIX.

Markov random field a graphic representation of two or more discrete states or stages in a MARKOV CHAIN with

M

directional lines between them to indicate the possible patterns of moving from one state to the next or back to earlier states. For example, consider a behavior change model in the context of quitting smoking, which could be represented in a Markov random field. A square may be used to depict one stage, smoking regularly, with a line drawn to a square representing the next stage, thinking about quitting, and so on through extended quitting. Lines also could be drawn from each of those stages back to earlier stages to represent the possibility of lapsing during the process. [Andrei **Markov**]

MARS acronym for MULTIVARIATE ADAPTIVE REGRESSION SPLINE.

martingale *n.* a STOCHASTIC process in which the probability of any future event is the same as that of the current event, such that knowledge of previous events does not help one to predict future events. For example, a game based on a series of coin tosses would be a martingale, as the probability of heads or tails remains the same (50%) at each toss. In contrast, a game involving the drawing of cards from a standard deck without replacement would not be a martingale, as the probability of drawing, say, a spade would change depending on the suits of the cards drawn previously.

masking *n.* the obscuring of the effect of one variable by the effect of another variable. For example, a researcher interested in whether risky sexual behavior is related to alcohol use might find that an experience of sexual abuse exerts a stronger influence on sexual behavior, thus masking the effect of alcohol use. —**mask** *vb.*

matched case-control study a CASE-CONTROL STUDY in which MATCHING is used to control for CONFOUNDS (e.g., age, sex). This approach is considered particularly appropriate where sample size is limited.

matched-pairs design a study involving two groups of participants in which each member of one group is paired with a similar person in the other group, that is, someone who matches them on one or more variables that are not the main focus of the study but nonetheless could influence its outcome. For example, a researcher evaluating the effectiveness of a new drug in treating Alzheimer's disease might identify pairs of individuals of the same age and intelligence and then randomly assign one person from each pair to the treatment condition that will receive the drug and the other to the control condition that will not. A **matched-groups design** (**matched-samples design**; **matched-subjects design**) is a similar approach but broader in that it allows for the inclusion of more than two groups of participants.

matched-pairs signed-ranks test see WILCOXON MATCHED-PAIRS SIGNED-RANKS TEST.

matched-pairs t test a statistical procedure used to test for significant differences between the two sets of data obtained from a MATCHED-PAIRS DESIGN. For example, a researcher could use a matched-pairs *t* test to assess whether relationship satisfaction significantly differs between two sets of individuals who have been matched for age and gender where one set has been married for 5 years and the other for 10 years. Also called **paired-samples t test**. See T TEST.

matching *n.* a procedure for ensuring that participants in different study conditions are comparable at the beginning of the research on one or more key variables that have the potential to influence results. After multiple sets of matched individuals are created, one member of each set is assigned at random to the EXPERIMENTAL GROUP and the other to the CONTROL GROUP. For example, a researcher could create two groups whose members are of the same sex and have the same family history of a disease; one group would be given a treatment while the other would not. Such an approach would enable the researcher to rule out sex and family history as potential explanations of the study outcome, thereby allowing greater validity to attributing any changes between the groups to the treatment. When individuals are paired according to their PROPENSITY SCORES, the process is referred to as **caliper matching**. See also MATCHED-PAIRS DESIGN.

matching coefficient an index of the correspondence between two sets of items, such as scores or other sample data. For example, a matching coefficient could be used during an investigation of possible plagiarism to assess how much overlap there is between an essay submitted by a student and an essay posted online.

mathematical statistics see THEORETICAL STATISTICS.

M **mathematico-deductive method** see HYPOTHETICO-DEDUCTIVE METHOD.

matrix *n.* a rectangular ordered arrangement (ARRAY) of numbers in rows and columns. The following is a simple example:

$$\begin{bmatrix} 1 & 6 & 3 \\ 4 & 1 & 5 \\ 3 & 7 & 1 \end{bmatrix}$$

Individual items in a matrix are called ELEMENTS or entries. Many different types of matrices are used in statistics, such as the CORRELATION MATRIX and the COVARIANCE MATRIX.

matrix algebra a set of mathematical rules for analyzing large numbers of variables arranged in matrices. Matrix algebra procedures may involve basic calculations, such as adding and subtracting matrices, and also more complex processes, such as multiplying and dividing matrices.

matrix decomposition in linear algebra, a process in which a complex matrix is broken down into its simpler component elements. See also CHOLESKY FACTORIZATION; SINGULAR VALUE DECOMPOSITION.

maturation *n.* naturally occurring time-related changes in a participant (e.g., growth, aging, fatigue, boredom, attention shifts) that pose a threat to the INTERNAL VALIDITY of a study, particularly a longitudinal one. These processes—as opposed to the specific treatment or intervention—may explain any changes in participants during the experiment. For example, a researcher may study substance use in a set of individuals from young adolescence to late adulthood. In the study, substance use may naturally decline as a function of the development of the participants rather than because of the influence of an experimental intervention. Thus, the investigator would want to assess and possibly control for this **maturation effect** in order to maintain the internal validity of the study.

Mauchly's sphericity test in WITHIN-SUBJECTS ANALYSES OF VARIANCE, a technique to determine whether there is HOMOGENEITY OF VARIANCE across all possible levels of the independent variable (a condition known as SPHERICITY). Sphericity is a basic assumption of such analyses and lack of it can distort the calculations of variance. The Mauchly test is based on the LIKELIHOOD RATIO criterion and involves a scaled comparison between the DETERMINANT and the TRACE of the sample covariance matrix. When the significance level of Mauchly's test is $< .05$ then equality of variance cannot be assumed. [John W. **Mauchly** (1907–1980), U.S. computer scientist]

maximin strategy in GAME THEORY or decision making, a tactic in which an individual chooses the best of a set of worst possible outcomes or payoffs. For example, participants in a study may need to choose whichever outcome would best maximize a minimum advantage: withdrawing from a scenario in which they are currently performing poorly, or continuing and possibly doing even worse. Compare MINIMAX STRATEGY.

maximum likelihood a statistical technique in which the set of possible values for the PARAMETERS of a distribution is estimated based on the most probable sample of observations that one might have obtained from that population. The values derived from this procedure are referred to as **maximum likelihood parameter estimates** or **maximum likelihood estimates** and can be used to obtain an overall estimate of how well a given model fits the data. Maximum likelihood techniques are used in several statistical methods, such as LOGISTIC REGRESSION, HIERARCHICAL LINEAR MODELING, and STRUCTURAL EQUATION MODELING. For example, when evaluating a pair of regression models, a **maximum likelihood ratio** of the overall estimates can be used to assess whether there is a significant difference between the two, which in turn can be used to identify the preferred model. Also called **maximum likelihood estimation** (**MLE**).

maximum likelihood–expectation maximization estimation (**ML-EM estimation**) a statistical method for calculating MAXIMUM LIKELIHOOD estimates for the parameters of a model that involves LATENT VARIABLES. The process uses the EM ALGORITHM to obtain the closest match between the sample data and the proposed model.

MCA abbreviation for multiple classification analysis. See MULTIPLE DISCRIMINANT ANALYSIS.

MCAR acronym for MISSING COMPLETELY AT RANDOM.

MCMC method abbreviation for MARKOV CHAIN MONTE CARLO METHOD.

MCML estimation abbreviation for MONTE CARLO MAXIMUM LIKELIHOOD ESTIMATION.

MCP abbreviation for MINIMUM CONVEX POLYGON.

MDA abbreviation for MULTIPLE DISCRIMINANT ANALYSIS.

MDL abbreviation for MINIMUM DESCRIPTION LENGTH.

MDS abbreviation for MULTIDIMENSIONAL SCALING.

mean *n.* the numerical average of a set of scores, computed as the sum of all scores divided by the number of scores. For example, suppose a health researcher sampled five individuals and found their numbers of hours of exercise per week to be 3, 1, 5, 4, and 7, respectively. The mean number of exercise hours per week thus would be $(3 + 1 + 5 + 4 + 7)/5 = 20/5 = 4$. The mean is the most widely used statistic for describing CENTRAL TENDENCY. Also called **arithmetic mean**; **arithmetic average**. See also GEOMETRIC MEAN; HARMONIC MEAN.

mean absolute deviation (**MAD**) a measure of DISPERSION, given as the typical distance of each score in a set from the mean of the set, irrespective of the positive or negative direction of the difference. For example, consider a set of five scores: 7, 1, 10, 8, and 4. To obtain the mean absolute deviation for the set, one first calculates the mean by summing all scores and dividing by the total number of scores: $30/5 = 6$. One then calculates the difference of each individual score from this average regardless of whether it is positive or negative, yielding the following: 1, 5, 4, 2, and 2. Summing these new values and dividing them by the total number of values provides the mean absolute deviation: $14/5 = 2.8$. Also called **average absolute deviation**; **average deviation** (**AD**); **mean deviation**. See also ABSOLUTE DEVIATION.

mean absolute percentage error (**MAPE**) a measure of variance in TIME-

M

SERIES values, given as the average difference of a set of such values from their expected values, regardless of the direction of that difference (i.e., whether it is positive or negative). For example, consider the following time series of the number of exercise hours per week for an individual over five weeks: 3, 1, 5, 4, and 7. If a researcher predicts the weekly exercise hours to be 2, 2, 5, 5, and 6, then he or she might wish to determine the general degree of inaccuracy of his or her predictions. Thus, the mean absolute percentage error would be calculated as follows: $(|3 - 2|/3 + |1 - 2|/1 + |5 - 5|/5 + 4 - 5|/4 + 7 - 6|/7)/5 = (.333 + 1 + 0 + .25 + .143)/5 = 1.726/5 = .35 \times 100 = 35\%$.

mean deviation see MEAN ABSOLUTE DEVIATION.

mean difference a measure of variability in a data set calculated as the average of the distances between each score and each of the other scores, disregarding whether the deviation is positive or negative. For example, consider the following three scores: 1, 3, and 9. The mean difference would be calculated as: $(|1 - 3| + |1 - 9| + |3 - 1| + |3 - 9| + |9 - 1| + |9 - 3|)/6 = (2 + 8 + 2 + 6 + 8 + 6)/6 = 32/6 = 5.33$.

mean effect size in a META-ANALYSIS, a measure of the average EFFECT SIZE across multiple studies. For example, an investigator analyzing several studies assessing a new treatment may determine a mean effect size by calculating the average standardized difference between treatment and control groups over all of the studies. Calculations of mean effect size often take variance and RELIABILITY into account by assigning different WEIGHTS to the values derived from different studies. A study with a large sample, for instance, or one that uses more precise measurement techniques may be weighted to have a greater impact in determining the mean effect size.

mean square (symbol: *MS*) an estimator of variance calculated as a SUM OF SQUARES divided by its DEGREES OF FREEDOM. It is used primarily in the ANALYSIS OF VARIANCE, in which an F RATIO is obtained by dividing the mean square between groups by the mean square within groups (see BETWEEN-GROUPS MEAN SQUARE; WITHIN-GROUPS MEAN SQUARE). The mean square also is used to determine the accuracy of REGRESSION ANALYSIS models, indicating the amount of variance explained by a model ($MS_{regression}$) compared to the amount of error or unexplained variance ($MS_{residual}$).

mean square between see BETWEEN-GROUPS MEAN SQUARE.

mean squared error (symbol: *MSE*) the average amount of ERROR VARIANCE within a data set, given as the typical squared distance of a score from the mean score for the set. Mean squared error may be calculated in both ANALYSIS OF VARIANCE and REGRESSION ANALYSIS. In the former it is referred to more specifically as the WITHIN-GROUPS MEAN SQUARE and used as the denominator when calculating an F RATIO; in the latter it is known as a **residual mean square** (or **mean-square residual**) and gives the mean difference between actual scores and those predicted by a regression model. A large mean squared error indicates that scores are not homogeneous within groups or are not consistent with prediction, such that there is more "noise" than "signal." For example, a large mean squared error in gender research would show no significant differences between groups of males and groups of females. Also called **error mean square**.

mean-square deviation the typical difference between a set of scores and the MEAN of those scores, raised to the second power. It is a measure of variability in a data set generally equivalent to the VARIANCE.

mean-square residual (symbol: *MSR*) see MEAN SQUARED ERROR.

mean-square successive difference (symbol: *MSSD*) the average varia-

M

tion between each score and the previous score in a LONGITUDINAL DESIGN. Used to obtain a more accurate estimate of a trend over time in situations when the mean shifts slightly and could cause bias, it is calculated in the same manner as VARIANCE except that scores at successive time points are used in place of the MEAN.

mean square within see WITHIN-GROUPS MEAN SQUARE.

mean substitution a method of IMPUTATION in which the average value for a set of scores is inserted for each missing score in the data set. Although this practice retains the original sample size, it can artificially reduce the variation among the scores. Mean substitution may involve inserting either the GRAND MEAN or the mean for a specific group; the latter approach typically yields a more accurate estimate of any given individual's score.

measure *n.* an item or set of items that provides an indication of the quantity or nature of the phenomenon under study. It is sometimes necessary in research to have more than one measure for each of the main variables of interest.

measurement *n.* the act of appraising the extent of some amount, dimension, or criterion—or the resultant descriptive or quantified appraisal itself. A measurement is often, but not always, expressed as a numerical value.

measurement equivalence the situation in which two instruments yield virtually the same results for the same group of individuals, such that either one could replace the other. For example, a researcher constructing ALTERNATE FORMS of the same test would want to ensure measurement equivalence for the FACTOR LOADINGS of each item within a subscale, as well as for each test as a whole. See also MEASUREMENT INVARIANCE.

measurement error in CLASSICAL TEST THEORY, any difference between an observed score and the TRUE SCORE. Measurement error may arise from flaws in the assessment instrument, mistakes in using the instrument, or random or chance factors. For example, an investigator may obtain biased results from a survey because of problems with question wording or response options, question order, variability in administration, and so forth.

measurement invariance the situation in which a scale or construct provides the same results across several different samples or populations. For example, an intelligence test could be said to have measurement invariance if it yields similar results for individuals of varying gender, ethnicity, or age. Measurement invariance may apply to a single relevant characteristic (e.g., gender only), several characteristics (e.g., gender and ethnicity), or all possible characteristics and situations. See also MEASUREMENT EQUIVALENCE. Compare SELECTION INVARIANCE.

measurement level the degree of specificity, accuracy, and precision in a particular set of observations or scores, as reflected in the MEASUREMENT SCALE used.

measurement model in STRUCTURAL EQUATION MODELING, a model that quantifies the association between observations obtained during research (indicators) and theoretical underlying constructs or factors. When carrying out a CONFIRMATORY FACTOR ANALYSIS, for example, one assesses a hypothesized measurement model that specifies the relationships between observed indicators and the LATENT VARIABLES that support or affect them.

measurement scale any of four common methods for quantifying attributes of variables during the course of research, listed in order of increasing power and complexity: NOMINAL SCALE, ORDINAL SCALE, INTERVAL SCALE, and

M

RATIO SCALE. More specifically, nominal scales consist of named categories with no numerical meaning (e.g., gender, birthplace), ordinal scales comprise rankings from highest to lowest or vice versa (e.g., birth order, contest winners), interval scales provide equal distance between numerical values but have an arbitrary zero point (e.g., degrees Fahrenheit, checkbook balance), and ratio scales provide equal distance between numerical values with an exact zero point (e.g., height, weight).

measurement theory a field of study that examines the attribution of values to traits, characteristics, or constructs. Measurement theory focuses on assessing the TRUE SCORE of an attribute, such that an obtained value has a close correspondence with the actual quantity, with high RELIABILITY and little MEASUREMENT ERROR. See also CLASSICAL TEST THEORY.

measure of agreement see COEFFICIENT OF AGREEMENT.

measure of association any of various indices of the degree to which two or more variables are related. One of the most common measures of association is the CORRELATION COEFFICIENT.

measure of central tendency any of a class of descriptive statistics that reflect the middle or central point of a set of scores. The most common measures of central tendency are the MEAN, MEDIAN, and MODE, which are the average, midpoint, and most frequently occurring scores in a distribution, respectively. Also called **measure of location**.

measure of correlation see CORRELATION COEFFICIENT.

measure of dispersion see DISPERSION MEASURE.

measure of fit see FIT INDEX.

measure of location see MEASURE OF CENTRAL TENDENCY.

measure of variability see DISPERSION MEASURE.

median *n.* the midpoint in a distribution, that is, the score or value that divides it into two equal-sized halves. The median is a MEASURE OF CENTRAL TENDENCY that is particularly useful when analyzing data that have SKEWNESS (i.e., lopsidedness), as it is more resistant to the influence of extreme values.

median absolute deviation (**MAD**) an index of the variance in a set of scores, given as the midpoint of the difference between each score in a set and the median of the set, irrespective of the positive or negative direction of the individual differences. For example, assume that five individuals spent the following number of hours per week using a computer: 6, 10, 15, 21, and 35. To obtain the median absolute deviation, one first identifies the median for the set as a whole—in this case, 15. Next, one calculates the difference of each individual score from this overall median irrespective of its direction—in this case, 9, 5, 0, 6, and 20. One then orders the differences—0, 5, 6, 9, and 20—and finds the midpoint of this new array, yielding a median absolute deviation of 6.

median test a NONPARAMETRIC method that assesses the equality of the midpoints (MEDIANS) in two or more samples of data to determine whether they come from the same population. Although previously used to indicate any of several alternative procedures, nowadays the term generally is used to refer to the WILCOXON–MANN–WHITNEY TEST.

mediational process a set of relationships in which an INDEPENDENT VARIABLE is linked to a MEDIATOR that in turn is linked with and influences a DEPENDENT VARIABLE. For example, the progression from childhood sexual abuse to adult risky behavior may be a mediational process that involves powerlessness.

mediator *n.* in statistical analyses, an intermediary or intervening variable that accounts for an observed relation between two other variables. For example, a researcher may posit a model involving an INDEPENDENT VARIABLE of ability, a mediator of self-efficacy, and a DEPENDENT VARIABLE of achievement. Thus, ability is hypothesized to influence self-efficacy, which in turn is thought to influence achievement.

member check a procedure used in QUALITATIVE RESEARCH whereby a researcher returns to a participant and requests feedback on his or her original responses as recorded and sometimes on their interpretation by others. Conducting a member check is intended to ensure the accuracy and INTERNAL VALIDITY of a qualitative study. However, some researchers question the merit of the process, viewing it as inconsistent with qualitative research in that it assumes participants' experiences are objective and finite. Also called **member validation**; **respondent validation**.

mesokurtic *adj.* describing a FREQUENCY DISTRIBUTION that is neither flatter nor more peaked than the NORMAL DISTRIBUTION.

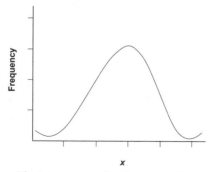

That is, a mesokurtic arrangement of values follows a bell-shaped curve, with the majority of scores clustered around a value at the midpoint and a few extreme scores tapering off on either side. See also PLATYKURTIC; LEPTOKURTIC.

M-estimator *n.* a type of ESTIMATOR used to calculate the minimum difference between an actual value obtained from a sample and the hypothesized value in the larger population or the estimated value obtained from a model. The estimators used in LEAST SQUARES REGRESSION and MAXIMUM LIKELIHOOD estimation are examples.

meta-analysis *n.* a quantitative technique for synthesizing the results of multiple studies of a phenomenon into a single result by combining the EFFECT SIZE estimates from each study into a single estimate of the combined effect size or into a DISTRIBUTION of effect sizes. For example, a researcher could conduct a meta-analysis of several studies on the association between self-efficacy and achievement, integrating the findings into an overall correlation. Although meta-analysis is ideally suited for summarizing a body of literature in terms of its impact, limitations, and future implications, there are conditions that limit its applicability. For example, there is no minimum number of studies nor participants required, and information of potential interest may be missing from the original research reports upon which the procedure must rely.

metaregression analysis a procedure similar to a META-ANALYSIS but conducted with two or more REGRESSION ANALYSES rather than experimental studies. For example, a researcher could conduct a metaregression analysis of relevant studies predicting college achievement from high school grades, integrating the findings into a single overall REGRESSION EQUATION. Thus, a metaregression analysis investigates the causes of heterogeneity (differences) across studies in order to determine when, where, and for whom a particular outcome will occur.

metatheory *n.* a higher order theory about theories, allowing one to analyze, compare, and evaluate competing bodies of ideas. The concept of a metatheory suggests that theories derive from other

M

theories such that there are always prior theoretical assumptions and commitments behind any theoretical formulation. It follows that these prior assumptions and commitments are worthy of study in their own right, and an understanding of them is essential to a full understanding of derivative theories. **—metatheoretical** *adj.*

method of least squares see LEAST SQUARES REGRESSION.

method of maximum likelihood see MAXIMUM LIKELIHOOD.

method of moments an alternative to MAXIMUM LIKELIHOOD estimation in which values describing basic characteristics of a sample (known as MOMENTS) are used to approximate the corresponding values for the larger population. For example, a researcher could use the method of moments to estimate the mean or variance for a population by inserting the appropriate sample value into an equation that calculates one from the other. Although simpler than maximum likelihood, the method of moments is less accurate.

methodological individualism a theory that emphasizes the importance of each person in determining his or her own circumstances and minimizes any possible influence from larger societal groups or structures. For example, a researcher who endorsed methodological individualism would be less apt to consider how socioeconomic status might contribute to the level of achievement for a sample of individuals, preferring instead to investigate variables believed to be under each person's control, such as motivation, determination, or ability.

methodological pluralism the belief that various approaches to conducting research, qualitative and quantitative, each have their respective strengths and weaknesses such that no one method is inherently superior to any other and no single method is best overall.

methodological triangulation the use of multiple quantitative and qualitative procedures to collect data so as to generate converging evidence on the topic of study. For example, a researcher studying alcohol consumption might employ methodological triangulation by measuring participants' blood alcohol levels, collecting self-reports on quantity of alcohol consumed, and obtaining input from peers on quantity of alcohol consumed.

methodology *n.* **1.** the science of method or orderly arrangement; specifically, the branch of logic concerned with the application of the principles of reasoning to scientific and philosophical inquiry. **2.** the system of methods, principles, and rules of procedure used within a particular discipline. For example, in research and experimental design the term refers to the techniques used to collect information, and in statistics it refers to the procedures used to analyze such data.

metric *n.* a scale or system used to express amount or quantity. For example, the Fahrenheit scale is a metric for assessing temperature and the system of IQ points is a metric for assessing intelligence.

Metropolis–Hastings algorithm a SIMULATION procedure for generating samples from a known PROBABILITY DISTRIBUTION. It is among the most commonly used MARKOV CHAIN MONTE CARLO METHODS. [Nicholas C. **Metropolis** (1915–1999), U.S. physicist; W. Keith **Hastings** (1930–), Canadian statistician]

MI abbreviation for MODIFICATION INDEX.

microdata *pl. n.* scores or other information collected on individual participants or units. In many research studies, microdata are consolidated into total scores, scale scores, or summary statistics known as AGGREGATE DATA.

microgenetic method a research approach that examines developmental change within a single set of individuals over relatively brief periods of time, usually days or weeks, in order to determine how it occurs. For example, health researchers could use a microgenetic method to study the weekly improvement of patients with traumatic brain injury during a one-year period.

middle-range theory an approach to the construction of THEORY that aims to combine existing formulations with experimental findings and in the process to generate new hypotheses that are open to empirical testing. Representing a level of investigation below that of a METATHEORY, middle-range theories often are used in sociology and psychology to identify the constructs and mechanisms that best explain relevant data. For example, a researcher could identify the main concepts related to organizational change by investigating previous formulations and findings in this area.

midpoint *n.* see MEDIAN.

midrange *n.* the average of the lowest and highest scores in a set of data. The midrange is a MEASURE OF CENTRAL TENDENCY more prone to bias than the MEAN, MEDIAN, and MODE since it relies solely upon the two most extreme scores, which potentially are OUTLIERS. For example, consider the following hours per week spent using a computer for five individuals: 6, 10, 15, 21, and 35. The midrange is 20.5, the mean is 17.4, and the median is 15. The midrange score thus is larger than the mean or median due to the influence of the outlier of 35 hours.

midspread *n.* see INTERQUARTILE RANGE.

MIMIC model acronym for MULTIPLE INDICATORS–MULTIPLE CAUSES MODEL.

minimax strategy in GAME THEORY or decision making, a tactic in which individuals attempt either to minimize their own maximum losses or to reduce the most an opponent will gain. For example, a health researcher may propose an intervention that would be the least aversive treatment for a serious disease, thereby minimizing the adverse effects patients may expect to experience as a result of the disease. Compare MAXIMIN STRATEGY.

minimum chi-square a method of identifying acceptable PARAMETER estimates that involves trying to find the smallest possible CHI-SQUARE value when assessing the differences between observed and expected data points. Minimum chi-square is an alternative to MAXIMUM LIKELIHOOD for finding population values that are close to observed sample values.

minimum convex polygon (**MCP**) a procedure for estimating the boundaries of an area in which a designated POPULATION may be found, based on sets of location points collected over a period of time for different individuals. For example, a health researcher may draw a minimum convex polygon around an area believed to hold the set of individuals who may have been exposed to a serious illness, based on reports about individuals with the illness.

minimum description length (**MDL**) in STRUCTURAL EQUATION MODELING, the principle that the best model for a given set of data is the one that provides the most compact description of this data. See also OCCAM'S RAZOR.

minimum variance bound see CRAMÉR–RAO LOWER BOUND.

minimum variance unbiased estimator (**MVUE**) see EFFICIENT ESTIMATOR.

minimum volume ellipsoid a statistical procedure for finding the smallest space that would encompass most of the points in a MULTIVARIATE data set, as in the generic depiction overleaf.

Identifying the minimum volume ellipsoid, for example, would help a re-

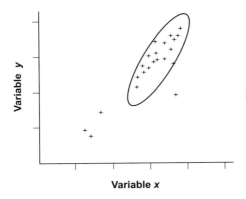

Variable *x*

searcher to observe the general location and DISPERSION of the main portion of the data and also ascertain any OUTLIER points outside the structure that may be considered for deletion due to their extremity.

misclassification cost an estimate of the costs that could arise from assigning an incorrect category or status to a situation or condition. For example, it would be worthwhile to estimate the misclassification cost of prematurely telling the public that previously contaminated town water is now safe to drink, versus waiting longer than needed to let people know they can drink the water. In this case, the misclassification cost of an early announcement would be much more serious—possibly involving severe illness or even loss of life—than that of a later announcement.

missing at random (**MAR**) the situation in which the absence of certain points from a data set is unrelated to the nature of the particular items but may be explained by other variables. For example, assume a researcher surveyed 100 students on a college campus about their weekly amount of alcohol, drug, and cigarette use but 12 individuals failed to note their use for an item. If all 12 people are male, and if there is no consistency as to which item was left blank by which person, then the pattern of responses on the survey could be related to sex (perhaps the men on campus are less likely to answer any type of evaluative

item than are the women). If so, the values would be missing at random. When data are missing at random but not MISSING COMPLETELY AT RANDOM there is a danger of biasing study results.

missing completely at random (**MCAR**) the situation in which the absence of certain points from a data set is unrelated to the nature of the variable being measured or to any other variables in the research. For example, assume a researcher identifies 100 items to ask young children in order to measure 10 conceptual variables. Given the still-developing cognitive skills of the participants, however, no more than 40 questions may be used with each child in order to obtain a sufficient response quality. Thus, if the researcher presents a computer-chosen set of 40 of the original items to each individual, the 60 dropped items would be missing completely at random—they have no systematic pattern and do not bias the study results.

missing values procedure any strategy for addressing the problem of empty items in a data set. A variety of alternatives exist, each having different merits and drawbacks. Traditional missing values procedures include LISTWISE DELETION, in which all of the data for a participant or case are deleted if even one item is left blank; PAIRWISE DELETION, in which certain data are retained for a participant even where some other items are missing; and MEAN SUBSTITUTION, in which each missing value is replaced by the average value of all points in the data set. More recent techniques include IMPUTATION, in which a value is inserted into the data to substitute for a missing one, and its many variations. Notable among them is MULTIPLE IMPUTATION, whereby several possible values are inserted into the data to replace omitted ones and then the average and standard deviation of those replacement values are obtained.

misspecification *n*. the situation in

which the number of variables, factors, PARAMETERS, or some combination of these was not correctly specified in a statistical model, with the result that the model does not offer a reasonable representation of obtained data. Misspecification is indicated by such things as large RESIDUALS between the data and that predicted by the model, large STANDARD ERRORS for the parameter estimates, values for the parameter estimates outside of the normal range (e.g., HEYWOOD CASES), or a nonsignificant result from a GOODNESS-OF-FIT TEST.

mixed design a study that combines features of both a BETWEEN-SUBJECTS DESIGN and a WITHIN-SUBJECTS DESIGN. Thus, a researcher examines not only the potential differences between two or more separate groups of participants but also assesses change in the individual members of each group over time. For example, a researcher might use a mixed design to study the influence of different types of music on relaxation. He or she could divide participants into a CONTROL GROUP (listening to no music) and two EXPERIMENTAL GROUPS (one listening to classical music and one listening to rock music). The researcher could administer a PRETEST to participants in all groups in order to determine the baseline level of physiological arousal prior to hearing any music and then introduce the music and test participants while they listen. After stopping the music, he or she could administer another test (a POSTTEST) to determine what specific reduction in arousal may have occurred throughout the listening period. In this situation, music type is a between-subjects factor (each participant hears only a single genre of music) and physiological arousal is a within-subjects factor (each participant is evaluated on this variable on multiple occasions and the different assessments compared).

mixed-design analysis of variance see MIXED-MODEL ANALYSIS OF VARIANCE.

mixed distribution a DISTRIBUTION in which the variables may take on both a DISCRETE and a CONTINUOUS range of values. This may occur when a continuously measured variable is abruptly topped off or bottomed out at an arbitrary value for a number of participants in the sample. For example, consider a health researcher studying the effects of a smoking cessation intervention who records the number of days since a participant quit smoking. For those participants who quit, the number of days will reflect an infinite series of potential values, whereas for those who continue to smoke the number of days will be the single finite value of zero.

mixed-effects design a vague term used to denote an approach to either research or analysis—the MIXED DESIGN or the MIXED-EFFECTS MODEL, respectively.

mixed-effects logistic regression a statistical procedure for analyzing a binary outcome in which at least one of the predictors is a FIXED EFFECT (i.e., specifically selected by the researcher for study) and one or more other predictors is a RANDOM EFFECT (i.e., chosen by chance from a range of possible choices). For example, an educational researcher might use mixed-effects logistic regression to examine the odds of a student selecting a quantitative major in college given his or her gender (a fixed predictor) and whether he or she has taken one or more specific quantitative classes in high school (random predictors), such as quantitative psychology or research methodology.

mixed-effects model any statistical procedure or experimental design that uses one or more independent variables whose levels are specifically selected by the researcher (FIXED EFFECTS; e.g., gender) and one or more additional independent variables whose levels are chosen randomly from a wide range of possible values (RANDOM EFFECTS; e.g.,

M

age). Also called **mixed model**. Compare FIXED-EFFECTS MODEL; RANDOM-EFFECTS MODEL.

mixed-methods research a study that combines aspects of both QUALITATIVE RESEARCH and QUANTITATIVE RESEARCH so as to more fully understand the phenomenon of interest. For example, a researcher studying a disease could conduct a focus group with a set of individuals who would share their experiences in dealing with the disease, and then supplement those qualitative findings by surveying a different set of individuals to obtain quantitative knowledge of risk factors for the disease.

mixed model see MIXED-EFFECTS MODEL.

mixed-model analysis of variance a TWO-WAY ANALYSIS OF VARIANCE in which one independent variable has fixed levels specifically chosen for investigation (e.g., gender) and the other has levels randomly selected from among many possible conditions (e.g., doses of a drug). It is one of many types of MIXED-EFFECTS MODELS. Also called **mixed-design analysis of variance**.

mixed sampling a method of collecting data that incorporates more than one sampling strategy. For example, a researcher initially may choose participants by RANDOM SAMPLING, in which each person in an identified population (e.g., cancer patients within a particular region) has an equal probability of being selected. However, the researcher may then need to switch to a STRATIFIED SAMPLING or CLUSTER SAMPLING approach if he or she discovered that certain subgroups (e.g., women with lung cancer, men with colon cancer) were not adequately represented in the sample and thus needed to be sampled more specifically. The two approaches together (e.g., simple random sampling and stratified random sampling) constitute mixed sampling.

mixture distribution see FINITE MIXTURE DISTRIBUTION.

MLE abbreviation for MAXIMUM LIKELIHOOD estimation.

ML-EM estimation abbreviation for MAXIMUM LIKELIHOOD–EXPECTATION MAXIMIZATION ESTIMATION.

modal class for grouped data, the interval or category containing the MODE (most frequently occurring score).

modal frequency the number of respondents who have the score that occurs most often in a set of data (i.e., the MODE). For example, in a small sample of college freshmen whose ages are 18, 18, 18, 19, 19, 20, 20, 21, 23, and 25, the modal frequency for age is 3: The most commonly occurring score is 18, and there are three people with such a score.

mode *n.* the most frequently occurring score in a set of data, which is sometimes used as a measure of CENTRAL TENDENCY. Also called **modal value**.

model *n.* a graphic, theoretical, or other type of representation of a concept or process that can be used for various investigative and demonstrative purposes, such as enhancing understanding of the concept, proposing hypotheses, showing relationships, or identifying patterns.

model I analysis of variance a rare synonym of FIXED-EFFECTS ANALYSIS OF VARIANCE.

model II analysis of variance a rare synonym of RANDOM-EFFECTS ANALYSIS OF VARIANCE.

model building the process of positing several alternative statistical models of a phenomenon by adding various PARAMETERS to or deleting various parameters from the model originally proposed and then comparing the different versions to identify the simplest way to accurately represent the data.

model calibration the process of improving the accuracy of a statistical model by adjusting the number or nature of its PARAMETERS until the output from the model is seen to match an observed sample of data.

model fit assessment the process of determining how close a proposed model of a relationship between variables is to the actual sample data obtained. Model fit assessment often involves a GOODNESS-OF-FIT TEST, an examination of the RESIDUALS between the proposed representation and the actual data, and an evaluation of whether the proposed representation is consistent with relevant theory. Statistical procedures, such as STRUCTURAL EQUATION MODELING and HIERARCHICAL LINEAR MODELING, use some or all of these various methods to gauge model fit.

model-free test a statistical procedure for identifying the underlying structure or pattern of associations for a phenomenon that does not require any initial assumptions about the nature of this pattern. A NONPARAMETRIC TEST is an example of a model-free test.

model identification see IDENTIFICATION.

modeling effect a type of EXPERIMENTER EFFECT in which a participant is unwittingly influenced to give responses similar to the responses the experimenter would give if the experimenter were a participant.

model misspecification see MISSPECIFICATION.

model-to-data fit see FIT.

moderated multiple regression a statistical procedure that is appropriate when there is a single CONTINUOUS outcome, two or more PREDICTOR VARIABLES, and one or more interactions between the predictor variables. For example, a researcher might use traditional MULTIPLE REGRESSION to predict mathematics performance from the variables of quantitative skill, gender, and teaching style. If the latter two predictors have a significant interaction between them, and this interaction changes the nature of the relationships (e.g., the REGRESSION COEFFICIENTS) among the other predictors when it is included in the analysis, then moderated multiple regression would be more appropriate.

moderating effect the effect that occurs when a third variable changes the nature of the relationship between a predictor and an outcome, particularly in analyses such as MULTIPLE REGRESSION. For example, STRUCTURAL EQUATION MODELING can be used to assess whether a predicted association between quantitative skill and performance fits equally well across different teaching style groups (e.g., lecture based vs. hands-on learning). If the prediction is different across the two groups, then teaching style is said to have produced a moderating effect. Also called **moderator effect**. See also MODERATED MULTIPLE REGRESSION.

moderator *n.* an INDEPENDENT VARIABLE that changes the nature of the relationship between other variables. For example, if a researcher examined the relationship between gender and math performance, a significant difference might emerge. However, if teaching style were taken into account, such that those who learned math by applied, hands-on methods performed better than those who learned with traditional lecture styles, regardless of gender, one could say that teaching style was a moderator of the relationship between gender and math performance. Also called **moderating variable**. See also MODERATING EFFECT.

modification index (**MI**) a measure that indicates the extent to which a model could be improved if a specific PARAMETER were added, or alternatively whether a parameter could be reasonably deleted without significantly altering model fit. Although procedures such as STRUCTURAL EQUATION MODELING

M

often provide a set of modification indexes as part of the output, researchers should only consider amending a model when using INDEPENDENT SAMPLES and when the modification is consistent with relevant theory.

modified replication see REPLICATION.

modulus *n.* see ABSOLUTE VALUE.

MOE abbreviation for MARGIN OF ERROR.

molar approach any theory or method that stresses comprehensive concepts or overall frameworks or structures. For example, METATHEORY uses a molar approach to understanding and developing ways of thinking about knowledge and research.

molecular approach any theory or method that stresses the components of a phenomenon, process, or system, making use of elemental units in its analysis. In a molecular approach the specific details are more important than the overall perspective.

moment *n.* the power to which the EXPECTED VALUE of a RANDOM VARIABLE is raised. Thus, $E(x^k)$ is the kth moment of x. The **first moment** is usually the MEAN of a variable, the **second moment** refers to VARIANCE, the **third moment** relates to SKEWNESS, and the **fourth moment** concerns KURTOSIS. Knowing each of these moments provides a complete picture of the DISTRIBUTION for a set of scores: A researcher knows the center point of the data, how spread out the values are, whether they are lopsided, and whether they are peaked (LEPTOKURTIC) or flat (PLATYKURTIC).

moment about the mean see CENTRAL MOMENT.

momentary time sampling a procedure in which the researcher indicates whether a particular behavior occurred during a designated interval of observation. It is important to collect momentary time sampling data for a large number of time periods in order to be able to draw accurate conclusions. For example, a researcher could conduct momentary time sampling to assess the occurrence of smoking at 100 specific time points during a month-long period, using a small portable device that prompts participants to record their smoking behavior at each point.

moment generating function a formula for calculating the various MOMENTS of a distribution for a random variable. The values obtained from a moment generating function describe the range and shape of the set of possible scores on that variable. See also CUMULANT GENERATING FUNCTION; PROBABILITY GENERATING FUNCTION.

monomethod bias the lack of RELIABILITY or VALIDITY that may occur when measuring a phenomenon with a single item, scale, or observation. For example, monomethod bias could be present if a researcher used only one questionnaire to measure a characteristic or trait, or if a teacher used scores on only one exam to evaluate students' performance for the entire academic year. Also called **mono-operation bias**.

monotonic *adj.* denoting a variable that either increases or decreases as a second variable either increases or decreases, respectively: The relationship is not necessarily LINEAR but there are no changes in direction. A **monotonically increasing** variable is one that rises consistently as a second variable increases, for example, level of performance in relation to amount of practice if this were observed to be the case. In contrast, depression would be a **monotonically decreasing** variable if its severity were found to fall consistently as a person's level of perseveration declined.

monotonic regression a NONPARAMETRIC method used when an outcome variable is expected to systematically increase or decrease as a FUNCTION of one or more predictor variables. For example, monotonic regression could be used

M

to assess the relationship between hours of exercise and body mass index, whereby the latter consistently decreases as the former consistently increases.

monotonic relationship any association between two variables in which increase or decrease in one produces a corresponding increase or decrease in the other.

monotrait–multimethod model see MULTITRAIT–MULTIMETHOD MODEL.

Monte Carlo maximum likelihood estimation (MCML estimation) in MONTE CARLO RESEARCH, a simulation procedure for obtaining a good approximation of a PARAMETER value (i.e., one that closely matches the sample values generated in the simulation). MCML estimation often is used in BAYESIAN INFERENCE.

Monte Carlo research a SIMULATION technique in which a large number of samples with specific selected properties (e.g., NORMALITY, size, model type) are generated by computer in order to assess the behavior of a statistical procedure or PARAMETER under varying conditions. For example, an investigator might conduct Monte Carlo research with a large number of normally distributed samples of various sizes (e.g., $N = 50, 100, 200, 400, 800$) in which a structural model is applied to characterize the data. Results would help the researcher determine the conditions under which the model behaves correctly (i.e., fits the data) as well as shows its limits (e.g., not fitting well with sample sizes less than 200). Also called **Monte Carlo method**.

morbidity rate the incidence of disease, expressed as a ratio denoting the number of people in a population who are ill or have a specific disease compared with the number who are well.

morphometrics *n.* the theory and technique associated with the physical measurement of living organisms and their component parts. Studies of size, shape, and structure are important not only in biology but also in neuropsychology and medical psychology. For example, researchers interested in morphometrics could study the form and structure of the brain in individuals who have various physical or psychological disorders. By contrast, PSYCHOMETRICS specifically focuses on the measurement of psychological phenomena.

mortality effect the degree to which circumstances or behavior increase or decrease the incidence of death. For example, a behavioral health researcher could study the mortality effects of a fatty diet and lack of exercise, which could lead to early death from heart disease.

mortality odds ratio a measure of the chance of dying from a specific illness as the result of a specific behavior or circumstance. For example, a medical psychology researcher could examine the ODDS RATIO for dying from cancer for individuals who smoke a pack or more of cigarettes per day. The mortality odds ratio will be greater than 1.0 (as in this example) when the chance of the outcome (i.e., death) occurring is high and less than 1.0 when the characteristic would lead to a smaller chance of death (e.g., as for the characteristic of a healthy diet).

mortality rate a measure of how often death occurs, usually with respect to a specific illness, characteristic, behavior, or population. For example, a researcher could estimate the mortality rate for individuals who have been diagnosed with cancer.

mortality table see LIFE TABLE.

moving average (MA) a form of average comprising the means of successive subsets of data within a longer set of observations. For example, a three-term moving average of the sequence 1, 3, 2, 4, 3, and 5 would be $(1 + 3 + 2)/3 = 2$, $(3 + 2 + 4)/3 = 3$, $(2 + 4 + 3)/3 = 3$, and $(4 + 3 +$

5)/3 = 4. Often plotted graphically, a moving average generally is used to describe or discern the pattern in TIME-SERIES data and may be adjusted (or smoothed) to allow for seasonal or cyclical trends. For example, a behavioral health researcher could plot moving average values for the occurrence of a specific behavior in several individuals with autism over a one-year period in order to identify a pattern that is less erratic than if individual values were plotted without grouping and averaging. Also called **rolling average**; **running average**.

moving-average model (**MA model**) a statistical depiction of the pattern of change over time for a series of mean (average) values on a variable, as collected in a LONGITUDINAL DESIGN.

moving medians a method of describing the pattern in a TIME SERIES in which different windows of *n* values are identified and the middle value from each is used to represent CENTRAL TENDENCY, with the process continuing until a SMOOTHED CURVE can be drawn to show the general trend in the data over time. Moving medians are less susceptible to the influence of OUTLIERS or shocks that exist in the series than are MOVING AVERAGES. Also called **running medians**.

Mozart effect a temporary increase in the affect or performance of research participants on tasks involving spatial–temporal reasoning after listening to the music of Austrian composer Wolfgang Amadeus Mozart (1756–1791). More generally, the term refers to the possibility that listening to certain types of music enhances inherent cognitive functioning. The notion of the Mozart effect has entered into popular culture to carry the as-yet-unsupported suggestion that early childhood exposure to classical music benefits mental development or intelligence.

MS symbol for MEAN SQUARE.

MSE symbol for MEAN SQUARED ERROR.

MSR symbol for MEAN-SQUARE RESIDUAL.

MSSD symbol for MEAN-SQUARE SUCCESSIVE DIFFERENCE.

MTMM 1. abbreviation for MULTITRAIT–MULTIMETHOD MATRIX. **2.** abbreviation for MULTITRAIT–MULTIMETHOD MODEL.

mu (symbol: μ) *n.* see POPULATION MEAN.

multicollinearity *n.* in MULTIPLE REGRESSION, the state that occurs when several INDEPENDENT VARIABLES are extremely highly interrelated, making it difficult to determine separate effects on the DEPENDENT VARIABLE and thus yielding unstable REGRESSION ESTIMATES with large STANDARD ERRORS. For example, if a researcher includes predictors of self-esteem, self-efficacy, and self-concept in an analysis with a dependent variable of achievement, multicollinearity most likely will be present.

multidimensionality *n.* **1.** the quality of a CONSTRUCT that cannot be adequately described by measuring a single trait or attribute. **2.** the quality of a scale, test, or so forth that is capable of measuring more than one DIMENSION of a construct. For example, a psychometrician may be interested in investigating the multidimensionality of a new scale to measure cognitive functioning. Compare UNIDIMENSIONALITY.

multidimensional scaling (**MDS**) a SCALING method that represents perceived similarities among stimuli by arranging similar stimuli in spatial proximity to one another, while disparate stimuli are represented far apart from one another. For example, a researcher may use multidimensional scaling to assess the dimensions underlying attributions for maternal behavior, as in the illustration opposite.

Multidimensional scaling is an alternative to FACTOR ANALYSIS for dealing with large matrices of data or stimuli.

multidimensional unfolding a MULTIDIMENSIONAL SCALING procedure for mapping, usually along two axes, how a set of individuals rate their preferences for or similarity to various characteristics, situations, or entities. For example, a researcher could use multidimensional unfolding to graph the preferences of a set of journal editors for research article characteristics such as experimental study, theoretical review, qualitative inquiry, and methodological application. Editors closer to one axis might prefer theoretical or qualitative articles, whereas those along the other axis would favor publishing articles that are experimental or methodological.

multidimensional variable a construct that cannot be fully described or measured using a single underlying FACTOR. For example, intelligence could be described as a multidimensional variable that involves verbal, quantitative, and other aspects.

multifactor design see FACTORIAL DESIGN.

multilevel design any research study involving two or more INDEPENDENT VARIABLES with multiple conditions (levels) of investigation. An example is a study examining how time of day (e.g., morning, afternoon, evening) and

amount of caffeine intake (e.g., 0 mg, 50 mg, 150 mg) affect rats' performance on a particular maze task. When only one independent variable with multiple conditions is involved, it is termed a SINGLE-FACTOR MULTILEVEL DESIGN.

multilevel model see HIERARCHICAL LINEAR MODEL.

multimethod approach a design that uses more than one procedure for measuring the main characteristic or construct of interest. For example, a researcher could use a multimethod approach to understanding relationship satisfaction by simultaneously collecting data from a survey, asking one or both of the partners to give their own self-report, and systematically observing the degree of relationship satisfaction. See also MULTITRAIT–MULTIMETHOD MODEL.

multimethod–multitrait model see MULTITRAIT–MULTIMETHOD MODEL.

M

multimodal distribution a set of data in which there is more than one MODE or score that occurs most frequently, as shown in the generic graphic overleaf.

For example, the ages of a sample of

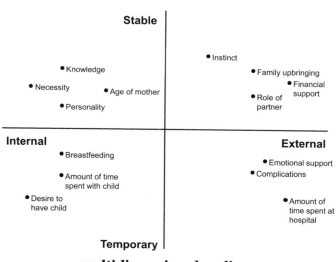

multidimensional scaling

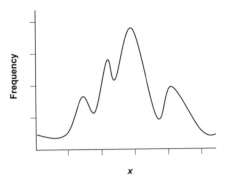

Frequency

x

college students would form a multimodal distribution since the largest number of people are either 18, 19, or 20 years old, with the remaining individuals aged 17 or 21 through 70. See also BIMODAL DISTRIBUTION; UNIMODAL DISTRIBUTION.

multinomial *adj.* describing a measurement that can have more than two categories or outcomes. For example, a professor assigning grades of A, B, C, D, or F to students in his or her course is making a multinomial decision, whereas assigning grades of pass or fail would be a binomial decision.

multinomial distribution a probability distribution that describes the theoretical distribution of *n* objects sampled at random from a population of *k* kinds of things with regard to the number of each of the kinds that appears in the sample. By contrast, a BINOMIAL DISTRIBUTION involves just two variables, categories, or objects.

multinomial expansion a mathematical procedure for finding the number of different ways in which a set of more than two events can occur when raised to a certain power. For example, a multinomial expansion could be used to determine the number of different ways a student could achieve grades of A, B, or C in three different courses. The outcome would be equal to $(A + B + C)^3 = A^3 + B^3 + C^3 + 3A^2B + 3A^2C + 3B^2A + 3B^2C + 3C^2A + 3C^2B + 6ABC$. That is, the outcomes would correspond to a sequence of all As (i.e., A^3); all Bs (i.e., B^3); all Cs

(i.e., C^3); three different ways of getting an A in two classes and a B in the other (e.g., AAB, ABA, BAA); and so on through the six different ways to get an A in one class, a B in another class, and a C in the other class (e.g., ABC, ACB, BAC, BCA, CAB, CBA). A similar process for only two events is called a BINOMIAL EXPANSION.

multinomial logistic regression a statistical procedure to characterize the relationship between a set of predictors and a single outcome with several categories, usually expressed as the odds of falling into one of the outcome categories (usually the most extreme) given each individual predictor. For example, a multinomial logistic regression could be conducted to assess the likelihood of being included in a high-risk category on a four-category risk outcome (where 1 = low and 4 = high) depending on predictors of smoking history, cholesterol level, and weight.

multinormal distribution see MULTIVARIATE NORMAL DISTRIBUTION.

multiple baseline design an experimental approach in which two or more behaviors are assessed to determine their initial, stable expression (i.e., baseline) and then an intervention or manipulation is applied to one of the behaviors while the others are unaffected. After a period, the manipulation is then applied to the next behavior while the remaining behaviors are unaltered, and so forth until the experimental manipulation has been applied in sequential fashion to all of the behaviors in the design. In successively administering a manipulation to different behaviors after initial behaviors have been recorded, a multiple baseline design allows for inferences about the effect of the intervention.

multiple-choice question see FIXED-ALTERNATIVE QUESTION.

multiple-choice test any test in which, for each item, the examinee chooses one of several given alternatives as being correct. A multiple-choice test contrasts with an ESSAY TEST, in which respondents are free to state answers in their own words. See FIXED-ALTERNATIVE QUESTION.

multiple classification analysis (MCA) see MULTIPLE DISCRIMINANT ANALYSIS.

multiple comparisons a set of comparisons made between samples to identify significant differences among their mean values. Multiple comparisons are generally done in a post hoc manner (i.e., are unplanned) in order to keep the TYPE I ERROR rate controlled at a pre-specified level. Also called **multiple contrasts**.

multiple comparison test any of various statistical procedures used to follow up on a significant result from an ANALYSIS OF VARIANCE by determining which groups in particular differ in their mean values. Examples include DUNCAN'S MULTIPLE RANGE TEST, the FISHER LEAST SIGNIFICANT DIFFERENCE TEST, the REGWQ TEST, the SCHEFFÉ TEST, and TUKEY'S HONESTLY SIGNIFICANT DIFFERENCE TEST. See also POST HOC COMPARISON.

multiple correlation coefficient (symbol: R) a numerical index of the degree of relationship between a particular variable and two or more other variables. Its value ranges from -1 to $+1$, with the former indicating a strong negative relationship and the latter a strong positive relationship. Also called **multiple R**.

multiple correlation coefficient squared see COEFFICIENT OF MULTIPLE DETERMINATION.

multiple covariates two or more correlated variables that are included in an ANALYSIS OF COVARIANCE to help rule out potential CONFOUNDS when examining group differences. For example, an educational researcher analyzing the covariance between an INDEPENDENT VARIABLE of phoneme training versus no training and an outcome variable of reading achievement might include multiple covariates of initial reading level, parents' education, and socioeconomic status. In this way, the researcher could determine whether a phoneme-trained group obtains significantly higher reading achievement than a nontrained control group, after ruling out the effects of the multiple covariates that could also be related to reading level.

multiple discriminant analysis (MDA) a MULTIVARIATE statistical procedure for examining the relationship between a set of more than two categories representing an outcome variable and a set of predictor variables. It often is used to verify that the predictors (e.g., family history, self-esteem, number of sleeping hours) are accurately classifying individuals into the appropriate categories of the outcome variable (diagnosis of depression). See DISCRIMINANT ANALYSIS. Also called **multiple classification analysis (MCA)**.

multiple imputation a method for addressing missing data in which several possible simulated values are inserted into a data set to replace omitted values, and then the mean and STANDARD DEVIATION of the set are calculated to arrive at an estimate to substitute for the missing value. Multiple imputation is considered less biased than other missing values procedures, such as LISTWISE DELETION, PAIRWISE DELETION, and single IMPUTATION.

multiple indicators–multiple causes model (MIMIC model) a MULTIVARIATE statistical procedure in which several INDEPENDENT VARIABLES are hypothesized to be predictors of one or more LATENT VARIABLES (factors). For example, a health researcher may hypothesize that measurements on several background variables—such as age, family history of illness, socioeconomic status, and amount of exercise per week—are linked to a latent factor of heart

M

health, which in turn has several indicators, such as systolic and diastolic blood pressure readings, pulse, and cholesterol level. This multiple indicators–multiple causes model would be depicted as four (predictor) measures having arrows pointing toward the factor, which in turn would have four lines emanating outward to represent its four indicators.

multiple linear regression see MULTIPLE REGRESSION.

multiple R see MULTIPLE CORRELATION COEFFICIENT.

multiple range test see DUNCAN'S MULTIPLE RANGE TEST.

multiple regression a statistical technique for examining the linear relationship between a continuous DEPENDENT VARIABLE and a set of two or more INDEPENDENT VARIABLES. It is often used to predict a single outcome variable from a set of predictor variables. For example, an educational psychology researcher could use multiple regression to predict college achievement (e.g., grade point average) from the variables of high school grade point average, Scholastic Assessment Test (SAT) reading score, SAT mathematics score, and SAT writing score. When a single predictor and a single outcome are involved the process is known as LINEAR REGRESSION. Also called **multiple linear regression**.

multiple regression equation a REGRESSION EQUATION generated from the process of MULTIPLE REGRESSION, which represents the relationship between a single outcome variable and the best LINEAR COMBINATION of a set of predictors. In the equation an outcome score (y) is presented as a function of a constant called an INTERCEPT, plus the products of a REGRESSION COEFFICIENT (B) times the values of various predictor variables (x), plus some prediction error. For example, assume a researcher is studying the relationship of college grade point average (GPA) to the predictors of high school GPA, Scholastic As-

sessment Test (SAT) reading score, and SAT mathematics score. The multiple regression equation would be

College GPA = intercept +
B_1(High School GPA) +
B_2(SAT Reading) +
B_3(SAT Mathematics) +
prediction error

Also called **multiple regression model**.

multiple time series a set of measures on two or more variables or individuals taken over numerous occasions. For example, a researcher could examine the daily recordings of speech and interaction for children with autism across a one-year period. The use of several parallel-running TIME SERIES to gather data in a LONGITUDINAL DESIGN is called a **multiple time-series design**, whereas the MULTIVARIATE ANALYSIS used to identify relationships among the variables in such data is called **multiple time-series analysis**. Alternatively, the researcher could use an INTERRUPTED TIME-SERIES DESIGN to see if the pattern of data for the two variables changed noticeably after the introduction of an intervention during the recording period. Also called **multivariate time series**.

multiple t test a T TEST used to make more than one comparison between pairs of group MEANS. The increased number of calculations results in an increased chance of making a TYPE I ERROR (i.e., of concluding there is a significant difference between groups when there is not).

multiplication rule a rule stating that the JOINT PROBABILITY of two independent events occurring together or in succession is equal to the probability of the first event times the probability of the second event. For example, the multiplication rule would indicate that the probability of drawing a heart followed by the probability of drawing a spade is equal to $13/52 \times 13/52 = .25 \times .25 = .0625$. Also called **and rule; multipli-

cation law; multiplicative law. Compare ADDITION RULE.

multiplicative model a description of the effect of two or more predictor variables on an outcome variable that allows for INTERACTION EFFECTS among the predictors. This is in contrast to an ADDITIVE MODEL, which sums the individual effects of several predictors on an outcome. For example, a health researcher could use a multiplicative model to examine the interaction effect of number of cigarettes smoked per day and length of smoking habit on the onset of cancer; the results might be compared to those obtained from an additive model that examines the separate effects of amount of cigarettes and length of a smoking habit on cancer onset.

multisite study research and data collection conducted over several locations or geographical areas; this allows greater generalization of findings than research conducted in a single place. Also called **cooperative study**.

multistage sampling a technique in which samples are drawn first from higher order groupings (e.g., states) and then from successively lower level groupings (e.g., counties within states, towns within counties) in order to avoid the necessity of having a SAMPLING FRAME for the entire population. That is, if subunits within a selected unit give similar results, one can select and measure a sample of the subunits in any chosen unit to avoid uneconomically measuring all of them. When two grouping sets are involved, the process is also known as **two-stage sampling**, when three sets are involved it is also called **three-stage sampling**, and so on.

multistate model a statistical representation of several possible stages for an event, either over the course of time or across a set of individuals; such models are often used to understand disease progression or health promotion. For example, a researcher may hypothesize a multistate model of behavior change, involving various stages from precontemplation, when an individual is not thinking of making a change, through to maintenance, when an individual has successfully made a behavior change (e.g., quitting smoking) for more than six months. A MARKOV CHAIN is similar to a multistate model but involves stages with some degree of dependence among them.

multitrait–multimethod matrix (MTMM) a matrix showing correlations among two or more measurement techniques used to assess two or more constructs or traits, as obtained from a MULTITRAIT–MULTIMETHOD MODEL. It includes correlations among the same traits with different methods (i.e., monotrait–heteromethod) and among different traits with the same method (i.e., heterotrait–monomethod). The for-

		Peer ratings				Association test			
		A_1	B_1	C_1	D_1	A_1	B_1	C_1	D_1
Peer ratings									
Courtesy	A_1	(.82)							
Honesty	B_1	.74	(.80)						
Poise	C_1	.63	.65	(.74)					
School drive	D_1	.76	.78	.65	(.89)				
Association test									
Courtesy	A_1	.13	.14	.10	.14	(.28)			
Honesty	B_1	.06	.12	.16	.08	.27	(.38)		
Poise	C_1	.01	.08	.10	.02	.19	.37	(.42)	
School drive	D_1	.12	.15	.14	.16	.27	.32	.18	(.36)

multitrait–multimethod matrix

mer are expected to be the largest, thus demonstrating CONVERGENT VALIDITY, whereas the latter are expected to be smallest, demonstrating DISCRIMINANT VALIDITY. Consider the example below, in which VALIDITY DIAGONALS are shown in italics and RELIABILITY DIAGONALS in parentheses.

HETEROTRAIT–MONOMETHOD COEFFICIENTS as large or larger than monotrait–heteromethod coefficients indicate that some method variance is present, suggesting that participants are responding similarly across different traits simply because they are being assessed with the same method.

multitrait–multimethod model (**MTMM**) a procedure for examining CONSTRUCT VALIDITY that assesses the correlations among two or more characteristics where these are each measured in two or more ways. For example, a researcher studying self-concept and achievement as measured by both self-reports and teacher evaluations could use a multitrait–multimethod model to evaluate the associations between the self-reports and teacher evaluations on each one of the characteristics. The set of correlations resulting from such an analysis is displayed in a MULTITRAIT–MULTIMETHOD MATRIX. In the related **monotrait–multimethod model**, a researcher examines a single characteristic using several different methods. Also called **multitrait–multimethod analysis**.

multivariate *adj.* consisting of or otherwise involving a number of distinct variables. For example, a multivariate study of ability could involve multiple measures of intelligence and achievement. Compare UNIVARIATE. See also BIVARIATE.

multivariate adaptive regression spline (**MARS**) a type of nonparametric REGRESSION ANALYSIS that examines NONLINEAR as well as LINEAR relationships among dependent and independent variables but without mak-

ing assumptions about their underlying functional relationships. For example, a researcher studying the relationship between achievement motivation and academic performance could use MARS to more accurately model the inverted U-shaped pattern expected to emerge. That is, individuals who have very low achievement motivation would be expected to have relatively low performance scores, which would increase as achievement motivation increases. After a certain point, however, performance scores could be expected to decline for individuals who have too much achievement motivation, thus forming a nonlinear pattern. See SPLINE FUNCTION.

multivariate analysis 1. a set of statistical procedures for studying the relationships between one or more predictors and several outcome or DEPENDENT VARIABLES. Examples include CANONICAL CORRELATION ANALYSIS for assessing the relationships among two sets of variables; FACTOR ANALYSIS for assessing the relationships among a large set of measures and a small set of underlying factors; MULTIVARIATE ANALYSIS OF VARIANCE and MULTIVARIATE ANALYSIS OF COVARIANCE for assessing potential group differences on several dependent variables; and STRUCTURAL EQUATION MODELING, which examines a theoretically based pattern of relationships among multiple independent, dependent, and even mediating variables. Also called **multivariate statistics**. Compare UNIVARIATE ANALYSIS. **2.** more generally, any procedure for understanding any large set of variables, whether dependent or independent.

multivariate analysis of covariance (**MANCOVA**) a statistical procedure for assessing possible group differences on a set of outcome or DEPENDENT VARIABLES, after taking into account the scores on one or more COVARIATES. For example, a researcher could conduct a multivariate analysis of covariance to assess whether two groups of participants in a teaching style study differ significantly on a set of achievement variables—such as quiz scores, homework scores, exam scores, and project scores—after taking into account the initial grade point average of each of the participants. It is an extension of the univariate ANALYSIS OF COVARIANCE, which examines a single dependent variable.

multivariate analysis of variance (MANOVA) a statistical procedure for assessing possible group differences on a set of outcome or DEPENDENT VARIABLES. For example, a researcher could conduct a multivariate analysis of variance to assess whether a group of participants who receive a new educational method differ significantly from another group of participants who are taught with a traditional method on a set of achievement variables, such as quiz scores, homework scores, exam scores, and project scores. It is an extension of the univariate ANALYSIS OF VARIANCE, which examines a single dependent variable.

multivariate distribution the DISTRIBUTION of scores obtained on several variables, as in the following example.

Participant	Exercise (hrs/day)	Cholesterol (mg/dL)	Blood pressure (mm/Hg)
A	1	233	160/100
B	5	175	100/75
C	3	192	105/80
D	1	216	122/85
E	1	221	135/86

A health researcher may want to examine these scores on level of exercise, cholesterol level, and blood pressure in a sample of individuals at risk for heart disease. Compare UNIVARIATE DISTRIBUTION.

multivariate distribution function a mathematical function giving the probability that certain values on several RANDOM VARIABLES will occur together. For example, a mathematical health researcher could examine the multivariate distribution function for the JOINT PROBABILITY of taking little exercise, having high cholesterol, and having heart trouble in a sample of middle-aged individuals. A **bivariate distribution function** is a form of multivariate distribution function specific to two variables.

multivariate generalizability theory a body of theory concerning the identification and control of one or more sources of error over several variables or measures. For example, a researcher may wish to assess the RELIABILITY of several measures of quantitative achievement, such as number of courses taken, mathematics score on the Scholastic Assessment Test or Graduate Record Examination, and score on a quantitative skills test. He or she could do so by identifying several possible sources of error, known as FACETS, and then examining the different VARIANCE and COVARIANCE components for the various facets. See GENERALIZABILITY THEORY.

multivariate kurtosis measure an index of the degree of KURTOSIS in a distribution of scores on several variables. It indicates the extent to which such a distribution differs from NORMALITY with respect to the presence of high peaks in the data (points at which many people or items obtain particular scores). An example is **Mardia's multivariate kurtosis measure**: A value of zero indicates normality, and increasingly larger values indicate increasingly greater peakedness or kurtosis.

multivariate normal distribution a pattern of values on several variables in which a graph of the data forms a bell-shaped NORMAL DISTRIBUTION. Evidence for a multivariate normal distribution may be obtained using a QUANTILE–QUANTILE PLOT, in which MAHALANOBIS DISTANCE scores are plotted against a set of points from a normal distribution. If

M

the plot shows a series of points along a diagonal line, indicating a lack of any discrepant scores (i.e., any MULTI-VARIATE OUTLIERS), then the data have a multivariate normal distribution. Also called **multinormal distribution**. See also MULTIVARIATE NORMALITY.

multivariate normality the situation in which the values for a set of variables have an even distribution, with most scores falling in the middle of the range and a smaller number of high and low scores. In other words, a set of scores demonstrating multivariate NORMALITY follows a MULTIVARIATE NORMAL DISTRIBUTION and lacks OUTLIERS or extreme scores.

multivariate outlier a data point whose values on several variables are very different from the others in a set, such that it may BIAS the results of a statistical analysis, particularly one based on an ASSUMPTION of NORMALITY. For example, an individual participating in a study who obtained an IQ score of 150 (when the mean IQ is 100 and the standard deviation is 15), a performance score of 100 (when the mean is 50 and the standard deviation is 20), and a social skills score of 1 (when the mean is 10 and the standard deviation is 5) would be a multivariate outlier. MAHALANOBIS DISTANCE, COOK'S DISTANCE, and other statistical procedures may be used to determine whether multivariate outliers are present in a data set. Compare UNIVARIATE OUTLIER.

multivariate research a study conducted to simultaneously assess the relationships among multiple DEPENDENT VARIABLES and INDEPENDENT VARIABLES. Compare UNIVARIATE RESEARCH.

multivariate statistics see MULTIVARIATE ANALYSIS.

multivariate t distribution the distribution of possible values for the statistic obtained from HOTELLING'S T^2 TEST

when comparing the mean values between two groups on two or more DEPENDENT VARIABLES. It is an extension of the T DISTRIBUTION used when testing for potential differences in situations that involve more than one outcome. For example, a researcher might consult a multivariate t distribution in order to find the CRITICAL VALUE that would indicate whether treatment and control groups differ in their physical health and psychological well-being outcomes.

multivariate test any of various statistical procedures involving two or more outcome or DEPENDENT VARIABLES. An example is the MULTIVARIATE ANALYSIS OF VARIANCE, which extends the ANALYSIS OF VARIANCE examining one dependent variable to include additional dependent variables. FACTOR ANALYSIS and MULTIPLE REGRESSION sometimes are considered multivariate tests as well, even though the former involves a single set of variables that are not necessarily independent or dependent and the latter allows for multiple INDEPENDENT VARIABLES but only one outcome.

multivariate time series see MULTIPLE TIME SERIES.

multivariate t test see HOTELLING'S T^2 TEST.

mundane realism the extent to which an experimental situation resembles a real-life situation or event. See also EXPERIMENTAL REALISM.

mutually exclusive events 1. two or more events that have no common elements, that is, they are disjoint (see DISJOINT SETS). **2.** in probability theory, two or more events that cannot co-occur: The occurrence of one precludes the simultaneous or subsequent occurrence of the other(s). For example, the alternatives "heads" and "tails" in a single toss of a coin are mutually exclusive events.

MVUE abbreviation for minimum variance unbiased estimator. See EFFICIENT ESTIMATOR.

Nn

n symbol for the number of scores or observations obtained from a particular experimental condition or subgroup.

N symbol for the total number of cases (participants) in an experiment or study.

naive participant a participant who has not previously participated in a particular research study and has not been made aware of the experimenter's hypothesis.

narrative analysis a type of QUALITATIVE ANALYSIS in which a researcher collects and examines stories from individuals about a variety of concrete life situations—ranging from first romantic involvements to larger issues, such as divorce, aging, and life satisfaction. The goal is to understand how individuals experience certain events, structure them into coherent sequences, and give them subjective meaning. Also called **narrative inquiry**; **narrative research**.

natural experiment the study of a naturally occurring situation as it unfolds in the real world. The researcher does not exert any influence over the situation but rather simply observes individuals and circumstances, comparing the current condition to some other condition. For example, an investigator might evaluate the influence of a new community policing program by observing neighborhood activities after it has been implemented and comparing the outcome to that for neighborhoods in which the policy has not yet been implemented. Since such real-life events cannot be manipulated or prearranged, natural experiments are QUASI-EXPERIMENTAL DESIGNS rather than true experiments. Also called **naturalistic design**; **naturalistic research**.

naturalistic observation data collection in a field setting, without laboratory controls or manipulation of variables. These procedures are usually carried out by a trained observer, who watches and records the everyday behavior of participants in their natural environments. Examples of naturalistic observation include an ethologist's study of the behavior of chimpanzees and a developmental psychologist's observation of playing children. See also SYSTEMATIC NATURALISTIC OBSERVATION. Compare ANALOGUE OBSERVATION; SELF-MONITORING OBSERVATION; STRUCTURED OBSERVATION.

natural logarithm (ln) see LOGARITHM.

nay-saying *n.* answering questions negatively regardless of their content, which can distort the results of surveys, questionnaires, and similar instruments. Also called **response deviation**. Compare YEA-SAYING.

NCE abbreviation for NORMAL CURVE EQUIVALENT.

N=1 design see SINGLE-CASE DESIGN.

nearest neighbor see SINGLE-LINKAGE CLUSTERING.

negative binomial distribution a THEORETICAL DISTRIBUTION of discrete values that describes the number of trials that will occur before a success in a sequence of n BERNOULLI TRIALS, with a given likeliness of failure and success across the sequence. Also called **Pascal distribution**. Compare POSITIVE BINOMIAL DISTRIBUTION.

negative case analysis see DEVIANT CASE ANALYSIS.

negative correlation a relationship between two variables in which the value of one variable increases as the value of the other decreases. For example, in a study about babies crying and being held, the discovery that those who are held more tend to cry less is a negative correlation. Also called **indirect correlation**; **inverse correlation**. Compare POSITIVE CORRELATION.

negative predictive power the proportion of cases correctly identified by a test as not having a particular condition, indicating the probability that someone predicted not to have a condition by this test in fact does not have that condition. For example, the negative predictive power of a diagnostic test for depression would be determined by dividing the percentage of people whose results correctly show they do not have the disorder (i.e., valid negatives) by the percentage of all people whose results are negative (i.e., both valid negatives and false negatives). Compare POSITIVE PREDICTIVE POWER.

negative relationship an association in which one variable decreases as the other variable increases, or vice versa. Also called **inverse relationship**. See also INDIRECT RELATIONSHIP. Compare DIRECT RELATIONSHIP.

negative skew see SKEWNESS.

negativistic-subject role behavior adopted by a participant in a research study who intentionally tries to be "bad," responding in a contrary or random fashion to obstruct the study. Compare APPREHENSIVE-SUBJECT ROLE; FAITHFUL-SUBJECT ROLE; GOOD-SUBJECT ROLE.

neighborhood control a group of individuals selected from the same region or area as a targeted study group to serve as a comparison group. The assumption is that such a group will share similar experiences, risk exposure, and other relevant characteristics to the study group, given their geographical proximity. Used especially in epidemiological or clinical research, neighborhood controls generally are chosen according to some rule-based procedure and matched to members of the target group on certain attributes, such as age or sex. For example, a researcher investigating cancer might go to every second house on the same city block as each person in the study group to identify similar individuals who do not have the disease to become part of a neighborhood control. Also called **community control**. Compare DISTAL CONTROL.

nested case-control study a research method in which individuals from a defined COHORT are sampled and divided into groups according to whether or not they have a disease or other condition. It is thus a combination of a CASE-CONTROL STUDY and a cohort study (see LONGITUDINAL DESIGN). For example, a researcher investigating a group of Vietnam War veterans (the cohort) might place participants who have attempted suicide (cases) into one subgroup and those with little to no suicidal ideation (controls) into another. Although an efficient strategy when the budget is limited or the condition or outcome of interest is rare, a nested case-control study has such disadvantages as greater risk of confounding (see CONFOUND) and reduced ability to generalize or make causal inferences.

nested design see HIERARCHICALLY NESTED DESIGN.

nested factor see NESTING.

nested model see HIERARCHICAL MODEL.

nesting *n.* in an experimental design, the appearance of the levels of one factor (the **nested factor**) only within a single level of another factor. For example, classrooms are nested within a school because each specific classroom is found only within a single school; similarly, schools are nested within school districts. See HIERARCHICALLY NESTED DESIGN.

network analysis the study of the relations among sampling units (e.g., individuals) within an interconnected group of such units (e.g., a friendship network) and the implications of these networks for the system in which they occur. In organizational contexts, for example, network analysis involves identifying patterns of communication, influence, liking, and other interpersonal behaviors and attitudes among employees and quantifying them in statistical and graphical models. Properties of systems are assumed to be emergent, that is, not immediately predictable from a knowledge of networks among individuals.

network sampling a sampling technique in which members of a study group recruit their peers to participate in the research. It is similar in process, benefits, and drawbacks to SNOWBALL SAMPLING but distinct in that new participants are acquired directly by existing ones according to certain rules (e.g., no more than four recruits per person) and that various incentives are provided for participation and recruitment.

Newman–Keuls multiple comparison test a statistical procedure in which sets of means are compared following a significant result from an ANALYSIS OF VARIANCE. The mean values of all experimental groups are arranged in order of size, formed into pairs, and the differences between members of each pair evaluated against a critical value known as the STUDENTIZED RANGE STATISTIC. Also called **Newman–Keuls multiple range test**; **Newman–Keuls test**. [D. **Newman**, British statistician; M. **Keuls**, Dutch horticulturalist]

Newton–Raphson method a technique for solving equations that is based on a process of linear approximation, that is, finding progressively closer approximations to the root of a function. Also called **Newton method**. [Isaac **Newton** (1642–1727), British physicist and mathematician; Joseph **Raphson** (1648–1715), British mathematician]

Neyman–Pearson theory an approach to formulating two competing hypotheses (the NULL HYPOTHESIS and an ALTERNATIVE HYPOTHESIS) and identifying appropriate statistical procedures for choosing between them. It focuses upon identifying CRITICAL REGIONS, minimizing errors in estimation, and obtaining an appropriate balance in the probability of committing TYPE I ERRORS and TYPE II ERRORS. [Jerzy **Neyman** (1894–1981), Russian-born U.S. statistician; Egon S. **Pearson** (1895–1980), British statistician]

NFI abbreviation for normed fit index. See BENTLER–BONETT INDEX.

NH abbreviation for NULL HYPOTHESIS.

NHST abbreviation for null hypothesis SIGNIFICANCE TESTING.

NNT abbreviation for NUMBER NEEDED TO TREAT.

N-of-1 design see SINGLE-CASE DESIGN.

no-intercept model see REGRESSION THROUGH THE ORIGIN.

nominal *adj.* denoting a number that indicates membership in a category, such as coding political party affiliations with a 0 for Democrat, a 1 for Republican, and a 2 for Independent. A nominal value is no indication of rank order or magnitude. Compare CARDINAL; ORDINAL.

nominal data numerical values that represent membership in specific categories. For example, the category male could be labeled 0 and the category female labeled 1, and each person within the population of interest (e.g., a particular town) assigned the number corresponding to their sex. Nominal data are similar to CATEGORICAL DATA, and the

N

two terms are often used interchangeably.

nominal scale a sequence of numbers that do not indicate order, magnitude, or a true zero point but rather identify items as belonging to mutually exclusive categories. For example, a nominal scale for the performance of a specific group of people on a particular test might arbitrarily use the number 1 to denote pass and the number 2 to denote fail. Since the numbers represent category labels, they cannot be manipulated mathematically or otherwise quantitatively compared. A nominal scale is one of four types of measurement scale, the others being an ORDINAL SCALE, an INTERVAL SCALE, and a RATIO SCALE. See also CATEGORICAL SCALE.

nominal variable a variable whose possible values are unordered categories or labels. For example, choice of college major is a nominal variable.

nomological network a conceptual network: a broadly integrative theoretical framework that identifies the key constructs associated with a phenomenon of interest and the associations among these constructs. For example, psychopathy is a complex notion involving a significant nomological network of knowledge and speculations about components, causes, correlates, and consequences as well as their interrelationships and means of measurement or evaluation.

nomological validity the degree to which a measure assesses the specific construct it is designed to assess, as formulated from the NOMOLOGICAL NETWORK for the construct being measured. See CONSTRUCT VALIDITY.

nomothetic *adj.* relating to the formulation of general laws as opposed to the study of the individual case. A **nomothetic approach** involves the study of groups of people or cases for the purpose of discovering those general and universally valid laws or principles that characterize the average person or case. Compare IDIOGRAPHIC.

nonadditive *adj.* describing values or measurements that cannot be meaningfully summarized through addition because the resulting total does not correctly reflect the underlying properties of and associations between the component values. For example, if two variables *a* and *b* interact to influence another variable *y*, the addition of the separate effects of *a* and *b* will not equal the total effect since the contribution of the interaction needs to be included. Compare ADDITIVE.

noncentral distribution a DISTRIBUTION in which the NONCENTRALITY PARAMETER is not equal to zero: In statistical SIGNIFICANCE TESTING, such a distribution is obtained when the NULL HYPOTHESIS under test is false. The noncentral version of a distribution has a different mean, SKEWNESS, and VARIANCE (among other properties) from its corresponding **central distribution**, as well as a larger proportion of numbers beyond the CRITICAL VALUES. For example, the CHI-SQUARE DISTRIBUTION, F DISTRIBUTION, and T DISTRIBUTION all have corresponding noncentral versions signified by a noncentrality parameter that is not equal to zero.

noncentrality parameter in many PROBABILITY DISTRIBUTIONS used in SIGNIFICANCE TESTING, a PARAMETER that has a value different from zero when the NULL HYPOTHESIS under test is false. This parameter is important in determining the POWER of a statistical procedure. See NONCENTRAL DISTRIBUTION.

nondirectional hypothesis a hypothesis that one experimental group will differ from another without specification of the expected direction of this effect. For example, a researcher might hypothesize that college students will perform differently from elementary school students on a memory task without predicting which group of students will perform better. Also called **nondirectional alternative hypothesis**; **two-tailed (alternative) hypothesis**. Compare DIRECTIONAL HYPOTHESIS.

nondirectional test a statistical test of an experimental hypothesis that does not specify the expected direction of an effect or a relationship. Also called **nondirectional alternative hypothesis test**; **nondirectional hypothesis test**; **two-tailed test**. See NONDIRECTIONAL HYPOTHESIS. Compare DIRECTIONAL TEST.

nondirective interview see UNSTRUCTURED INTERVIEW.

nonequivalent-groups design a QUASI-EXPERIMENTAL DESIGN in which the responses of a treatment group and a comparison group are compared on measures collected at the beginning and end of the research: In psychology and other social sciences, these designs often involve self-selection, in which the members of the treatment group are those who volunteer or otherwise seek the treatment whereas the comparison group members do not. For example, a researcher might wish to study the relative value of medication for patients participating in psychotherapy for depression. He or she might identify two groups of individuals—one currently receiving therapy only and the other receiving therapy plus a certain drug—and collect PRETEST data on their severity of depression. The investigator would then collect POSTTEST data on the severity of depression at some subsequent point (e.g., 12 weeks later) and compare the outcomes of the two groups in order to estimate the efficacy of the antidepressant medication. Since participants are not assigned to conditions at random, the two groups are likely to exhibit preexisting differences on both measured and unmeasured factors that must be taken into account during statistical analyses. Also called **nonequivalent comparison-group design**; **non-**

equivalent control-group design. Compare EQUIVALENT-GROUPS DESIGN.

nonexperimental *adj.* of a research project, lacking manipulation of INDEPENDENT VARIABLES by a researcher or RANDOM ASSIGNMENT of participants to treatment conditions, as in OBSERVATIONAL STUDIES and QUASI-EXPERIMENTAL DESIGNS for example.

nonexperimental research see QUASI-EXPERIMENTAL RESEARCH.

nonignorable missing value a piece of information whose loss from a data set is not random and consequently needs to be accounted for in parameter ESTIMATION and other statistical analyses. See IMPUTATION.

noninformative prior in BAYESIAN analysis, a theoretical set of feasible values for a parameter or unknown characteristic of interest in a population, where there is no specific or definite information about the parameter but certain values are assumed to be more likely to occur than others. One of two main types of PRIOR DISTRIBUTION, it is used to calculate an associated POSTERIOR DISTRIBUTION. Compare INFORMATIVE PRIOR.

nonlinear *adj.* describing any relationship between two variables (x and y) that cannot be expressed in the form $y = a + bx$, where a and b are numerical constants. The relationship therefore does not appear as a straight line when depicted graphically. Compare LINEAR.

nonlinear equation an equation in which the variables are related in an interactive fashion (e.g., x_1x_2) or are raised to powers greater than 1. For example, $y = a + b_1x_1 + b_2x_2^2$ is a nonlinear equation and will form a curve when depicted graphically. Compare LINEAR EQUATION.

nonlinear function see LINEAR FUNCTION.

nonlinear interpolation a method of constructing new data points within a

N

known range of such points that involves use of a NONLINEAR EQUATION. Compare LINEAR INTERPOLATION. See INTERPOLATION.

nonlinear model any model that attempts to relate the values of an outcome or dependent variable to the explanatory or independent variables using a NONLINEAR EQUATION. Compare LINEAR MODEL.

nonlinear regression a procedure for analyzing the relationship between an INDEPENDENT VARIABLE (x) and a DEPENDENT VARIABLE (y) where the REGRESSION EQUATION involves exponential forms of x. That is, the changes in y are not consistent for unit changes in the x variable(s) but are a function of the particular values of x. For example, a nonlinear regression model is given by $y = \alpha + b_1 x_1 + b_2 x_1^2 + \varepsilon$, where α indicates the place where the line of BEST FIT crosses the y-axis, b_1 indicates the number of units that y changes when x is changed by 1 point, and ε is error. Also called **curvilinear regression**. Compare LINEAR REGRESSION. See REGRESSION ANALYSIS.

nonlinear relationship an association between two variables in which the direction and rate of change fluctuate. That is, the amount of change in a DEPENDENT VARIABLE (y) varies as a function of the particular value or level of the INDEPENDENT VARIABLE (x). Compare LINEAR RELATIONSHIP.

nonlinear transformation a TRANSFORMATION of a data set that uses a function to change the linear relationship between variables. For example, a **normalizing transformation** creates a new set of scores that approximate a NORMAL DISTRIBUTION from the original non-normal data set, and a LOGARITHMIC TRANSFORMATION may be used to convert raw data into a form that more closely matches the ASSUMPTIONS required in particular statistical analyses. Compare LINEAR TRANSFORMATION.

nonmetric *adj.* describing data that are NOMINAL or ORDINAL, as opposed to INTERVAL DATA or RATIO DATA. Such data cannot be precisely quantified. Examples include yes/no answers or a list ranking individuals on some attribute.

nonmetric scaling an analytic technique in which similarities among data points are determined based on a relative ordering of their indexed difference values. A variation of standard (metric) MULTIDIMENSIONAL SCALING, which uses the actual quantified spatial distances among points (i.e., DISSIMILARITY COEFFICIENTS and SIMILARITY COEFFICIENTS), nonmetric scaling examines only the rankings of those distance values to identify similarities.

nonnormative *adj.* not conforming to or reflecting an established NORM. For example, an individual test score well above or well below the mean for a classroom of students is a nonnormative value. Compare NORMATIVE.

nonparametric *adj.* describing any analytic method that does not involve making ASSUMPTIONS about the data of interest. Compare PARAMETRIC.

nonparametric hypothesis test see NONPARAMETRIC TEST.

nonparametric regression a form of REGRESSION ANALYSIS in which the relationship between an outcome or DEPENDENT VARIABLE and one or more predictors or INDEPENDENT VARIABLES is analyzed without the assistance of a pre-existing model. KERNEL REGRESSION is an example. In contrast to traditional regression, in which the structure of the REGRESSION EQUATION is known and only the REGRESSION COEFFICIENTS are estimated from the data set, nonparametric regression requires that both the equation and coefficients be determined from the data.

nonparametric statistics statistical procedures in which the nature of the data being analyzed is such that certain common assumptions about the distribution of the attribute (or attributes) in the population being tested, such as normality and homogeneity of variance, are not necessary or applicable. Also called **distribution-free statistics**. Compare PARAMETRIC STATISTICS.

nonparametric test a type of HYPOTHESIS TEST that does not make any assumptions (e.g., of NORMALITY or HOMOGENEITY OF VARIANCE) about the population of interest. Nonparametric tests generally are used in situations involving NOMINAL or ORDINAL data. Also called **distribution-free test**; **nonparametric hypothesis test**. Compare PARAMETRIC TEST.

nonprobability sampling nonrandom selection: any process of choosing a subset of participants or cases from a larger population in which it is impossible to precisely determine each unit's likelihood of being selected. Examples include CONVENIENCE SAMPLING and QUOTA SAMPLING. Nonprobability sampling makes it difficult to determine how well the target population is represented by the subset, thus limiting the GENERALIZABILITY of findings. Compare PROBABILITY SAMPLING.

nonrandomized clinical trial a type of CLINICAL TRIAL in which the participants are not assigned by chance to the different treatment groups or interventions. For example, if participants choose whether to receive a new treatment or an existing standard of care then the trial would be nonrandomized. Compare RANDOMIZED CLINICAL TRIAL.

nonrandomized design any of a large number of research designs in which participants or cases are not assigned to experimental conditions via a chance process. For example, FIELD EXPERIMENTS often are nonrandomized. Compare RANDOMIZED DESIGN.

nonreactive measure see UNOBTRUSIVE MEASURE.

nonrecursive model a set of relationships in which a particular variable is sometimes a cause and sometimes an effect, thus suggesting there is a reciprocal relationship between that variable and others in the model. For example, high job satisfaction may lead to increased pay and job responsibility, which in turn may further enhance job satisfaction. Compare RECURSIVE MODEL.

nonresponse *n.* a participant's failure to answer one or more survey, questionnaire, or test items or to provide a measurement on some study variable. If data values are MISSING COMPLETELY AT RANDOM, then nonresponse does not distort results. In most research situations, however, nonresponse is not a purely random phenomenon; participants who do not answer questions differ in some important, systematic way from those who do answer. The basic method for compensating for such **nonresponse** (or **nonresponder**) **bias** involves estimating the probability that each sample case will become a respondent. See also MISSING VALUES PROCEDURE.

nonresponse rate see REFUSAL RATE.

nonsignificant *adj.* see NOT SIGNIFICANT.

nonsingular matrix a SQUARE MATRIX whose DETERMINANT is not equal to zero. Where **A** is a nonsingular matrix, **A** is an INVERSE MATRIX of the matrix **B**, **B** is an inverse of **A**, and the product of **AB** equals the product of **BA**. Also called **invertible matrix**. Compare SINGULAR MATRIX.

nonspecific effect a result or consequence whose specific cause or precipitating factors are unknown. An example would be the effect on a patient of the belief that he or she has received medication or some other intervention when no true treatment has been given (see PLACEBO EFFECT).

norm *n.* **1.** a standard or range of values that represents the typical performance

N

of a group or of an individual (of a certain age, for example) against which comparisons can be made. **2.** a conversion of a raw score into a scaled score that is more easily interpretable, such as percentiles or IQ scores. **—normative** *adj.*

normal approximation 1. a procedure in which part of an observed distribution of values is approximated to part of the symmetrical bell-shaped NORMAL DISTRIBUTION. Many sample data sets can be normally approximated, thus satisfying certain ASSUMPTIONS required for the use of particular analytic techniques and often simplifying the associated calculations. **2.** the distribution of values resulting from such a process.

normal curve equivalent (**NCE**) a standardized test score based on a NORMAL DISTRIBUTION with a mean of 50 and a STANDARD DEVIATION of 21.06. It is a measure of academic development or performance created by the U.S. Department of Education to allow test scores from different contexts and scales to be compared. NCEs range from 1 to 99 in value and are an alternative to T SCORES, Z SCORES, and other types of STANDARDIZED SCORES.

normal distribution a THEORETICAL DISTRIBUTION in which values pile up in the center at the MEAN and fall off into tails at either end. When plotted, it gives the familiar bell-shaped curve expected when variation about the mean value is random, as shown in the following generic depiction.

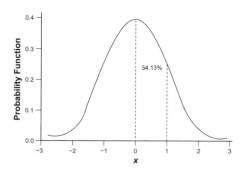

The normal distribution has several primary characteristics: It is symmetrical, it has both upper and lower ASYMPTOTES, and its mean, MEDIAN, and MODE are the same value. Perhaps most important, however, fixed proportions of values fall within defined sections of the distribution. For example, 34.13% of values fall between the mean and one STANDARD DEVIATION above the mean, and a corresponding 34.13% of values fall between the mean of the distribution and one standard deviation below the mean. Many statistical models are based on the assumption that data follow a normal distribution. For example, it is reasonable to expect that human height follows a normal distribution with a mean of 5 feet several inches, such that very few adults are less than 3 feet or greater than 7 feet tall. Also called **Gaussian curve**; **Gaussian distribution**; **normal curve**.

normality *n.* the condition in which a data set presents a NORMAL DISTRIBUTION of values.

normalize *vb.* to apply a TRANSFORMATION to data in order to produce a new set of scores that approximately follow the NORMAL DISTRIBUTION.

normal probability plot a type of PROBABILITY PLOT in which observed values are plotted against the values that would be consistent with a NORMAL DISTRIBUTION. If the observed values exhibit normality, they will appear on a diagonal line from the lower left to the upper right corner of the graph. Also called **full-normal plot**.

normal random variable any CONTINUOUS RANDOM VARIABLE whose values follow a NORMAL DISTRIBUTION that is centered around the MEAN for the population and that has a STANDARD DEVIATION matching that of the population. A STANDARD NORMAL VARIABLE is similar but has a mean of 0 and a standard deviation of 1.

normal range see REFERENCE INTERVAL.

normal score see STANDARDIZED SCORE.

normal variable see NORMAL RANDOM VARIABLE.

normative *adj.* relating to a particular NORM or norms generally. Thus, a **normative score** for a test (e.g., of language skills) reflects the average performance of a specific group (e.g., 10-year-old children) against which the score of a given individual from that group is evaluated. Similarly, **normative research** refers to any empirical investigation designed to determine such standards of comparison. Compare NONNORMATIVE.

normative scale any evaluative instrument on which the respondent provides ratings for a series of items or chooses scores to indicate his or her agreement with a series of statements. Unlike an IPSATIVE SCALE, there is no requirement for these scores to sum to a particular total (e.g., 100%). For example, a supervisor using a normative scale to assess an employee's job performance might be asked to choose a number from 1 to 5 to indicate how well the employee performed in each of several different areas, such as communication, timekeeping, and quality of work. The scores given in any area would not be affected by those given in any of the others (e.g., the supervisor could award all 5s or all 1s if he or she thought this was merited).

normed fit index (**NFI**) see BENTLER–BONETT INDEX.

norm group see STANDARDIZATION GROUP.

norm-referenced test any assessment in which scores are interpreted by comparison with a NORM, generally the average score obtained by members of a specified group. For example, a teacher might administer a norm-referenced reading test to the students in his or her classroom, with each person's score indicating how well that test taker reads relative to other examinees of that age.

Thus, if a student obtains a score of 70% but the standard test score (norm) for those of the same age is 90%, then the student has done relatively poorly. See also CRITERION-REFERENCED TEST; DOMAIN-REFERENCED TEST.

no-treatment control group a CONTROL GROUP who are not exposed to any experimental manipulation or intervention, thus serving as a neutral comparison for other study groups receiving the treatment under investigation. For example, a researcher investigating the effectiveness of a new antidepressant might divide participants into a treatment group that receives the new medication and a separate no-treatment control group that receives no medication whatsoever, and then compare the outcomes of each group to identify any significant differences. In contrast, an ordinary control group may be administered some standard treatment instead of the experimental one.

not significant (**NS**) denoting a result from a statistical hypothesis-testing procedure that does not allow the researcher to conclude that differences in the data obtained for different samples are meaningful and legitimate. In other words, a result that is not significant does not permit the rejection of the NULL HYPOTHESIS; any observed differences are considered to be due to chance or random factors. Also called **nonsignificant**.

nuisance parameter in statistical hypothesis testing, a population PARAMETER of secondary interest that must be accounted for in order to obtain an estimated value for a parameter of primary interest. For example, assume a researcher wishes to determine whether male and female schoolchildren differ in their mathematics ability. He or she might administer a math test to a sample of children at a particular school and use those data to estimate male and female means for all children. If, however, the researcher needed to calculate the variance of the scores before attempting to determine the means, the former would be a nuisance parameter.

nuisance variable a type of EXTRANE-OUS VARIABLE that does not differ systematically across levels or conditions of the independent variable under investigation but whose variation nonetheless may contribute to an increase in experimental error. Participant characteristics and environmental conditions often are nuisance variables. For example, individuals in a learning study who are distracted by noise in a nearby room may not perform as well as they would otherwise.

null distribution in statistical testing, the PROBABILITY DISTRIBUTION of values for a particular test statistic that is obtained when the NULL HYPOTHESIS is true. For example, the F RATIO from an ANALYSIS OF VARIANCE follows the F DISTRIBUTION if the null hypothesis is correct. Also called **null hypothesis distribution**. Compare ALTERNATIVE HYPOTHESIS DISTRIBUTION.

null finding the situation in which the outcome of a statistical hypothesis-testing procedure indicates that there is no relationship, or no significant relationship, between experimental variables. Also called **null result**.

null hypothesis (**NH**; symbol: H_0) a statement that a study will find no meaningful differences between the groups or conditions under investigation, such that there is no relationship among the variables of interest and that any variation in observed data is the result of chance or random processes. For example, if a researcher is investigating a new technique to improve the skills of children who have difficulty reading, the null hypothesis would predict no difference among the average reading performance of those children who receive the intervention and those who do not. The NH is contrasted with the ALTERNATIVE HYPOTHESIS, which is a pre-diction of a significant finding (e.g., a significant difference between sample means, a correlation that is significantly different from zero). Statistical procedures are applied to research data in an attempt to disprove or reject the NH at a predetermined SIGNIFICANCE LEVEL. See HYPOTHESIS TESTING.

null hypothesis significance testing (**NHST**) see SIGNIFICANCE TESTING.

null matrix a SQUARE MATRIX whose elements are all zeros. In MATRIX ALGEBRA null matrices serve many of the same functions that a zero does in other contexts. Also called **zero matrix**.

null result see NULL FINDING.

null set see EMPTY SET.

number needed to treat (**NNT**) the number of people who must receive a particular therapeutic intervention in order to prevent a single adverse outcome. An EFFECT SIZE commonly used in clinical research, it is the inverse of the absolute risk reduction (ARR). For example, if a new therapy for depression was found to reduce the risk of suicide from 50% to 30%, its ARR is .20. Thus, the NNT would be 1/.20 or 5, meaning that five people need to be treated for every one suicide that is avoided. Smaller NNTs indicate larger treatment effect sizes.

numerical variable see QUANTITATIVE VARIABLE.

Nuremberg code a set of 10 guidelines for conducting research with human participants that were established in 1949 following public discovery of the atrocities associated with the work of Nazi scientists during World War II. The Nuremberg code introduced several important principles, including INFORMED CONSENT procedures and the right of individuals to withdraw participation at any time. See INSTITUTIONAL REVIEW BOARD; RESEARCH ETHICS.

Oo

objective *adj.* **1.** having verifiable existence in the external world, independently of any opinion or judgment. **2.** impartial or uninfluenced by personal feelings, interpretations, or prejudices. Compare SUBJECTIVE.

objective examination see OBJECTIVE TEST.

objective prior see PRIOR DISTRIBUTION.

objective scoring scoring a test by means of a key or formula, so that different scorers will arrive at the same score for the same set of responses. It is contrasted with **subjective scoring**, in which the score depends on the scorer's opinion or interpretation of participant responses to items.

objective test a type of assessment instrument consisting of a set of items or questions that have specific correct answers (e.g., How much is 2 + 2?), such that no interpretation, judgment, or personal impressions are involved in scoring. Examples include MULTIPLE-CHOICE TESTS and TRUE–FALSE TESTS. In contrast, short-answer and essay examinations are SUBJECTIVE TESTS. Also called **objective examination**.

objectivism *n.* the position that judgments about the external world can be established as true or false independent of personal feelings, beliefs, and experiences. Compare SUBJECTIVISM. **—objectivist** *n., adj.*

objectivity *n.* **1.** the tendency to base judgments and interpretations on external data rather than on subjective factors, such as personal feelings, beliefs, and experiences. **2.** a quality of a research study such that its hypotheses, choices of variables studied, measure-ments, techniques of control, and observations are as free from bias as possible. Compare SUBJECTIVITY.

oblimin *n.* a class of OBLIQUE ROTATION methods used in FACTOR ANALYSIS.

oblique *adj.* describing a set of axes that do not form right angles; in graphical representations of mathematical computations (such as FACTOR ANALYSIS), this indicates correlated (not independent) variables. Compare ORTHOGONAL.

oblique rotation a transformational system used in FACTOR ANALYSIS when two or more factors (i.e., LATENT VARIABLES) are correlated. Oblique rotation reorients the factors so that they fall closer to clusters of vectors representing MANIFEST VARIABLES, thereby simplifying the mathematical description of the manifest variables. It is one of two types of FACTOR ROTATION used to identify a simpler structure pattern or solution, the other being ORTHOGONAL ROTATION.

oblique solution in FACTOR ANALYSIS, any of various FACTOR STRUCTURE patterns identified using OBLIQUE ROTATION methods.

observation *n.* **1.** the careful, close examination of an object, process, or other phenomenon for the purpose of collecting data about it or drawing conclusions. See CONTROLLED OBSERVATION; NATURALISTIC OBSERVATION; PARTICIPANT OBSERVATION. **2.** a piece of information (see DATA). **—observational** *adj.*

observational study research in which the experimenter passively observes the behavior of the participants without any attempt at intervention or manipulation of the behaviors being observed. Such studies typically involve observation of cases under naturalistic conditions rather than the random assignment of cases to experimental conditions: Specially trained individuals record activities, events, or processes as precisely and completely as possible without personal interpretation. Also called **observational design**; **observational method**; **observational research**. See also NATURALISTIC OBSERVATION.

observation coding system a scheme or list of mutually exclusive labels, categories, and so forth—each of which characterizes a coherent dimension of interest—used for classifying information obtained by observing others. It is an essential component of any OBSERVATIONAL STUDY as it clarifies what data should be collected and how, providing definitions of each code along with examples. For example, a researcher investigating infant behavior might develop the following observation coding system: (1) quietly alert, (2) crying, (3) fussing, and (4) sleeping. Thus, for every time during a specific observation period that an observer sees the baby acting alert, he or she would record a 1 on his or her data form; for every time the observer sees the baby crying, he or she would record a 2, and so forth.

observed distribution the DISTRIBUTION of values on a variable as actually obtained from a SAMPLE, as opposed to a THEORETICAL DISTRIBUTION based on the laws of probability. For example, one might draw a card from a standard deck of playing cards, note the suit, replace the card in the deck, and repeat the process 100 times. An observed distribution would show how many times a heart, a diamond, a club, and a spade were chosen in the trial of 100 draws.

observed frequency the counts of values or categories on a variable as obtained from a sample. For example, the number of people majoring in psychology at a particular college would be the observed frequency of that major, which may or may not match a theoretically EXPECTED FREQUENCY for the major. Indeed, in the CHI-SQUARE TEST and other statistical procedures observed frequencies are compared with expected frequencies, with large differences suggesting a poor fit for models or explanations proposed to describe the data. Also called **obtained frequency**.

observed score a data value recorded for a variable via actual measurement or observation, as opposed to an estimated or predicted score (or to a score on a LATENT VARIABLE, which is derived or approximated).

observed-score equating see SCORE EQUATING.

observed variable see MANIFEST VARIABLE.

observer bias any expectations, beliefs, or personal preferences of a researcher that unintentionally influence his or her recordings during an OBSERVATIONAL STUDY. See EXPERIMENTER EFFECT.

observer drift gradual, systematic changes over a period of time by a particular observer in his or her application of criteria for recording or scoring observations. See EXPERIMENTER DRIFT.

obtained frequency see OBSERVED FREQUENCY.

Occam's razor the maxim that given a choice between two hypotheses, the one involving the fewer assumptions should be preferred. In other words, one should apply the LAW OF PARSIMONY and choose simpler explanations over more complicated ones. [William of **Occam** or **Ockham** (c. 1285–1347), English Franciscan monk and Scholastic philosopher]

odd–even reliability a method of assessing the reliability of a test by correlating scores on the odd-numbered items with scores on the even-numbered items. The CORRELATION COEFFICIENT between the two halves is adjusted using the SPEARMAN–BROWN PROPHECY FORMULA, which accounts for the decreased size of the odd and even item sets compared to the test as a whole. Odd–even reliability is a special case of SPLIT-HALF RELIABILITY.

odds *n.* the ratio of the probability of an event occurring to the probability of the event not occurring, usually expressed as the ratio of two integers (e.g., 3:2).

odds ratio (**OR**) the quotient of two ODDS. For example, in a study on a drug, the odds ratio is calculated as the odds of an effect in a treated group divided by the odds of the same effect in a control group. A measure of EFFECT SIZE, it varies from 0 to infinity, with a value of 1 indicating no effect and a value of less than 1 indicating a negative effect.

ogive *n.* the somewhat flattened S-shaped curve typically obtained by graphing a CUMULATIVE FREQUENCY DISTRIBUTION. Consider the following hypothetical illustration of test results from students in a classroom.

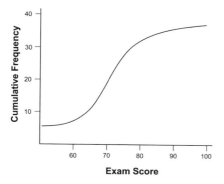

Cumulative frequency values are given along the vertical *y*-axis and obtained test scores are given along the horizontal *x*-axis. The plot increases slightly at either end, including that few students received very low or very high scores, but rises much more steeply in the center, indicating that the majority of students received average scores.

OLS abbreviation for ordinary least squares. See LEAST SQUARES REGRESSION.

omega squared (symbol: ω^2) a measure of the STRENGTH OF ASSOCIATION based

on the proportion of variance of one measure predictable from variance in other measures. In ANALYSIS OF VARIANCE it indicates how much variation in a DEPENDENT VARIABLE can be explained by variation in one or more INDEPENDENT VARIABLES.

omitted variable bias the situation in which values calculated from a statistical model systematically overestimate or underestimate a degree of relationship or other quantity of interest because an important variable has been left out of the model. For example, a researcher could hypothesize a linear REGRESSION EQUATION in which stressful life events and lack of social support predict depression. If coping skills also are highly relevant to predicting depression, the researcher's failure to include that element in his or her conceptualization would create an omitted variable bias. The exclusion of important variables from models may constrain the validity of study findings. See also BIASED ESTIMATOR.

omnibus test 1. any statistical test of significance in which more than two conditions are compared simultaneously or in which there are two or more INDEPENDENT VARIABLES. The ANALYSIS OF VARIANCE is an example. For instance, assume a researcher collects data from an experimental design having two independent variables, each of which has three different levels or conditions. He or she could conduct an analysis of variance to concurrently examine the mean values for all levels of each of the variables (and their combinations thereof) in order to determine whether there are any significant differences among them. **2.** a type of exam that simultaneously measures several different abilities. For example, a mathematics omnibus test may include items assessing numeracy, algebraic skills, geometric proficiency, and trigonometric competency.

one-bend transformation a sequence of POWER FUNCTIONS used to convert a MONOTONIC relationship between two variables into a linear one, such that a single bend in the curve depicting their values on a graph is straightened out. See also TWO-BEND TRANSFORMATION.

one-factor analysis of variance see ONE-WAY ANALYSIS OF VARIANCE.

one-group pretest–posttest design a variation of the PRETEST–POSTTEST DESIGN in which only a single set of participants is measured on a DEPENDENT VARIABLE of interest, exposed to a treatment or intervention, and then measured again to determine the change or difference between the initial (pre-) and second (post-) measurement. The lack of a CONTROL GROUP in this type of research design makes it difficult to attribute gains in the posttest score to the intervention, as other elements (e.g., participant MATURATION) may have contributed to any change observed. Also called **one-group pre–post design**.

one-parameter model see RASCH MODEL.

one-sample runs test see SINGLE-SAMPLE RUNS TEST.

one-sample test see SINGLE-SAMPLE TEST.

one-sample test for the median see SINGLE-SAMPLE TEST FOR THE MEDIAN.

one-sample t test see SINGLE-SAMPLE T TEST.

one-sample z test see SINGLE-SAMPLE Z TEST.

one-shot case study a research design in which a single group is observed on a single occasion after experiencing some event, treatment, or intervention. Since there is no CONTROL GROUP against which to make comparisons, it is a weak design; any changes noted are merely presumed to have been caused by the event.

one-sided confidence interval a CONFIDENCE INTERVAL in which only an upper or lower boundary is specified. For example, if a researcher has a negatively skewed data set (see SKEWNESS), most data points will be at the upper end of the range of values. Thus, he or she likely would focus upon that upper area and specify only a maximum value for the population PARAMETER (i.e., a value above which the parameter is not likely to fall).

one-tailed hypothesis see DIRECTIONAL HYPOTHESIS.

one-tailed test see DIRECTIONAL TEST.

one-way analysis of covariance an ANALYSIS OF COVARIANCE in which there is a single INDEPENDENT VARIABLE and one or more COVARIATES whose potential influence needs to be accounted for statistically. For example, assume a researcher is evaluating how three types of instructional methods (three levels of the independent variable) affect scores on an academic achievement test (the DEPENDENT VARIABLE). If the researcher believes general intelligence, gender, and other unmeasured factors could also affect scores, he or she might use a one-way analysis of covariance to control for such covariates when assessing the experimental data.

one-way analysis of variance an ANALYSIS OF VARIANCE that evaluates the influence of different levels or conditions of a single INDEPENDENT VARIABLE upon a DEPENDENT VARIABLE. The mean values of two or more samples are examined in order to determine the probability that they have been drawn from the same population. Also called **one-factor analysis of variance**; **single-factor analysis of variance**.

one-way blocked analysis of variance see RANDOMIZED BLOCK ONE-WAY ANALYSIS OF VARIANCE.

one-way design an experimental design in which a single INDEPENDENT VARIABLE is manipulated to observe its influence on a DEPENDENT VARIABLE. For example, a researcher could use a one-way design to examine the effect of different amounts of daily exercise (e.g., 0 minutes, 30 minutes, 60 minutes) on mood. Also called **single-factor design**.

open-ended interview an interview in which the interviewee is asked questions that cannot be answered with a simple *yes* or *no*. For example, a human resources staff member interviewing a candidate for employment might ask, "What were the major responsibilities of your most recent job?" Open-ended interviews encourage interviewees to talk freely and extensively, thus providing information that might not be obtained otherwise. The general questions and their order may be planned in advance (see STRUCTURED INTERVIEW) or a single initial question can be planned and the subsequent discussion allowed to pursue various areas of interest as they arise (see UNSTRUCTURED INTERVIEW).

open interval a set of numbers that falls between two defined endpoints. For example, an open interval (0, 3) around *x* indicates that the value of *x* will fall between 0 and 3 but not equal either. In contrast, the CLOSED INTERVAL [0, 3] (written with square brackets) indicates that *x* may be equal to 0 or 3 or assume any value in between.

open-label study a CLINICAL TRIAL in which both the researcher and the participant know the treatment the participant is receiving.

open question 1. in a test or survey, an item that does not come with any multiple-choice options for the respondent. Compare FIXED-ALTERNATIVE QUESTION. **2.** in an interview, a question that encourages the respondent to answer freely in his or her own words, providing as much or as little detail as desired. For example, a candidate in a job interview may be asked the open question, "How would you describe yourself?"

open study a research project in which new participants can be added after the project has begun.

operating characteristic curve for a given SIGNIFICANCE TESTING procedure, a plot showing the probability of the NULL HYPOTHESIS being correct at different values of a PARAMETER. Typically, the former is given along the vertical *y*-axis and the latter along the horizontal *x*-axis, as in the following generic depiction.

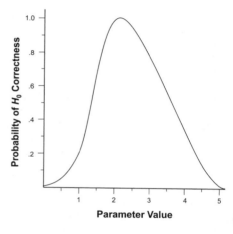

operational definition a description of something in terms of the operations (procedures, actions, or processes) by which it could be observed and measured. For example, the operational definition of anxiety could be in terms of a test score, withdrawal from a situation, or activation of the sympathetic nervous system. The process of creating an operational definition is known as **operationalization**.

operationalism *n.* the position that the meaning of a scientific concept depends upon the procedures used to establish it, so that each concept can be defined by a single observable and measurable operation. Also called **operationism**.

operational research see OPERATIONS RESEARCH.

operationism *n.* see OPERATIONALISM.

operations research the application of advanced analytical methods—such as mathematical modeling, OPTIMIZATION, and computer simulation—to the study of complex situations so as to obtain a comprehensive understanding that allows for accurate predictions of outcomes and estimates of risk and enables more rational, effective decision making. It is used particularly in management science and business contexts.

opinion survey a technique in which a large number of people are polled to determine their collective views, beliefs, or attitudes about a particular topic of interest. Information so obtained often is extrapolated to a broader population with a given MARGIN OF ERROR. For example, during an election year one might conduct an opinion survey in different states of preferences for potential U.S. presidential candidates. Also called **opinion poll**.

opinionnaire *n.* a type of measure for assessing the attitudes or beliefs of an individual about particular topics. It comprises a list of various statements that the respondent is asked to endorse or reject.

opportunity sampling see CONVENIENCE SAMPLING.

optimal design an approach to experimental design in which the conditions to be studied and the assignment of participants to those conditions are determined so as to best fulfill particular statistical criteria. See A-OPTIMAL DESIGN; D-OPTIMAL DESIGN; E-OPTIMAL DESIGN.

optimal scaling see DUAL SCALING.

optimization *n.* a statistical process in which ALGORITHMS are applied to data from a SAMPLE so as to obtain the best estimate of a value for a PARAMETER of interest in the broader population.

OR abbreviation for ODDS RATIO.

oral history background information about a person provided verbally by that individual during an interview. Oral histories may describe such things as perceptions and thoughts, experiences of important events, and family relationships. They can be collected, transcribed, and even analyzed as part of research studies.

oral test any assessment in which the questions are posed and answered verbally.

ordered scale see ORDINAL SCALE.

order effect 1. in WITHIN-SUBJECTS DESIGNS, the influence of the order in which treatments are administered, for example, the effect of being the first administered treatment (rather than the second, third, and so forth). As individuals participate in first one and then another treatment condition, they may experience increased fatigue, boredom, and familiarity with or practice with reacting to the independent variable. Any of these conditions could affect the participants' responses and CONFOUND the results of the study. Researchers often use COUNTERBALANCING to control for order effects. See also CARRYOVER EFFECT; SEQUENCE EFFECT. **2.** the influence of the order in which items or statements are listed on surveys and questionnaires. Three basic types of question order effect have been identified: (a) unconditional, in which the answer to a subsequent question is affected by having responded to the prior question but not by the response given on that prior question; (b) conditional, in which the answer to a subsequent question depends on the response given to the prior question; and (c) associational, in which the correlation between the prior and subsequent questions changes depending on which is asked first. Order effects present serious problems when measuring change over time—unless the question order is the same for each data collection it is difficult to know whether change reflects legitimate respondent differences or question effects.

order of magnitude the approximate degree or strength of a number or value within a range, usually to the nearest power of 10. For example, 2,500 (2.5×10^3) and 4,300 (4.3×10^3) are of the same order of magnitude, but both are one order of magnitude greater than 240 (2.4×10^2).

ordinal *adj.* pertaining to rank, order, or position in a series. Compare CARDINAL; NOMINAL.

ordinal data numerical values that represent rankings along a continuum from lowest to highest, as in a judge's assignment of a 2 to denote that a particular athlete's performance was fair and a 3 to denote that a subsequent athlete's performance was better. Ordinal data may be counted (i.e., how many athletes obtained a 2, how many a 3, etc.) and arranged in descending or ascending sequence but may not be manipulated arithmetically—such as by adding, subtracting, dividing, or multiplying any rank by any other—because the actual difference in performance between adjacent values is unspecified and may vary. In other words, one does not know how much better a rank of 3 is than a 2, and the difference between a 2 and a 3 may not be the same as the difference between a 3 and a 4.

ordinal interaction in a FACTORIAL ANALYSIS OF VARIANCE, a situation in which the effect of one INDEPENDENT VARIABLE is greater for certain conditions of another independent variable. It is indicated by a pattern of converging lines when plotting the MAIN EFFECTS from the analysis. For example, an ordinal interaction would exist if a researcher evaluating the effect of two dementia treatments (A and B) found that with both A and B functioning improved significantly in individuals with a slight to moderate degree of dementia but had little benefit for those with se-

vere dementia. It is important to note that although the results between groups vary depending on the levels of the variables under study, they do not reverse their direction of influence as they would in a DISORDINAL INTERACTION.

ordinal scale a sequence of numbers that do not indicate magnitude or a true zero point but rather reflect a rank ordering on the attribute being measured. For example, an ordinal scale for the performance of a specific group of people on a particular test might use the number 1 to indicate the person who obtained the highest score, the number 2 to indicate the person who obtained the next highest score, and so on. It is important to note that an ordinal scale does not provide any information about the degree of difference between adjacent ranks (e.g., it is not clear what the actual point difference is between the rank 1 and 2 scores). Compare INTERVAL SCALE; NOMINAL SCALE; RATIO SCALE.

ordinal variable a variable whose possible values have a clear rank order. For example, attitude is an ordinal variable as it may be denoted with ordered points indicating increasing or decreasing values, such as 1 = *strongly disagree*, 2 = *disagree*, 3 = *agree*, and 4 = *strongly agree*. Values on an ordinal variable indicate that one data point is higher or lower than another but do not define the extent of the difference between them. Compare INTERVAL VARIABLE.

ordinary least squares regression see LEAST SQUARES REGRESSION.

ordinate *n.* the vertical coordinate in a graph or data plot; that is, the *y*-axis. See also ABSCISSA.

or rule see ADDITION RULE.

orthogonal *adj.* **1.** describing a set of axes at right angles to one another, which in graphical representations of mathematical computations (such as FACTOR ANALYSIS) and other research in-

O

dicates uncorrelated (unrelated) variables. Compare OBLIQUE. **2.** denoting a research design in which there are an equal or proportional number of participants across study conditions. See ORTHOGONAL DESIGN.

orthogonal coding see CONTRAST CODING.

orthogonal contrast in a FACTORIAL ANALYSIS OF VARIANCE, a set of non-redundant comparisons among the mean values for different samples. In other words, the set contains no overlapping information, such that the results from one comparison provide no information about the results of the second comparison. Also called **orthogonal comparison**.

orthogonal design an experimental design involving multiple INDEPENDENT VARIABLES in which each level of one variable is combined with each level of every other and all of the resulting conditions contain an equal or proportional number of participants or observations.

orthogonal rotation a transformational system used in FACTOR ANALYSIS in which the different underlying or LATENT VARIABLES are required to remain separated from or uncorrelated with one another. It is one of two types of FACTOR ROTATION used to identify a simpler structure pattern or solution, the other being OBLIQUE ROTATION. Also called **rigid rotation**.

orthogonal solution in FACTOR ANALYSIS, any of various FACTOR STRUCTURE patterns identified using ORTHOGONAL ROTATION methods.

outcome *n.* **1.** the result of an experiment, treatment, intervention, or other event. For example, the test scores of students in a classroom who have been taught with a new lecture method comprise an outcome, as does any individual element from a SAMPLE SPACE. **2.** in GAME THEORY, the factor determining a particular set of payments, one set being paid to each participant.

outcome research a systematic investigation of the effectiveness of a type or technique of intervention (e.g., a new form of psychotherapy for treating depression) or of the comparative effectiveness of different intervention types or techniques (e.g., cognitive behavior therapy vs. drug therapy for depression). In other words, outcome research focuses on determining whether participants benefit from receiving the intervention. Compare PROCESS RESEARCH.

outcome variable see DEPENDENT VARIABLE.

outlier *n.* an extreme observation or measurement, that is, a score that significantly differs from all others obtained. For instance, assume a researcher administered an intelligence test to a group of people. If most individuals obtained scores near the average IQ of 100 yet one person had an IQ of 150, the latter score would be an outlier. Outliers can have a high degree of influence on summary statistics (e.g., the MEAN and STANDARD DEVIATION can be pulled severely toward outliers) and on estimates of PARAMETER values, and they may distort research findings if they are the result of error.

overdispersion *n.* in CATEGORICAL DATA ANALYSIS, a situation in which obtained observations display more variation (DISPERSION) than is predicted by a model. Overdispersion distorts STANDARD ERROR and CONFIDENCE INTERVAL estimates and often is associated with OUTLIERS or model MISSPECIFICATION.

overfitted model a model of a data set in which there are too many predictor variables or PARAMETERS relative to the number of sample observations. An overfitted model is unnecessarily complex for the amount of available data upon which it is based and does not replicate well nor accurately predict responses.

overidentification *n.* in STRUCTURAL EQUATION MODELING and similar statistical techniques, the presence of more PARAMETERS in a model than are required to correctly specify the relationships among the variables of interest. In other words, the number of known parameters exceeds the number of free parameters, allowing one or more values to be estimated in more than one way. Compare UNDERIDENTIFICATION.

overidentified model a model of a data set in which the number of PARAMETERS estimated exceeds the number of data points or pieces of unique information in the data. In other words, an overidentified model contains elements that are redundant, with more known than free parameter values. Compare JUST-IDENTIFIED MODEL; UNDERIDENTIFIED MODEL.

overmatching *n.* unnecessary MATCHING: the pairing of research participants on an excessive number of characteristics or on characteristics having little or no potential influence upon the outcome of interest. For example, a researcher investigating a new drug treatment for cancer might create two groups whose members are of the same age and sex, administering the drug to one group while the other receives a placebo. Such group comparability would allow the researcher greater validity in attributing any changes between them to the treatment rather than to sex or age differences. If, however, the researcher were to pair the groups on such additional factors as area of residence and household income, overmatching would be present and likely to mask the true nature of the relationship under investigation and lead to statistical BIAS, such as by reducing the POWER and EFFICIENCY of analyses.

oversampling *n.* a sampling strategy in which certain subsets of participants are overrepresented in a study group compared to the larger population from which they are drawn. Oversampling involves deliberately selecting greater numbers of such participants than would be obtained via RANDOM SAMPLING so as to enhance the accuracy of PARAMETER values estimated through statistical procedures. For example, a researcher selecting firefighters from a candidate pool might include equal numbers of males and females to ensure a sufficient sample of females for statistical analysis, even though males comprise the majority of firefighters in the pool.

oversaturated model see SATURATED MODEL.

O-X-O shorthand for a ONE-GROUP PRETEST–POSTTEST DESIGN, in which the researcher observes and measures a single set of participants (O), introduces an intervention (X), and then measures the participants (O) again to determine whether the intervention resulted in any change.

Pp

p symbol for PROBABILITY.

paired comparison method a systematic procedure for scaling and comparing a set of stimuli or other items. A pair of stimuli is presented to the participant, who is asked to compare them on a particular dimension: This is often a physical characteristic, such as size, loudness, or brightness, but may also include personal traits, abilities, or performance on some task. The process is continued until every item in the set has been compared with every other item; in a work setting, for example, the process would be complete when every employee has been evaluated relative to every other employee supervised by the rater. The number of pairs is found by the formula $n \times (n - 1)/2$, where n is the number of objects or people to be rated. Thus, if there are five objects or people to be compared, the number of pairs is 10; if there are 20 objects or people to be rated, the number of pairs is 190. This latter example illustrates a limitation of the procedure; when the number of objects to be rated becomes large, the number of paired comparisons becomes excessive and burdensome for the rater. See PAIRED COMPARISON EXPERIMENT.

paired comparison experiment a study design in which sets of paired alternatives are offered to respondents, who have to indicate which of the alternatives they prefer or rank more highly on a specified dimension. The alternatives offered may be real or hypothetical and judgments can be qualitative or quantitative. The purpose of the paired comparison experiment is to assess the importance of various attributes to the respondents and to determine the weights the respondents attach to the

different levels of these attributes. Also called **paired comparison design**. See PAIRED COMPARISON METHOD.

paired sample any sample in which each participant is matched on a particular variable to a participant in a second sample. This ensures that any differences on an outcome variable cannot be due to differences between participants on the matching variables. A simple example of a paired sample is a PRETEST–POSTTEST DESIGN in which a variable is measured before and after an intervention; in this case the participant is matched to him- or herself. More frequently, paired samples are achieved by matching individuals on personal characteristics such as age and gender. Typically, each member of the pair is randomly assigned to the treatment or control group. See MATCHED-PAIRS DESIGN.

paired-samples t test see MATCHED-PAIRS T TEST.

pairwise comparison in a FACTORIAL DESIGN where the variable being investigated has more than two levels, a procedure in which the data obtained from each level of the variable are compared separately to the data from every other level. For example, where the research interest is the differences in student achievement resulting from three different types of content presentation, statistical tests would be used to evaluate the different outcomes of each pair of content methods (i.e., Method 1 and Method 2, 1 and 3, and 2 and 3). DUNNETT'S MULTIPLE COMPARISON TEST, TUKEY'S HONESTLY SIGNIFICANT DIFFERENCE TEST, and the NEWMAN–KEULS MULTIPLE COMPARISON TEST all involve pairwise comparisons. See also MULTIPLE COMPARISONS.

pairwise deletion a method in which data for a variable pertinent to a specific assessment are included, even if values for the same individual on other variables are missing. For example, consider a researcher studying the influence of age, education level, and current salary on the socioeconomic status of a sample of employees. If assessing specifically how education and salary influence socioeconomic status, he or she could include all participants for whom that data had been recorded even if they were missing information on age, as the latter variable is not of interest in the current analysis. Also called **available-case analysis**. Compare LISTWISE DELETION.

panel data observations on multiple phenomena collected over multiple time periods for the same group of individuals or other units. Repeated observations permit the researcher to study the dynamics of change using techniques such as TIME-SERIES ANALYSIS. Panel data have characteristics of both LONGITUDINAL DATA and cross-sectional data (see CROSS-SECTIONAL ANALYSIS). For example, the values of the gross annual income for each of 500 randomly chosen households in New York City collected for each of 10 years would be panel data.

panel study see LONGITUDINAL DESIGN; PANEL DATA.

paper-and-pencil test a test in which the questions or problems are written, printed, or drawn and the answers are written down.

paradigm *n.* **1.** a model, pattern, or representative example, as of the functions and interrelationships of a process, a behavior under study, or the like. **2.** an experimental design or plan of the various steps of an experiment. **3.** a set of assumptions, attitudes, concepts, values, procedures, and techniques that constitutes a generally accepted theoretical framework within, or a general perspective of, a discipline.

parallel form see ALTERNATE FORM.

parallel-forms reliability see ALTERNATE-FORMS RELIABILITY.

parallel-groups design a research design that compares two conditions or treatments (e.g., relaxation training vs. no training) such that both groups are studied simultaneously and each participant receives one treatment only. A parallel-groups design thus contrasts with a CROSSOVER DESIGN, in which each individual participates in each condition.

parallelism *n.* **1.** in general, the quality or condition of being parallel, structurally similar, or having corresponding features. **2.** in philosophy, the proposition that, although mind and body constitute separate realities, they function in parallel such that responses seem holistic and the two realms seem to assert causal control over each other.

parallel research a study that examines an issue by simultaneously using two or more methods, such as using both focus groups and individual interviews.

parallel threshold method in CLUSTER ANALYSIS, a strategy in which several cluster centers are determined, then objects that are within a predetermined threshold of these centers are grouped together. Compare SEQUENTIAL THRESHOLD METHOD.

parameter *n.* **1.** a characteristic of a POPULATION, such as the mean or STANDARD DEVIATION, that is described or estimated by a STATISTIC obtained from sample data. For example, the mean score on a national exam for a sample of colleges provides an estimate of this parameter in the population of colleges. **2.** any of the variables in a statistical model that is studied or used to explain an outcome or relationship.

parameter estimation see ESTIMATION.

parameter space the set of experimental variables that are used as input into a model and serve as the basis for estimation of PARAMETERS in a population.

parametric *adj.* describing any analytic method that makes ASSUMPTIONS about the data of interest. Compare NONPARAMETRIC.

parametric hypothesis test see PARAMETRIC TEST.

parametric statistics statistical procedures that are based on assumptions about the distribution of the attribute (or attributes) in the population being tested, for example, that there is a NORMAL DISTRIBUTION of values. Compare NONPARAMETRIC STATISTICS.

parametric test a HYPOTHESIS TEST that involves one or more assumptions about the underlying distribution of the population (typically assumed to be a NORMAL DISTRIBUTION) from which the sample is drawn. Common parametric hypothesis tests include ANALYSIS OF VARIANCE, REGRESSION ANALYSIS, CHI-SQUARE TESTS, T TESTS, and Z TESTS. Also called **distribution-dependent test**. Compare NONPARAMETRIC TEST.

Pareto distribution a distribution whose values follow a POWER FUNCTION, such that there is a narrow peak at the extreme left of the x-axis and a long tail to the right. Pareto distributions occur in a diverse range of phenomena, such as the distribution of city populations or income, that are not adequately described by a NORMAL DISTRIBUTION. The marked SKEWNESS of the Pareto distribution is often summarized in the so-called 80:20 rule, which states that, for example, 20% of cities will have 80% of the total population, 20% of people will earn 80% of total income, and so on.

parsimony *n.* see LAW OF PARSIMONY.

part correlation the association between two variables, x and y, with the influence of a third variable, z, removed from one (but only one) of the two variables. This can help a researcher to get a clearer understanding of the relationship between x and y. Also called **semipartial correlation**. Compare PARTIAL CORRELATION; ZERO-ORDER CORRELATION.

partial autocorrelation in TIME-SERIES DATA, the relation between a measure at one time point and the same measure at a subsequent time point, controlling for study variables that are thought to affect the magnitude of the over-time relation. For example, mood ratings from one day to the next may be affected by whether or not a positive social interaction occurred. See AUTOCORRELATION; PARTIAL CORRELATION.

partial correlation the association between two variables, x and y, with the influence of one or more other variables (z_1, z_2) statistically removed, controlled, or held constant; the effect of the z variable is removed from both x and y. For example, partial correlation between salary and education level can be examined after the effects of age on each are removed. It is often of interest to learn whether a correlation is significantly reduced in magnitude once a third variable is removed. Also called **higher order correlation**; **higher order partial correlation**; **partial association**; **partial relationship**. Compare PART CORRELATION; ZERO-ORDER CORRELATION.

partial eta squared (symbol: η_p^2) in ANALYSIS OF VARIANCE, an EFFECT SIZE measure given as the ratio of the BETWEEN-GROUPS SUM OF SQUARES (SS_B) relative to the sum of the SS_B and the ERROR SUM OF SQUARES. It expresses the proportion of variance in the dependent or outcome variable that is accounted for by the factors or independent variables in the model. A higher value means that a higher proportion of the variance was accounted for by the factors included in the model. See also ETA SQUARED; GENERALIZED ETA SQUARED.

partial interaction a type of POST HOC TEST in which different aspects of a complex INTERACTION EFFECT are examined one at a time. The procedure makes use of CONTRAST CODING to determine whether the effect of one variable is the same across all levels or conditions of another variable. For example, a researcher whose study data show that diet, gender, and exercise jointly influence weight loss may use partial interactions to identify and characterize the specific contributions of each.

partial-interval recording a method for measuring or coding instances of behavior within particular time periods of observation. For frequently occurring behaviors or behaviors with a long duration, a researcher can identify time intervals in advance of the coding and have judges indicate whether a particular behavior occurs (or not) within each period. For example, in videos of mock ,job interviews the method could be used to record whether or not the candidate had eye contact with the interviewer within different periods of the interview. See also WHOLE-INTERVAL RECORDING.

partial least squares regression a statistical procedure that generalizes and combines features from PRINCIPAL COMPONENTS ANALYSIS and MULTIPLE REGRESSION. It is used when a researcher wants to estimate the outcomes on a set of dependent variables from a (very) large set of predictors, especially when these predictors have a high degree of MULTICOLLINEARITY or exceed the number of obtained observations. With this approach, a researcher can use varying measurement levels for both the independent and the dependent variables and can also use small samples. It is, however, particularly important to validate findings in independent data sets.

partialing *n.* an approach to the STATISTICAL CONTROL of the influence of a variable or set of variables on other variables of interest (typically, the dependent and independent variables). Partialing helps clarify a specific relationship by excluding the effects of other variables that may also be associated. In a MULTIPLE REGRESSION model, for example, a researcher may want to remove the effects of a set of COVARIATES before examining the final REGRESSION COEFFICIENTS of interest. This process can be accomplished using a hierarchical method, entering the covariates in the first step and the variables of interest in subsequent steps. Also called **partialing out**.

partially sequential sum of squares see TYPE II SUM OF SQUARES.

partial regression coefficient a measure of the relationship between an outcome variable and a particular independent variable with the effects of the other predictor variables in the equation controlled for. It gives the amount by which the outcome variable increases when one independent variable is increased by one unit and all the other independent variables are held constant. For example, a researcher may want to understand how several independent variables together predict salary and also how each variable explains salary while controlling for the influence of the other variables in the equation. The specific contribution of each independent variable to the REGRESSION EQUATION is assessed by the partial regression coefficient associated with each variable. This coefficient corresponds to the increment in EXPLAINED VARIANCE obtained by adding this variable to the regression equation after all the other independent variables already have been included. Also called **partial regression weight**; **partial slope coefficient**. See SIMULTANEOUS REGRESSION.

partial regression plot see ADDED-VARIABLE PLOT.

partial relationship see PARTIAL CORRELATION.

partial replication a REPLICATION of

P

an empirical study in which only a subset of the study's design and methodology are repeated. Often, a researcher will choose to conduct a partial replication to show that the general findings of a study remain the same, despite the methodological changes.

partial residual plot a graphical representation of the relationship between an INDEPENDENT VARIABLE (x_1) and a DEPENDENT VARIABLE (y) with the other independent variables in the model (x_2, x_3, ... x_v) statistically removed or controlled for. It allows the researcher to see the unique effects of an independent variable on the outcome. These plots are less informative when the independent variables are highly correlated. Also called **added-variable plot**; **component-plus-residual plot**.

participant *n.* a person who takes part in an investigation, study, or experiment, such as by performing tasks set by the experimenter or by answering questions set by a researcher. In an experimental design, the person may be further identified as an **experimental participant** (see EXPERIMENTAL GROUP) or a **control participant** (see CONTROL GROUP). Participants may also be referred to as SUBJECTS, although the former term is now often preferred when referring to humans rather than animals. See also RESPONDENT.

participant matching see MATCHING.

participant observation a QUASI-EXPERIMENTAL RESEARCH method in which a trained investigator studies a preexisting group by entering it as a member, while avoiding a conspicuous role that would alter the group processes and bias the data. The researcher's role may be known or unknown to the other members of the group. Cultural anthropologists become **participant observers** when they enter the life of a given culture to study its structure and processes. A downside to the approach is that the researcher can become enmeshed with the group to the extent that he or she is no longer able to document it in an unbiased way. Also called **participative research**; **participatory research**.

participant report a SELF-REPORT provided by an individual who takes part in a study. These data are useful because an individual has a unique access to his or her own thoughts, emotions, and behaviors. On the other hand, an individual may show biases due to memory recall and the desire to be seen in a particular light.

participants' rights in a study approved by an INSTITUTIONAL REVIEW BOARD, a set of conditions relating to participants in the study and their role in the research. Participants normally should be informed about the purpose of the study (but see DECEPTION RESEARCH), its procedures (i.e., what specifically is expected to occur) and the associated costs and benefits; that their data from the study will be kept confidential; whom they can contact if they have any concerns; and that they can leave the study at any time without penalty. Also called **subjects' rights**. See also INFORMED CONSENT; RESEARCH ETHICS.

participant variable see SUBJECT VARIABLE.

participative research see PARTICIPANT OBSERVATION.

participatory action research a form of ACTION RESEARCH that emphasizes collaboration between researchers and members of the disadvantaged community of interest.

participatory evaluation a type of PROGRAM EVALUATION in which the individuals who provide a service (e.g., professional staff) take a direct role in evaluating the service or program; clients of the service provided may also be involved. The official evaluator facilitates proceedings rather than actually

P

conducting the appraisal. Also called **collaborative evaluation**; **empowerment evaluation**.

participatory research see PARTICIPANT OBSERVATION.

partition 1. *vb.* in statistics and measurement, to divide VARIANCE observed in the DEPENDENT VARIABLE into component elements on the basis of its nature and origin. **2.** *n.* a specific component of the observed variance (e.g., variance due to a treatment effect and variance due to RANDOM ERROR).

Parzen window estimator see KERNEL DENSITY ESTIMATOR. [Emanuel **Parzen** (1929–), U.S. statistician]

Pascal distribution see NEGATIVE BINOMIAL DISTRIBUTION.

Pascal's triangle a set of numbers arrayed as a pyramid: Apart from the ones, each entry is the sum of the adjacent entries above.

```
            1
          1   1
        1   2   1
      1   3   3   1
    1   4   6   4   1
  1   5   10  10  5   1
```

It is used to calculate probabilities and binomial coefficients, which indicate the number of possible COMBINATIONS for a set of objects. [named after but not originated by Blaise **Pascal** (1623–1662), French mathematician]

passive deception the withholding of certain information from research participants, such as not informing them of the true focus of the study. As long as certain conditions are met (e.g., DEBRIEFING), this approach is generally considered acceptable, because researchers may not want to reveal their hypotheses to study participants in case this leads them—consciously or unconsciously—to adjust their behavior. Also

called **deception by omission**. Compare ACTIVE DECEPTION.

path analysis a type of STRUCTURAL EQUATION MODELING used to examine a set of simultaneous LINEAR RELATIONSHIPS between variables. Results are displayed using a figure in which boxes denote measured variables, bidirectional arrows show correlations, directional arrows show causal or predictive relations, and arrows coming from nowhere show error associated with the prediction model. Each variable is expressed as a LINEAR FUNCTION of the preceding variable as well as by a unique LATENT VARIABLE; the weights and STANDARD ERRORS for each coefficient provide information about the size of the PARAMETER. GOODNESS OF FIT is tested by comparing models with more pathways to models with fewer pathways. Also called **path modeling**. See PATH DIAGRAM.

path coefficient in PATH ANALYSIS, any of a set of weights (PARTIAL REGRESSION COEFFICIENTS) that reflect the strength of the different facets of the relationships among MANIFEST VARIABLES in a system. For example, if the model indicates that A→B→C, there would be a path coefficient for the relationship between A and B and another for the relationship between B and C; these would be direct effects, whereas the relationship between A and C would be an indirect effect, working through the impact of B. The size of the weight can be tested for STATISTICAL SIGNIFICANCE. If the weight is statistically significant, it is generally drawn as part of the PATH DIAGRAM, whereas if it is not, it is not included.

path diagram a figure describing the hypothesized relations tested in an analysis of simultaneous LINEAR RELATIONSHIPS among measured or MANIFEST VARIABLES; the object is to identify the causal relationships or logical ordering among variables. A diagram generally uses curved lines to represent un-

P

analyzed associations. Each measured variable is designated by a box and latent variables are represented by ovals. COVARIANCES or correlations between EXOGENOUS VARIABLES and between errors are represented by curved lines with arrowheads at both ends. Paths are represented by straight lines with an arrowhead pointing from the INDEPENDENT VARIABLE toward the DEPENDENT VARIABLE. Consider the generic example below. Notice that associated with each path is an asterisk or a number. The asterisks indicate free PARAMETERS, whose values will be estimated from the data, while the numbers indicate fixed parameters, whose values do not change as a function of the data. Also called **causal diagram**; **path model**. See also PATH ANALYSIS.

path modeling see PATH ANALYSIS.

pattern analysis a class of methods (e.g., CLUSTER ANALYSIS, FACTOR ANALYSIS, DISCRIMINANT ANALYSIS) that are used by researchers to recognize and find systematic regularity within a much larger field of data. Often these methods use computer modeling and simulation approaches and involve DATA MINING, image processing, and the study of networks.

pattern coefficient in EXPLORATORY FACTOR ANALYSIS, one of a set of variable WEIGHTS expressing the significance of the underlying factors: one of the individual elements in a FACTOR PATTERN MATRIX. The direction and magnitude of the weight help researchers to evaluate the factors.

pattern matrix see FACTOR PATTERN MATRIX.

pattern-mixture model an approach to analyzing LONGITUDINAL DATA or nested data (see NESTING) in which different strata of cases are identified and separate PARAMETER estimates obtained for each. Researchers also use this approach when accounting for missing data, including those that are not MISSING AT RANDOM.

pattern variable a variable consisting of two or more NOMINAL or CATEGORICAL items converted into a single item that includes all combinations of the relevant information. For two items, A and B, that can score either *correct* or *incorrect*, a single item can be created consisting of (a) zero items correct; (b) Item B correct, Item A incorrect; (c) Item A correct, Item B incorrect; and (d) both items correct.

PCA abbreviation for PRINCIPAL COMPONENTS ANALYSIS.

PDF abbreviation for PROBABILITY DENSITY FUNCTION.

Pearson chi-square test see CHI-SQUARE TEST FOR INDEPENDENCE. [Karl

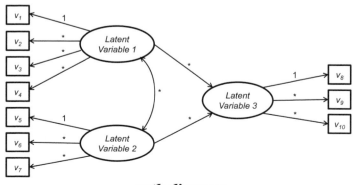

path diagram

Pearson (1857–1936), British mathematician]

Pearson product-moment correlation coefficient see PRODUCT-MOMENT CORRELATION COEFFICIENT. [Karl Pearson]

Pearson's r see PRODUCT-MOMENT CORRELATION COEFFICIENT. [Karl **Pearson**]

penalized maximum likelihood estimation (**PMLE**) a MAXIMUM LIKELIHOOD approach to the estimation of population PARAMETERS that is particularly useful in cases where the model may be overfitted (i.e., have too many parameters). For example, the accuracy of prediction models for drug benefits generally turns out to be lower than estimated when these drugs are given to new samples of patients. This may be because of differences between the new samples and those from which the predictions were generated, or because the developed model was overfitted, or both. The PMLE method makes an adjustment for overfitting that is directly built into the model development, instead of relying on strategies such as SHRINKAGE.

penalty function a WEIGHT applied to a statistic or index that lowers its value because of some undesired characteristic. In STRUCTURAL EQUATION MODELING, for example, several indices used to assess GOODNESS OF FIT include such a mechanism to downweight the index where a researcher's model exhibits a high level of complexity. See also SHRINKAGE ESTIMATOR.

percentage *n.* a fraction or ratio with 100 as the assumed denominator. For example, a national study of computer use might show that a high percentage of adolescents (89 for every 100 sampled) no longer use e-mail as their primary form of communication.

percentage of variance accounted for see PROPORTION OF VARIANCE ACCOUNTED FOR.

percent error see RELATIVE ERROR.

percentile *n.* the location of a score in a distribution expressed as the percentage of cases in the data set with scores equal to or below the score in question. Thus, if a score is said to be in the 90th percentile this means that 90% of the scores in the distribution are equal to or lower than that score. Also called **percentile rank**.

percentile norm see NORM.

percent point function see INVERSE DISTRIBUTION FUNCTION.

per-comparison error rate see TESTWISE ERROR RATE.

perfect correlation a relationship between two variables, *x* and *y*, in which the change in value of one variable is exactly proportional to the change in value of the other. That is, knowing the value of one variable exactly predicts the value of the other variable (i.e., $r_{xy} = 1.0$). When plotted graphically, a perfect correlation forms a perfectly straight line. If the variables change in the same direction (i.e., they both increase or both decrease), the correlation is **perfect positive**, whereas if the variables change in opposite directions (i.e., one increases as the other decreases or vice versa), the correlation is **perfect negative**. It is uncommon to observe this type of relationship in actual data. See also CORRELATION COEFFICIENT.

performance test any test of ability requiring primarily motor, rather than verbal, responses, such as a test requiring manipulation of a variety of different objects or completion of a task that involves physical movement.

period effect any outcome associated with living during a particular time period or era, regardless of how old one was at the time. Certain historical events, such as war, the introduction of social media, or the events occurring on September 11, 2001, may affect responses of participants in research studies. Period effects may be difficult to distinguish from AGE EFFECTS and CO-HORT EFFECTS in research.

periodicity *n.* **1.** the state of recurring more or less regularly, that is, at intervals. Phenomena that exhibit periodicity include the cycle of the seasons, human circadian rhythms, and consumer spending. **2.** in SYSTEMATIC SAMPLING, a problem that can arise when the process of selection (e.g., choosing every fifth unit from a list) interacts with a hidden periodic trait (e.g., gender) within the population. If the sampling technique coincides with the periodicity of the trait (e.g., every fifth person on the list is a male), the sampling technique will no longer be random and the representativeness of the sample is compromised.

periodic survey an assessment, often a questionnaire, that is administered with some regularity but not necessarily at equal time intervals and that generally includes new respondents each time. The national census is an example of a periodic survey with equal time intervals.

periodogram *n.* in SPECTRAL ANALYSIS or TIME-SERIES ANALYSIS, a plot that breaks down the complex sources of variance and noise in the function into component elements. A periodogram

can provide basic information about the underlying process that may otherwise be obscured.

period prevalence see PREVALENCE.

permutation *n.* an ordered arrangement of elements from a set. A permutation is similar to a COMBINATION but distinguished by its emphasis on order. For example, if there are three colored objects—red (R), white (W), and blue (B)—there are six possible permutations of these objects: RWB, RBW, WBR, WRB, BRW, and BWR.

permutation test see RANDOMIZATION TEST.

perpendicular *n.* a line that is at a right angle (90°) to another line or plane. Typically, in plotting a graph, the *y*-axis is perpendicular to the *x*-axis.

personality profile 1. a presentation of results from psychological testing in graphic form so as to provide a summary of a person's traits or other unique attributes and tendencies. Because various scores appear in one display, a researcher can see the pattern of high and low scale scores for a given person. For example, a profile of a client's test results from the Minnesota Multiphasic Personality Inventory would display his or her scores on measures of depression, hysteria, masculinity/femininity, paranoia, social

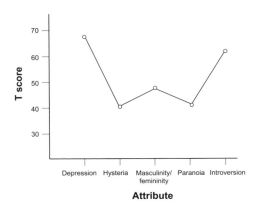

personality profile

introversion, and other attributes (as shown on the previous page). **2.** a summary of traits and behavioral tendencies that are believed to be typical of a particular group or category of individuals (e.g., people with a particular disorder, people employed in a particular profession).

personality study the study of the dynamic structure and processes that determine individuals' emotional and behavioral adjustments to their environment. Such research has focused on the structure of major trait constructs, on how traits affect actions and selection of social settings, and on the stability of processes. For example, a researcher might be interested in understanding how conscientiousness manifests itself from adolescence to late adulthood.

personal probability see SUBJECTIVE PROBABILITY.

person time 1. the sum of all of the years, months, days, and hours that all study participants have contributed to a piece of research. Usually the participants are an at-risk group for a certain disease and this value is used to calculate an incidence rate without any adjustment for dropouts in a study. When years are the unit of interest, the value is called **person-years at risk. 2.** the total amount of researcher time contributed to a project. For example, if there are two researchers who each devote 50 hours to a study, the project involves 100 hours of person time.

PGF abbreviation for PROBABILITY GENERATING FUNCTION.

phase I study in CLINICAL TRIALS, an initial study in which a new drug or treatment that showed promise in other settings is tested for basic safety on a small sample of patients. Should it pass this test, subsequent phases of the testing process will evaluate whether the drug or treatment works and whether it is better than the standard of care.

phenomenology *n.* **1.** the scientific study of human consciousness, perceptions, and experience. **2.** a movement in modern philosophy initiated by German philosopher Edmund Husserl (1859–1938), who argued for an approach to human knowledge in which both the traditional concerns of philosophy and the modern concern with scientific causation would be set aside in favor of careful attention to the nature of immediate conscious experience. The movement suggested that mental events should be studied and described in their own terms, rather than in terms of their relationship to events in the body or in the external world. However, phenomenology should be distinguished from introspection as it is concerned with the relationship between acts of consciousness and the objects of such acts. Husserl's approach proved widely influential in psychology and the social sciences. **—phenomenological** *adj.* **—phenomenologist** *n.*

phi coefficient (symbol: ϕ) a measure of association for two dichotomous or binary RANDOM VARIABLES. The phi coefficient is the PRODUCT-MOMENT CORRELATION COEFFICIENT when both variables are coded (0, 1). For example, the phi coefficient could be used to examine the relationship between gender (male [0] and female [1]) and left- (0) or right-handedness (1). A TWO-BY-TWO TABLE could be constructed to record the frequency of people with a 0 on both variables (i.e., left-handed males), a 1 on both variables (i.e., right-handed females), a 0 on the first variable and a 1 on the other (i.e., right-handed males), and vice versa (i.e., left-handed females). The pairs of responses on the variables could then be analyzed and a phi coefficient calculated to determine whether any relationship exists. The coefficient is interpreted in the same way as other coefficients of correlation. Also called **fourfold point correlation coefficient**. See also CRAMÉR'S V; TETRACHORIC CORRELATION COEFFICIENT.

Phillips–Perron test see UNIT ROOT

TEST. [Peter C. B. **Phillips** (1948–), British econometrician; Pierre **Perron** (1959–), Canadian econometrician]

phone survey see TELEPHONE INTERVIEW.

physical determinism see STATISTICAL DETERMINISM.

physiological measure any of a set of instruments that convey precise information about an individual's bodily functions, such as heart rate, skin conductance, skin temperature, cortisol level, palmar sweat, and eye tracking. Studies using these measures typically obtain measurements before and after the introduction of a stimulus condition as a way to document an individual's response to that stimulus.

pi *n.* (symbol: π) **1.** a ratio expressing the circumference of a circle to its diameter, given as 3.141592. **2.** a symbol denoting the probability of success on a trial, used often in ODDS RATIO calculations as well as in PROBIT ANALYSIS and LOGIT MODELS.

piecewise regression a variant on ordinary LEAST SQUARES REGRESSION in which a REGRESSION LINE consisting of several different lines is fitted to the data. The several pieces have different slopes and meet at nodal points to form a continuous line. This is an approach that is very useful for identifying abrupt changes or discontinuities in a process. For example, piecewise regression might be appropriate where a researcher is studying a group of participants before treatment, during treatment, and after treatment. Also called **segmented regression**.

pie chart a graphic display in which a circle is cut into wedges with the area of each wedge being proportional to the percentage of cases in the category represented by that wedge. For example, a researcher might present the results of a survey on sources of psychology-related literature used by the public in the manner shown below.

It generally works best when there are not many categories (with thin wedges) being shown. A downside of the graphic is that it is not very efficient because it uses significant space to show the frequencies of a single variable.

Pillai–Bartlett trace a statistic used in MULTIVARIATE ANALYSES OF VARIANCE and other procedures to determine the STATISTICAL SIGNIFICANCE of differences among levels of the INDEPENDENT VARIABLES while simultaneously taking into account multiple DEPENDENT VARI-

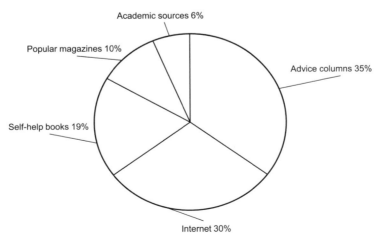

pie chart

ABLES. It is considered to be a robust statistic, even when assumptions of MULTIVARIATE NORMALITY, HOMOGENEITY OF VARIANCE, and COVARIANCE are not entirely met. Also called **Pillai's trace**. See also HOTELLING'S TRACE; WILKS'S LAMBDA. [K. C. Sreedharan **Pillai** (1920–1985), Indian statistician; M. S. **Bartlett** (1910–2002), British statistician]

pilot study a small, preliminary study designed to evaluate procedures and measurements in preparation for a subsequent, more detailed research project. Although pilot studies are conducted to reveal information about the viability of a proposed project and implement necessary modifications, they may also provide useful initial data on the topic of study and suggest avenues or offer implications for future research. Also called **feasibility study**; **pilot experiment**; **pilot research**; **pilot test**.

pivotal variable a quantity that is a function of a statistic (e.g., sample mean, sample size) and a parameter (e.g., population mean, variance) and is used in INFERENTIAL TESTS based on a NORMAL DISTRIBUTION. The Z SCORE, T SCORE, and F RATIO are all examples of pivotal variables. Also called **pivot**; **pivotal quantity**.

placebo *n.* (*pl.* **placebos**) **1.** a pharmacologically inert substance, such as a sugar pill, that is often administered as a CONTROL in testing new drugs. Formerly, placebos were occasionally used as diagnostic or psychotherapeutic agents, for example, in relieving pain or inducing sleep by suggestion, but the ethical implications of deceiving patients in such fashion makes this practice problematic. **2.** any medical or psychological intervention or treatment that is believed to have no effect, thus making it valuable as a control condition against which to compare the intervention or treatment of interest. See also PLACEBO EFFECT.

placebo control group a group of participants in a study who receive an inert substance (placebo) instead of the active drug under investigation, thus functioning as a CONTROL GROUP against which to make comparisons regarding the effects of the active drug. See also PLACEBO EFFECT.

placebo controlled trial a clinical research design that incorporates a PLACEBO CONTROL GROUP. Compare ACTIVE CONTROL TRIAL.

placebo effect a clinically significant response to a therapeutically inert substance or nonspecific treatment (PLACEBO), deriving from the recipient's expectations or beliefs regarding the intervention. It is now recognized that placebo effects accompany the administration of any drug (active or inert) and contribute to the therapeutic effectiveness of a specific treatment. For example, patients given a placebo to relieve headaches may report statistically significant reductions in headaches in studies that compare them with patients who receive no treatment at all. This term is also more generally used in nonclinical studies to indicate any effect arising from participants' expectations regarding the study.

placebo group see PLACEBO CONTROL GROUP.

planned comparison see A PRIORI COMPARISON.

platykurtic *adj.* describing a distribution of scores that is flatter than a NORMAL DISTRIBUTION, as in the general depiction overleaf.

Thus, it has more scores at the extremes and fewer in the center. See also MESOKURTIC; LEPTOKURTIC.

PLS abbreviation for partial least squares. See PARTIAL LEAST SQUARES REGRESSION.

pluralism *n.* the idea that any entity has many aspects and that it may have a variety of causes and meanings. —**pluralist** *adj.*

PMF abbreviation for PROBABILITY MASS FUNCTION.

P

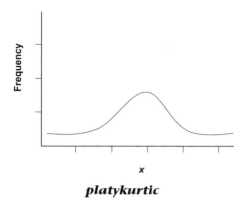

platykurtic

PMLE abbreviation for PENALIZED MAXIMUM LIKELIHOOD ESTIMATION.

point biserial correlation coefficient (symbol: r_{pbis}; r_{pb}) a numerical index reflecting the degree of relationship between two random variables, one CONTINUOUS and one dichotomous (binary). An example is the association between the propensity to experience an emotion (measured using a scale) and gender (male or female). The coefficient is interpreted in the same way as other CORRELATION COEFFICIENTS. Also called **point biserial**; **point biserial r**. Compare RANK BISERIAL CORRELATION COEFFICIENT.

point estimate a single estimated numerical value, determined from a sample, of a given population PARAMETER. Point estimates can often be tested for STATISTICAL SIGNIFICANCE if their STANDARD ERRORS are also known. Compare INTERVAL ESTIMATE.

point prevalence see PREVALENCE.

point process a random variable whose values are the locations in space or time at which a given type of event occurs. **Point process analyses** allow for modeling the occurrence of such events, for example when and where earthquakes occur or when and where bullying occurs in a school setting.

point sampling selecting units or cases from a region in space (e.g., on a computer screen, from a geographic region) using a random process. The selected cases may be used for research purposes or to estimate the average quantity that exists in a given area of the space.

point scale any scale for measuring some construct or attribute in which participants' responses to a series of multiple-choice questions are given numerical values (points). For example, a point scale with the values 1 (*poor*) through 5 (*excellent*) might be used to assess an employee's job performance. See also LIKERT SCALE; SEMANTIC DIFFERENTIAL.

Poisson distribution a DISCRETE DISTRIBUTION that generates the probability of occurrence of rare events that are randomly distributed in time or space. It is a type of THEORETICAL DISTRIBUTION. Count variables, such as the number of aggressive acts observed in a playground or the number of times a person attempts to stop smoking, take this form. When a variable is distributed in this way, a researcher needs to consider specialized statistical models. [Siméon D. **Poisson** (1781–1840), French mathematician]

Poisson process a STOCHASTIC PROCESS that governs the number of times that specific data are observed or counted within a specified period of time. In a study about communication among committed partners, for example, researchers might count the number of times that one member of the couple interrupts the other within a 10-minute problem-solving task. The distribution of a Poisson process at time *t* is the POISSON DISTRIBUTION. [Siméon D. **Poisson**]

Poisson regression an analytic model that has as its dependent variable a count variable and any of a number of predictor variables; in other words it is used when the outcome variable has a POISSON DISTRIBUTION. For example, a researcher may hypothesize that dyadic adjustment, number of years as a couple, and personality characteristics predict the number of times that one member of a couple interrupts the other during a problem-solving task. See also ZERO-INFLATED POISSON REGRESSION. [Siméon D. **Poisson**]

Poisson variable a study variable that is described by a count distribution within a particular time period. See POISSON DISTRIBUTION. [Siméon D. **Poisson**]

policy analysis a collection of techniques for synthesizing information (a) to specify alternative policy and program choices in cost–benefit terms, (b) to assess organizational goals in terms of input and outcome, and (c) to provide a guide for future decisions concerning research activities. Policy analysis is a useful approach for examining the implications of different potential scenarios. For example, an organization considering a flexible time option for its employees might choose to engage in this process before implementing the change.

policy research empirical studies conducted to guide the formulation of corporate or public policies. For example, a nonprofit organization might investigate how to help students from lower income urban areas gain access to higher education.

polychoric correlation coefficient an index showing the degree of association between two variables that are scored as ordered categories but assumed to be manifestations of underlying CONTINUOUS RANDOM VARIABLES. In other words, it is an alternative to the PRODUCT-MOMENT CORRELATION COEFFICIENT that is applied to ordered POLYCHOTOMOUS VARIABLES. For example, a researcher might use a polychoric correlation coefficient to assess the relationship between teacher ratings of student interest in a topic (none, moderate, substantial) and student self-reports of interest.

polychotomous *adj.* describing a single measurement or item scored with more than two unordered or ordered cat-

egories. For example, the quality of a training program could be described as polychotomous: poor, fair, good, or excellent. Also called **polytomous**. See also DICHOTOMOUS VARIABLE.

polychotomous variable a variable having more than two possible categories, either ordered or unordered. For example, college matriculation could be described as a polychotomous variable: freshman, sophomore, junior, or senior. Also called **polytomous variable**. See also DICHOTOMOUS VARIABLE.

polynomial *n.* a mathematical expression consisting of multiple terms, each of which is the product of a constant (a) and a variable (x) raised to a whole number exponent:

$$a_0 x^n + a_1 x^{n-1} \ldots + a_{n-1} x + a_n$$

See also BINOMIAL.

polynomial contrast a comparison of mean values for more than two different levels or time points of an INDEPENDENT VARIABLE to determine whether they follow a particular mathematical pattern, such as linear, quadratic, cubic, or quartic. For example, a researcher might have a specific prediction about how clients' average degree of motivation to attend therapy will differ over the course of treatment (e.g., will decrease, then increase, and then decrease again), and he or she could use a polynomial contrast to determine whether this is indeed the case. See also REPEATED CONTRAST.

polynomial function a mathematical function that relates one number, quantity, or entity to a POLYNOMIAL. For example, $y = 2x^5 + 4x^3 + x$ is a polynomial function.

polynomial regression a type of LINEAR REGRESSION analysis in which the relationship between an explanatory or INDEPENDENT VARIABLE and an outcome or DEPENDENT VARIABLE is modeled as a POLYNOMIAL. Polynomial regression is appropriate for expressing higher order NONLINEAR effects among variables (via

P

quadratic or cubic functions such as $y_i = \beta_0 + \beta_1 x_i + \beta_2 x_i^2 + \beta_3 x_i^3 + \dots$) while retaining all other aspects of linear approaches.

polynomial trend in TIME-SERIES ANALYSIS, a systematic pattern in the data that may be characterized by a POLYNOMIAL.

polytomous *adj.* see POLYCHOTOMOUS.

polytomous variable see POLYCHOTOMOUS VARIABLE.

pooled estimate a single estimated value for a population PARAMETER (e.g., a mean) obtained by averaging several independent estimates of that parameter.

pooling *n.* a procedure in which several independent estimated values of a population characteristic are averaged, with or without WEIGHTS, to obtain a single value. For example, the **pooled variance** is a single value for a variable's DISPERSION produced by combining several independent estimates of that dispersion. Consider a researcher examining correlations between children's educational performance and maternal depression who uses MULTIPLE IMPUTATION to fill in missing data. He or she could calculate the value of the VARIANCE using the data set that exists at each stage of the imputation procedure, and then average each of those individual variances to obtain a single overall value.

population *n.* a theoretically defined, complete group of objects (people, animals, institutions) from which a SAMPLE is drawn to obtain empirical observations and to which results can be generalized. Also called **universe**.

population-averaged model in the analysis of LONGITUDINAL DATA, a model that specifies a MARGINAL DISTRIBUTION, or averaged pattern of responses across cases, rather than a pattern conditional on a person-specific or cluster-specific effect. For example, consider a researcher investigating the characteristics of adults enrolled in distance learning classes, who are nested within families, which are further nested within neighborhoods and communities, and so forth. A population-averaged model would provide information about distance learners as a single entity, whereas a SUBJECT-SPECIFIC MODEL would focus on change in each distance learner individually, and a UNIT-SPECIFIC MODEL would describe the distinct groups of learners (e.g., at the family level, neighborhood level).

population correlation coefficient (symbol: ρ) an index expressing the degree of association between two continuously measured variables for a complete POPULATION of interest. For example, a researcher could obtain income and education information for all families in a town and calculate a population correlation coefficient for the entire town. In contrast, the SAMPLE CORRELATION COEFFICIENT indexes the association for a specific subset of those cases (e.g., every fourth family from a list of all those in the town).

population distribution the DISTRIBUTION of scores or responses on a variable for a complete POPULATION of interest. For example, a researcher could graph the income distribution of all families in a town; in contrast, the SAMPLE DISTRIBUTION would show the incomes of only a specific subset of families.

population mean (symbol: μ) the average (MEAN) value on a variable for a complete POPULATION of interest. In many research settings this value is estimated using the SAMPLE MEAN but in situations when information is known for all the units of interest it can be calculated directly. For example, the mean household income for an entire town may be determined by averaging the responses from a survey returned by all of the households in the town.

P

population parameter see PARAMETER.

population sampling see SAMPLING.

population standard deviation (symbol: σ) a value indicating the DISPERSION of scores in a complete POPULATION of interest, that is, how narrowly or broadly the scores deviate from the MEAN. In many research settings the population standard deviation is estimated from the sample STANDARD DEVIATION, but when information about the full set of units is known it can be calculated directly. See also POPULATION VARIANCE.

population validity the degree to which study results from a sample can be generalized to a larger target group of interest (the POPULATION). For example, consider an educational researcher wishing to characterize the academic motivation of students. If he or she conducts a study of only urban students then the investigator would need to demonstrate that the findings apply beyond the sample used in the study to the broader set of all students as a whole. Population validity is a type of EXTERNAL VALIDITY.

population variance (symbol: σ^2) the square of the POPULATION STANDARD DEVIATION. It is a measure reflecting the spread (DISPERSION) of scores in a complete POPULATION of interest (e.g., the test scores of all students at a school).

positive binomial distribution a theoretical set of discrete values that describes the probability of different numbers of successes occurring in a sequence of BERNOULLI TRIALS, such that there is zero probability of obtaining no successes and all other probabilities are scaled to add to one. Compare NEGATIVE BINOMIAL DISTRIBUTION. See BINOMIAL DISTRIBUTION.

positive correlation a relationship between two variables in which both rise and fall together. For example, one would expect to find a positive correlation between study hours and test performance. Also called **direct correlation**. Compare NEGATIVE CORRELATION.

positive definite describing a SYMMETRICAL MATRIX whose EIGENVALUES are all positive (i.e., > 0). In many modeling approaches, if a matrix does not possess this quality then the analysis cannot be conducted without model respecification.

positive predictive power a calculation of the probability that someone identified as having a particular condition by a specific test does in fact have that condition. It is the proportion of all people identified as having the condition who were correctly identified. Thus, the positive predictive power of a new mammography technology would be determined by dividing the percentage of women whose results correctly show they have breast cancer (i.e., valid positives) by the percentage of women whose results are positives (i.e., both valid positives and false positives). See also SENSITIVITY. Compare NEGATIVE PREDICTIVE POWER.

positive relationship see DIRECT RELATIONSHIP.

positive semidefinite describing a SYMMETRICAL MATRIX whose EIGENVALUES can include zeros as well as positive numbers. See also POSITIVE DEFINITE.

positive skew see SKEWNESS.

positivism *n.* a family of philosophical positions holding that all meaningful propositions must be reducible to sensory experience and observation, and thus that all genuine knowledge is to be built on strict adherence to empirical methods of verification. Its effect is to establish science and the scientific method as the model for all forms of valid inquiry and to dismiss the truth claims of religion, metaphysics, and speculative philosophy. Positivism, particularly LOGICAL POSITIVISM, was extremely influen-

P

tial in the early development of psychology and helped to form its commitment to empirical methods. Despite the advent of POSTPOSITIVISM, it continues to be a major force in contemporary psychology. **—positivist** *adj.*

postdictive validity see RETROSPECTIVE VALIDITY.

posterior distribution in BAYESIAN approaches, an estimated distribution of values for a population characteristic of interest that is obtained by combining empirical data with prior expectations based on existing knowledge or opinion (the PRIOR DISTRIBUTION).

posterior probability the probability that a certain event will occur given that other related events have been observed. For example, assume that Basket A contains 10 white cards and 20 red cards, while Basket B contains 20 white cards and 10 red cards. If one selects a card from a basket at random, without noting the color, the probability that it will be from Basket A is .5, since the only possibilities are A or B. If, however, the color of the card is noted then one must take this additional information into account in determining the probability that the card came from Basket A. For example, the probability that a white card will be pulled from Basket A would be revised downward from .5 according to BAYES THEOREM: Since there are fewer white cards in A, a white card is more likely to be drawn from B instead.

post hoc comparison any examination in which two or more quantities are compared after data have been collected and without prior plans to carry out the particular comparison. For example, after obtaining a significant F RATIO for a data set, a researcher may perform post hoc comparisons to follow up on and help explain the initial findings. Different statistical tests are required for post hoc comparisons than for A PRIORI COMPARISONS. Also called **a posteriori**

comparison (or **contrast**); **post hoc contrast**; **unplanned comparison** (or **contrast**).

post hoc power see RETROSPECTIVE POWER.

post hoc test a statistical procedure conducted on the basis of the findings obtained from previous analyses. Most commonly, the phrase refers to comparisons of the mean values obtained on a variable by different study groups that are made only after an overall ANALYSIS OF VARIANCE has revealed a significant F RATIO, indicating that there is some effect or difference across the groups that should be examined further. Also called **follow-up test**. See POST HOC COMPARISON.

postpositivism *n.* **1.** the general position of U.S. psychology since the mid-20th century, when it ceased to be dominated by LOGICAL POSITIVISM, HYPOTHETICO-DEDUCTIVE METHODS, and OPERATIONALISM. Postpositivistic psychology is a broader and more human endeavor, influenced by such developments as social constructionism and PHENOMENOLOGY. **2.** more generally, any approach to science and the philosophy of science that has moved away from a position of strict POSITIVISM. **—postpositivist** *adj.*, *n.* **—postpositivistic** *adj.*

posttest 1. *n.* an assessment carried out after the application of some intervention, treatment, or other condition to measure any changes that have occurred. Posttests often are used in research contexts, in conjunction with PRETESTS, to isolate the effects of a variable of interest. For example, in a study examining whether a new therapy helps to alleviate depression, participants might receive the therapy and then complete a short symptom inventory, the results of which would be compared to those from an inventory taken prior to the treatment. **2.** *vb.* to administer a posttest.

posttest-only control-group design a research design in which an EXPERIMENTAL GROUP and a CONTROL GROUP are compared on a POSTTEST measure only. It is assumed that participants' results on any PRETEST administered before the introduction of the experimental manipulation would be essentially equivalent across the groups due to the RANDOM ASSIGNMENT of individuals to conditions. A posttest-only control-group design is distinct from a **posttest-only design**, in which all groups receive some treatment and there is no neutral comparison.

power *n.* **1.** a measure of how effective a statistical procedure is at identifying real differences between populations: It is the probability that use of the test will lead to the NULL HYPOTHESIS of no effect being rejected when the ALTERNATIVE HYPOTHESIS is true. For example, if a given statistical test has a power of .70, then there is a 70% probability that its use will result in the null hypothesis correctly being rejected as false, with a corresponding 30% chance that its use will lead to a TYPE II ERROR. Power ranges from 0 to 1, with values of .80 or above generally considered acceptable. Researchers try to maximize power in their study designs prior to data gathering. Also called **statistical power**. **2.** a mathematical notation that indicates the number of times a quantity is multiplied by itself.

power analysis the process of determining the number of cases or observations that a study would need to achieve a desired level of POWER with a certain EFFECT SIZE and a certain SIGNIFICANCE LEVEL. This information is particularly important because it enables a researcher to plan what resources will be needed to enroll or select the desired number of individuals.

power function 1. a relationship in which the values for one variable vary according to the values of another variable raised to a power. In mathematics,

it is expressed by the equation $y = ax^b$, where x and y are the variables and a and b are numerical constants. Power functions have been used to characterize the scales relating perceived and physical intensity, for example, as well as to characterize the relationship between response speed and practice. **2.** a formula relating different factors, such as sample size, EFFECT SIZE, and SIGNIFICANCE LEVEL, to the likelihood that use of a particular statistical procedure will lead to rejection of the NULL HYPOTHESIS when it is in fact false (see POWER). For example, a researcher may plan to use a specific statistical test to detect a medium-sized effect, evaluate the effect at the .001 significance level, and reach a desired statistical power level of .80. Using a power function, the researcher could determine the sample size needed under those conditions. Power functions may be presented in tabular form or plotted graphically as **power curves**.

power transformation a class of TRANSFORMATIONS used to make the distribution of values on a variable more closely resemble that of a NORMAL DISTRIBUTION and to have more stable VARIANCE. In this approach, the obtained values are raised to some exponential quantity (e.g., squared), which preserves their original order. The BOX–COX TRANSFORMATION is an example of a power transformation.

P-P plot abbreviation for probability–probability plot. See PROBABILITY PLOT.

practical significance the extent to which a study result has meaningful applications in real-world settings. An experimental result may lack STATISTICAL SIGNIFICANCE or show a small EFFECT SIZE and yet potentially be important nonetheless. For example, consider a study showing that the consumption of baby aspirin helps prevent heart attacks. Even if the effect is small, the finding may be of practical significance if it saves lives over time. Also called **substantive significance**. See also CLINI-

CAL SIGNIFICANCE; PSYCHOLOGICAL SIGNIFICANCE.

practice effect any change or improvement that results from practice or repetition of task items or activities. The practice effect is of particular concern in experimentation involving WITHIN-SUBJECTS DESIGNS, as participants' performance on the variable of interest may improve simply from repeating the activity rather than from any study manipulation imposed by the researcher.

practice trial the first of a series of opportunities to respond to a test or an experimental setting, which is given to participants to acquaint them with the procedures used and is therefore not scored. The use of practice trials is believed to ensure that the initial measurements of the study proper will provide more accurate assessments of participants' performance.

pragmatic analysis 1. in a CLINICAL TRIAL, an analysis that seeks to determine which treatments will be beneficial to individuals in real-life settings, rather than how or why a treatment is effective, as in an EXPLANATORY ANALYSIS. **2.** a loose synonym of INTENTION-TO-TREAT ANALYSIS.

pragmatic trial see EXPLANATORY TRIAL.

pragmatism *n.* a philosophical position holding that the truth value of a proposition or a theory is to be found in its practical consequences: If, for example, the hypothesis of God makes people happy, then it may be considered true. Although some forms of pragmatism emphasize only the material consequences of an idea, more sophisticated positions recognize conceptual and moral consequences. Arguably, all forms of pragmatism tend toward RELATIVISM, because they can provide no absolute grounds—only empirical grounds—for determining truth and no basis for judging whether the consequences in question are to be considered good or bad. See also INSTRUMENTALISM. **—pragmatist** *adj., n.*

PRE abbreviation for PROPORTIONAL REDUCTION OF ERROR.

precision *n.* a measure of accuracy. In statistics, an estimate with a small STANDARD ERROR is regarded as having a high degree of precision. **—precise** *adj.*

precision matrix a SQUARE MATRIX that is the RECIPROCAL of the COVARIANCE MATRIX. Each element in a precision matrix thus is a PARTIAL CORRELATION, showing the relationship between two variables with the influence of all other variables removed.

predicted value (symbol: $\hat{y}$) in REGRESSION ANALYSIS, the estimated value of the outcome or DEPENDENT VARIABLE (y) for a case in a data set, as calculated from the specified mathematical model of the relationship between predictor variables (i.e., from the REGRESSION EQUATION). The differences between predicted values and observed data are known as RESIDUALS. Also called **Y hat**.

prediction *n.* an attempt to estimate, forecast, or project what will happen in a particular case, generally on the basis of past instances or accepted principles. In science, the use of prediction and observation to test hypotheses is a cornerstone of the empirical method. See also STATISTICAL PREDICTION. **—predict** *vb.* **—predictable** *adj.* **—predictive** *adj.*

predictive criterion-related validity see PREDICTIVE VALIDITY.

predictive discriminant analysis a multivariate procedure that distinguishes between two or more categories of a future outcome on the basis of several current assessments of predictor or explanatory variables. More specifically, the technique combines variables measured at one point in time to produce the highest possible association with different levels or categories of an outcome measured at a subsequent point in time. For example, a researcher might measure daily amounts of exercise, cholesterol levels, and average stress and use this information to predict which individuals will have a diagnosis of serious, mild, or no heart disease six months later. Compare DESCRIPTIVE DISCRIMINANT ANALYSIS.

predictive efficiency 1. the number or proportion of correct predictions that can be made from a particular test or model. **2.** the gain in utility (explanatory information) obtained by adding more predictor or independent variables to a REGRESSION EQUATION. For example, the accuracy of a student's predicted college grade point average may be increased if one considers high school grade point average in addition to Scholastic Assessment Test score.

predictive research empirical research concerned with forecasting future events or behavior: the assessment of variables at one point in time so as to predict a phenomenon assessed at a later point in time. For example, a researcher might collect high school data, such as grades, extracurricular activities, teacher evaluations, advanced courses taken, and standardized test scores, in order to predict such college success measures as grade point average at graduation, awards received, and likelihood of pursuing further education. Compare EXPLANATORY RESEARCH.

predictive validity evidence that a test score or other measurement correlates with a variable that can only be assessed at some point after the test has been administered or the measurement made. For example, the predictive validity of a test designed to predict the onset of a disease would be strong if high test scores were associated with individuals who later developed that disease. It is one of three types of CRITERION VALIDITY. Also called **predictive criterion-related validity**; **prospective validity**. See also CONCURRENT VALIDITY; RETROSPECTIVE VALIDITY.

predictive value 1. the ability of a test or scale to correctly classify items into mutually exclusive categories or states. Predictive value often is determined using DECISION THEORY methods, such as RECEIVER-OPERATING CHARACTERISTIC CURVES. **2.** the percentage of times that the obtained value on a given test is the true value. Also called **predictive power**. See also NEGATIVE PREDICTIVE POWER; POSITIVE PREDICTIVE POWER.

predictor variable a variable used to estimate, forecast, or project future events or circumstances. In personnel selection, for example, predictors such as qualifications, relevant work experience, and job-specific skills (e.g., computer proficiency, ability to speak a particular language) may be used to estimate an applicant's future job performance. In REGRESSION ANALYSIS and other models, predictor variables are investigated to assess the strength and direction of their association with an outcome, criterion, or DEPENDENT VARIABLE. When more than one variable is included in the analysis, the relative weights of each in determining the outcome are evaluated as well. This term sometimes is used interchangeably with INDEPENDENT VARIABLE. Also called **predictor**.

preexperimental design a research design or study with no CONTROL GROUP and no random assignment of participants to experimental conditions. Examples include the ONE-SHOT CASE STUDY and the ONE-GROUP PRETEST–POSTTEST DESIGN. Although such a design is of minimal value in establishing causality, it may be used when it is not possible to identify an appropriate control and circumstances prohibit randomization.

pre–post design see PRETEST–POSTTEST DESIGN.

pretest 1. *n.* an initial assessment designed to measure existing characteristics (e.g., knowledge, ability) before some intervention, condition, manipulation, or treatment is introduced. Pretests often are given to research participants before they take part in a study. For example, in a study examining whether training helps math performance, participants might be administered a short math test to assess their original knowledge prior to undergoing the training. See also POSTTEST. **2.** *n.* a test administered before the main study to ensure that participants understand the instructions and procedures. See PILOT STUDY; PRACTICE TRIAL. **3.** *vb.* to administer a pretest.

pretest–posttest design a research design in which the same assessment measures are given to participants both before and after they have received a treatment or been exposed to a condition so as to determine if there are any changes that could be attributed to the treatment. The A-B DESIGN and A-B-A-B DESIGN are examples. A more complete version in which participants are randomly assigned to a treatment group or a CONTROL GROUP is a **pretest–posttest control-group design**: All individuals are assessed at the beginning of the study, the intervention is presented to the treatment group but not the control, and then all individuals are measured again. The presence of the control group allows the researcher to identify any pre-existing disparities between the groups and thus more definitely attribute differences between the pre- and posttest scores to the treatment of interest. Also called **before–after design**; **pre–post design**.

pretest sensitization an effect in which the administration of a PRETEST affects the subsequent responses of a participant to experimental treatments. For example, if a researcher administers a mood measure prior to treatment conditions, participants may realize that the study is about mood and be more attuned to the mood induction occurring as part of the experimental condition.

Pretest sensitization is important to consider in the interpretation of research findings, as it may make a treatment appear more effective than it actually is. Also called **pretest–treatment interaction**.

prevalence *n.* the total number or percentage of cases (e.g., of a disease or disorder) existing in a given population, either at a given time (**point prevalence**) or during a specified period (**period prevalence**). For example, health researchers may want to investigate the prevalence of a new disease in an area, whereas education researchers may be interested in the prevalence of bullying or cheating among students of a certain age group.

prevention research research directed toward finding interventions to reduce the likelihood of future pathology (e.g., cancer, substance abuse). Such research often concentrates on individuals or populations considered to be particularly at risk of developing a condition, disease, or disorder. It involves one or more of the following: (a) analyzing risk and protective factors and assessing susceptibility; (b) identifying markers for those at risk and developing screening methods; (c) developing and implementing interventions to promote health and prevent the disease; and (d) conducting **prevention analysis**, the methodological and statistical evaluation of the effects of such interventions.

prevention trial a clinical study in which a new intervention to avert a particular disease or disorder is evaluated or compared with an existing intervention. For example, a researcher might investigate whether daily engagement in cognitively challenging tasks (e.g., crossword puzzles) is more effective than medication in preventing Alzheimer's disease. If so, standards of preventive care for Alzheimer's could be changed to benefit older adults.

primary data 1. information cited in a

study that was gathered directly by the researcher, from his or her own experiments or from first-hand observation. Compare SECONDARY DATA. **2.** original experimental or observational data, that is, RAW DATA.

primary factor see FIRST-ORDER FACTOR.

primary sampling unit an item or case chosen in the initial stage of a multistep process for selecting elements for study from a larger group. For example, in a national study of medical school students, the first major step might be choosing a random pool of medical schools from among those available throughout the country; each medical school so identified is a primary sampling unit. Compare SECONDARY SAMPLING UNIT; TERTIARY SAMPLING UNIT.

principal-axis factor analysis in EXPLORATORY FACTOR ANALYSIS, an extraction method in which the COEFFICIENT OF MULTIPLE DETERMINATION of one variable with all other variables in the system is used as the initial COMMUNALITY estimate for that variable.

principal component a single linear combination extracted as part of a PRINCIPAL COMPONENTS ANALYSIS.

principal components analysis (**PCA**) a data reduction approach in which a number of independent linear combinations of underlying explanatory variables are identified for a larger set of original observed variables. PCA reproduces all of the information in the original CORRELATION MATRIX and does not assume that variables are measured with any degree of error. Thus, the result is a new set of variables that are uncorrelated with each other and ordered in terms of the percentage of the total variance for which they account. The technique is similar in its aims to FACTOR ANALYSIS but has different tech-

nical features. Also called **principal-components factor analysis**.

principal components regression a prediction model that uses a set of uncorrelated variables obtained from a PRINCIPAL COMPONENTS ANALYSIS as predictor or INDEPENDENT VARIABLES. The benefit of this approach is that the original set of predictors in the model may have been so highly interrelated as to result in COLLINEARITY. The drawback is that if the uncorrelated variables are not interpretable then the problem of collinearity is not solved.

principal factor analysis an approach to identifying the dimensions underlying associations among a set of variables using a COVARIANCE MATRIX of estimated COMMUNALITIES as input. Principal factor analysis assumes that all variables have been measured with some degree of error and requires that dimensions be extracted in a particular way. Specifically, the first dimension extracted must account for the maximum possible variance, having the highest squared correlation with the variables it underlies; the second dimension must account for the next maximal amount of variance and be uncorrelated with the previously extracted dimension; and so forth. The researcher retains a certain number of dimensions based on various criteria, including interpretations of FACTOR LOADINGS.

principle of beneficence in RESEARCH ETHICS, the requirement of INSTITUTIONAL REVIEW BOARDS that studies "do good" with respect to the work being conducted, the benefits to society at large, and the treatment of participants. Thus, the researcher should maximize the possible benefits of each study and consider its potential impact in the broadest sense. For example, in a study of implicit attitudes a researcher might note that understanding more about the measurement of attitudes regarding sensitive topics may lead to reduced societal prejudice.

P

principle of nonmaleficence in RE-SEARCH ETHICS, the requirement of IN-STITUTIONAL REVIEW BOARDS that studies "do no harm" to participants. When a person considers taking part in a study, there is an expectation that he or she will leave the study in a state that is no worse than when the study began. Where negative consequences are not entirely avoidable—as in an experiment in which a participant is required to recall painful memories, for example—researchers have a duty to minimize the impact of such consequences.

principle of parsimony see LAW OF PARSIMONY.

prior distribution a PROBABILITY DIS-TRIBUTION of possible values for an unknown population characteristic that is formulated before one obtains any current data observations about the phenomenon of interest. It may be a **subjective prior** (based on a researcher's knowledge of the specific field) or an **objective prior** (based on evidence obtained from other studies). In BAYESIAN methods the prior distribution is combined with the LIKELIHOOD FUNCTION to yield the POSTERIOR DISTRIBUTION from which inferences are made. Also called **prior; prior probability distribution**. See also INFORMATIVE PRIOR.

prior probability in BAYESIAN methods, the likelihood of a certain event occurring as determined from current accumulated knowledge about the phenomenon. For example, a researcher could calculate the prior probability of a couple divorcing within five years of marriage based on estimates obtained from census data and previously conducted studies. See also BAYES THEOREM; POSTERIOR PROBABILITY.

probability (symbol: *p*) *n*. the degree to which an event is likely to occur. See also CONDITIONAL PROBABILITY; PROBABILITY LEVEL. —**probabilistic** *adj*.

probability curve a graphic represen-tation of a PROBABILITY DISTRIBUTION. Also called **density curve**.

probability density function (**PDF**) the mathematical representation of the shape of a PROBABILITY DISTRIBUTION: It gives the likelihood that a CONTINUOUS VARIABLE of interest will assume any specific value from the given range. Also called **density function; probability function**. See also PROBABILITY MASS FUNCTION.

probability distribution a distribu-tion describing the probability that a random variable will take certain values. The best known example is the bell-shaped NORMAL DISTRIBUTION; others include the CHI-SQUARE DISTRIBUTION, Student's T DISTRIBUTION, and the F DIS-TRIBUTION. A probability distribution is a THEORETICAL DISTRIBUTION.

probability generating function (**PGF**) a formula giving the coefficients of a sequence of exponential terms de-scribing the likely values of a random variable. It is the summative sequence of the individual PROBABILITY MASS FUNC-TIONS for each possible value of that variable. See GENERATING FUNCTION. See also CUMULANT GENERATING FUNCTION; MOMENT GENERATING FUNCTION.

probability judgment a decision made by an individual about the likeli-hood that an event will occur. Often based on a personal feeling or estimate and thus highly subjective in nature, such decisions are a common area of study, for example by researchers seek-ing to understand why some individuals engage in risky health behaviors. See SUBJECTIVE PROBABILITY.

probability level (**p value**) in statisti-cal SIGNIFICANCE TESTING, the likeli-hood that the observed result would have been obtained if the NULL HYPOTH-ESIS of no real effect were true. Small *p* values (conventionally, those less than .05 or .01) suggest that the chance of ex-perimental results mistakenly being at-tributed to the independent variables

P

present in the study (rather than to the random factors actually responsible) is small. Traditionally, the null hypothesis is rejected if the value of p is no larger than the SIGNIFICANCE LEVEL set for the test. Also called **probability value**.

probability mass function (PMF) the mathematical expression that relates a given value to the probability that a discrete RANDOM VARIABLE will take that value. It is thus the equivalent for a DISCRETE DISTRIBUTION of the PROBABILITY DENSITY FUNCTION for continuous variables.

probability matrix see TRANSITION MATRIX.

probability plot a graphic that compares probability values from two data sets; typically, one set will be a series of experimental findings and the other a theoretical set. Good examples are the **probability–probability plot** (P-P plot), depicting the CUMULATIVE PROBABILITIES of one data set against those of the other, and the QUANTILE–QUANTILE PLOT.

probability ratio the likelihood that a randomly selected unit will have a particular quality as derived from the known or expected frequency of this quality in the population. For example, if a bag contains 300 red balls and 500 white balls, then the probability ratio of drawing a red ball is 300 out of 800 = 3:8.

probability sampling any process in which a sample of participants or cases are chosen from a larger group in such a way that each item has a known (or calculable) likelihood of being included. This requires a well-defined POPULATION and an objective selection procedure, as in RANDOM SAMPLING. Additionally, all members of the population must have some (i.e., nonzero) chance of being selected, although this probability need not be the same for all individuals. Compare NONPROBABILITY SAMPLING.

probability table 1. a chart showing all possible outcomes of a situation under specified conditions and their likelihoods of occurrence. For example, one could create a probability table for the number of boys born into a family. **2.** a display of CRITICAL VALUES for various statistical tests (e.g., Z TEST, T TEST, F TEST, CHI-SQUARE TEST) at different SIGNIFICANCE LEVELS and with different DEGREES OF FREEDOM. Probability tables traditionally were presented as appendixes in the back of statistics textbooks but currently are widely available via computer software.

probability theory the branch of mathematics and statistics concerned with the study of probabilistic phenomena.

probability value see PROBABILITY LEVEL.

probable error an estimated range of error for the value of a population characteristic as calculated from a sample of that population. The probable error of a mean, for example, is obtained by multiplying the STANDARD DEVIATION by 0.6745.

probit n. *prob*ability un*it*: the inverse of the normal CUMULATIVE PROBABILITY DISTRIBUTION. It is used as the LINK FUNCTION in PROBIT ANALYSIS and other techniques for modeling values of binary variables.

probit analysis a type of REGRESSION ANALYSIS in which a dichotomous outcome variable is related to any of a number of different predictor or independent variables. The technique assumes that a latent process generated the observed binary data and uses a LINK FUNCTION to generate a mathematical representation of relationships. Probit analysis and LOGISTIC REGRESSION often produce very similar results. Also called **probit regression**.

probit transformation a method by which a nonlinear arrangement of val-

P

ues, such as those forming an S-shaped curve, is converted into probability units (see PROBIT) through a formula that involves addition, subtraction, multiplication, or division with a constant. It is thus a type of LINEAR TRANSFORMATION.

procedure *n.* a specific sequence of steps or actions delineating the manner in which a study is to be conducted or has been conducted. Procedural descriptions enable other researchers to understand the conditions of a study and replicate it if desired. —**procedural** *adj.*

process research the study of the various mechanisms that influence the outcome of a treatment or intervention. A basic goal of such research is to identify those therapeutic methods and processes that are most effective in bringing about positive change, as well as any inadequacies or other limitations. In other words, process research focuses on the means by which participants benefit from receiving an intervention. Compare OUTCOME RESEARCH.

Procrustes analysis an approach in which empirical data are superimposed onto some fixed target matrix or other structure of theoretical interest. The name derives from the robber in Greek mythology who forced his victims to fit his bed by stretching them or cutting off their limbs.

Procrustes rotation a LINEAR TRANSFORMATION of the points represented in a MATRIX to best conform, in a least squares sense (see LEAST SQUARES CRITERION), to the points in another target matrix. Usually the points in the target matrix represent some theoretical factor structure or the results of a FACTOR ANALYSIS on a different population. It is performed as part of a PROCRUSTES ANALYSIS. See also PROMAX ROTATION.

proctored test a test that is administered with an observer present to monitor the security of the administration and address any issues that might arise, such as a need to clarify instructions. Compare SELF-ADMINISTERED TEST.

product-limit estimator see KAPLAN–MEIER ESTIMATOR.

product-moment correlation coefficient (symbol: *r*) an index of the degree of linear relationship between two variables. Devised by British statistician Karl Pearson (1857–1936), it is often known as the **Pearson product-moment correlation coefficient (Pearson's *r*)** and is one of the most commonly used SAMPLE CORRELATION COEFFICIENTS.

product vector the result of multiplying two matrices each of which comprises a single column or row. Product vectors are relevant to the calculation of COVARIANCES and other statistics. Also called **vector product**. See also CROSS-PRODUCT.

profile *n.* see PERSONALITY PROFILE; TEST PROFILE.

profile analysis a multivariate statistical technique that compares independent groups of individuals across several constructs or dimensions (e.g., of personality) that are measured on the same scale in terms of their mean level or elevation, their shape, and their scatter or variability. The data can be depicted graphically with the scale name on the *x*-axis, the scale score on the *y*-axis, and different lines reflecting the different groups being examined.

profile similarity coefficient any of several indices used in multivariate analyses to describe the similarity in elevation, shape, and scatter of sets of scores from different groups of cases. Some measures, such as the PRODUCT-MOMENT CORRELATION COEFFICIENT, describe the consistency of scores across groups but not the mean level or elevation of the scores. Other indices, such as the INTRACLASS CORRELATION coefficient, describe whole score sets well but are not able to distinguish extreme or av-

P

erage individual scores. Also called **profile proximity measure**.

prognostic variable in medical research, a BASELINE CHARACTERISTIC of an individual that may lead to a clinical diagnosis in the future. It is important for researchers to define such characteristics early in a study to help customize interventions to be as effective as possible for each person. For example, childhood obesity is a prognostic variable for adult-onset diabetes, such that many interventions focus on promoting healthy eating and exercise in youth.

program evaluation an appraisal process that contributes to decisions on installing, continuing, expanding, certifying, or modifying social programs, depending on their effectiveness. Program evaluation also is used to obtain evidence to rally support or opposition for the organization providing services and to contribute to basic knowledge in the social and behavioral sciences about social interventions and social experimentation. See EVALUATION RESEARCH.

projection *n.* in linear algebra and EXPLORATORY FACTOR ANALYSIS, the mapping of a set of points in multidimensional space. —**project** *vb.*

projection pursuit in EXPLORATORY DATA ANALYSIS, a method for identifying the most interesting clusters in LINEAR COMBINATIONS of variables in a multivariate data set. If a nonnormal cluster is identified, its corresponding data are removed and a subsequent cluster is obtained. The process continues until no further clusters can be found.

projective technique any assessment procedure that consists of a fixed series of relatively ambiguous stimuli designed to elicit unique, sometimes highly idiosyncratic, responses that reflect the personality, cognitive style, and other psychological characteristics of the respondent. Examples of this type of procedure are the Rorschach Inkblot Test and the Thematic Apperception Test, as well as sentence completion, word association, and drawing tests. The use of projective techniques has generated considerable discussion among researchers, with opinions ranging from the belief that personality assessment is incomplete without data from at least one or more of these procedures to the view that such techniques lack important psychometric features such as RELIABILITY and VALIDITY. Also called **projective method**.

promax rotation in EXPLORATORY FACTOR ANALYSIS, a type of PROCRUSTES ROTATION used to fit a solution to a simpler structure or target. More specifically, it is a form of OBLIQUE ROTATION in which a researcher starts with a solution from a VARIMAX ROTATION and raises the FACTOR LOADINGS to a certain power to make them more extreme; he or she then finds the rotation to the target using the LEAST SQUARES CRITERION. A researcher subsequently interprets the loadings of the variables on the factors and also a correlation matrix of the factors.

proof *n.* **1.** the establishment of a proposition or theory as true, or the method by which it is so established. There is much debate as to whether propositions or theories can ever be truly proven. In logic and philosophy, even a valid argument can be untrue if its first premise is false. For example, it is a valid argument to say that *All trees are pines: I have a tree in my garden: Therefore my tree is a pine.* In empirical sciences such as psychology, both logical and methodological problems make it impossible to prove a theory or hypothesis true. Disciplines that rely on empirical science must settle for some type of probabilism based on empirical support of its theories and hypotheses. See also FALSIFIABILITY. **2.** in mathematics and logic, a sequence of steps formally establishing the truth of a theorem or the validity of a proposition.

propensity score in an experimental design lacking RANDOM ASSIGNMENT, a measure of the probability that a participant will be part of the treatment group. It is a type of BALANCING SCORE used to adjust for SAMPLING BIAS by matching differences among participants across conditions. Several different algorithms exist for determining propensity scores.

prophecy formula see SPEARMAN–BROWN PROPHECY FORMULA.

proportion *n.* a decimal value that expresses the size of a subset of cases of interest relative to the set as a whole. For example, if 10 students out of 40 students in a class complete their assignments on time then the proportion of students who are not late is 10/40 = .25.

proportional *adj.* having a constant ratio between quantities, such that the overall relationship does not change. For example, consider a researcher who is examining the differences between two treatments among males and females as follows: 10 males in Treatment A and 20 males in Treatment B, and 20 females in Treatment A and 40 females in Treatment B. Although there are unequal numbers of people in each treatment condition, the ratio or proportion between them remains the same—twice as many females as males. In UNBALANCED DESIGNS, the presence or absence of such **proportional cell frequency** is critical to a researcher's choice of analytic strategy.

proportional hazards assumption in COX REGRESSION ANALYSIS, the situation in which two individuals with similar COVARIATES have the same ratio of estimated hazards over time. A variety of tests of proportionality exist for researchers to evaluate whether this assumption holds.

proportional hazards model see COX REGRESSION ANALYSIS.

proportional odds model a type of LOGISTIC REGRESSION used when the outcome variable has more than two ordered response categories. The researcher calculates an ODDS RATIO for each category, which indicates the likelihood of that specific outcome occurring according to the values of the predictors and COVARIATES of interest. For example, one might use the proportional odds model to determine employees' likely degree of job satisfaction (poor, fair, or good) according to such variables as salary, work hours, length of commute, work responsibilities, decision-making authority, age, and sex.

proportional reduction of error (PRE) an index of the extent to which the addition of one or more INDEPENDENT VARIABLES in a REGRESSION EQUATION reduces inaccuracy in predicting scores on the DEPENDENT VARIABLE. It is based on a LOSS FUNCTION and generally ranges from 0 to 1 in value. The concept may be applied to GENERALIZED LINEAR MODELS and other statistical approaches as well. Also called **proportional reduction of prediction error**.

proportional sampling an approach in which one draws cases for study from certain groups (e.g., gender, race/ethnicity) in the amounts that are observed in the larger population. For example, if a university has 60% female students and 40% male students, a researcher would obtain a sample comprising the same percentages or proportions, such as 120 females and 80 males in a 200-student subset. A significant drawback of this form of STRATIFIED SAMPLING is that small sample sizes may limit statistical modeling and inference. Also called **proportionate sampling**.

proportion of variance accounted for the extent to which certain factors or INDEPENDENT VARIABLES in a proposed model are associated with the outcome or DEPENDENT VARIABLE of interest. The total amount of possible variance in an outcome is 1.00 or 100%, hence the proportion of variance accounted for indicates what fraction of that 100% is explained by the model. For example, in a REGRESSION EQUATION predicting propensity to help someone in distress, an individual's level of agreeableness and confidence may explain .14, or 14%, of the variance in the propensity to help measure.

proportion of variance index any of several measures describing the amount of variability in an outcome variable that is explained by the independent variables. In MULTIPLE REGRESSION, for example, the COEFFICIENT OF MULTIPLE DETERMINATION is a commonly used proportion of variance index. The larger the value of this index, the greater the amount of variance that is accounted for by the independent variables, with 1.00 (100%) being the theoretical upper bound.

prosecutor's fallacy see DEFENDER'S FALLACY.

prospective research research that starts with the present and follows participants forward in time to examine trends, predictions, and outcomes. Examples include randomized experiments and LONGITUDINAL DESIGNS. Also called **forward-looking study**; **prospective study**. Compare RETROSPECTIVE RESEARCH.

prospective sampling a sampling method in which cases are selected for inclusion in experiments or other research on the basis of their exposure to a risk factor. Participants are then followed to see if the condition of interest develops. For example, young children who were exposed to lead in their drinking water and those who were not exposed to this risk factor could be included in a study and then followed through time to assess health problems that emerge when they are adolescents. Compare RETROSPECTIVE SAMPLING.

prospective validity see PREDICTIVE VALIDITY.

protected t test see FISHER LEAST SIGNIFICANT DIFFERENCE TEST.

protocol *n.* see RESEARCH PROTOCOL; VERBAL PROTOCOL.

protocol violation any intentional deviation by a researcher or study personnel from the research procedures as approved by an INSTITUTIONAL REVIEW BOARD. For example, an investigator who begins participant recruitment before the board has authorized the study has committed a protocol violation.

prototheory *n.* a working HYPOTHESIS or starting set of assumptions about a phenomenon of interest. If empirical data from independent studies do not support the prototheory, it must be revised or rejected. See THEORY.

proximate cause the most direct or immediate cause of an event. For example, the proximate cause of Smith's aggression may be an insult, but the ULTIMATE CAUSE may be Smith's early childhood experiences.

proximity matrix a general term denoting either a SIMILARITY MATRIX or a DISSIMILARITY MATRIX.

proxy variable a variable, *b*, used in place of another, *a*, when *b* and *a* are substantially correlated but scores are available only on variable *b*, often because of the difficulty or costs involved in collecting data for variable *a*. In other words, *b* is a substituted measure of *a*. For example, rather than reporting the precise income levels of their parents or guardians, survey respondents instead may be asked to indicate the highest level of education of each parent or guardian; in this case, education is a proxy for income. Also called **surrogate variable**.

pseudoinverse *n.* see GENERALIZED INVERSE.

pseudorandom *adj.* describing a process that is close to being RANDOM but is not perfectly so. For example, so-called RANDOM NUMBER GENERATORS are often described as pseudorandom because their algorithms do not achieve the ideal of producing a flawlessly random process. Also called **quasi-random**.

pseudoscience *n.* a system of theories and methods that has some resemblance to a genuine science but that cannot be considered such. Examples range from astrology, numerology, and esoteric magic to such modern phenomena as Scientology. Various criteria for distinguishing pseudosciences from true sciences have been proposed, one of the most influential being that of FALSIFIABILITY. On this basis, certain approaches to psychology and psychoanalysis have sometimes been criticized as pseudoscientific, as they involve theories or other constructs that cannot be directly or definitively tested by observation. —**pseudoscientific** *adj.*

pseudovalue *n.* an estimated PARAMETER value used as a temporary placeholder in analytic approaches that require intensive iterative calculations, such as BOOTSTRAPPING, the JACKKNIFE, and other RESAMPLING techniques.

psychogram *n.* see TRAIT PROFILE.

psychological scale 1. a system of measurement for a cognitive, social, emotional, or behavioral variable or function, such as personality, intelligence, attitudes, or beliefs. **2.** any instrument that can be used to make such a measurement. A psychological scale may comprise a single item measured using a variety of response formats (e.g., SEMANTIC DIFFERENTIAL, multiple choice, checklist) or be a collection of items with similar formats. Also called **psychometric scale**. See also PSYCHOLOGICAL TEST.

psychological significance the extent to which an effect found in a research study is relevant to the attitudes, cognitions, beliefs, and behavior of humans. For example, a finding that describes how individuals function in a variety of different settings would have psychological significance. See also CLINICAL SIGNIFICANCE; PRACTICAL SIGNIFICANCE; STATISTICAL SIGNIFICANCE.

psychological statistics the area within psychology and the behavioral sciences that is concerned with research design and methodology, addressing issues of measurement, SAMPLING, data collection, data analysis, and reporting of findings. See also QUANTITATIVE PSYCHOLOGY.

psychological test any standardized instrument, including scales and self-report inventories, used to measure behavior or mental attributes, such as attitudes, emotional functioning, intelligence and cognitive abilities (reasoning, comprehension, abstraction, etc.), aptitudes, values, interests, and personality characteristics. For example, a researcher might use a psychological test of emotional intelligence to examine whether some managers make better decisions in conflict situations than others. Also called **psychometric test**.

psychological testing see PSYCHOMETRICS.

psychometrician *n.* **1.** an individual with a theoretical knowledge of measurement techniques who is qualified to develop, evaluate, and improve psychological tests. **2.** an individual who is trained to administer psychological tests and interpret their results, under the supervision of a licensed psychologist. Also called **psychometrist**.

psychometric model any theoretical and statistical framework describing how respondents generate their answers to items on a scale or instrument and explaining associated sources of error, which in turn provides a means to determine the reliability of test scores across different testing situations. There are three major approaches: CLASSICAL TEST THEORY, GENERALIZABILITY THEORY, and ITEM RESPONSE THEORY.

psychometric research studies in the field of psychological measurement. Such

P

research includes the development of new measures and appropriate methods for their scoring, the establishment of RELIABILITY and VALIDITY evidence for measures, the examination of item and scale properties and their dimensions, and the evaluation of DIFFERENTIAL ITEM FUNCTIONING across subgroups. For example, psychometric research could be used to determine whether a new scale is appropriately administered and scored in a specific subpopulation of respondents.

psychometrics *n.* the branch of psychology concerned with the quantification and measurement of human attributes, behavior, performance, and the like, as well as with the design, analysis, and improvement of the tests, questionnaires, and so on used in such measurement. Also called **psychometric psychology**; **psychometry**.

psychometric scale see PSYCHOLOGICAL SCALE.

psychometric scaling the creation of an instrument to measure a psychological concept through a process of analyzing responses to a set of test items or other stimuli. It involves identifying item properties, noting whether responses match theoretical formats, reducing the larger set of items into a smaller number (e.g., through EXPLORATORY FACTOR ANALYSIS), and determining appropriate scoring methods. THURSTONE SCALING is an example.

psychometric test see PSYCHOLOGICAL TEST.

psychophysical research empirical studies, often conducted in a laboratory setting, linking properties of a physical stimulus to a sensory response. For example, in a study of hearing, a participant might be requested to distinguish a number of different sounds by their loudness.

psychophysical scaling any of the techniques used to construct scales relating physical stimulus properties to perceived magnitude. For example, a respondent in a study may have to indicate the roughness of several different materials that vary in texture. Methods are often classified as direct or indirect, based on whether the observer directly judges magnitude.

psychophysiological research empirical studies, often conducted in a laboratory setting using functional magnetic resonance imaging and other neuroscientific tools, that link an individual's bodily responses (e.g., change in heart rate, palmar sweat, eye blink) and mental processes (e.g., memory, cognitive processing, brain function). For example, in addition to collecting data on several performance measures, a psychophysiological researcher might examine cortisol levels in adolescents with a diagnosis of conduct disorder and compare them to levels in those without the disorder.

psychosocial effect any effect upon an individual's attitudes and interactions that involves the influence of a particular social environment. For example, a study might show a psychosocial effect in which lack of social support lowers one's likelihood of seeking mental health treatment.

P-technique factor analysis a method in EXPLORATORY FACTOR ANALYSIS for understanding the major underlying dimensions of variables for a given person over time. In this approach, a single individual or unit is measured repeatedly on a broad range of variables, the variables are correlated over the series of occasions sampled, and the correlation factor is analyzed. For example, a set of memory tests may be administered to a person at several points in his or her life; P-technique factor analysis could then be used to identify dimensions of change or patterns of covariation among the variables across occasions. Compare Q-TECHNIQUE FACTOR ANALYSIS; R-TECHNIQUE FACTOR ANALYSIS.

P

publication bias the tendency for study results that are published in journals or other outlets to differ from study results that are not published. In particular, published studies are more likely to show positive or statistically significant findings. Thus, when conducting a META-ANALYSIS it is important to gather the full range of available research, both published and unpublished, to ensure the analysis does not provide unrepresentatively large EFFECT SIZES. See FILE-DRAWER PROBLEM.

publication ethics the principles and standards associated with the process of publishing the results of scientific research or scholarly work in general. These include such matters as giving the appropriate credit and authorship status to those who have earned it; ensuring that appropriate citations are given to ideas, methodology, or findings from another study; not submitting the same article to more than one journal simultaneously; and not submitting for republication results that have already been published elsewhere without indicating that fact.

pure research see BASIC RESEARCH.

pure science see BASIC SCIENCE.

purposive sampling a SAMPLING method that focuses on very specific characteristics of the units or individuals chosen. For example, a researcher investigating a specific type of amnesia may select for study only those individuals who have specific lesions in their brains. Although the final subset of cases is extreme and not random, valuable information nonetheless may be obtained from their study. See NONPROBABILITY SAMPLING.

p value *n.* see PROBABILITY LEVEL.

Pygmalion effect a consequence or reaction in which the expectations of a leader or superior engender behavior from followers or subordinates that is consistent with these expectations: a form of SELF-FULFILLING PROPHECY. For example, raising a manager's expectations regarding the performance of subordinate employees has often been found to enhance the performance of those employees. See UPWARD PYGMALION EFFECT.

P

Qq

q 1. symbol for STUDENTIZED RANGE STATISTIC. **2.** symbol for the probability of failure in a BINARY TRIAL: $q = 1 - p$.

Q 1. see COCHRAN Q TEST. **2.** see YULE'S Q. **3.** symbol for a specific QUARTILE (e.g., Q_1, first quartile; Q_3, third quartile).

QDA abbreviation for QUADRATIC DISCRIMINANT ANALYSIS.

QI abbreviation for QUASI-INDEPENDENCE.

Q methodology a set of research methods used to study how people think or feel about a topic. It includes, among other methods, Q-TECHNIQUE FACTOR ANALYSIS, which attempts to identify shared ways of thinking; and Q SORTS, in which participants are given statements about people and topics and asked to sort them into categories. Compare R METHODOLOGY.

Q-Q plot abbreviation for QUANTILE–QUANTILE PLOT.

Q sort a data-collection procedure, often used in personality measurement, in which a participant or independent rater sorts a broad set of stimuli into categories using a specific instruction set. The stimuli are often short descriptive statements (e.g., of personal traits) printed on cards. Examples of the instruction set are "describe yourself"; "describe this child"; and "describe your friend." In the classic or **structured Q sort**, raters are constrained to use a predetermined number of stimuli in each category. Often, general categories are used to reflect the NORMAL DISTRIBUTION with raters assigning fewer stimuli to the extreme categories and many more stimuli to the middle categories. See Q METHODOLOGY.

Q-technique factor analysis a type of FACTOR ANALYSIS used to understand the major dimensions or "types" of people by identifying how they perceive different variables. Instead of describing how variables group together, as in R-TECHNIQUE FACTOR ANALYSIS, this approach examines how people group together, with a correlation of people across a broad range of variables. For example, types of students could be identified based on how participants describe themselves academically (e.g., "hard working," "procrastinating"); individual descriptors of academic behavior (e.g., "Plans projects in advance of due dates") would have FACTOR LOADINGS on each of the underlying person factors. Also called **inverse factor analysis**; **Q-technique factoring**. Compare P-TECHNIQUE FACTOR ANALYSIS.

quadrant *n.* one of four divisions of a two-dimensional *x–y* plot of psychological variables, as shown in the generic depiction overleaf. The quadrants correspond to (A) positive scores on both dimensions (upper right corner of plot), (B) negative scores on both dimensions (lower left corner of plot), and (C and D) positive scores on one dimension and negative scores on the other dimension (upper left corner and lower right corner, respectively, of the plot).

quadrant sampling a method for selecting units of analysis (e.g., participants, organizations) from different areas of a space. The space is divided into four sections and units are drawn from each. In psychology, units may be drawn from psychological space, such as personality variables that are thought of as arrayed in two-dimensional space. See QUADRANT.

quadratic discriminant analysis (QDA) a method used to classify vari-

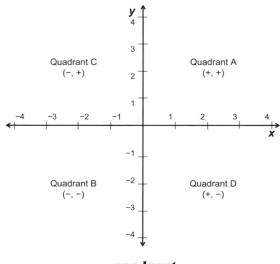

quadrant

ables into two or more groups. A set of PREDICTOR VARIABLES is combined optimally to maximize the association with a particular grouping outcome (e.g., different clinical diagnostic groups) without the strong assumptions required of other, more simple linear versions of the model (see DISCRIMINANT ANALYSIS). These assumptions include MULTIVARIATE NORMALITY and HOMOGENEITY OF VARIANCE.

quadratic discriminant function the set of optimal PREDICTOR VARIABLE weights that emerge from QUADRATIC DISCRIMINANT ANALYSIS. The weights help the researcher understand and interpret which of the predictor variables in the analysis are particularly strong in accounting for membership in a particular outcome group and which variables have little or no influence in this prediction.

quadratic form 1. a specific mathematical form that is central to MULTIVARIATE ANALYSIS. If x is a vector and A a square matrix, then the quadratic form is given by $x'Ax$. **2.** a POLYNOMIAL of degree two; for example, $4x^2 + 2xy - 3y^2$ is a quadratic form of the variables x and y.

quadratic loss function a commonly used process in statistical procedures involving the LEAST SQUARES CRITERION or other principles for minimizing error; it sequentially determines the difference between a provisional estimate and a final estimate until some stopping point. See LOSS FUNCTION.

quadrature *n.* the numerical computation of an integral of a function, either by traditional rules or by an adaptive process involving approximation. It is used extensively during estimation in modeling approaches, such as ITEM RESPONSE THEORY and GENERALIZED LINEAR MODELS.

qualitative *adj.* referring to a variable, study, or analysis that involves a method of inquiry based on descriptive data without the use of numbers. Qualitative methods and approaches focus on understanding open-ended responses, such as those found in written narratives, interviews, focus groups, observation, and case studies (see QUALITATIVE RESEARCH). Compare QUANTITATIVE.

qualitative analysis the investigation of open-ended material and narratives by researchers or raters who describe dominant themes that emerge in the data. In many cases specialized computer programs are used to identify these themes with researcher-provided search terms. A major component of describing the data is trying to understand the reasons behind the observed themes. Compare QUANTITATIVE ANALYSIS.

qualitative data information that is not expressed numerically, such as descriptions of behavior, thoughts, attitudes, and experiences. If desired, qualitative data can often be expressed quantitatively through a CODING process. See QUANTITATIVE RESEARCH. Compare QUANTITATIVE DATA.

qualitative observation a formal description of a phenomenon that takes into account the context in which that phenomenon occurs but does not rely on numbers in the description. See QUALITATIVE RESEARCH.

qualitative research a method of research that produces descriptive (nonnumerical) data, such as observations of behavior or personal accounts of experiences. The goal of gathering this QUALITATIVE DATA is to examine how individuals can perceive the world from different vantage points. A variety of techniques are subsumed under qualitative research, including CONTENT ANALYSES of narratives, in-depth INTERVIEWS, FOCUS GROUPS, PARTICIPANT OBSERVATION, and CASE STUDIES, often conducted in naturalistic settings. Also called **qualitative design; qualitative inquiry; qualitative method; qualitative study**. Compare QUANTITATIVE RESEARCH.

qualitative variable a descriptive characteristic or attribute, that is, one that cannot be numerically ordered. Examples are gender, eye color, and preferred sport. Compare QUANTITATIVE VARIABLE.

quality adjusted survival analysis in controlled clinical trials, a type of SURVIVAL ANALYSIS that not only predicts time to an event (e.g., number of years to death, time to relapse) but also recognizes aspects of the treatment that affect a patient's quality of life. For example, the analysis would identify a treatment condition (e.g., introduction of a new drug) that might lead to longer but much lower quality of life for the patient.

quality adjusted survival time in QUALITY ADJUSTED SURVIVAL ANALYSIS, a patient's days of survival in good health, that is, discounting days with side effects, sickness, or low productivity due to the treatment.

quality assurance in health administration or other areas of service delivery, a systematic process that is used to monitor and provide continuous improvement in the quality of health care services. It involves not only evaluating the services in terms of effectiveness, appropriateness, and acceptability but also offering feedback and implementing solutions to correct any identified deficiencies and assessing the results.

quality control processes associated with research, production, or services that are designed to reduce the number of defective measurements and products.

quality control angle chart a pictorial representation of a TIME SERIES in which a change in the mean or variability is indicated by a change in angular direction. It shows the behavior of a statistic (on the y-axis) across many different samples over time (on the x-axis). A researcher can see whether the statistic settles to a particular point over time and where extreme values of that statistic are over samples. The figure usually includes the average of the statistic over the samples and upper (UCL) and lower (LCL) control limits shown as lines that are two or three standard deviations from the mean.

Consider the hypothetical example overleaf, which depicts mood change for a group of 25 individuals undergoing 12 weeks of psychotherapy for depression.

Q

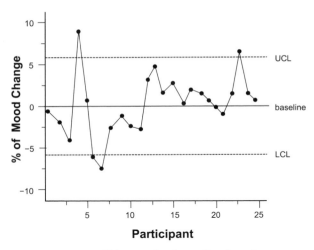

quality control angle chart

quantification *n.* the process of expressing a concept or variable in numerical form, which may aid in analysis and understanding.

quantile *n.* a value in a series of values in ascending order below which a given percentage of values lies; for example, a 50% quantile (also called a MEDIAN) is the point at which 50% of the values fall below that value (and 50% above). Other types of quantile are QUARTILES, dividing the series into four equal-sized groups; DECILES, dividing it into 10 groups; and PERCENTILES (or centiles), dividing it into 100 groups. Also called **fractile**.

quantile–quantile plot (**Q-Q plot**) a plot of the QUANTILES of one set of data against the quantiles of a second set, used to determine if the two data sets follow a common distribution. A 45° line on the plot shows where a perfect match of distributions would be.

quantitative *adj.* involving the use of a numerical measurement system to analyze data. Compare QUALITATIVE.

quantitative analysis the investigation of data empirically using numerical variables. Quantitative analysis includes both DESCRIPTIVE STATISTICS—such as summaries of MEANS and STANDARD DEVIATIONS of variables—and INFERENTIAL STATISTICS—such as ANALYSIS OF VARIANCE, REGRESSION ANALYSIS, and HIERARCHICAL LINEAR MODELS. Compare QUALITATIVE ANALYSIS.

quantitative data information expressed numerically, such as test scores or measurements of length or width. These data may or may not have a real zero but they have order and often equal intervals. Compare QUALITATIVE DATA.

quantitative psychology the study of methods and techniques for the measurement of human attributes, the statistical and mathematical modeling of psychological processes, the design of research studies, and the analysis of psychological data. Researchers in this area develop new methodologies and evaluate existing methodologies under particular conditions (e.g., with small samples).

quantitative research a method of research that relies on measuring variables using a numerical system, analyzing these measurements using any of a variety of statistical models, and reporting relationships and associations among the studied variables. For example, these variables may be test scores or measurements of reaction time. The goal of gathering this QUANTITATIVE DATA is to understand, describe, and predict the nature of a phenomenon, particularly through the development of models and theories. Quantitative research techniques include experiments and surveys. Also called **quantitative design**; **quantitative inquiry**; **quantitative method**; **quantitative study**. Compare QUALITATIVE RESEARCH.

quantitative variable a characteristic or attribute that can be measured numerically using a score obtained from any of a variety of data sources. Examples are age, height, and weight. Compare QUALITATIVE VARIABLE.

quartile *n.* one of the three values in a series of values that divide it into equal-sized fourths. For example, the **first** (or **lower**) **quartile** of a distribution is the data value below which are the lowest 25% of scores, the **second quartile** is the data value below which are 50% of scores, and the **third** (or **upper**) **quartile** is the data value below which are 75% of scores (or, conversely, above which are 25% of scores). These values provide information to researchers about the relative spread of the distribution. See Q; QUANTILE.

quartile coefficient of dispersion a descriptive index that allows researchers to compare the spread of two data distributions. It is computed by finding the difference between the first and third QUARTILES for each of the distributions and then comparing the values in a ratio: $(Q_1 - Q_3)/(Q_1 - Q_3)$. For example, if the quartile coefficient of dispersion is 10 for the first set and 4 for the second set, then the quartile coefficient of dispersion is 2.5 times as great for the first set as for the second set ($10/4 = 2.5$).

quartile coefficient of skewness a descriptive index of SKEWNESS in a data set that is a ratio between a function of the first, second, and third quartiles over the difference between the first and third

quartiles: $(Q_3 + Q_1 - 2Q_2)/(Q_3 - Q_1)$. The value is negative (or positive) if few values are at the negative (or positive) side of the distribution and is zero when the data distribution is symmetric.

quartile deviation a measure of DISPERSION that is defined as the value halfway between the first and third QUARTILES (i.e., half the INTERQUARTILE RANGE). Also called **semi-interquartile range**.

quartimax rotation in FACTOR ANALYSIS, an ORTHOGONAL ROTATION that maximizes the variance across the rows of the factor matrix by raising the loadings to the fourth power; the effect is to make large loadings especially large and small loadings especially small. The objective is to increase the interpretability of a factor solution by satisfying the SIMPLE STRUCTURE ideal.

quasi-experimental control group in a QUASI-EXPERIMENTAL DESIGN, any group of participants who are assigned to a condition in which the treatment is not introduced. These individuals will receive the standard of care, receive a placebo, or participate in an activity that involves them in the study but does not include the treatment in any way.

quasi-experimental design an experimental design in which assignment of participants to an EXPERIMENTAL GROUP or to a CONTROL GROUP cannot be made at random for either practical or ethical reasons; this is usually the case in FIELD RESEARCH. Assignment of participants to conditions is usually based on self-selection (e.g., employees who have chosen to work at a particular plant) or selection by an administrator (e.g., children are assigned to particular classrooms by a superintendent of schools). Such designs introduce a set of assumptions or threats to INTERNAL VALIDITY that must be acknowledged by the researcher when interpreting study findings. A study using this design is called a **quasi-experiment**. Examples include

Q

studies that investigate the responses of large groups to natural disasters or widespread changes in social policy.

quasi-experimental research research in which the investigator cannot randomly assign units or participants to conditions, cannot generally control or manipulate the INDEPENDENT VARIABLE, and cannot limit the influence of extraneous variables. FIELD RESEARCH typically takes the form of quasi-experimental research. Also called **nonexperimental research**. See QUASI-EXPERIMENTAL DESIGN.

quasi–F ratio in ANALYSIS OF VARIANCE and REGRESSION ANALYSIS, a substitute for the F RATIO that can sometimes be obtained when the denominators for an exact F ratio cannot be completed. The quasi–F ratio is obtained by determining the MEAN SQUARED ERROR using certain estimated components of variation when these cannot be calculated directly.

quasi-independence (QI) *n.* in a CONTINGENCY TABLE, the situation in which only a subset of entries or frequencies are independent or uninfluenced by one another. Entries may not be independent for a variety of reasons: They may be invalid, missing, or not counted in the analysis.

quasi-independent variable in experimental design, personal attributes, traits, or behaviors that are inseparable from an individual and cannot reasonably be manipulated. These include gender, age, and ethnicity. Such attributes may be modeled and treated as statistically independent but are not subject to RANDOM ASSIGNMENT, as are INDEPENDENT VARIABLES.

quasi-interval scale a rating scale that classifies responses using ordered options but lacks equal distances between all scale points. For example, some response items could show equal distances between scale points, whereas for others respondents could have a difficult time differentiating among options, leading

to compression or stretching between scale points. See INTERVAL SCALE.

quasi-likelihood function a function used to obtain estimates for count or binary data that show more DISPERSION than the statistical model can handle. An advantage of quasi-likelihood models is that they permit an increased flexibility in the data types and research situations to which they may be applied. A limitation is that the function does not derive from a known population distribution. Also called **quasi-score estimating function**.

quasi-observation *n.* **1.** the process of collecting data about a person from a close source, rather than directly from the subject. An example is asking an individual to report on the job satisfaction of his or her partner. **2.** the use of mechanical means, such as video surveillance or audiotaping, to record behaviors as a substitute for real-time observation and questioning by a researcher. In marketing research, an example would be the use of surveillance cameras to monitor shopper behavior in stores. This would cost less than paying a trained researcher to observe and interview shoppers in situ. There is also the advantage that such data can be viewed, stored, and analyzed at the researcher's convenience.

quasi-random *adj.* see PSEUDORANDOM.

quasi-random sampling see SYSTEMATIC SAMPLING.

quasi-score estimating function see QUASI-LIKELIHOOD FUNCTION.

questionnaire *n.* a set of questions or other prompts used to obtain information from a respondent about a topic of interest, such as background characteristics, attitudes, behaviors, personality, ability, or other attributes. A questionnaire may be administered with pen and paper, in a face-to-face interview, or via interaction between the respondent and a computer or website.

quick-and-dirty *adj.* describing a research design or data analysis that is admitted to be informal and imperfect. The researcher who adopts such an approach recognizes that there is a more refined way to set up the experiment or to analyze the findings. In research, a quick-and-dirty approach is more informal than a PILOT STUDY; in data analysis, it is regarded as a first peek at data from a specific analysis.

quintile *n.* one of four values in a score distribution that divides it into five equal parts. For example, the first quintile of a distribution is the value below which are the lowest 20% of scores. See QUANTILE.

quota control in survey methodology, an approach that imposes a limit on the number of respondents that are obtained either in the total sample or in substantively meaningful subgroups, such as gender or ethnicity. The approach is efficient because it does not overuse resources, such as respondent time or good will, by obtaining more individuals than are needed for a study. It also allows a researcher to obtain a desired balance of sample sizes across groups for statistical testing. Most computerized surveys include an automatic quota control function. See also QUOTA SAMPLING.

quota sampling a method of forming a sample in which a prespecified number of individuals with specific background characteristics, such as a particular age, race, ethnicity, sex, or education, are selected for inclusion. Often, participants are recruited as they arrive; once the quota for a given demographic group is filled, the researcher stops recruiting subjects from that group. A researcher who uses this approach can obtain a final study sample that has the same proportional characteristics as the target population, enabling statistical testing to be performed on a subset of cases that is appropriately representative of the larger group of interest. See DELIBERATE SAMPLING. See also QUOTA CONTROL.

quotient *n.* the value that is the result of dividing one number or quantity by another.

Q

Rr

r symbol for SAMPLE CORRELATION COEFFICIENT, which is typically in the form of a PRODUCT-MOMENT CORRELATION COEFFICIENT.

r^2 symbol for COEFFICIENT OF DETERMINATION.

R 1. abbreviation for RESPONSE or respondent. **2.** symbol for MULTIPLE CORRELATION COEFFICIENT.

R^2 symbol for COEFFICIENT OF MULTIPLE DETERMINATION.

radial plot a SCATTERPLOT used in META-ANALYSIS to assess whether there is HETEROGENEITY in the findings from different studies, which could limit interpretation of results. It depicts an EFFECT SIZE divided by its STANDARD ERROR on the vertical *y*-axis and the ratio of 1 divided by the standard error on the horizontal *x*-axis, as in the hypothetical example below.

Each point represents the strength of the effect, relative to the standard error

for each study involved in the meta-analysis. If an effect is large and the standard error is small, the point for that study will appear in the upper right corner of the radial plot. A wide range of points indicates that effect sizes and standard errors vary across studies (i.e., there is heterogeneity), which could limit conclusions regarding the average effect size in the meta-analysis and suggests that variables potentially causing this heterogeneity should be explored. Also called **Galbraith plot**.

radian (rad) *n.* a unit of angular measure. It is calculated as the length of an arc divided by its radius. 1 rad = $180°/\pi$.

R^2_{adj} symbol for ADJUSTED R^2.

random *adj.* **1.** without order or predictability. **2.** determined by chance alone, as in RANDOM SAMPLING or a RANDOM ERROR.

random assignment in experimental design, the assignment of participants or

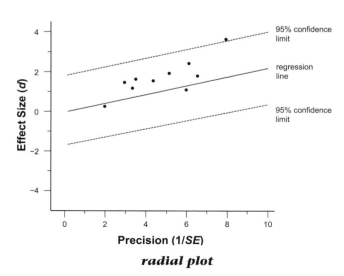

radial plot

units to the different conditions of an experiment entirely at random, so that each unit or participant has an equal likelihood of being assigned to any particular condition. In clinical trials this decreases the CONFOUNDING of the treatment factor with other factors by making the treatment and control groups approximately comparable in all respects except for the treatment. Also called **randomization; random allocation**. See also RANDOMIZED GROUP DESIGN.

random coefficient model see RANDOM INTERCEPT MODEL.

random-digit dialing (RDD) a survey strategy in which participants are contacted randomly by telephone. Usually, the researcher selects the area code(s) and then uses a computer program to select the last digits at random. This increases the likelihood of contacting participants with unlisted numbers. A concern with this strategy is that nonresponders may differ from responders in ways that introduce bias. The approach also assumes that potential respondents have telephones that are in service.

random digits a series of numbers generated by a process that relies on chance for each value, so that the occurrence of any number in the list is unrelated to the occurrence of any other. Such lists are often used in RANDOM SAMPLING. Potential participants are each given a number and the sample is drawn by choosing those with numbers in the randomly generated list. This ensures that selections are not driven by any known or unknown biases on the part of the researchers. Lists of random digits are now produced mainly by computer program (see RANDOM NUMBER GENERATOR). Formerly, they were often printed as tables in the back of statistics textbooks. Also called **random numbers**.

random effect an INDEPENDENT VARIABLE in an experimental design whose values or levels are drawn randomly from some larger (conceptual) population of levels that could (in principle) have been selected. For example, a health researcher investigating the relationship between exercise and weight may select a few levels of daily exercise for study (e.g., 0 hours, between 0 and 1 hour, between 1 and 2 hours, between 2 and 3 hours) from a wide range of possible options. Results involving a random effect can be generalized to values beyond those observed and modeled in the study analysis. Also called **random factor**. Compare FIXED EFFECT.

random-effects analysis of variance a statistical procedure in which the variability of an outcome (typically a continuously measured variable) is accounted for by several different factors or predictors, each of which reflects a sampling of possible factor levels. The focus in a random-effects analysis of variance is upon identifying differences in the mean values obtained on an outcome variable at the different levels of the predictors sampled. Compare FIXED-EFFECTS ANALYSIS OF VARIANCE.

random-effects model any statistical procedure or experimental design that involves RANDOM EFFECTS. For example, a researcher wishing to investigate the effects of temperature on frequency of aggressive behavior could not easily examine each temperature value and so instead examines a random sample of such values and their effects. Although random-effects models tend to be less powerful than FIXED-EFFECTS MODELS, they enable generalization to be made to levels of the independent variable not actually employed in the study. Also called **random model; variance components model**. Compare MIXED-EFFECTS MODEL.

random error error that is due to chance alone. Random errors are nonsystematic and occur arbitrarily when unknown or uncontrolled factors affect the variable being measured or the process of measurement. Such errors are generally assumed to form a NORMAL DISTRIBUTION around a TRUE SCORE. Also called **unbiased error**; **unreliability**; **unsystematic error**; **variable error**. See also ABSOLUTE ERROR; CONSTANT ERROR. Compare SYSTEMATIC ERROR.

random error variance that part of the variability of a test or other score that is not accounted for by other modeled factors. It reflects RANDOM ERRORS in measurement arising from the respondent, the situation, evaluator idiosyncrasies, the measure itself, or interactions among these factors. Different statistical frameworks handle this type of variation differently; some combine it with SYSTEMATIC ERROR VARIANCE whereas others treat it separately. See ERROR VARIANCE.

random event an EVENT that is generated by a chance process and cannot be predicted from any other event.

random event generator (**REG**) see RANDOM NUMBER GENERATOR.

random factor see RANDOM EFFECT.

random group design see RANDOMIZED GROUP DESIGN.

random intercept model a type of HIERARCHICAL LINEAR MODEL used to describe the correlations among observations or scores within a cluster. For example, a researcher examining the average number of work hours and burnout among nurses at several different hospitals might use this approach to account for dependence among certain variables, determining both the overall score variation across all nurses and the variation among the nurses in each of the individual hospitals. When plotted, the data for each nurse grouping have a different INTERCEPT, thus providing a more accurate and comprehensive description of relationships that corrects for the underestimated STANDARD ERRORS obtained when other models are applied to nested data and that parti-

tions components of VARIANCE at several levels. The similar **random coefficient model** (or **random slope model**) allows each data cluster to have its own SLOPE, indicating the explanatory variable has a different effect upon each.

randomization *n*. see RANDOM ASSIGNMENT.

randomization test an inferential approach that combines observed data across all participants and experimental conditions and then randomly sorts the data into new samples. A test of STATISTICAL SIGNIFICANCE is performed, and the value obtained is compared with the value that was obtained when the data were in their original form. This process is repeated many times, theoretically for all possible rearrangements (permutations) of the data, although the sheer number of possible permutations generally precludes this and a subset of permutations (10,000 often is recommended) is used instead. For example, suppose there were 1,000 recalculated mean differences between the experimental (E) and control (C) groups, derived from 1,000 permutations. Comparison of the 1,000 recalculated means to the original means provides an exact probability of getting the original means. If 25% of the mean differences between the E and C group permutations differ by as much or more than the difference between the original E and C means, then the probability value for the original mean difference is $p = .25$. A randomization test is a NONPARAMETRIC approach; that is, it does not make assumptions about the distribution of the data. Also called **permutation test**.

randomized block design (**RBD**) an approach to assigning participants to treatment conditions in which meaningful discrete strata within the sample (e.g., gender, experience) are used to identify homogeneous subsamples; individuals from each subsample or "block" are then assigned randomly to the different conditions. In this way, participants are initially matched on a "blocking variable" that the researcher wishes to control. The acknowledgment of heterogeneity within the sample enables the researcher to reduce within-group variance and to use that information when evaluating treatment effects. The variable on which participants are stratified is assessed prior to the study. Also called **randomized complete block design**; **treatment-by-blocks design**.

randomized block one-way analysis of variance a model used to evaluate mean differences on an outcome variable across three or more levels of a factor, while allowing for an additional variable used in assigning participants to conditions (e.g., gender). It is assumed that the additional variable will not interact with the main factor of interest. Also called **one-way blocked analysis of variance**. See ONE-WAY ANALYSIS OF VARIANCE; RANDOMIZED BLOCK DESIGN.

randomized clinical trial (**RCT**) an experimental design in which patients are randomly assigned to either a group that will receive an experimental treatment, such as a new drug, or to one that will receive a comparison treatment, standard-of-care treatment, or a PLACEBO. The RANDOM ASSIGNMENT occurs after recruitment and assessment of eligibility but before the intervention. There may be multiple experimental and comparison groups, but each patient is assigned to one group only. Also called **randomized controlled clinical trial**; **randomized controlled trial**. Compare NONRANDOMIZED CLINICAL TRIAL.

randomized complete block design see RANDOMIZED BLOCK DESIGN.

randomized consent design see ZELEN'S DESIGN.

randomized controlled clinical trial see RANDOMIZED CLINICAL TRIAL.

randomized controlled trial see RANDOMIZED CLINICAL TRIAL.

randomized design any of various experimental designs in which individual participants are assigned to different conditions (groups) using a purely chance process, such as rolling a die. A crucial assumption underlying randomized designs is that any systematic differences between treatment groups will be due to the experimental conditions themselves and not to any other unmeasured factors. Compare NONRANDOMIZED DESIGN.

randomized field trial a design that tests the effectiveness of a social intervention in settings outside the laboratory and incorporates RANDOM ASSIGNMENT of participants to different study conditions. Such designs trade the control of the laboratory for the chance to observe the actual behavior of participants in their everyday settings.

randomized group design an experimental design that involves the use of a purely chance process, such as the toss of a coin, to assign participants to the different study conditions.

randomized-response technique (**RRT**) a procedure for reducing SOCIAL DESIRABILITY bias when measuring sensitive attitudes (e.g., racial attitudes) or behaviors (e.g., drug use, eating behavior) at an aggregate group level. Respondents are presented with a pair of questions that have dichotomous response options (e.g., agree or disagree, yes or no), one question being the target question (sensitive question) and the other an innocuous filler question. They are instructed to roll a die (or use a similar randomization procedure) to determine which question they should answer and to conceal the result of this roll from the interviewer; they then provide the answer to that question but do not tell the interviewer which one it is. The ambiguity regarding which question has been answered is assumed to re-

R

duce participants' concerns about the social desirability of their answers. Despite the fact that the interviewer does not know which question each person has answered, PROBABILITY THEORY can be used to estimate the distribution of responses to the target question in the population.

random model see RANDOM-EFFECTS MODEL.

random number generator (RNG) a device or system used to produce a random output of numbers. Such RANDOM DIGITS have various experimental uses, including the RANDOM ASSIGNMENT of participants to treatment conditions, thereby taking the decision of assignment out of the hands of the researcher. Most current RNGs operate by computer program; strictly speaking, such programs produce a "pseudorandom" output because the algorithms that they use rely on a nonrandom system. Also called **random event generator (REG)**.

random numbers see RANDOM DIGITS.

random number table a table of RANDOM DIGITS. Historically, before the widespread use of computers to generate random values, such tables were often printed as an appendix in statistics textbooks. A researcher requiring random numbers for a study would close his or her eyes and point to a start place on the page. Next, with eyes open, he or she would use a predetermined way of moving through the table to select values (e.g., skip every other value). The researcher could then be assured that a chance process characterized the selection of values for the study.

random observation any observation that results from a chance process (such as a flip of a coin), is uncontrolled, or is not part of a schedule or pattern of organized observation.

random process a process that relies on chance alone, such that outcomes

may be analyzed according to their probability but not otherwise predicted. See STOCHASTIC.

random response set the tendency for certain research participants to answer study questions in a way that is or appears to be based on a chance process. This can occur when participants are not taking the study seriously (e.g., in a rush, tired, distracted, experiencing low motivation). If this is detected, a researcher may decide to discard these responses because they were generated by a chance process only and not for any reasons that are related to the constructs under study.

random sampling a process for selecting a SAMPLE of study participants from a larger potential group of eligible individuals, such that each person has the same fixed probability of being included in the sample and some chance procedure is used to determine who specifically is chosen. A group selected in this way is known as a **random sample**. The main value of this form of PROBABILITY SAMPLING is its positive impact on GENERALIZABILITY and EXTERNAL VALIDITY.

random selection any procedure for sampling a set of participants or units from a larger set that relies on the use of a chance process to minimize risk of researcher bias, either conscious or unconscious.

random series a series of values that are produced by a chance process, such as a flip of a coin. The WALD–WOLFOWITZ TEST is an inferential test for evaluating whether a string of numbers is indeed demonstrating this chance process. See RANDOM DIGITS; RANDOM NUMBER TABLE.

random set a set of items (e.g., measures, experimental stimuli) that are chosen by a chance process, such as a flip of a coin. For example, to save time and reduce participant burden, a researcher might ask participants to complete a subset of possible items rather

R

than the entire set; the subset might be chosen for each participant using a process determined by chance.

random slope model see RANDOM INTERCEPT MODEL.

random variable a variable that takes on different values according to a chance process. These values cannot be predicted with certainty and are assumed to vary across studies; however, their frequency can be described in terms of probability. Also called **stochastic variable**. Compare FIXED VARIABLE.

random variation differences in a DEPENDENT VARIABLE that are due to chance, rather than to the factors being studied. Causes of random variation in test results may include respondent factors, such as health, motivation, attention, concentration, and fatigue; situational factors, such as room temperature, noise, and working environment; or respondent-by-situation factors, such as a respondent not being prepared for the specific rating task. Researchers try to estimate the extent to which these factors may be involved in the study (see RANDOM ERROR VARIANCE) to understand the true impact of the factors being assessed. See also CHANCE DIFFERENCE.

random walk a series of values plotted over time that reflects the workings of a chance process, such that each value has an unpredictable relation to the preceding value and the series has no definable pattern. The concept is used in many research settings, including simulation studies and models of price movements on the stock market. Compare MARKOV CHAIN. See also DRUNKARD'S WALK; STOCHASTIC.

range *n.* a measure of DISPERSION obtained by subtracting the lowest score from the highest score in a distribution. For example, if the highest score on a test is 100 and the lowest score is 10, then the range is $(100 - 10) = 90$ points. Because it describes a raw dis-

crepancy between the low and high scores, the range is generally perceived as less informative than other measures of dispersion, such as the STANDARD DEVIATION.

range restriction see RESTRICTION OF RANGE.

rank 1. *n.* a relative position along an ordered continuum. See RANK ORDER. **2.** *vb.* to arrange items in a graded order, such as from highest to lowest value. In a peer nomination study, for example, a child might be asked to order individuals in a class from *most disruptive* to *least disruptive*. See also ORDINAL DATA. **3.** *n.* the maximum number of linearly independent row vectors or column vectors in a CORRELATION MATRIX: These values are always equal. For example, a 10×10 correlation matrix of personality scores might have a rank of 6, indicating that there are not 10 independent pieces of information present in the 10 scores.

rank biserial correlation coefficient an index of association between a DICHOTOMOUS VARIABLE and an ORDINAL VARIABLE. Its interpretation is the same as for other standardized measures of association. For example, a researcher might relate experimental condition (experimental vs. control group) to an ordinal measure of task performance. Compare POINT BISERIAL CORRELATION COEFFICIENT.

rank correlation coefficient a numerical index reflecting the degree of relationship between two variables that have each been arranged in ascending or descending order of magnitude (i.e., ranked). It does not reflect the association between the actual values of the variables but rather that between their relative position in the distribution. For example, placement in a marathon race could be correlated with the runners' heights but in this case the two variables—race outcome and height—would take the form first place, second place, and so on; and tallest, next tallest, and

R

so on, respectively (rather than actual times run in the race and specific heights in feet and inches). Among the most commonly used such indexes are the SPEARMAN CORRELATION COEFFICIENT and KENDALL'S TAU. Also called **rank-order correlation coefficient**.

rank-difference correlation a specific approach to calculating the SPEARMAN CORRELATION COEFFICIENT, which involves computing discrepancies between the relative positions of an individual on two variables.

ranked data see ORDINAL DATA.

ranked distribution a set of values on a variable sorted in magnitude from lowest to highest. The entries in a CUMULATIVE FREQUENCY table are an example of a ranked distribution.

ranking experiment a study in which the researcher asks participants to make a series of comparisons among stimuli (such as pictures, words, or emotions) so that the stimuli can be ordered on some dimension of interest (e.g., size, preference, cost, importance). For example, a researcher conducting a marketing study might ask respondents about their preferences among certain products by ranking these from *most likely to buy* to *least likely to buy*, or by comparing two products at a time and indicating which one of the two would be preferred.

rank order the arrangement of a series of items (e.g., scores, individuals) in order of magnitude.

rank-order data see ORDINAL DATA.

rank-order method a procedure in which a participant sorts various study stimuli (e.g., cards, pictures, words, people) from highest to lowest on a dimension of interest. See RANKING EXPERIMENT.

rank-order scale see ORDINAL SCALE.

rank-order statistic test any NONPARAMETRIC TEST that allows researchers to evaluate hypotheses related to

group differences or associations between ranked variables. Such tests make use of a RANK CORRELATION COEFFICIENT, such as the SPEARMAN CORRELATION COEFFICIENT or KENDALL'S TAU.

rank regression a type of REGRESSION ANALYSIS in which independent variables are used to predict the rank (as opposed to the actual value) of a dependent or response variable. This approach is particularly useful for distributions of errors that lack NORMALITY in their end values. The relative efficiency of a rank regression as compared to a LEAST SQUARES REGRESSION is more than 95%. See NONPARAMETRIC REGRESSION.

rank-sum test any NONPARAMETRIC TEST that involves combining the data points from two or more samples in a single data set and ranking these values in ascending order. See MANN–WHITNEY U TEST; WILCOXON–MANN–WHITNEY TEST; WILCOXON RANK-SUM TEST.

rank transformation a class of TRANSFORMATION in which a participant's score on a variable is replaced by the rank position of the score relative to the other scores in the data set. For example, an instructor might modify an original distribution of exam scores for a class into a listing that is ordered from highest to lowest. Rank transformations serve as the basis for a wide variety of NONPARAMETRIC TESTS.

Rasch model in ITEM RESPONSE THEORY, a model in which only one parameter, item difficulty, is specified. This is thought to be a parsimonious way to describe the relation between an item response and an underlying dimension and is thus preferred in some cases. Also called **one-parameter model**. See TWO-PARAMETER MODEL; THREE-PARAMETER MODEL. [proposed in 1960 by Georg **Rasch** (1901–1980), Danish statistician]

ratee *n.* an individual who is being rated on a particular dimension. Compare RATER.

rate of change the amount of change in a variable per unit time divided by the value of the variable before the change. If a score rises from 20 to 30 in unit time, for example, the rate of change is $(30 - 20)/20 = 10/20 = 0.5$.

rate of response see RESPONSE RATE.

rater *n.* a judge or evaluator who assesses a person or other unit on a characteristic of interest. To understand bullying on the playground, for example, a researcher might ask three independent and trained individuals to rate a specific child's behavior during school recess, usually on a particular scale (e.g., type of interactions in which the child is engaged). The consistency of the judgments made by these three individuals could then be evaluated (see INTER-RATER RELIABILITY). Compare RATEE.

rater reliability see INTERRATER RELIABILITY.

rating *n.* a score assigned to a person or object on a numerical scale (e.g., 1 to 5) or a verbal scale (e.g., *very good* to *very poor*). See RATING SCALE.

rating error an incorrectly assigned RATING. Error of this kind may be owing to several types of bias, including END-AVERSION BIAS, HALO EFFECTS, leniency effects, and primacy effects. For example, if a rater always describes the first of two targets presented in more favorable terms, then a primacy effect may account for these assigned responses.

rating scale an instrument that is used to assign scores to persons or items along some numerical dimension, such as agreement with an attitude statement or frequency of occurrence. Rating scales can be classified according to the number of points along the dimension that is being assessed (e.g., a 5-point scale, 7-point scale) and the way in which the response labels are ordered along the dimension. See BIPOLAR RATING SCALE; LIKERT SCALE; SEMANTIC DIFFERENTIAL.

rating scale checklist a list of items characterized by a particular attribute that a respondent judges to be present (often scored as 1) versus absent (often scored as 0). The number of items can be summed to reflect the extent that the attribute is present for the respondent. For example, a daily hassles checklist might list "flat tire," "visit from mother-in-law," or "difficult work project due," and a sum of this list might reflect the amount of stress that a person is experiencing.

ratio *n.* the quotient of two numbers, that is, one number divided by the other number.

ratio data numerical values that indicate magnitude and have a true, meaningful zero point. Ratio data represent exact quantities of the variables under consideration, and when arranged consecutively they have equal differences among adjacent values (regardless of the specific values selected) that correspond to genuine differences between the physical quantities being measured. Income provides an example: The difference between an income of $40,000 and $50,000 is the same as the difference between $110,000 and $120,000, and an income of $0 indicates a complete and genuine absence of earnings. Ratio data are continuous in nature (i.e., able to take on any of an infinite variety of amounts) and of the highest MEASUREMENT LEVEL, surpassing INTERVAL DATA, ORDINAL DATA, and NOMINAL DATA in precision and complexity.

rationalism *n.* **1.** any philosophical position holding that (a) it is possible to obtain knowledge of reality by reason alone, unsupported by experience, and (b) all human knowledge can be brought within a single deductive system. This confidence in reason is central to classical Greek philosophy, notably in its mistrust of sensory experience as a source of truth and the preeminent role it gives to reason in epistemology. However, the term "rationalist" is chiefly applied to thinkers in the Continental philosophi-

R

cal tradition initiated by French philosopher René Descartes (1596–1650), most notably Dutch Jewish philosopher Baruch Spinoza (1632–1677) and German philosopher Gottfried Wilhelm Leibniz (1646–1716). Rationalism is usually contrasted with EMPIRICISM and POSITIVISM, which hold that knowledge comes from or must be validated by sensory experience. In psychology, psychoanalytical approaches, humanistic psychology, and some strains of cognitive theory are heavily influenced by rationalism. **2.** in general language, any position that relies on reason and evidence rather than on faith, intuition, custom, prejudice, or other sources of conviction. —**rationalist** *adj., n.*

rational number any value that can be expressed as the ratio between two integers (e.g., 2/3 or 8/1). A ratio with zero as the denominator would not be a rational number.

ratio scale a measurement scale having a true zero (i.e., zero on the scale indicates an absence of the measured attribute) and a constant ratio of values. Thus, on a ratio scale an increase from 3 to 4 (for example) is the same as an increase from 7 to 8. The existence of a true zero point is what distinguishes a ratio scale from an INTERVAL SCALE.

ratio score 1. formerly, in the early days of the aptitude testing of children, a score expressed as a ratio of the child's mental age to his or her chronological age multiplied by 100. Thus, a child who was 8 years old but solved problems that normally could be solved only by children of 10 years old had a ratio score or **ratio IQ** of 120 [(12/10) × 100]. **2.** any score that is expressed as a ratio of one value to another.

ratio variable a variable that is measured with a RATIO SCALE (e.g., height or weight). See RATIO DATA.

raw data the original measurements on a variable as collected by the researcher, prior to data cleaning, RECODING,

TRANSFORMATIONS, and quantitative or qualitative analysis. For example, a survey may ask respondents to enter their annual income in dollars: The figures supplied by respondents would be the raw data. For the purposes of analysis, however, the researcher may prefer to use data that have been cleaned to account for improbable entries or individuals who prefer not to answer and then recoded to create a smaller set of income categories.

raw score a participant's score on a test before it is converted to other units or another form or subjected to quantitative or qualitative analysis. For example, a score may be transformed into a percentage (e.g., 45 correct answers out of 50 = 90%) or into a standardized metric such as a Z SCORE (mean of 0; standard deviation of 1) or a T SCORE (mean of 50; standard deviation of 10). Also called **unstandardized score**.

raw score partial regression coefficient in REGRESSION ANALYSIS, the average or expected change in the DEPENDENT VARIABLE for each increase in the INDEPENDENT VARIABLE, with all other independent variables in the model held constant. It is expressed in the units of the variable being measured, whereas a PARTIAL REGRESSION COEFFICIENT is derived from data that have undergone STANDARDIZATION.

Rayleigh distribution a special type of CONTINUOUS DISTRIBUTION often used in the analysis of data having both speed and direction components. For example, in psychology it may be applied in the assessment of human auditory processing. [John William Strutt, Lord **Rayleigh** (1842–1919), British physicist]

Rayleigh test a test for SIGNIFICANCE of directional data that form a circular pattern (e.g., movements of captive animals away from a point of release into the wild). The test involves calculating the mean of a number of circular means; the results are the mean angle, the length of the mean vector, and a CONFIDENCE IN-TERVAL around the mean angle. [Lord **Rayleigh**]

r_b symbol for BISERIAL CORRELATION CO-EFFICIENT.

RBD abbreviation for RANDOMIZED BLOCK DESIGN.

r_{bis} symbol for BISERIAL CORRELATION COEFFICIENT.

R_c symbol for CANONICAL CORRELATION COEFFICIENT. A further subscript may be added to show which canonical variates are being correlated.

R correlation see MULTIPLE CORRELA-TION COEFFICIENT.

RCT abbreviation for RANDOMIZED CLIN-ICAL TRIAL.

RDD 1. abbreviation for RANDOM-DIGIT DIALING. **2.** abbreviation for REGRES-SION-DISCONTINUITY DESIGN.

reaction time (RT) the time that elapses between the onset or presenta-tion of a stimulus and occurrence of a specific response to that stimulus. There are several types, including simple reac-tion time (single stimulus and single re-sponse) and choice reaction time (two or more stimuli, each with a different re-sponse). Reaction time can be used to as-sess various psychological constructs. To assess negative affect, for example, a re-searcher might measure the time be-tween presentation of various words with emotional connotations and a par-ticipant's indication that the word was either "positive" or "negative." Also called **response latency; response time**.

reactive measure a measure that alters the response under investigation. For ex-ample, if participants are aware of being observed, their reactions may be influ-enced more by the observer and the fact of being observed than by the stimulus object or situation to which they are os-tensibly responding. Compare UNOB-TRUSIVE MEASURE.

reactivity *n.* the condition in which a participant being observed is changed in some way by the act of observation. Within an experimental setting reactiv-ity is viewed as a threat to INTERNAL VA-LIDITY because the change in behavior is not due to the experimental manipula-tion. See also REACTIVE MEASURE.

reactivity effect any of several specific ways in which a target's performance may change as a result of being observed or receiving increased attention within a research setting. Examples include EX-PERIMENTER EFFECTS, the HAWTHORNE EFFECT, the PYGMALION EFFECT, and SELF-FULFILLING PROPHECY effects.

real limit the lower or upper bound of a given value for a continuous variable measured on a RATIO SCALE. For exam-ple, a test score of 95 has the **lower real limit** of 94.5 and the **upper real limit** of 95.5 since any value within that range will equal 95 when rounded to a whole number.

real-world setting conditions for data collection that closely resemble condi-tions in the natural flow of life (e.g., ob-serving workers at their workplace rather than having them report about what oc-curs at work). A study conducted in a real-world setting is often viewed as more ecologically valid and gen-eralizable than one conducted in a labo-ratory setting.

recall bias the type of BIAS that often occurs when an individual reports about a past behavior or event. Although such retrospective reporting may have accu-rate features, it also tends to include in-accurately remembered aspects, such as a systematic undercount or overcount of the frequency with which a certain be-havior occurred. This type of distortion is discussed in the literatures associated with survey methodology and eyewit-ness testimony.

recall data responses to questions that ask what a participant can remember about something. For example, a partici-

R

pant may be asked to read a passage and later list specific features of it from memory. Another type of memory task might involve asking the participant whether or not specific items have been presented before (the **recognition method**).

receiver-operating characteristic curve (**ROC curve**) in a detection, discrimination, or recognition task, the relationship between the proportion of correct "yes" responses (hit rate) and the proportion of incorrect "yes" responses (false alarm rate). This is plotted on a graph to show an individual's sensitivity on the particular task: The axes are hit and false alarm rates, points are marked to denote the different rates obtained under different conditions, and the points are connected to form a smooth area (see illustration below).

For example, an ROC curve may be used to indicate how well a person detects a specific tone in the presence of noise. A single quantitative INDEX of performance may be calculated from the curve as well. Also called **isosensitivity function**.

reciprocal *n.* the number that when multiplied by another number gives a result of 1. The reciprocal of *x* is therefore $1/x$ and that of $1/x$ is *x*. So, for example, 1/4 is the reciprocal of 4.

reciprocal relationship 1. a correlation between two variables such that the value on one variable is the RECIPROCAL of the value on the other. For example, if a researcher is studying the average time taken to complete a task, then tasks completed per unit time (e.g., two per hour) has a reciprocal relationship with unit time taken per task (0.5 hours). **2.** the situation in which two variables can mutually influence one another, that is, each can be both a cause and an effect.

reciprocal transformation a TRANSFORMATION of raw data that involves (a) replacing the original data units with their RECIPROCALS and (b) analyzing the modified data. It can be used with nonzero data and is commonly used when distributions have SKEWNESS or clear OUTLIERS. Unlike other transformations, a reciprocal transformation changes the order of the original data. For example, if the original unit of a study variable is time, a researcher might transform the raw data to produce an analysis of rate. Also called **inverse transformation**.

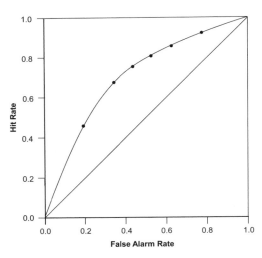

receiver-operating characteristic curve

recoding *n.* a manipulation of an original variable in a data set so that it can be used in a different way in future analysis (e.g., reverse keying items, collapsing many categories into just a few categories). See also TRANSFORMATION. **—recode** *vb.*

recruitment bias see SAMPLING BIAS.

rectangular axes two coordinate lines (the *x*-axis and *y*-axis) that cross at the origin (the point at which *x* and *y* are both 0), are at right angles, have a single unit length, and create a two-dimensional plane. See CARTESIAN CO-ORDINATE SYSTEM.

rectangular distribution see UNIFORM DISTRIBUTION.

rectilinear *adj.* moving in or formed by straight lines. For example, a **rectilinear polygon** is a figure whose edges all meet at right angles and a **rectilinear path** refers to motion or progress in a straight line. In memory research, pictures or photographs presented as stimuli are referred to as **rectilinear views**.

recursive *adj.* describing a rule or procedure that is applied repeatedly for a finite number of times, with the output of each application becoming the input to the next. For example, a **recursive algorithm** might be used to help identify the set of predictors that relate maximally to a specific outcome variable.

recursive model a set of relationships in which the effects flow in one direction only and there are no feedback loops such that effects are sometimes also causes. In STRUCTURAL EQUATION MODELING, for example, a recursive model in which independent variables lead to dependent variables without feedback loops is generally more easily estimated. Compare NONRECURSIVE MODEL.

recursive partitioning regression a CLASSIFICATION TREE strategy that uses a systematic algorithm (the CHI-SQUARE AUTOMATIC INTERACTION DETECTOR or CHAID) to identify predictor variables that differentiate high from low values on a response variable or outcome of interest. A researcher can identify through this systematic search which predictors from a larger set are most associated with different mean splits on an outcome. The statistical significance of each split is described using an F TEST and can be corrected for MULTIPLE COMPARISONS. The analysis generates a tree, with the outcome at the top and branches showing various splits based on the different predictors and their association with the outcome.

reduced maximum likelihood see RESTRICTED MAXIMUM LIKELIHOOD.

reduced model in the GENERAL LINEAR MODEL, a model that has fewer parameters than the most highly parameterized model in a set of models to be compared. Usually, the smaller model is said to be "nested" within the larger, more highly parameterized model.

reductionism *n.* the strategy of explaining or accounting for some phenomenon or construct, A, by claiming that, when properly understood, it can be shown to be some other phenomenon or construct, B, where B is seen to be simpler, more basic, or more fundamental. The term is mainly applied to those positions that attempt to understand human culture, society, or psychology in terms of animal behavior, physical laws, or biological phenomena.

redundancy analysis a multivariate statistical model for examining the degree to which one set of variables or scores may maximally relate to a second such set. A researcher derives a number of CANONICAL VARIATES of interest from the first set of variables and examines the relation between these variates and the variance in the second set. Redundancy analysis is an alternative to CANONICAL CORRELATION ANALYSIS.

redundancy coefficient in MULTIVARIATE ANALYSIS, an asymmetric index

R

showing the proportion of variance in the outcome or dependent variables that is accounted for by a set of predictor or independent variables. It can be differentiated from the CANONICAL CORRELATION COEFFICIENT, which assumes that the two sets of variables are symmetric. The redundancy coefficient is highly affected by the unit of measurement; therefore, common metrics need to be established before it is applied.

reference axis in FACTOR ANALYSIS, any of a set of AXES that create a coordinate frame depicting the spatial configuration of the dimensions underlying the relationships among a group of variables. This frame can be rotated to improve the interpretability of the configuration, using either ORTHOGONAL or OBLIQUE methods.

reference database a database of bibliographic information in a particular field of study. Among other uses, such a resource may be invaluable for developing a comprehensive review of the literature in a particular field or for supporting an empirical synthesis of studies in a meta-analysis.

reference distribution see THEORETICAL DISTRIBUTION.

reference interval a range of expected values regarding behavior, performance, or clinical levels (e.g., blood pressure). The limits of the interval are generally established through a systematic process, such as examination of past empirical studies. Also called **normal range**; **reference range**. See also NORM.

reference population 1. a subset of a TARGET POPULATION that serves as a standard against which research findings are evaluated. For example, consider an investigator examining the effectiveness of eating disorder prevention programs at four-year colleges and universities in the United States. In such a situation, the portion of educational institutions that have not implemented any program would serve as the compar-

ison reference population. **2.** the target population itself.

reference prior a set of values based on expectation or belief that is used as a standard starting point in certain multivariate problems, especially in the BAYESIAN tradition. See PRIOR DISTRIBUTION.

$r_{effect\ size}$ symbol for EFFECT-SIZE CORRELATION.

reflexivity *n.* **1.** a bidirectional relationship of cause and effect. **2.** in QUALITATIVE RESEARCH, the self-referential quality of a study in which the researcher reflects on the assumptions behind the study and especially the influence of his or her own motives, history, and biases on its conduct. See EPISTEMOLOGICAL REFLEXIVITY.

refusal rate the proportion of potentially eligible respondents for a survey or study who have been successfully contacted but will choose not to participate for a variety of reasons (e.g., survey takes too much time, respondent lacks interest in topic or surveys in general, respondent tires of answering questions and breaks off the interview midway). The refusal rate must be taken into account when calculating the likely RESPONSE RATE for a survey. Also called **nonresponse rate**.

REG abbreviation for random event generator. See RANDOM NUMBER GENERATOR.

region of acceptance see ACCEPTANCE REGION.

region of rejection see CRITICAL REGION.

regressed change-score analysis a REGRESSION ANALYSIS in which DIFFERENCE SCORES (scores based on two or more measurements over time) are used as the outcome variables. For example, in a PRETEST–POSTTEST DESIGN a researcher could "remove" the pretest score from the posttest score to create a difference score: This could then be used as the outcome variable in a regression analysis.

regression analysis any of several statistical techniques that are used to describe, explain, or predict (or all three) the variance of an outcome or DEPENDENT VARIABLE using scores on one or more predictor or INDEPENDENT VARIABLES. Regression analysis is a subset of the GENERAL LINEAR MODEL. It yields a REGRESSION EQUATION as well as an index of the relationship (R or r) between the dependent and independent variables. In addition, the regression weights obtained for the various independent variables provide information about their relative predictive contribution to the outcome. For example, a regression analysis could show the extents to which first-year grades in college (outcome) are predicted by such factors as standardized test scores, courses taken in high school, letters of recommendation, and particular extracurricular activities. Also called **slope analysis**.

regression artifact an experimental finding that has been distorted by extreme measurements and the associated influence of REGRESSION TOWARD THE MEAN.

regression calibration 1. an approach in which a researcher uses specific values of a DEPENDENT VARIABLE to determine the associated values of an INDEPENDENT VARIABLE when the relationship between the two variables is already known. For example, a researcher studying university faculty salaries might choose a very high salary (dependent variable) to see how many years it takes for a new faculty member at that institution to achieve such a rate of pay (independent variable). **2.** a method of adjusting POINT ESTIMATES and INTERVAL ESTIMATES for COEFFICIENTS in a prediction model to account for known MEASUREMENT ERROR.

regression coefficient in a REGRESSION ANALYSIS, the WEIGHT associated

with a unit change in a specific independent (predictor) variable on the dependent (outcome) variable, given the relationship of that predictor to other independent variables already in the model. This value may be standardized (see STANDARDIZATION) with a variance equal to 1 (in which case it is called a BETA COEFFICIENT), or it may be unstandardized and expressed in the units of the outcome variable being measured (in which case it is called a **B coefficient**). Also called **regression weight**. See also PARTIAL REGRESSION COEFFICIENT.

regression constant the value of a response or DEPENDENT VARIABLE in a REGRESSION EQUATION when its associated predictor or INDEPENDENT VARIABLES equal zero (i.e., are at baseline levels). Graphically, this is equivalent to the Y-INTERCEPT, or the point at which the REGRESSION LINE crosses the y-axis.

regression curve see REGRESSION LINE.

regression diagnostics a set of graphical and numerical techniques routinely used by researchers to check for VIOLATIONS OF ASSUMPTIONS in the application of REGRESSION ANALYSIS to particular data sets. For example, one assumes that the relationship between the INDEPENDENT VARIABLES and the DEPENDENT VARIABLE is linear, that the variables have been measured accurately, and that any prediction errors resulting from the REGRESSION EQUATION are independent and normally distributed with equal variance and a mean of zero. If the data do not possess such characteristics, the analysis may not be appropriate and thus its results may not be valid. See DIAGNOSTICS; RESIDUAL ANALYSIS.

regression-discontinuity design (RDD) a type of QUASI-EXPERIMENTAL DESIGN in which a specific threshold value or CUTOFF SCORE is used to assign participants to treatment conditions. Theoretically, individuals near the threshold value are comparable and

R

only differ on the basis of their treatment assignment, which enables a researcher to estimate treatment effects. For example, a researcher might use a regression-discontinuity design to investigate worker performance, assigning employees who work more than a certain number of hours to receive a reward while those below that threshold number do not. The analysis of such a design involves examining the REGRESSION LINES for those receiving the treatment (e.g., receiving a reward) versus those not receiving the treatment (e.g., no reward). A continuous straight line for the two groups indicates no effect of reward on performance, whereas any break or jump (discontinuity) in the line across the groups indicates a treatment effect.

regression effect see REGRESSION TOWARD THE MEAN.

regression equation the mathematical expression of the relationship between a dependent (outcome or response) variable and one or more independent (predictor) variables that results from conducting a REGRESSION ANALYSIS. It often takes the form $y = a + bx + e$, in which y is the dependent variable, x is the independent variable, a is the INTERCEPT, b is the REGRESSION COEFFICIENT, and e is the ERROR TERM. Also called **regression formula; regression model**.

regression estimate an EXPECTED VALUE for an outcome or DEPENDENT VARIABLE that is calculated from a REGRESSION EQUATION. For a typical univariate linear model, in which multiple INDEPENDENT VARIABLES predict a single outcome, this value is obtained using LEAST SQUARES REGRESSION.

regression formula see REGRESSION EQUATION.

regression imputation see IMPUTATION.

regression line a straight or curved line fitting a set of data points and usually obtained by a LEAST SQUARES REGRESSION. A graphic representation of the REGRESSION EQUATION expressing the hypothesized relation between an outcome or DEPENDENT VARIABLE and one or more predictors or INDEPENDENT VARIABLES, a regression line summarizes how well the proposed model actually fits the sample data obtained.

Data points that do not fall exactly on the line indicate deviations in model fit, as in the hypothetical example below showing parent ratings of aggressive behavior in their children as a function of

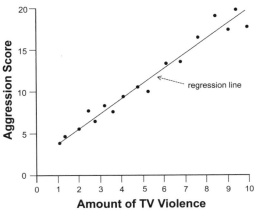

regression line

amount of violence watched on television.

regression model see REGRESSION EQUATION.

regression of x on y a method that "reverses" the typical model of REGRESSION ANALYSIS by treating the INDEPENDENT VARIABLES (xs) as DEPENDENT VARIABLES (ys). In other words, one uses a REGRESSION EQUATION to estimate an x score from one or more y scores. Regression of x on y typically is conducted to better understand possible MULTICOLLINEARITY among the independent variables. Also called **inverse prediction**. Compare REGRESSION OF Y ON X.

regression of y on x a typical REGRESSION ANALYSIS, in which one predicts values of a DEPENDENT VARIABLE, y, from values of one or more INDEPENDENT VARIABLES, x, using a REGRESSION EQUATION. Compare REGRESSION OF X ON Y.

regression plane the plane in three-dimensional space created when graphing data points from a REGRESSION EQUATION in which more than one predictor or INDEPENDENT VARIABLE is associated with an outcome or DEPENDENT VARIABLE. The regression plane is flat and slices through EUCLIDEAN SPACE when the relationship between the variables is linear but becomes curved and flowing for nonlinear relationships. A REGRESSION LINE is used for situations involving a single independent variable.

regression sum of squares (symbol: $SS_{regression}$) a number indicating the amount of variance in a DEPENDENT VARIABLE that can be explained by the variance in one or more associated INDEPENDENT VARIABLES. It thus describes how well a particular model fits the observed data. For example, in LINEAR REGRESSION it is used to calculate a COEFFICIENT OF DETERMINATION or a COEFFICIENT OF MULTIPLE DETERMINATION, and in ANALYSIS OF VARIANCE it is used to determine the total SUM OF SQUARES and calculate an F RATIO. Also called **explained sum of squares**. Compare ERROR SUM OF SQUARES.

regression through the origin an approach to REGRESSION ANALYSIS in which the REGRESSION CONSTANT is removed from the REGRESSION EQUATION and the Y-INTERCEPT is zero rather than nonzero as it is in ordinary LEAST SQUARES REGRESSION. Thus, when the value of one or more predictor or independent variables (xs) equals zero, the mean value of an outcome or dependent variable (y) also equals zero (i.e., the REGRESSION LINE goes through the origin). Use of regression through the origin is justified only in certain circumstances, such as when the dependent variable has a true baseline value of zero (e.g., zero dollars, zero cigarettes smoked, zero words recalled). Also called **no-intercept model**; **regression without intercept**.

regression toward the mean the tendency for extremely high or extremely low scores to become more moderate (i.e., closer to the MEAN) upon retesting over time. In experimental studies this tendency threatens INTERNAL VALIDITY in that shifts of scores may be for reasons unrelated to study manipulations or treatments. For example, regardless of the interventions a researcher is investigating to improve mathematics performance (e.g., extra study sessions, providing positive or negative reinforcement), low scoring students will tend to perform slightly better on the next math exam, while high scoring students will tend to perform slightly worse. RANDOM ASSIGNMENT to treatment and control conditions may be used to minimize the influence of regression toward the mean upon experimental results. Also called **regression effect**. See REGRESSION ARTIFACT; THREATS TO VALIDITY.

regression tree a diagram displaying a set of conditions and their associations with a particular outcome variable as determined via a REGRESSION ANALYSIS.

An initial node represents the outcome of interest (e.g., annual income under $15,000), from which branches extend to additional nodes according to the values of a studied predictor variable (e.g., level of education). Further branches extend from these subnodes based on additional predictors (e.g., area of residence, type of employment), with the process continuing until no more predictors are available in the data set or until a predetermined number of nodes is obtained. Regression trees provide a convenient, visually appealing method for examining large amounts of data. See also CART ANALYSIS.

regression weight see REGRESSION COEFFICIENT.

regression without intercept see REGRESSION THROUGH THE ORIGIN.

regress on to determine the extent to which a given DEPENDENT VARIABLE (y) can be explained or predicted by a number of INDEPENDENT VARIABLES (xs). For example, a researcher may be interested in learning how scores on a measure of relationship commitment vary as a function of age, relationship status, time in relationship, and shared experiences. That is, the researcher may regress y on x. See REGRESSION ANALYSIS.

regressor variable see INDEPENDENT VARIABLE.

regularized discriminant analysis a procedure for classifying individuals or units into discrete groups based on a set of variables under study that represents a compromise between linear DISCRIMINANT ANALYSIS and QUADRATIC DISCRIMINANT ANALYSIS. In general terms, it involves the adjustment of two PARAMETERS to yield different combinations or ways of classifying the units, with the overall goal being to minimize the risk of misclassification.

REGWQ test Ryan–Einot–Gabriel–Welsch multiple range test: a procedure used to evaluate if there are statistically significant differences between independent groups in a ONE-WAY ANALYSIS OF VARIANCE of a BALANCED DESIGN. It is one of many such MULTIPLE COMPARISON TESTS. Also called **Ryan's method**. [Thomas A. **Ryan** Jr., U.S. statistician; Israel **Einot**, Israeli statistician; K. Ruben **Gabriel** (1929–2003), German-born U.S. statistician; Roy E. **Welsch**, U.S. statistician]

reinforcer effect a situation in which one variable strengthens the relationship between two other variables. For example, if performance on a free recall task is enhanced when participants are in a positive mood when studying words for the memory task, positive mood has demonstrated a reinforcer effect on study recall. See also INTERACTION EFFECT; MEDIATOR. Compare SUPPRESSOR EFFECT.

Reinsch spline an approach that fits a curve to TIME-SERIES DATA while minimizing noise around the data points. It is a useful nonparametric strategy for SMOOTHING a REGRESSION LINE representing change over time, which typically contains many bends or turns. Also called **Demmler–Reinsch spline**. See SPLINE FUNCTION. [A. **Demmler**; Christian H. **Reinsch**]

reinterviewing *n.* collecting LONGITUDINAL DATA by interviewing the same participants at several different points in time. For example, a researcher investigating familial interactions might conduct multiple home visits to obtain numerous details about the parent–child relationship and how it evolves over time. Potential problems with this approach include participant REACTIVITY, participant ATTRITION, and decreased INTERNAL VALIDITY. See also RETEST RELIABILITY.

rejection error see TYPE I ERROR.

rejection method a technique that uses an algorithm to generate and select random values for a study (see RANDOM DIGITS). Values are automatically included in or excluded from the study sample depending on whether they fall within a particular range. Also called **acceptance–rejection method**; **rejection sampling**.

rejection region see CRITICAL REGION.

rejection value see CRITICAL VALUE.

related-measures design see WITHIN-SUBJECTS DESIGN.

related samples see DEPENDENT SAMPLES.

related-samples design see WITHIN-SUBJECTS DESIGN.

related-samples t test see DEPENDENT-SAMPLES T TEST.

relational research see CORRELATIONAL RESEARCH.

relationship *n.* an association or connection between objects, events, variables, or other phenomena. Research often involves the study of associations between and among variables. See also CORRELATION.

relative efficiency 1. for two tests (A and B) of the same hypothesis operating at the same SIGNIFICANCE LEVEL, the ratio of the number of cases needed by Test A compared to the number needed by Test B for each to have the same statistical POWER. The relative efficiency value enables a researcher to determine whether there is a preferred statistical approach for evaluating a particular phenomenon. For example, when hypothesis testing involves NORMAL DISTRIBUTIONS, parametric inferential statistics have a more favorable ratio than nonparametric inferential statistics. **2.** for two parameter ESTIMATES (A and B), a value reflecting the ratio of the STANDARD ERROR of Estimate A compared to the standard error of Estimate B. See RELATIVELY EFFICIENT ESTIMATOR.

relative error in measurement, the ratio of the ABSOLUTE ERROR (i.e., the positive difference between an exact measured value and the estimated value)

to the measured value. For example, if the value of a particular characteristic in the population is known to be .7 but a recently developed statistical procedure estimated a value of .5, the relative error would be $(.7 - .5)/.7 = .2/.7 = .286$. A relative error may be converted to a **percent error** by multiplying by 100—thus, for the example given, the percent error is $.286 \times 100$, or 28.6%.

relative frequency the frequency of a type or category of event expressed as a proportion of the total frequency of all types or categories. For example, if 47 out of 100 participants answered "yes" to a particular question on a survey, the relative frequency of "yes" responses would equal .47 (i.e., the number of "yes" responses divided by the total number of "yes," "no," and "I don't know" responses).

relative frequency distribution a tabular display of the number of observations at each level of a variable compared to the total number of observations obtained. For example, a researcher asks 200 participants to describe their level of extraversion on a 5-point scale and obtains the following results: 32 individuals indicated they are extremely introverted; 24 individuals indicated they are somewhat introverted; 50 individuals indicated they are neither introverted nor extraverted; 38 individuals indicated they are somewhat extraverted; and 56 individuals indicated they are extremely extraverted. These values can be expressed as both proportions—the number of observations per level divided by all observations (i.e., .16, .12, .25, .19, and .28)—and as percentages—the number of observations per level divided by all observations multiplied by 100 (i.e., 16%, 12%, 25%, 19%, and 28%). Thus, in the corresponding relative frequency distribution overleaf, the first column lists the different extraversion levels, the second column lists the number of people at each of the different extraversion levels, the third col-

R

Extraversion level	Frequency (*f*)	Relative frequency (proportion)	Relative frequency (%)
Extremely introverted	32	.16	16
Somewhat introverted	24	.12	12
Neither introverted nor extraverted	50	.25	25
Somewhat extraverted	38	.19	19
Extremely extraverted	56	.28	28

relative frequency distribution

umn lists each value in the second column as a proportion of the total, and the fourth column lists each value in the second column as a percentage of the total.

This type of table is useful in identifying which scores or values are most likely to occur at which variable level, and it provides an organized display of data that could also be graphed in a REL-ATIVE FREQUENCY POLYGON. Also called **relative distribution; relative frequency table**. See FREQUENCY DISTRIBUTION.

relative frequency polygon a graphical representation of a RELATIVE FREQUENCY DISTRIBUTION, conveying the number of individuals responding in a particular manner on a given variable as compared to the total number of people responding. For a CONTINUOUS VARIABLE, the polygon is constructed by (a) creating intervals of scores and identifying each interval midpoint; (b) labeling

the horizontal *x*-axis with the interval midpoints from lowest to highest; (c) labeling the vertical *y*-axis with the range of proportional score values; (d) plotting the specific proportion associated with each midpoint; and (e) connecting all of the plotted points with lines. A hypothetical example is given below.

Also called **relative frequency curve**; **relative frequency diagram**; **relative frequency function**; **relative frequency graph**. See FREQUENCY POLYGON.

relatively efficient estimator given two ESTIMATORS (approximated population values) for a given model, the estimator that has the smallest variance in its sampling distribution and thus provides a more precise estimate of the parameter. See RELATIVE EFFICIENCY.

relative measurement a context-specific assessment approach in which the value of an individual score depends on its comparison to other scores within

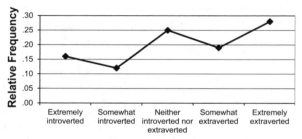

relative frequency polygon

a group or subgroup. For example, one might evaluate beauty by assigning a person a number that reflects his or her attractiveness compared with others of the same age, the same occupation, and so forth. Comparison of scores within subgroups can sometimes be useful but also may produce bias. Compare ABSOLUTE MEASUREMENT.

relative risk see RISK RATIO.

relative standing the position of a particular score in the context of a distribution of scores. There are several ways to describe relative standing, including PERCENTILES (e.g., deciles, quartiles), STANDARDIZED SCORES (e.g., T SCORES, Z SCORES), and status as an OUTLIER. Graphical approaches such as BOX-AND-WHISKER PLOTS and FREQUENCY POLYGONS also can provide valuable information about relative standing.

relative survival a value indicating the number of people with a specific disease who are alive compared to the number of surviving people who are disease free but otherwise have the same characteristics (age, sex, etc.). Relative survival often is calculated for several different time points, such as one year since a significant milestone (e.g., diagnosis, treatment, remission), five years since the milestone, and 10 years since the milestone.

relative variability an assessment of the DISPERSION within a sample, typically expressed as a COEFFICIENT OF VARIATION or a DIVERSITY INDEX.

relativism *n.* any position that challenges the reality of absolute standards of truth or value. In EPISTEMOLOGY, relativism is the assertion that there are no absolute grounds for truth or knowledge claims. Thus, what is considered true depends solely on individual judgments and local conditions of culture, reflecting individual and collective experience. Such relativism challenges the validity of science except as a catalog of experience and a basis for ad hoc empirical pre-

diction. In ethics, relativism is the claim that there are no moral absolutes. Thus, judgments of right and wrong are based on local culture and tradition, on personal preferences, or on artificial principles. Standards of conduct vary enormously across individuals, cultures, and historical periods, and it is impossible to arbitrate among them or to produce universal ethical principles because there can be no means of knowing that these are true. In this way, relativism in epistemology and relativism in ethics are related. —**relativist** *adj.*

relevance–sensitivity tradeoff in research, the balance struck between measuring dependent variables accurately and specifically and obtaining results with applicability to contexts beyond the original study. The relevance–sensitivity tradeoff should be considered by a researcher when designing a study.

reliability *n.* the trustworthiness or consistency of a measure, that is, the degree to which a test or other measurement instrument is free of RANDOM ERROR, yielding the same results across multiple applications to the same sample. See ALTERNATE-FORMS RELIABILITY; INTERNAL CONSISTENCY; RELIABILITY COEFFICIENT; RETEST RELIABILITY.

reliability coefficient (symbol: r_{xx}) an index describing the consistency of scores across contexts (e.g., different times, items, or raters). Its value, ranging from 0 to 1, provides an estimate of the amount of obtained score variance that is due to TRUE VARIANCE rather than to error. The larger this coefficient, the more confident a researcher may be that scores obtained at different times under similar conditions with the same participants will be alike. Typically, reliability coefficients are considered to be acceptable if they are above .80. Also called **coefficient of reliability**; **index of reliability**; **reliability index**.

reliability diagonal the MAIN DIAGO-

NAL in a CORRELATION MATRIX where the values of 1 that are typically given along this diagonal are replaced by RELIABILITY COEFFICIENTS indicating the consistency of each measure used. This allows a researcher to evaluate the reliability of each measure quickly and easily.

reliability index see RELIABILITY COEFFICIENT.

reliability of components the average RELIABILITY of scores obtained from the component subsets that make up a test. Components are identified by grouping a large set of items into clusters with similar content through rational or intuitive approaches or through the use of an empirical method (e.g., FACTOR ANALYSIS, PRINCIPAL COMPONENTS ANALYSIS). The INTERNAL CONSISTENCY of each of the component sets is determined and then used to estimate the overall reliability of the larger test. For example, a researcher might factor analyze a 20-item social support questionnaire, identify three content subscales, calculate the internal consistency of scores for those three subscales, and then use that information to determine the test's overall reliability. The concept is a form of COMPOSITE RELIABILITY specific to testing contexts, although the two terms nonetheless are often used interchangeably. See SPEARMAN–BROWN PROPHECY FORMULA.

reliability of composites see COMPOSITE RELIABILITY.

reliability sampling a form of ACCEPTANCE SAMPLING in which samples of, say, a consumer product are inspected to determine their acceptability against quality specifications at some future date. This is often a test of the product's future life.

reliability theory any of various conceptualizations about why scores on a test or performance task are consistent across contexts. Three prominent reliability theories are CLASSICAL TEST THEORY, GENERALIZABILITY THEORY, and ITEM RESPONSE THEORY. Each considers error differently and thus it is important for a researcher to specify which conceptualization underlies his or her study.

remitted-disorder study an empirical investigation of patients with a disorder whose condition has improved. Because the trajectories of certain disorders (e.g., schizophrenia, bipolar disorder, chronic pain, cancer) include periods of relapse and abatement, researchers seek to identify the conditions under which each occurs so as to predict these transitions in severity more accurately and develop better treatments.

REML abbreviation for RESTRICTED MAXIMUM LIKELIHOOD.

remote cause see ULTIMATE CAUSE.

remote effect any outcome that results indirectly from a cause, such as some manipulation in a system or experiment. For example, a remote effect of a head trauma might be a reduced sense of taste. See also ULTIMATE CAUSE. Compare LOCAL EFFECT.

removing harmful consequences an ethical principle requiring researchers to ensure that participants in DECEPTION RESEARCH or other potentially detrimental practices leave a study in the same emotional state as when they arrived. Investigators thus are obligated to alleviate any feelings of alienation, resentment, negativity, and so forth by minimizing study risks before the study begins and providing an in-depth DEBRIEFING after the study is complete. For example, at the conclusion of a study in which participants were induced into negative moods, the experimenters would need to take steps to induce a positive mood in participants and explain the reasons for the methods used in the study. See also FREEDOM FROM HARM.

reparameterization *n.* the process of redefining the PARAMETERS necessary for the complete specification of a model, usually for the purpose of removing technical difficulties in an analytic solution that stem from the original parameterization. For example, in STRUCTURAL EQUATION MODELING a researcher may decide to add another pathway between a MANIFEST VARIABLE and a LATENT VARIABLE because of a new insight gained from theory or an empirical result.

repeatability *n.* the degree to which specific research studies obtain similar results when they are conducted again. Study or measurement conditions (e.g., instructions, assessments, setting) must be identical on both occasions. See REPLICATION; REPRODUCIBILITY.

repeated contrast in a WITHIN-SUBJECTS ANALYSIS OF VARIANCE, a comparison of means conducted across different levels of the INDEPENDENT VARIABLE. For example, assume a researcher is interested in how commitment to therapy changes over the course of the process. He or she could assess participant commitment at the start of therapy (Month 1) and at the beginning of each of the four months thereafter, and then evaluate how the mean commitment scores at Months 2, 3, 4, and 5 differ from the mean baseline commitment score obtained at Month 1. There are several types of repeated contrasts available, such as SIMPLE COMPARISONS and POLYNOMIAL CONTRASTS.

repeated event an episode or occurrence that happens at multiple points in time. For example, a study designed to prevent falls in older adults might document each time participants experience a fall as well as all of the features of the fall (e.g., surface conditions, location, time of day). SURVIVAL ANALYSIS may be used to examine such recurrent data and model the episode as a function of any number of independent variables (e.g., age, health status, treatment condition).

repeated factor an INDEPENDENT VARIABLE for which multiple scores are recorded for an individual research participant. For example, in a study examining political attitudes a researcher may collect approval ratings for a candidate at four time points before the election. Thus, the variable of candidate approval would be a repeated factor having four levels corresponding to the four different points at which ratings were obtained. See also REPEATED MEASURES DATA; WITHIN-SUBJECTS DESIGN.

repeated measures analysis of variance see WITHIN-SUBJECTS ANALYSIS OF VARIANCE.

repeated measures data in a WITHIN-SUBJECTS DESIGN, scores generated from observing a sample of individuals multiple times (e.g., across experimental trials, therapy sessions, grades in school) on a given outcome measure. These multiple assessments can be analyzed using REPEATED CONTRASTS as part of approaches such as WITHIN-SUBJECTS ANALYSIS OF VARIANCE and LATENT GROWTH CURVE ANALYSIS.

repeated measures design see WITHIN-SUBJECTS DESIGN.

repeated measures t test see DEPENDENT-SAMPLES T TEST.

replacement sampling see SAMPLING WITH REPLACEMENT.

replication *n.* the repetition of an original experiment or research study to verify or bolster confidence in its results. In **exact replication** (or **literal replication**), a researcher uses procedures that are identical to the original experiment or duplicated as closely as possible. In **modified replication**, a researcher incorporates alternative procedures and additional conditions. In **conceptual replication**, a researcher introduces different techniques and manipulations to gain theoretical information. See also BALANCED REPLICATION.

representational validity the extent to which a SIMULATION accurately replicates the real-world situation that it is intended to represent (**external representational validity**) and functions in the intended manner (**internal representational validity**).

representative conclusion a single finding from an empirical study that represents the entire set of results obtained. For example, researchers might summarize a set of findings from a multiyear study of women in midlife with the statement, "Women who experience high role conflict in their work change jobs more often and show lower resilience." In many research settings it is not possible to derive a representative conclusion because there is some uncertainty in the findings or the number of findings is too small.

representative design an experimental design that includes processes and variables that might be found outside the laboratory setting. In representative designs, the participants, situations, constructs, and assessments are sampled in a way that permits generalization beyond the specific research setting, and background variables are intentionally not controlled so that research results will apply more realistically to the real world. See ECOLOGICAL VALIDITY.

representative measure an instrument, assessment, or procedure that adequately reflects a broader group of available options, having characteristics or features that enable it to serve as an appropriate indicator for the larger set. For example, a representative measure of general job satisfaction would be applicable to multiple types of jobs and settings and systematically cover a full range of associated topics, such as satisfaction with pay, with coworkers, with the work itself, with supervision, with company policies, and so forth.

representativeness *n.* the correspondence between a sample and the larger population from which it is drawn such that the sample accurately reflects its population, reproducing the essential characteristics and constitution in correct proportions and allowing for GENERALIZABILITY.

representative sampling the selection of study units (e.g., participants, homes, schools) from a larger group (population) in an unbiased way, such that the sample obtained accurately reflects the total population. For example, a researcher conducting a study of university admissions would need to ensure he or she used a **representative random sample** of schools—in other words, each school would have an equal probability of being chosen for inclusion, and the group as a whole would provide an appropriate mix of different school characteristics (e.g., private and public, student body size, cost, proportion of students admitted, geographic location).

reproduced correlation in FACTOR ANALYSIS, the correlation between the LATENT VARIABLES or factors that have been extracted and the MANIFEST VARIABLES. Reproduced correlations are calculated for all extracted factors and then displayed in a tabular format called a **reproduced correlation matrix**. This is compared to the original CORRELATION MATRIX to determine whether their values are similar: If so, the proposed factors are a good fit for the obtained data.

reproducibility *n.* the extent to which a study produces the same findings when it is conducted again by a different independent researcher. A given research finding is thought to be stronger when it can be both repeated and reproduced. See REPEATABILITY; REPLICATION.

resampling *n.* an analytic method in which a researcher repeatedly chooses subgroups of observations from a larger overall data set in order to estimate various characteristics of that larger set. The smaller subsets of observations may be drawn through random SAMPLING WITH REPLACEMENT or without replacement, with either strategy having implications

R

for the different analytic approaches that may be used.

research *n*. the systematic effort to discover or confirm facts, to investigate a new problem or topic, or to describe events and understand relationships among variables, most often by scientific methods of observation and experimentation. Research is essential to science in contributing to the accumulation of generalizable knowledge.

research design a strategic plan of the procedures to be followed during a study in order to reach valid conclusions, with particular consideration given to participant selection and assignment to conditions, data collection, and data analysis. Research designs may take a variety of forms, including not only experiments but also quasi-experiments (see QUASI-EXPERIMENTAL RESEARCH), OBSERVATIONAL STUDIES, LONGITUDINAL DESIGNS, surveys, focus groups, and other nonexperimental methods. See also EXPERIMENTAL DESIGN.

research diary an investigator's documentation of the activities undertaken during a study, including its overall design and conceptualization, sampling and measurement procedures, data collection and analysis, and reporting of findings as well as reflections, notes, and observations of a more personal nature. Research diaries may be reviewed to understand the nuances of a project and often provide ideas that form the basis of future studies.

researcher *n*. the investigator who is conducting a study or experiment. This person may be working on the project independently or be part of a larger collaborative team. A researcher's involvement in the study may range from designing the research procedure to collecting and analyzing data or reporting findings. In the context of a traditional experimental design, a researcher often is referred to more specifically as an EXPERIMENTER.

researcher bias any unintended errors in the research process or the interpretation of its results that are attributable to an investigator's expectancies or preconceived beliefs. The term essentially is synonymous with EXPERIMENTER BIAS but is applied to all types of investigative projects rather than to experimental designs only.

research ethics the values, principles, and standards that guide the conduct of individual researchers in several areas of their professional lives, including the design and implementation of studies and the reporting of findings. For example, research ethics stipulate that studies involving data collection from human participants must be evaluated by INSTITUTIONAL REVIEW BOARDS.

research hypothesis a statement describing the investigator's expectation about the pattern of data that may result from a given study. By stating specific expectations before the data are collected, the investigator makes a commitment about the direction (e.g., Method A will yield higher final exam scores than Method B) and magnitude (e.g., participants' income will increase with more education) of potential relationships based on the study's theoretical framework and related prior studies. See also ALTERNATIVE HYPOTHESIS; NULL HYPOTHESIS.

research method a procedure for the formulation and evaluation of hypotheses that is intended to reveal relationships between variables and provide an understanding of the phenomenon under investigation. In psychology, this generally involves empirical testing and takes the form of the SCIENTIFIC METHOD. See also QUALITATIVE RESEARCH; QUANTITATIVE RESEARCH.

research program a set of planned, interrelated empirical studies that an investigator conducts, usually on a general topic of interest. For example, a researcher interested in the effectiveness

R

of elementary-school teachers may study several different classrooms using a different method in each, such as in-school visits, online surveys, observations of students, and interviews with teachers, parents, and peers.

research protocol the complete description of one's outline or plan for conducting a study. It should be as detailed as possible, including such elements as the RESEARCH HYPOTHESIS to be addressed and the rationale for doing so; the materials and resources that will be required; the timeline or duration; the precise sampling, measurement, and analysis procedures that will be used; a discussion of any ethical considerations; a description of strengths and limitations; and so forth.

research risk the potential costs to participants or to society at large associated with a particular study, which must be clearly specified to an INSTITUTIONAL REVIEW BOARD by an investigator prior to conducting the research. Examples of potential risk to participants include embarrassment at being involved in DECEPTION RESEARCH, side effects from a treatment, time and resource commitments, and emotional upset (e.g., from exposure to unpleasant or painful memories). An investigator must discuss how the costs will be minimized to the fullest extent possible and how the study benefits outweigh the costs.

research strategy see RESEARCH DESIGN.

research synthesis the systematic use of established data-gathering methods and statistical approaches to evaluate a body of empirical literature on a topic. An investigator must be careful to include both published and unpublished studies, to document the methods that each study uses, to provide detail about the findings and obtained EFFECT SIZES, and to summarize commonalities and account for differences across studies. See META-ANALYSIS.

residual *n.* in REGRESSION ANALYSIS, the difference between the value of an empirical observation and the value of that observation as predicted by a model. Analysis of residuals allows a researcher to judge the fit or appropriateness of the model for the data.

residual analysis a diagnostic review of the discrepancies between specific observations and their respective values predicted by a model (see RESIDUAL). Summarizing these discrepancies in several different ways can help a researcher identify problems in the application of a model to a particular data set. For example, a residual analysis might show large discrepancies for one group but not another, suggesting the model is not appropriate for that specific group. See REGRESSION DIAGNOSTICS.

residual degrees of freedom the total number of cases in a REGRESSION ANALYSIS minus the number of groups or conditions into which they have been placed (i.e., the number of PARAMETERS being estimated). It is equivalent to the WITHIN-GROUPS DEGREES OF FREEDOM in an ANALYSIS OF VARIANCE.

residual error see ERROR VARIANCE.

residual matrix a MATRIX displaying the discrepancies between observed data and the corresponding values predicted by a researcher-specified model. For example, in FACTOR ANALYSIS a residual matrix reflects what remains after factors or dimensions are removed from a CORRELATION MATRIX or COVARIANCE MATRIX. Large values in the matrix show where the model did not fit the data well and can provide clues about its MISSPECIFICATION. Researchers often prefer to standardize the values in a residual matrix so that they are directly interpretable, with values greater than 1.96 considered statistically significant at the $p < .05$ level (see PROBABILITY LEVEL) and values greater than 2.58 considered statistically significant at the $p < .01$ level,

Variable	1	2	3	4	5	6	7	8	9	10	11	12	13	14	15	16	17	18
1. JobSat1	0.20																	
2. JobSat2	1.04	1.89																
3. JobSat3	−0.49	0.87	0.33															
4. HlCon1	−0.09	0.56	0.09	0.02														
5. HlCon2	−1.81	−0.04	−0.35	6.39	0.01													
6. HlCon3	0.41	0.54	0.81	−3.00	−2.98	0.02												
7. Psych1	−1.25	−0.69	−0.51	**−8.55**	**−4.73**	**−8.36**	0.70											
8. Psych2	−2.30	−1.41	−1.21	**−8.46**	**−4.57**	**−9.05**	0.67	0.35										
9. Psych3	−1.38	−0.60	−0.56	**−7.93**	**−4.77**	**−8.79**	0.86	0.34	0.43									
10. HelSat1	1.50	1.49	1.92	−1.45	−1.79	1.88	**−8.19**	**−8.00**	**−8.29**	0.04								
11. HelSat2	0.05	0.22	0.26	−2.82	−0.55	2.10	**−6.47**	**−6.53**	**−5.93**	1.79	0.02							
12. HelSat3	1.72	0.29	0.54	0.51	−2.16	3.77	**−9.36**	**−9.37**	**−8.62**	−0.86	−1.02	0.02						
13. Jwith1	**−3.04**	**−3.31**	**−3.58**	1.44	1.25	1.40	0.45	2.12	0.75	1.01	0.15	−0.27	0.00					
14. Jwith2	**−5.54**	**−5.67**	**−5.49**	−0.16	0.09	−0.20	4.43	4.78	4.54	−1.05	−0.65	−1.00	−0.02	0.00				
15. Jwith3	**−5.74**	**−6.01**	**−5.66**	1.69	0.50	1.09	2.99	3.96	2.61	0.63	−1.16	−0.44	1.14	−0.88	0.00			
16. Wwith1	−0.30	1.34	0.02	−3.36	−2.81	−3.93	**5.99**	**6.19**	**6.15**	**−5.63**	**−4.26**	**−4.80**	2.30	1.96	2.33	0.00		
17. Wwith2	−2.60	−1.68	−2.20	−3.37	−2.10	−4.71	**7.52**	**7.00**	**6.70**	**−4.75**	**−3.99**	**−4.51**	2.98	4.41	3.51	0.00	0.00	
18. Wwith3	−0.30	1.81	1.23	−4.15	−3.21	−4.37	**6.12**	**6.72**	**5.99**	**−5.50**	**−4.29**	**−5.15**	2.03	2.26	1.76	0.00	−0.40	0.00

residual matrix

as indicated by boldface in the example above.

JobSat1, JobSat2, and JobSat3 are the three indicators for the latent construct job satisfaction. Each of the subsequent sets of three variables are the three indicators for the latent constructs health conditions, psychological conditions, health satisfaction, job withdrawal, and work withdrawal, respectively. Also called **residual correlation matrix**.

residual maximum likelihood see RESTRICTED MAXIMUM LIKELIHOOD.

residual mean square see MEAN SQUARED ERROR.

residual path coefficient in PATH ANALYSIS, a value reflecting the amount of error in an equation linking measured variables to an outcome of interest. In other words, the residual path coefficient indicates the degree of variance in a DEPENDENT VARIABLE that is not accounted for by the INDEPENDENT VARIABLES included in the model.

residual score see ERROR SCORE.

residual sum of squares see ERROR SUM OF SQUARES.

residual term see ERROR TERM.

residual variance see ERROR VARIANCE.

resistant estimator an ESTIMATOR for an unknown characteristic in a popula-tion that is less likely to be influenced by the presence of OUTLIERS (extreme scores) in the sample upon which it is based. See also ROBUST ESTIMATOR.

respondent *n.* a study participant who is interviewed as part of a research design or who completes a survey or questionnaire.

respondent validation see MEMBER CHECK.

responders-versus-nonresponders analysis an empirical review of research data to understand potential differences between those who choose to participate in a survey and those who choose not to participate. For example, a responders-versus-nonresponders analysis might show that people who complete a questionnaire about mood exhibit fewer symptoms of depression than those who opt not to do so. See ATTRITION. See also MISSING VALUES PROCEDURE.

response *n.* any glandular, muscular, neural, or other reaction to a stimulus. A response is a clearly defined, measurable unit of behavior discussed in terms of its result (e.g., pressing a lever, indicating *yes* vs. *no* on a survey item) or its physical characteristics (e.g., raising an arm, sharing a toy).

response acquiescence see YEA-SAYING.

R

response bias the tendency for a study participant to give one answer or type of answer more than others, regardless of the stimulus condition. There are several different types of response bias, including the HALO EFFECT, NAY-SAYING, and YEA-SAYING. See also RESPONSE SET; RESPONSE STYLE.

response deviation 1. the difference between an individual's score and the average value for the total set of scores. **2.** see NAY-SAYING.

response effect the influence of some attribute of the MEASUREMENT SCALE or administration context on a participant's answers to survey or interview items. For example, the order in which response options are presented may affect how a participant will answer, as might the inclusion of a middle or neutral point on an agreement scale or whether a survey is conducted in person, via the Internet, or over the telephone.

response-feature analysis any of several methods of evaluating LONGITUDINAL DATA that involve calculating the same SUMMARY STATISTICS, such as the MEAN, STANDARD DEVIATION, SLOPE, and AREA UNDER THE CURVE, for a data set at different time points.

response latency see REACTION TIME.

response rate the number of individuals who complete an interview, answer a survey, or join a research study compared to the number who were contacted to participate, often expressed as a PERCENTAGE. Compare REFUSAL RATE.

response scale any of various types of instrument provided to a respondent to express an answer to an item. Examples of different response scales include FIXED-ALTERNATIVE QUESTIONS, LIKERT SCALES, VISUAL ANALOGUE SCALES, and SEMANTIC DIFFERENTIALS.

response set a tendency to answer questions in a systematic manner that is unrelated to their content. An example is the SOCIAL DESIRABILITY response set. See also RESPONSE BIAS; RESPONSE STYLE.

response style a RESPONSE SET arising from dispositional factors that appear across contexts and over time rather than from situational factors.

response surface methodology (**RSM**) a set of procedures used to model and analyze the relationships between one or more outcome or DEPENDENT VARIABLES and multiple predictor or INDEPENDENT VARIABLES posited in a particular REGRESSION EQUATION. The analysis involves graphing a function in three-dimensional space (i.e., creating a **response surface**), examining the contours of the resulting plot, and using the information so obtained to optimize and refine the model by adding or deleting predictors, identifying OUTLIERS, and considering NONLINEAR terms. Consider the following example.

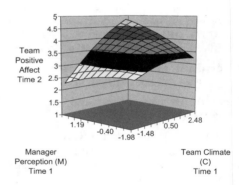

This response surface depicts team average perception of climate for organizational support, manager perception of team climate, and levels of team positive affect for employees in different branches of three savings banks in the same geographical region. Also called **response surface analysis**.

response time see REACTION TIME.

response variable see DEPENDENT VARIABLE.

restricted maximum likelihood (**REML**) a technique for estimating the

PARAMETERS of a distribution, often used in HIERARCHICAL LINEAR MODELS, GENERALIZABILITY THEORY, and VARIANCE COMPONENTS ANALYSIS. It is a form of MAXIMUM LIKELIHOOD that uses less information than other related approaches (i.e., it does not use all of the available observations in a very large data set) to produce coefficients with desirable characteristics (e.g., UNBIASED estimates). Also called **residual maximum likelihood**; **reduced maximum likelihood**.

restriction of range the limitation—via sampling, measurement procedures, or other aspects of experimental design—of the full range of total possible scores that may be obtained to only a narrow portion of that total. For example, in a study of the grade point averages of university students, restriction of range occurs if only students from the dean's list are included. Range restriction on a particular variable may lead to such negative effects as failing to observe or improperly characterizing a relationship between the variables of interest.

retest 1. *n.* the administration of a test, assessment instrument, or other measurement procedure to the same participants at a point in time subsequent to the original administration (e.g., two weeks later, one year later). **2.** *vb.* to readminister such a test, assessment instrument, or measurement procedure.

retest reliability a measure of the consistency of results on a test or other assessment instrument over time, given as the correlation of scores between the first and second administrations. It provides an estimate of the stability of the construct being evaluated. Also called **test–retest reliability.**

retrospective cohort study research that compares outcomes for groups of individuals who differ on a single identified characteristic that occurred in the past. For example, a researcher studying exposure to secondhand tobacco smoke might use existing survey data to divide a sample into groups or cohorts based on reported exposure in their childhood homes (no smoking, one person smoked, more than one person smoked) before examining current reported health problems. Because the research relies on reports of past occurrences, inaccuracies may arise due to poor recall. See also RETROSPECTIVE RESEARCH.

retrospective power an assessment of the probability that a study will detect a statistically significant effect that is conducted after the study has been completed. Researchers sometimes use this approach to provide evidence of whether a study had a sufficient likelihood of detecting an effect at a certain p value (see PROBABILITY LEVEL), given the sample size used and the EFFECT SIZE obtained. Generally, the more appropriate strategy is to conduct a POWER ANALYSIS prior to collecting study data so as to determine if the planned research design is sufficient to produce significant results at a certain statistical level. Also called **post hoc power**.

retrospective research observational, nonexperimental research that tries to explain the present in terms of past events; that is, research that starts with the present and follows participants backward in time. For example, an investigator may select a group of individuals who exhibit a particular problematic symptom and then study them to determine if they had been exposed to a risk factor of interest. Also called **retrospective study**. Compare PROSPECTIVE RESEARCH.

retrospective sampling a technique in which participants or cases from the general population are selected for inclusion in experiments or other research based on their previous exposure to a risk factor or the completion of some particular process. Participants are then examined in the present to see if a particular condition or state exists, often in

R

comparison to others who were not exposed to the risk or did not complete the particular process. Compare PROSPECTIVE SAMPLING.

retrospective validity the extent to which an instrument that purports to measure a particular behavior or phenomenon of interest can be shown to correlate with past behaviors or occurrences that demonstrate this behavior. For example, a researcher evaluating a new measure of accident proneness might administer it to a sample of respondents and then check the individuals' archived medical records to determine if higher test scores correlate with the number of actual treated incidents. It is one of several types of CRITERION VALIDITY. Also called **postdictive validity**. See also CONCURRENT VALIDITY; PREDICTIVE VALIDITY.

reversal design an experimental design, generally used when only a single group is being studied, that attempts to counteract the confounding effects (see CONFOUND) of sequence, order, and treatment by alternating baseline conditions with treatment conditions. Examples include the A-B-A DESIGN, A-B-A-B DESIGN, and other similar combinations. See also ALTERNATING TREATMENTS DESIGN.

reverse counterbalancing a specific procedure for ordering stimulus materials in a research study that involves administering one order (A-B-C) for one half of the participants and the opposite order (C-B-A) for the other half of the participants. Reverse counterbalancing is used to minimize any potential influence of presentation upon results, so as to ensure it is the stimuli themselves that are producing any effect that may be seen.

rho correlation (symbol: ρ) **1.** see POPULATION CORRELATION COEFFICIENT. **2.** see SPEARMAN CORRELATION COEFFICIENT.

ridge regression a variant on ordinary LEAST SQUARES REGRESSION designed to remedy problems that arise from MULTICOLLINEARITY. It involves modifying the MAIN DIAGONAL of the CORRELATION MATRIX before calculating the coefficients, thus eliminating the associations among the INDEPENDENT VARIABLES. A researcher can use the information obtained from this analysis to determine whether certain independent variables should be removed from the final model. Also called **damped regression**.

right censoring inability of a researcher to document when all participants have reached a target event (e.g., achieving a specific milestone, experiencing a relapse) at the conclusion of the study period. This may occur for one of three reasons: A participant may never experience the target event or experience it after the observation period has ended; a participant may experience a competing event that prevents him or her from experiencing the target event; or a participant may be lost to ATTRITION. Compare LEFT CENSORING.

rigid rotation see ORTHOGONAL ROTATION.

risk level the probability of making a TYPE I ERROR that one is willing to accept in null hypothesis SIGNIFICANCE TESTING.

risk ratio the comparison of one group's probability of experiencing an event (e.g., being diagnosed with lung cancer) to a second group's probability of experiencing that event. It is often used to describe health status following exposure to some stimulus (e.g., lead in water) or clinical intervention. A value greater than 1 indicates the group under study has a higher probability than the control group of experiencing the event; a value less than 1 indicates the group under study has a lower probability of experiencing the event; and a value of exactly 1 indicates the two groups are equally likely to experience the event. Also called **relative risk**.

risk set in SURVIVAL ANALYSIS, the number of individuals or cases who are at risk of experiencing a specific event (e.g., first drink, birth of a child, promotion) during a particular time period.

R methodology a collection of various methods used to evaluate individuals' scores on a set of objective measures, such as intelligence tests. Examples include FACTOR ANALYSIS and PRINCIPAL COMPONENTS ANALYSIS. Compare Q METHODOLOGY.

RMS abbreviation for ROOT MEAN SQUARE.

RMSE abbreviation for ROOT-MEAN-SQUARE ERROR.

RMSR abbreviation for ROOT-MEAN-SQUARE RESIDUAL.

RNG abbreviation for RANDOM NUMBER GENERATOR.

Robinson matrix in TIME-SERIES ANALYSIS, a SYMMETRICAL MATRIX containing CORRELATIONS of early time points with later time points. Correlations are arranged such that those closest to the MAIN DIAGONAL are the largest and the ones furthest away are the smallest. [W. S. **Robinson**]

robust estimator an ESTIMATOR for an unknown characteristic in a population that is less likely to be influenced by VIOLATIONS OF ASSUMPTIONS about the sample data upon which it is based. For example, rather than using a mean to describe CENTRAL TENDENCY in a distribution with OUTLIERS, a researcher might choose a MEDIAN, a TRIMMED MEAN, or a WINSORIZED MEAN. Each option reflects a different way of handling the outliers, such as downweighting them, replacing them with a new value, or ignoring them. Also called **sturdy statistic**. See also RESISTANT ESTIMATOR.

robustness *n.* the ability of a statistical

procedure to produce valid estimated values for a population characteristic (PARAMETER) despite violations of the ASSUMPTIONS upon which the technique is based.

ROC curve abbreviation for RECEIVER-OPERATING CHARACTERISTIC CURVE.

role-playing research a design in which participants are asked to assume a specific character in a defined situation and to behave as if that character were really theirs and the situation were actual. It is a type of SIMULATION, often used in therapeutic and organizational contexts, that enables researchers to assess how individuals think, feel, and act under certain circumstances.

rolling average see MOVING AVERAGE.

root mean square (RMS) the square root of the sum of the squares of a set of values divided by the number of values. For a set of values $x_1, x_2, \ldots x_n$, the root mean square value is

$$\sqrt{[(x_1^2 + x_2^2 + \ldots x_n^2)/n]}$$

and describes the average size of the values in the set. In the physical sciences the term is used as a synonym for STANDARD DEVIATION under certain circumstances.

root-mean-square deviation the square root of a MEAN-SQUARE DEVIATION.

root-mean-square error (RMSE) the square root of a MEAN SQUARED ERROR.

root-mean-square residual (RMSR) the square root of a mean-square residual (see MEAN SQUARED ERROR). A standardized version of this value commonly is used to assess model fit in STRUCTURAL EQUATION MODELING.

rootogram *n.* a HISTOGRAM modified to show the response or outcome variable on the horizontal x-axis and the square root of the response frequencies (or counts) on the vertical y-axis, as in the hypothetical example overleaf.

Alternatively, the square root of RELA-

R

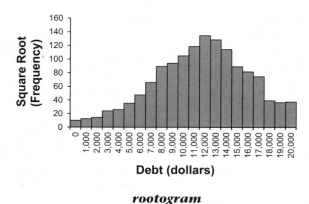

rootogram

TIVE FREQUENCIES, CUMULATIVE FREQUENCIES, or CUMULATIVE RELATIVE FREQUENCIES may be given along the *y*-axis. See also HANGING ROOTOGRAM.

Rosenbaum's test of unidimensionality a statistical procedure to evaluate whether the associations among a set of items or variables are generally described by a single dominant factor rather than by several factors (i.e., are unidimensional instead of multidimensional). It is a NONPARAMETRIC method that assesses conditional associations within CONTINGENCY TABLES. Also called **Holland–Rosenbaum test of unidimensionality**. [Paul W. Holland and Paul R. Rosenbaum, U.S. statisticians]

Rosenthal effect the situation in which an investigator's expectations about the outcome of a given study unwittingly affect the actual study outcome. A researcher may use BLINDS to prevent the Rosenthal effect from occurring and biasing study results. This term is often used synonymously with EXPERIMENTER EXPECTANCY EFFECT and SELF-FULFILLING PROPHECY. See also DEMAND CHARACTERISTICS. [Robert **Rosenthal** (1933–), U.S. psychologist]

rotation *n.* in statistics, movement around the origin in a multidimensional space. Rotation is commonly used in FACTOR ANALYSIS to enhance interpretability of a factor solution. For ex-

ample, it may be used to maximize loadings on certain factors while minimizing these loadings on other factors, thereby showing SIMPLE STRUCTURE. See OBLIQUE ROTATION; ORTHOGONAL ROTATION; PROCRUSTES ROTATION; QUARTIMAX ROTATION; VARIMAX ROTATION. —**rotational** *adj.*

rotation sampling a technique used when conducting surveys in which after specified time periods some proportion of respondents or cases is replaced with new units. Rotation sampling helps to reduce the burden on respondents and allows for better prediction from past samples.

row marginal a summary of the values across each horizontal row of cells in a table. For a table containing frequency counts it is a sum of the number of counts in each row, whereas for a table of averages it is the mean value of data observations across each row. Compare COLUMN MARGINAL.

row sum of squares 1. in an ANALYSIS OF VARIANCE for two independent variables *a* and *b*, the amount of VARIANCE that is associated with either *a* or *b*, as derived from the values given in the relevant row of the data table. It is obtained by determining the average of all observations in the row, calculating how much each score deviates from that average, multiplying the resulting value by itself, and adding it to the similarly obtained values for all other cases in the row. The calculated quantities for each row are then used to compute the BETWEEN-GROUPS SUM OF SQUARES, which in turn is used to compute an F RATIO. See also TOTAL SUM OF SQUARES. Compare COLUMN SUM OF SQUARES. **2.** in EXPLORATORY FACTOR ANALYSIS, the variance accounted for by each variable across factors (see COMMONALITY ANALYSIS). It is determined by raising the FACTOR LOADINGS for each variable in a factor loading matrix to the second power and then totaling the values.

row vector a data matrix with a single row of values. In other words, it has the dimensions $1 \times c$, where 1 denotes the single row and c refers to the number of columns. Compare COLUMN VECTOR.

Roy's greatest characteristic root see GREATEST CHARACTERISTIC ROOT.

Roy's largest-root test see GREATEST-CHARACTERISTIC-ROOT TEST.

r_{pb} symbol for POINT BISERIAL CORRELATION COEFFICIENT.

r_{pbis} symbol for POINT BISERIAL CORRELATION COEFFICIENT.

RRT abbreviation for RANDOMIZED-RESPONSE TECHNIQUE.

r_s symbol for SPEARMAN CORRELATION COEFFICIENT.

RSM abbreviation for RESPONSE SURFACE METHODOLOGY.

RT abbreviation for REACTION TIME.

R-technique factor analysis a type of FACTOR ANALYSIS performed on a CORRELATION MATRIX: It examines associations between variable measurements in order to understand how the variables themselves group together and are related. Compare P-TECHNIQUE FACTOR ANALYSIS; Q-TECHNIQUE FACTOR ANALYSIS.

r_{tet} symbol for TETRACHORIC CORRELATION COEFFICIENT.

r to z transformation see FISHER'S R TO Z TRANSFORMATION.

Rubin's causal model a model used to estimate the magnitude of an intervention's effect relative to a comparison condition. Used primarily in economics, medicine, and public health research, the model unrealistically assumes that participants experience multiple conditions simultaneously (e.g., the same participant was in a treatment and control condition at the same time) in order to envision all possible potential outcomes of the intervention. [Donald B. **Rubin** (1943–), U.S. statistician]

Rudas–Clogg–Lindsay index of fit a quantitative measure of how well a statistical model corresponds to data in a CONTINGENCY TABLE that exhibit a FINITE MIXTURE DISTRIBUTION. It relies on the idea that for part of the population the model is true and for part it is not true. The measure, which does not depend on sample size as does the CHI-SQUARE GOODNESS-OF-FIT TEST, ranges in value from 0 to 1, with the latter indicating good fit. [Tamás **Rudas**, Hungarian mathematician; Clifford C. **Clogg** (1950–1995), U.S. sociologist; Bruce G. **Lindsay** (1947–), U.S. mathematician]

rugplot *n.* a HISTOGRAM or SCATTERPLOT of data for one or more groups of a CATEGORICAL VARIABLE that has been modified to include each group's distribution of values on another CONTINUOUS VARIABLE, as in the generic example overleaf.
It is so named because the short horizontal lines along the x-axis showing the density of observations at different points along the continuously measured variable resemble a rug in cross section.

run-in period in an experiment or SIMULATION, an initial period of time that is included to allow the phenomenon of interest to stabilize before any treatment or manipulation is administered. A run-in period helps a researcher identify problems with the protocol or treatment.

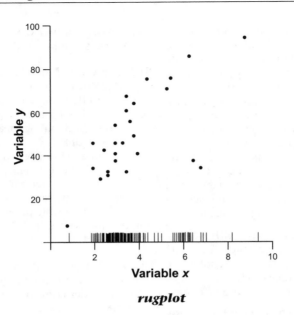

rugplot

running average see MOVING AVER-
AGE.

running medians see MOVING MEDI-
ANS.

runs test see WALD–WOLFOWITZ TEST.

Ryan's method see REGWQ TEST.

$R^2_{yy'}$ symbol for CROSS-VALIDATED MUL-
TIPLE CORRELATION.

R

Ss

s² symbol for SAMPLE VARIANCE.

S abbreviation for a SUBJECT (i.e., individual or case) in a study. People partaking in research are now more commonly referred to as PARTICIPANTS.

St. Petersburg paradox a paradox often cited in PROBABILITY THEORY and DECISION THEORY, which shows how a decision criterion that only takes an EXPECTED VALUE into account may result in a recommended course of action that no rational person would follow. The paradox involves a theoretical game called the St. Petersburg Lottery, which is played by flipping a coin until it comes up tails, and the total number of flips, n, determines the prize, which equals $\$2 \times n$. Thus, if the coin comes up tails the first time, the prize is \$2 and the game ends. If the coin comes up heads the first time, it is flipped again. If it comes up tails the second time, the prize is \$4 and the game ends. If it comes up heads the second time, it is flipped again, and so forth. The expected value of the game is the sum of the potential payoffs; since the payoff of each possible consequence is $\$2/2 = \$1$, and since there are potentially an infinite number of payoffs, the sum is an infinite number of dollars. In theory, because the amount one could win is infinite, a rational gambler should be willing to pay any finite amount to play (i.e., any price of entry is smaller than the expected value of the game). In practice, however, this would clearly not be the case.

sample *n.* a subset of a POPULATION of interest that is selected for study with the aim of making inferences to the population. It is important to ensure that a sample is representative of the larger population. Characteristics that describe observations in this subset, such as the mean, median, or STANDARD DEVIATION, are called STATISTICS.

sample correlation coefficient (symbol: r) an index of the degree of association between two variables based on the data in a studied subset (sample) of cases from a larger group of interest. It is a variant of the PRODUCT-MOMENT CORRELATION COEFFICIENT, such that the same symbol is used for both statistics. See also POPULATION CORRELATION COEFFICIENT.

sample distribution the DISTRIBUTION of scores in a particular subset (sample) drawn from the wider population. Of interest is the general shape of the distribution, reflecting the frequency of particular scores (its KURTOSIS, SKEWNESS, etc.). Compared to the theoretical POPULATION DISTRIBUTION, the distribution of scores in a sample is often jagged and not smooth.

sample mean (symbol: $\bar{X}$, M) the arithmetic average (MEAN) of a set of scores from cases or observations in a subset from a wider population. Because each score contributes equally to this index of CENTRAL TENDENCY, it can be affected greatly by OUTLIERS. Many widely used STATISTICAL TESTS are based on the comparison of sample means.

sample of convenience see CONVENIENCE SAMPLING.

sample overlap the situation in which two or more subsets drawn from a population feature items in common (i.e., the same individual or observation features in more than one sample). A researcher can design a selection strategy in which the probability of finding the same individuals across two studies is maximized, thereby reducing costs associated with data collection. Alternatively, this probability could be minimized, thereby ensuring independence across studies and reducing respondent burden.

sample reliability the degree to which a SAMPLE is representative of the POPULATION from which it is drawn. It is typically indexed by the STANDARD ERROR OF THE MEAN.

sample size the number of observations (cases, individuals, units) included in the sample to be studied. This is usually denoted N (for the study as a whole) or n (for subgroups from the study).

sample space the collection of all possible outcomes of an experiment of chance. For example, for a toss of a single coin the sample space is heads and tails, whereas for a toss of two coins the sample space is heads–heads, heads–tails, tails–tails, and tails–heads.

sample standard deviation (symbol: s) see STANDARD DEVIATION.

sample variance (symbol: s^2) the dispersion of scores within a group selected for study, as opposed to the POPULATION VARIANCE. It is calculated by determining each score's difference from the average for the set, squaring and summing these differences, and then dividing by the total number of scores minus one.

sampling *n.* the process of selecting a limited number of units from a larger set for a study. The term most often refers to the selection of respondents, observations, or cases for inclusion in experiments, surveys, interviews, or other research. However, sampling can also involve selecting theoretical constructs to study, selecting measurement instruments from a broad set of potential options, or selecting time points at which to observe individuals or cases. There are various different methods of selecting participants for a study, including SIMPLE RANDOM SAMPLING, STRATIFIED SAMPLING, CONVENIENCE SAMPLING, and QUOTA SAMPLING. Each approach has a different potential of obtaining a sample appropriately representative of the POPULATION under study.

sampling bias a systematic and directional error involved in the choice of units, cases, or participants from a larger group into a research study. This is a potential problem whenever the researcher has latitude in selecting individual units for the sample. Selection bias can pose a threat to the INTERNAL VALIDITY of a study if there is a possibility that pre-existing differences arising from the sampling process may interact with the variable of interest. Similarly, if the procedure used to choose participants tends to favor specially motivated individuals or people from a certain segment of society, there would be a threat to the study's EXTERNAL VALIDITY (i.e., inferences to a larger population would not be viable). Selection bias is associated with a lack of RANDOM SAMPLING and with nonrandom assignment to conditions. Also called **selection bias**; **recruitment bias**. See also SELF-SELECTION BIAS.

sampling design the specific approach, method, or strategy that a researcher decides to use to select a sample from the larger population. Formulating a design involves determining the nature of the target population, a suitable SAMPLING FRAME for drawing the cases, the desired sample size, whether random or nonrandom selection will be used, and whether there are any important variables on which to stratify selection. Also called **sampling plan**.

sampling distribution the distribution of a statistic, such as the mean, over repeated samples drawn from a population. SIMULATION studies allow researchers to specify known population information, conduct a very large number of repeated draws on the population, and build an empirical distribution of the statistic based on these draws (e.g., t, F, or χ^2 distributions). For example, the means calculated from samples of 100 observations, repeatedly and randomly drawn from the population, yield a sampling distribution for the mean. Knowledge about the distribution of a statistic allows researchers to say when a finding from a sample is unusual (e.g., statistically significant) and when it would be expected from the statistic's known behavior, thus enabling the sampling distribution of a statistic to be used in testing hypotheses about variables and their relationships. See also INFERENTIAL TEST.

sampling error the predictable MAR-GIN OF ERROR that occurs in studies that draw samples of cases or observations from a larger POPULATION: It indicates the possible variance between the true value of a parameter in the population and the estimate of that value made from the sample data. The larger the sample, the smaller the sampling error (if the entire population was sampled, there would be no error in the sample estimate). Large national surveys, such as those reporting political attitudes, state the sampling error along with their findings. For example, a survey finding that 65% prefer a particular policy with a margin of error of 3% means that the true figure could be anywhere between 62% and 68%.

sampling frame the specific source used in drawing a subset of cases or individuals from the larger POPULATION. In many cases the sampling frame will be a complete list of all the elements in a population (e.g., the electoral register). In other cases this will be impossible or the issue may be less straightforward than it appears. In a study of college students' aspirations for life after graduation, for example, the researchers might decide to use a listing of students obtained from the institution's office of evaluation and assessment and randomly select from this list every fifth student. In this example, however, the researcher would need to be assured of the completeness of the institution's re-cords in light of the inferences that will be made: Some relevant questions would be whether part-time as well as full-time students are included in the institution's files and whether students currently on leave are included. The key point is that any sampling frame should be representative of the target population as a whole.

sampling interval in SAMPLING DE-SIGNS that involve the researcher selecting every nth case from a list or table, the value of n. The chosen interval will usually depend on the nature of the SAMPLING FRAME. For example, if the researcher has access to an alphabetized list, he or she might want to ensure that all parts of the alphabet are represented and select a value to maximize that goal. Alternatively, for a study conducted in the field that involves the researcher approaching individuals in an office building, the value could be selected based on the average number of people who are likely to be available and eligible for selection.

sampling plan see SAMPLING DESIGN.

sampling theory the body of principles underlying the drawing of SAMPLES that accurately represent the population from which they are taken and to which inferences will be made. This conceptualization of the sampling process provides guidance to researchers about which SAMPLING DESIGN to choose in the particular circumstances and how best to account for subsets of cases that are not well represented (or are overrepresented) in the population (e.g., by using WEIGHTS).

sampling unit any of the elements selected from a population to make up a sample. For instance, if classrooms are selected at random from the population, then the classroom, not the individual student, is the sampling unit. See UNIT OF ANALYSIS.

sampling variability the extent to which the value of a statistic differs across a series of samples, such that there is some degree of uncertainty involved in making inferences to the larger POPULA-TION. See SAMPLING ERROR.

sampling without replacement a SAMPLING technique that involves selecting an item from the larger set and removing it from the general pool; thus, this particular case cannot be redrawn. Compare SAMPLING WITH REPLACEMENT.

sampling with replacement a SAMPLING technique in which each item selected from the larger set is returned to the general pool so that it may subsequently be redrawn. This means that a particular case may be drawn more than once for a given sample. Compare SAMPLING WITHOUT REPLACEMENT.

saturated model a model that fits the data perfectly because it has as many estimated parameters as there are values to be fitted. In STRUCTURAL EQUATION MODELING this type of model is called a JUST-IDENTIFIED MODEL: It poses a problem as a researcher cannot evaluate fit, as would be the case with the preferred OVERIDENTIFIED MODEL (or **oversaturated model**), in which there are fewer estimated parameters than DEGREES OF FREEDOM. Relatedly, the underidentified model (or **unsaturated model**) has more parameters than can be estimated from the available data. In FACTOR ANALYSIS, the problem of **saturation** occurs when the number of factors that will be estimated is the same as the number of variables in the data set.

saturated test in EXPLORATORY FACTOR ANALYSIS, a scale that is highly correlated with one of the factors being measured. Such a test helps define the meaning of the factor.

saturation *n.* see SATURATED MODEL.

scalability *n.* the ability of an item on a test or scale to elicit responses that represent identifiable positions on an ordered progression of scores or values describing an underlying construct, such as an ability or attitude. See GUTTMAN SCALE.

scalar 1. *n.* a quantity having only mag-nitude and not direction. Compare VECTOR. **2.** *n.* in MATRIX ALGEBRA, a quantity that can multiply a vector in a vector space to produce another vector. **3.** *adj.* describing a variable that can be represented by positions on a scale. **4.** *adj.* describing a matrix in which the entries in the MAIN DIAGONAL are equal and all other entries are zero.

scalar analysis the evaluation of data obtained from a test or measure using an ITEM RESPONSE THEORY model, often a RASCH MODEL.

scale *n.* **1.** a system for ordering test responses in a progressive series, so as to measure a trait, ability, attitude, or the like. For example, an agreement scale used on an attitude survey might have seven response options ranging from *strongly disagree* (1) to *strongly agree* (7), with *neither disagree nor agree* (4) as the middle point. See LIKERT SCALE; RATING SCALE. **2.** a sequence of ordered values used as a reference in measuring a physical property (e.g., weight, temperature). See INTERVAL SCALE; RATIO SCALE. See also MEASUREMENT LEVEL. **3.** more generally, any test or other assessment instrument as a whole.

scale attenuation the situation in which the response format on a measure includes too few options to reflect a respondent's actual behavior, opinion, or belief. For example, if an item asks about average time spent watching television each day and a scale ranging from *none* (1) to *1 hour or more* (5) is used, the upper end of the scale is likely to be selected by the great majority of respondents, some of whom will watch many hours per day; this results in little ability to differentiate the sample in terms of how many hours are actually watched. See CEILING EFFECT; FLOOR EFFECT.

scale development the process of creating a new INSTRUMENT for measuring an unobserved or latent construct, such as depression, sociability, or fourth-grade mathematics ability. The process includes defining the construct and test specifications, generating items and RE-SPONSE SCALES, piloting the items in a large sample, conducting analyses to fine-tune the measure, and then re-administering the refined measure to develop NORMS (if applicable) and to assess aspects of RELIABILITY and VALIDITY.

scale homogeneity see INTERNAL CONSISTENCY.

scale parameter see DISPERSION PARAMETER.

scale value a number that represents an individual's position on an underlying construct (trait, ability, attitude, etc.), as measured by an item on a SCALE or the scale as a whole.

scaling *n.* the process of constructing an instrument to measure, assess, and order some quantity or characteristic (e.g., height, weight, happiness, empathy). A researcher must evaluate how a given CONSTRUCT of interest should be measured and how optimally to obtain scores for individuals on these measures. See SCALE DEVELOPMENT.

scalogram *n.* see GUTTMAN SCALE.

scatter *n.* **1.** the tendency of data points to diverge from each other. An example is the variation in scores across a set of tests on the same individual; another is the variation among test takers on a particular test. See also DISPERSION; VARIANCE. **2.** in PROFILE ANALYSIS, the tendency for a set of scores for an individual to vary from the average of scores.

scatter analysis 1. a study of the relationship between two variables carried out using a SCATTERPLOT. **2.** any study of SCATTER, especially in intelligence testing and PROFILE ANALYSIS.

scatterplot *n.* a graphical representation of the relationship between two continuously measured variables in which one variable is arrayed on each axis and a dot or other symbol is placed at each point where the values of the variables intersect. For instance, the hypothetical example below depicts the weight and average daily calorie consumption for a sample of individuals.

The overall pattern of dots provides an indication of the extent to which there is a LINEAR RELATIONSHIP between variables. A round mass of points shows no linear relation, an elliptical cloud of points with a positive slope shows a positive relation, and an elliptical cloud with a negative slope shows a negative relation. OUTLIER points are also clearly visible. Also called **dot plot**; **scattergram**. See also REGRESSION LINE.

scatterplot matrix a matrix in which all variables being studied are arrayed as both rows and columns, so that each cell reflects the relationship between two variables and the values along the MAIN DIAGONAL reflect the distribution of each variable. For example, the scatterplot matrix overleaf shows respondent age, respondent gender, and

S

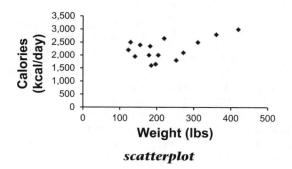

scatterplot

AGE   SEX   INCOME   CHILDREN   TOGETHER

number of years in current relationship for a survey of counseling clients. All pairwise displays (e.g., in a study with 8 variables, Variables 1 with 2, Variables 1 with 3, … Variables 7 with 8) are shown so that the researcher can easily and efficiently see the associations among variables and other characteristics of the data.

scedasticity *n.* the distribution of ERROR TERMS in a set of random variables. The pattern of errors may be due to chance and have constant variance (homoscedasticity), or there may be some distinct pattern, such as a clustering of greater error with certain points on the independent variable (heteroscedasticity). REGRESSION ANALYSIS generally assumes homoscedasticity (homogeneity of variance).

Scheffé test a POST HOC TEST used after a researcher obtains a significant F RATIO in an ANALYSIS OF VARIANCE that has more than two levels (i.e., more than two conditions of an independent variable that are being examined for differences among their mean values). It allows for the testing of all possible contrasts (weighted comparisons of any number of means) while controlling the probability of a TYPE I ERROR for the set of contrasts at a prespecified level. The Scheffé test is considered to be one of the most stringent MULTIPLE COMPARISON TESTS because it is conservative in its identification of statistically significant mean differences between groups. [Henry Scheffé (1907–1977), U.S. mathematician]

schematization *n.* the act or process of reducing very rich information to a simpler scheme or outline, often with the help of graphical tools.

Schemper's measures a set of indices that measure the amount of EXPLAINED VARIANCE in COX REGRESSION ANALYSIS or other SURVIVAL MODELS in which the time to an event is predicted by a set of independent variables. [Michael Schemper, Austrian biostatistician]

Schoenfeld residual in a COX REGRESSION ANALYSIS of time to an event, the RESIDUAL for each individual case for each predictor in the model. These residuals are not defined for CENSORED DATA. Also called **score residual**. [David A. Schoenfeld, U.S. biostatistician]

science *n.* the systematic study of structure and behavior in the physical, natural, and social worlds, involving the generation, investigation, and testing of HYPOTHESES, the accumulation of data, and the formulation of general laws and theories. There are several major branches, including physical, biological, and social sciences. The subdisciplines of psychology are themselves divided among the different branches. For example, neuroscience and the study of the biological bases for behavior can be classed with the natural sciences, whereas social psychology and many aspects of clinical psychology can be seen as belonging to the social sciences. See SCIENTIFIC EXPLANATION; SCIENTIFIC METHOD.

scientific explanation an account of an event, behavior, or thought that is couched in terms of an established set of scientific principles, facts, and assumptions. Typical forms of explanation may be reductionistic, analyzing phenomena into components and describing how they combine to produce the phenomenon; ontogenic, relating the phenomenon to a universal set of developmental stages; empiricistic, describing a phenomenon in terms of the conditions that have been observed to produce it; or metaphoric or categorical, identifying a phenomenon as similar in some important respects to other phenomena already understood. Such an explanation stated systematically is generally known as a THEORY.

scientific hypothesis see HYPOTHESIS; RESEARCH HYPOTHESIS.

scientific method a set of procedures, guidelines, assumptions, and attitudes required for the organized and systematic collection, interpretation, and verification of data and the discovery of reproducible evidence, enabling laws and principles to be stated or modified. See also SCIENCE; SCIENTIFIC EXPLANATION.

scientific notation a compact way of reporting very large or very small numbers in which the reported number is represented by a value multiplied by 10 raised to either a positive or negative number. For example, $p = .0025$ would be expressed as 2.5×10^{-3}.

scientific theory see THEORY. See also SCIENCE; SCIENTIFIC EXPLANATION; SCIENTIFIC METHOD.

scientism *n.* an uncritical commitment to a particular view of science and scientific methods that leads its adherents to dismiss all other approaches as intellectually invalid. The term is mainly used by those who criticize the assumptions of Western science as arrogant or flawed, who maintain that scientific methods are inappropriate in certain fields or incapable of apprehending certain kinds of truth, or who reject the implication that all philosophical questions will one day reduce to scientific questions. **—scientistic** *adj.*

score 1. *n.* a quantitative value assigned

to test results or other measurable responses. **2.** *vb.* to assign scores to responses using some predetermined criteria.

score equating the process of ensuring that results from one version or administration of a test have the same distribution as those obtained from another version or administration, so that the interpretation of the results can be as fair as possible to all test takers. Also called **observed-score equating**.

score residual see SCHOENFELD RESIDUAL.

scorer reliability see INTERRATER RELIABILITY.

scoring *n.* the application of an answer key to a test or survey for the purpose of obtaining a value (SCORE) that reflects an individual's position on an underlying construct. The answer key would typically indicate individual scores for the different responses on each item (e.g., from 1 to 7), such that the values per item can then be summed or averaged to obtain a composite score. Some instruments may have multiple subscales yielding separate values.

screener *n.* see SCREENING TEST.

screening experiment a preliminary study in which a large number of factors are examined with the aim of filtering out those that show little association with the studied outcome. This allows researchers to narrow the field of potentially important factors before devoting resources to further study. See PILOT STUDY.

screening sample in survey methodology, a large group of individuals who are asked a preliminary set of questions in order to identify a much narrower subset of the population with an attribute of interest. For example, a nationwide survey of businesses might allow researchers to identify and then study in greater depth those companies that were started by

S

business owners over 60 years of age. See also SCREENING TEST.

screening test any testing procedure designed to separate out people or items with a given characteristic or property. Screening tests are typically used to distinguish people who have a disease, disorder, or predisease condition from those who do not; they may be used, for example, in primary health care settings at intake to identify people who are depressed and need further clinical attention. Screening tests are designed to be broadly sensitive, and subsequent highly specific or focused testing is often required to confirm the results. They are often designed to be brief to facilitate broad classifications. Also called **screener**; **screening study**.

scree plot in EXPLORATORY FACTOR ANALYSIS, a graphic that shows (in descending order) the EIGENVALUES of the COMMUNALITY-adjusted correlation matrix. Consider the generic example below.

Researchers examine the plot to identify a "break" in the curve between strong, dominant factors at the top and other smaller factors at the bottom: In this way they can determine which factors to retain in the analysis. The plot was named by Raymond B. Cattell, in analogy with the sloping heaps of differ-

ently sized rocks (screes) that form at the foot of a mountain. Also called **Cattell's scree test**.

SD symbol for STANDARD DEVIATION.

SDT abbreviation for SIGNAL DETECTION THEORY.

SE symbol for STANDARD ERROR.

seasonal adjustment in TIME-SERIES ANALYSIS, the removal of that component of the variance that is associated with a systematic pattern occurring at regular intervals over time. For example, if highway accidents occur about 5% more in the winter than in the summer months, winter figures would have to be **seasonally adjusted** to give a true increase that may be caused by other factors. See SEASONAL COMPONENT.

seasonal component in TIME-SERIES DATA, that element of the variance that can be accounted for by patterns reoccurring regularly over time (e.g., certain months of the year, days of the week, times of day). Usually the variance associated with this component can be described and modeled. For example, researchers studying substance use in college students might need to account for the days in the week (Thursday, Friday, and Saturday) that are associated with most use.

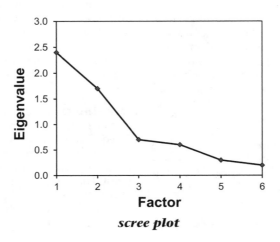

scree plot

secondary data information cited in a study that was not gathered directly by the current investigator but rather was obtained from an earlier study or source. The data may be archived or may be accessed through contact with the original researcher. When consulting or analyzing this information, the investigator should be sensitive to the original research questions and the conditions under which the observations were gathered. Compare PRIMARY DATA.

secondary sampling unit in MULTI-STAGE SAMPLING, a grouping of elements selected from a larger population (the PRIMARY SAMPLING UNIT). For example, in a study of college student attitudes, a researcher might first sample small, medium, and large colleges and institutions and then specify four geographic regions that need to be represented within those larger units. Compare TERTIARY SAMPLING UNIT.

second moment see MOMENT.

second-order factor a latent construct that emerges from a further FACTOR ANALYSIS (i.e., a **second-order factor analysis**) of the primary dimensions derived from correlations among a set of items or variables. The higher order dimensions so derived are held to generate the FIRST-ORDER FACTORS that in turn generate observed responses at the level of the individual item or scale.

second-order interaction in ANALYSIS OF VARIANCE or REGRESSION ANALYSIS, an effect in which three independent variables combine to have a nonadditive influence on a dependent variable. See HIGHER ORDER INTERACTION.

second-order Markov model see FIRST-ORDER MARKOV MODEL.

second-order partial correlation the correlation between two variables (e.g., x and y), with the effects of two additional variables (e.g., a and b) removed. It is often useful to see whether an association between two variables is reduced once other factors or variables that might also be related are removed or controlled for (i.e., are held constant for all participants in the data set). For example, a researcher might want to examine the extent of the association between conservatism and political behavior once the effects of age and education level are removed. Compare FIRST-ORDER PARTIAL CORRELATION. See also PARTIAL CORRELATION.

second-order stationarity the quality of a TIME SERIES such that the MEAN, VARIANCE, and PROBABILITY DISTRIBUTION remain constant over time and the AUTOCOVARIANCE depends only on the lag, or distance between pairs of time points. See STATIONARITY.

second quartile see QUARTILE.

sectional bar graph see COMPONENT BAR GRAPH.

SEE symbol for STANDARD ERROR OF ESTIMATE.

segmented bar graph see COMPONENT BAR GRAPH.

segmented regression see PIECEWISE REGRESSION.

segregation analysis a statistical method to examine the probability that offspring will have certain inherited attributes, traits, or phenotypes. For example, a clinical study of a disorder may examine families of the affected person seeking treatment.

selected group a SAMPLE explicitly chosen with respect to specific criteria related to the purpose of the research. For example, in a study of attitudes of older adults a researcher might choose a sample of citizens ages 65 and over from four geographic regions in the United States. Also called **selected sample**.

selection *n.* the process of choosing an item (e.g., an individual, an object, a measurement) from a larger universe of units for a purpose, such as study, testing, classifying, or working (hiring employees).

selection bias see SAMPLING BIAS.

selection invariance in choosing among applicants for, say, employment or admission to college, the property of a selection procedure such that it is equally efficient (i.e., makes a similar number of errors) for all subgroups of applicants (e.g., ethnic or income groups). Selection invariance is the empirically testable assumption that there is equal SENSITIVITY and equal SPECIFICITY across all groups. Compare MEASUREMENT INVARIANCE.

selection methods in regression in the GENERAL LINEAR MODEL, various sets of decision rules that help researchers determine which predictors or INDEPENDENT VARIABLES are related to the outcome or DEPENDENT VARIABLE. Some methods are theory driven and involve entering variables into the model in a preconceived order (i.e., HIERARCHICAL REGRESSION). Other approaches apply a rule (usually based on STATISTICAL SIGNIFICANCE) for the inclusion of a variable into the model or its exclusion from the model (i.e., STEPWISE REGRESSION). For example, FORWARD-SELECTION approaches begin with no variables in the model and proceed by including the variable (or variables) with the strongest association with the outcome until there is no increase in EXPLAINED VARIANCE by the addition of remaining variables. Conversely, BACKWARD-ELIMINATION approaches begin with all possible variables in the model and proceed by successive deletion of the variable (or variables) that contribute least to the prediction or explanation of the outcome.

selection model a two-stage REGRESSION ANALYSIS used to estimate PARAMETERS and STANDARD ERRORS in an unbiased way when scores for one aspect of the sample may be affected by a nonrandom selection process. An exam-

ple of data that could be appropriate for this method is women's salaries: Some aspects of the data could be modeled using standard regression methods, but the preponderance of zero salaries (reflecting a decision by some women not to work) would also need to be incorporated into the analysis. In such cases the two-stage regression method uses a model that relies on BIVARIATE NORMALITY to estimate the selection equation and an ordinary LEAST SQUARES REGRESSION to estimate the remainder. See also TRUNCATED DISTRIBUTION; ZERO-INFLATED POISSON REGRESSION.

selection ratio the proportion of all those eligible to be selected for a purpose who actually are selected. In personnel selection, for example, it is the number of applicants hired to perform a job divided by the total number of applicants. The lower the selection ratio, the more competitive the hiring situation will be and the more useful, all other factors being held constant, any given predictor will be in making selection decisions.

selection threat the THREAT TO VALIDITY arising from any form of SAMPLING BIAS (i.e., nonrandomly selecting units for a study).

selective dropout the nonrandom loss of participants from a study that occurs when an identified feature of the study design (e.g., topic studied, number of tasks) interacts with respondent characteristics (e.g., depression, education level). See ATTRITION.

selective observation a process in which an individual attends to behaviors, attitudes, and interpersonal settings that correspond to his or her current beliefs or self-interests. When listening to a speech by a presidential candidate, for example, a person with strong views on national spending for social programs may listen for aspects of the speech that address those specific beliefs. Compare UNSELECTIVE OBSERVATION. See also CONFIRMATION BIAS.

S

self-administered test a test in which the instructions are sufficiently self-evident not to require further clarification (e.g., by the researcher), enabling the respondent to complete it by him- or herself. Compare PROCTORED TEST.

self-fulfilling prophecy a belief or expectation that helps to bring about its own fulfillment, as, for example, when a person expects that nervousness will impair his or her performance during a job interview or when a teacher's preconceptions about a student's ability influence the pupil's achievement for better or worse. See PYGMALION EFFECT; UPWARD PYGMALION EFFECT. See also DEMAND CHARACTERISTICS; EXPERIMENTER EXPECTANCY EFFECT.

self-monitoring observation the study of one's own behaviors, attitudes, or emotions over time. In research studies and clinical interventions focused on weight loss, for example, participants are encouraged to keep track of their eating patterns, their feelings related to their eating, and triggers for not maintaining their diet. This enables a clinician or researcher to review periods when the participant is outside the clinical setting or laboratory. Compare ANALOGUE OBSERVATION; NATURALISTIC OBSERVATION.

self-rating scale any questionnaire, inventory, survey, or other instrument in which participants are asked to assess their own characteristics (e.g., attitudes, interests, abilities, performance). See also SELF-REPORT; SELF-REPORT INVENTORY.

self-report *n.* a statement or series of answers to questions that an individual provides about his or her state, feelings, thoughts, beliefs, past behaviors, and so forth. Self-report methods rely on the honesty and self-awareness of the participant and are used especially to measure behaviors or traits that cannot easily be directly observed by others.

self-report inventory a type of questionnaire on which participants indicate the degree to which the descriptors listed apply to them. Also called **self-report scale**.

self-selected groups design an experimental design in which participants choose their group or the condition to which they will be exposed. Because the assignment of participants to research conditions is nonrandom, causal inference from data gleaned in such experiments is questionable. See QUASI-EXPERIMENTAL DESIGN.

self-selection bias a type of BIAS that can arise when study participants choose their own treatment conditions, rather than being randomly assigned. In such cases it is impossible to state unambiguously that a study result is due to the treatment condition and not to the pre-existing characteristics of those individuals who chose to be in this condition. Also called **self-selection effect**. See also SAMPLING BIAS.

SEM 1. abbreviation for STRUCTURAL EQUATION MODELING. **2.** symbol for STANDARD ERROR OF MEASUREMENT. **3.** symbol for STANDARD ERROR OF THE MEAN.

semantic differential a type of scale that researchers use to assess a respondent's views on a certain topic (e.g., a stimulus such as a word or photograph, the quality of some experience). Participants are asked to rate the topic or stimulus on a scale that has pairs of opposites, such as *bad–good*, *unpleasant–pleasant*, or *competitive–cooperative*, as ANCHORS or reference points. For example, the bipolar opposites of *bad* to *good* may be scaled along 7 points and the respondent asked to position him- or herself on the 7-point continuum. Generally, the anchors are focused on three dimensions—evaluation, activity, and potency. Responses to items are then scaled in some way (theory, EXPLORATORY FACTOR ANALYSIS) so that items can be averaged or summed to arrive at a final index of attitudes. This procedure

S

is one of the most widely used methods of assessing attitudes and may be used in psychometric testing or in a wide array of settings, such as marketing and politics, to gauge public reactions to a product, issue, or personality.

semi-interquartile range see QUARTILE DEVIATION.

semi-Markov process a STOCHASTIC PROCESS with a finite set of states in which the "jump" (transition) from each state to the next is memoryless but the process as a whole is not.

semiparametric model a model that combines a PARAMETRIC component that has strict assumptions relating to the distribution of the variables and a NONPARAMETRIC component that does not rely on distribution parameters. An example of this flexible hybrid model is the Cox proportional hazards model (see COX REGRESSION ANALYSIS).

semipartial correlation see PART CORRELATION.

semistructured interview an interview format that involves the interviewer asking a specified set of questions in a particular order, while also allowing for open-ended responses by the interviewee and a more natural conversational style. In a study of health professionals, for example, interviewers might follow a guide that includes several open-ended questions in which the professionals are asked to reflect on their patients' use of their medications. By using prompts such as "Tell me more" and "Why is that?", the interviewers would encourage a full and rich response. This approach recognizes that a researcher may still learn valuable information even when the interviewee moves away a little from the topic at hand. See also STRUCTURED INTERVIEW.

sensitivity *n.* **1.** the capacity to detect and discriminate differences. In SIGNAL DETECTION THEORY, sensitivity is measured by the index D PRIME (d'). **2.** the

probability that a test gives a positive diagnosis given that the individual actually has the condition for which he or she is being tested. Compare SPECIFICITY.

sensitivity analysis an analysis that measures the extent to which the overall outcome of a model or system will be affected by potential changes to the input. This type of analysis is often used where the values of key variables are uncertain or subject to change: In financial planning, for example, it might be used to determine whether a potential change in mortgage rates, cash flow, local house prices, or all of these might alter the decision to purchase a new home. In research studies, sensitivity analysis enables researchers to understand the boundaries of their statistical models and design updated models that can account for the data at hand.

Sen's slope estimator see THEIL–SEN ESTIMATOR.

separate-variances t test a variant on the INDEPENDENT-SAMPLES T TEST used where the samples being compared have differing VARIANCES. It involves making a special adjustment to the DEGREES OF FREEDOM.

sequence effect in WITHIN-SUBJECTS DESIGNS, a difference in scores that emerges because of a particular arrangement of treatments; that is, the presentation of one level of the independent variable has an effect on responses to another level of that variable. A researcher can test for a sequence effect by administering the treatments in various different arrangements (e.g., the arrangement ABC vs. ACB, vs. BCA, etc.). The sequence effect is not to be confused with the ORDER EFFECT.

sequential analysis a class of statistical procedures in which decisions about sample size and the type of data to be collected are made or modified as the study proceeds, based on the cumulative findings to date. This approach contrasts with one in which the sample size is determined in advance and data are not analyzed until the entire sample is collected. A common form of sequential analysis is one in which data are collected until a desired outcome or level of precision is reached; also, some clinical trials require an approach that allows researchers to stop data collection if the treatment is clearly not working or if participants are being harmed in some way. Also called **sequential hypothesis testing**.

sequential design 1. a research design that allows for termination of the study at various points of data collection if the results do not conform to a desired pattern or if there is danger or cost to participants. Also called **sequential test design**. See SEQUENTIAL ANALYSIS. **2.** see COHORT-SEQUENTIAL DESIGN.

sequential probability ratio test (**SQRT**) a form of SEQUENTIAL ANALYSIS in which samples of units are drawn in sequence and tested to see if units meet some specified criterion. Inferential approaches allow researchers to determine the exact point at which the attribute of interest reaches a required level and no more sampling is needed. The SQRT was developed in QUALITY CONTROL studies but has been extended to many other areas.

sequential regression see HIERARCHICAL REGRESSION.

sequential sampling a method of NONPROBABILITY SAMPLING in which the researcher draws a group of units from the larger population, conducts a study within a specified time frame, analyzes the data, and then determines whether another sample is needed. The process can be repeated several times. The sequential approach enables a researcher to determine when enough data have been collected and to fine-tune his or her methodology over repeated studies.

sequential sum of squares see TYPE I SUM OF SQUARES.

sequential test design see SEQUENTIAL DESIGN.

sequential threshold method a form of CLUSTER ANALYSIS that involves identifying the center of the variables being analyzed (the CENTROID), grouping all variables within a certain distance of that point into a cluster, and then repeating the process several times for progressively larger distances. The method emphasizes some clusters over others by prioritizing those that are closest to the center point. See also K-MEANS CLUSTERING. Compare PARALLEL THRESHOLD METHOD.

serial correlation see AUTOCORRELATION.

serial dependence see AUTOCORRELATION.

set theory the branch of mathematics and logic that is concerned with the properties of sets (i.e., collections of entities that are themselves treated as entities).

setwise regression see ALL-POSSIBLE-SUBSETS REGRESSION.

sex-specific rate the RATIO of the number of instances of some variable (e.g., birth, mortality, incidence of disease) to the total population in some specified period, as reported separately for males and females. Because many diseases and life processes differ for men and women, it is more useful in most cases to obtain the sex-specific rate.

Shannon index a DIVERSITY INDEX widely used in ecological studies, where it provides important information about the rarity or abundance of species in a community. It is calculated by identifying the PROBABILITY of each species in the system, multiplying each probability value by the LOGARITHM (usually the natural logarithm), and taking the negative sum of those numbers. Also called **Shannon's information measure**.

S

Compare SIMPSON INDEX. [Claude **Shannon** (1916–2001), U.S. mathematician]

Shapiro–Wilk test an INFERENTIAL TEST to determine whether a random sample comes from a population with a NORMAL DISTRIBUTION. If the test statistic, W, is significant, then the NULL HYPOTHESIS that the distribution is normal should be rejected. Because so many of the most common statistical tests are designed for normally distributed data, Shapiro–Wilk is a useful test to identify those data sets that require a different approach. [Samuel S. **Shapiro** (1930–   ), U.S. statistician; Martin **Wilk** (1922–2013), Canadian statistician]

short-answer test a test that uses such item types as multiple choice, fill-in-the-blanks, true–false, and matching alternatives, as opposed to one requiring lengthy, open-ended answers. Short-answer tests can be quickly scored and are generally preferred when time and resources are limited.

shotgun approach an unsystematic way of conducting research in which the investigator examines a large number of variables, often without a theoretical basis, in the hopes that some relationships will be found. Any study effects that emerge are unlikely to be cross-validated and may not be stable.

shrinkage *n.* the situation in which the strength of a CORRELATION COEFFICIENT or REGRESSION EQUATION decreases when it is applied to a new data set. Such shrinkage occurs when the initial estimate of the correlation reflects unique characteristics of the initial sample, which are not replicated in subsequent samples.

shrinkage estimator a PENALTY FUNCTION used to reduce the value of a statistic: The estimator reflects some known aspect of the model, such as a high number of independent variables (i.e., its complexity). In MULTIPLE REGRESSION, the R^2 value is often the target of this reduction, yielding an ADJUSTED R^2 value.

shrinkage formula any of various formulae used to estimate the degree of SHRINKAGE that will occur when a statistic or REGRESSION EQUATION is applied to a new data set. The degree of shrinkage will generally depend on the size of the initial sample used to obtain the statistic and the number of predictors in the model.

shrunken R² see ADJUSTED R^2.

Šidák test see DUNN–ŠIDÁK PROCEDURE.

Siegel–Tukey test a NONPARAMETRIC TEST that evaluates any difference in VARIANCE across two independent samples to determine whether they represent two different populations. Data values for the two groups are first ordered in a single list from lowest to highest and then ranked in terms of alternate extremes, so that, for example, the highest and lowest values are both ranked 1, the next highest and next lowest 2, and so on. Finally, the ranked values in each group are summed. If final sums per group do not differ, there is no evidence that the dispersion differs across groups. The test has relatively low statistical POWER when data have a NORMAL DISTRIBUTION.

sigma *n.* **1.** (symbol: Σ) the sum of a list of values. **2.** (symbol: σ) see POPULATION STANDARD DEVIATION.

sigmoid curve an S-shaped curve that describes many processes in psychology, including learning and responding to test items. The curve starts low, has a period of acceleration, and then approaches an ASYMPTOTE. Often the curve is characterized by the LOGISTIC FUNCTION.

signal detection theory (SDT) a body of concepts and techniques from communication theory, electrical engineering, and DECISION THEORY that were applied during World War II to the detection of radar signals in noise. The same concepts were applied to auditory and visual psychophysics in the late 1950s and are now widely used in many areas of psychology. An important methodological contribution of SDT has been the refinement of psychophysical techniques to permit the separation of SENSITIVITY from criterial, decision-making factors. SDT has also provided a valuable theoretical framework for describing perceptual and other aspects of cognition and for quantitatively relating psychophysical phenomena to findings from sensory physiology. A key notion of SDT is that human performance in many tasks is limited by variability in the internal representation of stimuli due to internal or external noise. See D PRIME; RECEIVER-OPERATING CHARACTERISTIC CURVE.

signed-ranks test see WILCOXON SIGNED-RANKS TEST.

significance *n.* the extent to which something is meaningful or of consequence. In statistics and related fields, the term usually denotes STATISTICAL SIGNIFICANCE. See also CLINICAL SIGNIFICANCE; PRACTICAL SIGNIFICANCE; PSYCHOLOGICAL SIGNIFICANCE.

significance level (symbol: α) in SIGNIFICANCE TESTING, a fixed probability of rejecting the NULL HYPOTHESIS of no effect when it is in fact true. It is set at some value, usually .001, .01, or .05, depending on the consequences associated with making a TYPE I ERROR. When a particular effect is obtained experimentally, the PROBABILITY LEVEL (p) associated with this effect is compared to the significance level. If the p value is less than the α level, the null hypothesis is rejected. Small p values suggest that obtaining a statistic as extreme as the one obtained is rare and thus the null hypothesis is unlikely to be true. The smaller the α level, the more convincing is the rejection of the null hypothesis. Also called **alpha level**.

significance testing in HYPOTHESIS TESTING, a set of procedures used to determine whether the differences between two groups or models are statistically significant (i.e., unlikely to arise solely from chance). In its most common form, significance testing is used to decide whether the NULL HYPOTHESIS of no effect should be rejected. A comparison of the probability statistic obtained from the test to the chosen SIGNIFICANCE LEVEL determines whether an observed effect may be due to chance variance and hence whether the null hypothesis is or is not likely to be correct. This approach may also be used to differentiate between two models that differ in terms of the number of parameters specified in them (as in MULTIPLE REGRESSION analysis).

significant difference the situation in which a SIGNIFICANCE TESTING procedure indicates the statistical differences observed between two groups (e.g., a treatment group and a control group) are unlikely to reflect chance variation.

sign test a NONPARAMETRIC procedure for testing the hypothesis that two related samples have come from two different populations. The procedure is appropriate to ORDINAL DATA, that is, scores that have a meaningful order but lack equal distances between points. The scores within each sample are first ranked. For each pair of corresponding scores (e.g., a participant's score in the first set and its pair from the second set) the sign of the difference (either positive or negative) in the rankings is recorded. If the proportion of participants who obtain a positive sign is significantly different from those obtaining a negative sign, then the data are considered to come from different populations.

Simes modified Bonferroni procedure a method for providing strong control of the FAMILY-WISE ERROR RATE in multiple POST HOC COMPARISONS of means. It is a less conservative variant of the DUNN–BONFERRONI PROCEDURE. [R. J. **Simes**, Australian medical statistician; Carlo Emilio **Bonferroni** (1892–1960), Italian mathematician]

S

SIMEX abbreviation for SIMULATION AND EXTRAPOLATION PROCEDURE.

similarities test a test in which the participant must either state the likenesses between items or arrange items in categories according to their similarities. Some neuropsychological batteries include these assessments.

similarity coefficient any index that allows a researcher to assess the similarity of two or more samples. In EXPLORATORY FACTOR ANALYSIS, for example, such an index is used to compare FACTOR STRUCTURES across studies. See also CONGRUENCE COEFFICIENT. Compare DISSIMILARITY COEFFICIENT.

similarity matrix a matrix whose elements measure pairwise similarities of items—the greater the similarity of two items, the greater the value entered in the matrix at this point. A variety of METRICS can be used to measure similarity, including proximities and correlations. Compare DISSIMILARITY MATRIX.

simple analysis of variance an ANALYSIS OF VARIANCE involving one DEPENDENT VARIABLE and one INDEPENDENT VARIABLE that has two or more levels.

simple comparison a contrast between two means, usually in the context of multilevel analyses of data from a FACTORIAL DESIGN. For example, consider a researcher examining the influence of three different amounts of caffeine (0 mg, 50 mg, and 100 mg) on student test performance. His or her evaluation of the differences between 0 mg and 50 mg would represent one possible simple comparison. Compare COMPLEX COMPARISON.

simple correlation the linear association of one variable with one other variable, as quantified by a CORRELATION COEFFICIENT.

simple-effects analysis where an ANALYSIS OF VARIANCE or MULTIPLE REGRESSION analysis has identified an INTERACTION EFFECT among two independent variables, an examination of the effect of one variable at one level of the other variable. For example, if there were two levels of a factor, a_1 and a_2, and two levels of a second factor, b_1 and b_2, the comparison of a_1 vs. a_2 at b_1 would represent one simple-effects analysis; another would be a comparison of a_1 vs. a_2 at b_2. In this way a series of simple-effects analyses can be used to break down an interaction into its component parts.

simple event see ELEMENTARY EVENT.

simple hypothesis a hypothesis that specifies all the parameters of a population distribution. For example, consider a researcher who wants to examine the hypothesis that graduates from a particular institution have higher than average overall grade point averages if they have studied abroad. If the researcher specified the population mean and standard deviation of grades in the full population of students at that institution, this would be a simple hypothesis. Compare COMPOSITE HYPOTHESIS.

simple random sampling the most basic approach to drawing a RANDOM SAMPLE of cases, observations, or individuals from a population, in which the cases are selected individually using a fair process, such as the toss of a coin or a table of RANDOM DIGITS. Also called **independent random sampling**.

simple regression a type of REGRESSION ANALYSIS that has only one predictor or independent variable and one outcome or dependent variable. See also MULTIPLE REGRESSION.

simple structure in EXPLORATORY FACTOR ANALYSIS, a set of criteria for determining the adequacy of a FACTOR ROTATION solution. These criteria require that each factor show a pattern of high FACTOR LOADINGS on certain variables and near-zero loadings on others and that each variable load on only one factor. This minimizes the complexity of the factor solution, allows each variable to be most strongly identified with a specific factor, and increases interpretability.

simplex model a model stating that when *v* variables are ordered by time, severity, or some other attribute, their associations in a *v* × *v* CORRELATION MATRIX will have a particular structure. The variables will have stronger relations the closer they are to one another and weaker relations the further they are apart. Also called **simplex pattern**.

Simpson index a commonly used DIVERSITY INDEX that measures the probability that two randomly selected individuals from a sample will be from different groups or categories. It is calculated as the sum of the squared probabilities (*p*) of each group. For example, if a sample of students contained freshmen (*p* = .30), sophomores (*p* = .10), juniors (*p* = .40), and seniors (*p* = .20), the Simpson index would be .30 (.09 + .01 + .16 + .04), meaning that two randomly selected individuals have a 30% chance of being from different classes. Compare SHANNON INDEX. [Edward H. **Simpson** (1922–   ), British statistician]

Simpson's paradox a phenomenon that can occur when data from two or more studies are merged, giving results that differ from those of either study individually. For example, two studies, each showing a correlation of .00 between two variables, *x* and *y*, may show a strong positive correlation between variables *x* and *y* when the data are merged. This paradoxical effect could occur if the mean values of each variable in one study are both substantially different (e.g., lower) than their mean values in the second study. Simpson's paradox highlights the fact that important relations can be masked under certain conditions. Also called **Yule–Simpson effect**; **Yule's paradox**. [Edward H. **Simpson**; George Udny **Yule** (1871–1951), British statistician]

simulation *n.* **1.** an experimental method that is used to investigate the behavior and psychological processes and functioning of individuals in social and other environments, often those to which investigators cannot easily gain access, by reproducing those environments in a realistic way. For example, simulations are often used in personnel selection, where various exercises have been developed to tap job-related dimensions or behaviors; such exercises need to be pretested to ensure that the techniques are objective and relevant for the assessment of a candidate's potential for, say, a management position. **2.** the artificial creation of experimental data through the use of a mathematical or computer model. The purpose is usually to test the behavior of a statistic or model under controlled conditions.

simulation and extrapolation procedure (**SIMEX**) a method used to estimate a CUMULATIVE FREQUENCY DISTRIBUTION for an entire population in the presence of MEASUREMENT ERROR. It involves adding extra measurement error in known quantities, establishing a relationship between the bias thus induced and the variance of the error, and extrapolating back to the case in which there is no measurement error.

simulator *n.* a training device that simulates the conditions or environment of the actual operating situation or that resembles the actual equipment to be used, such as a flight simulator for pilots. The training allows for a safe, lower cost experience with the conditions under study but in most cases lacks realism.

simultaneous comparison method a strategy used in sensory discrimination research, such as color or sound discrimination, in which the stimuli for comparison are viewed simultaneously. This is in contrast to the **successive comparison method**, in which stimuli are successively presented.

simultaneous confidence intervals joint CONFIDENCE INTERVALS that are formed for estimating multiple parameters simultaneously from the same set of data. Various techniques have been developed for obtaining confidence intervals for a finite or infinite set of parametric functions, such that the probability of the parametric functions of the set being simultaneously covered by the corresponding intervals is a preassigned value.

simultaneous equations a set of equations containing two or more variables, the values for which are to be found simultaneously. Many MULTIVARIATE problems in psychology that express complex relationships among constructs require such an approach to obtain parameter estimates. See STRUCTURAL EQUATION MODELING.

simultaneous regression a type of REGRESSION ANALYSIS in which all predictors or INDEPENDENT VARIABLES are entered into the equation at the same time. Each independent variable's coefficient or WEIGHT is interpreted in the context of all of the other independent variables in the model at that time, some of which may be correlated. Also called **simultaneous multiple regression**. Compare HIERARCHICAL REGRESSION; STEPWISE REGRESSION.

single blind see BLIND.

single-case design an approach to the empirical study of a process that tracks a single unit (e.g., person, family, class, school, company) in depth over time. It is a WITHIN-SUBJECTS DESIGN with just one UNIT OF ANALYSIS. Such studies are useful for generating ideas for broader studies and for focusing on the micro-level concerns associated with the particular unit. However, data from these studies need to be evaluated carefully given the many potential threats to INTERNAL VALIDITY; there are also issues relating to the sampling of both the one unit and the process it undergoes.

Also called **N-of-1 design; N=1 design; single-participant design; single-subject (case) design**.

single-factor analysis of variance see ONE-WAY ANALYSIS OF VARIANCE.

single-factor design see ONE-WAY DESIGN.

single-factor multilevel design a research design involving one INDEPENDENT VARIABLE (e.g., treatment modality) with more than two conditions or levels (e.g., clinical therapy plus medication, medication only, clinical therapy only). See ONE-WAY ANALYSIS OF VARIANCE.

single-group validity the notion that some measures may be valid for certain groups (e.g., Caucasians) but not others (e.g., minority ethnic groups). See also DIFFERENTIAL VALIDITY.

single-linkage clustering in HIERARCHICAL CLUSTERING, a method in which the proximity between one group of x items (e.g., people, objects) and another group of y items is computed as the distance between the two closest elements of the groups. Also called **nearest neighbor**. Compare AVERAGE-LINKAGE CLUSTERING; COMPLETE-LINKAGE CLUSTERING.

single masked see BLIND.

single-participant design see SINGLE-CASE DESIGN.

single-sample runs test a statistical analysis to detect if there is a nonrandom pattern in a sequence of dichotomous outcomes. For example, suppose one flipped a coin multiple times and observed the outcomes of heads (H) and tails (T). Defining a run as a succession of identical outcomes that is followed and preceded by different outcomes, for the series of flips yielding HTTTTHTT there are two runs of length one for heads, a run of four tails, and a run of two tails. The single-sample runs test is concerned with whether there are fewer or more

S

runs than would be expected by chance. Also called **one-sample runs test**.

single-sample test any of various statistical procedures used to analyze data from one sample and determine whether the distribution of values differs significantly from a known or theoretical distribution for the larger POPULATION from which the sample is believed to derive. Also called **one-sample test**. Compare TWO-SAMPLE TEST.

single-sample test for the median any of a variety of statistical procedures used to determine whether the middle value (MEDIAN) for a given SAMPLE differs significantly from a hypothesized value of the median in the larger POPULATION. Also called **one-sample test for the median**.

single-sample t test a statistical procedure used to determine whether there is a significant difference between the observed mean of a SAMPLE and the known or hypothetical mean of the larger POPULATION from which the sample is randomly drawn. In the single-sample t test, one calculates a t value using (a) the mean of the sample (observed average); (b) the mean of the population (known or theoretically expected average); (c) the STANDARD DEVIATION of the sample; and (d) the total number of sample observations taken. The t value obtained is then compared to a standard table of values, arranged by sample size, to determine whether it exceeds the threshold of STATISTICAL SIGNIFICANCE. Also called **one-sample t test**.

single-sample z test a statistical procedure used to determine how closely the MEAN value on a variable for a given SAMPLE corresponds to the mean of the same variable for a larger POPULATION with a known mean. Also called **one-sample z test**. See also Z TEST.

single-subject case design see SINGLE-CASE DESIGN.

single-subject design see SINGLE-CASE DESIGN.

singly censored data a set of CENSORED DATA in which there is only one censoring point (i.e., one threshold beyond which values are unknown). Most often, single censoring results from the nonoccurrence of the event of interest during the study observation period: It is therefore particularly common in SURVIVAL ANALYSIS. See also DOUBLY CENSORED DATA.

singular matrix a SQUARE MATRIX whose inverse does not exist. The following is an example.

$$\begin{bmatrix} 7 & 7 \\ 1 & 1 \end{bmatrix}$$

A singular matrix has a zero DETERMINANT and cannot be used within FACTOR ANALYSIS and other multivariate procedures. Compare NONSINGULAR MATRIX.

singular value decomposition (SVD) a specialized form of MATRIX DECOMPOSITION, a process used in linear algebra to break a complex matrix down into its simpler component elements.

situational differences any distinction arising from environmental characteristics, as opposed to INDIVIDUAL DIFFERENCES. For example, in a study of men and women in social settings versus business settings, the amount of positive emotion displayed by the participants may be explained not only by gender (e.g., females tending to exhibit more positive emotion) but also by the situation (more positive emotions in a social setting regardless of whether the participant is male or female).

skewness *n.* the degree to which a set of scores, measurements, or other numbers are asymmetrically distributed around a central point (see example overleaf).

A normal FREQUENCY DISTRIBUTION of data is shaped like a bell, with equal values for each of its three indices of CENTRAL TENDENCY—the MEAN, the MEDIAN, and

S

skewness

the MODE. Approximately 68% of the scores lie within 1 STANDARD DEVIATION of the mean and approximately 95% of the scores lie within 2 standard deviations of the mean. When a distribution has a few extreme scores toward the high end relative to the low end (e.g., when a test is difficult and few test takers do well), it has a **positive skew** (or is **positively skewed**), such that the mean is greater than the mode. When a distribution has a few extreme scores toward the low end relative to the high end (e.g., when a test is easy and most test takers do well), it has a **negative skew** (or is **negatively skewed**).

skew-symmetrical matrix a SQUARE MATRIX whose TRANSPOSE is equal to its negation.

original			skew-symmetrical		
0	1	2	0	−1	−2
−1	0	1	1	0	−1
−2	−1	0	2	1	0

It is symmetrical about its MAIN DIAGONAL, with each element negated, as shown in the example above. See also SYMMETRICAL MATRIX.

slope *n.* the steepness or slant of a line on a graph, measured as the change of value on the Y-AXIS associated with a change of one unit of value on the X-AXIS. In a REGRESSION EQUATION, slope is represented by the variable b, with $+b$ indicating an upward slope to the line and $-b$ indicating a downward slope. See also ACCELERATION.

slope analysis see REGRESSION ANALYSIS.

smallest space analysis (SSA) a statistical technique for creating a visual representation of data, in which more closely correlated variables are grouped together. Smallest space refers to the fewest number of geometric dimensions (e.g., one dimension may be denoted by a line, two by a square, three by a cube) by which a body of data may be adequately represented. Similar in purpose to FACTOR ANALYSIS and PRINCIPAL COMPONENTS ANALYSIS, smallest space analysis may be applied to the assessment of objects, persons, attitudes, test constructs, and other similar variables.

small expected frequencies an issue that arises when the CHI-SQUARE TEST is used to study GOODNESS OF FIT for variables in a CONTINGENCY TABLE. The chi-square test is based on the assumption that the obtained frequencies within any cell of the table will be distributed normally around the theoretically EXPECTED FREQUENCY. If the expected frequency is small, however, the observed frequencies cannot be normally distributed and thus the chi-square test is inappropriate. Generally, the expected frequency for a cell should be five or more.

small-N design a research approach in which only a few participants are studied in order to focus attention upon the individual rather than the group as a whole. Typically, such designs are conducted over a longer period of time, to allow for the behavior of interest to stabilize, and employ QUALITATIVE ANALY-SES as opposed to INFERENTIAL STAT-ISTICS in analyzing results. Although small-*N* designs have several advantages—including reduced cost since fewer participants are involved, better control of EXTRANEOUS VARIABLES, and more comprehensive records of participant performance—a significant disadvantage is that EXTERNAL VALIDITY may be lower if participants are not representative of the larger population from which they are drawn. Compare LARGE-N DESIGN.

small-sample theory the understanding and application of appropriate methods for analyzing data from groups (samples) comprising 30 or fewer individuals or cases. Although there is some SAMPLING ERROR in any group under study, the theory accounts for the fact that this error tends to be greatest in smaller samples.

Smirnov test see KOLMOGOROV–SMIRNOV GOODNESS-OF-FIT TEST; KOLMOGOROV–SMIRNOV TWO-SAMPLE TEST.

smoothed curve a graphical representation of the relationship between two variables that has been adjusted to eliminate erratic or sudden changes in SLOPE, so that its fundamental shape and direction will be evident. Also called **smooth curve**.

smoothing *n.* a collection of techniques used to reduce the irregularities (RANDOM VARIATION) in a data set or in a plot (curve) of that data, particularly in TIME-SERIES analyses, so as to more clearly see the underlying trends. The use of a MOVING AVERAGE is one example of smoothing. See SMOOTHED CURVE.

Snedecor's F distribution see F DISTRIBUTION. [George W. **Snedecor** (1881–1974), U.S. statistician]

snowball sampling a technique to identify and recruit candidates for a study in which existing participants recommend additional potential participants, who themselves are observed and asked to nominate others, and so on until a sufficient number of participants is obtained. Researchers generally use snowball sampling if the population of interest is hard to locate, rare (e.g., people who have an infrequent condition or disease), or otherwise limited. Although this nonprobability strategy of chain referral is simple and cost efficient, there is the potential for SAMPLING BIAS in that initial participants may tend to nominate people they know well and thus are likely to share the same traits and characteristics.

social desirability the bias or tendency of individuals to present themselves in a manner that will be viewed favorably by others. In an experiment, for example, it manifests as the **social desirability response set**, which is the tendency of participants to give answers that are in accordance with social norms or the perceived desires of the researcher rather than genuinely representative of their views. This is a CONFOUND to be controlled for in certain research, as it often reduces the validity of interviews, questionnaires, and other self-reports.

social indicator any feature of a society that can be measured over time and is presumed to reveal some underlying aspect of social reality and quality of life. For example, the retail price index is used as a measure of inflation, which in turn is taken as a key indicator of economic performance. Other commonly used indicators are derived from unemployment figures, per capita income, poverty levels, labor conditions, housing costs, mental health, general health and mortality data, nutrition information, pollution levels, crime rates, education levels, opportunities for leisure and recreation, and the status of the elderly. Researchers and policymakers frequently use social indicators to assess the extent to which a society is "progressing" as well as make predictions about its future.

socially sensitive research research

on topics likely to evoke controversy in the community or strong emotional responses from participants. Such topics would include those that have ethical implications affecting subgroups or cultures within society (e.g., ethnic minorities) or that involve potential costs and consequent problems for the participants, investigators, or sponsors. For example, a study that examines the relative merits of day care for infants versus full-time care by the mother can have broad social implications and thus be considered socially sensitive.

social science 1. any of a number of disciplines concerned with the common elements and collective dimensions of human experience, studied from a scientific and research perspective. These disciplines traditionally have included anthropology, economics, geography, history, linguistics, political science, psychiatry, psychology, and sociology, as well as associated areas of mathematics and biology. Additional fields include related psychological studies in business administration, journalism, law, medicine, public health, and social work. The focus of analysis ranges from the individual to institutions and entire social systems. The general goal is to understand social interactions and to propose solutions to social problems. **2.** these disciplines collectively.

sociometry *n.* a field of research in which various techniques or **sociometric measures** are used to analyze the patterns of intermember relations within groups and to summarize these findings in mathematical and graphic form. In most cases researchers ask the group members one or more questions about their fellow members, such as "Whom do you most like in this group?", "Whom in the group would you like to work with the most?", or "Whom do you like the least?". These choices can then be summarized in a **sociogram**, in which each member is represented by a numbered or lettered symbol and the various choices are identified by lines between them

with arrows indicating the direction of relationships. In most cases the diagram is organized into a meaningful pattern by placing those individuals who are most frequently chosen (**stars**) in the center of the diagram and the **isolates** about the periphery. The method also yields various indices of group structure and group cohesion, including choice status (the number of times a person is chosen by the other group members), rejection status (the number of times a person is rejected by others), the relative number of mutual pairs in a group, and so on. —**sociometric** *adj.*

soft data subjective data that lack the rigor of HARD DATA. Soft data usually result from informal collection methods, such as those lacking RANDOM ASSIGNMENT to conditions, those lacking formal RANDOM SAMPLING, or those based only on anecdote. Soft data may be descriptive or qualitative and are used to help interpret hard data.

Solomon four-group design an experimental design that assesses the effect of having been pretested on the magnitude of the treatment effect. Participants are randomly divided into four groups and each group experiences a different combination of experimental manipulations: The first group (A) receives the pretest, the treatment, and the posttest; the second group (B) receives only the treatment and posttest; the third group (C) receives the pretest, no treatment, and a posttest; and the fourth group (D) receives only a posttest. The major advantages of the Solomon four-group design over a traditional two-group PRE-TEST–POSTTEST DESIGN are that it reduces the influence of CONFOUNDS and that it can pinpoint whether changes in the dependent variable are due to some INTERACTION EFFECT between the pretest and the treatment. A major disadvantage, however, is that its analysis and statistics are complex. [Richard L. **Solomon** (1919–1992), U.S. psychologist]

Somers's d (Somers's d_{BA}) a NONPARA-

METRIC TEST of whether there is an association between two ORDINAL VARIABLES when the data are presented in a CONTINGENCY TABLE. The focus of the analysis is on the number of agreements and disagreements in the set of data. For example, suppose a researcher interested in the relationship between age and attitudes conducted a study in which the former were measured as ranges (e.g., 20–25 years, 26–30 years, etc.) and the latter were measured as good, neutral, or poor. Somers's *d*, which ranges from –1 to +1, could then be used to obtain a measure of association between the two. Also called **Somers's delta**. [Robert H. Somers]

sorting test a format for assessing the ability to conceptualize, often used in adult neuropsychological assessments or in determining a child's level of cognitive development. The participant is asked to arrange an assortment of common objects by category. A common example is the **Wisconsin Card Sorting Test**, in which the participant is asked to match a set of cards depicting shapes of differing color, quantity, and design; he or she is given no matching rules but is told whether a particular match is correct or incorrect. During the course of the test the matching rules are changed and the time taken for the participant to learn the new rules and the mistakes made during this learning process are analyzed to arrive at a score.

soundproof room a room designed to balance the absorption of sound with its controlled reflection. Mostly used for the study of acoustic issues, soundproof rooms eliminate unwanted outside noise and ensure sounds are sufficiently confined to and evenly distributed throughout the space within.

space–time autoregressive integrated moving-average model (STARIMA model) an extension of the AUTOREGRESSIVE INTEGRATED MOVING-AVERAGE MODEL to STATIONARY PROCESSES. The model is used in TIME-SERIES ANALYSIS, where the purpose is to identify the nature of the phenomenon represented by a sequence of measurements, typically taken at successive points in time under the assumption that the sequence is not random, and to forecast or predict future values. In a STARIMA model, the value of each observation in the series depends, at least in part, on the value of one or more of the immediately preceding observations, and each observation in the series is predicted by a linear combination of prior observations as well as RANDOM ERROR. When a variable, such as the number of unemployed, is plotted over time there are likely to be considerable seasonal or cyclical components to the variation that make it difficult to see the underlying pattern. These components can be eliminated by taking a suitable moving average, which reduces random fluctuations and makes long-term trends clearer.

space–time autoregressive moving-average model (STARMA model) an extension of the AUTOREGRESSIVE MOVING-AVERAGE MODEL to include additional spatial and temporal dimensions in the exploration and forecasting of relationships in a TIME SERIES. For example, a researcher could apply a STARMA model to predict traffic flow at several adjacent intersections in a neighborhood using data gathered throughout a particular year. There are likely to be multiple associations among multiple variables at multiple points in time that must be accounted for in such a situation, which can best be understood using a STARMA model.

spatial autocorrelation a measurement of a variable's association with itself throughout space. Although statistical approaches often assume that measured outcomes are independent of each other, this may not be true for observations made at different locations. For example, measurements made at nearby locations may be closer in value than measurements made at locations farther apart. Spatial autocorrelation thus provides an index of the similarity of objects within an area, the level of interdependence between the variables, and the nature and strength of that interdependence. Suppose one wanted to study the relationships among cultures. In this research the distance between societies could be either spatial (based on physical distance) or cultural (based on language). Thus, spatial autocorrelation models would examine the relationship among values of a single variable that arises from the geographic arrangement of the areas in which these values occur. Spatial autocorrelation may be positive or negative. Positive spatial autocorrelation occurs when similar values occur near one another, whereas negative spatial autocorrelation occurs when dissimilar values occur near one another. When no statistically significant spatial autocorrelation exists, the pattern of spatial distribution is considered random. See also AUTOCORRELATION.

spatial data any observations or measurements with a direct or indirect reference to a specific location or geographical area.

spatial experiment a research design that studies variables with respect to their physical distance or separation from one another. For example, a spatial experiment might examine the rates of maltreatment referrals for children of a specific age across different residential areas.

Spearman–Brown prophecy formula the mathematical formulation of a basic tenet of CLASSICAL TEST THEORY concerning the length (number of items) of a test and its influence on reliability, whereby increasing the number of items with similar content results in increased reliability for the test; similarly, decreasing the number of items leads to decreased reliability. The formula allows a researcher to estimate the gains or losses in reliability that would occur with changes in test size. Also called **Spearman–Brown prediction formula**. [Charles Edward **Spearman** (1863–1945), British psychologist and psychometrician; W. **Brown**, 20th-century British psychologist]

Spearman correlation coefficient (symbol: r_s; ρ) a nonparametric measure of statistical dependence between two variables that were measured on an ORDINAL SCALE; that is, the individual observations (cases) can be ranked into two ordered series. The Spearman correlation coefficient assesses how well the relationship between the variables can be described using a MONOTONIC function. It ranges in value from +1 to –1. Also called **Spearman's rank correlation coefficient**; **Spearman's rho**. [Charles Spearman]

Spearman footrule a simpler version of the SPEARMAN CORRELATION COEFFICIENT: a procedure for measuring rank association that assesses the absolute difference (D) between pairs of values. For example, one supervisor ranks a set of employees as 1, 2, 3, and 4, respectively, on overall performance while another supervisor rates the same set of employees as 2, 3, 1, and 4, respectively. The absolute sum of the differences for the sets of ranks is obtained by subtracting one rank in a pair from the other, disregarding the sign of the difference, and adding the values together. Thus, $[1 - 2 = 1; 2 - 3 = 1; 3 - 1 = 2; 4 - 4 = 0]$, yielding a $D = 4$. The lower the absolute value of D, the closer the relationship between the two sets of data. [Charles **Spearman**]

Spearman's rho see SPEARMAN CORRELATION COEFFICIENT.

speciesism *n.* discriminatory, prejudicial, or exploitative practices against nonhuman animals, often on the basis of an assumption of human superiority. See also ANIMAL RIGHTS. —**speciesist** *n., adj.*

specification error in REGRESSION ANALYSIS, a type of error that may occur when converting a theory into a regression model, which involves selecting an appropriate functional form for the model and choosing which variables to include. In specification error, an INDEPENDENT VARIABLE becomes correlated with the ERROR TERM through use of an incorrect functional form; through omitting a variable from the model that has a relationship with both the DEPENDENT VARIABLE and one or more of the independent variables; or through including an irrelevant variable in the model. If an estimated model is misspecified, it will be biased and inconsistent.

specification search a strategy used to find a statistical model that correctly describes a population of interest. The researcher first constructs artificial data for which there is a known correct model, then fits a misspecified model to the data (see SPECIFICATION ERROR), and finally adjusts this as necessary until the "search" yields the combination of variables that best explains the phenomenon under study. The likelihood of success in a specification search is optimal when (a) the investigator's initial model corresponds closely to the true model, (b) the search is allowed to continue even when a statistically plausible model is obtained, (c) the investigator can place valid restrictions on permissible modifications, and (d) a large sample is used.

specific factor in FACTOR ANALYSIS, a LATENT VARIABLE that is significant only to a single MANIFEST VARIABLE. In contrast, a **common factor** pertains to multiple manifest variables.

specificity *n.* **1.** the quality of being unique, of a particular kind, or limited to a single phenomenon. For example, a stimulus that elicits a particular response is said to have specificity. **2.** the probability that a test yields a negative diagnosis given that the individual does not have the condition for which he or she is being tested. Compare SENSITIVITY.

specific variance in FACTOR ANALYSIS, the systematic variability that is specific to a particular variable and not shared with other variables. Specific variance contrasts with COMMUNALITY, the variability that a single variable shares with one or more of the other variables in the analysis, and RANDOM ERROR, the unsystematic variability specific to a particular variable.

specimen record a data collection strategy in which a trained observer documents the activities of a particular individual within a particular context for a specific period. For example, a specimen record of a child's gross motor skills might involve creating a detailed description of the child's behavior while watching him or her play on recreational equipment for 15 minutes.

spectral analysis in TIME-SERIES ANALYSIS, a strategy used to decompose a complex cycle of data into a small number of underlying sine and cosine functions of different frequencies. For example, if the cycle to be studied is one year—12 monthly collections of data on the same variable—spectral analysis examines the fluctuations that occur over that 12-month period and then determines which appear to be particularly strong or important. Also called **spectrum analysis**.

spectral density function a mathematical description of how the periodic variation in a TIME SERIES may be accounted for by cyclic components at different frequencies. The procedure for estimating the spectral densities at various frequencies is called SPECTRAL ANALYSIS.

spherical data observations or measurements that involve direction, distance, or both in three dimensions. Spherical data are most common in the earth sciences but are also analyzed in neuroscience. For example, investigations of how the nervous system processes auditory information to create spatial rep-

S

resentations may involve quantifying the direction and distance from an observer of a sound presented to him or her.

sphericity *n.* an assumption, encountered in a WITHIN-SUBJECTS ANALYSIS OF VARIANCE of data obtained from the same individuals on multiple occasions, requiring the variations among each individual's set of scores to be equal or the correlations among all time points to be constant. Results from analyses of variance that violate sphericity require adjustments, such as the **Greenhouse–Geisser correction**, the **Huynh–Feldt correction**, or the **lower-bound correction**, to compensate for an increased propensity of the researcher to draw invalid conclusions by making a TYPE II ERROR. See WITHIN-SUBJECTS DESIGN.

sphericity test see BARTLETT TEST OF SPHERICITY; MAUCHLY'S SPHERICITY TEST.

spike *n.* in a TIME-SERIES ANALYSIS, a point in time at which there is a sharp increase followed by a rapid decrease in measurements of the DEPENDENT VARIABLE.

Spjøtvoll–Stoline test in an ANALYSIS OF VARIANCE, a statistical examination of POST HOC COMPARISONS among means for groups that contain an unequal number of cases (observations). The NULL HYPOTHESIS is that there are no pairwise comparisons that are significantly different; the ALTERNATIVE HYPOTHESIS is that at least one pair of means is different. The Spjøtvoll–Stoline test is an extension of TUKEY'S HONESTLY SIGNIFICANT DIFFERENCE TEST, which is restricted to cases in which each sample mean is based on an equal number of observations. [Emil **Spjøtvoll** (1940–2002), Norwegian mathematician and statistician; Michael R. **Stoline**, U.S. statistician]

spline function a smoothed mathematical representation of a disjointed or disaggregated relationship between an INDEPENDENT VARIABLE (x) and a DEPENDENT VARIABLE (y), in which values of y vary sharply for different intervals of x. Each range of x thus has a different SLOPE, and spline functions are formed by joining piecewise polynomials at fixed points called **knots**. An essential feature of a spline function is that it is continuous; in other words, it has no breaks on the boundaries between two adjacent intervals. Spline functions (or **splines** for short) are useful for fitting data that have random components and are widely used for interpolation and approximation of data sampled at a discrete set of points (e.g., for TIME-SERIES interpolation).

spline regression a nonparametric technique in which a SPLINE FUNCTION is used to model an x variable that has CATEGORICAL DATA.

split-ballot technique a procedure in which a sample is randomly divided into halves and each half receives a slightly different version of a questionnaire or survey designed to measure the same construct. The technique can be used to determine whether different versions of the survey have different outcomes (e.g., whether position of a particular item on the questionnaire makes a difference in the outcomes obtained from the two administrations). Also called **split-half method**; **split-sample test**.

split-half reliability a measure of the internal consistency of surveys, psychological tests, questionnaires, and other instruments or techniques that assess participant responses on particular constructs. Split-half reliability is determined by dividing the total set of items (e.g., questions) relating to a construct of interest into halves (e.g., odd-numbered and even-numbered questions) and comparing the results obtained from the two subsets of items thus created. The closer the correlation between results from the two versions, the greater the INTERNAL CONSISTENCY of the survey or instrument. The RELIABILITY of the total survey can be determined by applying the SPEARMAN–BROWN PROPHECY FORMULA.

split-plot design a variation of a full FACTORIAL DESIGN in which one of the INDEPENDENT VARIABLES is held constant while all other combinations of conditions are examined, often using different sample sizes or different randomization schemes. For example, consider a researcher examining the influence on crop yield of four different types of corn seed, three different types of fertilizer, and two different types of planting technique. If each planting technique requires its own specialized set of expensive equipment, such that it is not financially feasible to provide all of the equipment to all participants, the investigator instead could have half of the participating farmers plant all of the seed types in a random order using one technique and the other half plant all of the seed types in a different random order using the second technique. Indeed, split-plot designs are particularly common in agricultural and industrial contexts, in which certain conditions may be difficult to manipulate or change for experimental purposes. Data from such designs may be examined with a **split-plot analysis of variance**.

split-sample test see SPLIT-BALLOT TECHNIQUE.

spread *n.* see DISPERSION.

spurious correlation a situation in which variables are associated through their common relationship with one or more other variables but not through a causal mechanism. For example, assume that the data show a relationship between the total amount of loss in a fire and the number of firefighters at the scene. One cannot infer from this that calling fewer firemen would lower loss: There is a third variable—the initial size of the fire—that influences both the amount of loss and the number of firefighters present. The main problem with spurious correlations is that one typically does not know what other variable is influencing the obtained relationship. If, however, one has some insight into possible other variables, PARTIAL CORRELATIONS can be used to control for their influence. See THIRD-VARIABLE PROBLEM.

spurious precision a value or outcome stated with more precision than can be justified, considering the procedures used to obtain it. The statistics cited in advertising or journalism often show spurious precision.

SQRT abbreviation for SEQUENTIAL PROBABILITY RATIO TEST.

squared correlation coefficient see COEFFICIENT OF DETERMINATION.

squared multiple correlation coefficient see COEFFICIENT OF MULTIPLE DETERMINATION.

square matrix a MATRIX that has the same number of rows as columns. The number of rows and columns determines the order of the matrix (e.g., 3 rows by 3 columns is an order of 3), and any two square matrices of the same order can be added and multiplied. Square matrices are used in REGRESSION ANALYSIS, FACTOR ANALYSIS, and other multivariate analytical techniques.

square-root transformation a procedure for converting a set of data in which each value, x_i, is replaced by its **square root**, another number that when multiplied by itself yields x_i. Square-root TRANSFORMATIONS often result in HOMOGENEITY OF VARIANCE for the different levels of the INDEPENDENT VARIABLE (x) under consideration. As with transformations generally, the goal is to obtain data that more closely meet the assumptions of a statistical procedure that is to be applied.

SS symbol for SUM OF SQUARES.

SSA abbreviation for SMALLEST SPACE ANALYSIS.

SSCP symbol for SUM OF SQUARES OF CROSS-PRODUCTS.

SSE symbol for sum of squared errors. See ERROR SUM OF SQUARES.

S-shaped curve see OGIVE.

SS$_{regression}$ symbol for REGRESSION SUM OF SQUARES.

stability *n.* see STATISTICAL STABILITY.

stability coefficient an index of RELIABILITY determined via a test–retest method, in which the same test is administered to the same respondents at two different points in time. For example, the stability coefficient of a psychological test may be estimated by determining the degree of similarity between participants' scores across time: The more the two scores for each participant are alike, the higher the correlation between the two administrations and the greater the stability coefficient of the test. A critical issue in using this strategy is the interval of time between the two administrations. It should not be so long that participants are likely to change on the construct being assessed nor so short that memory of responses on the initial administration influences responses on the second administration (see PRACTICE EFFECT). Also called **coefficient of stability**.

stable rate 1. a constant change in the value of a DEPENDENT VARIABLE as the value of an INDEPENDENT VARIABLE changes. **2.** in a REGRESSION ANALYSIS, the relative consistency of a BETA COEFFICIENT over time and across populations, conditions, and so forth.

stacked bar graph see COMPONENT BAR GRAPH.

stage sampling see MULTISTAGE SAMPLING.

staggered entry design in SURVIVAL ANALYSIS, a research design that allows for the entry or exit of participants at any time throughout the course of the study. In a typical survival analysis design, all samples have a common origin—they start at the same time—and there is a single, terminal event (typically, death). By contrast, in a staggered entry design each participant begins the study at a particular time zero and has an ending point corresponding to the length of time that he or she was part of the study (i.e., until he or she experienced the event of interest or otherwise ceased participation). For example, consider a study of a new treatment method implemented at a specific hospital: There will be patients who survived over the entire study period, others who survived but entered the hospital after the study had already begun, and still others who moved away and lost contact with the researcher. Although the latter two groups of patients contributed only partial, incomplete information to the research (see CENSORED OBSERVATION), their data nonetheless should not be excluded from the study since those individuals are "survivors" and therefore reflect on the success of the new treatment method. Staggered entry allows for increased precision in estimating the SURVIVAL FUNCTION.

Stahel–Donoho robust multivariate estimator in FACTOR ANALYSIS, DISCRIMINANT ANALYSIS, and other statistical techniques for examining multivariate data, a strategy for handling OUTLIERS that weights each observation according to its overall "outlyingness." The Stahel–Donoho estimator is necessary since the most common methods for identifying averages and variances, the sample MEAN and the sample COVARIANCE MATRIX, are sensitive to outliers and thus tenable only when the data follow a NORMAL DISTRIBUTION. [Werner **Stahel**, Swiss statistician; David **Donoho** (1957–), U.S. statistician]

stalactite plot a graphical display of the pattern of extreme values found in a set of numbers during MINIMUM VOLUME ELLIPSOID or other search procedures specifically used to detect masked

Observation Number

```
                    1                   2                   3                   4
  1 2 3 4 5 6 7 8 9 0 1 2 3 4 5 6 7 8 9 0 1 2 3 4 5 6 7 8 9 0 1 2 3 4 5 6 7 8 9 0
 6  X X       X                       X       X               X X   X X X X X X X
 8  X X       X                       X       X               X X   X X X X X X X
10  X X X     X                       X       X               X X   X X X X X X X
12  X   X   X X                       X       X         X     X X   X X X X   X X
14  X X X   X X                       X       X         X     X X   X X X X X X X
16  X X X   X X           X X         X       X         X X     X X X X X X X
18  X X X   X X           X X         X       X         X X       X X X X X X X
20  X X X   X X           X X         X       X         X X     X X X X X X
22  X X X   X                         X               X X     X X X X X X
24  X X X   X X           X X         X       X         X X     X X X X X X
26  X X X   X X           X X         X       X         X X     X X X X
28  X X X   X X           X X         X               X X     X X X X
30  X X X   X X           X X         X         X     X X     X X X
32    X X   X                                   X       X     X   X
34      X   X X           X X         X         X       X     X X X
36    X     X                                   X       X       X X
38      X     X           X X         X               X     X X X X
40    X   X               X                     X       X   X X X
42    X X                           X                         X X
44      X   X             X           X       X                   X
46      X   X                         X
48              X                     X
50                                    X
```

stalactite plot

OUTLIERS in MULTIVARIATE data. In the hypothetical example above, xs are used to denote those observations that can be considered outliers within each subset size, with observation 23 emerging as the most extreme outlier.

standard Cox regression model see COX REGRESSION ANALYSIS.

standard deviation (symbol: *SD*) a measure of the variability of a set of scores or values, indicating how narrowly or broadly they deviate from the MEAN. A small *SD* indicates data points that cluster around the mean, whereas a large standard deviation indicates data points that are dispersed across many different values. It is expressed in the same units as the original values in the sample or population, so that the *SD* of a series of measurements of weight would be in pounds, for example. The *SD* is equal to the square root of the VARIANCE. If a population of *n* values has a mean μ, then the *SD* is

$$\sqrt{[\Sigma(X_i - \mu)^2/n]}$$

For a sample of the population, with a mean value $\bar{X}$, the **sample standard deviation** is taken to be

$$\sqrt{[\Sigma(X_i - \bar{X})^2/(n - 1)]},$$

that is, the divisor is $(n - 1)$ rather than n. See also ROOT MEAN SQUARE.

standard error (symbol: *SE*) in statistical analysis, a quantification of the inherent inaccuracy of a calculated POPULATION value that is attributable to random fluctuations within the SAMPLE data upon which it is based. Some degree of imprecision is present whenever a value for a large group (the population) is estimated by studying a subset of that group (the sample), and the standard error provides a numerical description of that variability. It is expressed as the STANDARD DEVIATION of the SAMPLING DISTRIBUTION. For example, the SAMPLE MEAN is the usual estimator of a POPULATION MEAN yet different samples drawn from that same population nonetheless will yield different values for the mean. Thus, to determine how much sample variability exists the STANDARD ERROR OF THE MEAN may be obtained by taking the standard deviation of all of the means over all of the samples taken. Standard error is expressed in units given in the same scale of measurement that was used for the sample data (e.g., for a set of means that are given in weight the standard error unit is also a weight). The more samples involved in determining the standard error, the smaller its value; the smaller the standard error, the more reliable the calculated population value.

standard error of estimate (symbol: *SEE*) for a relationship between two variables (*x* and *y*) given by a REGRESSION EQUATION, an index of how closely the predicted value of *y* for a specific value of *x* matches its actual value. If y' is an estimated value from a regression line and *y* is the actual value, then the standard error of estimate is

$$\sqrt{[\Sigma(y - y')^2/n]},$$

where *n* is the number of points. The smaller the standard error of estimate, the better the degree of relationship (CORRELATION) between *x* and *y* and the more confident one can be in the accuracy of the estimated (predicted) *y* value. It is one of several types of STANDARD ERROR that may be calculated. Also called **standard error of prediction**.

standard error of measurement (symbol: *SEM*) an index of the RELIABILITY of an assessment instrument, representing the variation of an individual's scores across multiple administrations of the same test. A perfectly reliable instrument will have a standard error of measurement of 0, which means that an individual will have the same score upon repeated testings with the instrument. Otherwise, the standard error of measurement will be between 0 and 1 and the individual will have different scores on different occasions; the larger the error the greater the variation across administrations. In essence, the standard error of measurement provides an indication of how confident one may be that an individual's obtained score on

any given measurement opportunity represents his or her TRUE SCORE. It is one of several types of STANDARD ERROR that may be calculated.

standard error of prediction see STANDARD ERROR OF ESTIMATE.

standard error of the difference an index of the degree to which statistical distinctions between two SAMPLES from a larger POPULATION reflect real disparities between those samples. For example, suppose a researcher analyzes two samples, A and B, randomly drawn from the same normally distributed source population and obtains a different MEAN for Sample A than for Sample B. The standard error of the difference between the two means is used to determine whether those sample values truly are different or instead reflect random, irrelevant data fluctuations. It is equal to

$$\sqrt{[(SD^2/n_a) + (SD^2/n_b)]},$$

where SD^2 = the population variance (i.e., the square of the STANDARD DEVIATION for the source population); n_a = the size of Sample A; and n_b = the size of Sample B. It is one of several types of STANDARD ERROR that may be calculated.

standard error of the difference between two proportions an index of the degree to which percentage distinctions between two SAMPLES from a larger POPULATION reflect real disparities between those samples. For example, suppose a researcher is interested in whether the percentage of college graduates in Sample A (males) differs from the percentage of college graduates in Sample B (females). Both samples are randomly drawn from the same normally distributed source population of all college graduates from a particular university. The difference between the percentages of the two samples, A and B, is given by

$$SE = \sqrt{\{[p * (1 - p) * [(1/n_1) + (1/n^2)]\}}$$

where *p* is the pooled sample proportion

of college graduates. See also STANDARD ERROR OF THE DIFFERENCE.

standard error of the mean (symbol: *SEM*; σ_M) a statistic that indicates how much the average value (MEAN) for a particular SAMPLE is likely to differ from the average value for the larger POPULATION from which it is drawn. It is equal to $\sigma/\sqrt{n}$, where σ is the standard deviation of the original distribution and n is the sample size. Less commonly called **standard error of the population mean**.

standard gamma distribution see GAMMA DISTRIBUTION.

standardization *n.* **1.** the process of establishing NORMS for a test. **2.** the use of uniform procedures in test administration to ensure that all participants take the same test under the same conditions and are scored by the same criteria, which in turn ensures that results can be compared to each other. **3.** the transformation of data into a distribution of STANDARDIZED SCORES, often one having a mean of 0 and a STANDARD DEVIATION of 1, which produces derived measures of relative standing and allows comparison of raw scores from different distributions. The Z-SCORE TRANSFORMATION is an example of standardization.

standardization group a sample used to establish reliable norms for the population that it represents. This is done by analyzing the results of the test administered to the sample and ascertaining the average performance level and the relative frequency of each deviation from the mean. The NORMAL DISTRIBUTION thus created is then used for comparison with any specific future test score. For example, the standardization group for a new test of computer literacy in older adults might comprise a large set of test takers above age 60 whose characteristics (e.g., sex, demographics, ethnicity, race) reproduce those of the larger population for whom the test is

intended. The arrangement of scores obtained by such a standardization group subsequently provides a point of comparison for the scores of other older adults who take the test. It is important to note, however, that the standardization group must be representative of the intended population of test takers in order to yield valid information. Also called **norm group**; **standardization sample**.

standardized coefficient any index derived from an analysis of two or more variables that have been transformed via STANDARDIZATION, which ensures their value RANGES and VARIANCES are equivalent and thus appropriate for comparison. The term is most commonly used to denote the standardized regression coefficient or BETA COEFFICIENT.

standardized distribution a NORMAL DISTRIBUTION whose values have undergone TRANSFORMATION so as to have a MEAN of 0 and a STANDARD DEVIATION of 1. Also called **standard normal distribution**; **unit normal distribution**.

standardized instructions directions for a measuring instrument that are to be presented to all participants exactly as prepared as part of the standard experimental or assessment procedure. See STANDARDIZATION.

standardized interview see STRUCTURED INTERVIEW.

standardized mean difference a summary statistic used in a META-ANALYSIS of studies that assess the same outcome but measure it in a variety of ways. For example, many studies measure the construct of anxiety and its relationship to school performance, but they do so using different psychometric scales. In order to examine the anxiety–school performance effects found across these multiple studies, it is necessary to first standardize the results of each of the studies to a uniform scale and then combine the results. The standardized mean difference therefore expresses the size of the effect in each study relative to the variability observed in that study; it is the difference in mean outcomes between the groups divided by the STANDARD DEVIATION of the outcome among participants in the study. COHEN'S D and HEDGES'S G are two commonly used types of standardized mean difference. Also called **standardized mean effect**.

standardized measure see STANDARDIZED TEST.

standardized regression coefficient see BETA COEFFICIENT.

standardized regression equation in REGRESSION ANALYSIS, a formula showing the average change in the DEPENDENT VARIABLE (y) that occurs with one unit change in an INDEPENDENT VARIABLE (x) after each has been converted into a form whose distribution has a MEAN of 0 and a STANDARD DEVIATION of 1. The use of a standardized regression equation allows for direct comparison of the variables despite differences in their measurement scales. See also REGRESSION EQUATION.

standardized residual in a REGRESSION ANALYSIS, the error in the DEPENDENT VARIABLE (y) score not explained by the INDEPENDENT VARIABLE (x) when the x and y variables have undergone STANDARDIZATION.

standardized score a value derived from a raw score by subtracting the mean value of all scores in the set and dividing by the STANDARD DEVIATION of the set. The advantage of standardized scores is that they are not reflective of the units of the measuring device from which they were obtained and thus can be compared to one another regardless of the device's scale values. Several types of standardized score exist, including STANINES, T SCORES, and Z SCORES. Also called **normal score; standard score**. See also STANDARDIZATION.

standardized test 1. an assessment instrument whose VALIDITY and RELIABILITY have been established by thorough empirical investigation and analysis. It has clearly defined norms, such that a person's score is an indication of how well he or she did in comparison to a large group of individuals representative of the population for which the test is intended. Also called **standardized measure. 2.** an assessment instrument administered in a predetermined manner, such that the questions, conditions of administration, scoring, and interpretation of responses are consistent from one occasion to another.

standard normal distribution see STANDARDIZED DISTRIBUTION.

standard normal variable any random variable whose probable value follows a NORMAL DISTRIBUTION with a MEAN of 0 and a STANDARD DEVIATION of 1. Also called **standard normal deviate; standard normal variate; unit normal variable**.

standard observer in color vision research, a hypothetical typical human visual system that is described in terms of mathematical functions and equations relating its quantitative visual responses to measurable physical statistics of light stimuli. The descriptions are therefore psychophysical and used to achieve a shared technical description of the perceptual effects of light stimuli on human observers. The equations that define the standard observer are based on averages of laboratory measurements of the visual responses of human participants to particular light stimuli under particular viewing conditions.

standard stimulus an item used as the basis of comparison in the quantitative investigation of physical stimuli and the sensations and perceptions they produce. For example, in the method of adjustment, a participant may be presented with a sound of a particular intensity (the standard stimulus) and asked to change the intensity of another sound to match.

standard treatment control in a CLINICAL TRIAL, a type of CONTROL CONDITION in which participants receive the treatment typically administered to a group of participants with a given medical problem. Another group of participants receives the experimental treatment. After the trial, the outcomes of the two groups are compared to see if the experimental treatment is better than, as good as, or worse than the standard treatment.

stanine *n.* a method of scaling scores on a nine-point scale that ranges from a low of 1 to a high of 9, with a mean of 5 and a STANDARD DEVIATION of 2. A stanine is a **standard ninth**, referring to the interval used in dividing the results into nine more or less equal parts. A stanine score of 1, 2, or 3 is below average; 4, 5, or 6 is average; and 7, 8, or 9 is above average. A stanine is a type of STANDARDIZED SCORE and is mainly used with school achievement tests.

STARIMA model abbreviation for SPACE–TIME AUTOREGRESSIVE INTEGRATED MOVING-AVERAGE MODEL.

STARMA model abbreviation for SPACE–TIME AUTOREGRESSIVE MOVING-AVERAGE MODEL.

state space 1. multidimensional space, particularly as related to the depiction of the results of classification methods that group objects with similar characteristics and patterns of behavior. **2.** in system behavior, an abstract representation of the potential states of the system that emerges from the complex interactions of the variables that make up the system. The interactions are based on a set of nonlinear relations.

stationarity *n.* in TIME-SERIES ANALYSIS, the property of being unchanging or "flat," such that the data are without trends or periodic fluctuations and the MEAN, VARIANCE, and AUTOCORRELA-

TION structure remain constant over time. Most statistical forecasting methods are based on the assumption that the time series of interest can be mathematically transformed into approximate stationarity (i.e., can be "stationarized").

stationary distribution a distribution describing an invariant equilibrium state in a MARKOV CHAIN. The process being modeled is associated with a single, time-independent MATRIX.

stationary process a STOCHASTIC PROCESS whose joint probability distribution does not change when shifted in time or space. In other words, the parameters of a stationary process, such as the mean and the variance, do not change over time or position. See also STATIONARITY.

statistic *n.* **1.** a number measuring some characteristic, construct, variable, or other item of interest. **2.** any function of the observations in a SAMPLE that may be used to estimate the unknown but corresponding value in the POPULATION. Examples include measures of CENTRAL TENDENCY (e.g., the MEAN, MEDIAN, MODE), measures of DISPERSION (e.g., STANDARD DEVIATION, VARIANCE), and distributional attributes (e.g., SKEWNESS, KURTOSIS). Statistics often are assigned Roman letters (e.g., M, s), whereas the equivalent values in the population (called PARAMETERS) are assigned Greek letters (e.g., μ, σ).

statistical analysis any of a wide range of techniques used to describe, explore, understand, explain, predict, and test HYPOTHESES about data. It involves the examination of data collected from SAMPLES within POPULATIONS as well as the use of probabilistic models to make inferences and draw conclusions.

statistical conclusion validity the degree to which the conclusions drawn from statistical analyses of data are accurate and appropriate. In other words, statistical conclusion validity addresses whether inferences about relationships (i.e., whether the independent variable and dependent variable covary and, if so, how strongly) are reasonable or not, given the observed data. It is related to but distinct from INTERNAL VALIDITY, which is concerned with the causality of the relationship. Statistical conclusion validity is enhanced when there is good statistical POWER, RELIABILITY of measures, and use of good experimental methods and procedures. Conversely, it is threatened by such factors as (a) violations of the ASSUMPTIONS embedded in a statistical test; (b) problems associated with the EXPERIMENT-WISE ERROR RATE; (c) RESTRICTION OF RANGE; (d) use of inappropriate EFFECT-SIZE measures; and (e) extraneous variation in the experimental setting.

statistical control the use of statistical procedures to remove the influence of a particular factor that could not be eliminated or controlled by the experimental design in order to better analyze the relationship between two variables. For example, the relationship between age (x) and income earned (y) could be influenced by a third variable, years of education (z). Thus, if a researcher did not first remove the effects of education he or she might derive erroneous conclusions about the influence of age on income from his or her analysis. One type of statistical control is PARTIAL CORRELATION, which shows the association between two quantitative variables after statistically controlling for one or more extraneous variables. A second type of statistical control is ANALYSIS OF CO-VARIANCE, a technique that shows the relationship between a categorical independent variable and a quantitative dependent variable after statistically controlling for one or more extraneous variables.

statistical decision theory a branch of statistical science concerned with the use of data to arrive at decisions. It focuses upon identifying the values, uncertainties, and other issues relevant to a given decision. Specific equations are used to calculate the degree of loss associated with each course of action in order to determine the most advantageous choice.

statistical dependence the situation in which the conditional probability of one event given another event is greater than the probability of that first event. In other words, knowing information about one variable provides information about the other. Compare STATISTICAL INDEPENDENCE. See also DEPENDENT EVENTS.

statistical determinism the position that the laws of probability can predict the likely number of events of a given kind that will occur in a given population under certain defined conditions (e.g., the number of coin tosses per 1,000 that will be heads; the number of male Americans age 70 who will die in a 12-month period). This is analogous to, but logically distinct from, **physical determinism**, which is the proposition that all events—including human behaviors—are caused by prior events, conditions, and natural laws.

statistical difference see SIGNIFICANT DIFFERENCE.

statistical error see ERROR.

statistical evaluation see STATISTICAL TEST.

statistical hypothesis a research question posed in a statistically testable form. For example, if a researcher is interested in whether one treatment leads to a more positive outcome than another treatment, he or she could reframe the question in terms of mean differences, such that the NULL HYPOTHESIS is 0 (no difference between treatments) and the ALTERNATIVE HYPOTHESIS is not 0 (the difference between treatments is greater or lesser than zero). See also HYPOTHESIS TESTING.

statistical independence the condition in which the occurrence of one event makes it neither more nor less probable that another event will occur. In other words, knowing information about one variable provides no information about the other variable. Compare STATISTICAL DEPENDENCE. See also INDEPENDENT EVENTS.

statistical inference see INFERENCE.

statistical model a formal description of the relationships between two or more variables in the form of a mathematical equation. It is statistical in that the variables are related in a STOCHASTIC rather than a deterministic manner, with each set of possible observations on a variable linked to a set of probability distributions. Many STATISTICAL TESTS involve comparing a particular model with the observed data.

statistical power see POWER.

statistical prediction the process of using correlations between variables to hypothesize about future events and outcomes. For example, a university administrator may use a REGRESSION EQUATION to predict a student's college grade point average with reasonable accuracy from measures of performance in high school, such as scores on tests and final grades in classes.

statistical procedure see STATISTICAL TEST.

statistical psychology the application of statistical methods and models to organize, summarize, and interpret data so as to derive descriptions and explanations of cognitive, behavioral, social, and other psychological phenomena.

statistical sequential test any statistical procedure in which the sample size is not fixed in advance but rather the process of collecting more data (more observations or more participants) is continued until there is enough information available either to accept or to reject the NULL HYPOTHESIS. A particular benefit of this approach is that fewer participants might be required than in alternative strategies.

statistical significance the degree to which a research outcome cannot reasonably be attributed to the operation of chance or random factors. It is determined during SIGNIFICANCE TESTING and given by a critical p value, which is the probability of obtaining the observed data if the NULL HYPOTHESIS (i.e., of no significant relationship between variables) were true. Significance generally is a function of sample size—the larger the sample, the less likely it is that one's findings will have occurred by chance. See also CLINICAL SIGNIFICANCE; PRACTICAL SIGNIFICANCE; SIGNIFICANCE LEVEL.

statistical significance testing see SIGNIFICANCE TESTING.

statistical stability consistency of results across samples, study designs, and analyses. A META-ANALYSIS may be used to examine the stability of means, CORRELATIONS, and other PARAMETER estimates obtained from different studies of the same population. See also STABILITY COEFFICIENT.

statistical surveillance continuous observation and analysis of a set of data with the goal of detecting any important changes (e.g., in the direction of a process) as soon as they occur. For example, a statistical surveillance system to determine the end of the influenza season might rely upon NONPARAMETRIC methods to identify the decline in incidence that signals the season's end.

statistical table any table of values used by a researcher to plan experiments or interpret results. For example, there are tables of CRITICAL VALUES in HYPOTHESIS TESTING, tables to estimate the sample size needed to obtain a desired level of POWER, and tables to convert one distribution to another (e.g., from a correlation to a standardized value). A CONTINGENCY TABLE is often used in the CROSS-CLASSIFICATION of items: For ex-

S

ample, a 2×2 table might show the average scores on a test according to individuals' gender (male and female) and education level (high school and college graduates).

statistical test any mathematical technique or procedure used to evaluate the correctness of an empirical hypothesis by determining the likelihood of the sample results occurring by chance. Statistical testing will reveal the probability of committing a TYPE I ERROR if the NULL HYPOTHESIS is rejected. See HYPOTHESIS TESTING; STATISTICAL SIGNIFICANCE.

statistical uncertainty the degree of inaccuracy inherent to the process of estimating PARAMETERS from sampled data. When researchers make such estimates they generally assume that some exact or TRUE SCORE exists and often specify a CONFIDENCE INTERVAL or range of values that they expect this true value to fall within. For example, an estimate of 8 ± 2 means that the researcher is confident that the actual parameter value lies between 6 and 10. The uncertainty is the experimenter's best estimate of how far an estimated quantity might be from the true value.

statistics *n.* the branch of mathematics that uses data descriptively or inferentially to find or support answers for scientific and other quantifiable questions. It involves various techniques and procedures for recording, organizing, analyzing, and reporting quantitative information. See also DESCRIPTIVE STATISTICS; INFERENTIAL STATISTICS; SUMMARY STATISTICS. —**statistical** *adj.* —**statistician** *n.*

steepest ascent when conducting a study with repeated runs, that region of the INDEPENDENT VARIABLE in which there is maximum response or improvement on the DEPENDENT VARIABLE of interest. If research is being carried out in a new area, it is likely that initial levels of the independent variable will not provide a satisfactory level of response on the dependent variable. Repeated runs are therefore undertaken and the path of steepest ascent is identified via the use of a REGRESSION EQUATION. Where improvement is defined as the minimizing of a particular variable, then the **steepest descent** will be sought in the same way.

stem *n.* the introductory part of a FIXED-ALTERNATIVE QUESTION, often an incomplete statement that the respondent is asked to complete. It is followed by a set of response options consisting of the correct answer and several plausible but incorrect choices (DISTRACTORS).

stem-and-leaf plot a graphical method of presenting data that have been measured on an INTERVAL SCALE. A basic stem-and-leaf plot comprises two columns separated by a vertical line; the right column lists the last digit of each data point (the "leaves") and the left column lists all of the other digits from each data point (the "stems"). Each stem is listed only once and no numbers are skipped, even if that means some stems have no leaves. The leaves are listed in increasing order of magnitude in a row to the right of each stem. For example, consider the following hypothetical values for participants measured on a particular variable:

55 57 58 59 74 75 77 79 79 83 83 86 87 92 95 99 107

The stem-and-leaf plot for these values is

5 | 5 7 8 9

6 |

7 | 4 5 7 9 9

8 | 3 3 6 7

9 | 2 5 9

10 | 7

Also called **stem-and-leaf diagram**; **stem-and-leaf display; stemplot**.

stepdown selection see BACKWARD ELIMINATION.

stepup selection see FORWARD SELECTION.

stepwise correlation see STEPWISE REGRESSION.

stepwise discriminant analysis a type of DISCRIMINANT ANALYSIS in which a model that can differentiate maximally between categories is built step by step. In **forward stepwise discriminant analysis**, all possible predictor variables are reviewed and evaluated at each step to determine which one contributes most to the discrimination between groups. That variable is then included in the model, and the process starts again. In **backward stepwise discriminant analysis**, all variables are initially included in the model and then, at each step, the variable that contributes least to the prediction of group membership is eliminated. The stepwise procedure is structured so that the respective F-TO-ENTER and F-TO-REMOVE values of each variable can be isolated, thereby determining its unique contribution to the prediction of group membership.

stepwise regression a group of REGRESSION ANALYSIS techniques that enter predictor (independent) variables into (or delete them from) the REGRESSION EQUATION one variable (or block of variables) at a time according to some predefined criterion. It is contrasted with SIMULTANEOUS REGRESSION, which enters all variables at the same time. Also called **stepwise correlation**; **stepwise multiple regression**.

stimulus sampling a procedure for increasing the generalizability of research results by using multiple stimuli within a category as representative of an experimental condition, as opposed to selecting a single stimulus whose unique characteristics may distort results. For example, a study investigating the effects of gender on monetary generosity would demonstrate stimulus sampling if it employed a variety of different males and females to elicit donations from participants instead of using a single male and a single female.

stimulus value 1. the strength of a given stimulus, measured in standard units (e.g., a shock of 40 volts). **2.** a theoretical characteristic of a stimulus said to index its effectiveness as a reinforcer.

stochastic *adj.* **1.** random or undetermined; arising from chance. **2.** describing a system or process that follows a probability pattern, such that events may be analyzed according to their statistical probability but not accurately predicted.

stochastic matrix a SQUARE MATRIX in which all of the rows or all of the columns sum to 1. A **right stochastic matrix** is one in which the rows contain nonnegative real numbers summing to 1, whereas a **left stochastic matrix** is one in which the columns contain nonnegative real numbers summing to 1. See also DOUBLY STOCHASTIC.

stochastic model a model in which one or more of the inputs allow for random variation, thus generating a range of potential outcome values. The random variation is usually based on fluctuations observed in historical data. Stochastic models are used to estimate the probabilities of various outcomes occurring under varying conditions. They are widely used in the social and behavioral sciences and also in the financial world. Compare DETERMINISTIC MODEL.

stochastic process a random process: a sequence of events with a random probability pattern such that the occurrence of any event in the sequence is independent of past events. For example, the number of people in a doctor's office who have colds during a one-month period could be said to follow a stochastic process. In contrast to **deterministic processes**, stochastic processes involve some indeterminacy, such that their development over time may only be described by probability distributions. A

S

MARKOV CHAIN is a stochastic process. Also called **discrete-time stochastic process**.

stochastic variable see RANDOM VARIABLE.

stooge *n.* a colloquial name for a CONFEDERATE.

stopping rule a criterion stated at the outset of a research project for ending the study early, as when one treatment clearly has been shown to be more effective than another.

strata *pl. n.* see STRATUM.

stratified log-rank test a nonparametric statistical procedure used to compare the time to an event in two samples where each sample has component layers or strata. For example, if there are two preventative treatments to be compared according to the time from initial use until a patient's heart attack, and low-risk, medium-risk, and high-risk individuals are in each treatment group, application of the stratified log-rank test controls for the difference between treatments as a function of risk. The stratified log-rank test is appropriate when there are CENSORED DATA or when the data have positive SKEWNESS.

stratified sampling the process of selecting a sample from a population comprised of various subgroups (strata) in such a way that each subgroup is represented. For example, in a study of college students a researcher might wish to examine people from the different majors (e.g., social sciences, physical sciences, humanities). The selection procedure within each of these strata may be random or systematic. In **stratified random sampling**, a chance process (e.g., a RANDOM NUMBER GENERATOR) is used to select individuals, whereas in **stratified systematic sampling** an objective, orderly procedure is applied to choose individuals (e.g., listing all of the students within each major alphabetically and choosing every 10th case).

Stratified sampling often improves the representativeness of the selected cases by reducing SAMPLING ERROR. The proportion of the sample to be selected from each subgroup is decided in advance.

stratum *n.* (*pl.* **strata**) a layer (typically one of a number of parallel layers) in a structure, such as any of the subpopulations in SAMPLING. For example, if the variable of interest is gender, the two subgroups (strata) would be male and female, and members of each subgroup would be chosen separately for research participation.

stratum chart see BAND CHART.

streaky hypothesis see HOT-HAND HYPOTHESIS.

strength of association in statistics, the degree of relationship between two or more variables, as measured by such indices as a CORRELATION COEFFICIENT, COEFFICIENT OF DETERMINATION, ETA SQUARED, or OMEGA SQUARED.

strength-of-effect index see EFFECT SIZE.

stress test in MULTIDIMENSIONAL SCALING, a measure that indicates the RELIABILITY or GOODNESS OF FIT of the solution. The KRUSKAL STRESS test is an example. Stress tests also are used to determine the number of dimensions to be included in the scaling solution.

strong inference an inductive argument based on systematic, controlled investigation. It involves a cyclic process of developing several different testable hypotheses, devising and carrying out an experiment to exclude one or more of these, and devising and testing additional hypotheses to refine the possibilities that remain. Compare WEAK INFERENCE.

strong law of large numbers see LAW OF LARGE NUMBERS.

structural coefficient in STRUCTURAL EQUATION MODELING, a measure of the amount of change expected in an outcome or DEPENDENT VARIABLE given a one-unit change in the causal or INDEPENDENT VARIABLE and no change in any other variable.

structural equation modeling (**SEM**) any of a broad range of multivariate analysis methods, including FACTOR ANALYSIS and PATH ANALYSIS, that examine VARIANCES and COVARIANCES in order to find interrelationships among LATENT VARIABLES. For example, assume a researcher states that job satisfaction leads to happiness. Both are latent variables that are not directly observable but are defined in terms of other measurable variables, such as judgments of job performance from supervisors and peers; self-reports about attitudes toward pay, supervision, type of work, and other job characteristics; results from PSYCHOLOGICAL TESTS; and so forth. The researcher could use the measurable data to generate an equation representing the strength and nature of the links among the latent variables. Also called **structural modeling**.

structural time-series model a REGRESSION EQUATION in which the explanatory variables are functions of time and the REGRESSION COEFFICIENTS associated with the interval of time are allowed to vary. For example, a researcher could study changes in emotional behavior as a person grows older. Structural time-series models are used not only to describe trends and patterns but also to FORECAST outcomes.

structural validity see FACTORIAL VALIDITY.

structural zero an entry in a table that is certain to be zero because it corresponds to an impossible outcome, as opposed to an entry that has an empirical value of zero. The occurrence of zeros may be inherent to the issue of interest or, in some applications, introduced intentionally through the experimental design. For example, in studying friendships, one might ask each of 15 people to indicate who among the others is a friend. This would yield a 15×15 contingency table or matrix, with 1 representing "is a friend" and 0 representing "is not a friend." Although there would be empirical zeros in some cells to represent not-a-friend responses, all entries along the diagonal of the matrix are structural zeros since they represent one person's response with regard to himself or herself rather than another person.

structure coefficient 1. in REGRESSION ANALYSIS, a CORRELATION COEFFICIENT indicating the extent of relationship between scores on a particular MANIFEST VARIABLE and scores on a latent or predicted variable derived from the entire set of variables. It is used to quantify the importance of an observed variable. **2.** in DISCRIMINANT ANALYSIS, a value representing the association between a particular variable being considered as a differentiator of group membership and the DISCRIMINANT FUNCTION scores derived from the full set of predictor variables.

structured interview a method for gathering information, used particularly in surveys and personnel selection, in which questions, their wordings, and their order of administration are determined in advance. The choice of answers tends to be fixed and determined in advance as well. With structured interviews, answers can be aggregated and comparisons can be made across different samples or interview periods; interviewees can be assessed consistently (e.g., using a common rating scale); and ORDER EFFECTS, whereby the answer to a particular question can depend on the preceding questions, are minimized. Also called **standardized interview**. Compare UNSTRUCTURED INTERVIEW. See also SEMISTRUCTURED INTERVIEW.

structured observation a systematic method of collecting behavioral data within a controlled environment, often used in research with infants and young

S

children, in which observers measure overt actions and interpersonal processes. In structured observation, researchers (a) select which behaviors are of interest and which are not, (b) clearly define the characteristics of each behavior so that observers all agree on the classification, and (c) note the occurrence and frequency of these targeted behaviors in the situation under analysis. Observers may monitor situations unobtrusively or from within as active participants (see PARTICIPANT OBSERVATION). Structured observation differs from NATURALISTIC OBSERVATION, which involves observing individuals outside of the laboratory in their own environments.

structured Q sort see Q SORT.

structured stimulus a well-defined, well-organized stimulus, the perception of which is influenced more by the characteristics of the stimulus than by those of the perceiver. Compare UNSTRUCTURED STIMULUS.

Stuart test see COX–STUART TEST FOR TREND.

stub factor in FACTOR ANALYSIS, that part of a FIRST-ORDER FACTOR that remains after the variance due to a second-order or other HIGHER ORDER FACTOR has been removed.

Studentization *n.* a procedure to eliminate a NUISANCE PARAMETER in particular calculations. It transforms a statistic whose distribution of probable values relies upon the unknown parameter into one whose distribution relies on quantities that can be derived from the sample data. Such transformed statistics are described as "Studentized." [**Student**, pseudonym of William S. Gosset (1876–1937), British statistician]

Studentized deletion residual in REGRESSION ANALYSIS, a statistic computed to determine if any observations or cases are significantly different from the others and thus can be considered OUTLIERS. It is the difference (after STAN-DARDIZATION) between the observed value and the value predicted by the REGRESSION EQUATION when the potential outlier is included, minus the same difference when the potential outlier is excluded. A large Studentized deletion residual (e.g., greater than 2) provides evidence that the observation in question is indeed an outlier biasing the results of the analysis. Also called **Studentized deleted residual**. [**Student**, pseudonym of William S. Gosset]

Studentized maximum modulus distribution a distribution of *p* values (see PROBABILITY LEVEL) used when an INDEPENDENT VARIABLE has multiple conditions (e.g., *very high*, *high*, *average*, *low*, and *very low*) that a researcher wishes to compare two at a time (e.g., *very high* to *high*, *very high* to *average*, etc.). The Studentized maximum modulus distribution adjusts the *p* values needed to indicate significance in order to minimize the possibility that a PAIRWISE COMPARISON will be found significant simply because multiple comparisons are being made. [**Student**, pseudonym of William S. Gosset]

Studentized range distribution a theoretical PROBABILITY DISTRIBUTION that is used in MULTIPLE COMPARISON TESTS when assessing differences between pairs of means for significance. It is similar to the T DISTRIBUTION but differs in accounting for the number of means under consideration: The more means being considered, the larger the CRITICAL VALUE of the STUDENTIZED RANGE STATISTIC must be in order to reject the NULL HYPOTHESIS. [**Student**, pseudonym of William S. Gosset]

Studentized range statistic (symbol: *q*) a statistic used in TUKEY'S HONESTLY SIGNIFICANT DIFFERENCE TEST and other MULTIPLE COMPARISON TESTS to establish CRITICAL VALUES for rejecting the NULL HYPOTHESIS. It is the RANGE of a sample expressed in units of the standard distribution for that sample. [**Student**, pseudonym of William S. Gosset]

S

Studentized residual in REGRESSION ANALYSIS, a standardized statistic describing the variation between obtained and predicted values. It is calculated by obtaining the difference between the empirical value of an observation and the value of that observation predicted by a model, and then dividing that difference (called a RESIDUAL) by an estimated STANDARD DEVIATION. Studentized residuals are used to identify REGRESSION EQUATIONS that are a poor fit for the observed data. [**Student**, pseudonym of William S. Gosset]

Student's t distribution see T DISTRIBUTION. [**Student**, pseudonym of William S. Gosset]

Student's t test see T TEST. [**Student**, pseudonym of William S. Gosset]

study *n.* a research investigation conducted for the purpose of understanding, explaining, describing, or predicting some phenomenon of interest. It may be conducted in the laboratory or natural environment, and it may yield quantitative or qualitative data.

study artifact see ARTIFACT.

sturdy statistic see ROBUST ESTIMATOR.

Sturges's rule a rule for determining the width of CLASS INTERVALS or bars on a HISTOGRAM, that is, for deciding the number of groups into which a distribution of observations should be classified. It is given as $1 + \log_2 n$, where n is the number of observations. [Herbert A. **Sturges** (1882–1958), mathematician]

subgroup analysis the division of a sample into smaller groups for the purpose of evaluating differences among those subgroups. For example, if the variable of interest is gender, subgroups of males and females could be created in order to examine differences between them on a dependent variable.

subject (S) *n.* generally, the individual human or animal who takes part in an experiment or research study and whose responses or performance are reported or evaluated; less frequently, the subject may also be an institution, group, or other entity. PARTICIPANT is now often the preferred term for human subjects, because the word *subject* is held to be depersonalizing and to imply passivity and submissiveness on the part of the experimentee.

subject attrition see ATTRITION.

subject bias the influence of participants' knowledge of the purpose of the research upon their responses to experimental conditions and manipulations. For example, a participant who knows he or she is in the treatment group as opposed to the control group might behave differently than he or she would otherwise. See DEMAND CHARACTERISTICS.

subject history 1. background information about a participant in a study, such as sociological, occupational, and educational data. **2.** events that a research participant experiences outside of the controlled environment of the study, which may threaten its INTERNAL VALIDITY. See HISTORY EFFECT.

subjective *adj* **1.** taking place or existing only within the mind. **2.** particular to a specific person and thus intrinsically inaccessible to the experience or observation of others. **3.** based on or influenced by personal feelings, interpretations, or prejudices. Compare OBJECTIVE.

subjective error any systematic deviation of an individual's OBSERVED SCORE from the TRUE SCORE that can be attributed to individual variations in perception or particular interpretive biases held by that person.

subjective examination see SUBJECTIVE TEST.

subjective method any of various approaches to the collection, evaluation, and interpretation of data that depend upon the researcher's or analyst's personal judgments, feelings, attitudes, or intuitions.

subjective prior see PRIOR DISTRIBUTION.

subjective probability a person-specific estimate, derived from individual experience, of the likelihood of a given event or outcome. Also called **personal probability**.

subjective scoring see OBJECTIVE SCORING.

subjective test an assessment tool that is scored according to personal judgment or to standards that are less systematic than those used in OBJECTIVE TESTS, as in some essay examinations. Although there are no necessarily right or wrong answers, responses are scored based on appraisals of their appropriateness or quality. Also called **subjective examination**.

subjectivism *n.* in general, any position holding that judgments of fact or value reflect individual states of mind rather than states of affairs that can be said to be true or false independently of individuals. Compare OBJECTIVISM. —**subjectivist** *n., adj.*

subjectivity *n.* the tendency to interpret data or make judgments in the light of personal feelings, beliefs, or experiences. Compare OBJECTIVITY.

subject matching see MATCHING.

subject maturation see MATURATION.

subject role a coherent set of behaviors assumed by a research participant in response to his or her perceptions of what is required or expected in the situation. See APPREHENSIVE-SUBJECT ROLE; FAITHFUL-SUBJECT ROLE; GOOD-SUBJECT ROLE; NEGATIVISTIC-SUBJECT ROLE.

subject selection effect see SAMPLING BIAS.

subject sophistication a familiarity with general research procedures that may influence a person's behavior as a participant in a study. It is an issue of particular concern in DECEPTION RESEARCH, as participants may significantly modify their behavior (e.g., specifically searching for any evidence of deceit in the experimental procedure) as they become increasingly knowledgable about the nature of deception in experiments. Sources of sophistication include participating in research previously, talking to participants from other studies, and reading about studies in the mass media.

subject-specific model in the analysis of LONGITUDINAL DATA—for example, via REGRESSION ANALYSIS or TIME-SERIES ANALYSIS—a mathematical representation in which the PARAMETERS are fit to a given person's data. Compare POPULATION-AVERAGED MODEL.

subjects' rights see PARTICIPANTS' RIGHTS.

subjects-to-variables ratio the number of research participants compared to the number of research variables (e.g., 5 to 1) in a study. The subjects-to-variables ratio provides a guideline for determining what size of sample to use to ensure the greatest POWER when conducting a statistical analysis, such as MULTIPLE REGRESSION or FACTOR ANALYSIS.

subject variable an experience or characteristic of a research participant that is not of primary interest but nonetheless may influence study results and thus must be accounted for during experimentation or data analysis. Examples include age, marital status, religious affiliation, and intelligence. A variable of this type is neither manipulated by the experimenter, as an INDEPENDENT VARIABLE might be, nor is it usually changed in the course of the experiment, as a DEPENDENT VARIABLE might be. Also called **background variable**; **individual-difference variable**; **participant variable**.

subpopulation *n.* a subgroup of a larger POPULATION of individuals or cases. For example, if the population of interest is all U.S. college undergraduates, one could divide the students into subpopulations by state (e.g., individuals attending college in California, New York, etc.).

subsample *n.* a subset of a SAMPLE of individuals or cases selected for study. For example, if one chooses a random group of college students for research purposes, one could divide the students into subsamples by major (e.g., individuals from the group who are majoring in psychology, mathematics, etc).

subscale *n.* a SCALE that taps some specific constituent or otherwise differentiated category of information as part of a larger, overall scheme. For example, a test of intelligence might consist of several subscales (or subtests) assessing verbal and performance aspects or dimensions of intelligence, which in combination yield a verbal intelligence score, a performance intelligence score, and an overall intelligence score.

subset *n.* in mathematics and logic, a set (collection of entities) that is part of a larger set. See also VENN DIAGRAM.

substantive hypothesis a statement, derived from a theory being tested, that indicates expectations about the type, strength, or direction of relationship among variables. The substantive hypothesis is not empirically testable until each of its terms is given an OPERATIONAL DEFINITION. For example, if the substantive hypothesis is that those interested in biology will do better in medical school, the concept of "interest in biology" could be operationally defined as the score on a questionnaire assessing one's curiosity about and experiences in this area, and "doing better" could be operationally defined as one's grade point average in medical school. See also RESEARCH HYPOTHESIS.

substantive significance see PRACTICAL SIGNIFICANCE.

substitution matrix see TRANSITION MATRIX.

substitution test any examination in which the test taker exchanges one set of symbols for another. For example, a person might be required to substitute numbers with letters according to a specific code or to substitute a word in a sentence with a grammatically equivalent alternative. Substitution tests often are used in neuropsychology to evaluate cognitive function and identify individuals with brain damage, dementia, and other conditions.

subtest *n.* a separate division of a test or instrument, usually with an identifiable content (e.g., the multiplication subtest of a mathematics test).

successive comparison method see SIMULTANEOUS COMPARISON METHOD.

sufficient estimator an ESTIMATOR that utilizes all the relevant or useful information from a sample in order to approximate a population parameter. For example, the SAMPLE MEAN is a sufficient estimator for the POPULATION MEAN. Also called **sufficient statistic**.

summary statistics a set of statistics used to communicate the most important descriptive information about a collection of raw data in succinct form. For example, the VARIANCE, CENTRAL TENDENCY, SKEWNESS, and KURTOSIS may be used to summarize a sample data set.

summary table any tabular presentation of crucial descriptive information about a data set. An ANOVA SUMMARY TABLE is an example.

summated rating scale a series of statements measuring the same construct or variable to which respondents indicate their degree of agreement or disagreement. The number of response options for each item varies, often from 5 to 7 points (e.g., from *strongly agree* to *strongly disagree*). The response values for individual items may be summed to obtain a total or average score that reflects

S

a person's general attitude toward the construct of interest. A LIKERT SCALE is the most commonly used summated rating scale. Also called **summated rating method**; **summated scale**.

summative evaluation in evaluation research, an attempt to assess the overall effectiveness of a program in meeting its objectives and goals after it is in operation. This is in contrast to FORMATIVE EVALUATION, which is used to help in the development of the program.

sum of cross-products a statistical value obtained for two sets of variables x_i and y_i defined by the summation

$$\Sigma (x_i - \bar{x}) (y_i - \bar{y}),$$

where $\bar{x}$ is the mean value of x_i and $\bar{y}$ the mean value of y_i. It is used in MULTIVARIATE ANALYSIS OF VARIANCE.

sum of products the value obtained by multiplying each pair of numbers in a set and then adding the individual totals. For example, for the set of number pairs

2, 4
3, 5
6, 6
1, 4

the sum of cross products is $(2 \times 4) + (3 \times 5) + (6 \times 6) + (1 \times 4) = 8 + 15 + 36 + 4 = 63$.

sum-of-ranks test see RANK-SUM TEST.

sum of squared errors (symbol: *SSE*) see ERROR SUM OF SQUARES.

sum of squares (symbol: *SS*) the number obtained by determining the deviation of each point in a data set from some value (such as a mean or predicted value), multiplying each deviation by itself, and adding the resulting products. Thus, for a set of variables x_i,

$$\Sigma(x_i - \bar{x})^2,$$

where $\bar{x}$ is the mean value of x_i. For example, if an analysis yields a mean score of 5 but a person's actual score is 7, the squared deviation for that individual is

$(7 - 5)^2 = 2^2 = 4$: This would be added to the squared deviations of all other individuals in the sample. Various types of sums of squares are calculated in ANALYSIS OF VARIANCE, REGRESSION ANALYSIS, and other statistical procedures. Also called **sum of the squared deviations**. See BETWEEN-GROUPS SUM OF SQUARES; REGRESSION SUM OF SQUARES; ERROR SUM OF SQUARES; WITHIN-GROUPS SUM OF SQUARES.

sum of squares of cross-products (symbol: *SSCP*) the value obtained by first multiplying the squared differences of individual x and y scores in a sample from their respective means and then adding all of the results. It is used in certain statistical analyses to determine the COVARIATION between two sets of scores for a group. For example, if a participant in a sample has x and y scores of 4 and 7, respectively, and the means of the x and y variables are 2 and 4, respectively, the squared cross-product for the participant would be $(4 - 2)^2 \times (7 - 4)^2 = 4 \times 9 = 36$; this deviation would then be added to the deviations for all other participants in the sample to yield the sum of squares of cross-products.

sum of the squared deviations see SUM OF SQUARES.

supersaturated design a type of FACTORIAL DESIGN in which dozens of INDEPENDENT VARIABLES that influence a single DEPENDENT VARIABLE of interest are assessed simultaneously to identify those vital few that are most influential. In a supersaturated design, the number of variables being investigated exceeds the number of runs or trials conducted; algorithms and other criteria exist to determine the appropriate number of runs to conduct. Such designs commonly are used for screening purposes, wherein the goal is to identify a small number of dominant active factors with minimal cost.

suppressor effect a reduction in the correlation between two variables due to the influence of a third variable. Compare REINFORCER EFFECT.

suppressor variable 1. a condition or characteristic that is associated with an INDEPENDENT VARIABLE, such that the correlation between the independent variable and the DEPENDENT VARIABLE is less than what it would be otherwise. **2.** in REGRESSION ANALYSIS, a predictor variable that is highly correlated with other predictors but that has a small correlation with the outcome variable. The suppressor variable thus serves to remove the other predictors' variance that is irrelevant to the outcome, resulting in stronger relationships with the dependent variable of interest. See also PARTIALING.

surrogate end point in CLINICAL TRIALS, a measure that is intended to substitute for or predict a particular outcome. Surrogate end points often are used when the primary end point is undesirable or rare, thus making it unethical or impractical to conduct a clinical trial to gather a statistically significant number of end points. For example, a researcher testing a drug to decrease the likelihood of death from heart disease may use blood pressure as a surrogate end point.

surrogate variable see PROXY VARIABLE.

survey *n.* a study in which a group of participants is selected from a population and some selected data about or opinions of those participants are collected, measured, and analyzed. Information typically is gathered by interview or self-report questionnaire, and the results thus obtained may then be extrapolated to the whole population.

survey error the degree to which the results of a SURVEY are inaccurate, due to such factors as SAMPLING BIAS, content or measurement flaws, or the RESPONSE BIASES of participants. See MEASUREMENT ERROR; SAMPLING ERROR.

survival analysis a family of statistical methods used to model a variety of time-related outcomes. The simplest application of survival analysis involves estimating the amount of time until the occurrence of an event (e.g., death, illness, graduation, marriage) for a group of individuals, but the technique also may be applied to compare durations for two or more groups and to build multivariate models that explain variation in duration. Survival analysis can be more informative than other techniques because it gives insight into the relationship between time and the outcome of interest. That is, it enables the researcher to determine not just whether an outcome is likely to occur but whether it will occur early or late and whether the chances of event occurrence increase gradually or sharply over time. Also called **duration analysis; event history analysis**.

survival curve in SURVIVAL ANALYSIS, a graph showing the probability of an event's occurrence at specific points in time, as in the illustration overleaf using hypothetical data.
In this example, the survival curve depicts the number of individuals who died from a disease of interest at various points in time relevant to the study of the specific disease. Also called **survival plot**.

survival function in SURVIVAL ANALYSIS, a mathematical formula that describes the relationship between the likelihood of a particular event occurring and a given time frame.

survival model in SURVIVAL ANALYSIS, a model that shows the probability of the occurrence of a well-defined event at different time points while taking into account the influence of certain predictors or explanatory variables. See CONTINUOUS-TIME SURVIVAL MODEL; DISCRETE-TIME SURVIVAL MODEL.

survival plot see SURVIVAL CURVE.

survival probability in SURVIVAL ANALYSIS, the likelihood of experiencing

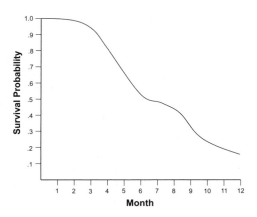

survival curve

the event of interest as a function of time. It often is computed using the KAPLAN–MEIER ESTIMATOR.

survival rate in SURVIVAL ANALYSIS, a value used to indicate the frequency of a particular event's occurrence at a specific point in time. For example, in a health study, the survival rate (i.e., occurrence of death) may be lower within the first year of the diagnosis of a moderately serious disease but become progressively higher over time as the disease becomes more serious.

survival ratio in SURVIVAL ANALYSIS, a value used to indicate the elapsed time prior to an event of interest (e.g., disease onset, death) in relation to the total amount of time studied. Larger survival ratios indicate a longer time until the event's occurrence.

survival time in SURVIVAL ANALYSIS, the amount of time that elapses until the occurrence of a negative event (e.g., death, disease). Also called **failure time**.

suspended rootogram see HANGING ROOTOGRAM.

SVD abbreviation for SINGULAR VALUE DECOMPOSITION.

switchback design a type of WITHIN-SUBJECTS DESIGN in which participants are assigned to multiple experimental conditions in a specific pattern that controls for personal- and time-related variations that may influence individuals' responses. The pattern can be expressed as a combination of rows and columns. The number of columns usually equals the number of unique pairs of experimental conditions and the number of rows tends to be three or four, regardless of the total number of conditions being studied. For example, suppose a researcher is investigating the effect of three types of instruction (A, B, and C) on the performance of six participants, each of whom has a different learning curve. A switchback arrangement for such a study might be

A C B A C B

C B A B A C

A C B A C B

C B A B A C

Each row represents a distinct time period and each column represents a specific participant, with only two instruction types switching back and forth for any given participant.

symmetrical confidence interval an estimated range of values (CONFIDENCE INTERVAL) for an unknown population PARAMETER that follows a NORMAL DISTRIBUTION. Each side of the interval mirrors the other, such that half of the values are in the left tail of the distribution and the other half are in the right tail. Compare ASYMMETRICAL CONFIDENCE INTERVAL.

symmetrical distribution a distribution in which the frequency of values above the MEAN are a mirror image of those below the mean. Compare ASYMMETRICAL DISTRIBUTION.

symmetrical matrix a SQUARE MATRIX in which the values above the MAIN DIAGONAL are a mirror image of the values below the diagonal. It has the property $A = (a_{ij})$, or $a_{ij} = a_{ji}$, with i denoting rows and j denoting columns.

$$\begin{bmatrix} 2 & 1 & 2 \\ 1 & 2 & 1 \\ 2 & 1 & 2 \end{bmatrix}$$

Thus, in the example matrix above the third value in column 2 is the same as the second value in column 3 (i.e., 1).

symmetry *n.* equality relative to some axis. More specifically, it is a condition in which values are arranged identically above and below the middle of a data set (see NORMAL DISTRIBUTION) or above and below the diagonal of a matrix (see SYMMETRICAL MATRIX). Many standard statistical techniques are appropriate only for symmetrical data, such that nonsymmetrical data often are transformed into a roughly symmetrical form prior to analysis. Compare ASYMMETRY. —**symmetrical** *adj.*

symmetry test a method of determining whether a graphical representation of a data set demonstrates SYMMETRY about its *x*-axis, *y*-axis, or origin, such that knowing the arrangement of values for one portion of the graph (e.g., values above the mean) enables one to determine the values for the opposite, mirror-image portion of the graph (i.e., values below the mean). If the data do possess such symmetry, they can be analyzed using statistical techniques that assume a NORMAL DISTRIBUTION.

synchronic *adj.* describing research that focuses on events or other phenomena at a given point in time. For example, a synchronic approach to linguistics would seek to characterize linguistic features at a particular time, without reference to their historical development. Synchronic research contrasts with **diachronic** research, which focuses on processes of change over time.

synergism *n.* the joint action of different elements such that their combined effect is greater than the sum of their individual effects. For example, synergism occurs in organizational behavior when a work group's overall performance exceeds the aggregate performance of its individual members. See also INTERACTION EFFECT. —**synergistic** *adj.*

synthetic approach the combining (synthesizing) of various processes, systems, skills, or other components into a more complex whole as a means of learning or better understanding the whole. For example, a synthetic approach to learning to read is one in which the child first learns to recognize written letters and understand their associated sounds before learning to combine letters into syllables and words. Compare ANALYTIC APPROACH.

synthetic risk map a graphical display of the results of a HAZARD ANALYSIS, which uses multivariate statistical procedures to identify and understand hazardous or risky situations. Synthetic risk maps provide an estimate of what the prevalence rate of the hazard (e.g., cancer mortality from airborne toxins) in a given area is expected to be given the demographics of the area.

Consider the example overleaf from the 2002 National-Scale Air Toxics Assessment of the U.S. Environmental Protection Agency.

synthetic variable see LATENT VARIABLE.

systematically biased sampling any sampling method that consistently

Average Risk Level

☐ <1 in a Million
☐ 1 - 25 in a Million
☐ 25 - 50 in a Million
☐ 50 - 75 in a Million
■ 75 - 100 in a Million
■ >100 in a Million

synthetic risk map

favors some outcomes or characteristics over others, such that the resulting sample does not accurately represent the larger population from which it was drawn. For example, suppose a researcher conducts a phone survey using telephone directories to identify participants. This sampling approach would be systematically biased in not including in the sample those who do not have phones, those who have opted out of receiving calls of certain types, and those who have unlisted numbers.

systematic error error in which the data values obtained from a sample deviate by a fixed amount from the true values within the population. For example, a scale that repeatedly provides readings 0.5 g lower than the true weight would be demonstrating systematic error. Systematic errors tend to be consistently positive or negative and may occur as a result of SAMPLING BIAS or MEASUREMENT ERROR. Also called **systematic bias**. Compare RANDOM ERROR.

systematic error variance a consistent directional discrepancy in scores that is produced by extraneous factors (e.g.,

measurement imprecision). Systematic error variance is generally positive or generally negative and makes it more difficult to identify the unique effects of the INDEPENDENT VARIABLE in experimental manipulations. Compare RANDOM ERROR VARIANCE.

systematic naturalistic observation an objective, consistent method for recording behavior as it occurs in the natural environment, without any intervention or manipulation of variables by the researcher. It is a more focused form of NATURALISTIC OBSERVATION in that it employs a structured system to examine a single behavior of interest (or one specific aspect thereof), measuring its frequency, duration, latency, or other characteristics as applicable.

systematic observation an objective, well-ordered method for close examination of some phenomenon or aspect of behavior so as to obtain reliable data unbiased by observer interpretation. Systematic observation typically involves specification of the exact actions, attributes, or other variables that are to be recorded and precisely how they are to be recorded. The intent is to ensure that, under the same or similar circumstances, all observers will obtain the same results.

systematic random sampling see SYSTEMATIC SAMPLING.

systematic replication the process of conducting a study again but with certain consistent differences, often in an attempt to extend the original research to different settings or participants. For example, a systematic replication could refine the design (e.g., by using more participants) or the methodology (e.g., by using more standardized procedures or objective measures). Compare DIRECT REPLICATION.

systematic review an organized method of locating, assembling, and evaluating a body of literature on a particular topic using a specific set of criteria. Standards for inclusion, the search strategy, the coding and analysis of the included studies, and other procedures are explicitly defined in advance in order to ensure that the process is transparent and can be replicated, with the aim of minimizing bias in terms of what is reviewed and the conclusions that are drawn.

systematic sampling a type of sampling process in which all the members of a population are listed and then some objective, orderly procedure is used to randomly choose specific cases. For example, the population might be listed alphabetically and every seventh case selected. Also called **quasi-random sampling; systematic random sampling**.

systematic variance see UNSYSTEMATIC VARIANCE.

systems theory see GENERAL SYSTEMS THEORY.

S

Tt

T symbol for the statistic obtained from the WILCOXON SIGNED-RANKS TEST.

T² see HOTELLING'S T² TEST.

table *n.* a presentation of data in the form of an ordered arrangement of overlaid vertical columns and horizontal rows. As with a GRAPH, the purpose of a table is to communicate information (either in words or numerical values) in a concise, space-efficient manner that can be assessed at a glance and interpreted easily. The columns have headings (the leftmost column, which usually lists the independent variable, is referred to as the **stub column**). The intersection of a column and row is called a CELL. Tables are often accompanied by explanatory notes. —**tabular** *adj.*

tachistoscope *n.* a device that displays (usually by projecting) visual material on a screen for a specific amount of time, usually at very brief intervals. Words, numbers, pictures, and symbols can be rapidly presented in the right or left visual field. The device is used in experiments that are concerned with visual perception, recognition speed, and memory. It is also widely used in market research concerned with advertising, logos, branding, and so forth. Also called **T-scope**.

tactile test any test designed to measure how people perceive something through the sense of touch.

tail of a distribution in a PROBABILITY DISTRIBUTION, especially one that is graphically displayed, the region (or regions) of least frequently occurring values. This is often the CRITICAL REGION in tests of STATISTICAL SIGNIFICANCE.

tally sheet an instrument, usually a simple printed form, used for checking, counting, or scoring a variable. For example, a researcher might use a tally sheet to record the frequency of occurrence of various behaviors or other events. Also called **tally chart**.

TAR abbreviation for THRESHOLD AUTOREGRESSION.

target *n.* **1.** an area or object that is the focus of a process, inquiry, or activity. **2.** the goal object in a task. For example, the target in a visual search might be to find a letter *S* in a randomly arranged array of letters. In some concept-discovery tasks, the target is the rule that classifies objects as belonging or not belonging to a category. Where a search has more than one item as its goal, these are known as the **target set**.

target group the specific group of people within a TARGET POPULATION that is the focus of research. The target group may be defined by age, gender, marital status, or other similar background variables. Often, a particular combination of variables, such as men ages 20 to 50, may define the target group.

target population the population that a study is intended to research and to which generalizations from samples are to be made. Also called **reference population**. See also TARGET GROUP.

target stimulus a specific stimulus to which participants in a test or experimental procedure must attend or respond. For example, in tests of hearing the target stimulus may be a specific tone that must be identified.

Tarone–Ware test in SURVIVAL ANALYSIS, a test that can be used to determine whether two survival curves are equivalent when there are reasons to think that the traditional survival test may not give useful results. This may be because test assumptions have been violated, such as the assumption of independence of CENSORING, or because there are factors unaccounted for in the analysis that affect survival or censoring times or both. The Tarone–Ware test is designed to be used with a large percentage of censored data and with nonnormal distributions. [Robert E. **Tarone**, U.S. epidemiologist; James H. **Ware**, U.S. statistician]

task analysis 1. the breakdown of a complex task into component tasks to identify the different skills needed to correctly complete the task. In education, for example, it entails the breakdown of a subject or field of study to identify the specific skills the student must possess in order to master it. **2.** a method of evaluating a product or system in which researchers interview actual or target users in order to find out information such as (a) what tasks are performed, (b) which of these are most frequently performed and which are most important, (c) how and in what sequence the tasks are performed, (d) what standards of performance apply, and (e) how different categories of user vary in their answers to the above. Although some scripted questions are asked, the interviews are otherwise unstructured, the better to reflect users' actual experience.

tau test see KENDALL'S TAU.

Taylor series an infinite sum of terms that are calculated from the values of a function's DERIVATIVES at a single point a. The process provides for a **Taylor expansion** of the function $f(x)$ about $x = a$. [Brook **Taylor** (1685–1731), British mathematician]

Tchebechev's inequality see CHEBYSHEV'S INEQUALITY.

t distribution a theoretical PROBABILITY DISTRIBUTION that plays a central role in testing hypotheses about population means, among other parameters. It is the sampling distribution of the statistic $(M - \mu_0)/s$, where μ_0 is the mean of the population from which the sample is drawn, M is the estimate of the mean of the population as obtained from sample data, and s is the standard deviation of the data set. Also called **Student's t distribution**.

telephone interview an interview that is conducted by telephone rather than face to face. QUESTIONNAIRES and surveys involving large numbers of geographically dispersed participants are often carried out in this way. Sometimes, telephone interviews may be used to screen participants in order to narrow the pool of those who will be invited for in-person interviews.

temporal consistency the CORRELATION between measurements obtained when the same test or instrument is administered to the same sample on two different occasions. Temporal consistency is an index of the RETEST RELIABILITY of an instrument. This approach assumes that there is no substantial change in the CONSTRUCT being measured between the two occasions. The longer the time gap, the greater the likelihood of a lower correlation. Also called **temporal stability**. See RELIABILITY.

temporal frequency the number of occurrences of a repeating event per unit time. For example, if 80 repeating events occur within 20 seconds, the frequency, f, is $80/20 = 4$.

temporal precedence in establishing cause–effect relationships between two variables, the principle that the cause must be shown to have occurred before the effect. Two other requirements are those of COVARIATION and nonspuriousness (i.e., there are no plausible alternative explanations for the observed relationship).

temporal stability see TEMPORAL CONSISTENCY.

temporal validity a type of EXTERNAL

T

VALIDITY that refers to the generalizability of a study's results across time. Also called **temporal external validity**.

terminal event in a series of related events, an event that can occur only once and after which no other event of interest can occur. In many clinical and observational studies the terminal event is death, whereas the nonterminal or recurrent events include hospitalizations, relapses, repeat of behaviors and symptoms, and the like. For the analysis of such situations and data, one must take into account the dependence among different types of recurrent events and that between the recurrent events and the terminal event.

tertiary sampling unit a unit selected in the third stage of sampling. For example, suppose the job satisfaction of employees in a supermarket chain is being studied. The first sampling could be drawn by identifying stores geographically across the United States; this would be the PRIMARY SAMPLING UNIT. Then, within each geographical location, stores from large urban areas would be selected for possible inclusion in the research; this would be the SECONDARY SAMPLING UNIT. Finally, cashiers from within the urban stores would be selected to complete the job satisfaction survey; this last sample would be the tertiary sampling unit.

test 1. *n.* any procedure or method to examine or determine the presence of some factor or phenomenon. **2.** *n.* a standardized set of questions or other items designed to assess knowledge, skills, interests, or other characteristics of an examinee. See PSYCHOLOGICAL TEST. **3.** *n.* a set of operations, usually statistical in nature, designed to determine the VALIDITY of a hypothesis. **4.** *vb.* to administer a test.

testability *n.* the degree to which a hypothesis or theory is capable of being evaluated empirically.

testable hypothesis a HYPOTHESIS that generates predictions of what is likely to occur (or not occur) that are capable of being evaluated empirically. To be truly testable, a prediction must be capable of being operationalized such that reliable measures to collect unbiased data are available.

test administration the giving of a test for the purpose of obtaining information, especially in a standardized manner that can be replicated.

test age see AGE EQUIVALENT.

test analysis a detailed statistical analysis of a test's PSYCHOMETRIC properties, including an evaluation of the quality of the test items and of the test as a whole. It usually includes information such as the MEAN and STANDARD DEVIATION for the test scores in the population used to develop the test as well as data on the test's RELIABILITY; it may also include data on such factors as item DIFFICULTY VALUE, ITEM DISCRIMINABILITY, and the impact of ITEM DISTRACTORS.

test battery a group, series, or set of several tests designed to be administered as a unit in order to obtain a comprehensive assessment of a particular factor or phenomenon. For example, a health researcher may administer a battery of health surveys to a group of individuals diagnosed with a particular disease to assess multiple facets of the disease. Depending on the purpose of testing, individual tests may measure the same or different areas (or both) and may be scored separately or combined into a single score.

test bias the tendency of a test to systematically over- or underestimate the true scores of individuals to whom that test is administered, for example because they are members of particular groups (e.g., ethnic minorities, genders). See also CULTURAL TEST BIAS.

test construction the creation of a test, usually with a clear intent to meet the usual criteria of VALIDITY, RELIABIL-ITY, NORMS, and other elements of test standardization.

test data 1. any data gathered from a TEST. **2.** data that have been specifically identified for use in testing models, programs, or assumptions. For example, data may be used in a confirmatory way, typically to verify that a given set of input to a given function produces some expected result. Other data may be used in order to challenge the ability of the program to respond to unusual, extreme, exceptional, or unexpected input.

test for contrasts any procedure used to determine which of the specific groups examined in an ANALYSIS OF VARIANCE are significantly different from each other, whether this takes the form of a POST HOC COMPARISON carried out after the data have been observed or an A PRIORI COMPARISON formulated before observation. For example, suppose one wished to analyze the outcomes from three different modes of training: (a) video-based instruction, (b) live lecture by an instructor, and (c) text reading only. After conducting an analysis of variance and obtaining results indicating there is a significant difference between the three modes, one could use a test for contrasts to evaluate various combinations of modes to identify where exactly the differences lie. More specifically, one comparison could be between video-based testing versus lecture, which assesses two modes that involve an instructor explaining content to the students; another comparison could be the video and live lecture groups versus the text reading, which assesses an instructor presenting information against learning via reading; and so on until all possible combinations have been evaluated. Examples of specific tests for contrasts include the SCHEFFÉ TEST, TUKEY'S HONESTLY SIGNIFICANT DIFFERENCE TEST, and the FISHER LEAST SIGNIFICANT DIFFERENCE TEST.

test for equality of variance any procedure used to test for HOMOGENEITY OF VARIANCE. Examples include the BARTLETT TEST FOR EQUALITY OF VARIANCE and the LEVENE TEST FOR EQUALITY OF VARIANCE. The assumption that the VARIANCES in the populations sampled are substantially equal is basic to many statistical procedures. If this assumption is violated, it may be necessary to transform the data or use NONPARAMETRIC TESTS. Also called **test of homogeneity**.

test for independence a procedure used to test the hypothesis of association or relationship between two variables. The test compares the observed frequencies of a variable with the frequencies that would be expected if the NULL HYPOTHESIS of no association (i.e., statistical independence) were true. The CHI-SQUARE TEST is often used for this purpose.

test for normality any procedure used to test whether a data set follows a NORMAL DISTRIBUTION. Many statistical procedures are based on the assumption that the RANDOM VARIABLE is normally distributed. When this assumption is violated, interpretation and inference from the statistical tests may not be warranted. Often normality is most conveniently assessed using graphical methods, such as a STEM-AND-LEAF PLOT, to visualize the differences between an empirical distribution and the standard normal distribution. Alternatively, numerical methods can be used to present summary statistics, such as SKEWNESS and KURTOSIS, which indicate the degree of nonnormality. In addition, there are statistical tests of normality, such as the KOLMO-GOROV–SMIRNOV GOODNESS-OF-FIT TEST, the SHAPIRO–WILK TEST, the DARLING TEST, and the CRAMÉR–VON MISES GOODNESS-OF-FIT TEST.

test for two independent proportions a statistical test used to determine whether a PROPORTION created by a random sample represents the proportion for the entire population or whether

T

the difference between two proportions, measured in two samples, is statistically significant. An example is the z TEST for a population proportion.

testing effect the research finding that the long-term retention of information is significantly improved by testing learners on the information. Exams or tests seem to activate retrieval processes that facilitate the learning of study material and cause knowledge to be stored more effectively in long-term memory.

test interpretation the clinical, educational, vocational, or other practical implications and inferences given to a particular test result. Such conclusions are typically drawn by an expert in testing or by suitable computer software.

test item a constituent part, or the smallest scoreable unit, of a test. It is the stimulus (question or task) to which a test taker responds.

test norm the standard of performance typically attained in a test, as established by testing a large group of people (the STANDARDIZATION GROUP) and analyzing their scores. In NORM-REFERENCED TESTING, subsequent test takers' scores on the test are compared with the test norm to provide an estimate of the position of the tested individual in a predefined population, with respect to the trait being measured.

test of association any of a category of STATISTICAL TESTS that examines the degree of relationship or dependence between variables. An example is the CHI-SQUARE TEST.

test of extreme reactions a procedure used to test for differences in range between the responses (scores) of a treatment group and those of the control group. In some experiments, the treatment is likely to increase the scores of some participants and at the same time decrease the scores of other participants; in contrast, the control group does not experience such reactions. A situation in which some treated participants are likely to experience extreme reactions in either direction is one that generally is subject to intentional distortion of responses. Tests of extreme reactions are typically tests of ranks and are used when there is an indication beforehand that the experimental condition may cause such reactions.

test of homogeneity see TEST FOR EQUALITY OF VARIANCE.

test of significance any statistical test or procedure, such as a T TEST, Z TEST, F TEST, or CHI-SQUARE TEST, used in SIGNIFICANCE TESTING.

test of simple effects in an ANALYSIS OF VARIANCE, a test to determine the effect of one INDEPENDENT VARIABLE on the DEPENDENT VARIABLE at a single level of a second independent variable; the test examines the effects of one of the independent variables with the other independent variable held constant. When a statistically significant interaction is found, in which, for example, there are two independent variables, a and b, with each independent variable having two levels, a_1 and a_2 and b_1 and b_2, the question of interest turns to a systematic examination of the nature of the interaction. In this case, a test of simple effects involves two statistical tests: one of the difference between a_1 and a_2 at b_1, and a second of the difference between a_1 and a_2 at b_2. The comparisons can also be undertaken by examining the difference between b_1 and b_2 at a_1 and the difference between b_1 and b_2 at a_2.

test power see POWER.

test profile an overall description that summarizes an individual's relative standing or characteristics by collating the findings from a series of tests or subtests. For example, a personality profile may present the data gathered on personality and other tests of interest and be used to evaluate the individual in areas related to his or her personal, edu-

T

cational, and professional lives, including temperament, decision-making methods and communication style, and general attitude toward work and life.

test reliability see RELIABILITY.

test–retest correlation the degree of association between measurements of the same variable when the same test is applied on separate occasions. It is a simple estimator of the RELIABILITY of a test or instrument and is indexed by the **test–retest coefficient**.

test–retest reliability see RETEST RELIABILITY.

tests and measurements in psychology, a field of interest that focuses on psychological testing and assessment. It encompasses the knowledge and skills required in understanding, selecting, scoring, and interpreting individual and group-administered psychological, educational, and employment tests. The field also includes the principles necessary to develop tests and to evaluate their usefulness.

test score a numerical value assigned as a measure of performance on a test.

test sensitization the design of a classification test so that it achieves optimum accuracy in identifying those participants who fall into particular categories. For example, a test may be sensitized by including certain items that are designed specifically to identify the highest performing students or employees.

test statistic 1. the numerical result of a STATISTICAL TEST, which is used to determine STATISTICAL SIGNIFICANCE and evaluate the viability of a hypothesis. **2.** any of the statistics relating to a test or its components, such as indices of item difficulty, item RELIABILITY, DISCRIMINABILITY, and so on. See TEST ANALYSIS.

test theory the body of theory underlying the interpretation and use of test scores. Of central concern is the concept of RELIABILITY—its definition and

measurement. Theoretical frameworks include CLASSICAL TEST THEORY, GENERALIZABILITY THEORY, and ITEM RESPONSE THEORY.

testwise *adj.* describing a test taker who has developed skills and strategies that are not related to the construct being measured in the test but facilitate an increased test score. Experience with similar tests, coaching, or the ability to respond advantageously to items that contain extraneous clues and suggestions may yield a score that is higher than the "true" ability of the test taker.

testwise alpha level in HYPOTHESIS TESTING, the SIGNIFICANCE LEVEL (i.e., the level of risk of a TYPE I ERROR) selected for each individual test within a larger experiment. This is in contrast to the EXPERIMENT-WISE ALPHA LEVEL, which sets the total risk of Type I error for the experiment. As more significance tests are conducted, the experiment-wise alpha level goes up, unless there is an adjustment to lower the testwise alpha level. See TESTWISE ERROR RATE.

testwise error rate in a test involving MULTIPLE COMPARISONS, the probability of making a TYPE I ERROR on any specific test or comparison. FACTORIAL DESIGNS allow for the possibility of performing many such individual contrasts, and the related FAMILY-WISE ERROR RATE reflects the possibility of Type I error across the entire set of comparisons. Also called **comparison-wise error rate**; **per-comparison error rate**. See TESTWISE ALPHA LEVEL. See also EXPERIMENT-WISE ERROR RATE.

tetrachoric correlation coefficient (symbol: r_{tet}) an index reflecting the degree of relationship between two continuous variables both of which have been dichotomized. For example, a researcher may need to correlate pass–fail on a test and graduate–nongraduate from school, where pass–fail is the dichotomization of continuous scores

T

on a test and graduate–nongraduate is a dichotomization of grade point average.

tetrad difference criterion in FACTOR ANALYSIS, a procedure used to study the intercorrelations among tests, particularly intelligence tests. Suppose there are five tests presumed to be measuring five specific abilities (e.g., numerical ability, verbal ability, perceptual ability, spatial ability, memory), thus yielding 10 possible intercorrelations. With the tetrad difference criterion, one examines four elements of the CORRELATION MATRIX at a time for each of the possible tetrads, cross-multiplying them and determining whether the differences between the products approximate to zero. With five tests, there are a total of 15 tetrads. If all of the differences between tetrads approximate to zero, the assumption is that there is one underlying factor and five specific factors. Also called **tetrad difference method**.

Theil's method a NONPARAMETRIC approach to fitting a straight REGRESSION LINE to a set of data; it is typically used to reduce the effect of OUTLIERS on the SLOPE and INTERCEPT estimates and when the assumption of NORMALITY is not required. There are two versions of the method, **Theil's incomplete method** and **Theil's complete method**, which differ in the amount of data that enter into the calculations. [Henri **Theil** (1924–2000), Dutch econometrician]

Theil's test for linearity a test to determine whether a linear or nonlinear fit is best for a REGRESSION LINE. [Henri **Theil**]

Theil–Sen estimator a popular rank-based NONPARAMETRIC procedure for fitting a straight line to data. It is efficient in conditions of HETEROGENEITY OF VARIANCE and resistant to OUTLIERS. The procedure is based on choosing the median slope among all lines through pairs of data points. Also called **Kendall robust line-fit method**; **Sen's slope**

estimator. [Henri **Theil**; Pranab K. **Sen** (1937–), Indian-born U.S. statistician]

thematic analysis a QUALITATIVE research strategy that identifies, analyzes, and reports recurrent identifiable patterns or themes within data. There are multiple phases to this process: The researcher (a) familiarizes him- or herself with the data; (b) generates initial codes or categories for possible placement of themes; (c) collates these codes into potential themes, gathering all data relevant to each potential theme; (d) reviews the chosen themes and checks that these work in relation to the coded extracts and the entire data set, effectively generating a thematic "map" of the analysis; (e) defines and names the themes, using continuous ongoing analysis to refine the specifics of each theme and to generate clear definitions and names for each one; and (f) produces the report, which should aim to be a vivid and compelling account of the data. See also GROUNDED THEORY; THEORETICAL SAMPLING.

theorem *n.* in mathematics and logic, a statement or formula that can be deduced from previously established or accepted statements.

theoretical construct an explanatory concept that is not itself directly observable but that can be inferred from observed or measurable data. In psychology, many hypothesized internal processes are of this kind, being presumed to underlie specified overt behaviors. For example, a personality dimension, such as neuroticism, might be described as a theoretical construct that is measured by means of a questionnaire.

theoretical distribution a DISTRIBUTION that is derived from certain principles or assumptions by logical and mathematical reasoning, as opposed to one derived from real-world data obtained by empirical research. Examples of such distributions include the NORMAL DISTRIBUTION, the BINOMIAL DIS-

TRIBUTION, and the POISSON DISTRIBUTION. In general, the procedures of INFERENTIAL STATISTICS involve taking one or more EMPIRICAL DISTRIBUTIONS and referring these to an appropriate theoretical distribution. When there is correspondence between an empirical and a theoretical distribution, the latter may be used to make inferences (predictions) about the probability of future empirical events. Also called **reference distribution**.

theoretical frequency distribution the FREQUENCY DISTRIBUTION that would result if data conformed to the values predicted by a theory or law as opposed to their actual observed values.

theoretical probability the mathematical PROBABILITY of a particular event occurring, as determined by dividing the number of positive outcomes by the total number of possible outcomes. For example, when flipping a coin, the theoretical probability that a tail will occur is 1 divided by 2 (the number of possible outcomes), giving a probability of .5 or 50%. Compare EMPIRICAL PROBABILITY.

theoretical relative frequency distribution for a discrete variable x, a hypothesized or expected distribution of observations or scores that will be obtained at each of the possible values of x in relation to the total number of observations to be made (i.e., their **theoretical relative frequencies**). In contrast to a RELATIVE FREQUENCY DISTRIBUTION, which indicates the relative frequencies with which the values of x actually occur in a chosen sample, a theoretical relative frequency distribution specifies the likely number of occurrences of each of the possible values of x with reference to the anticipated total.

theoretical sampling a sampling strategy, often adopted in QUALITATIVE RESEARCH, that involves the PURPOSIVE SAMPLING of further data while a theoretical framework is still under construction. In order to gain a deeper understanding of the constructs involved, the researcher samples new research sites, cases, incidents, time periods, or data sources to compare with those that have already been studied. In this way he or she seeks to build a theory from the emerging data while continuing to select new samples to examine and elaborate on the theory. See GROUNDED THEORY.

theoretical statistics the study of statistics from a mathematical and theoretical perspective involving PROBABILITY THEORY, DESCRIPTIVE STATISTICS, INFERENCES, and MODEL BUILDING. For example, a researcher could use theoretical statistics to describe a set of achievement data, conduct HYPOTHESIS TESTING, and create models assessing possible predictors of achievement. Also called **mathematical statistics**. Compare APPLIED STATISTICS.

theory *n.* **1.** a principle or body of interrelated principles that purports to explain or predict a number of interrelated phenomena. See CONSTRUCT; MODEL. **2.** in the philosophy of science, a set of logically related explanatory hypotheses that are consistent with a body of empirical facts and that may suggest more empirical relationships. See SCIENTIFIC EXPLANATION. —**theoretical** *adj.*

theory-led thematic analysis a form of THEMATIC ANALYSIS in which a specific theoretical or epistemological approach is used to provide a direction for the analysis.

theory trimming in PATH ANALYSIS or STRUCTURAL EQUATION MODELING, deleting nonsignificant paths from the model to improve model fit.

theory verification the process of developing and citing empirical evidence to increase or bolster the tenability of theories.

therapeutic trial see CLINICAL TRIAL.

therapy outcome research research

T

that investigates the end results of treatment or other interventions to which patients are exposed. The focus is primarily on the "cure" (or not) of patients, but the research also evaluates their experiences, preferences, and values, as well as the wider impact on society. The aim is to identify shortfalls in practice and to develop strategies to prevent or mitigate problems and improve care. See also TREATMENT OUTCOME RESEARCH; TREATMENT PROCESS RESEARCH.

thick description in QUALITATIVE RESEARCH, a strategy that aims to describe and interpret observed behavior within its particular context so that the behavior becomes meaningful to an outsider. The context may be a small unit (a family or work environment) or a larger unit (a community or general culture). The researcher not only accurately describes observed behavior or social actions but also assigns purpose, motivations, and intentionality to these actions by explaining the context within which they took place; thick description conveys the thoughts and feelings of participants as well as the complex web of relationships among them. In contrast, **thin description** is a superficial account that does not explore underlying meanings.

third moment see MOMENT.

third quartile see QUARTILE.

third variable see HIDDEN VARIABLE.

third-variable problem the fact that an observed correlation between two variables may be due to the common correlation between each of the variables and a third variable rather than because the two variables have any underlying relationship (in a causal sense) with each other. In other words, when two variables, *a* and *b*, are found to be positively or negatively correlated, it does not necessarily mean that one causes the other: It may be that changes in an unmeasured or unintentional third variable, *c*, are causing a random and co-incidental relationship between the two variables, or changes independently in variable *a* and variable *b*. For example, as the sales of air conditioners increase, the number of drownings also increases: The unintentional third variable in this case would be the increase in heat. See HIDDEN VARIABLE.

thought experiment a mental exercise in which a hypothesis, theory, or idea is put to the test without actually conducting an experiment or research project. The purpose is to explore the logical consequences of a hypothesis or principle. Thought experiments often involve arguments about events or states of affairs of a hypothetical or counterfactual nature, which nevertheless have implications for the actual world. They can be used to challenge the intellectual status quo, correct misinformation, identify flaws in an argument, or generate ideas as part of a problem-solving exercise. Thought experiments are most familiar in philosophy but are also used in the physical sciences, generally as a step toward designing a physical experiment. Also called **idealized experiment**.

threats to validity factors that may threaten the VALIDITY of inferences drawn from the results of an experiment or research program. For example, common threats to the INTERNAL VALIDITY of an experiment include (a) lack of clear TEMPORAL PRECEDENCE among variables, leading to confusion of cause and effect; (b) SAMPLING BIAS or other nonrandom factors in the assignment of participants to the different conditions of the experiment; (c) the possibility that events extraneous to the experiment, including REGRESSION TOWARD THE MEAN and naturally occurring changes over time, could cause the observed effect; and (d) ATTRITION of participants, especially where differential attrition rates between groups produce artificial effects.

Common threats to the converse EX-

TERNAL VALIDITY of an experiment (i.e., the extent to which its results can be generalized) include (a) the possibility that an effect found with certain units or participants may not hold if other units had been studied; (b) the possibility that the results obtained in one situation, such as studying the effects of a treatment program over one year, will not be the same in another situation (e.g., if the program was extended to two years); (c) the possibility that the results obtained with one measure or observation may not hold if other measures or observations were used; and (d) the possibility that an effect found in one setting (e.g., an inner city) may not hold in another setting (e.g., a rural area). See also CONSTRUCT VALIDITY; STATISTICAL CONCLUSION VALIDITY.

three-mode factor analysis an extension of classical two-mode FACTOR ANALYSIS to **three-mode data**, that is, data classified by three characteristics at once. It enables the researcher to perform a simultaneous factor analysis of all three modes. For example, the scores of a sample of individuals on a battery of tests could be classified by the individuals in the sample as well as by the tests in the battery: The sample of individuals would constitute one mode of the data and the battery of tests a second mode. If the battery of tests were administered to the sample of individuals on several occasions, the set of occasions would constitute a third mode. A three-mode factor analysis would identify factors appearing from correlations in each of the different modes and those extending across modes.

three-parameter model in ITEM RESPONSE THEORY, a model that specifies three parameters affecting an individual's response to a particular test item: (a) the difficulty level of the item; (b) the DISCRIMINATING POWER of the item; and (c) in multiple-choice items, the effect of guessing. The probability of a correct response to the item is held to be a mathematical function of these parameters.

three-period crossover design a specific CROSSOVER DESIGN that is used in treatment research. As in other such designs, part way through the experiment, all participants "cross over" or are switched to another experimental condition. A three-period design usually involves two different treatments and a control. For example, a researcher may be interested in studying the effects of a low dose (D1) and high dose (D2) drug on the behavior of participants; the experiment will also involve administration of a placebo (D0). A three-period crossover design would involve the following sequences of drug intervention: sequence #1 as D0, D1, D2; sequence #2 as D1, D0, D2; and sequence #3 as D1, D2, D0. Observations are collected before treatment and after treatment in each of the dosage conditions.

three-quarters high rule a general rule of thumb stating that the height (y-axis) of a graph should be roughly three fourths the length (x-axis) of the graph. This is to avoid the distortion of the data that can result from choosing arbitrary (or deliberately misleading) scales of measurement along the x- and y- axes. The representation of numbers on the graph should be directly proportional to the numerical quantities that are being represented.

three-sigma rule a rule of thumb stating that in a NORMAL DISTRIBUTION nearly all (approximately 99%) of the values will lie within three STANDARD DEVIATIONS (or sigmas) of the mean. In certain problems in probability theory and mathematical statistics, an event is considered to be practically impossible if it lies outside this region of values.

three-stage sampling see MULTISTAGE SAMPLING.

three-way analysis of variance an ANALYSIS OF VARIANCE that isolates the MAIN EFFECTS of three independent vari-

T

Stress level	Television violence		
	None	Moderate	High
	Sugar		
High	20	30	51
Low	17	15	16
	No sugar		
High	10	20	32
Low	10	12	8

three-way table

ables, *a*, *b*, and *c*, on a dependent variable and their INTERACTION EFFECTS— one THREE-WAY INTERACTION, $a \times b \times c$, and three two-way interactions, $a \times b$, $a \times c$, and $b \times c$.

three-way classification 1. a classification of observed data into groups or classes based on a consideration of three characteristics at the same time. For example, a college population could be classified by gender, year in college, and major. The correlations in such data can be analyzed using a THREE-MODE FACTOR ANALYSIS. **2.** a three-way CHI-SQUARE TEST used to determine the significance of the difference between the frequencies of occurrence in three categories.

three-way design an experimental design in which three INDEPENDENT VARIABLES are examined simultaneously to observe their separate MAIN EFFECTS and their joint INTERACTION EFFECTS on a DEPENDENT VARIABLE of interest. Data from such designs often are evaluated with a THREE-WAY ANALYSIS OF VARIANCE.

three-way interaction in a THREE-WAY ANALYSIS OF VARIANCE, the joint effect of all three independent variables, *a*, *b*, and *c*, on a dependent variable. A statistically significant three-way interaction indicates that one or more of the three possible two-way interactions ($a \times b$, $a \times c$, and $b \times c$) differ across the levels of a third variable. For example, the $a \times b$ interaction may differ for one level of *c* compared to another level of *c*. A three-

way interaction is a type of HIGHER ORDER INTERACTION.

three-way mixed design an experimental design in which there are three variables of interest and where at least one variable is a BETWEEN-SUBJECTS FACTOR (e.g., gender) and at least one variable is a WITHIN-SUBJECTS FACTOR (e.g., pretest and posttest scores for the same participants); the third factor can be either within subjects or between subjects. Data from such designs often are evaluated with a **three-way mixed design analysis of variance**.

three-way repeated measures design see THREE-WAY WITHIN-SUBJECTS DESIGN.

three-way table in THREE-WAY CLASSIFICATION, a tabular presentation of the values for the three classes or variables. This typically takes the form of a set of two-way tables, as in the above hypothetical example of aggression ratings in a sample of 120 children as a function of stress levels, level of violence in a television program, and sugar intake.

three-way within-subjects design an experimental design in which there are three variables or factors of interest and the same participants are studied in each of the levels of each of the factors. For example, suppose *a*, *b*, and *c* represent type of training (lecture vs. reading), type of content (physics vs. psychology), and multiple tests over a nine-month training course (tests at 3, 6, and 9 months). All participants receive all treatment conditions of all three factors; that is, all participants receive both types of training, for both contents, and are tested three times. Data from such designs often are evaluated with a **three-way within-subjects analysis of variance**. Also called **three-way repeated measures design**.

threshold autoregression (TAR) an AUTOREGRESSIVE MODEL used in the analysis of nonlinear TIME SERIES. Nonlinear time-series models have the advantage of being able to capture asymmetries, jumps, and time irreversibility in complex empirical phenomena, such as financial and economic data (e.g., changes in interest rates). The TAR model allows for changes in the model parameters when the value of an exogenous variable (i.e., one from outside the time series of interest) crosses a particular threshold.

threshold-crossing data in a THRESHOLD MODEL, data used to determine the point in time at which a THRESHOLD EFFECT occurs in the dependent variable. This may have to be imputed (see IMPUTATION) if observation has not been continuous.

threshold-crossing model see THRESHOLD MODEL.

threshold effect an effect in a DEPENDENT VARIABLE that does not occur until a certain level, or threshold, is reached in an INDEPENDENT VARIABLE. For example, a drug may have no effect at all until a certain dosage level (the threshold value) is reached. The change in the dependent variable can be either an irreversible dichotomous change, for example, from "functional" to "not functional," or it can be continuous, such that the dependent variable changes each time the independent variable crosses the threshold in either direction.

threshold model any model specifying that there is a value in a range of values on an INDEPENDENT VARIABLE at which the DEPENDENT VARIABLE (e.g., the behavior or action of a participant) changes from one state (e.g., unwilling to buy a product) to another (e.g., willing to buy the product). Also called **threshold-crossing model**.

Thurstone scaling a method for developing a scale to assess attitudes toward a single subject of interest. There are six basic steps in the general approach: (a) identify the CONSTRUCT of interest (e.g., attitudes toward providing public funds for charter schools); (b) generate statements that describe specific attitudes that people might have toward such a construct; (c) have judges or subject matter experts rate each statement on a numerical scale in terms of how far each statement indicates a favorable attitude toward public funding for charter schools (e.g., the rating 1 = *extremely unfavorable attitude toward public funding for charter schools* and the rating 11 = *extremely favorable attitude toward public funding for charter schools*); (d) compute scale score values for each item, together with the mean or median and some measure of VARIANCE; (e) select the final scale items, choosing statements that are at equal intervals across the range of means or medians—for example, select one statement for each of the 11 mean values, with the constraint that there be little variance in ratings for the statements; and (f) administer the scale by asking participants to agree or disagree with each statement. To get an individual's total scale score, the scale scores of all the items that the person agreed with are averaged. [Louis Leon **Thurstone** (1887–1955), U.S. psychologist]

tied ranks in a NONPARAMETRIC TEST that involves ranking data, the ranks assigned to two or more data points that have the same values. Such data are usually given a rank that is the mean of their positions in the ascending order of ranks. For example, suppose the data reveal that Case 1 has the lowest value, followed by Cases 2, 3, and 4, each of

T

which yields the same value; Cases 5 and 6 have the next-to-highest and highest values, respectively. Here Cases 2, 3, and 4 can be awarded the tied rank of 3, as this is the mean value of 2 + 3 + 4.

time-constant covariate see TIME-INDEPENDENT COVARIATE.

time-dependent covariate a PREDICTOR VARIABLE whose values change over time or the course of the study for an individual (e.g., blood pressure, dose of drug). Time-dependent variables are relevant in SURVIVAL ANALYSIS. Also called **time-varying covariate**. Compare TIME-INDEPENDENT COVARIATE.

time-dependent Cox regression model see COX REGRESSION ANALYSIS.

time-homogeneous Markov chain a TIME-SERIES model in which an event's probability is dependent only upon the immediately preceding event in the series and the transition probabilities do not change over time (i.e., the probability of going from State A to State B today is the same as it will be at any time in the future). Also called **time-homogeneous stationary chain**. See MARKOV CHAIN.

time-independent covariate a PREDICTOR VARIABLE that is measured at the outset of a study and whose values do not change over time or the course of the study for an individual (e.g., gender, year of birth). Time-independent covariates are relevant in SURVIVAL ANALYSIS. Also called **time-constant covariate**. Compare TIME-DEPENDENT COVARIATE.

time-lag design a type of QUASI-EXPERIMENTAL RESEARCH in which participants of the same age are compared at different time periods. It is typically used in developmental, educational, and social psychological research to study whether there are differences in a given characteristic for samples of equal age but drawn from different cohorts measured at different times. For example, a time-lag study of intelligence might compare a group of people who were 20 years old in 2005 with groups who were 20 years old in 2006, 2007, and 2008. Time-lag designs have the benefit of controlling for time-of-testing effects. Thus, although no differences between ages are examined, the researcher can determine differences due to changes in the environment over time. However, there are drawbacks of low INTERNAL VALIDITY and the difficulty in separating COHORT EFFECTS from AGE EFFECTS.

time-lagged correlation the correlation of a measure at one point in time with the value of that same measure at a different point in time. An example is the correlation of IQ scores of individuals at 5 years of age with their IQ scores when they are 10 years of age. See STABILITY COEFFICIENT.

time-lag study a LONGITUDINAL DESIGN in which participants are measured on two variables at two or more different points of time, with a view to determining whether one is more likely to "cause" the other. Ideally, the measurements of the variables are separated by the length of time it takes for the cause to influence the effect. There are limitations to the procedure for inferring causality, particularly the OMITTED-VARIABLE BIAS or the THIRD-VARIABLE PROBLEM.

time–location sampling a method of finding research participants in which members of a hard-to-reach target population (e.g., homeless persons, migrant workers) are recruited from specific locations at which they may be found during specific time periods when they are likely to be present. The sample is selected in stages: (a) The SAMPLING FRAME is determined, comprising all of the locations at which there is sufficient attendance by persons in the population of interest to make sampling worthwhile. (b) A random sample of locations is chosen from this frame. If attendance depends on day of the week and time of day, a sampling period is then chosen for each location in the sample. (c) A sample of participants is chosen, usually randomly, during each sampling event. Also called **time–location cluster sampling**; **time–space sampling**; **venue-based sampling**; **venue sampling**; **venue time-based sampling**.

time-reversible Markov chain a MARKOV CHAIN in which it is not possible to determine, given the states at a number of points in time after running the STOCHASTIC PROCESS, which state came first and which state arrived later.

time sampling in DIRECT OBSERVATION, a data collection strategy that involves noting and recording the occurrence of a target behavior whenever it is seen during a stated time interval. The process may involve fixed time periods (e.g., every 5 minutes) or random time intervals. For example, a researcher may observe a group of children for 10 seconds every 5 minutes for a specific 30-minute period each day, noting the occurrence or nonoccurrence of particular behaviors (overt actions). Observations taken during these periods are known as **time samples**. An individual score is made on the basis of one or more of the following: (a) number of time units in which the defined behavior occurs, (b) total frequency of occurrence of the defined behavior in the total observational time, and (c) average frequency of the defined behavior per unit of time. See PARTIAL-INTERVAL RECORDING; WHOLE-INTERVAL RECORDING.

time score a score based on the amount of time used to complete a particular task. An example is the number of minutes a 3-year-old child requires to solve a simple puzzle.

time-sequential design an experimental design to separate AGE EFFECTS from time of measurement and COHORT EFFECTS (i.e., to determine if the results

obtained are age-related only). In a time-sequential design a second age group is added to a TIME-LAG STUDY, and two or more cross-sectional comparisons are made at different times of testing.

time series a set of measures on a single attribute, variable, or construct obtained repeatedly over time.

time-series analysis a branch of statistics that involves the analysis of changes in a single variable recorded repeatedly over time. The data may have an internal structure (such as AUTOCORRELATION, trend, or seasonal variation) that should be accounted for and that provides input allowing for the prediction of future values of the variable. Compare CROSS-SECTIONAL ANALYSIS.

time-series data a sequence of measurements taken at successive times separated by specified time intervals. The data have a natural temporal ordering (e.g., chronological order).

time-series design an experimental design that involves the observation of units (e.g., people, countries) over a defined time period. Data collected from such designs may be evaluated with TIME-SERIES ANALYSIS.

time-series plot a graph on which TIME-SERIES DATA are connected by straight lines, used to show the changes of the measured variable (y-axis) relative to the different measurement times (x-axis).

time-varying covariate see TIME-DEPENDENT COVARIATE.

Tobit analysis a type of REGRESSION ANALYSIS used when a DEPENDENT VARIABLE with values above or below a certain threshold takes on the value of that threshold; that is, the exact value of the variable is unknown or ignored (see CENSORED DATA). For example, in an analysis of aptitude in college students, the dependent variable could be a score on a standardized aptitude test that has an upper limit of 500 (the threshold value).

T

Students who answer all questions on the test correctly receive a score of 500, even though these students may not have equal aptitude. In such a case the influence of INDEPENDENT VARIABLES, such as reading and math scores, on the dependent variable of academic aptitude is more appropriately studied with Tobit regression analysis than with ordinary LEAST SQUARES REGRESSION because the threshold values would bias the slope of the obtained REGRESSION LINE. Also called **censored regression**; **Tobit model**. [James **Tobin** (1918–2002), U.S. economist]

tolerance *n.* permissible or allowable deviation from a specified value or standard. —**tolerant** *adj.*

tolerance interval a range of values within which, with some probability, a specified proportion of a population falls. For instance, one may be 95% confident that 90% of the population will fall within the range specified by the tolerance interval. It differs from a CONFIDENCE INTERVAL, which bounds a single population parameter (e.g., the mean or variance).

tolerance limit the upper or lower value of a TOLERANCE INTERVAL.

topastic error of measurement the partly random, partly systematic error or variance that results when the taker of a multiple-choice test has the opportunity to get some of the answers correct by guessing.

top-down clustering (top-down hierarchical clustering) see DIVISIVE CLUSTERING.

total degrees of freedom the total number of observations in an analysis minus one. For example, in an experiment in which there are four conditions, with 20 participants randomly assigned to each condition, there are 80 independent observations: The total degrees of freedom is 79 (80 – 1) observations, as there is one constraint on any value that

will be computed to describe the sample, such as the MEAN. Relatedly, each individual condition has its own DEGREES OF FREEDOM as well: 20 – 1 = 19.

total effect in the study of causal effects, the total extent to which the dependent (or outcome) variable is changed by the independent (or predictor) variable, including any indirect effect through a MEDIATOR. In a simple example, if the independent variable, *x*, is presumed to cause the outcome variable, *y*, the PATH COEFFICIENT of this direct effect, *A*, is the total effect. If there is an intervening variable, linked by two path coefficients, *B* and *C*, this indirect effect is *BC*, and the total effect is *A* + *BC*. See also PATH ANALYSIS.

total probability law a law relating to BAYES THEOREM and conditional probabilities, stating that, for two events, A and B, the probability of A occurring is equal to the probability that both A and B occur plus the probability that A occurs and B does not.

total sum of squares (symbol: *TSS*) in ANALYSIS OF VARIANCE and REGRESSION ANALYSIS, the SUM OF SQUARES due to the effects of treatment plus the sum of squares due to error.

total variance in ANALYSIS OF VARIANCE and REGRESSION ANALYSIS, the variability that is due to the effects of treatment (TRUE VARIANCE) plus the variability that is due to error (ERROR VARIANCE).

trace *n.* in multivariate statistics and linear algebra, the sum of the elements on the MAIN DIAGONAL of a SQUARE MATRIX.

training sample a representative sample of a larger population that is typically used to develop a model or to obtain conditional probabilities in BAYESIAN analysis.

training set a portion of a TIME SERIES used to predict future values, that is, to train (fit) a model for prediction.

Training sets are used in artificial intelligence (e.g., for neural networks), statistical modeling, and other areas of information science.

trait *n.* **1.** an enduring personality characteristic that describes or determines an individual's behavior across a range of situations. **2.** in ITEM RESPONSE THEORY, an individual's level of competence on a certain task or aptitude measurement.

trait profile a graphic display of test scores in which each score represents an individual TRAIT. These scores or ratings are often arranged on a common scale to enable them to be interpreted quickly. The hypothetical example below shows a respondent's results (given in T SCORES) on a personality questionnaire assessing neuroticism, extraversion, openness, agreeableness, and conscientiousness. Also called **psychogram**. See TEST PROFILE.

trait rating a technique in which a given behavioral feature or trait (e.g., a character trait or attribute) is observed, rated, and recorded.

trait–treatment interaction (**TTI**) the interaction between traits (e.g., gender, aptitude) and conditions of treatments (e.g., methods of instruction) as it affects a dependent variable (e.g., scores on an academic test). Using ANALYSIS OF VARIANCE or MULTIPLE REGRESSION analysis, it is possible to determine the best type of treatment for people with different traits. Also called **aptitude–treatment interaction** (**ATI**).

trait validity the degree to which a test is capable of measuring a trait. A test has trait validity if it demonstrates an association between the test scores and the prediction of an underlying trait. See also MULTITRAIT–MULTIMETHOD MATRIX.

transfer function model in TIME-SERIES ANALYSIS, a type of model used to forecast a time series that is influenced by present and past values of other time series.

transformation *n.* the conversion of data to a different form through a rule-based, usually mathematical process, for example, changing Fahrenheit to Celsius. In statistics, a RAW SCORE is often transformed into a STANDARDIZED SCORE for purposes of comparison. See also LINEAR TRANSFORMATION; NONLINEAR TRANSFORMATION. **—transform** *vb.* **—transformational** *adj.*

transformed score a score that has been changed into another scale to allow direct comparison and meaningful interpretation with other scores. For example, a RAW SCORE of 44 on a first test might not mean the same thing as a raw score of 44 on the second test. The transformation could be to percentages: 44 on the first test could be out of 100 items, and thus represent 44%, while on the second test it could be out of 50 items, and thus have a transformed

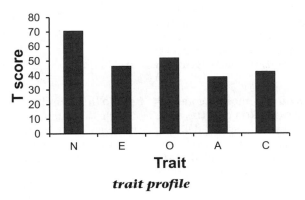

trait profile

Initial behavior	Subsequent behavior									
	1	2	3	4	5	6	7	8	9	10
1. Change talk	.24	.06	.16	.11	.49	.36	.04	.04	.01	.30
2. Question positive	.15	.15	.17	.30	.32	.25	.02	.04	.02	.25
3. Question negative	.06	.02	.08	.10	.22	.09	.02	.01	.01	.32
4. Question neutral	.12	.02	.36	.32	.15	.05	.01	.01	.01	.02
5. Simple reflection	.09	.05	.28	.02	.10	.28	.00	.02	.00	.02
6. Complex reflection	.26	.36	.32	.02	.12	.31	.00	.00	.00	.02
7. Raise concern	.04	.06	.40	.10	.04	.02	.00	.03	.02	.10
8. Give affirmation	.10	.06	.26	.09	.03	.02	.00	.01	.03	.09
9. Give advice	.07	.03	.01	.01	.02	.01	.01	.01	.00	.11
10. Other	.06	.01	.03	.02	.02	.04	.01	.01	.00	.50

transition matrix

score of 88%. Similarly, STANDARDIZED SCORES also can be transformed. For example, a Z SCORE can be transformed to a T SCORE.

transient state in MARKOV CHAIN analysis, a state (*i*) that can be left for another state (*j*) from which there is no possible return to *i*. Compare ABSORBING STATE.

transition matrix a SQUARE MATRIX used to describe the transitions of a MARKOV CHAIN and the probabilities of moving from one state to another. Each row contains the probabilities of moving from the state represented by that row to the other states.

For example, a researcher might construct a transition matrix similar to the hypothetical example above to represent conversational exchange during a therapy session.

The numbers give the probabilities that if the speech act in the row category occurs—from either the therapist or the client—the response by the other person will be the speech act in the column category. Also called **Markov matrix; probability matrix; substitution matrix**.

transition model a model representing the TRANSITION PROBABILITIES from one state to another, thereby defining the possible changes in state for the events being studied. Also called **state transition model**. See also MARKOV CHAIN.

transition probability the probability of moving from one state of a system into another state. If a MARKOV CHAIN is in state *i*, the transition probability, p_{ij}, is the probability of going into state *j* at the next time step.

translation and back-translation a method of ensuring that the translation of an assessment instrument into another language is adequate, used primarily in cross-cultural research. A bilingual person translates items from the source language to the target language, and a different bilingual person then independently translates the items back into the source language. The researcher can then compare the original with the back-translated version to see if anything important was changed in the translation.

transpose *n.* in matrix algebra, a matrix formed by interchanging the rows and columns of the original matrix.

$$
\begin{array}{cc}
\text{original} & \text{transpose} \\
(\mathbf{X}) & (\mathbf{X}^T) \\
\begin{bmatrix} 1 & 2 & 3 \\ 4 & 5 & 6 \\ 7 & 8 & 9 \end{bmatrix} &
\begin{bmatrix} 1 & 4 & 7 \\ 2 & 5 & 8 \\ 3 & 6 & 9 \end{bmatrix}
\end{array}
$$

t ratio the formula used for the T TEST, in which the numerator is the difference between the two means of the groups and the denominator is a measure of the DISPERSION of the scores. The *t* value is compared to a T DISTRIBUTION table to determine if the difference between the means is significant or likely to have been a chance finding.

treatment *n.* the intervention to which some participants in an experimental design (the EXPERIMENTAL GROUP or treatment group) are exposed, in contrast to a CONTROL GROUP, who do not receive the intervention. Also called **treatment condition**. See TREATMENT LEVEL.

treatment-by-blocks design see RANDOMIZED BLOCK DESIGN.

treatment-by-subjects design see WITHIN-SUBJECTS DESIGN.

treatment combination 1. the particular combination of treatments administered to a participant in a study. **2.** the combination of levels of different FACTORS in a FACTORIAL DESIGN.

treatment condition see TREATMENT.

treatment effect the magnitude of the effect of a treatment (i.e., the INDEPENDENT VARIABLE) upon the response variable (i.e., the DEPENDENT VARIABLE) in a study. It is usually measured as the difference between the level of response under a control condition and the level of response under the treatment condition in standardized units. See EFFECT SIZE.

treatment group see EXPERIMENTAL GROUP; TREATMENT.

treatment level the specific condition to which a group or participant is exposed in a study or experiment. For example, in a design employing four groups, each of which is exposed to a different dosage of a particular drug, each dosage amount represents a level of the treatment factor.

treatment outcome research research designed to evaluate the efficacy of interventions and to investigate the mechanism by which effective interventions produce change. It is designed to answer such questions as the following: Is treatment better than no treatment? Is

one treatment better than another? If a treatment is effective, do some levels of the treatment produce better outcomes than others? Are the benefits of treatment worth the cost? See also THERAPY OUTCOME RESEARCH.

treatment population the larger group to which the results obtained from the EXPERIMENTAL GROUP (or treatment group) in a study will be generalized.

treatment process research research, usually of a clinical nature, that investigates how interventions activate mechanisms of behavior change. See also TREATMENT OUTCOME RESEARCH.

treatment-received analysis assessment of the outcome of a RANDOMIZED CLINICAL TRIAL that focuses only on participants who actually received the treatment, rather than those to whom it was prescribed (see INTENTION-TO-TREAT ANALYSIS). Also called **efficacy subset analysis**.

treatments-by-subjects analysis of variance see WITHIN-SUBJECTS ANALYSIS OF VARIANCE.

treatment trial a research study designed to evaluate the effectiveness of an experimental intervention or procedure, its possible adverse effects, and other information that would contribute to the decision to use the procedure in the future. During the trial the experimental procedure is compared with an existing one, which acts as a control. When the intervention being evaluated is a new drug the term CLINICAL TRIAL is used instead.

treatment validity the extent to which an instrument is of value in identifying those individuals who are likely to benefit from a particular treatment or intervention. The term is used particularly in the field of special needs education.

treatment variability the degree to which the response of participants to *tree diagram*

a treatment differs according to the domain being assessed, the setting in which the treatment occurred, and the intensity of the treatment. See GENERALIZABILITY.

treatment variable the INDEPENDENT VARIABLE, whose impact on a DEPENDENT VARIABLE is studied in a research project.

tree diagram 1. a diagram for generating and depicting a probability distribution. It shows all the possible outcomes of an event and is used to determine the probability of getting specific results where the possibilities are nested. For example, consider an experimental memory task in which participants view multiple target stimuli one at a time and then determine whether subsequently presented cues are targets or distractors. The researcher may use a simple tree diagram similar to the one above to illustrate the recall process.
  Here, θ_s represents the proportion of recall trials where there is sufficient storage and, across all such trials in which there is sufficient storage, θ_r represents the proportion of times with successful retrieval. **2.** see DENDROGRAM. **3.** more generally, any branching depiction of a process or condition. A DECISION TREE is an example.

trend analysis any of several analytic techniques designed to uncover systematic patterns (trends) in a set of variables, such as linear growth over time or qua-

dratic increases in response to increases in the level of an INDEPENDENT VARIABLE (e.g., increased dosage levels). Such analysis is often used to predict future events. Also called **trend test**. See CHI-SQUARE TEST FOR TREND; COX–STUART TEST FOR TREND; CUZICK'S TREND TEST.

trend correlation coefficient a CORRELATION COEFFICIENT that describes a trend in TIME-SERIES DATA. If there is a positive correlation, then the trend is for increases in the variable of interest over time; a negative correlation represents a decrease in the variable over time.

trend line a line on a graph that depicts the overall pattern of relationship between variables. See also TREND ANALYSIS.

trend study a LONGITUDINAL DESIGN in which data are collected at periodic intervals on samples drawn from a particular population and used to reveal trends (systematic tendencies or patterns) over time.

trend test see TREND ANALYSIS.

trial *n.* **1.** in testing, conditioning, or other experimentation, one performance of a given task (e.g., one run through a maze) or one presentation of a stimulus (e.g., an ordered list of three-letter words). **2.** see CLINICAL TRIAL; TREATMENT TRIAL.

trial design the strategy or design used to conduct a CLINICAL TRIAL for the purpose of evaluating the efficacy of a new treatment.

triangular contingency table a special class of incomplete CONTINGENCY TABLE that contains structural zeros in one or more cells above or below the MAIN DIAGONAL.

triangular matrix a SQUARE MATRIX in which the values of all numbers either above or below the MAIN DIAGONAL are zero (a **lower triangular matrix** or **upper triangular matrix**, respectively).

triangular test a test involving SE-QUENTIAL ANALYSIS that can be stopped when a particular POWER is reached and results can be evaluated. It is typically used in clinical trials when it is difficult to recruit participants.

triangulation *n.* the process of confirming a hypothesis by collecting evidence from multiple sources. There are several different types of triangulation. In **data triangulation** various sampling methods are used: The data are collected at different times, from different groups of people, and so forth. **Investigator triangulation** involves multiple researchers in an investigation; **theory triangulation** involves using more than one theoretical scheme to interpret the phenomenon; and METHODOLOGICAL TRIANGU-LATION involves using interviews, observations, questionnaires, documents and other data-collection methods.

triggered causal variable an INDE-PENDENT VARIABLE, causally related to the DEPENDENT VARIABLE, that does not produce any change in the dependent variable unless preceded by another causal variable.

trigram *n.* any three-letter combination, particularly a nonsense syllable used in studies of learning and memory. **2.** in studies of language processing, a sequence of three words, syllables, or other items in which the identity of the first two items is used as a basis for predicting the third.

trimmed mean a mean calculated by averaging the scores in a distribution after removing equal numbers of the highest and lowest values. For example, a researcher may decide to exclude the top and bottom 10% of the distribution; the mean is then calculated on the 90% remaining scores.

trimming *n.* **1.** the exclusion of a fixed percentage of cases at each end of a distribution before calculating a statistic on the set of data. This is done to eliminate the influence of extreme scores on the estimate. See TRIMMED MEAN. **2.** in PATH ANALYSIS, the removal of nonsignificant paths after the first run of analyses. The analysis is then rerun until the best fitting model is obtained. The ultimate model should then be CROSS-VALIDATED on another data set.

triple blind see BLIND.

true experiment a study in which participants are assigned at random to two or more experimentally manipulated treatment conditions or to a treatment group and a control group. This type of experiment is in contrast to QUASI-EXPERIMENTAL DESIGNS, such as NATURAL EXPERIMENTS and FIELD EXPERIMENTS.

true–false test a test in which the participant must respond to statements, words, and the like with either "true" or "false."

true score in CLASSICAL TEST THEORY, that part of a measurement or score that reflects the actual amount of the attribute possessed by the individual being measured.

true variance naturally occurring variability within or among research participants. This VARIANCE is inherent in the nature of the participant and is not due to measurement error, imprecision of the model used to describe the variable of interest, or other extrinsic factors. It represents the variance of the TRUE SCORES among the participants taking the measure.

T

true zero see ABSOLUTE ZERO.

truncated data a set of data in which some values are excluded as a matter of deliberate selection. For example, if the distribution of age being studied focuses on 21 to 65 years of age, those under 21 and over 65 are excluded from the analyses. Truncated data can be contrasted to CENSORED DATA, in which certain values in the data sample are unknown owing to some random cause.

truncated distribution a set of scores lacking values beyond a specific maximum point, below a specific minimum point, or both. See TRUNCATED DATA.

truncated Poisson distribution a POISSON DISTRIBUTION in which a value is excluded. For example, this may occur when the count variable cannot take on the value zero (**zero-truncated Poisson distribution**).

T-scope see TACHISTOSCOPE.

T score a STANDARDIZED SCORE based on a score distribution that has a mean of 50 and a STANDARD DEVIATION of 10. For example, a RAW SCORE that is 1 standard deviation above its mean would be converted to a T score of 60. See TRANSFORMED SCORE.

T-squared test see HOTELLING'S T^2 TEST.

TSS symbol for TOTAL SUM OF SQUARES.

t test any of a class of statistical tests based on the fact that the test statistic follows the T DISTRIBUTION when the NULL HYPOTHESIS is true. Most t tests deal with hypotheses about the mean of a population or about differences between means of different populations, where the populations show NORMAL DISTRIBUTIONS and the variances are unknown and need to be estimated. The test can be used with independent groups (e.g., test scores of those who were given training vs. a control group without training) or dependent groups (e.g., test scores before vs. after training). Also called **Student's t test**.

TTI abbreviation for TRAIT–TREATMENT INTERACTION.

Tukey–Kramer procedure an extension of TUKEY'S HONESTLY SIGNIFICANT DIFFERENCE TEST (HSD test) so that it can be used with samples of unequal size. Whereas the HSD test computes a single CRITICAL DIFFERENCE (CD) for each pair of means, the Tukey–Kramer test uses a different CD as required to evaluate the significance of the difference between each pair of means. [John Wilder **Tukey** (1915–2000 and Clyde Y. **Kramer**, U.S. statisticians]

Tukey lambda distribution a CONTINUOUS DISTRIBUTION that is defined by a particular shape parameter known as lambda (λ): It is used mainly to generate a CORRELATION COEFFICIENT for a PROBABILITY PLOT of a data set. On the basis of the coefficient, a model can be suggested for the set; in particular, it can be used to identify whether a distribution has a long or a short tail. This technique is not appropriate for a distribution (such as the normal distribution) that has only location and scale parameters and no shape parameter. [John Wilder **Tukey**]

Tukey line a procedure for fitting a straight line to data that reduces the impact of OUTLIERS. The data are divided into three groups and the fitted line is determined from the group medians. [John Wilder **Tukey**]

Tukey quick test a NONPARAMETRIC test used to compare two independent samples and to test the NULL HYPOTHESIS of no differences in population medians or means. The test does not require that any special assumptions are met. Also called **Tukey pocket test**. [John Wilder **Tukey**]

Tukey's honestly significant difference test (**Tukey's HSD test**) a MULTIPLE COMPARISON procedure that is used to test for significant differences between all possible pairs of mean values on a variable for groups of research participants; it is generally applied after an ANALYSIS OF VARIANCE has determined that there is a significant difference among three or more means. The procedure simultaneously compares all possible pairs of means based on a single quantity, called the honestly significant difference (HSD), such that if the difference between any two group means exceeds the HSD the corresponding population means are said to be significantly different from each other as well. Tukey's HSD test preserves the FAMILY-WISE ERROR RATE by adjusting the overall SIGNIFICANCE LEVEL to take into account the fact that multiple T TESTS are being conducted. Also called **Tukey's range test**. [John Wilder **Tukey**]

Tukey test of additivity an approach used in TWO-WAY ANALYSIS OF VARI-ANCE to assess whether the independent variables are additively related to the EX-PECTED VALUE of the dependent variable, or whether there is an INTER-ACTION EFFECT. Also called **Tukey's one-degree-of-freedom test**; **Tukey test of nonadditivity**. [John Wilder **Tukey**]

twin control in a TWIN STUDY, a method in which the target twin—that is, the one who has had certain experiences or training or has been exposed to the experimental conditions—is compared against the twin who has not had the experiences, training, or treatment and therefore serves as a CONTROL. Also called **cotwin control**.

twin study research utilizing twins. The purpose of such research is usually to assess the relative contributions of heredity and environment to some attribute. Specifically, twin studies often involve comparing the characteristics of identical and fraternal twins and comparing twins of both types who have been reared together or reared apart. For example, two types of study have been used to investigate intelligence in twins: (a) Identical twins reared apart. Here the genotypes (genetic makeups) are identi-cal but as there is no shared environment any disparity in intelligence must result from the different environments. (b) Comparisons between identical twins reared together and fraternal twins reared together. Here one can assume that each pair of twins shares the same environment, but while the identical twins have 100% of their genes in common, the fraternal twins share only 50% of their genes. The assumptions made in these studies are, however, never completely fulfilled. For example, the identi-cal twins reared apart have had some common environment, if only their intrauterine experiences. Moreover, identical twins reared together usually have more similar environments than fraternal twins raised together. These differences can make the estimations of heritability of intelligence open to some doubts.

two-bend transformation the use of a TRANSFORMATION to stretch out the tails of a distribution, on a graph, when the relationship between two variables produces an S-shaped line, thus eliminating the two bends in the line. The ARC SINE TRANSFORMATION, LOGIT transformation, and PROBIT TRANSFOR-MATION can be used for this purpose. See also ONE-BEND TRANSFORMATION.

two-by-two chi-square test see TWO-WAY CHI-SQUARE TEST.

two-by-two contingency table see TWO-BY-TWO TABLE.

two-by-two crossover design see CROSSOVER DESIGN.

two-by-two factorial design an experimental design in which there are two INDEPENDENT VARIABLES each having two levels. When this design is depicted as a matrix, two rows represent one of the independent variables and two columns represent the other independent variable. Also called **two-by-two design**; **two-way factorial design**. See FACTORIAL DESIGN.

T

two-by-two table a type of TWO-WAY TABLE used to display and analyze data for two DICHOTOMOUS VARIABLES. For example, suppose a survey of a group of 100 participants reported information on two variables: (a) gender (male or female) and (b) major in college (social sciences or humanities).

Major	Male	Female	Total
Humanities	20	40	60
Social sciences	15	25	40

The results could be shown in a two-by-two table similar to the one above. Also called **fourfold table**; **two-by-two contingency table**.

two-factor analysis of variance see TWO-WAY ANALYSIS OF VARIANCE.

two-factor design see TWO-WAY DESIGN.

two-mode data information that records patterns of relationship among two classes of entities (typically actor and event) in such a way that it is possible to describe ties between two sets of nodes at two different levels of analysis. For example, data can be collected on which of 50 women were present at events sponsored by the local rotary club (e.g., 15 events) during the course of the social season in a community. By examining patterns of which women were present (or absent) at which events, it would be possible to infer an underlying pattern of social ties, factions, and groupings among the women. This would be one mode of analysis. At the same time, by examining which events were attended by which women, it would be possible to infer underlying patterns in the similarity of the events. This would be a second mode of analysis.

two-parameter model in ITEM RESPONSE THEORY, a model that specifies two parameters affecting an individual's response to a particular test item: (a) the difficulty level of the item and (b) the ITEM DISCRIMINABILITY. See also RASCH MODEL; THREE-PARAMETER MODEL.

two-period crossover design see CROSSOVER DESIGN.

two-sample runs test see WALD–WOLFOWITZ TEST.

two-sample test any procedure in which data are collected on two samples and then subjected to a test for SIGNIFICANT DIFFERENCES between the two samples. Compare SINGLE-SAMPLE TEST.

two-sample t test a type of T TEST in which the mean value on a variable obtained by one group is compared to the mean value obtained by another distinct group. In other words, two discrete experimental groups are evaluated against one another. By contrast, in the SINGLE-SAMPLE T TEST, the results of only one experimental group are compared to some standard of reference.

two-sigma rule a rule of thumb stating that in a NORMAL DISTRIBUTION approximately 95% of the values lie within two STANDARD DEVIATIONS (or sigmas) of the mean. Thus, if the mean is 50 and the standard deviation is 5, then approximately 95% of the scores will lie between the values of 40 and 60 (i.e., 50 +/– 2 standard deviations or 10 points).

two-stage least squares regression an extension of ordinary LEAST SQUARES REGRESSION (OLS) to cover models that violate some of the assumptions of OLS, such as correlation among ERROR TERMS, error in the dependent variable, reciprocal causality, or the correlation of one or more independent variables with UNMEASURED VARIABLES affecting the dependent variable. In the first stage, the dependent variable is regressed on all of the independent variables in the model and the predicted values from the regression are obtained. The purpose of the first stage is to create new dependent variables that do not violate the assumptions of OLS regression. In the second stage, a standard OLS regression is carried out using the predicted values from the first-stage regression analysis in place of the original dependent variable. The new dependent variable will be uncorrelated with the error term of the original dependent variable because it is a function of the independent variables.

two-stage sampling see MULTISTAGE SAMPLING.

two-stage stopping rule in a CLINICAL TRIAL comparing two treatments, a strategy in which results are examined after only a fraction of the planned number of participants in each group have completed the trial (usually either half or two thirds of the patients). At this point, the test statistic is computed and the trial stopped if the difference between treatment means is significant at the SIGNIFICANCE LEVEL set for this first stage. If not, the remaining participants in each group are studied, the test statistic is recomputed, and the means compared at a significance level set for the second stage. The significance levels for the two stages should be such that they equal the overall significance level for the trial, usually .05 or .01.

two-tailed alternative hypothesis see NONDIRECTIONAL HYPOTHESIS.

two-tailed confidence interval in statistical testing, a CONFIDENCE INTERVAL that specifies both upper and lower limits to the population parameter (see CONFIDENCE LIMIT).

two-tailed hypothesis see NONDIRECTIONAL HYPOTHESIS.

two-tailed p value in a NONDIRECTIONAL TEST of significance, a probability value for making a TYPE I ERROR that falls below the SIGNIFICANCE LEVEL for the test, leading to the rejection of the NULL HYPOTHESIS. In other words, assuming the null hypothesis to be true, the p value is the probability that randomly selected samples would have means that are different, with either sample having the larger mean (see NON-

DIRECTIONAL HYPOTHESIS). For a significance value of .05, .025 marks the CRITICAL REGION at each end of the distribution.

two-tailed test see NONDIRECTIONAL TEST.

two-way analysis of covariance an ANALYSIS OF COVARIANCE in which there are two INDEPENDENT VARIABLES and a COVARIATE whose effects the researcher wishes to bring under statistical control.

two-way analysis of variance an ANALYSIS OF VARIANCE that isolates the MAIN EFFECTS of two independent variables, a and b, and their INTERACTION EFFECT, $a \times b$, on a dependent variable. Also called **two-factor analysis of variance**.

two-way chi-square test a CHI-SQUARE TEST used to determine whether there is a significant relationship between the variables summarized in a TWO-WAY TABLE. Also called **two-by-two chi-square test**.

two-way design a type of FACTORIAL DESIGN in which two INDEPENDENT VARIABLES are manipulated. Also called **two-factor design**.

two-way factorial design see TWO-BY-TWO FACTORIAL DESIGN.

two-way interaction in a TWO-WAY ANALYSIS OF VARIANCE, the joint effect of both independent variables, a and b, on a dependent variable. A statistically significant two-way interaction indicates that there are differences in the influence of each independent variable at their different levels (e.g., the effect of a_1 and a_2 at b_1 is different from the effect of a_1 and a_2 at b_2). See also HIGHER ORDER INTERACTION.

two-way mixed design an experimental design in which there are two independent variables of interest, where one variable is a BETWEEN-SUBJECTS FACTOR (e.g., gender) and the other variable is a WITHIN-SUBJECTS FACTOR (e.g., pre-

T

test and posttest scores for the same participants). Data from such designs may be evaluated with a **two-way mixed-design analysis of variance**.

two-way repeated measures design see TWO-WAY WITHIN-SUBJECTS DESIGN.

two-way table a table in which the joint FREQUENCY DISTRIBUTION of two INDEPENDENT VARIABLES is arrayed. See also TWO-BY-TWO TABLE.

two-way within-subjects design a type of WITHIN-SUBJECTS DESIGN in which there are two variables or factors of interest, *a* and *b*, and the same participants are studied in each of the levels of each of the factors. For example, suppose *a* and *b* represent type of training (lecture vs. reading) and type of content (physics vs. psychology), respectively. All participants receive all treatment conditions of both factors; that is, all participants receive both types of training and are exposed to both contents. Data from such designs may be evaluated with a **two-way within-subjects analysis of variance**. Also called **two-way repeated measures design**.

Type 0 error see TYPE III ERROR.

Type I error the error of rejecting the NULL HYPOTHESIS when it is in fact true. Investigators make this error when they believe they have detected an effect or a relationship that does not actually exist. The projected probability of committing a Type I error is called the SIGNIFICANCE LEVEL or alpha (α) level. Also called **alpha error**; **rejection error**.

Type II error the error of failing to reject the NULL HYPOTHESIS when it is in fact not true. Investigators make this error if they conclude that a particular effect or relationship does not exist when in fact it does. The probability of committing a Type II error is called the beta (β) level of a test. Conversely, the probability of not committing a Type II error (i.e., of detecting a genuinely significant difference between samples) is

called the POWER of the test, where power = $1 - \beta$. Also called **beta error**.

Type III error 1. the error that occurs when there is a discrepancy between the research focus and the hypothesis actually tested. For example, a Type III error would be committed if a researcher collected data on INDIVIDUAL DIFFERENCES within a sample and determined the causes of variation when the question of interest concerned differences between populations. In other words, a Type III error involves providing the right answer for the wrong question. Also called **Type 0 error**. **2.** the error that occurs when a researcher correctly rejects the NULL HYPOTHESIS of no difference between samples but then makes an incorrect inference about the direction of the difference. Researchers investigating the direction of a relationship (e.g., "Which is more?" or "Which is better?") will make a Type III error if they use a NONDIRECTIONAL TEST to make a directional decision. **3.** in clinical tests, attributing a lack of results to the weakness of a treatment when, in fact, the problem was that the treatment was not administered properly.

Type I sum of squares the reduction in the ERROR SUM OF SQUARES obtained by adding a particular factor (e.g., Factor A) to a fit that already includes the other factors in the model (e.g., Factors B, C, and D): In other words, it is the amount of the sum of squares attributable only to Factor A. A Type I sum of squares depends on the order in which factors are listed in the model statement. For some data sets, there would be different results for a model that states B then A than for a model that states A then B; this is because each factor is adjusted only for the factors that were entered before it. If one fits two models, one with A then B, the other with B then A, not only can the Type I sum of squares for Factor A be different under the two models, but there is no way to predict whether the sum of squares will go up or down when A comes second instead of first. Also called **sequential sum of squares**. Compare TYPE II SUM OF SQUARES; TYPE III SUM OF SQUARES.

Type II sum of squares the reduction in the ERROR SUM OF SQUARES obtained by adding a particular factor (e.g., Factor A) to a model consisting of all other factors (e.g., Factors B, C, and D) that do not contain the factor in question. The Type II sum of squares is appropriate for model-building procedures in which one would adjust, for example, B for A, A for B, and then AB (the INTERACTION EFFECT) for A and B. Examination of the different reductions provides insight into the best model. Also called **hierarchical sum of squares**; **partially se-quential sum of squares**. Compare TYPE I SUM OF SQUARES; TYPE III SUM OF SQUARES.

Type III sum of squares the SUM OF SQUARES for a particular factor (e.g., Factor A) after correcting, controlling for, or taking into account all of the other factors in a model (e.g., Factors B, C, and D). The Type III sum of squares does not depend upon the order in which effects are specified in the model. It is also unaffected by the frequency of observations, making it appropriate for designs in which there are unequal numbers of observations in each group. Also called **marginal sum of squares**. Compare TYPE I SUM OF SQUARES; TYPE II SUM OF SQUARES.

T

Uu

ultimate cause the underlying reason for some observed result or event, as compared to the PROXIMATE CAUSE directly preceding it. For example, in a study of the link between a social factor, such as socioeconomic status, and an outcome behavior, such as health behavior, the data may show that lower socioeconomic groups practice poorer health behaviors. However, the ultimate cause may be that lower socioeconomic groups are subject to greater hazard or environmental harm, which in turn discourages healthy behavior. Also called **distal cause; remote cause**.

UMP test abbreviation for UNIFORMLY MOST POWERFUL TEST.

unbalanced design an experimental design having multiple INDEPENDENT VARIABLES in which the number of measurements or observations obtained is different for each condition under study. Although BALANCED DESIGNS generally are preferred for their greater POWER in statistical analyses, unbalanced designs nonetheless may arise due to participant ATTRITION or other unavoidable factors. For example, if a researcher is investigating how sleep and diet influence academic performance and only 35 of the 40 college undergraduates recruited to participate were able to do so through the full term of the project, certain data will be missing for the five people who left the study prematurely and the design will become unbalanced.

unbalanced longitudinal data see BALANCED LONGITUDINAL DATA.

unbiased *adj.* impartial or without net error. In unbiased procedures, studies, and the like any errors that do occur are RANDOM ERROR and therefore self-canceling in the long run.

unbiased error see RANDOM ERROR.

unbiased estimator a quantity calculated from sample data whose value is representative of the true quantity in the larger population. In other words, when data from samples are used to make inferences about unknown quantities (parameters) in populations, an unbiased estimator is one that over repeated sampling has an average equal to the true value of the parameter in the population. For example, an **unbiased estimator of variance** provides an accurate index of the variability of measurements for a given phenomenon in a given population of interest based on calculations made from the SAMPLE VARIANCE. Also called **unbiased statistic**. Compare BIASED ESTIMATOR.

unbiased sampling selecting individuals for a study using a process that yields a group exemplifying the larger population from which it derives. In practice, no strategy produces a completely **unbiased sample** but RANDOM SAMPLING yields a good approximation, as it introduces the minimum possible amount of error in representing the population. Compare BIASED SAMPLING.

unbiased statistic see UNBIASED ESTIMATOR.

uncertainty analysis in an experiment or study, an analysis used to assess the accuracy of measurements and model predictions, taking into account such possible sources of error as instrumentation, methodology, and the presence of CONFOUNDS.

unconditional model a type of HIER-

ARCHICAL LINEAR MODEL that amalgamates the effect of explanatory or PREDICTOR VARIABLES across the different levels of analysis. For example, imagine a study having three levels of analysis: students (Level 1), nested within classrooms (Level 2), further nested within schools (Level 3). An unconditional model would represent variation in the outcome measure or DEPENDENT VARIABLE across the three levels (student, classroom, and school), whereas a CONDITIONAL MODEL would explain the individual influence of each predictor variable on the dependent variable.

unconditional variance the long-term trend in a sequence of observations made over time. Unconditional variance implies that knowledge of individual fluctuations between previous observations is irrelevant to identifying and understanding the overall variability of the sequence as a whole. Compare CONDITIONAL VARIANCE.

unconfounded comparison a comparison of two or more groups of research participants that yields an unbiased estimate of the effect of the treatment or other condition under investigation. For comparisons to be unconfounded, studies must be designed to ensure identical handling of all participants, in addition to their RANDOM ASSIGNMENT to different experimental groups, such that any differences between the groups may be attributed solely to the experimental manipulation rather than the influence of other related factors. Compare CONFOUNDED COMPARISON.

uncontrolled variable a characteristic factor that is not regulated or measured by the investigator during an experiment or study, such that it is not the same for all participants in the research. For example, if the investigator collects data on participants having varying levels of education, then education is an uncontrolled variable. If the investigator, however, were to collect data only on participants with college degrees then education would be identical for all individuals and thus serve as a CONTROL VARIABLE.

uncorrected moment a MOMENT calculated on the basis of the raw data in a distribution, rather than from the same data after CORRECTION for error or some unwanted effect. The term is often applied to moments calculated from a GROUPED FREQUENCY DISTRIBUTION (as in a **corrected moment**).

underdetermination *n.* a situation in which the available evidence is insufficient to know what beliefs to hold in response. For example, if one knows that a person spent $10 on apples and oranges and that apples cost $1 while oranges cost $2, then one knows that the person did not buy six oranges but not whether the person bought one orange and eight apples, two oranges and six apples, and so forth. —**underdetermined** *adj.*

underestimation *n.* a situation in which systematic discrepancies between measurements and model outputs lead researchers to calculate a PARAMETER of interest as being significantly lower than its true value. For example, applying a REGRESSION ANALYSIS in which there are BIASED ESTIMATORS could lead a medical researcher to obtain a lower value for the presence of a particular illness in the general population than is actually the case.

underidentification *n.* a situation, such as may occur during STRUCTURAL EQUATION MODELING, in which it is not possible to estimate all of the model's parameters based on the sample data being analyzed. Compare OVERIDENTIFICATION.

underidentified model a theoretically identified model in which one or more PARAMETER estimates cannot be made because of an insufficient number of available data points. This may occur, for example, when there is high MULTICOLLINEARITY among the variables studied. Empirically underidenti-

U

fied parameters are very unstable. Compare JUST-IDENTIFIED MODEL; OVER-IDENTIFIED MODEL.

underlying dimension an explanatory or descriptive concept, inferred from empirical evidence or theory, that is used to interpret observed outcomes. For example, researchers studying infant attachment may conclude that the different attachment styles demonstrated can be explained by two underlying dimensions of avoidance and anxiety. In FACTOR ANALYSIS and other contexts, such underlying dimensions are called LATENT VARIABLES.

underlying distribution the THEORETICAL DISTRIBUTION for a given population of interest.

underspecified model in CAUSAL MODELING, a predictive formula from which relevant explanatory variables have been excluded, such that the effect estimates it provides are both biased and inefficient. See OMITTED VARIABLE BIAS.

undirected graph a display in which various points (**nodes**) of information are connected by lines (**edges**) having no direction. The value between two nodes often is called a WEIGHT. Thus, the following example has several nodes (e.g., A, B, F, E) and several weights (e.g., 5, 9, 12, 18).

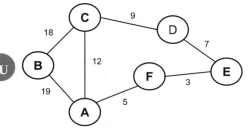

In contrast, a DIRECTED GRAPH uses arrows or numbered nodes to show directionality, such as A leading to B, which in turn leads to E, and so forth.

unequal probability sampling a strategy for selecting a sample of units from a larger population in which different units have different likelihoods of being chosen for inclusion. In SAMPLING WITHOUT REPLACEMENT, for example, each time a unit is chosen to be part of the sample it is removed from further consideration, thus altering the likelihood of inclusion for the remaining units. This contrasts with **equal probability sampling**, in which all population units have the same likelihood of being selected for the sample.

unexplained variance see ERROR VARIANCE.

unfolding *n.* a unidimensional SCALING procedure in which respondents evaluate a set of items and their choices are used to construct a continuum along which their relative preferences are placed. For example, consider a scale measuring attitudes toward marijuana sales. A person who wholeheartedly favors the item "The city should legalize the sale of marijuana" would be located at a different point along the continuum from a person who completely opposes the sale of marijuana, and a person who endorses the item to some extent would be located at yet another point along the continuum. See also MULTIDIMENSIONAL UNFOLDING.

unidimensionality *n.* the quality of measuring a single construct, trait, or other attribute. For example, a unidimensional personality scale, attitude scale, or other scale would contain items related only to the respective concept of interest. Compare MULTIDIMENSIONALITY. —**unidimensional** *adj.*

uniform association model a model for a CONTINGENCY TABLE in which a constant ODDS RATIO is assumed across all of the component cells.

uniform distribution a theoretical CONTINUOUS DISTRIBUTION in which the probability of occurrence is the same for all values of x, represented by $f(x) = 1/(b-a)$, where a is the lower limit of the distribution and b is its upper limit. For example, if a fair die is thrown, the probability of obtaining any one of the six possible outcomes is 1/6. Since all outcomes are equally probable, the distribution is uniform. If a uniform distribution is divided into equally spaced intervals, there will be an equal number of members of the population in each interval. Also called **rectangular distribution**.

uniformly most powerful test (UMP test) a statistical test of one hypothesis against another that has the greatest POWER among all tests available at a given ALPHA value. Suppose the two hypotheses are the NULL HYPOTHESIS of no difference between two groups (Sample 1 mean = Sample 2 mean) and the ALTERNATIVE HYPOTHESIS of some difference between the groups (Sample 1 mean ≠ Sample 2 mean). Since the latter actually is a composite of several possibilities, a UMP test is one defined by a CRITICAL REGION that is best suited to test the null hypothesis against each of the simple hypotheses comprising the larger alternative hypothesis.

unimodal distribution a set of scores with a single peak, or MODE, around which values tend to fluctuate, such that the frequencies at first increase and then decrease. See also BIMODAL DISTRIBUTION; MULTIMODAL DISTRIBUTION.

unipolar rating scale a type of instrument that prompts a respondent to evaluate the degree to which a single quality or attribute is present. For example, consider a five-point scale with the following anchors or benchmarks: (1) *not at all satisfied*, (2) *slightly satisfied*, (3) *moderately satisfied*, (4) *very satisfied*, and (5) *completely satisfied*. Since there is no anchor that represents the opposing quality of dissatisfaction, the scale has one pole. Also called **unipolar scale**. Compare BIPOLAR RATING SCALE.

uniqueness *n.* in FACTOR ANALYSIS, that part of the variance of a variable that it does not share with any other variable in the system. It is given as $1 - h_j^2$, where h_j^2 is the COMMUNALITY of the *j*th variable. Each of the observed variables in the data set being analyzed can be expressed as a combination of a common factor shared among all variables plus a unique factor associated with a measurement error or another specific, individual source of variation.

unit matrix see IDENTITY MATRIX.

unit normal distribution see STANDARDIZED DISTRIBUTION.

unit normal variable see STANDARD NORMAL VARIABLE.

unit of analysis in research, the group of people, things, or entities that are being investigated or studied. For example, in organizational contexts, data can be collected from employees, who in turn are part of departments, which in turn are part of the larger organization, which may have multiple sites in several countries. The unit of analysis chosen influences the methodological and analytical procedures used (e.g., studying groups within organizations may require a HIERARCHICALLY NESTED DESIGN). Also called **analysis unit**; **level of analysis**.

unit root test a statistical procedure that uses an AUTOREGRESSIVE MODEL to determine whether TIME-SERIES DATA exhibit systematic trends, which must be mathematically removed before any analyses may be conducted. Two commonly used unit root tests are the **Dickey–Fuller test** and the **Phillips–Perron test**.

unit-specific model a HIERARCHICAL LINEAR MODEL that aims to identify those outcomes specifically associated with a particular level, magnitude, or category of the independent variable being analyzed. For example, a researcher may be investigating students, who are nested within classrooms, who are further nested within schools. A unit-specific model would address questions about

U

one of these three levels or units of analysis: students (Level 1), classrooms (Level 2), or schools (Level 3). Compare POPULATION-AVERAGED MODEL.

unity *n.* a synonym for the value of 1. Statisticians often state that the statistic or value they are working with "approaches unity," which means it approaches the value of 1.

univariate *adj.* characterized by a single variable. For example, a researcher may collect univariate data by recording how many hours a day students in a particular course spend outside of class on completing their homework. Compare BIVARIATE; MULTIVARIATE.

univariate analysis a statistical examination of data for only one variable of interest. For example, a univariate analysis of study habits for a sample of college students would examine habits across all individuals without taking into account whether a particular student was a freshman, sophomore, junior, or senior. Also called **univariate statistics**. Compare MULTIVARIATE ANALYSIS.

univariate distribution a distribution of values on a single RANDOM VARIABLE according to their observed or expected frequency. If this is a NORMAL DISTRIBUTION it is known as a **univariate normal distribution**. Compare MULTIVARIATE DISTRIBUTION.

univariate outlier an extreme or unusual value occurring for a single variable. For example, if a student in a college course obtains a score of 100 points on an exam when all other students in the course score below 80 points his or her perfect score would be a univariate outlier. Compare MULTIVARIATE OUTLIER.

univariate research research that employs only one DEPENDENT VARIABLE. Compare MULTIVARIATE RESEARCH.

universal set in SET THEORY, the entire collection of elements currently under consideration.

universe *n.* see POPULATION.

universe of admissible generalization in GENERALIZABILITY THEORY, the entire set of conditions to which a researcher wishes to generalize from a subset of actual measurements obtained under specific conditions. It is important when specifying the universe of admissible generalization to isolate and estimate as many potential sources of MEASUREMENT ERROR as is reasonably and economically feasible. Otherwise, unreliable findings may be used to make improper generalizations. Also called **universe of generalization**.

universe of admissible observations in GENERALIZABILITY THEORY, the set of all possible measurements or scores that could reasonably be substituted for one that was actually obtained by a researcher. In other words, any actual behavioral measurement (e.g., a test score) is considered to be a sample from a larger universe of potentially interchangeable measurements. Although research participants cannot be exposed to all possible levels or conditions of a measure (e.g., an infinite pool of test items about a topic), the goal is to characterize the variability of a participant's score over all possible combinations of such levels or conditions.

universe score in GENERALIZABILITY THEORY, an average score for a given person derived from an actual sample of observations and a given UNIVERSE OF ADMISSIBLE OBSERVATIONS.

unmeasured variable 1. in PATH ANALYSIS, any hypothetical variable, LATENT VARIABLE, or unobservable variable. **2.** in REGRESSION ANALYSIS, any variable that is not specifically assessed or evaluated but that is presumed to influence the relationship observed between two other variables, x and y. The influence of such an unmeasured variable is subsumed in the ERROR TERM for y. In many statistical models of relationships, causal estimates may be biased because relevant variables have not been included in the causal systems investigated, a problem generally referred to as OMITTED VARIABLE BIAS. See THIRD-VARIABLE PROBLEM.

unnumbered graphic rating scale see VISUAL ANALOGUE SCALE.

unobtrusive measure a measure obtained without disturbing the participant or alerting him or her that a measurement is being made. For example, a researcher may observe passersby in a public park from a nearby café and document their activities. The behavior or responses of such participants are thus assumed to be unaffected by the investigative process or the surrounding environment. Also called **concealed measure**; **nonreactive measure**. Compare REACTIVE MEASURE.

unobtrusive observation the process of collecting UNOBTRUSIVE MEASURES, such as by the use of hidden cameras.

unplanned comparison see POST HOC COMPARISON.

unpredicted variance see ERROR VARIANCE.

unrelated t test see INDEPENDENT-SAMPLES T TEST.

unrestricted model see FULL MODEL.

unsaturated model see SATURATED MODEL.

unselected sample an informal name for a random sample. See RANDOM SAMPLING.

unselective observation a process in which an individual watches and records all occurrences of a prespecified event within a given period of time. For example, if a researcher wishes to determine whether drivers who have cars of a certain color tend to exceed the speed limit more often, he or she could note the speed and color of every car that passes a particular point within a 5-minute period and then compare the different percentages of speeding cars by

color. Unselective observation is a more objective strategy than SELECTIVE OBSERVATION.

unstandardized score see RAW SCORE.

unstructured interview an interview that is highly flexible in terms of the questions asked, the kinds of responses sought, and the ways in which the answers are evaluated across interviewers or across interviewees. For example, a human resource staff member conducting an unstructured interview with a candidate for employment may ask open-ended questions so as to allow the spontaneity of the discussion to reveal more of the applicant's traits, interests, priorities, and interpersonal and verbal skills than a standard predetermined question set would. Also called **nondirective interview**. Compare STRUCTURED INTERVIEW.

unstructured stimulus a vague, poorly organized, and not clearly identifiable stimulus, such as an inkblot in the Rorschach Inkblot Test. The perception of unstructured stimuli is often thought to be influenced more by the characteristics of the perceiver than by those of the stimulus. Compare STRUCTURED STIMULUS.

unsystematic error see RANDOM ERROR.

unsystematic variance the haphazard or random fluctuation of data for individuals over time. It is one of two types of variance identified in research, the other being **systematic variance** arising from the effects of the INDEPENDENT VARIABLES studied.

U

unweighted means analysis in ANALYSIS OF VARIANCE, a strategy for handling missing data in which the actual sample size in each of the different conditions or levels of the INDEPENDENT VARIABLE is replaced by the average sample size. When participants become ill, withdraw, or otherwise fail to complete a research study, there are no longer equal numbers of cases in each experimental condition. An unweighted means analysis takes this inequality into account by applying an adjusted sample size value across all conditions, thus ensuring that data from all experimental groups contribute equally to the determination of treatment effects. Also called **unweighted means procedure**.

up-and-down method a strategy in which the administration of a stimulus event or item depends on a participant's response to the previous item. The up-and-down method employs fixed, discrete levels and sequential transition rules of moving one level up, moving one level down, or remaining at the current level. For example, in PSYCHO-PHYSICAL RESEARCH, a participant who correctly detects a stimulus during one trial would be presented with a reduced value of the same stimulus in the next trial; conversely, if he or she did not detect the original stimulus its value would be increased in the next trial. Thus, the stimulus value that is presented varies sequentially until a stable estimate is obtained of the individual's sensitivity to the stimulus. Similarly, in computer adaptive testing there is a finite set of possible items with known difficulty levels, and depending on the individual's response to the initial item the next item administered will have the same difficulty or be slightly more or less difficult. The process continues until an estimate of the individual's ability on the trait being measured can be obtained.

upper hinge the point in a distribution of values above which lie one fourth of the data and below which lie the other three fourths of the data. It is equivalent to the third QUARTILE. Compare LOWER HINGE.

upper quartile see QUARTILE.

upper real limit see REAL LIMIT.

upper-tail probability the value at

the extreme right on the x-axis in the plot of a FREQUENCY DISTRIBUTION, denoting the probability of obtaining the highest value in the distribution. Upper-tail probabilities are useful when conducting statistical tests of experimental hypotheses. Compare LOWER-TAIL PROBABILITY.

upper whisker in a BOX-AND-WHISKER PLOT, the line extending from the value at the 75th PERCENTILE to the largest value within one INTERQUARTILE RANGE of that percentile score. Compare LOWER WHISKER.

upward Pygmalion effect an effect in which the expectations of followers or subordinates lead to behavior on the part of the leader or superior that is consistent with these expectations. The behavior of the leader does not reflect his or her true abilities or personality traits, but rather the perception of the leader by subordinates. Compare PYGMALION EFFECT. See SELF-FULFILLING PROPHECY.

urn model a THOUGHT EXPERIMENT in which objects of interest (e.g., people, events) are represented as colored balls placed in an urn or other container. In imagination, the experimenter randomly removes one "ball" from the urn, notes its color, and places it back before repeating the process; the goal is to determine the probability of drawing one color or another. The urn model is a convenient way to calculate certain basic probabilities using CONDITIONAL PROBABILITIES.

U-shaped distribution a graphical representation of a FREQUENCY DISTRIBUTION that is shaped more or less like the letter U, with the maximum frequencies at both ends of the range of the variable. For example, the number of people infected by the flu each year may have a U-shaped distribution by age, with those who are very young or very old having the highest frequency of occurrence, as shown in the hypothetical illustration opposite.

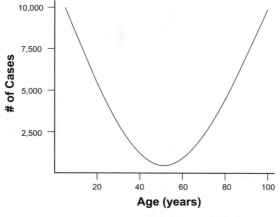

U-shaped distribution

In an **inverted U-shaped distribution**, the most frequent values are in the middle of the distribution and the least frequent values are at the extremes.

Vv

vague prior in BAYESIAN statistics, an imprecise probability specification applied in the estimation of a population parameter when more conclusive information about its true value is lacking. For example, a researcher may use a mean obtained previously for another population to construct a CONFIDENCE INTERVAL within which the mean for the current population of interest may be considered to lie.

validation *n.* the process of establishing the truth or logical cogency of something. An example is determining the accuracy of a research instrument in measuring what it is designed to measure. **—validate** *vb.*

validity *n.* the degree to which empirical evidence and theoretical rationales support the adequacy and appropriateness of conclusions drawn from some form of assessment. Validity has multiple forms, depending on the research question and on the particular type of inference being made. For example, the three major types of test validity are CRITERION VALIDITY, based on correlation with an accepted standard; CONSTRUCT VALIDITY, based on the conceptual variable underlying a test; and CONTENT VALIDITY, based on the subject matter of a test. Other forms of validity prominent in the social sciences include ECOLOGICAL VALIDITY, EXTERNAL VALIDITY, INTERNAL VALIDITY, and STATISTICAL CONCLUSION VALIDITY. See also THREATS TO VALIDITY. **—valid** *adj.*

validity check the process of verifying that a data set is free of errors and adheres to standard or intended rules. Performed manually or using software, a validity check may involve such things as verifying the accuracy of calculations and the legitimacy of included values (e.g., impossible values are not present), confirming that information is consistent across records, and confirming that no records are missing.

validity coefficient an index, typically a CORRELATION COEFFICIENT, that reflects how well an assessment instrument predicts a well-accepted indicator of a given concept or criterion. For example, if a measure of criminal behavior is valid, then it should be possible to use it to predict whether a person (a) will be arrested in the future for a criminal violation, (b) is currently breaking the law, and (c) has a previous criminal record. A validity coefficient could be used to relate scores on the measure to each of these criteria and thus determine how useful the measure actually is for behavioral forecasting.

validity criterion an external concept or standard of comparison that is used to define the attribute an instrument is purported to measure and that is applied in estimating how well the measurement instrument actually fulfills its intended purpose. See CRITERION VALIDITY.

validity diagonal the MAIN DIAGONAL in a MULTITRAIT–MULTIMETHOD MATRIX, which represents correlations between the same construct or trait measured using different methods. See CONVERGENT VALIDITY.

validity generalization the use of META-ANALYSIS and other statistical procedures to assess the evidence of a test's adequacy and appropriateness in multiple situations and settings. Validity generalization typically involves correcting all of the correlations being examined for methodological and statistical limitations and flaws and providing estimates of correlations or results that would have been obtained in the absence of such limitations.

value analysis a type of CONTENT ANALYSIS of written material consisting of a table, or other systematic notation, documenting the frequency of appearance in the material of all expressions referring to specified values.

variability *n.* the degree to which members of a group or population differ from each other, as measured by such statistics as the RANGE, STANDARD DEVIATION, and VARIANCE.

variable *n.* a condition in an experiment or characteristic of an entity, person, or object that can take on different categories, levels, or values and that can be quantified (measured). For example, test scores and ratings assigned by judges are variables. Numerous types of variables exist, including CATEGORICAL VARIABLES, DEPENDENT VARIABLES, INDEPENDENT VARIABLES, MEDIATORS, MODERATORS, and RANDOM VARIABLES. Compare CONSTANT.

variable error see RANDOM ERROR.

variable stimulus in PSYCHO-PHYSICAL RESEARCH, any one of a set of experimental stimuli that are to be systematically compared to a constant stimulus.

variance (symbol: σ^2) *n.* a measure of the spread, or DISPERSION, of scores within a sample or population, whereby a small variance indicates highly similar scores, all close to the sample MEAN, and a large variance indicates more scores at a greater distance from the mean and possibly spread over a larger range. See also STANDARD DEVIATION.

variance analysis see ANALYSIS OF VARIANCE.

variance-balanced design a type of CROSSOVER DESIGN in which the possible sequences of treatments are arranged in such a manner that all PAIRWISE COM-PARISONS can be made with equal precision. In other words, the amount of variation or inaccuracy involved when estimating the average effect for one treatment will be the same as that involved when estimating the average effect for all other treatments.

variance components analysis any statistical procedure for examining MIXED-EFFECTS MODELS and RANDOM-EFFECTS MODELS that decomposes the total variance on a DEPENDENT VARIABLE into that stemming from the effects of the INDEPENDENT VARIABLE (the TRUE VARIANCE) and that produced by extraneous factors (the ERROR VARIANCE). An ANALYSIS OF VARIANCE provides an example. Assume a researcher is studying whether caffeine and gender influence students' test performance. The former is a random variable, as it has numerous possible levels from which to choose a subset to study (e.g., 0 mg, 50 mg, 100 mg, 150 mg), and the latter is a fixed variable, as it may assume only one of two values (male or female). The researcher might use an analysis of variance to apportion the variance in the response measure—test performance—among the two different factors—level of caffeine and being male or female. The central output is a table that shows the proportion of variance attributable to the main effects of the factors, the proportion attributable to interactions between the factors, and the proportion attributable to error and other external factors.

variance components model see RANDOM-EFFECTS MODEL.

variance–covariance matrix see COVARIANCE MATRIX.

variance estimate an index of variation in a population that has been calculated using a sample of that population. For example, a sample STANDARD DEVIATION is an estimate of the deviation in the larger population.

variance explained an indication of

how well variation in one variable (or set of variables) can be accounted for by the variation in another variable. For example, if the CORRELATION COEFFICIENT between a PREDICTOR VARIABLE (x) and a DEPENDENT VARIABLE (y) is 0.25, then 25% of the variability in y is explained by the variability in x.

variance inflation factor (**VIF**) an index of the degree to which the variability of an estimated REGRESSION CO-EFFICIENT is increased because of interrelationships among the variables in an ordinary LEAST SQUARES REGRESSION model. A variance inflation factor exists for each of the k PREDICTOR VARIABLES in the model. A VIF of 1 means that there is no correlation among the kth predictor and the remaining predictor variables (and hence the variance is not inflated at all), a VIF exceeding 4 warrants further investigation, and a VIF exceeding 10 indicates serious MULTI-COLLINEARITY requiring correction.

variance-preservation model a method of conducting a META-ANALYSIS to determine EFFECT SIZES that accounts for variation among study designs. For example, some studies included in the analysis may involve a single INDEPENDENT VARIABLE (a) with a single level while others may involve two independent variables (b, c) with two levels each. To ensure that single-factor effect-size measures are comparable to multiple-factor effect-size measures, a researcher may use a variance-preservation model to treat the multiple-variable design as two single-variable designs (i.e., the treatment effect for a is measured at Level 1 of b and again at Level 2 of b). Variances within each level are then compared to ensure that they do not differ significantly between the two types of designs. Alternatively, a researcher may use a **variance-reduction model**, in which the participants in the single-variable design are stratified into two homogeneous subpopulations (e.g., males and females), such that the vari-

ability within each of the smaller, more homogeneous groups is less than that for the undivided larger group.

variance ratio a comparison of two indices of variance, expressed as a quotient. The F RATIO, which compares effect variances to error variances, is an example.

variance-ratio test see F TEST.

variance-reduction model see VARI-ANCE-PRESERVATION MODEL.

variance-stabilizing transformation in REGRESSION ANALYSIS or ANALYSIS OF VARIANCE, any of a class of mathematical processes that convert data showing HETEROGENEITY OF VARIANCE to a different form, so as to enable the application of specific analytical techniques or to simplify considerations.

variate *n.* **1.** a specific value of a particular VARIABLE. **2.** a RANDOM VARIABLE itself.

variation *n.* fluctuation: the degree of VARIANCE or DISPERSION of values that is obtained for a specific variable.

variation coefficient see COEFFI-CIENT OF VARIATION.

variation ratio a measure of VARIABILITY for numerical values that represent membership in specific categories (i.e., for CATEGORICAL DATA). It indexes the proportion of cases that deviate from the MODE.

varimax rotation a statistical procedure applied within FACTOR ANALYSIS and PRINCIPAL COMPONENTS ANALYSIS to simplify solutions and enhance interpretation of the results. It is a type of OR-THOGONAL ROTATION intended to make each factor have a small number of large FACTOR LOADINGS and a large number of zero (or small) factor loadings. Thus, following a varimax rotation, each original variable tends to be associated with a small number of factors, and each factor represents only a small number of variables. See FACTOR ROTATION.

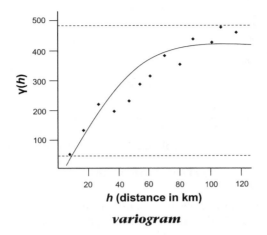

variogram

variogram *n.* a graphical representation of the degree of correlation between values separated by particular distances, providing information about whether values that are closer together in geographic space are more similar than observations that are farther apart. Consider the generic example above, in which the diamonds represent observed data points, the solid curve represents estimated data values, and the dashed line represents VARIANCE.

One may use a variogram, for instance, to examine whether adolescents living in close proximity have more similar perceptions of their neighborhoods than do more widely dispersed adolescents.

varying-coefficient model a model that provides information on the association between a DEPENDENT VARIABLE and a PREDICTOR VARIABLE over time. An extension of MULTIPLE REGRESSION techniques to data that have been collected over multiple occasions (i.e., LONGITUDINAL DATA), varying-coefficient models substitute functional coefficients that reflect the time-dependent relationships between the variables of interest for the constant coefficients used in typical multiple regression.

vector *n.* **1.** a mathematical entity with magnitude and direction. Compare SCALAR. **2.** in MULTIVARIATE ANALYSIS, a one-dimensional arrangement in which the scores of *n* individuals on a particular measure are arrayed. **3.** in MATRIX ALGEBRA, a column or row of a matrix.

vector analysis a branch of mathematics concerned with the study of entities having both magnitude and direction in three-dimensional space.

vector product see PRODUCT VECTOR.

Venn diagram a visual depiction of elements and relations. Consider the following generic example.

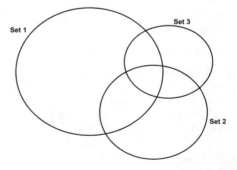

Circles represent the elements of a set, and the union and intersection between or among the circles represent relationships between the sets (i.e., the degree to which they are mutually inclusive or exclusive). [John **Venn** (1834–1923), British logician]

venue sampling see TIME–LOCATION SAMPLING.

vertical line graph

verbal protocol a method of eliciting verbal reports of individuals' thoughts as they perform a set of specified research tasks. Participants are asked to describe whatever they are seeing, thinking, doing, and feeling as it occurs during task performance. Rather than capturing mere summaries of a task's results, the method provides the researcher with insight about the cognitive processes involved in task completion and the representations on which they operate.

verisimilitude *n.* the appearance of being true. In scientific investigation, a theory or model is said to have verisimilitude if it can be shown to be more consistent with empirically verified fact than its predecessors or competitors.

vertical axis see Y-AXIS.

vertical line graph a way of displaying data that is similar to a BAR GRAPH but uses discrete lines of varying height to represent the different values of a variable. For example, the above hypothetical illustration shows the political affiliations of Americans.

video-recall technique a research procedure in which participants review a video recording of their behavior in a previous situation and report what they were thinking, feeling, or otherwise experiencing at that time. The video-recall technique is intended to reduce distortion in SELF-REPORTS, the premise being that reimmersion in the situation generates a more representative set of recollec-

tions with less defensive justification than memory alone.

VIF abbreviation for VARIANCE INFLATION FACTOR.

violation of assumptions a situation in which the theoretical ASSUMPTIONS associated with a particular statistical or experimental procedure are not fulfilled. Common assumptions for statistical tests include NORMALITY of the distribution, equal VARIANCES within the cells of treatment levels, HOMOGENEITY OF VARIANCE, and LINEARITY. Research designs also need to meet certain assumptions, such as RANDOM SAMPLING and RANDOM ASSIGNMENT, sample REPRESENTATIVENESS, and the like. Because violation of assumptions introduces bias, the validity of assumptions must be confirmed prior to data analysis to ensure that the methods and strategies chosen are appropriate and will yield valid results.

violation-of-expectation method a technique for studying infant cognition, based on habituation and dishabituation procedures, in which increases in an infant's looking time at an event or other stimulus are interpreted as evidence that the outcome he or she expected has not occurred. For example, while a baby watches, a researcher may repeatedly return a toy to a blue box. If the researcher sometime later retrieves the same toy from a nearby red box (after a CONFEDERATE surreptitiously moved it) and the baby

**Employee overall performance
during past year**

poor ┃━━━━━━━━━━━━━━━━━━━━━━━┃ excellent

visual analogue scale

looks longer at that red box, it is assumed that he or she has some understanding of object permanence and was not expecting the toy to be there.

visual analogue scale a psychometric instrument used to evaluate subjective characteristics that extend over a range of continuous values: Respondents specify their level of the characteristic of interest by indicating a position along a continuous line anchored at its end points by word descriptors. For example, a visual analogue scale for performance might have *poor* on the left end with a blank line across to *excellent* on the right end, as shown above.

The respondent would mark a place along that line to indicate his or her perceived performance level. Also called **unnumbered graphic rating scale**.

visual test any test intended to measure or study vision, involving stimuli that are viewed. For example, a test of visual function in newborn infants might have items requiring the infants to fixate on a target of black and white concentric circles or track a colorful object as it moves past their eyes.

voice key an electronic device that interfaces between a microphone and a computer, used for recording vocal response times in language-production tasks, such as word or picture naming. When a stimulus is presented the voice key is activated and begins to monitor the sound level from the microphone; if the sound level then exceeds a specific threshold level, indicating speech, the voice key records the amount of time that has elapsed since it was activated.

volunteer bias any systematic difference between individuals who volunteer to be in a study versus those who do not, which may potentially render the resulting group or sample of participants unrepresentative of the larger population.

V

Ww

W 1. symbol for the COEFFICIENT OF CON-
CORDANCE. **2.** symbol for the statistic
obtained from the WILCOXON RANK-
SUM TEST.

W^2 symbol for the statistic obtained from
the CRAMÉR–VON MISES GOODNESS-OF-
FIT-TEST.

wait-list control group a group of research participants who receive the
same intervention or treatment as those
in the EXPERIMENTAL GROUP but at a
later time. Wait-list CONTROL GROUPS
commonly are used in therapy outcome
and similar studies to account for the
potential influence of elapsed time upon
treatment effectiveness; they may also
be used to address the ethical ramifica-
tions of withholding treatment from individuals.

Wald distribution see INVERSE GAUS-
SIAN DISTRIBUTION. [Abraham **Wald**
(1902–1950), Hungarian-born mathe-
matician]

Wald's test a PARAMETRIC statistical
procedure used to evaluate the signifi-
cance of individual coefficients (β) in a
LOGISTIC REGRESSION model. It yields
estimated values of population PARAME-
TERS that are compared to a CHI-SQUARE
DISTRIBUTION having one DEGREE OF
FREEDOM in order to determine their
theoretical occurrence under the NULL
HYPOTHESIS. [Abraham **Wald**]

Wald–Wolfowitz test a nonparametric test of the NULL HYPOTHESIS that
two samples have been taken from identical populations, based on whether or
not the number of runs or sequences in
an ordering is random. For instance,
consider the following ordering of males

(M) and females (F) from 1 to 27 according to their performance on a task:

MMMFFFMMMMFFMMMMFFFFFFFMMFMM

In this data set there are nine runs. If
the two samples are from the same population, then the males and females will
be well mixed and the number of runs
thus will be large (e.g., close to 25); if the
number of runs is small, as it is in this example, the ordering cannot be caused by
chance fluctuation and the NULL HY-
POTHESIS thus is rejected. Indeed, visual
inspection of the data shows that the
males tend to cluster toward the left-
hand side of the scale and the females
toward the right-hand side. Also called
runs test; **two-sample runs test**.
[Abraham **Wald**; Jacob **Wolfowitz** (1910–
1981), U.S. psychologist]

Ward's method an approach to HIER-
ARCHICAL CLUSTERING that attempts to
minimize the SUM OF SQUARES of any
two (hypothetical) clusters that may be
formed at each step of the data analysis.
In other words, Ward's method reveals
the cost in increased sum of squares that
arises from merging clusters, such that
only those clusters that yield the smallest increases should be merged to
achieve the optimum grouping of cases.
[Joe H. **Ward** (1927–2011), U.S. statisti-
cian]

wash-out period the time frame allot-
ted for an administered drug to be eliminated from the body or for a previously
administered intervention to become
ineffective. Wash-out periods are particularly important in medical and other
clinical research since the CARRYOVER
EFFECT between treatments might otherwise confound the estimates of treatment effects.

wave *n.* an individual measurement session in panel studies and other LONGITUDINAL DESIGNS in which the same participants are measured repeatedly over time.

wavelet analysis a mathematical method used in TIME-SERIES ANALYSIS to decompose variation into simpler, individual **wavelets**, or functions that have specific frequencies, amplitudes, and temporal characteristics. The process generates information about periodicity within the series.

weak inference a conclusion based upon correlations drawn from observational studies or QUALITATIVE RESEARCH, as opposed to experimental hypothesis testing. Compare STRONG INFERENCE.

weak law of large numbers see LAW OF LARGE NUMBERS.

weight *n.* a coefficient or multiplier used in an equation or statistical investigation and applied to a particular variable to reflect the contribution to the data. For example, a **weighted sample** is one in which different values are applied to its different constituent subgroups to reflect their representation within the larger population from which it was taken. Thus, if a population is 50% male and 50% female but the sample studied is 40% and 60%, respectively, different multipliers could be used to adjust the individual subsample results to match the makeup of the population. Similarly, a weighted least squares regression is a version of ordinary LEAST SQUARES REGRESSION in which different variables contribute differentially to the analysis process according to their relative importance. See WEIGHTING.

weighted average an average calculated to take into account the relative importance of the items making up the average: Different values or WEIGHTS are assigned to different data points to reflect their relative contribution. For example, in examining grade point average, one might give grades A through F the weights of 4, 3, 2, 1, and 0, respectively. One would multiply the number of A grades a student obtained by 4, the number of B grades by 3, and so forth, and then divide the resulting sum by the total number of grades to obtain the student's overall weighted average. Also called **weighted mean**.

weighted kappa an index of interrater agreement that takes into account the degree of disparity between the categorizations assigned by different observers. Thus, different levels of agreement contribute more or less heavily to the overall value of kappa than others. For example, if two raters differ by two categories, that difference is assigned more importance (i.e., given a greater WEIGHT) in the analysis than if they differ only by one category. See also COHEN'S KAPPA.

weighted mean see WEIGHTED AVERAGE.

weighted multidimensional scaling (WMDS) see INDIVIDUAL-DIFFERENCES SCALING.

weighting *n.* the process of multiplying test items, subtests, tests that are part of a test battery, or other measures that are components of a total score by a value or WEIGHT other than 1. If all components were to be weighted by 1, the result would be **equal weighting**, which is essentially no weighting.

Welch test see ASPIN–WELCH–SATTERTHWAITE TEST.

Wherry's formula an equation used to estimate SHRINKAGE, or the degree to which REGRESSION COEFFICIENTS derived from one sample are applicable to another sample. It is given as

$$\hat{R}^2 = 1 - \frac{N-1}{N-p}(1-R^2),$$

where N is the sample size, p is the number of predictor variables, and R^2 is the COEFFICIENT OF MULTIPLE DETERMINATION. The formula yields an index called the ADJUSTED R^2 that itself has been adjusted according to the number of par-

W

ticipants and the number of predictors that were used to generate the regression equation. [R. J. **Wherry** Sr. (1904–1981), U.S. statistician]

whisker *n.* see BOX-AND-WHISKER PLOT.

whole-interval recording a strategy for observing behavior that provides information about the specific timing and duration of the behavior. In whole-interval recording, the length of an observation session is identified (e.g., 1 hour) and then broken down into smaller, equal-length time periods (e.g., 10-minute intervals). An observer then records whether the behavior of interest occurs throughout an entire interval, counts the total number of intervals in which the behavior was present, and calculates what percentage of intervals that number represents. See also PARTIAL-INTERVAL RECORDING.

wide-range test a brief screening instrument administered to gauge ability quickly and determine if a more comprehensive test is needed. Its items vary widely in difficulty so as to measure performance at very broad levels. For example, a wide-range test of vocabulary given to ninth-grade students might include simple words typically known by elementary-school students as well as complex words generally familiar only to college students.

Wilcoxon–Mann–Whitney test a NONPARAMETRIC TEST, used when data are rank-ordered, to determine whether two INDEPENDENT SAMPLES have been drawn from the same population, based on comparison of their median values. It combines the MANN–WHITNEY U TEST and WILCOXON RANK-SUM TEST into a single statistical procedure. [Frank **Wilcoxon** (1892–1965), Irish-born U.S. statistician; Henry Berthold **Mann** (1905–2000), Austrian-born U.S. mathematician; Donald Ransom **Whitney** (1915–2001), U.S. statistician]

Wilcoxon matched-pairs signed-ranks test an extension of the WILCOXON SIGNED-RANKS TEST used to determine whether two DEPENDENT SAMPLES have been drawn from the same population. Each member of a sample has two scores from some RATIO SCALE (e.g., a pre- and postscore), which allow for the computation of a difference score. The difference scores are then ranked and computations performed to determine whether the median of the difference scores equal 0. The test takes into account the direction of the differences and gives more weight to large differences than to small differences. The Wilcoxon matched-pairs signed-ranks test is a NONPARAMETRIC equivalent of the DEPENDENT-SAMPLES T TEST. [Frank **Wilcoxon**]

Wilcoxon rank-sum test a statistical test of centrality for ranked data that compares the median values of two INDEPENDENT SAMPLES to determine whether they have been drawn from the same population. In this NONPARAMETRIC equivalent of the T TEST, one combines the data points from the different groups into a single pool and ranks their values in ascending order. The ranks that have been assigned are in turn used to determine the test statistic, *W*, which is evaluated for statistical significance. The calculations involved in the Wilcoxon rank-sum test are nearly identical to those for the MANN–WHITNEY U TEST. [Frank **Wilcoxon**]

Wilcoxon signed-ranks test a NONPARAMETRIC statistical procedure used to determine whether a single sample is derived from a population in which the median equals a specified value. The data are values obtained using a RATIO SCALE, and each is subtracted from the hypothesized value of the population median and the difference scores are then ranked. The test takes into account the direction of the differences and gives more weight to large differences than to small differences. The symbol for the test statistic is *T*. Also called **Wilcoxon T test**. [Frank **Wilcoxon**]

Wilks's lambda (symbol: Λ) a statistic used in MULTIVARIATE ANALYSIS OF VARIANCE to determine whether there are significant differences between the means of groups on a combination of DEPENDENT VARIABLES. It may be converted to an F RATIO to obtain a SIGNIFICANCE LEVEL or used to calculate ETA SQUARED, which is a measure of the proportion of variance in the combination of dependent variables that is explained by the INDEPENDENT VARIABLE. [Samuel Stanley **Wilks** (1906–1964), U.S. mathematician]

Wilks's multivariate outlier test a statistical procedure for identifying extreme measurements or observations within MULTIVARIATE data. Essentially, it is a sequential application of WILKS'S LAMBDA: Potential OUTLIERS are studied in a forward fashion, with the most extreme point being removed at each step, until the test fails to indicate the presence of outliers. [Samuel Stanley **Wilks**]

Williams's agreement measure (symbol: I_n) a numerical index that measures the degree of similarity between the judgments of a specific rater and the judgments of the whole set of raters. Specifically, it measures whether the rater of interest agrees with the set as often as others in that set do. Williams's agreement measure is similar to COHEN'S KAPPA but distinguished by its focus on a particular rater. [George W. **Williams**, U.S. biostatistician]

Winsorized mean a measure of CENTRAL TENDENCY that is less sensitive to OUTLIERS than is a standard mean. To obtain a Winsorized mean, one replaces the highest and lowest values from a set of data with less extreme values, sums the values in the modified set, and calculates the average. [Charles P. **Winsor** (1895–1951), U.S. statistician]

Winsorizing *n.* an IMPUTATION strategy, intended to reduce the influence of OUTLIERS, in which extreme values in a data set are replaced with the highest and lowest remaining values before any calculations are performed. Typically, an equal number of high and low values are replaced, comprising from 10% to 25% of the total distribution. [Charles P. **Winsor**]

Wishart distribution a generalization of the univariate CHI-SQUARE DISTRIBUTION to two or more variables. It is often used as a model for the distribution of the sample COVARIANCE MATRIX for normal random data pertaining to multiple variables. [John **Wishart** (1898–1958), British statistician]

withdrawal design an experimental design in which the treatment or other intervention is removed during one or more periods. A typical withdrawal design consists of three phases: an initial condition for obtaining a baseline, a condition in which the treatment is applied, and another baseline condition in which the treatment has been withdrawn. Often, the baseline condition is represented by the letter A and the treatment condition by the letter B, such that this type of withdrawal design is known as an A-B-A DESIGN. A fourth phase of reapplying the intervention may be added, as well as a fifth phase of removing the intervention, to determine whether the effect of the intervention can be reproduced (see A-B-A-B DESIGN; A-B-A-B-A DESIGN).

within-groups analysis of variance see WITHIN-SUBJECTS ANALYSIS OF VARIANCE.

within-groups degrees of freedom in an ANALYSIS OF VARIANCE for a WITHIN-SUBJECTS DESIGN, the number of scores or observations obtained for a treatment level minus one, added across all treatment levels. For example, in a 60-participant study examining three dosages or levels of a drug treatment, the DEGREES OF FREEDOM would be calculated by determining the number of participants observed within each level minus one and them summing those

W

values: $(20-1)+(20-1)+(20-1)=19+19+19=57$. The within-groups degrees of freedom is used to calculate the WITHIN-GROUPS MEAN SQUARE. Also called **within-conditions degrees of freedom**; **within-subjects degrees of freedom**; **within-treatments degrees of freedom**. Compare BETWEEN-GROUPS DEGREES OF FREEDOM.

within-groups design see WITHIN-SUBJECTS DESIGN.

within-groups mean square an index of random variability or error in an ANALYSIS OF VARIANCE. It is calculated as the WITHIN-GROUPS SUM OF SQUARES divided by the WITHIN-GROUPS DEGREES OF FREEDOM, and it forms the denominator of the F RATIO. Also called **mean square within**; **within-conditions mean square**; **within-groups variance**; **within-subjects mean square**; **within-subjects variance**; **within-treatments error**; **within-treatments mean square**; **within-treatments variance**. Compare BETWEEN-GROUPS MEAN SQUARE.

within-groups sum of squares an index of variability in an ANALYSIS OF VARIANCE that is used to determine the WITHIN-GROUPS MEAN SQUARE. It is calculated by adding together the squared deviations of the individual observations (scores) on the DEPENDENT VARIABLE from the relevant group mean. Also called **within-conditions sum of squares**; **within-subjects sum of squares**; **within-treatments sum of squares**. Compare BETWEEN-GROUPS SUM OF SQUARES.

within-groups variance see WITHIN-GROUPS MEAN SQUARE.

within-subjects analysis of variance a variation of the standard ANALYSIS OF VARIANCE that is applied to data from a study in which the independent variable has multiple levels and each participant experiences each treatment level or is otherwise measured more than once (see WITHIN-SUBJECTS DESIGN). Because such designs involve recording multiple responses from the same person, it is necessary to examine how each individual varies in his or her responses, so as to separate such unique fluctuation from variation that is due to the influence of the treatment under investigation. For example, a researcher studying how amount of daily walking (e.g., none, 30 minutes, 60 minutes, 90 minutes) affects quality of sleep might have participants walk each length of time across consecutive weeks and then evaluate the results using a within-subjects analysis of variance. Also called **dependent-groups analysis of variance**; **dependent-samples analysis of variance**; **within-groups analysis of variance**; **repeated measures analysis of variance**; **treatments-by-subjects analysis of variance**. Compare BETWEEN-SUBJECTS ANALYSIS OF VARIANCE.

within-subjects degrees of freedom see WITHIN-GROUPS DEGREES OF FREEDOM.

within-subjects design an experimental design in which the effects of treatments are seen through the comparison of scores of the same participant observed under all the treatment conditions. For example, teachers may want to give a pre- and postcourse survey of skills and attitudes to gauge how much both changed as a result of the course. Such a design could be analyzed with a DEPENDENT-SAMPLES T TEST, a WITHIN-SUBJECTS ANALYSIS OF VARIANCE, or an ANALYSIS OF COVARIANCE. Also called **correlated-groups design**; **correlated-samples design**; **dependent-groups design**; **dependent-samples design**; **related-measures design**; **related-samples design**; **repeated measures design**; **treatment-by-subjects design**; **within-groups design**. Compare BETWEEN-SUBJECTS DESIGN.

within-subjects factor the independent variable under study in a WITHIN-

SUBJECTS ANALYSIS OF VARIANCE. This variable has multiple levels to which each participant is exposed. For example, if a researcher is interested in job performance differences as a function of workshift length (e.g., 8 hours, 12 hours, 24 hours) and has each participant work each shift length during the study, then workshift length is a within-subjects factor. Also called **within-subjects variable**.

within-subjects mean square see WITHIN-GROUPS MEAN SQUARE.

within-subjects sum of squares see WITHIN-GROUPS SUM OF SQUARES.

within-subjects variable see WITHIN-SUBJECTS FACTOR.

within-subjects variance see WITHIN-GROUPS MEAN SQUARE.

within-treatments error see WITHIN-GROUPS MEAN SQUARE.

WMDS abbreviation for weighted multidimensional scaling. See INDIVIDUAL-DIFFERENCES SCALING.

work decrement in an experiment, a decline in the magnitude of responses as a function of frequency of the response.

working hypothesis a provisional but empirically testable statement about the relationship between two or more variables that is readily subject to revision upon further experimentation. See HYPOTHESIS.

worm plot a visual examination of the differences between two GROWTH CURVE distributions, used for assessing the GOODNESS OF FIT of the data. It is a general diagnostic tool for the analysis of RESIDUALS. The vertical y-axis displays the difference between each observation's location in the theoretical and empirical distributions, while the horizontal x-axis depicts the Z SCORES for different age groups, as in the following generic example.

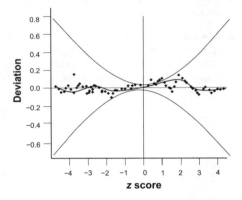

A well-fitting plot for a given age group is linear with zero SLOPE and zero curvature.

Xx

x a letter used to symbolize a variable of interest. For example, in a REGRESSION EQUATION, *x* may represent a particular predictor or INDEPENDENT VARIABLE.

x′ symbol for X PRIME.

X̄ (X bar) symbol for SAMPLE MEAN.

x-axis *n.* the horizontal axis on a graph. See ABSCISSA.

x-coordinate *n.* the horizontal value in a pair of graph coordinates (*x*, *y*), which indicates how far to move left or right from the origin along the X-AXIS. For example, in the ordered pair (4, 8), the *x*-coordinate is 4 and the corresponding vertical Y-COORDINATE value is 8. See CARTESIAN COORDINATE SYSTEM.

x-intercept *n.* in an equation representing a straight-line relationship between two variables, the value of variable *x* when the value of variable *y* equals zero. For example, in the general LINEAR EQUATION format $x = a + by$, *a* represents the *x*-intercept.

x prime (symbol: *x′*) the predicted or EXPECTED VALUE of a given variable of interest, *x*.

Yy

y symbol for a variable of interest. For example, in a REGRESSION EQUATION, y may represent a particular outcome or DEPENDENT VARIABLE.

y′ symbol for Y PRIME.

Yates's correction for continuity an adjustment made to a CHI-SQUARE TEST of data from a CONTINGENCY TABLE having only two columns and two rows of information. The Yates's correction yields a more conservative chi-square statistic and improves the test's accuracy by accounting for the fact that it uses a CONTINUOUS DISTRIBUTION to approximate a DISCRETE DISTRIBUTION. To apply the correction, one takes each value within the table (i.e., the observed frequency) and subtracts the value predicted to occur by a theoretical model (i.e., the expected frequency). One then takes the difference so obtained and subtracts 0.5, squares the total, and divides the resulting number by the expected frequency. When such a correction is applied, the term **Yates-corrected chi-square test** or **Yates chi-square test** is used to refer to the test itself. [Frank **Yates** (1902–1994), British statistician]

y-axis *n.* the vertical axis on a graph. See ORDINATE.

y-coordinate *n.* the vertical value in a pair of graph coordinates (x, y), which indicates how far to move up or down from the origin along the Y-AXIS. For example, in the ordered pair (4, 8), the y-coordinate is 8 and the corresponding horizontal X-COORDINATE value is 4. See CARTESIAN COORDINATE SYSTEM.

yea-saying *n.* answering questions positively regardless of their content, which can distort the results of surveys, questionnaires, and similar instruments. Also called **acquiescence bias**; **acquiescent response set**; **response acquiescence**. Compare NAY-SAYING.

y-intercept *n.* in an equation representing a straight-line relationship between two variables, the value of variable y when the value of variable x equals zero. For example, in the general LINEAR EQUATION format $y = a + bx$, a represents the y-intercept.

yoked-control group a CONTROL GROUP in which each participant is paired with a participant in another group (see MATCHED-PAIRS DESIGN); the paired individuals are then exposed to precisely the same experiences except for the specific treatment or other condition under study. This procedure is intended to make the control group as similar as possible to the experimental group. For example, in a study of the effectiveness of rewards upon children's learning, matched individuals in the control and experimental groups would complete the same tasks under the same conditions but only those in the experimental group would be praised for good performance.

Youden's index a measure of the capacity of a diagnostic test to correctly identify individuals with a certain illness and to correctly identify those who do not have the illness. It ranges from 0 to 1, with values closer to 1 indicating both greater SENSITIVITY and SPECIFICITY of the test. Also called **Youden's J.** [William John **Youden** (1900–1971), Australian-born U.S. chemist and statistician]

y prime (symbol: $y′$) the predicted or EXPECTED VALUE of a given variable of interest, y.

Yule–Simpson effect see SIMPSON'S PARADOX.

Yule's paradox see SIMPSON'S PARADOX. [George Udny **Yule** (1871–1951), British statistician]

Yule's Q a measure of the strength of the relationship between two DICHOTO-MOUS VARIABLES, such as a person's sex (male or female) and graduation from college (yes or no). It ranges from –1 to +1, with values close to either negative or positive 1 indicating a very strong relation and values around 0 indicating little to no relation. Also called **Yule's coefficient of association**. [George Udny **Yule**]

Zz

z-axis *n.* the third dimension in a CARTESIAN COORDINATE SYSTEM or graph. It is perpendicular to both the horizontal X-AXIS and the vertical Y-AXIS.

Zelen's design a type of RANDOMIZED CLINICAL TRIAL in which patients are assigned to experimental conditions before they have consented to participate in the research. In a typical trial, patients are first informed of the nature of the study and then decide whether to participate, which may result in certain biases that Zelen's design attempts to overcome. There are two versions of the design, both of which remain ethically controversial: In the single-consent strategy, patients assigned to the experimental treatment are told there is an alternative (the control) available and offered the option to switch or remain in the experimental group; those in the control group are not informed of their study participation and their agreement to participate thus is not obtained. In the double-consent strategy, both the experimental and control groups are offered the option to switch from the treatment to which they initially were assigned. Also called **randomized consent design**. [Marvin **Zelen** (1927–), U.S. biostatistician]

zero-inflated Poisson regression (**ZIP**) a model for analyzing a data set with an excessive number of zero outcomes. An alternative to regular POISSON REGRESSION for explaining outcome variability, it assumes that with probability p the only possible observation is zero (0), and with probability $1 - p$, a POISSON VARIABLE is observed. For example, consider a study of 100 teams selling boxes of cookies on a weekend. In this data set, there could be excessive counts of zero (i.e., no boxes sold) because several teams did not go out to sell due to inclement weather in their neighborhoods; however, zero counts also could occur because of nonsuccess in selling. Consequently, the number of zeros may be inflated and the number of teams not selling boxes cannot be explained in the same manner as the number of teams selling more than one box.

zero matrix see NULL MATRIX.

zero-order correlation a simple association between two variables that does not control for the possible influence of other variables. For example, consider the relationship between success selling computers and knowledge of how the Internet works. A zero-order correlation would examine the direct relationship between these two variables without taking into account other explanatory information, such as education level, sales experience, and so forth. The actual index of the magnitude or degree of such a relationship is called the **zero-order correlation coefficient**; it ranges in value from –1 to +1, with the former indicating a perfect negative relationship and the latter a perfect positive relationship. Compare PART CORRELATION; PARTIAL CORRELATION.

zero-sum game in GAME THEORY, a type of game in which the players' gains and losses add up to zero. The total amount of resources available to the participants is fixed, and therefore one player's gain necessarily entails the others' loss. The term is used particularly in analyses of bargaining and economic behavior but is sometimes also used in other sociocultural contexts (e.g., politics).

zero-truncated Poisson distribution see TRUNCATED POISSON DISTRIBUTION.

ZIP abbreviation for ZERO-INFLATED POISSON REGRESSION.

z score the STANDARDIZED SCORE that results from applying a Z-SCORE TRANSFORMATION to raw data. For purposes of comparison, the data set is converted into one having a distribution with a mean of 0 and a standard deviation of 1. For example, consider a person who scored 30 on a 40-item test having a mean of 25 and a standard deviation of 5, and 40 on an 80-item test having a mean of 50 and a standard deviation of 10. The resulting z scores would be +1.0 and –1.0, respectively. Thus, the individual performed better on the first test, on which he or she was one standard deviation above the mean, than on the second test, on which he or she was one standard deviation below the mean. A tabular or graphical arrangement of several z scores is called a **z-score distribution**.

z-score transformation a statistical procedure used to convert raw data into z SCORES, dimensionless quantities that may be interpreted without reference to the original units of measurement. It is performed by subtracting each data point from a reference value (the sample average) and dividing the difference by the STANDARD DEVIATION of the sample. The primary purpose of the z-score transformation is to allow comparisons of scores with different underlying characteristics by converting them into values that have a distribution with a mean of 0 and a standard deviation of 1. It is distinct from FISHER'S R TO Z TRANSFORMATION, which is specific to PRODUCT-MOMENT CORRELATION COEFFICIENTS.

z test a type of statistical test that compares the means of two different samples to determine whether there is a significant difference between them (i.e., one not likely to have occurred by chance). Generally, this involves comparing the mean from a sample of a population to the mean for the whole population but may also involve comparing the means of two different populations. The z test is based on the NORMAL DISTRIBUTION and is used when a population's STANDARD DEVIATION is known or the sample is large (greater than 30). The equivalent T TEST is used with unknown standard deviations or smaller samples. Different variations of the basic z test exist, such as the **z test for a population proportion**, which compares differences between PROPORTIONS as opposed to means; the **z test for two dependent samples**, which compares differences between two samples whose members have been matched on certain characteristics; and the **z test for two independent samples**, which compares differences between two distinct, unrelated groups of participants.

z transformation see FISHER'S R TO Z TRANSFORMATION.

Appendixes

Abbreviations and Acronyms

ACE	alternating conditional expectation
ACES	active control equivalence study
ACF	autocorrelation function
AD	average deviation
AEq	age equivalent
AH	alternative hypothesis
AIC	Akaike's information criterion
AID	automatic interaction detector
AML	asymmetric maximum likelihood
ANCOVA	analysis of covariance
ANOVA	analysis of variance
ARIMA model	autoregressive integrated moving-average model
ARMA model	autoregressive moving-average model
AR model	autoregressive model
ATI	aptitude–treatment interaction
AUC	area under the curve
AWS test	Aspin–Welch–Satterthwaite test
BCa or BC_a	bias-corrected accelerated percentile interval
BIC	Bayesian information criterion
BLUE	best linear unbiased estimator
BMA	Bayesian model averaging
BRR	balanced repeated replication
CART analysis	classification and regression tree analysis
CDF	cumulative distribution function
CF	cumulative frequency
CFA	confirmatory factor analysis
CFI	Bentler comparative fit index
CGF	cumulant generating function
CHAID	chi-square automatic interaction detector
CI	confidence interval
CLT	central limit theorem
Co	comparison stimulus
CTT	classical test theory
CuSum chart	cumulative sum chart
DA	data augmentation
DAG	directed acyclic graph

DFBETAS	differences in beta values
DFFITS	difference in fits
DIC	deviance information criterion
DIF	differential item functioning
DS	dual scaling
Duncan's MRT	Duncan's multiple range test
DV	dependent variable
e	exponent; error
ECM algorithm	expectation-conditional maximization algorithm
ECME algorithm	expectation-conditional maximization either algorithm
EDA	exploratory data analysis
EFA	exploratory factor analysis
EMA	ecological momentary assessment
EM algorithm	expectation-maximization algorithm
EPSEM	equal probability of selection method
erf	error function
ESM	experience-sampling method
exp	exponential function
FA	factor analysis
FDA	functional data analysis
FU plot	follow-up plot
GAM	generalized additive model
GAMM	generalized additive mixed model
GARCH	generalized autoregressive conditional heteroscedasticity
GCR	greatest characteristic root
GEE	generalized estimating equation
GIGO	garbage in, garbage out
g inverse	generalized inverse
GLM	general linear model; generalized linear model
GLMM	generalized linear mixed model
GLS	generalized least squares
GMM	generalized mixed model
HLM	hierarchical linear model
HSD test	honestly significant difference test
ICC	intraclass correlation coefficient; item characteristic curve
IDA	initial data analysis
IID	independent and identically distributed
INDSCAL	individual-differences scaling
IPA	interpretive phenomenological analysis
IQR	interquartile range
IRB	institutional review board
IRT	item response theory
ITI	intertrial interval

IV	independent variable
KMO test	Kaiser–Meyer–Olkin test of sampling adequacy
K-R 20	Kuder–Richardson formula 20
K-R 21	Kuder–Richardson formula 21
LCA	latent class analysis
LLR	log-likelihood ratio
ln	natural logarithm
LOCF	last observation carried forward
loess	local regression
log	logarithm
lowess	local regression
LR	likelihood ratio; logistic regression
LSD	least significant difference
LSD test	Fisher least significant difference test
LTA	latent transition analysis
MA	moving average
MAD	mean absolute deviation; median absolute deviation
MA model	moving-average model
MANCOVA	multivariate analysis of covariance
MANOVA	multivariate analysis of variance
MAPE	mean absolute percentage error
MAR	missing at random
MARS	multivariate adaptive regression spline
MCA	multiple classification analysis
MCAR	missing completely at random
MCMC method	Markov chain Monte Carlo method
MCML estimation	Monte Carlo maximum likelihood estimation
MCP	minimum convex polygon
MDA	multiple discriminant analysis
MDL	minimum description length
MDS	multidimensional scaling
MI	modification index
MIMIC model	multiple indicators–multiple causes model
MLE	maximum likelihood estimation
ML-EM estimation	maximum likelihood–expectation maximization estimation
MOE	margin of error
MTMM	multitrait–multimethod matrix; multitrait–multimethod model
MVUE	minimum variance unbiased estimator
NCE	normal curve equivalent
NFI	normed fit index
NH	null hypothesis
NHST	null hypothesis significance testing

NNT	number needed to treat
NS	not significant
OLS	ordinary least squares
OR	odds ratio
O-X-O	one-group pretest–posttest design
PCA	principal components analysis
PDF	probability density function
PGF	probability generating function
PLS	partial least squares
PMF	probability mass function
PMLE	penalized maximum likelihood estimation
P-P plot	probability–probability plot
PRE	proportional reduction of error
p value	probability level
QDA	quadratic discriminant analysis
QI	quasi-independence
Q-Q plot	quantile–quantile plot
R	response or respondent
rad	radian
RBD	randomized block design
R correlation	multiple correlation coefficient
RCT	randomized clinical trial
RDD	random-digit dialing; regression-discontinuity design
REG	random event generator
REGWQ test	Ryan–Einot–Gabriel–Welsch multiple range test
REML	restricted maximum likelihood
RMS	root mean square
RMSE	root-mean-square error
RMSR	root-mean-square residual
RNG	random number generator
ROC curve	receiver-operating characteristic curve
RRT	randomized-response technique
RSM	response surface methodology
RT	reaction time
S	subject
SDT	signal detection theory
SEM	structural equation modeling
SIMEX	simulation and extrapolation procedure
SQRT	sequential probability ratio test
SSA	smallest space analysis
STARIMA model	space–time autoregressive integrated moving-average model
STARMA model	space–time autoregressive moving-average model
SVD	singular value decomposition

TAR	threshold autoregression
TTI	trait–treatment interaction
UMP test	uniformly most powerful test
VIF	variance inflation factor
WMDS	weighted multidimensional scaling
ZIP	zero-inflated Poisson regression

Entry Illustrations

Overview of Research Design Considerations

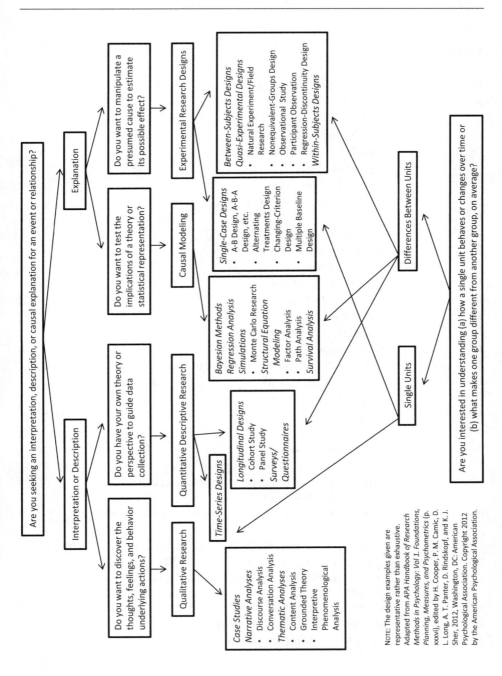

Are you seeking an interpretation, description, or causal explanation for an event or relationship?

Explanation

Interpretation or Description

Do you want to manipulate a presumed cause to estimate its possible effect?

Do you want to test the implications of a theory or statistical representation?

Do you have your own theory or perspective to guide data collection?

Do you want to discover the thoughts, feelings, and behavior underlying actions?

Experimental Research Designs

Causal Modeling

Quantitative Descriptive Research

Qualitative Research

Between-Subjects Designs
Quasi-Experimental Designs
- Natural Experiment/Field Research
- Nonequivalent-Groups Design
- Observational Study
- Participant Observation
- Regression-Discontinuity Design
Within-Subjects Designs

Single-Case Designs
- A-B Design, A-B-A Design, etc.
- Alternating Treatments Design
- Changing-Criterion Design
- Multiple Baseline Design

Bayesian Methods
Regression Analysis
Simulations
- Monte Carlo Research
Structural Equation Modeling
- Factor Analysis
- Path Analysis
Survival Analysis

Time-Series Designs

Longitudinal Designs
- Cohort Study
- Panel Study
Surveys/Questionnaires

Case Studies
Narrative Analyses
- Discourse Analysis
- Conversation Analysis
Thematic Analyses
- Content Analysis
- Grounded Theory
- Interpretive Phenomenological Analysis

Differences Between Units

Single Units

Are you interested in understanding (a) how a single unit behaves or changes over time or (b) what makes one group different from another group, on average?

NOTE: The design examples given are representative rather than exhaustive. Adapted from *APA Handbook of Research Methods in Psychology: Vol 1. Foundations, Planning, Measures, and Psychometrics* (p. xxxvi), edited by H. Cooper, P. M. Camic, D. L. Long, A. T. Panter, D. Rindskopf, and K. J. Sher, 2012, Washington, DC: American Psychological Association. Copyright 2012 by the American Psychological Association.

Symbols

Latin

adj R^2	adjusted R^2
C	coefficient of contingency
d	Cohen's d; Glass's d
d'	d prime
D	Cook's distance; difference score
D^2	Mahalanobis distance
df	degrees of freedom
E	expected value
f	an effect size index; frequency
F	F ratio
G^2	likelihood-ratio chi-square
h^2	communality coefficient
H_0	null hypothesis
H_1	alternative hypothesis
H_a	alternative hypothesis
H	hat matrix
I_n	Williams's agreement measure
I	identity matrix
k	coefficient of alienation; number of units in a statistical analysis
K^2	D'Agostino test statistic
M	sample mean
MS	mean square
MSE	mean squared error
MSR	mean-square residual
$MSSD$	mean-square successive difference
n	number of scores or observations from a particular experimental condition
N	total number of cases (participants) in an experiment
p	probability
q	Studentized range statistic; probability of failure in a binary trial
Q	Cochran Q test statistic; Yule's Q; quartile
r	product-moment correlation coefficient; sample correlation coefficient
r^2	coefficient of determination
R	multiple correlation coefficient
R^2	coefficient of multiple determination

R^2_{adj}	adjusted R^2
r_{b}	biserial correlation coefficient
r_{bis}	biserial correlation coefficient
R_{c}	canonical correlation coefficient
$r_{\text{effect size}}$	effect-size correlation coefficient
r_{pb}	point biserial correlation coefficient
r_{pbis}	point biserial correlation coefficient
r_{s}	Spearman correlation coefficient
r_{tet}	tetrachoric correlation coefficient
r_{xx}	reliability coefficient
$R^2_{yy'}$	cross-validated multiple correlation
s	sample standard deviation
s^2	sample variance
SD	standard deviation
SE	standard error
SEE	standard error of estimate
SEM	standard error of measurement; standard error of the mean
SS	sum of squares
$SSCP$	sum of squares of cross-products
SSE	sum of squared errors
$SS_{\text{regression}}$	regression sum of squares
T	Wilcoxon signed-ranks test statistic
T^2	Hotelling's T^2 test
TSS	total sum of squares
U	Mann–Whitney U test statistic
V	Cramér's V
W	coefficient of concordance; Wilcoxon rank-sum test statistic
W^2	Cramér–von Mises goodness-of-fit test statistic
x	a variable of interest
x'	x prime
$\bar{X}$	sample mean
$\mathbf{X}$	data matrix
y	a variable of interest
y'	y prime
$\hat{y}$	predicted value of an outcome or dependent variable

Greek

α	alpha
β	beta
χ^2	chi-square
χ^2 distribution	chi-square distribution
Δ	change in a parameter; Glass's d

ε	a small value
ε^2	proportion of shared variance
η	correlation ratio; a latent variable
η^2	amount of explained variance
η_G^2	generalized eta squared
η_p^2	partial eta squared
γ	Goodman–Kruskal's gamma
κ	Cohen's kappa
λ	eigenvalue
Λ	Wilks's lambda
μ	population mean
ω^2	omega squared
ϕ	phi coefficient
ϕ_c	Cramér's V
π	ratio expressing the circumference of a circle to its diameter; probability of success in a trial
ρ	population correlation coefficient; Spearman correlation coefficient
σ	population standard deviation
σ^2	population variance
σ_M	standard error of the mean
Σ	sum
τ	Kendall's tau
θ	ability parameter